Psychology of Physical Activity

In today's urbanised and technologised society, physical activity is becoming an increasingly peripheral part of our daily lives.

Psychology of Physical Activity is a comprehensive account of our psychological knowledge about physical activity, covering:

- motivation and the psychological factors associated with activity or inactivity
- the 'feel-good' factor: the psychological outcomes of exercising, including mental illnesses and clinical populations
- interventions and applied practice in the psychology of physical activity
- current trends and future directions in research and practice.

This new edition is updated to reflect new findings and current research directions, and includes full textbook features. A dedicated accompanying website (www.routledge.com/textbooks/9780415366656) provides lecturers and students with extensive supporting materials, including slide presentations and self-test questions.

Stuart J. H. Biddle is Professor of Exercise and Sport Psychology at Loughborough University, UK.

Nanette Mutrie is Professor of Exercise and Sport Psychology at Strathclyde University, UK.

Psychology of Physical Activity

Determinants, well-being and interventions

2nd edition

Stuart J. H. Biddle
and Nanette Mutrie

Routledge
Taylor & Francis Group

LONDON AND NEW YORK

First edition published 2001
This edition published 2008 by Routledge
2 Park Square, Milton Park, Abingdon, Oxon, OX14 4RN

Simultaneously published in the USA and Canada
by Routledge
270 Madison Avenue, New York, NY 10016

Reprinted 2008, twice

Routledge is an imprint of the Taylor & Francis Group, an informa business

© 2001, 2008 Stuart J. H. Biddle and Nanette Mutrie

Typeset in Times by
GreenGate Publishing Services, Tonbridge, Kent
Printed and bound in Great Britain by
The Cromwell Press, Trowbridge, Wiltshire

British Library Cataloguing in Publication Data
A catalogue record for this book is available from the British Library

Library of Congress Cataloging in Publication Data
Biddle, Stuart.
Psychology of physical activity: determinants, well-being, and interventions / Stuart J. H.
Biddle and Nanette Mutrie. -- 2nd ed.
p. cm.
Includes bibliographical references and index.
ISBN 978-0-415-36664-9 (hardcover) -- ISBN 978-0-415-36665-6 (softcover) 1. Exercise--
Psychological aspects. 2. Clinical health psychology. 3. Health promotion. I. Mutrie, Nanette,
1953- II. Title.
RA781.B486 2007
613.7'1--dc22
2007005420

ISBN-10: 0 415 36664 X (hbk)
ISBN-10: 0 415 36665 8 (pbk)
ISBN-10: 0 203 01932 6 (ebk)

ISBN-13: 978 0 415 36665 6 (pbk)
ISBN-13: 978 0 415 36664 9 (hbk)
ISBN-13: 078 0 203 01932 0 (ebk)

Contents

Figures

Tables

Boxes

Preface

Developments in physical activity and health have been significant since the publication of our first text in 1991 (*Psychology of Physical Activity and Exercise*, London: Springer-Verlag). For example, there has been a huge increase in the study of physical activity and health from a psychological point of view which can be illustrated by the number of meta-analytic reviews in the sub-field of physical activity and mental health. The increase in the available evidence led to us to write a new version of the book, published in 2001 by Routledge and what you see now is our second edition of that book. One obvious factor accommodated in the current edition is the need to update the evidence again. Many of the key areas or topics – attitudes, the transtheoretical model, psychological well-being, interventions – now have a substantial evidence base and often significant systematic review data.

In addition, since the 2001 edition, there has been a greater recognition of the 'bigger picture' of the influences on physical activity. This has usually resulted in the use of the ecological framework whereby factors associated with, or directly influencing, physical activity are placed within a wider framework of psychological, social, environmental and policy environments. Far from diminishing the role of psychological factors, it shows how important 'cognitive mediation' is in physical activity decision-making. For example, even when a workplace is well served with dedicated cycle routes and safe walking routes, creating an incentive system for people to cycle or walk to work still requires the development of beliefs and attitudes, as well as decision-making, choice, motivation and, ultimately, behaviour on the part of the individual. Explaining this behaviour without reference to individual or social psychological processes would be strange indeed. Conversely, to expect psychology to have all of the answers, or to expect studies of individual thoughts and beliefs to be sufficient to explain some physical or sedentary behaviours, is equally misguided. In short, in this edition of the book, we place psychological frameworks within wider social–environmental frameworks – we provide one piece of the jigsaw. We have expanded coverage of social and environmental influences on physical activity, although the book remains clearly focused on psychology per se.

Another area of change that has continued during the period of the writing of this second edition is that of research methods. These are evolving and developing rapidly, including greater recognition of systematic review methods, sophisticated statistical techniques, such as multi-level modelling, and greater use of qualitative methods. Our plea is for all those interested in physical activity and health to recognise the appropriate use of *certain* methods to answer *certain* questions and to provide us with different kinds of evidence. To dismiss 'qualitative' or 'quantitative' methods because of personal bias or preference is bad research.

Stuart acknowledges Loughborough University for granting a study leave during his period as Head of School. This assisted in the completion of this book. The growing physical activity and health agenda and excellent environment at Loughborough are particularly appreciated. Nanette would like to thank the University of Strathclyde and the rapidly expanding physical activity and health research team for providing a supportive environment. Finally, we thank the excellent work of the staff at Routledge for their support and encouragement.

Stuart Biddle,
Loughborough University
Nanette Mutrie,
University of Strathclyde
January 2007

Acknowledgements

Stuart would like to acknowledge colleagues, students, friends and family who have been so important during this writing period and, in some cases, made huge contributions to my thinking in the field of physical activity. During the period of revising this text I have been the Head of the School of Sport and Exercise Sciences at Loughborough and I could not have managed the task of writing the book without help and support. A study leave period granted by the university was particularly helpful, and the Loughborough environment generally is supportive and inspirational in my field. There is no better place to be!

During the writing of this revision, my father, Jim, died. In addition to being a wonderful father, Jim was a great physical educator. He taught physical education teacher education students for twenty-six years and was universally recognised as a great mentor and educator. He had a love for physical activity and passed this on to generations of teachers: great intervention, great psychology! Jim, this book is for you. I hope I get close to having the impact you had.

Nanette would like to acknowledge how much her colleagues, students, friends and family have contributed (even if they do not know it) to the completion of this revision of our 2001 text. There are at least three groups:

- colleagues with whom discussions (the best ones over a glass of wine or a game of golf!) have helped me think forwards and whose published work has helped us update this text: Stuart Biddle (of course!), Precilla Choi, Andy Smith, Adrian Taylor, Guy Faulkner, Ken Fox, Joan Duda, Amanda Daley, Frank Eves, Madeleine Grealy, Anna Campbell, Ruth Lowry, Carol Emslie, Sally Macintyre, Dan Landers, Celia Brackenridge, Avril Blamey, Fiona Crawford, Vicki Trim, David Ogilvie and the SPARColl (www.sparcoll.org.uk) advisory board
- current and former PhD and MSc students who have added to the knowledge base in physical activity psychology and who have been such a joy to work with over the years: Liz Marsden, Marie Donaghy, Chris Loughlan, Mathew Lowther, Alison Kirk, Adrienne Hughes, Ann McPhail, Roseanne McKee, Graham Baker, Jo Smith, Chloe Hughes, Kate Hefferon, Catherine Woods, Jean Rankin, Annemarie Wright
- friends and family who have provided in equal measure distraction, challenge, support and humour: Kay, Jock and Cal; the Pitlochry Six; Dog's Dinners; the families Mutrie and Munro and my squash and golf buddies. Thanks folks! I know I have been a pain in the neck to most of you – constantly making you walk up stairs and count steps on your pedometer – bad news – I am going to continue to do that! For Kay special thanks for being a wonderfully civil partner and also for her information skills that helped me update this text.

Nanette would like to dedicate this book to the memory of Precilla Choi (Krane, 2005).

Part I
Introduction and rationale

1 Introduction and rationale

Why you should take your dog for a walk even if you don't have one!

Purpose of the chapter

The purpose of this chapter is to introduce key concepts in the study of physical activity, exercise and health as a prelude to a more extensive discussion in subsequent chapters of physical activity, psychological correlates, psychological well-being, and interventions to promote physical activity. Specifically, in this chapter we aim to:

- provide a brief synopsis of human evolution and history that is relevant to current physical activity and health behaviours in contemporary society
- define key terms
- highlight recent policy and position statements and guidelines on physical activity
- summarise the evidence linking physical activity with various health outcomes and risks
- review the prevalence and trends in physical activity and sedentary behaviour in selected countries.

Many forms of physical activity are healthy! As a result we have been interested in the promotion of physical activity for some time and our first text on the subject was published in the early 1990s (Biddle and Mutrie 1991). It is pleasing to see that physical activity for health is now very high priority for governments and other agencies. Initially, a great deal of time was spent on identifying the biological mechanisms of the health effects of activity – indeed an essential aspect of our knowledge – but rather less energy was devoted to the issues of why people do or do not exercise much, what the psychological benefits might be, or the best ways of promoting physical activity. But we are glad to report a significant increase in interest in 'exercise psychology', 'behavioural' interventions and related topics in the past few years. When writing our book in 1991 there were few textbooks giving more than cursory attention to the behavioural aspects of physical activity and health. Today, however, nearly all works in the field address at least some aspect of psychology, behaviour change or behavioural interventions.

Even within the field of physical activity psychology, there has been a greater recognition of exercise for health whereas in the past the vast majority of the literature focused on competitive sport. For example, one of the key research journals, the *Journal of Sport Psychology*, became the *Journal of Sport and Exercise Psychology* (*JSEP*) in 1988 to better reflect the field, and now nearly all such journals have the word 'exercise' in their title. Similarly, in a review of trends in sport and exercise psychology (Biddle 1997), two journals (*JSEP* and the *International Journal of Sport Psychology*) were analysed for content over the ten-year period 1985–94 and exercise studies were the most popular overall in comparison with sport-related constructs and showed the most significant increase over the time period studied (nearly 250 per cent). A recently established journal – *Psychology of Sport and Exercise* – published 37 per cent of its first five volumes (2000–4) on exercise psychology. This would have been unheard of some time ago. Indeed, there are new journals emerging, covering behavioural aspects of physical activity and health, such as the *International Journal of Behavioral Nutrition and Physical Activity* and the *Journal of Physical Activity and Health*. Moreover, established journals, such as the *American Journal of Preventive Medicine, Annals of Behavioral Medicine,* and *Preventive Medicine* all give substantial coverage to physical activity research.

This book, therefore, provides a review of contemporary psychological knowledge in physical activity, with the focus exclusively on physical activity for health rather than sport performance. Although usually referred to as 'exercise psychology', we feel that this may reflect only structured bouts of physical activity, as we discuss in the definitions section shortly. We therefore prefer to broaden the discussion to 'physical activity' in its widest sense, at least as far as health is concerned. However, as you will see, a great deal of the literature does actually refer to exercise as this is often a behaviour that is easier to quantify and study.

The behavioural epidemiological and ecological frameworks

We adopt a 'behavioural epidemiological' framework advocated by Sallis and Owen (1999). Applying this to physical activity, the framework proposes that a five-stage model in which physical activity correlates build on an understanding of the relationship between physical activity and health and the measurement of physical activity. Correlates then inform the development of interventions, the results of which are translated into action. The framework is illustrated in Figure 1.1.

The five-phase behavioural epidemiological framework is a useful way of viewing various processes in the understanding of physical activity and health. Behavioural epidemiology considers the link between behaviours and health and disease, such as why some people are physically active and others are not. The five main phases are:

1   *to establish the link between physical activity and health.* This is now well documented for many diverse conditions as well as well-being (Bouchard, Shephard and Stephens 1994; Dishman, Washburn and Heath 2004). Many of these are described in this chapter. Psychological outcomes of physical activity are dealt with in detail in Part III

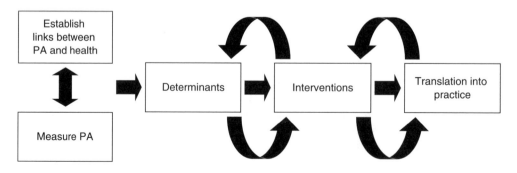

Figure 1.1 A behavioural epidemiological framework (Sallis and Owen 1999)

2 *to develop methods for the accurate assessment of physical activity.* This remains a problematic area. Large-scale surveillance of population trends inevitably relies on self-report, a method that is fraught with validity and reliability problems. Recent 'objective' methods, such as movement sensors, heart rate monitors or pedometers, are useful but do not necessarily give all of the information required, such as intensity or type of activity or the setting in which activity took place. Until we have better measures of the behaviour itself – that is, physical activity – the field will struggle to progress in many respects. We report on prevalence and trends in this chapter

3 *to identify factors that are associated with different levels of physical activity.* Given the evidence supporting the beneficial effects of physical activity on health, it is important to identify factors that might be associated with the adoption and maintenance of the behaviour. This area is referred to as the study of 'correlates' or 'determinants' of physical activity. This is the main theme in Part II of the book

4 *to evaluate interventions designed to promote physical activity.* Once a variable is identified as a correlate of physical activity (for example, self-efficacy), then interventions can manipulate this variable to test if it is, in fact, a determinant. The number of intervention studies in physical activity is increasing (Kahn *et al.* 2002). We discuss interventions in Part IV

5 *to translate findings from research into practice.* If interventions work, it is appropriate to translate such findings into ecologically valid 'real-world' settings.

It is important to realise that the above sequence is not linear. For example, measures of physical activity are developed and refined alongside tests of outcomes, and often community projects are established prior to convincing evidence, but may include a monitoring and evaluation element to test the efficacy of such an intervention before refining future interventions (see Figure 1.1). The whole process then becomes iterative.

In this introductory chapter, we present a rationale for the study of physical activity, outline briefly some of the health benefits of physical activity, and summarise initiatives and statements from key organisations that illustrate the importance of the topic. Finally, we overview the evidence on how active, or inactive, people are in contemporary Western societies. The chapter provides a background on which to judge and assess the role of behavioural and psychological factors in physical activity. Specifically, in this book we address:

- psychological correlates (determinants) of physical activity
- psychological well-being and physical activity
- behavioural interventions to increase physical activity.

The book is focused on psychological and behavioural factors. However, physical activity can also be viewed from the perspective of an ecological framework. This approach recognises that individual approaches take us only so far and that behaviour is also affected by wider social and environmental influences. An ecological framework recognises *intra*personal (individual), *inter*personal (social), physical/environmental and societal/legislative influences on behaviour. Although we do address environmental, policy and social issues, we can only give these brief coverage. However, we fully acknowledge that psychological factors are but one set of influences, or potential influences, on physical activity. Our preference, at this stage, however, is to review these issues to provide a more focused analysis, while recognising the powerful influence of many other factors.

Key point: Physical activity can be influenced by many factors. Psychological influences coexist with social, environmental, and wider policy/legislative influences.

Physical activity, evolution and history

In the wonderful animated film *The Wrong Trousers,* Wallace buys his dog Gromit a pair of 'techno-trousers': automatically walking trousers that allow Wallace to sit at home while the techno-trousers take Gromit for a walk. Is this the shape of things to come, seeking ways of allowing our pets to exercise without moving ourselves? As Wallace said, 'I think you will find these a valuable addition to our modern lifestyle.' It is ironic that we wouldn't dream of depriving our dogs of their walk!

From Gromit to Astrand: 'There is virtually no way of reverting to our "natural" way of life, but with insight into our biological heritage we may be able to modify the current, self-destructive, elements of our modern lifestyle' (Astrand 1994: 103). Astrand's fascinating analysis of evolutionary history in relation to current lifestyles highlights the central issue – we are now living our lives, at least in developed countries, in ways that are largely unhealthy and different from what we have done for most of our past. As some have expressed it, we are living twenty-first century lifestyles with hunter–gatherer genes. Indeed, Astrand's analysis of lifestyles of humans since we first appeared on Earth some four million years ago led him to conclude 'during more than 99 per cent of our existence we were hunters and food gatherers. Now we are exposed to an enormous experiment – without control groups' (Astrand 1994: 101).

From Astrand to Gromit: Professor Astrand often finishes his eloquent lectures with the statement 'you should always take your dog for a walk – even if you don't have one!'

Blair (1988), for example, suggests that four evolutionary periods are important in understanding the relationship between physical activity and health. The pre-agricultural period (up until about 10,000 years ago) was characterised by hunting and gathering activities. Exercise levels were high and diet was low in fat. The agricultural period (from 10,000 years ago until about the beginning of the nineteenth century) was characterised again by reasonably high physical activity levels and relatively low-fat diets, although the fat content probably increased during this time.

The industrial period (1800–1945) saw the development of the 'industrialised society' with the accompanying problems of overcrowding, poor diet, poor public health measures and inadequate medical facilities and care. Infectious diseases were responsible for a high proportion of premature deaths. However, this trend became reversed in the 'nuclear/technological' period, which Blair (1988) identified as from 1945 until the present. The major improvement in public health measures and medical advances meant that infectious diseases were becoming less common in 'advanced' societies. However, health problems were merely shifted in terms of causes and outcomes. The major causes of premature mortality have now become 'lifestyle related', such as coronary heart disease, with risk factors such as cigarette smoking, poor diet and lack of physical activity (Paffenbarger *et al.* 1994). As Paffenbarger *et al.* put it, 'both energy intake and energy output are determined primarily by individual behavior' (1994: 119).

In short, humans have now adopted lifestyles in industrialised countries that were quite unknown until very recently in terms of human evolution (see Box 1.1 and Figure 1.2). This is not to say, of course, that 'health' has necessarily deteriorated; far from it in some cases, although this depends on the definition and measurement of health. Lifespan itself has increased dramatically. In developed Western societies males can expect to live well beyond seventy years of age, with females exceeding a life expectancy of eighty years in at least seventeen countries, according to Dishman, Washburn and Heath (2004). Average life expectancy was less than fifty only in the middle of the last century in the USA (Malina 1988). Similarly, other indicators of physical and mental health have shown improvements, although Malina (1988) says that these are largely restricted to the 'developed' countries. Indeed, it has been an explicit health objective for many international and national organisations and governments to increase both longevity and quality of life.

Box 1.1 Living today as we did 150 years ago: the case of the Amish community

Many people claim that we are 'less active then previous generations'. While this may be true, it is quite difficult to demonstrate because we do not have data from many years ago. A recently published study by David R. Bassett and colleagues from the USA provides a fascinating view on what physical activity levels might have been some 100–150 years ago by studying a community of Amish people in Ontario, Canada, in 2002 (Tudor-Locke and Bassett 2004). The Amish – known to many through Harrison Ford's film 'Witness' – shun modern 'conveniences' and motorised transport and essentially live rural, farming-based lives.

Although not all women in the sample led highly active lives, often due to the traditional roles of women in Amish communities centred on cooking, they still had greater physical activity than one might expect today. The men, however, showed exceptionally high levels of physical activity by today's standards. For example, as Figure 1.2 shows, the average number of steps per day for men and women easily exceeded the 12,500 considered 'highly active' for contemporary Western societies (Tudor-Locke and Bassett 2004). Overweight and obesity levels were also much lower than in traditional Western communities. If the Amish community studied here is similar to that of many communities in the UK and other Western countries 150 years ago, it suggests that physical activity levels have declined markedly.

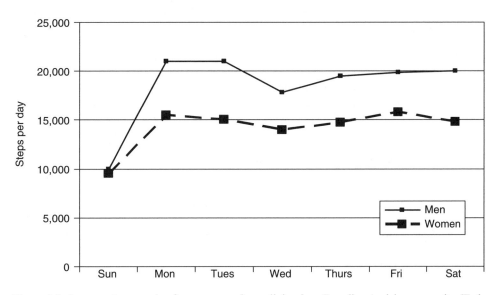

Figure 1.2 Average steps per day for women and men living in a Canadian Amish community (Tudor-Locke and Bassett 2004; reprinted with permission)

But the change in lifestyle, particularly through and beyond the latter part of the twentieth century, has brought its own health problems. Some have referred to a selection of these as 'hypokinetic diseases', or health problems caused by, or related to, a lack of physical activity (Kraus and Raab 1961). Such hypokinetic problems can include poor mental health, coronary heart disease (CHD), obesity, low back pain, osteoporosis, hypertension, diabetes and some cancers. The UK Government's Chief Medical Officer states that 'there are few public health initiatives that have a greater potential for improving health and well-being than increasing the activity levels of the population' (Department of Health 2004a). The evidence linking physical activity patterns with such health measures is increasing rapidly and will be reviewed in brief shortly.

Key point: We are living our lives now in totally different ways from what we have done as humans for more than 99 per cent of our existence.

Box 1.2 Some do, some don't: observations of physical activity

In addition to analysing the increasing amount of data we have on physical activity in our society, it is informative and certainly interesting to note a few observations of everyday life that relate to physical activity. To support the claims made in this opening chapter that some forms of physical activity have increased over the past decade or so, it is quite obvious that there are more exercise classes available in the community and more joggers on the street in comparison with, say, fifteen years ago. Even the social climate seems to have changed. Joggers on the street are no longer a strange sight and are accepted by passersby. Cycling has become a fashionable pursuit in respect of clothes, styles of bikes, etc. Sports shops are numerous and sports/leisure wear is fashionable, although whether this reflects increased participation, of course, is another matter.

The mass media are content to carry the exercise message too. Exercise videos and 'shape up' books, however dubious the content in some, reach the top ten lists of best sellers, usually when promoted by some 'celebrity'. Of course, many are bought for Christmas presents and the recipients never get past the first few days of involvement.

On the other hand, we can also observe many people *actively pursuing inactivity!* Arriving back at London's Heathrow airport one time, Stuart came across the amusing sight of a passenger deciding whether to walk to the *right* about twenty metres in order to get on the moving walkway which was travelling *left* back to the baggage claim area! Have you noticed how many people stand still on these walkways, even after long haul flights of many hours of seated inactivity? Moreover, I was struck by how many 'health professionals'(!) took the escalators rather than the stairs at the American College of Sports Medicine meeting in San Francisco when I attended in 2003, and then stood still! A wide set of stairs was available immediately adjacent to the escalators.

And surely we have far more labour-saving devices that a few years ago (who needs an electric toothbrush?) and we use motorised transport far more than we need. Yet, at the same time, local planning officers are attempting to integrate more cycle paths into our communities, reduce private car use, and increase public transport. Although these are often for environmental and life quality reasons, rather than to increase physical activity per se, they are a move in the right direction and suggest that inter-agency collaboration is both possible and desirable.

Defining key terms

With the increasing interest being shown in the sport and exercise sciences, and the links now being made between various medical and non-medical disciplines in relation to physical activity, the terminology adopted in the study of health and physical activity has not always been consistent. This section will give operational definitions and clarifications to key words and terms.

Physical activity

Caspersen, Powell and Christenson (1985) define physical activity in terms of the following three elements:

- movement of the body produced by the skeletal muscles
- resulting energy expenditure which varies from low to high
- a positive correlation with physical fitness.

As far as health outcomes are concerned, the energy expenditure is usually required to be well above resting levels (Bouchard and Shephard 1994). For example, while I could be classified as being physically active while writing this book (fingers are moving fairly rapidly across the keyboard), this type of physical activity is largely irrelevant for health. However, in special cases such manipulative skills are encouraging the maintenance of functional capacity and life quality, such as in very old or activity-impaired individuals.

Given the decline in the amount of physical activity that most people have to perform in work duties (as illustrated by the example of the Amish community lifestyle in Box 1.1), and the increase in motorised transport, a great deal of the physical activity that has become necessary for health must be freely chosen in leisure time or consciously integrated into one's normal daily routine. This, in itself, justifies the increasing importance of studying psychological processes, such as motivation and decision-making, in physical activity, alongside other influences such as social and environmental factors.

Exercise

Given that physical activity includes all movement, it is helpful also to recognise subcomponents, or elements, of physical activity. Caspersen *et al.* (1985: 127) define exercise with reference to the following factors:

- body movement produced by skeletal muscles
- resulting energy expenditure varying from low to high (so far, these points are the same as for physical activity);
- 'very positively correlated with physical fitness'
- 'planned, structured and repetitive bodily movement'
- the objective is to maintain or improve physical fitness.

Exercise may also have the objective of health enhancement or improving performance (Bouchard and Shephard 1994). However, the distinction between physical activity and exercise is not always easy and one should recognise an overlap between the two constructs. In this book, exercise will usually refer to more structured leisure-time physical activity, such as participation in jogging, swimming, 'keep-fit' activities and recreational sports.

It has been recognised that, for many, exercise is perceived as being hard work, vigorous and possibly unpleasant. Consequently, the need to promote 'active living' (Killoran, Cavill and Walker 1994; Quinney, Gauvin and Wall 1994) or an 'active lifestyle' has been recognised in an effort to produce a more acceptable or palatable message and may be more cost-effective (Sevick *et al.* 2000b).

Box 1.3 On the road to nowhere ... more observations on physical activity

On my (SJHB) way home from work I cycle past the commercial fitness club in Loughborough. It is an interesting building with a glass-sided circular room perched above ground level. I can clearly see people cycling, walking, running and stepping on their machines. I find it quite amusing as I cycle somewhere with a purpose to see these people (many of whom will have driven there), moving nowhere (literally). I understand why some have to do this (indeed I enjoy my treadmill walking at home with music), but it does illustrate the problems of modern life whereby many have to seek out exercise machines or else they will be very sedentary. I also wonder how often these people could be active by walking and cycling more without the gym, and by driving less.

Sport

Philosophers have argued long and hard over the word 'sport', but for our purposes we define it as a sub-component of exercise whereby the activity is rule-governed, structured, competitive and involves gross motor movement characterised by physical strategy, prowess and chance (Rejeski and Brawley 1988). The competitive nature of sport has sometimes been difficult to clarify. Indeed, the Sports Councils in the UK (for example, 'Sport England') have jurisdiction over activities that are non-competitive (for example, keep-fit and yoga), and 'Sport for All' campaigns have often included a wider range of activities than 'traditional' competitive sports. Moreover, not all sports will necessarily be 'health-related' in the sense we adopt in this book. For example, playing darts or pool may be enjoyable and require great skill, but provide minimal physical activity.

Health and well-being

Health is multifactorial in nature and includes dimensions of the physical, mental and social, and some might argue the 'spiritual'. It involves enhancement of well-being as well as absence of disease. High positive health is sometimes referred to as 'wellness' or high level well-being. This is positive physical and emotional well-being with a high capacity for enjoying life and challenges, and possessing adequate coping strategies in the face of difficulties. Negative health is characterised by disease, morbidity and possibly premature death (Bouchard and Shephard 1994).

Physical fitness

Physical fitness refers to the ability of the individual to perform muscular work. Caspersen *et al.* define it as 'a set of attributes that people have or achieve that relates to the ability to perform physical activity' (Caspersen *et al.* 1985: 129). This suggests that physical fitness is partly related to current physical activity levels ('attributes that people *achieve*') and partly a function of heredity ('attributes that people *have*').

In recent years it has become more usual to refer to health-related and performance (skill)-related components of physical fitness (Caspersen *et al.* 1985). The performance-related aspects of fitness are associated with athletic ability and are sometimes referred to as 'motor fitness'. The components include agility, balance, coordination, power, reaction time and speed. There is no evidence linking the development of such qualities to 'health' outcomes in the sense of risk for chronic disease. However, they may have more indirect or less tangible health benefits such as through the development of independence for older people. Generally speaking, though, they are separated from health-related components of fitness, and epidemiological evidence supports such a distinction (Dishman, Washburn and Heath 2004). The skill-related aspects of fitness are important, of course, for sport and other activities relying on motor skills and abilities.

The health-related components of physical fitness have traditionally been identified as cardiovascular fitness, muscular strength and endurance, muscle flexibility, and body composition (fatness) (Caspersen *et al.* 1985). The development of these components of health-related fitness (HRF) has been related to specific 'health' or disease outcomes. Indeed, Pate (1988) has argued that 'physical fitness' should be defined solely in terms of the health-related aspects by stating that the following criteria should be met in such a definition:

- fitness should refer to the functional capacities required for comfortable and productive involvement in day-to-day activities
- it should 'encompass manifestation of the health-related outcomes of high levels of habitual activity' (Pate *et al.* 1988: 177).

Bouchard and Shephard (1994), however, broaden the definition of HRF by referring to morphological, muscular, motor, cardiovascular and metabolic components. Given the public health perspective adopted in this book, the types and forms of exercise and physical activity that have been reviewed in relation to psychological principles and research are generally health-related. Competitive sport, except where it sheds some light on the wider public health aspects of exercise and physical activity, is not covered.

Correlates and determinants

We have used the word 'correlates' to reflect the factors that affect, or are thought to affect, participation in exercise and physical activity. Sometimes the word 'determinants' is also used. Correlates has now become the standard term to use for this in the literature, mainly because it is recognised, when using the term determinants, that many of the factors discussed are not, or may not be, true determinants. In other words, data may show associations but information cannot necessarily be gleaned as to causality. The word correlates, therefore, seems more appropriate. Buckworth and Dishman refer to correlates as 'reproducible associations that are potentially causal' (Buckworth and Dishman 2002: 191).

Policy and position statements on physical activity and exercise

A growing number of organisations are producing position statements and policy documents on health-related behaviours, including physical activity. This reflects the increasing concern regarding the changes in morbidity and premature mortality that face many contemporary societies. Two of the largest projects undertaken in this respect emanate from the World Health Organization and the Department of Health and Human Services in the United States. In addition, many other national organisations have made statements or been involved in substantial promotion of physical activity, including the UK Government's Chief Medical Officer's (CMO) Report (Department of Health 2004a).

The World Health Organization

The World Health Organization (WHO) published its targets for 'health for all' in their European region in 1985. The 1986 revision of their book *Targets for health for all* 'set out the fundamental requirements for people to be healthy, to define the improvements in health that can be achieved by the year 2000 for the peoples of the European Region of WHO, and to propose action to secure these improvements' (World Health Organization 1986: 1). Broadly, WHO lists four dimensions of health outcomes it wishes to achieve. These are equity in health, adding 'life to years', adding 'health to life', and adding 'years to life'. Specifically, thirty-eight targets were outlined up until the year 2000.

In 2004, WHO endorsed a global strategy on diet, physical activity and health indicating that inactivity is not just a problem for developed countries (World Health Organization 2004). WHO recognised that physical activity levels worldwide were falling as a result of industrialisation, urbanisation and economic development. The global strategy has adopted a broad-ranging approach and was developed from a May 2002 mandate from member states. The evidence for the need for a global strategy presented by WHO is summarised in Table 1.1.

The strategy calls for WHO member states to develop national strategies, tailored to local cultural needs, that seek to increase the level of physical activity and healthy eating. In addition, nations are encouraged to improve the evidence base about what policies and interventions will create behaviour change, engage with the key stakeholders that would be interested in such change and advocate the importance of such changes at policy levels.

Initiatives in the UK

The 'Health of the Nation' (HON) initiative in England by the British government of the time (Department of Health 1993b) marked a significant change in approach in health care and promotion in England. This is discussed more fully in Chapter 13 when we consider legislative initiatives in physical activity promotion, but for the sake of continuity we shall outline a few key points here also.

Table 1.1 Evidence for the need for a global strategy concerning diet and physical activity

- Appropriate regular physical activity is a major component in preventing the growing global burden of chronic disease.
- At least 60 per cent of the global population fail to achieve the minimum recommendation of thirty minutes moderate intensity physical activity daily.
- The risk of getting cardiovascular disease increases by 1.5 times in people who do not follow minimum physical activity recommendations.
- Inactivity greatly contributes to medical costs – by an estimated $75 billion in the USA in 2000 alone.
- Increasing physical activity is a societal, not just an individual problem, and demands a population-based, multi-sectoral, multi-disciplinary and culturally relevant approach.

The overall aims of the HON were:

- 'adding years to life' – reduce premature mortality and improve life expectancy
- 'adding life to years' – improve the quality of life.

Physical activity was identified as an important element to combat coronary heart disease and stroke, one of the five priority areas of the HON initiative. A 'Physical Activity Task Force' (PATF) was established with the remit of recommending targets and strategies for physical activity for the English population. However, the government later decided that they did not want targets, leaving the PATF to consider strategies. This led to the Health Education Authority's 'Active for Life' campaign (Hillsdon *et al.* 2001) and other local initiatives.

The Labour government developed the HON through the 'Our Healthier Nation' paper early in 1998 (Department of Health 1998). This sought to tackle the 'root causes' of ill health and was explicit about the need to address social inequalities as a contributing factor to health and health inequalities. This approach remains a key element of UK government policy today.

In the UK, ambitious targets for increasing the percentage of the Scottish and English populations who are regularly active have recently been set. In Scotland the goal is to have 50 per cent of the adult population regularly active by the year 2022 (Scottish Executive 2003) and in England the suggested target was 70 per cent by 2020 with an interim target of 50 per cent by 2011 (Department for Culture, Media and Sport 2002). These targets represent an approximate 20 per cent increase for Scotland and a 40 per cent increase for England in the number of people achieving the recommended minimum activity levels. To put this another way, in Scotland there is an expectation that a year-on-year increase of 1 per cent of the population reaching the recommended minimal levels can be achieved, whereas the English target aimed for a 2 per cent year-on-year increase. These targets are highly ambitious given that:

- it is not yet clear exactly how we should intervene to achieve these increases
- there is little evidence that this rate of increase is achievable
- there is no clear resourcing model in either country for ensuring that money will be made available to ensure the target can be met
- increasing physical activity is a task that does not fall easily to one agency such as schools, sport organisations, health boards or transport planners.

The more recent English document *Choosing activity: a physical activity action plan* has been written by the Department of Health after consultation and in an attempt to bring together all government efforts to promote activity (Department of Health 2005). It is notable that the foreword to this document is signed by both the Minister of Sport and the Minister for Public Health – thus emphasising that the task of increasing physical activity in the population does not fall naturally to one agency. The aim of the action plan is to provide a summary of the various means by which physical activity is being promoted in England across different departments and organisations. The action plan noted that, after considering the consultation responses, the goal of achieving 70 per cent of the English population being sufficiently active by the year 2020 was seen to be unachievable and described this goal as 'aspirational'.

The Wanless Report is a landmark document that provided advice to the government about how to ensure good health for the whole population (Wanless 2004). It focuses on prevention and tries to move away from a model of health care that is wholly focused on delivery of acute services. It is encouraging reading for those who have been calling for a change of resourcing from downstream (dealing with acute medical concerns) to upstream (preventing the development of disease) (Naidoo and Wills 1994).

The Wanless Report applauds the setting of national targets for changing the prevalence of all major determinants of health, such as reducing the percentage of the population who smoke or who are overweight and increasing the percentage that eat in a healthy way and take appropriate levels of activity. However, Wanless recommends that while long-term targets are needed, shorter-term interim targets are also needed so that progress can be checked. For physical activity, Wanless recommended that the aspirational target of 70 per cent of the English population achieving minimum activity recommendations by 2020 should be replaced by more realistic targets. However, as yet, these exact targets have yet to emerge from the Department of Health in the UK government.

The American experience: Health Objectives for the Nation and Healthy People 2000/2010

A more specific set of goals was established by the Department of Health and Human Services (DHHS) of the United States government (Department of Health and Human Services 1980, 1986, 1991, 2000). Initially, the DHHS set 223 'health objectives for the nation' by the year 1990. As with the WHO targets these included many objectives unrelated to physical activity. However, the DHHS did set eleven objectives for 1990 that were concerned specifically with exercise and physical fitness. A review in 1985 revealed a mixed pattern of success in moving towards the objectives and targets set (Powell *et al.* 1986).

Consequently, a revision of the 1990 objectives was made in a 'midcourse review'. New proposals (Department of Health and Human Services 1986) suggested that thirty-six exercise and fitness objectives be stated for the year 2000. Of particular importance from the point of view of the psychological approach adopted in this book are the following two objectives:

- 'by 2000, the relationship between participation in various types of physical activities during childhood and adolescence and the physical activity practices of adults will be known'
- 'by 2000, the behavioural skills associated with a high probability of adopting and maintaining a regular exercise programme will be known' (Dishman 1988: 435).

The American Healthy People 2000 project (Department of Health and Human Services 1991), has rationalised these thirty-six objectives into twelve. These include national objectives for physical activity levels, physical education provision, workplace physical activity promotion, availability of community facilities and primary care interventions to increase physical activity. With the increased recognition of the health benefits of physical activity levels below the threshold thought to be necessary for cardiovascular fitness, the Healthy People 2000 objectives place greater emphasis than the 1990 objectives on reducing inactivity and increasing participation in moderate physical activity.

Position statements

A number of position statements have emerged that address the issues of physical activity, exercise and physical fitness. One of the first statements addressed adults. The American College of Sports Medicine (ACSM) produced the standard guidelines for the development of cardiovascular fitness in healthy adults (American College of Sports Medicine 1978). This has now been revised and extended into a new position paper concerning cardiovascular fitness, as well as muscular strength and endurance and body composition (American College of Sports Medicine 1990). The recommended parameters for cardiovascular fitness are:

- frequency: 3–5 days per week
- intensity: 60–90 per cent of maximum heart rate, or 50–85 per cent $VO_{2\ max}$ or heart rate reserve
- duration: 20–60 minutes of continuous aerobic activity
- mode: large muscle groups activities that are continuous, rhythmic and aerobic.

Subsequent research now shows that a graded dose–response relationship exists between physical activity and health, consequently it makes better sense not to 'prescribe' exercise only for the development of cardiovascular fitness but for other health outcomes as well. This can be done through more moderate levels of physical activity and has led to the recent statement by Pate *et al.* (1995) for the Centers for Disease Control and Prevention and ACSM that stated that adults should accumulate thirty minutes or more of moderate intensity physical activity on most, and preferably all, days of the week. This has now been adopted in other countries too, such as the UK (Department of Health 2004a).

The ACSM made initial statements about the physical fitness and activity for children and youth a little after they addressed the issue for adults (American College of Sports Medicine 1988). They made eight specific recommendations, including the development of appropriate school physical education programmes that emphasise lifetime exercise habits, enhanced knowledge about exercise, and behaviour change; the encouragement of a greater role in the development of children's activity levels from parents, community organisations and health care professionals; the adoption of a scientifically sound approach to fitness testing in schools whereby the emphasis is placed on health-related aspects assessed in relation to acceptable criteria rather than normative comparison; and finally award schemes for fitness should encourage individual exercise behaviour and achievement rather than superior athletic ability.

A similar statement on children was issued by the Sports Council, in conjunction with the Health Education Authority (HEA), in England, and covered the physical growth and development of the child, promotion of health and prevention of disease, body weight, children with special needs, and ten recommendations for the future. From the standpoint of this book, the most important recommendation was that more research was required on the development of effective strategies for promoting exercise habits in children. Despite the date of the statement, we have made slow progress in the intervening years. Nevertheless, in 1998, the HEA convened a meeting of experts. Reviews of evidence were written, discussed and revised, and recommendations made for research and policy (Biddle, Sallis and Cavill 1998), as shown in Box 1.4.

Other comprehensive statements on exercise and health are also available. One of the first was the 'Workshop on epidemiologic and public health aspects of physical activity and exercise' arranged by the US Centers for Disease Control in 1984 (published as a special issue of *Public Health Reports,* 1985, volume 100, issue 2), a position statement from the American Heart Association (Fletcher *et al.* 1992), and the comprehensive volumes stemming from the 1988 and 1992 physical activity consensus conferences in Toronto, Canada (Bouchard, Shephard and Stephens 1994; Bouchard *et al.* 1990). Readers are strongly encouraged to see the consensus statement in Bouchard *et al.* (1994) which contains nearly

Box 1.4 Guidelines for physical activity for youth in England (Biddle, Sallis and Cavill 1998)

Primary recommendations

- all young people should participate in physical activity of at least moderate intensity for one hour per day
- young people who currently do little activity should participate in physical activity of at least moderate intensity for at least half an hour per day

Secondary recommendation

- at least twice per week, some of these activities should help to enhance and maintain muscular strength and flexibility, and bone health.

seventy topics and 355 'important research topics'. While now over a decade old, it is still a highly valuable source.

A statement was also endorsed by the World Health Organization and UNESCO as part of the World Forum on Physical Activity and Sport in Quebec City, in May 1995 (Research Quarterly for Exercise and Sport 1995). The statement is a succinct consensus on physical activity, health and well-being.

The Chief Medical Officer's report

In 2004, the Chief Medical Officer (CMO) in the UK published a position paper about physical activity titled *At least five a week* (Department of Health 2004a). The aim of this publication was to provide information on the evidence of the relationship between physical activity and health. The report was compiled from comprehensive reviews of various aspects of the physical activity and health relationship and provides a substantial evidence base which should inform practice and policy. In many ways this report replaces the US Surgeon General's report (Department of Health and Human Services 1996) as the most recent evidence base that the world should use as a reference point for developing new knowledge.

The landmark report by the CMO makes a very strong statement about the importance of physical activity for public health. Physical inactivity is a major public health concern because it is very prevalent, and more so than smoking, hypertension or high levels of cholesterol and, at least for cardiovascular disease, is as risky as these other behaviours and conditions. It is the combination of prevalence and risk that makes the strong case for physical activity as a public health concern. Physical activity is a relatively new topic for public health. This is partly because the evidence was not readily available – even now we only have a small amount of population data concerning physical activity compared with smoking and we have not been collecting physical activity data as long as we have been collecting smoking data.

The CMO report documents the evidence for lack of sufficient physical activity contributing to at least twenty chronic diseases and disorders, and these shown in Table 1.2. The recommendations for how much activity to do for health are also clearly stated in this report. The recommendations for young people are as stated in Box 1.4. For adults, we adopted the guidelines from the US, as shown in Box 1.5.

Table 1.2 Level of strength of evidence for a relationship between physical activity and contemporary chronic conditions (Department of Health 2004a) (reprinted with permission)

Condition	Preventive effects			Therapeutic effects	
	Level of evidence[a]	Strength of effect	Evidence of a dose–response relationship	Level of evidence[a]	Strength of effect
Cardiovascular disease:					
Coronary heart disease	High	Strong	Yes	Medium	Moderate
Stroke: Occlusive	High	Moderate		Low	Weak
Stroke: Haemorrhagic	Medium	Weak		Low	Weak
Peripheral vascular disease	No/insufficient data			Medium	Moderate
Obesity and overweight	Medium	Moderate		Medium	Moderate
Type 2 diabetes	High	Strong	Yes	Medium	Weak
Musculoskeletal disorders:					
Osteoporosis	High	Strong		Medium	Weak
Osteoarthritis	No/insufficient data			Medium	Moderate
Low back pain	Medium	Weak		High	Moderate
Psychological well-being and mental illness:					
Clinical depression	Low	Weak		Medium	Moderate
Other mental illness	No/insufficient data			Low	Weak
Mental well-being				Medium	Moderate
Mental function	Low	Moderate		Low	Weak
Social well-being	No/insufficient data			Low	Weak
Cancer:					
Overall	Medium	Moderate	Yes	No/insufficient data	
Colon	High	Strong	Yes	No/insufficient data	
Rectal	Medium	No effect		No/insufficient data	
Breast	High	Moderate	Yes	No/insufficient data	
Lung	Low	Moderate		No/insufficient data	
Prostate	Medium	Equivocal		No/insufficient data	
Endometrial	Low	Weak	Yes	No/insufficient data	
Others	Low	Equivocal		No/insufficient data	

Note
a Volume and quality of data

Box 1.5 Physical activity guidelines for adults, as recommended in the UK (Department of
         Health 2004a)

- For general health benefit, adults should achieve a total of at least thirty minutes a day of
  at least moderate intensity physical activity on five or more days of the week.
- The recommended levels of activity can be achieved either by doing all the daily activity in
  one session, or through several shorter bouts of activity of ten minutes or more. The activity can be lifestyle activity or structured exercise or sport or a combination of these.
- More specific activity recommendations for adults are made for beneficial effects for individual diseases and conditions. *All* movement contributes to energy expenditure and is
  important for weight management. It is likely that for many people, 45–60 minutes of
  moderate intensity physical activity a day is necessary to prevent obesity. For bone health,
  activities that produce high physical stresses on the bones are necessary.
- The recommendations for adults are also appropriate for older adults. Older people should
  take particular care to keep moving and retain their mobility through daily activity.
  Additionally, specific activities that promote improved strength, coordination and balance
  are particularly beneficial for older people.

Key point: The importance of physical activity for health is now recognised throughout the
industrialised world and is supported in many cases by governmental and other inter-agency
collaborations.

Health-related outcomes of physical activity and exercise

To understand behavioural aspects of physical activity, it is important to identify the proposed
links between physical activity and health that have emerged over recent years. Comprehensive
overviews can be found in Bouchard *et al.* (1994), Dishman *et al.* (2004) and Hardman and
Stensel (2003), and in a summary in the CMO's Report (Department of Health 2004a).

Physical activity, physical fitness and chronic disease

Much of the literature dealing with the health outcomes of physical activity has been associated with chronic diseases and health risks such as coronary heart disease (CHD) and
obesity. The CMO's report in England (Department of Health 2004a) summarised the level
and strength of evidence for a relationship between physical activity and cardiovascular disease, overweight and obesity, Type 2 diabetes, musculo-skeletal disorders, psychological
well-being and mental illness, and cancer (see Table 1.2).

All-cause mortality

Large studies in Finland (Salonen *et al.* 1983) and the USA (Paffenbarger *et al.* 1986) have
shown that those who are physically more active are less likely to suffer premature death and
thus have greater longevity. Prospective epidemiological studies have established that sedentary living carries at least twice the risk of morbidity and all-cause mortality (Powell and
Blair 1994). This is also the case when physical fitness is assessed, rather than just physical
activity. For example, Blair *et al.* (1989) split their sample of over 10,000 men and 3,000

women from the Aerobics Center Longitudinal Study in Dallas, into five fitness categories based on scores on a maximal treadmill test. Age-adjusted all-cause death rates showed significantly greater risk for the lower fitness groups. This is illustrated in Figure 1.3 where the highest fitness group (5) is represented by the relative risk of 1.0.

Lee and Skerrett (2001) identified papers investigating the nature of the relationship between physical activity and all-cause mortality. They included only those with at least three levels of physical activity in order to test a dose–response relationship and this yielded forty-four studies. Evidence for an inverse dose–response relationship was found for physical activity in thirty-four (77 per cent) of the studies. The authors concluded that there is 'clear evidence' for this association (Lee and Skerrett 2001: S469).

Coronary heart disease and stroke

Most interest, if volume of research is considered, has been focused on the proposed link between CHD risk and physical activity. The CMO report (Department of Health 2004a) describes the level of evidence as 'high' (see Table 1.2). CHD is known to be a major health problem in many industrialised countries. For example, in England and Wales CHD is the leading cause of mortality in males and females and is the condition leading to the second highest number of hospital admissions after cancers. Cardiovascular disorders rank second in terms of certified days lost at work. Countries of the United Kingdom are very high in the international league table for premature deaths from CHD, with large costs to the National Health Service (Barker and Rose 1990).

EPIDEMIOLOGY AND THE CAUSAL LINK

Powell *et al.* (1987) selected forty-three studies having the criterion of sufficient data to calculate relative risk or 'odds ratio' for CHD at varying levels of physical activity. They concluded that:

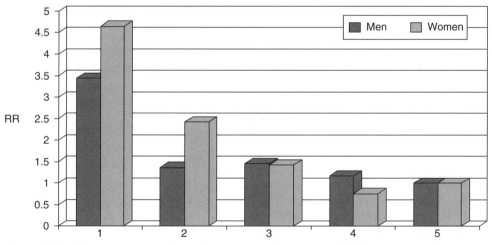

Figure 1.3 Relative risk for age-adjusted all-cause death rates per 10,000 person-years by physical fitness group, indicating the importance of low physical fitness as a risk factor (adapted from Blair *et al.* 1989)

Note
(Most fit group is the reference category with relative risk (RR) = 1) (1 = low fitness group, 5 = high fitness group)

> the inverse association between physical activity and incidence of CHD is consistently observed, especially in the better designed studies; this association is appropriately sequenced, biologically graded, plausible and coherent with existing knowledge. Therefore, the observations reported in the literature support the inference that physical activity is inversely and causally related to the incidence of CHD.
>
> (Powell *et al.* 1987: 283)

This was the first time that such respected researchers had stated their belief that the relationship is causal. Powell *et al.* went on to say that the 'relative risk of inactivity appears to be similar in magnitude to that of hypertension, hypercholesterolemia, and smoking' (Powell *et al.* 1987: 283).

The bulk of the evidence associating CHD and physical inactivity has been accumulated using epidemiological methods. These involve the quantification of health-related behaviours and disease in the population. Specifically, epidemiology attempts to establish the magnitude of the health problem, the causes and modes of transmission, the scientific base for prevention, and evaluation of the effectiveness of preventive or curative measures (Caspersen 1989). The emergent field of 'physical activity epidemiology' can now be identified (Caspersen 1989; Dishman, Washburn and Heath 2004).

The initial studies on CHD and physical activity investigated activity at work, with the studies of Morris in Britain and Paffenbarger in the USA forming the basis of a demonstrated link (Morris *et al.* 1953; Morris *et al.* 1966; Paffenbarger *et al.* 1986; Paffenbarger, Wing and Hyde 1978). For reviews, see Blair (1993, 1994), Dishman *et al.* (2004), Kohl (2001), Leon (1997) and Paffenbarger *et al.* (1994).

Although epidemiologic studies can be criticised for problems of self-selection, as was the case with the early Morris *et al.* studies, the establishment of a plausible cause–effect relationship is possible but requires a number of criteria to be satisfied first, such as temporal sequencing, consistency, specificity and a dose–response relationship (see Caspersen 1989). The weight of evidence is now supportive of such a relationship for physical inactivity and CHD risk. Kohl (2001), for example, reviewed thirty-one studies that investigated at least three levels of physical activity and CHD and concluded that a causal dose–response relationship exists.

VIGOROUS OR MODERATE, FITNESS OR ACTIVITY?

The nature and type of exercise necessary to affect CHD risk positively has also been debated. Morris's work has tended to support the notion that aerobic activity of a relatively 'vigorous' nature is the key to reduced CHD risk (although the activities referred to, such as brisk walking and cycling, are probably 'moderate' level activities). He has suggested that the activity should be of the intensity requiring energy expenditure of 7.5 kcal/min sustained for three periods of twenty minutes per week. Alternatively, Paffenbarger and his co-workers have stressed total leisure-time energy expenditure rather than exercise intensity per se. Paffenbarger's study of Harvard alumni showed that those who expended less than 2,000 kcal per week in leisure time were significantly more at risk of premature mortality from CHD than those who expended more than 2,000 kcal/week (see Paffenbarger *et al.* 1994).

Whether it is physical fitness or habitual physical activity that is critical in the reduction of CHD risk has remained an issue for discussion for some time now. Blair and colleagues (2001) conducted a review of sixty-seven papers that investigated dose–response relationships between either fitness or activity and health outcomes and concluded that both showed a consistent gradient. They were unable to conclude which was more important.

Changes in physical activity have also been shown to be associated with reduced risk of CHD. For example, Paffenbarger *et al.*'s (1993) follow-up of men in the Harvard alumni study showed that for those who were sedentary in 1962 or 1966, but later (1977) took up moderate to vigorous sports/activities, the health effects were strong. Using 1.0 as the adjusted relative risk index for 1962/66, those active in 1977 had reduced their CHD risk index to less than 0.6 – as important to risk reduction as stopping smoking. Similar results were obtained from the Aerobics Center Study.

Other health outcomes

One of the advantages of physical activity is that it can affect many different health parameters. We shall briefly review the areas of hypertension, obesity, diabetes, immune function, musculo-skeletal health and mental health.

Hypertension

Reviews suggest that favourable effects of exercise can be found for hypertension and lack of physical activity is a primary risk factor of hypertension (Department of Health 2004a; Fagard 2001). Moderate aerobic exercise can reduce systolic/diastolic blood pressures by 2.6/1.8 mmHg in normotensives, and 7.4/5.8 mmHg in hypertensives (Fagard 2001). If such reductions were made in large sections of the population, particularly for hypertensives, significant public health benefits would accrue.

Obesity

Based on defining obesity as a body mass index (BMI; weight in kg divided by height in m squared) of 30 or above (British Nutrition Foundation 1999), 22.1 per cent of men and 22.8 per cent of women in English are obese (Department of Health 2004a). Targets for changes in obesity in England for 2005, published in 1992, sought declines of at least 25 per cent in men and 33 per cent in women, leaving only 6 per cent of men and 8 per cent of women classified as obese; figures which equate to obesity levels in 1980 (Rennie and Jebb 2005). Unfortunately, current trends are going in completely the opposite direction and at some speed. With a decline in energy consumption between 1970 and 1990 (Prentice and Jebb 1995), the obesity figures suggest that physical inactivity is a primary cause. Increase in overweight and obesity is a worldwide problem for developed countries. However, even in countries not noted previously for their overweight, similar changes are taking place. For example, China has shown that recent increases in car ownership are associated with increases in obesity (Bell, Ge and Popkin 2002). Obesity trends for children in England are shown in Figure 1.4.

Despite physical activity being the principal discretionary component of energy expenditure, the relationship between exercise and body fat is complex. Nevertheless, the use of exercise in the control of body fat levels is supported despite the small caloric expenditure associated with exercise in comparison with normal dietary intake (Fox 1999).

Hill *et al.* (1994) conclude that physical activity helps prevents moderate obesity in some individuals, and inactivity contributes to the development of obesity in some also. However, they believe it is erroneous to say that physical inactivity is the sole cause of obesity but

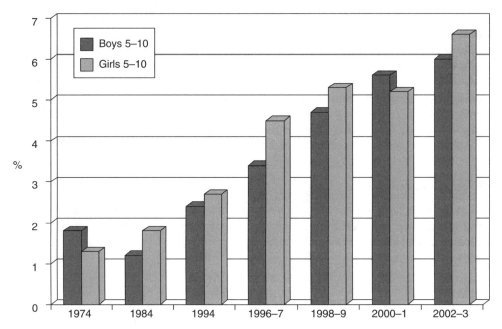

Figure 1.4 Prevalence (per cent) of obesity for English boys and girls 1974–2003 (Stamatakis *et al.* 2005)

physical activity may be most important in preventing weight increase. Moreover, Prentice and Jebb state that 'there is still an overwhelming case in favor of the conclusion that physical activity (especially discretionary leisure-time and recreational physical activity) is strongly related to successful weight maintenance' (Prentice and Jebb 2000: 259).

Type 2 diabetes

Type 2 diabetes, or non-insulin-dependent diabetes mellitus (NIDDM), is a disorder in which cells are 'insulin resistant', resulting in less glucose being cleared from the blood into the cells (Hardman and Stensel 2003). Current trends predict that many industrialised countries will see a doubling of rates of NIDDM over the next twenty years, mainly due to the rise in obesity. This also means that childhood cases of NIDDM, previously non-existent, are now apparent.

Berg (1986) reports that even prior to the discovery of insulin in 1921, exercise was recommended in the treatment of diabetes. Indeed, the 'treatment triad' of diet, insulin and exercise is a frequent term in the control of diabetes (Cantu 1982). Bouchard and Despres (1995) conclude that physical activity and exercise can increase insulin sensitivity, reduce plasma insulin levels, improve glucose tolerance and thus reduce the risk of developing adult-onset diabetes, even for those who are overweight. Glucose tolerance decreases with increased age and obesity, and exercise has been shown to slow this effect (Fentem, Bassey and Turnbull 1988). Similarly, lifestyle interventions, including increases in physical activity, have been effective in reducing the incidence of NIDDM in adults (Diabetes Prevention Program Research Group 2002). The CMO's report concludes that the level of evidence for the effects of physical activity on NIDDM is 'high' and the strength of effects 'strong' (Department of Health 2004a).

Diabetes and obesity tend to cluster with other CHD risk factors. These include raised blood pressure and low HDL cholesterol. This has been termed the 'metabolic syndrome' or 'insulin resistance syndrome' and is associated with low physical activity and fitness (Hardman and Stensel 2003).

Immune function and cancers

There is now evidence linking physical activity with some forms of cancer (Batty and Thune 2000; Hardman 2001; Lee 1994). However, the complexities of the numerous forms and aetiologies of cancers provide researchers with a difficult problem in identifying links and potential causes. Nevertheless, Lee (1995) concluded that there is now good, possibly causal, evidence showing an inverse relationship between physical activity and colon cancer and that physical activity has been associated with reduced risk of breast cancer in superior research studies. Similarly, Thune and Furberg (2000) reported a comprehensive review of the dose–response effects of physical activity on site-specific cancers and reported the clearest effects for colon and breast cancer.

In addition to a great deal of interest being shown in cancer and physical activity, the relationship between immune function and physical activity is now also attracting attention (Lee 1995; Mackinnon 1989). It appears that moderate exercise can enhance the immune system, but high levels of training may depress immune function and increase the risk of infection, such as in the upper respiratory tract (Hardman and Stensel 2003; Lee 1995).

Functional capacity and musculo-skeletal health

Vuori (1995) states that an adequately functioning musculo-skeletal system is very important for functional capacity and quality of life and that a substantial part of the age-related decline in functional capabilities is due to decreased or insufficient physical activity. Moreover, increased or maintained flexibility and strength will help prevent falls and associated fractures. As the populations of developed countries show extended life expectancies, skeletal health is likely to become increasingly important over the coming years. Maintenance or improvement in functional capacity may be a critical factor in improving life quality for older adults in particular.

OSTEOPOROSIS

The excessive loss of bone mineral content, often resulting in fractures, is the condition known as osteoporosis. It is common in older people, particularly in women when 15 per cent of bone mass can be lost within the first decade after menopause (Hardman and Stensel 2003). Weight-bearing activities, such as walking, are considered the most appropriate for reducing the risk of osteoporosis, although weight-bearing activity is recommended at all ages, including young people (Biddle, Sallis and Cavill 1998).

Physical activity does not appear to prevent bone loss post-menopause but it may be effective in maximising and maintaining bone mass. A comprehensive review by Vuori (2001) concluded that physical activity has a strong relationship with bone mass but a clear dose–response relationship cannot be identified.

LOW BACK PAIN

It has been reported that over 80 per cent of adults will suffer from back pain at some time in their lives, although only about 10 per cent will seek medical attention. Approximately

10 per cent of certified days of absence from work in England and Wales are attributed to back pain.

Vuori (2001) reports that there is strong evidence that physical activity can have a preventive effect on low back pain, a conclusion that is more optimistic than that in the CMO's report, where preventive effects are described as 'medium' level with 'weak' strength (Department of Health 2004a). Typical recommendations include the improvement of strength, endurance and flexibility of muscles in the trunk, but that prolonged, heavy and repetitive activity can cause low back pain in susceptible individuals.

Mental health and psychological well-being

A link between exercise and mental health has been suggested for centuries. Data have now been accumulated on the complex processes involved and a clearer picture has emerged over the past few years. Although this topic is dealt with specifically in several chapters in this book (see Part III), summary statements will be made here also.

Drawing on clinical and epidemiological studies, as well as narrative and meta-analytic reviews, it can be concluded that physical activity, usually of a moderate level:

- has a small-to-moderate beneficial effect on anxiety reduction and stress reactivity
- has a moderate-to-large beneficial effect on mild to moderate depression
- has a small effect on self-esteem and a moderately favourable effect on self-perceptions, mood and psychological well-being
- has been associated with positive effects on selected measures of cognitive function and psychological adjustment (Biddle, Fox and Boutcher 2000; Morgan 1997).

Some of these statements will be moderated by age, gender or other factors.

> Key point: The benefits of physical activity are numerous and affect multiple health outcomes and conditions. More evidence is required to assess potential causal links between activity and health, including the dose–response effects and the size of effects.

Risks of exercise and physical activity

Although the evidence supports quite clearly the beneficial health effects of physical activity, there are some aspects that may be contraindicated for some groups, or situations in which a particular health risk is elevated during physical activity. The most commonly cited risks of exercise are sudden cardiac death and musculo-skeletal injury.

Although the risk of sudden cardiac death is elevated with exercise, the balance of cardiac benefit and risk as a result of being an exerciser is positive (Hardman and Stensel 2003). Siscovick *et al.* (1984) reported that men who exercised vigorously for more than twenty minutes each week had an overall risk of primary cardiac arrest only 40 per cent of their sedentary counterparts. It appears, therefore, that despite a temporary rise in risk during exercise, this is outweighed by the long-term effects of exercise on cardiac risk.

Knowledge on the musculo-skeletal risks of exercise is not extensive, although clinical studies have been conducted on swimming, running, cycling, callisthenics and racket sports and have identified a number of injuries (Koplan, Siscovick and Goldbaum 1985; Pate and

Macera 1994). Blair, Kohl and Goodyear (1987) reported three population studies on the rates of running injuries. In their first study, they found that 24 per cent of runners reported an injury during the previous year and the rate increased with body weight and weekly distance run. In their second study, Blair *et al.* found that when comparing runners with non-runners at a preventive medicine clinic, only knee injuries were significantly higher in runners. Finally, a worksite population study found that risk of injury was associated with a number of factors, including increased age and body mass index. Few studies have assessed control groups, hence our knowledge of physical activity-related injuries relative to sedentary cohorts is poor (Dishman, Washburn and Heath 2004).

Some mental health problems have been identified with exercise, such as eating disorders or dependence on exercise. Polivy (1994) located only eleven studies on addiction to exercise and concluded that exercise could indeed be a compulsive behaviour for some individuals. This is likely to be unhealthy due to increased risk of injury, fatigue, illness and psychological ill health. However, the prevalence of exercise dependence is not known and is likely to be very small (Szabo 2000). The issue of negative psychological outcomes from physical activity is discussed more fully in Chapter 10.

Physical activity and its relationship with other health behaviours

A question that has interested physical activity researchers in recent years is whether involvement in physical activity is associated with the adoption of other health behaviours, such as good nutrition and no smoking. In a review of the literature on leisure-time physical activity, Wankel and Sefton (1994) concluded the following:

- there is a small negative association between physical activity and smoking behaviours
- moderate increases in physical activity levels of non-obese individuals have been shown to be associated with corresponding increases in caloric intake
- more active groups tend to have better nutritional habits and this is strongest in most active groups, such as runners
- no relationship exists between physical activity and alcohol consumption
- a small positive association exists between physical activity and some preventive health behaviours, such as seat belt use.

A large-scale study of health behaviours of 2,400 Belgian adults showed that physical activity was not associated with other health behaviours (De Bourdeaudhuij and Van Oost 1999). A review of correlates of physical activity in adults found weak or mixed evidence of an association with alcohol consumption, whereas smoking as negative correlate of activity was supported for adolescent girls (Biddle *et al.* 2005), but only by some studies in adults (Trost *et al.* 2002).

Patterns of physical activity across developed countries

The proposed health outcomes of physical activity suggest that considerable public health benefits could be achieved through physical activity, although some risks are also evident. However, the impact on public health is dependent on people being physically active and avoiding prolonged periods of sedentary behaviour. The identification of patterns of physical activity and sedentary living is important in any effort to plan public health initiatives in this field.

Measurement and surveillance of physical activity and sedentary behaviours

We believe it is important to assess both physically active and sedentary behaviours. Indeed, although studying sedentary behaviour as a concept distinct from physical activity has been advocated recently (Owen *et al.* 2000), one factor that has confounded our understanding is the conceptual and definitional ambiguity over what inactivity actually is.

Many large-scale epidemiologic surveys have attempted to assess the prevalence of sedentariness in a population by measuring against a minimum criterion for physical activity or energy expenditure thought necessary to obtain health benefits. While a central function of these surveys is simply to provide a description of patterns of (in)activity in a population, these measures often fail to capture the diversity of physical inactivity behaviour and tell us nothing about what inactive people are actually doing. It is therefore proposed that 'physical inactivity' is an inadequate label to describe patterns of sedentariness because the definitional premise is one of 'activity absence', thus failing to capture the complexity of sedentary behaviour. It is suggested that a typology of sedentary behaviour be developed and conceptualised as a distinct class of behaviours characterised by low energy expenditure. This definition acknowledges that both the topography of movement (what they are actually doing) and the energy cost are equally important features for understanding behaviour (Marshall *et al.* 2002).

Few studies have assessed physical activity and sedentary behaviours, although a meta-analysis suggests that for children and adolescents the relationship between physical activity and TV viewing (the most prevalent sedentary behaviour) is very small, suggesting that the two behaviours may be able to co-exist (Marshall *et al.* 2004).

The problems in determining the activity levels of the population should not be underestimated. The measurement of physical activity becomes less reliable as techniques more suited to large-scale surveys are used (Sallis and Saelens 2000). In a review of physical activity assessment in epidemiological research, LaPorte, Montoye and Caspersen (1985) identified over thirty different techniques. For large-scale population-based research, however, the use of some variation on survey recall of activity is inevitable. However, so-called 'objective' measures, such as heart rate monitors or movement sensors, are possible in smaller samples, although with the development of cheap pedometers, larger cohorts can now be assessed (Tudor-Locke and Bassett 2004). There is no agreed 'gold standard' technique for assessing physical activity (Ainsworth, Montoye and Leon 1994).

In an effort to obtain greater standardisation of self-reported physical activity levels across countries, a group of researchers have developed the International Physical Activity Questionnaire (IPAQ) for both international surveillance trends monitoring and more focused research projects (Craig *et al.* 2003). In the late 1990s, an international group of physical activity specialists developed several forms of the IPAQ. These included long and short forms, self-administered and those administered by telephone, and those that referred to the 'last seven days' and a 'usual week'. The long form of IPAQ allows for assessment of different types of activity, including occupational, transport, yard/garden, household, leisure and sitting.

Satisfactory reliability and validity, at least comparable with other self-report measures, were reported and it was recommended that the short form (seven-day version) be used for national physical activity monitoring purposes. In addition, it was proposed that the long form be used for research purposes where more detailed assessing is required (Craig *et al.* 2003). Further details are available at www.ipaq.ki.se.

Prevalence of physical activity and sedentary behaviour

The estimates of activity levels of the population will partly be dependent on the method used. Similarly, the criteria defining the quantification of 'activity' will likely be inversely related to the activity levels reported. In other words, the more stringent the criterion adopted for classifying people as 'active', the fewer people will be classified as active. This accounts for why Stephens, Jacobs and White (1985), in their analysis of eight national leisure-time physical activity surveys, found that estimates of population physical activity levels varied from 15 per cent to 78 per cent. They concluded, however, that in North America approximately 20 per cent of the population take part in leisure-time physical activity of sufficient intensity and frequency that cardiovascular benefits are likely to result, while 40 per cent may be considered to be sedentary. The other 40 per cent would appear to be moderately or intermittently active with the possibility of some health benefits.

An international analysis, however, shows that prevalence of 'aerobic activity' across Australia, Canada, England and the USA varies between 5 per cent and 15 per cent, whereas 'moderate activity' varies between 29 per cent and 51 per cent (including data from Finland). Similarly, estimates of sedentary adults in these countries varies from 43 per cent to 15 per cent (Stephens and Caspersen 1994). A pan-European study of adults showed that 'inactivity', defined as no leisure-time physical activity, was most prevalent in Portugal (60 per cent) and least so in Finland (8 per cent) (de Almeida *et al.* 1999).

Surveillance of physical activity patterns usually shows that levels of activity are highest for males, for the young, and for those with higher educational/socio-economic status (de Almeida *et al.* 1999; Stephens and Caspersen 1994). In a summary of data from Canada, England, Finland, Germany and Sweden, Oja (1995) concluded that 'health-enhancing physical activity' varied from about 20 per cent in Sweden to nearly 50 per cent in Canada and England, with Finland at about 30 per cent. International recommendations now state that adults should seek to be active at moderate intensity for thirty minutes on most (at least five) days of the week (Department of Health 2004a; Pate *et al.* 1995). This means a target of 150 mins/week. According to de Almeida *et al.* (1999), many European countries have the majority of their adult population participating in more than 210 mins/week of leisure-time physical activity, with only Portugal and Spain below 50 per cent. However, most countries showed two extremes with many either doing very little or quite a lot of activity.

Recent trends for young people

Concern has been expressed about the levels of physical activity of young people even though they are the most active group in Western societies. Interest is high for reasons of increasing obesity (see Figure 1.4) and the belief that if children are not active enough then serious health problems will accrue in later life.

Reviews of physical activity participation studies conducted in Europe, Australia and North America during the late 1980s and early 1990s have concluded that at least 50 per cent of children and adolescents are insufficiently active for health (Armstrong and Van Mechelen 1998; Stone *et al.* 1998) with girls less active than boys. These findings, as well as a steep decline across the adolescent period, are robust and appear to hold across Westernised countries despite measurement and methodological differences.

Several nationally representative studies have been published. A large pan-European survey of approximately 1,300 eleven, thirteen and fifteen year olds in each of twenty-five European countries (World Health Organization 2000) found that patterns of involvement were similar across countries and that about 65 per cent of boys and 47 per cent of girls participate in vigorous exercise two or more times per week and about 80 per cent of boys and 63 per cent of girls participate in vigorous exercise for two or more hours per week. Gender differences noted in previous reviews were also found. These results are somewhat encouraging as they show relatively good levels of participation in vigorous exercise, but data for participation in moderate exercise were not collected, so it is not possible to comment on the proportion who are sufficiently active for health. The 1992 US National Health Interview Survey – Youth Risk Behavior Survey (NHIS-YRBS) conducted with over 10,000 Americans aged 12–21 years found that around 12 per cent of young males and 15 per cent of young females had not participated in vigorous or moderate physical activity during the last week, and the prevalence of inactivity increased with age. In contrast, about 60 per cent of young males and 49 per cent of young females had participated in vigorous activity on three or more days during the last week (Department of Health and Human Services and Centers for Disease Control and Prevention 1996).

In the 1995 school-based US Youth Risk Behavior Survey (YRBS) of nearly 11,000 15–18 year olds, 7 per cent of males and 14 per cent of females reported no vigorous or moderate physical activity in the preceding week but 76 per cent of males and 57 per cent of females had participated in vigorous physical activity on at least three days in the last week (Department of Health and Human Services and Centers for Disease Control and Prevention 1996). A national survey in New Zealand (Sport & Recreation New Zealand (SPARC), 2002) showed that only about 30 per cent of young people were insufficiently active for health (defined as less that two and a half hours of sport or active leisure in the last week), suggesting that in some countries at least, participation rates, while not ideal, are better.

Sedentary behaviours

Data from the Allied Dunbar National Fitness Survey (ADNFS) in England (Sports Council and Health Education Authority 1992) showed a dramatic increase in physical inactivity with age (Figure 1.5). However, this tells us little about what people are choosing to do. Data on sedentary behaviours in young people worldwide suggests that total media-use among Western adolescents is approximately forty hours per week, or just over five and a half hours per day (Roberts *et al.* 1999; Robinson and Killen 1995; Stanger 1997, 1998; Stanger and Gridina 1999; Woodard and Gridina 2000). Of this, approximately two and half to three hours per day is devoted to TV viewing (A.C. Nielson Company 1990; Gordon-Larsen, McMurray and Popkin 1999; Kimm *et al.* 1996; Roberts *et al.* 1999; Stanger 1997, 1998; Stanger and Gridina 1999; Woodard and Gridina 2000). Estimates of other media use in North American youth suggest they spend time watching videos (about one hour per day), reading books (just under one hour), playing video games (about thirty-five minutes), using the computer/internet (about forty-five minutes), talking on the telephone (thirty minutes) and reading magazines and newspapers (twenty minutes) (Stanger 1997, 1998; Stanger and Gridina 1999; Woodard and Gridina 2000). Comparable data outside of the USA are lacking. However, two cross-national studies of youth aged 11–15 years in Europe and Canada have found that approximately 30 per cent of boys and 10 per cent of girls play video games for more than four hours per week and that 23 per cent of boys and 16 per cent of girls watch more than four hours of video-tapes in a week (World Health Organization 1996, 2000).

North American data suggest that approximately 23 per cent of girls and 29 per cent of boys aged 8–16 years watch TV more than four hours per day (Andersen *et al.* 1998). Similar estimates are evident in European countries (World Health Organization 1996,

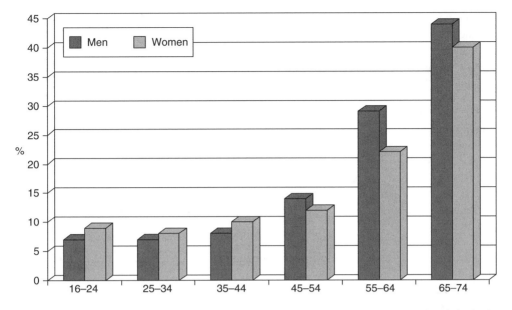

Figure 1.5 Percentage of English adults in different age groups reporting no physical activity in the Allied Dunbar National Fitness Survey

2000). Together, these trends suggest that less than one-third of adolescents watch television for more than four hours per day, a level twice that recommended by the American Academy of Pediatrics (1986). However, there is recent evidence that there is time for both physical activity and TV viewing for young people (Marshall *et al.* 2004; Marshall *et al.* 2002).

Temporal trends in physical activity and sedentary behaviours

Stephens and Caspersen (1994) studied trends in physical activity and concluded that sedentary people have become more involved in moderate activity, but that vigorous activity has not markedly increased in recent times. However, Caspersen *et al.* (1994) point out that the greatest increases in Australia and Canada have been in vigorous activity. Oja (1995) supports the view that the main increases have been in moderate activities, such as walking, golf, cross-country skiing and swimming. More vigorous pursuits in Finland, for example, have decreased in popularity. UK data suggests that the proportion of adults meeting national guidelines for moderate activity have remained stable, although leisure-time trends in the UK show a slight increase in those choosing to walk and in cycling for pleasure. Nevertheless, rates remain low for cycling, particularly for women (Department of Health 2004a). These trends may be explained by people taking less physical activity as part of their daily work, possible work-related, routine, but doing more activity in leisure time. This might be a behavioural challenge because of the greater choice, intention and effort required for free-time behaviours over those required in daily routines.

A frequent assumption in both the academic and popular media is that young people today are less active than in previous generations. There are insufficient direct data at both the behavioural (for example, participation rates) and physiological (for example, aerobic fitness) level to argue convincingly in favour of this assumption (Cavill, Biddle and Sallis 2001; Sallis *et al.* 1992), although personal transport patterns are changing and energy expenditure appears to have declined in children (Durnin 1992). For example, male teenagers now cycle half the distance they did twenty years ago, while 20 per cent of motorised traffic during the immediate pre-school period is involved with transporting children to school. This reflects a dramatic decline in physically active transport to school and a general decline in children's walking and cycling (DiGiuiseppi, Roberts and Li 1997). On the other hand, time-use trend data suggests that organised sports participation has increased in young people (Sturm 2005).

A survey by Sport England showed no change in the number of hours of weekly TV viewing for young people between 1999 and 2002, a trend confirming systematic review data over many years (Marshall, Gorely and Biddle 2006), but there was a slight increase in hours devoted to sport and exercise (Sport England 2003). Sturm (2005), using time-use data from the United States, shows a decline in TV viewing, alongside a small increase in sport and outdoor activities and decreases in playing. A shift has also occurred from free discretionary time to more time spent in structured environments such as school and day care (see Figure 1.6).

In conclusion, despite favourable trends in the past decade or so, the majority of adults in developed countries appear not to be active enough for optimal health benefits (Oja 1995). In addition, those identified as inactive are more likely to be older, less well educated and have lower incomes (Owen and Bauman 1992). Data on young people show them to be reasonably active but a clear downward trend is evident as adolescents age.

> Key point: Despite the difficulties in assessing physical activity accurately at population levels, there seems little doubt that many people are not active enough for health benefits.

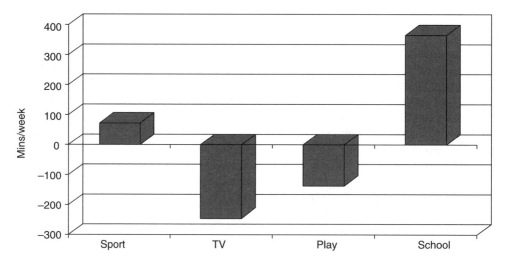

Figure 1.6 Time use trends for 3–12 yr olds: 1981–1997 (Sturm 2004)

Notes
'Sport' includes sport and outdoor activities; 'play' includes hobbies; 'school' includes school, day care, studying, arts and reading

Chapter summary and conclusions

Evidence supports the view that appropriate physical activity can have significant health benefits for all sectors of the population. This book, therefore, will consider psychological and wider behavioural factors likely to influence the participation of individuals in physical activity, as well as the likely psychological outcomes of such involvement. Through a better understanding of these outcomes, correlates (determinants) and interventions we should be able to increase participation rates, decrease sedentary behaviour and bring about significant public health benefits.

In this chapter, as a prelude to a discussion of the psychological issues affecting correlates and determinants of physical activity, and psychological well-being and interventions in physical activity, we have introduced key topics.

Specifically, we have:

- used the behavioural epidemiology framework to structure the study of physical activity
- sketched a brief synopsis of the issues associated with human evolution and history that impact on current physical activity and health behaviours and outcomes
- defined key terms, including physical activity, exercise, fitness and health
- highlighted key statements and policies on physical activity and exercise
- summarised the evidence linking physical activity with various health outcomes and risks
- provided information on the prevalence and trends in physical activity and sedentary behaviours

In summary, therefore, we conclude that:

- humans in developed Western societies have lifestyles quite dissimilar to that which our evolution has prepared us for and that this is likely to be a major factor in modern disease patterns
- a number of national and international organisations have supported the promotion of physical activity as an important health behaviour through the publication of policy and position statements
- physical activity has been shown to be beneficial for many health outcomes, including all-cause mortality, CHD, hypertension, obesity, diabetes and metabolic syndrome, some cancers, immune function, functional capacity and capabilities, musculo-skeletal health and psychological well-being
- physical activity in the form of vigorous exercise does have risks, such as injury and occasional sudden cardiac death, but the evidence shows clearly that people are at greater risk if they are inactive
- some physically active people may be more likely to adopt other health behaviours, such as non-smoking and healthy nutrition, but evidence is mixed
- data from developed countries show that the majority of the adult population is not active enough for health benefits, although the trends over the past ten years or so suggest that leisure-time physical activity may have increased in adults
- sedentary behaviours are highly prevalent but evidence shows TV viewing in youth is not strongly associated with a lack of physical activity and rates of viewing may have actually declined.

Part II

Physical activity

Why we do, why we don't

Part II introduction

Correlates of physical activity are multi-faceted and are not confined to psychological variables. It is important to understand the different types of correlates. These are:

- personal and demographic
- psychological
- social
- environmental.

Typically, psychologists have addressed more individually based issues, such as psychological and social psychological correlates of behaviour, with less emphasis being placed on wider environmental and policy environments. The place of individual psychological approaches alongside these others is shown in Figure P2.1. To understand physical activity fully, we need to combine knowledge across these different environments, although the emphasis in this book is firmly psychological. Nevertheless, we do address social and environmental correlates of physical activity in Chapter 7, and have provided some policy background in Chapter 1.

Personal/demographic correlates

There are consistent positive trends for leisure-time physical activity in adults associated with male gender and higher levels of education and socio-economic status (SES), but negatively associated with non-white ethnicity and age (Trost *et al.* 2002), with similar trends in youth (Sallis, Prochaska and Taylor 2000). Such gender differences are highly reproducible and one of the most consistent findings in the literature. Promoting physical activity in girls

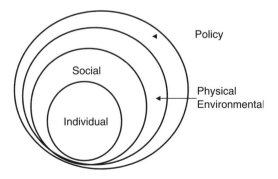

Figure P2.1 Representation of the ecological framework for understanding different 'environments' for physical activity

seems a particular challenge although trials with adults suggest that more women than men show interest in taking part (Mutrie *et al.* 2002).

Psychological correlates

Psychological correlates of physical activity have been studied quite extensively and form the basis for much of this section of the book. There are two main types of studies: those using descriptive approaches whereby psychological variables are assessed alongside physical activity (Chapter 2), and those that use a theoretical model (Chapters 3–6). The latter enable us to build knowledge and understanding of how and why people might be motivated or not ('amotivated') to adopt and/or maintain a physically active lifestyle. Descriptive studies can be helpful in developing more explanatory research designs.

The development of exercise psychology as a thriving research field has led to the proliferation of theories borrowed from other areas of psychology. In particular, theories tested in social and health psychology have been utilised. To help make sense of the different approaches, it is useful to view theories as falling into five categories (see Figure P2.2). There are theories focused on:

- beliefs and attitudes (Chapter 3)
- perceptions of control (Chapter 4)
- perceptions of competence (Chapter 5)
- stage-based theories (Chapter 6)
- hybrid approaches (Chapters 3 and 6).

Although these divisions are not always clear-cut, they may help readers better organise the field (Biddle *et al.* 2007; Biddle and Nigg 2000).

Belief/attitude theories test the links between beliefs, attitudes, intentions and physical activity, such as the theory of planned behaviour. Evidence shows that intentions are predicted best by attitudes and perceived behavioural control, and rather less so by subjective (social) norms (Hagger Chatzisarantis and Biddle 2002). However, research shows that intentions are far from perfect predictors of behaviour, and one could argue that greater emphasis is needed on how to

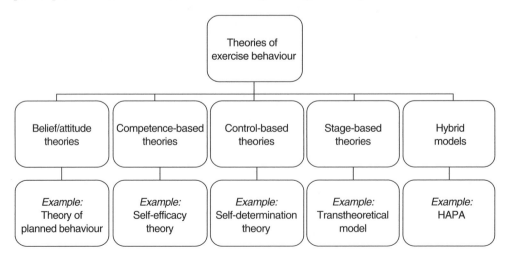

Figure P2.2 A framework for classifying theories of physical activity

translate intentions into behaviour. Competence-based theories focus on perceptions of competence and confidence as a prime driver of behaviour, such as in self-efficacy approaches (Bandura 1997; McAuley and Blissmer 2000). Early attempts in exercise psychology favoured theories of perceived control, such as locus of control (Rotter 1966). These yielded small effects or were inadequately tested so researchers searched for other control-related constructs (Biddle 1999; Biddle and Mutrie 2001). One that has been popular is the self-determination theory advocated by Deci, Ryan and colleagues (Deci and Flaste 1995; Deci and Ryan 1985; Ryan and Deci 2000a, 2000b; Williams *et al.* 2000), and applied to physical activity by others (Chatzisarantis *et al.* 2003). Research shows that motivation for physical activity is likely to be more robust if it involves greater choice and self-determination rather than external control. In addition, such an approach is likely to lead to feelings of higher well-being.

Stage-based theories have recently been favoured, and the transtheoretical model (TTM) of behaviour change has grown in popularity (Marshall and Biddle 2001). The TTM was developed as a comprehensive model of behaviour change and was initially applied to smoking cessation (Prochaska and DiClemente 1982). It incorporates cognitive, behavioural and temporal aspects of changing behaviour. The TTM applied to physical activity consists of the stages of change, the processes of change, decisional balance (weighing up the pros and cons of change) and self-efficacy. The stage of change is the time dimension along which behaviour change occurs. The stages are:

- precontemplation – no intention to start physical activity on a regular basis
- contemplation – intending to start physical activity on a regular basis, usually within the next six months
- preparation – immediate intention (within the next thirty days) and commitment to change (sometimes along with small behavioural changes, such as obtaining membership at a fitness club)
- action – engaging in regular physical activity but for less than six months
- maintenance – engaging in regular physical activity for some time (more than six months).

The processes of change are the strategies used to progress along the stages of change. The processes are divided into cognitive (thinking) and behavioural (doing) strategies. For example, people might seek information on physical activity and mood enhancement (cognitive strategy) or post a note on the fridge door to remind them to walk that day (behavioural strategy). We found that both types of strategies tend to be used throughout the change cycle (Marshall and Biddle 2001), probably due to individual preferences.

The health action process approach (HAPA) is becoming a popular framework to understand both the intentional and behavioural aspects of physical activity. It combines constructs from stage-based and linear models (Biddle *et al.* 2007).

Social correlates

Social support appears to be associated with physical activity in adults and youth. Trost *et al.*'s (2002) review suggested that social support from friends/peers and family/spouse was particularly important. In addition, the influence of one's GP (family physician) plays a role, particularly for adults, as may the leader of group exercise sessions. The 'motivational climate' created by such a leader may be vital in determining whether people return for future sessions (Ntoumanis and Biddle 1999). Evidence suggests that the most positive climate will be when the exercise leader encourages cooperation and rewards effort over comparative performance. Social correlates are covered in Chapter 7.

Environmental correlates

Environmental correlates of physical activity have only been studied quite recently. Trost *et al.*'s (2002) review showed that eleven new environmental variables had been studied since a review of correlates published in 1999. There was weak or mixed support for an association of most variables with physical activity. A recent review of environmental correlates of walking in adults (Owen *et al.* 2004) found eighteen studies. From these, it was concluded that walking was associated with aesthetic attributes; convenience of facilities, such as trails; accessibility of destinations, such as shops; and perceptions of traffic and busy roads. However, the authors concluded that the current evidence is 'promising, although at this stage limited' (Owen *et al.* 2004: 75). It is likely that facilities, including open spaces and parks, are only part of a solution to increase physical activity levels. Other factors include previous experiences of physical activity and current level of fitness.

2 Introduction to correlates of physical activity

Things that might be related to being active

Why we do what we do

Title of prominent motivational researcher Edward L. Deci and
R. Flaste's 1995 book on 'understanding self-motivation'

Purpose of the chapter

The purpose of this chapter is to introduce key concepts of motivation, including early research efforts made in an attempt to understand exercise participation. In particular, these concepts will be placed in the wider context of different types of correlates of physical activity. Subsequent chapters will deal with specific motivational theories in more detail. Specifically, we have the following objectives for this chapter:

- to define motivation and its subcomponents
- to put psychological constructs into the wider context of different types of correlates of physical activity
- to discuss the literature dealing with descriptive approaches to motivation, such as that addressing children's and adults' participation motives and reasons for ceasing participation, as well as the identification of barriers to physical activity
- to describe and comment on early approaches to the study of exercise and physical activity correlates.

The initiation, maintenance and resumption of many health behaviours are rarely easy. Physical activity is certainly no exception to this. The complex psychological, social, environmental and biological influences on involvement in physical activity merely highlight the difficulty of singling out one perspective, theory or approach in attempting to understand the field. Nevertheless, discussion of physical activity inevitably touches the topic of 'motivation'. For this reason, and coupled with the fact that many exercise and sport researchers have devoted a great deal of time and energy to the topic, an understanding of motivation would appear critical if progress is to be made in the study and promotion of physical activity as a health behaviour. This chapter, and those that follow in this section of the book, will cover key issues in physical activity motivation. This chapter will highlight definitions, delimitations and, briefly, historical trends as a precursor to subsequent chapters dealing with central theoretical perspectives in more detail.

The need for a motivational perspective

Few topics can claim to be more central to human behaviour than motivation. For example, we acknowledge that many behaviours can contribute significantly to an individual's healthy lifestyle but, at the same time, considerable difficulties are often faced by people when attempting to start, maintain or resume involvement in such activities. The study of motivation in this context, therefore, would appear to be more than just of academic interest. It is also central to the understanding of behavioural choice and decision-making.

In introducing his report on physical activity and health, the UK Government's Chief Medical Officer, Professor Sir Liam Donaldson, said that 'we now need a culture shift' to achieve national physical activity goals and that 'current levels of physical activity are a reflection of personal attitudes about time use and of cultural and societal values' (Department of Health 2004a: iii–iv). Understanding personal attitudes, motivations and barriers – individual, social, cultural and environmental – represents our own challenge as researchers.

Definition and trends in motivation

The study of human motivation has been central to psychology since its earliest days and has developed through many different perspectives (Weiner 1992). Maehr and Braskamp's (1986) components of motivation will be offered as an operational definition of motivation. In particular, we find the following components helpful:

- direction (choice)
- persistence
- continuing motivation
- intensity.

Choice

The first indicator of motivation, according to Maehr and Braskamp, is that of direction. This implies that a choice has been made and so decision-making is central to understanding motivation. In the context of physical activity, for example, there is the basic choice of whether to be active or not, as well as choices of alternative leisure-time activities. Two important issues arise here. First, to what extent is habitual physical activity consciously chosen? Some may be forced into walking or cycling through a lack of personal resources to travel in any other way. Different psychological processes may be involved here. Given that exercise is mostly structured and likely to take place in particular locations, such as exercise facilities, and at certain times, choice is important for this type of activity. For more 'active living' behaviours, this may not be the case. Second, one needs to consider the issue of alternative behavioural choices. Someone may not be rejecting exercise in any conscious way, but merely choosing activities that are seen as higher priorities. Some physical activity choices are likely to be made in an effort to reinforce personal perceptions of competence, or behaviours that are coherent with one's sense of self.

It is also noteworthy, however, that we are faced with physical activity choices throughout a normal day, and often quite unrelated to self-perceptions of competence. Will I climb the stairs or take the lift? Will I walk or drive? Some choices may be made relatively subconsciously and this in itself provides a challenge to health professionals.

Persistence

Maehr and Braskamp's second motivation factor, persistence, refers to the degree of sustained concentration on one task. Persistence, and hence motivation, might be inferred about someone who walks to work alongside a bus route. Lack of persistence is inferred when the walker gives up after five minutes and takes the first available bus. Of course, persistence is also a reflection of choice and decision-making and is likely to be correlated with how important something is to the individual. In addition, such persistence at a task may be high in order to enhance positive self-presentational aspects – 'I want to be seen walking to work as this confirms my identity (to me and others) that I am an active person'.

Continuing motivation

This is when people regularly return to a task after a break. Indeed, Maehr and Braskamp suggest that 'it is almost as if a certain tension exists when a task is left incomplete; the person simply cannot leave it alone' (Maehr and Braskamp 1986: 4). There is some evidence that a few individuals feel highly committed in this way to structured exercise (Szabo 2000) – the so-called phenomenon of exercise dependence. At a more moderate level, many people report 'feeling good' from physical activity and less good when they have missed their activity for several days.

One aspect of motivation for physical activity that is currently poorly understood involves continuing motivation. Although we have accumulated information on activity maintenance, we know much less about the processes involved in resuming activity after a break – the 'relapse' or 'stop–start' syndrome (Sallis and Hovell 1990). Seeing that few people adopt physical activity without periods of 'relapse', this would appear to be an important area for future study.

Intensity

Behavioural intensity is another indicator of motivation. This is important in relation to the debate about how much physical activity is enough for health gains, since more moderate forms of activity require less intense levels of motivation. Certainly we have argued many times before that promoting physical activity on the basis of 'vigorous' exercise, regardless of any physiological rationale, is often doomed to failure due to the perceived, or actual, motivational effort (intensity) required – namely, it's too much like hard work!

> Key point: Motivation involves which behaviours you choose to do, how persistent you are, whether you continue over time, and how intensive is your involvement in the behaviour.

Putting motivation in an historical context

Weiner (1992) suggests that the fundamental motivational question concerns the 'why?' of human action rather than the 'how?' Certainly this is a central theme reflected in this book – why is physical activity adopted, maintained, shunned or resumed?

As with much psychological research and theorising, the dominant themes, perspectives or paradigms in the study of human motivation have shifted a great deal over time. Initial perspectives emphasised people's motivation more in terms of mechanistic processes or 'drives', or what Weiner (1992) has described in terms of 'the machine' metaphor. Many behaviours were seen to be largely involuntary and predetermined, fixed and routine, and described in terms of energy transmission. Should the 'machine' be out of balance, movement takes place to restore the balance.

More contemporary views are 'social cognitive' in orientation. Bandura says that in the social cognitive view, people are 'neither driven by internal forces nor automatically shaped and controlled by external stimuli' (Bandura 1986: 18). In other words, we operate cognitive evaluations of behaviours, cognitions and environmental events in a reciprocal way ('reciprocal determinism') and anticipate future consequences. In this approach Bandura discusses the importance of self-regulatory and self-reflective aspects of behaviour:

> Another distinctive feature of social cognitive theory is the central role it assigns to self-regulatory functions. People do not behave just to suit the preferences of others. Much of their behavior is motivated and regulated by internal standards and self-evaluative reactions to their own actions.
>
> (Bandura 1986: 20)

By this process, people evaluate their actions, often against some expectation or desire, and then modify their actions accordingly. For example, some people may be motivated to exercise for weight control if they perceive a discrepancy between what they are currently like and what they want to be. The self-reflective elements of Bandura's social cognitive approach are central to human action. This operation of 'meta-cognition' (thinking about our own thoughts) is recognised through Bandura's seminal work on self-efficacy, and this will be discussed in more detail in Chapter 5.

Descriptive approaches to the study of physical activity motivation

A common approach to the study of motivation in physical activity settings has been to look at participation motives. This is a descriptive approach using self-reported perceived reasons for starting, maintaining or ceasing involvement in some form of physical activity. It could be argued that this atheoretical approach is limited in scope, but it does provide a useful starting point for understanding people's 'surface' motivation. It does not, of course, help explain physical activity involvement in more detailed or theoretical terms.

A great deal of the literature on motives has dealt with children, usually in volunteer sport situations (Gould 1987). A more limited literature exists looking at adults, although this includes more on exercise and health-related physical activity (Biddle 1995). Given the differences in both activities and perceptions that exist between children and adults, these two groups will be reviewed separately.

Descriptive research on adults

Typically, researchers in this field have asked questions concerning motives for participation and also about reasons for dropping out of activity. Questionnaires and structured interviews have been used.

Motives for participation

Several population surveys have addressed issues associated with participation motivation. With some exceptions, such as the Campbell's Survey of Well-Being (Wankel and Mummery 1993), the breadth of data collection attempted has precluded much theoretical work taking place. Consequently, the majority of such surveys provide descriptive data on beliefs, attitude statements and motives. Nevertheless, given the large samples often included in these works, these can provide valuable descriptive data.

In 1992, the results of the Allied Dunbar National Fitness Survey (ADNFS) (Sports Council and Health Education Authority 1992) were published. This was an ambitious project involving over 4,000 16–74 year olds from thirty regions of England. Home interviews took place on 1,840 men and 2,109 women for up to one and a half hours, with subsequent physical measures taken in the home and in mobile laboratories.

The home interview involved questions on involvement in physical activities as well as health, lifestyle and health-related behaviours, barriers and motivation for exercise, social background, personal attributes and general attitudes. The most important motivational factors for physical activity were 'to feel in good shape physically', 'to improve or maintain health', and 'to feel a sense of achievement'. Motives associated with weight control and physical appearance were also important for women. Motives of 'fun' were more likely to be reported by younger people whereas older respondents reported the factor of 'independence' to be more important than others.

A study of over 15,000 people from fifteen countries in the European Union found that the most frequently given reason for physical activity participation was to maintain good health, whereas socialisation and weight control were less likely to be endorsed (see results for the EU alongside the UK in Figure 2.1).

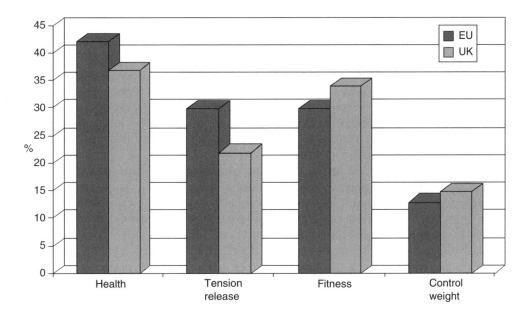

Figure 2.1 Responses (percentage of people) concerning selected motivating factors for participation from the EU (an average of fifteen countries, including the UK), and the UK (Zunft *et al.* 1999)

Reasons for ceasing participation

'Dropping out' of physical activity and exercise should not be seen as an 'all or none' phenomenon (Sonstroem 1988) but as an on-going process of change. For example, Sallis and Hovell (1990) have proposed a process model of exercise – the 'natural history model' (see Chapter 6) – in which at least two different routes could be taken by adults who cease participation. One route is to become sedentary while the other is to cease participation temporarily but return at a later date. Motivational factors affecting these routes may be different. Indeed, why some adults resume participation after a period of inactivity is still poorly understood.

One of the problems with research in this area is that once again only 'surface' reasons are offered, although one could argue that such responses are important to document. The ADNFS reported the reasons given for stopping regular participation in moderate to vigorous sport, exercise and active recreation. The three most frequently cited reasons were associated with work, loss of interest and the need for time for other things. The factors of marriage/change in partnership and having or looking after children were also important factors, but more so for women than men.

THE STUDY AND MEASUREMENT OF EXERCISE/PHYSICAL ACTIVITY BARRIERS

In discussing motives for participation, we have suggested differentiating motives for adoption from those of maintenance. Similarly, when discussing reasons for ceasing participation one could identify barriers that prevent people from being more active as well as the reasons why those who were previously active are no longer so.

Perceived lack of time is frequently cited as the major barrier to physical activity. Owen and Bauman (1992) reported on just over 5,000 sedentary Australians and found that the reason 'no time to exercise' was much more likely to be reported by those in the 25–54 age group compared with those over fifty-five years of age, data confirmed in a subsequent study in Australia (Booth *et al.* 1997) as well as the ADNFS.

In the ADNFS, reported barriers to preventing adults from taking more exercise were classified into five main types: physical, emotional, motivational, time and availability. This is a useful way of analysing barriers for large population surveys as it gives a wider picture of barriers and some information for possible interventions. Figure 2.2 shows the main gender differences for the main barriers in each of the categories, except 'availability'. Figure 2.3 shows age differences for women, and Figure 2.4 for men. Each barrier category is explained in more detail in Table 2.1.

Time barriers appeared to be the most important for both men and women, although women were likely to report emotional barriers to exercise (for example 'I'm not the sporty type') more than men. This is likely to be related to perceptions of competence (see Chapter 5). On a more anecdotal note, it is sad to think that participation in something as simple as cycling or jogging might be avoided on the basis of self-presentational concerns. It makes one wonder how people developed such self-presentations and whether early experiences of 'exercise' in school were not as appropriate as perhaps they should have been. Certainly one can understand the self-presentational concerns in sport where competence levels are so clearly displayed. Interestingly, Australian data show that where the cost of physical activity was seen as a barrier to participation, participants were more likely to adopt walking, showing the potential ease of involvement in this form of activity (Salmon *et al.* 2003).

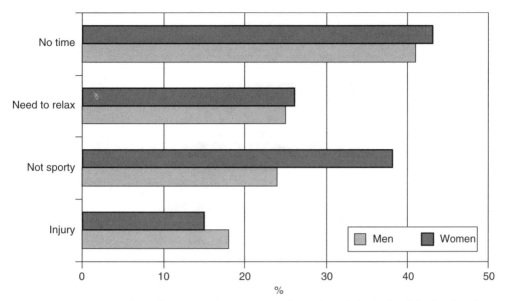

Figure 2.2 Percentage of English men and women reporting selected physical activity barriers from the ADNFS

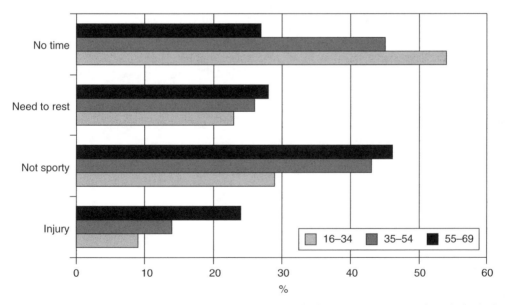

Figure 2.3 Percentage of three different age groups of English women reporting selected physical activity barriers from the ADNFS

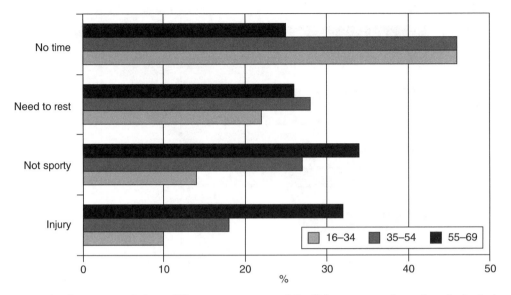

Figure 2.4 Percentage of three different age groups of English men reporting selected physical activity barriers from the ADNFS

Table 2.1 Factors given as barriers by people aged 16–69 years in the Allied Dunbar National Fitness Survey for England (Sports Council and Health Education Authority 1992)

Barrier label	Barriers
Physical	I have an injury or disability that stops me I'm too fat My health is not good enough I'm too old
Emotional	I'm not the sporty type I'm too shy or embarrassed I might get injured or damage my health
Motivational	I need to rest and relax in my spare time I haven't got the energy I'd never keep it up I don't enjoy physical activity
Time	I haven't got the time I don't have time because of my work I've got young children to look after
Availability	There is no one to do it with I can't afford it There are no suitable facilities nearby I haven't got the right clothes or equipment

Predictably, in the ADNFS, the physical and emotional barriers increased across the age groups, while, as reported, time barriers decreased, at least for those over fifty-five years of age. This again shows the importance of a lifespan approach.

Useful though the approach used in the ADNFS is, it does not provide a replicable instrument that has been psychometrically validated. In attempting to address this inconsistency in measurement, both Sechrist, Walker and Pender (1987) and Steinhardt and Dishman (1989) developed scales for the assessment of exercise barriers, as well as perceived benefits. Initial psychometric work by Steinhardt and Dishman revealed the barriers of time, effort, obstacles and 'limiting health'. Sechrist *et al.* identified barriers labelled exercise milieu, time expenditure, physical exertion and family encouragement. Little research has been done to further validate the scales although they do appear to reflect the barriers reported in population surveys.

Other personal correlates of physical activity in adults

Sallis and Owen (1999) and Trost *et al.* (2002) reviewed the demographic, biological, psychological and behavioural correlates of physical activity in adults. Key demographic correlates suggested that higher levels of physical activity were associated with higher levels of income and education, and with being male. Negative predictors were non-white ethnicity and age.

Psychological correlates were enjoyment of exercise, expected benefits, stronger intentions, fewer barriers and a positive and stable mood. In addition, they found that greater self-efficacy and self-motivation were positive for activity involvement. Behavioural correlates were activity during adulthood (but not childhood, suggesting weak or no tracking of physical activity) and the quality of dietary habits. In addition, they found that activity was more likely in those undertaking exercise programmes in the past and using processes (strategies) of behaviour change.

Descriptive research on children and youth

Much of the research on children's participation motivation tends to focus on competitive sport rather than more diverse aspects of exercise and physical activity. However, this is not surprising as children are less likely to participate in fitness pursuits currently favoured by adults, at least not until mid to late adolescence. Nevertheless, it is important that we understand more fully the reasons children give for participation or non-participation in recreational play or the taking of non-motorised forms of transport.

Motives for participation

Interviews with young people and their parents in England (Mulvihill, Rivers and Aggleton 2000) have shown that children aged 5–11 years are often physically active and are enthusiastic about activity. They are motivated by enjoyment and social elements of participation, while for those aged 11–15 years, enjoyment was important, itself enhanced when an element of choice was evident, and feelings of well-being. Motives for weight control started to emerge in girls at this age.

Research in Finland (Telama and Silvennoinen 1979) of over 3,000 11–19 year olds showed clear changes in motivation for physical activity as a function of age and gender. Boys and younger adolescents were more interested in achieving success in competition but by late adolescence very few showed interest in this factor. This trend was reversed for motives associated with relaxation and recreation. Fitness motivation was strongest among those who often thought about sport and took part in sports club activities. This fitness motive was unimportant for 18–19 year olds, or for those uninterested or inactive in sport. This has important implications for the way we promote fitness in youth and illustrates the need to distinguish between sport and exercise.

Data from over 3,000 children in Northern Ireland (Van Wersch 1997; Van Wersch, Trew and Turner 1992) have shown that 'interest in physical education' remains relatively constant for boys from age eleven to nineteen years, whereas during the same period interest declines sharply for girls. 'Interest' was assessed by questionnaire items pertaining to attitude, behaviour, motivation and perceptions of fun in the PE setting.

Data from the English Sports Council's survey of young people and sport (Mason 1995) shows that from a sample of over 4,000 6–16 year olds, motives are diverse, ranging from general enjoyment to fitness and friendships. Similar results have been reported in North American research such as the Canada Fitness Survey (1983a) which sampled over 4,500 young people aged 10–19 years of age.

North American research (Canada Fitness Survey 1983a; Gould and Petlichkoff 1988; Wankel and Kreisel 1985) generally confirms reports from Europe that children are motivated for a variety of reasons. Reviews have concluded that children are motivated for diverse reasons, including fun and enjoyment, learning and improving skills, being with friends, success and winning, and physical fitness and health. The latter factor might also include weight control and body appearance for older youth. However, more research is needed to understand the differences in motives across activities, levels of participation, and developmental stages, although so far the research shows some similarity in motives across settings and groups.

Barriers to physical activity in young people

As with motives for participation, there appear to be numerous barriers to physical activity in children and youth. For example, Coakley and White (1992) conducted sixty in-depth interviews with 13–23 year olds, half of whom had decided to participate in one of five different sports initiatives in their local town. The others had either ceased involvement or had decided not to participate at all. The decision to participate or not appeared to be influenced by perceptions of competence, by external constraints, such as money and opposite sex friends, degree of support from significant others and past experiences, including school PE. Negative memories of school PE included feelings of boredom and incompetence, lack of choice and negative evaluation from peers. Feelings of embarrassment in sport settings, mainly due to perceived incompetence or concerns over self-presentation associated with their physique during puberty, have been reported elsewhere (Mason 1995).

Time has even been reported as a barrier for 5–11 year olds (Mulvihill, Rivers and Aggleton 2000), perhaps reflecting less discretionary time being allowed by parents (Sturm 2005). Environmental barriers, such as road traffic and fear of safety may be interrelated with such barriers (Davis and Jones 1996, 1997; Gomez *et al.* 2004). However, somewhat surprisingly, Sallis *et al.* (2000) found only 33 per cent of studies of barriers with adolescents to show associations with physical activity. All three studies they located for children, however, did show the expected relationship. Our own review of correlates of physical activity for adolescent girls (Biddle *et al.* 2005) showed that time barriers were associated with less physical activity, as were barriers related to school work and the perceived effort required to be active.

Box 2.1 Media portrayals and perceptions of sport and physical activity for girls

We recently conducted focus group interviews with adolescent girls in Scotland to study the influences on their participation in physical activity. One theme that emerged concerned images generated through the media. Girls spoke of two problems relating to females in the media. First, they spoke of a lack of media coverage of females in sport. Choi (2000) reported that media coverage is low and remains so (less than 11 per cent in national newspaper sports coverage) at a time when more women are taking part in high level sport. Even when high profile performances of women are reported, they receive less coverage than equivalent performances of their male counterparts. One girl from our focus group interviews said '... and there could be a brilliant women's football player out there and you don't know, you only know about someone who isn't any good but he's a guy and everyone advertises it on TV and everything'. Does this affect levels of physical activity or just those wanting to play sport?

The girls also spoke of the media representation of the ideal girl as being thin and beautiful. Overall, the poor and uneven nature of representation of women in sports media provides a clear message that women in sport are less important than men.

Key point: Correlates of physical activity can involve simple reasons for getting involved as well as barriers to involvement. These are useful but superficial psychological constructs that may not fully explain participation.

Other personal correlates of physical activity in young people

Results for demographic and biological variables in children from the review by Sallis *et al.* (2000) showed that greater physical activity was associated with being male and, surprisingly, having an overweight parent. This gender difference is a highly consistent finding (Van Mechelen *et al.* 2000; Vilhjalmsson and Kristjansdottir 2003; Wold and Hendry 1998). Inconsistent findings were reported for age and body weight/fatness, while SES and ethnicity were unrelated to physical activity in this age group. However, English children in lower socio-economic groups do show more rapid increases in obesity (Stamatakis *et al.* 2005). For adolescents, greater physical activity was found for boys compared with girls and non-Hispanic whites compared with all other ethnic groups. Less physical activity was associated with increasing age. Body weight/fatness was inconsistently associated and SES unrelated to physical activity. Biddle *et al.*'s systematic review showed that the physical activity of adolescent girls was less for those from families with lower incomes and parental education (Biddle *et al.* 2005). Recent qualitative research (Mulvihill, Rivers and Aggleton 2000) suggests that body weight per se may be less important than perceptions of body image and self-presentation in physical activity settings.

The finding that SES, in Sallis *et al.*'s (2000) analysis, is not consistently related to physical activity is surprising and differs from other sources, such as Biddle *et al.* (2005). Wold and Hendry (1998) report on the social inequalities in participation that are likely to be reproduced across generations. This social reproduction may be accounted for through the social position of parents and their level of physical activity, as well as the link between education and access to sports clubs.

For children, less physical activity was associated with greater perceived barriers while greater activity was related to intentions and preferences for physical activity. For adolescents, only achievement orientation, perceived competence and intention to be active were positively associated, and depression negatively associated, with physical activity. A consensus statement from the UK (Cavill, Biddle and Sallis 2001) suggested that activity may also be related to perceptions of enjoyment, self-efficacy, competence, control and autonomy, positive attitudes towards activity and a perception of few barriers and many benefits. However, much of this research is cross-sectional using self-report measures of unknown validity. Better research designs are required.

For children, Sallis *et al.* (2000) found that only healthy diet and previous physical activity had consistent positive associations with activity, whereas for adolescents it was sensation seeking, previous activity and participation in community sports. No consistent association was found between physical activity and sedentary behaviours in children (for example, TV viewing), but time in sedentary pursuits in adolescents after school and at weekends was inversely related to physical activity. Meta-analytic data show that, overall, the association between physical activity and TV viewing in young people is very small (Marshall *et al.* 2004), suggesting that there may be time for the two behaviours to co-exist.

> Key point: Individual 'personal' correlates are best categorised as demographic, biological, psychological and behavioural.

Early studies of physical activity correlates

Subsequent chapters address theoretical approaches to the study of physical activity behaviour. In this section we discuss early research that did not rely on known theoretical approaches of the time. This is not necessarily to single out such studies as weak but merely to differentiate them from those based on theories developed in other settings and branches of psychology. In fact, some of these studies could be labelled as 'pioneering' and have laid the foundation for research in 'exercise psychology'.

Comparisons of adherers and dropouts

A number of studies attempted to differentiate exercise adherers from non-adherers on the basis of psychological and other variables (Dishman and Gettman 1980). For example, data from the Ontario Exercise Heart Collaborative Study showed that adherence to a post-coronary exercise programme was related to the convenience of the exercise facility, perceptions of the exercise programme and family/lifestyle factors (Andrew *et al.* 1981; Andrew and Parker 1979). In particular, spouse support was a significant predictor of adherence. Interestingly, social support remains an underdeveloped area of research in physical activity.

One of the earliest attempts to characterise the exercise 'dropout' was reported by Massie and Shephard (1971). They found that both physiological and psychological factors at entry to a fitness programme differed between adherers and dropouts such that dropouts tended to be overweight, but stronger, were more likely to smoke (a finding supported by Andrew *et al.* 1981) and were more extroverted. Other studies have also reported physiological differences between adherers and dropouts at entry to a programme, and factors such as muscle fibre type (Inger and Dahl 1979), functional capacity (Blumenthal *et al.* 1982), and body composition

(Dishman 1981) have been significant. In all cases the most likely explanation is that biological factors which make exercise a more difficult or less reinforcing experience will predict dropout. For example, exercisers with greater amounts of body fat will experience more discomfort in exercise, and may also experience some embarrassment.

Such notions led to the development of a 'psychobiological model' through a widely cited study of the discriminating power of physiological and psychological variables in predicting adherence to exercise (Dishman and Gettman 1980). These researchers investigated the predictive utility of both psychological and biological variables in a prospective design. A twenty-week exercise programme was used whereby all participants were assessed at entry on a variety of psychological measures, including self-motivation, physical activity attitudes, health locus of control, perceived competence and attraction to physical activity. Biological variables assessed were metabolic capacity (predicted oxygen consumption), body weight and percentage body fat.

Results showed that both psychological and biological factors predicted adherence after twenty weeks. This led the authors to propose a 'psychobiological model' of adherence. Specifically, adherers and dropouts could be significantly discriminated from each other on the basis of body fat, self-motivation and body weight. Further analysis showed that just under 80 per cent overall (and slightly less for dropouts) could be classified correctly as adherers or dropouts based on their scores on these three variables.

Although a psychobiological model retains some intuitive appeal, it has not been possible to support it fully since the Dishman and Gettman (1980) research. While psychological and physiological variables may interact to predict participation, which variables become important may differ across exercise settings. For example, adherence to a high intensity aerobic endurance programme is likely to require high self-motivation and favourable physiological

---

Box 2.2 Adherence or compliance?

When discussing the topic of involvement in physical activity and exercise, one can often get into a definitional minefield. Early on in the study of exercise psychology it was quite common to refer to exercise 'compliance', a term borrowed from medical settings where people were under some compulsion to follow a medical programme of rehabilitation or other treatment. However, is exercise the same thing? Should we talk about 'compliance' to exercise? It creates images of compulsion that we want to avoid in exercise promotion.

Other researchers have used the word 'adherence'. For example, whereas exercise psychologists use the word adherence to mean staying with (or dropping out of) an exercise programme, others have broadened the construct to refer to the study of participation in exercise from a multidisciplinary approach. Using it in this way means that it goes beyond the construct of 'motivation'. For example, adhering to an exercise programme has physiological effects that can then legitimately be studied under the title 'adherence'. Motivation, as we discuss here, is more focused on choice, persistence, etc. and reflects a psychological approach to involvement.

Finally, if compliance, adherence and motivation are discussed mainly in the context of structured exercise, where does this leave habitual physical activity, such as walking to the shops or cycling to work? This now opens up a difficult issue. How volitional is this behaviour? You may cycle to work because there is no other alternative. The increasing study of habitual physical activity, to complement that of exercise programmes, needs to address this issue more closely. Certainly, the use of the word 'compliance' seems inappropriate here also. We would recommend that the word 'adherence' is best and that it encompasses various determinants, one set of which are psychological.

factors such as a high percentage of Type I ('slow twitch') muscle fibres and low body fat. However, this may not be true for other exercise regimes or habitual physical activity of an unstructured nature. Similarly, the psychobiological model was only developed on sixty-six people and is therefore in need of validation with larger and more diverse samples.

Correlates of sedentary behaviour

Although studies of correlates of physical activity make the assumption that little or no physical activity is the same as being 'sedentary', we prefer to argue that it is equally or more important to identify actual sedentary behaviours and their correlates. For example, much has been said about the apparent negative effect of excessive television (TV) viewing in young people (American Academy of Pediatrics 1986; Australian College of Paediatrics 1994; Kaiser Family Foundation 2004), although some of the data and claims can be debated (Biddle and Gorely 2005; Marshall *et al.* 2004). Given that TV viewing is highly prevalent in young people (Marshall, Gorely and Biddle 2006), it might be informative to understand the correlates of this one sedentary behaviour. In a systematic review of sixty-eight studies (Gorely, Marshall and Biddle 2004), we found that consistent positive associations with the amount of TV viewing were for the variables of non-white ethnicity, body weight, between-meal snacking, parents' TV viewing habits, weekend and having a TV in the bedroom. Negative associations were found for parental income and education, and the number of parents in the house. Many of these are largely non-modifiable. Gender, other markers of SES, body fatness, cholesterol levels, aerobic fitness, strength, other indicators of fitness, self-perceptions, emotional support, physical activity, other diet variables and being an only child all had a consistent lack of association with TV viewing. Although surprising in some cases, other data on physical activity, body fatness and TV viewing in young people (Marshall *et al.* 2004) support these conclusions. TV viewing may be part of a wider sedentary or active lifestyle and may be better studied alongside other behaviours rather than in isolation (Biddle and Gorely 2005; Jago and Baranowski 2004; Marshall *et al.* 2002).

> Key point: Correlates of physical activity may not be the same as correlates of sedentary behaviours.

Chapter summary and conclusions

Central to our understanding of physical activity is motivation. Clearly such an all-embracing construct cannot explain all that we do, but it remains at the core of the psychology of physical activity correlates. In this chapter, therefore, we have:

- defined motivation
- reviewed the literature on descriptive approaches to participation motives for both adults and young people
- described key barriers to physical activity
- summarised key demographic, biological, psychological and behavioural correlates of physical activity and sedentary behaviour for children and adults
- described some early exercise determinants research, including studies of comparisons of adherers and dropouts and a psychobiological model.

The chapter has been necessarily broad to allow for a more focused discussion in the subsequent chapters on physical activity correlates. In summary, we conclude:

- despite well-known benefits, only a minority of people in industrialised countries are sufficiently physically active to have a beneficial effect on their health. This necessitates a greater understanding of the determinants (correlates) of involvement in exercise and physical activity, including motivation
- motivation involves different behaviours, including choice, persistence, continuing motivation and intensity
- descriptive research on participation motives has tended to reflect motives for children's involvement in sport and adults' involvement in exercise and recreational physical activity. For children and youth common motives are fun, skill development, affiliation, fitness, success and challenge, whereas for adults motives change across stages of the lifecycle. Younger adults are motivated more by challenge, skill development and fitness, whereas older adults are more interested in participation for reasons of health, relaxation and enjoyment
- key barriers are lack of time and, for young people, issues of safety and feelings of incompetence
- early research on exercise determinants involved static comparisons of profiles of exercisers and non-exercisers, but did identify some potentially important variables, such as self-motivation. Such studies usually lacked a theoretical focus
- a psychobiological model was proposed but results have been equivocal. However, the concept of both psychological and biological variables explaining exercise participation is still valid
- correlates of sedentary behaviour in the form of TV viewing can be identified, but they are largely non-modifiable. TV viewing may be better studied alongside other sedentary and active behaviours rather than in isolation.

3 Theories based on attitudes and beliefs

Active people have attitude!

The first letter of the psychological alphabet is A for Attitude.

(Jung, quoted by Hamilton 1929)

Purpose of the chapter

The purpose of this chapter is to review key attitude-based theories used in research on physical activity. Specifically, in this chapter we aim to:

- define and delimit the attitude construct
- briefly overview the early descriptive approach to the study of physical activity attitudes
- review the theoretical foundations and contemporary physical activity research of the Theory of Planned Behaviour
- summarise the Health Belief Model and research findings from physical activity
- briefly discuss the Health Action Process Approach and Protection Motivation Theory in the light of physical activity and health research
- reach a consensus on the role of attitudes in physical activity.

Health promotion campaigns are often aimed at changing beliefs or knowledge on the assumption that such changes are necessary to bring about a change in behaviour. Unfortunately, changes in awareness, attitudes, beliefs and knowledge far from guarantee changes in behaviour, although they may be an important first step in such a process. Although any inference of a causal link between beliefs and behaviour cannot usually be sustained, it does seem reasonable that beliefs and attitudes will have some influence on our actions. Indeed, such an assumption has occupied social psychologists for many years in health research (Conner and Norman 1996; Stroebe and Stroebe 1995).

A number of theoretical models have been proposed that attempt to explain the role of attitudes in human behaviour. The purpose of this chapter, therefore, is to outline the major integrating theories in health-related attitudes, and to report research findings that have a bearing on physical activity behaviours.

Defining attitudes

It is often seen to be a statement of the obvious that attitudes are about feelings and behaviour. However, the study of attitudes in social psychology has a long, yet controversial, history, particularly when attempting to predict behaviours from stated attitudes. Even so, Olson and Zanna report that 'attitude and attitude change remain among the most extensively researched topics by social psychologists' (Olson and Zanna 1993: 118). Unfortunately, the extensive usage of the word attitude in everyday speech has rendered it prone to misinterpretation, or to be used in a way that is ill-defined or too vague. For example, the Allied Dunbar National Fitness Survey (ADNFS) (Sports Council and Health Education Authority 1992) uses the sub-heading 'Attitudes to exercise and fitness' to cover a range of psychological factors associated with exercise participation. In one sense they do cover 'attitudes', but they do not refer to well-known social psychological theories of attitude prominent in the health and exercise literature.

Attitude has been defined as 'a psychological tendency that is expressed by evaluating a particular entity with some degree of favour or disfavour' (Eagly and Chaiken 1993: 1), suggesting that the affective element of attitude is key. However, a three-component model of attitude (Hovland and Rosenberg 1960) suggests that in addition to attitudes having an affective (emotional) component, they can also have a belief (cognitive) and behavioural component (see Figure 3.1).

Attitude, like personality, motivation and some other psychological constructs, is hypothetical and not open to direct observation. The responses often used to infer attitudes can be either verbal or non-verbal in each of the cognitive, affective and behavioural categories of the three-component model. These are illustrated in Table 3.1, with examples from physical activity. In addition, Olson and Zanna (1993) propose that most attitude theorists agree that attitudes are represented in memory.

Early attitude-based research in health concerned the nature of beliefs. Indeed, the question of why people do, or do not, seek health care has been an important one for health psychologists and other social scientists over the past few decades. The field was initially typified by diverse findings and an apparently irreconcilable set of behavioural predictors. However, in the 1950s a group of American social psychologists attempted to integrate the work on health behaviours by developing an attitude-based model of health decision-making – the Health Belief Model (HBM) (Becker *et al.* 1977; Conner and Norman 1994; Janz and Becker 1984; Sheeran and Abraham 1996).

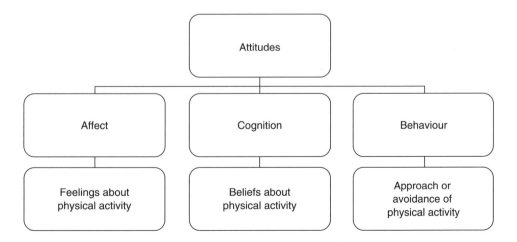

Figure 3.1 The three-component view of attitudes applied to physical activity

Table 3.1 Inferring physical activity attitudes from different responses (adapted from Ajzen 1988)

Response mode	Response category		
	Cognitive	*Affective*	*Behavioural*
Verbal	Expressions of *beliefs* concerning physical activity	Expressions of *feelings* (likes, dislikes, etc.) concerning physical activity	Expressions of intention to be physically active or inactive
Non-verbal	Perceptual reactions to physical activity	Physiological reactions (independent of effort) to physical activity	Approach or avoidance of physical activity and related contexts

Key point: Attitude is usually about feelings but it will also involve beliefs and behaviour.

The Health Belief Model

The HBM developed from Kurt Lewin's 'field theory' and an expectancy-value approach to motivation and behaviour. This means that people often make decisions about behaviours based on the *expectations* of what might happen if they do or do not act in that way (outcomes) and also on what *value* (importance) they place on such outcomes. Lewin's phenomenological perspective advocated that behaviour is influenced by the individual's characteristics and the environment. Lewin's 'field theory' stated that we exist in a 'life space' of regions of both positive and negative value, and forces attract and repel us from these. Illness is a region of negative value and hence we are motivated to avoid it most of the time and this formed a central tenet of the HBM.

The HBM was devised in an attempt to predict health behaviours, primarily in response to low rates of adoption and adherence of preventive health care behaviours. Becker *et al.* (1977) stated that the HBM was adopted as an organising framework for four main reasons:

- the model has potentially modifiable variables
- the model is derived from sound psychological theory
- although the HBM was first developed to account for preventive health behaviours, it has also been employed successfully to account for 'sick-role' and 'illness' behaviours. 'Sick-role' behaviours are primarily associated with seeking treatment or a remedy for illness, whereas 'illness' behaviours are primarily associated with seeking advice or help on the nature and/or extent of the illness
- the HBM is consistent with other health behaviour models.

The HBM has been applied to a wide variety of health behaviours, including physical activity, although the literature on physical activity is not extensive. The model hypothesises that people will not seek (preventive) health behaviours unless:

- they possess minimal levels of health motivation and knowledge
- view themselves as potentially vulnerable
- view the condition as threatening

- are convinced of the efficacy of the 'treatment'
- see few difficulties in undertaking the action.

These factors can be modified by socio-economic and demographic factors, as well as prompts (referred to as 'cues to action' in the model), such as media campaigns or the illness of a close friend or relative. The HBM is illustrated in Figure 3.2.

The majority of the HBM research has involved illness, sick-role or preventive behaviours and has 'a clear-cut avoidance orientation' (Rosenstock 1974: 333) and has often involved the study of one-shot behaviours such as clinic attendance. Its applicability to physical activity, therefore, is questionable, but it may apply to activity contexts that involve one-off decisions, as we discuss later.

In 1984, after a decade of systematic research using the HBM, a state-of-the-art review was published (Janz and Becker 1984). It was reported that 'the HBM has continued to be a major organising framework for explaining and predicting acceptance of health and medical care recommendations' (Janz and Becker 1984: 1). They concluded that:

- there was substantial support for the model across more than forty studies
- the HBM is the most extensively researched model of health-related behaviours
- 'perceived barriers', when studied, were the most consistently powerful predictor
- beliefs associated with susceptibility appeared to be more important in preventive health behaviours

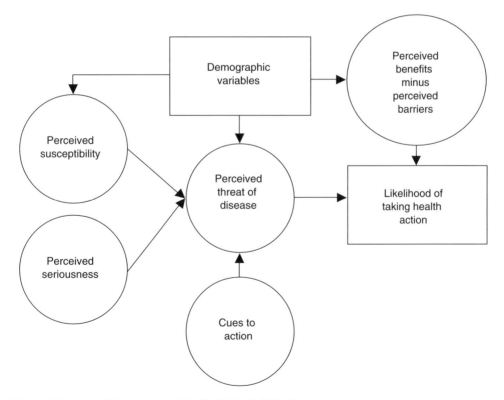

Figure 3.2 A simplified version of the Health Belief Model

- beliefs in the perceived benefits of action seemed more important in sick-role and illness behaviours
- despite the variability of measuring instruments, the HBM has remained robust across a wide variety of settings and with a wide variety of research techniques.

Despite this optimistic view, Harrison, Mullen and Green (1992) went further and tested the HBM with adults using meta-analysis but with much stricter criteria for inclusion of studies than Janz and Becker (1984). From 147 research studies, Harrison *et al.* excluded all but sixteen on various criteria, including lack of a behavioural dependent variable, not measuring susceptibility, severity, benefits and costs in the same study, and lack of information about scale reliability. Overall, small but significant effect sizes were found for all four dimensions of the model but effect sizes varied greatly across the dimensions. In addition, they reported that prospective studies had significantly smaller effect sizes than retrospective ones, thus further weakening the case in favour of the HBM.

From evidence on physical activity and the HBM (for example, Biddle and Ashford 1988; Lindsay-Reid and Osborn 1980), it appears that the optimistic conclusions of Janz and Becker (1984) and, to a certain extent the low but significant effect sizes reported in Harrison *et al.*'s (1992) meta-analysis, do not necessarily hold true for physical activity. Although isolated variables, such as barriers, may relate to some physical activity behaviours, the model as a whole has been relatively unsuccessful in predicting the adoption and/or maintenance of physical activity and exercise. Indeed, it could be argued that there is greater support for beliefs about health concerns and worries from the HBM predicting non-participation. For example, some people may believe that exercise will cause more harm than good, with such beliefs often based on myths and stereotyping.

There is little doubt about the general heuristic appeal of the HBM. However, a number of points can be made in criticism of the model and associated research, and in particular in relation to its use in physical activity settings (Godin 1994; Sonstroem 1988; Stroebe and Stroebe 1995; Wallston and Wallston 1985).

First, one must question the holistic nature of the model. Is it one model or merely a collection of individual variables? Indeed some have argued that because the list of potential variables is so large, the model is untestable (Wallston and Wallston 1985). Similarly, what relationships exist between the variables and how should the model variables be tested? Some research studies test the variables in linear combination while others test interactions. In addition, Harrison *et al.*'s (1992) meta-analysis tested the effect of individual variables only.

Second, there has been a lack of consistency in the operationalising of variables and the measuring tools used. Psychometric developments have been made in the measurement of exercise benefits, outcomes and barriers (Sechrist, Walker and Pender 1987; Steinhardt and Dishman 1989) but these instruments were not developed as tools for the direct assessment of the HBM.

The illness-avoidance orientation of the model is generally not appropriate for the explanation or prediction of physical activity. However, the increasing recognition of physical activity as a health behaviour, manifesting itself in promotion schemes such as family doctor-initiated 'exercise on prescription' schemes (Fox *et al.* 1997; Taylor 1999) may mean that the HBM is an appropriate framework for some physical activity contexts.

Key point: The Health Belief Model has intuitive appeal, but its application to physical activity has not been clearly demonstrated.

Attitudes towards physical activity:
early descriptive approaches

The study of attitudes has interested sport and exercise scientists for a long time, although the initial research efforts were primarily descriptive (Kenyon 1968) and failed to specify clear behavioural targets for the attitudes. For example, it is unlikely that agreement with a general statement concerning one's 'liking' for physical activity will predict specific physical activity behaviours such as swimming or walking. Disaffection with such limitations led to the development of the theory of reasoned action by American social psychologists Icek Ajzen (latterly changing the spelling of his name to Aizen) and Martin Fishbein (Ajzen and Fishbein 1980; Fishbein and Ajzen 1975). Ajzen's modification of this model – the Theory of Planned behaviour – has been tested extensively in the physical activity and health literature and will be discussed later.

Models and theories linking attitudes
and behaviour in physical activity research

The descriptive approach to attitude measurement inevitably led researchers to question whether attitudes actually did predict behaviours at all – the 'attitude–behaviour discrepancy'. Indeed, Eiser states that this discrepancy is 'essentially an artefact of the haphazard selection of *specific* behavioural indices which researchers have tried to relate to *general* verbal measures of attitudes' (emphasis added), but goes on to say that 'if we are as selective in our choice of behavioural indices as we are at present in our choice of verbal indices, the "attitude–behaviour discrepancy" may disappear as a substantive problem' (Eiser 1986: 60). Ajzen and Fishbein sought to increase the strength of association between attitudes and behaviours by not only stating hypothesised predecessors of attitude, but also saying that attitudes and behaviour measures must be compatible, thus having a degree of correspondence. For example, generalised attitudes towards physical activity will predict participation in jogging less well (if at all) than attitudes towards jogging. Of course, better measure will not ensure perfect associations between attitudes and behaviour, but correspondence between measures is a prudent approach to research in this area.

The Theory of Reasoned Action (TRA)

Proposed by Ajzen and Fishbein (Ajzen and Fishbein 1980; Fishbein and Ajzen 1975), the TRA is concerned with 'the causal antecedents of volitional behaviour' (Ajzen 1988: 117). It is based on the assumption that intention is an immediate determinant of behaviour, and that intention, in turn, is predicted from attitude and subjective (social) normative factors. The TRA, however, was proposed to predict 'volitional behaviour' – behaviour where essentially the motivation of the individual was paramount and no external barriers existed (Eagly and Chaiken 1993). The TRA is illustrated in Figure 3.3 and has been used extensively in early research on physical activity and exercise.

Ajzen and Fishbein suggested that the attitude component of the model is a function of the beliefs held about the specific behaviour, as well as the evaluation, or value, of the likely outcomes. The measurement of such variables, they suggest, should be highly specific to the behaviour in question in order to achieve correspondence, or compatibility, between assessed attitude/subjective norm questions and the behaviour being predicted. It is recommended that questionnaire item content for testing the TRA be derived from interview

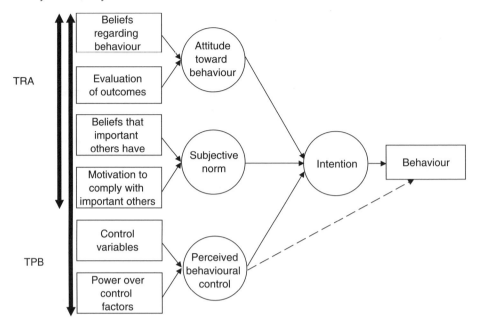

Figure 3.3 Theories of Reasoned Action (TRA) and Planned Behaviour (TPB)

material gathered from the population to be studied. Four factors should be considered in terms of achieving correspondence:

- action: attitude and behaviour need to be assessed in relation to a specific action, such as taking part in an exercise class, rather than a general attitude object such as physical activity
- target: reference should be made to specific target groups, such as exercisers, or specified significant others
- context: reference should be made to the context in which the behaviour takes place (for example '... at this health club')
- time: time should be clearly specified (for example 'attending this exercise class three times/week over the next two months').

Ajzen (1988) proposed that these four factors should be assessed at the same level of generality/specificity. Of course, very high correspondence, such as predicting attendance at the fitness club on Tuesdays from items that refer only to exercising at the club on Tuesdays, will have limited generalisability and, indeed, may appear trivial. While vague attitude measures about 'exercise' may be less than precise and be weak predictors, we also want to have the ability to generalise, thus some compromise between the two may sometimes be necessary, depending on what it is we wish to predict. Kenyon's (1968) 'attitude toward physical activity' (ATPA) scale, for example, assesses only the target (physical activity) and not the action, context or time. Perhaps this has led to some researchers being confused about the role of attitudes in physical activity. For example, Dishman and Sallis (1994) concluded, in their review of studies of supervised and unsupervised settings, that 'attitudes' are largely unrelated to physical activity. This is a surprising conclusion given the clear evidence showing that both intentions and attitudes are related to physical activity when appropriate theoretical models, such as the TRA, are used (Hagger, Chatzisarantis and Biddle 2002; Hausenblas, Carron and Mack 1997). Similarly, King *et al.* (1992) say that intentions do not predict actual behaviour in adult studies of exercise. This also is not correct and, indeed, intentions are even better predictors of physical activity than attitudes (Hagger, Chatzisarantis and Biddle 2002). Correlations between intention and physical activity are consistently positive and statistically significant. Indeed, Sallis and Owen, in reference to meta-analytic evidence from Hausenblas *et al.* (1997), describe the correlations between intentions and exercise as 'substantial' (Sallis and Owen 1999: 118).

The subjective norm component of the TRA ('normative component') is comprised of the beliefs of significant others and the extent that one wishes or is motivated to comply with such beliefs or people. The relative importance of the attitudinal and normative components will depend on the situation under investigation. For example, one might hypothesise that adolescent health behaviours, in some contexts, will be more strongly influenced by the normative component (expressed through peer influence) than the attitudinal component, but that this trend may be reversed with adults.

The Theory of Reasoned Action and physical activity

The TRA has received a great deal of attention in social psychology generally (Ajzen 1988; Sheppard *et al.* 1988) and in health contexts (Conner and Armitage 1998; Conner and Sparks 1996; Stroebe and Stroebe 1995). Although not without its critics, particularly in respect of the causal structure of the model and emphasis on volitional behaviour (Liska 1984), it has also been recommended and used in physical activity research (Doganis and Theodorakis 1995; Godin 1993, 1994; McAuley and Courneya 1993a).

The work of Gaston Godin and co-workers in Canada has provided the most extensive test of the TRA in exercise settings and he was the first to review the research on physical activity. Godin (1993) reported that about 30 per cent of the variance in intention is explained by the attitudinal and normative components of the TRA, although the attitudinal component is nearly always the stronger of the two predictors. Indeed, the normative component has been inconsistently associated with physical activity participation.

Subsequently, two meta-analyses have been conducted using the TRA and the Theory of Planned Behaviour (TPB). Hausenblas *et al.* (1997) analysed thirty-one exercise studies, yielding 162 effect sizes (ES) with over 10,000 participants, and they found that intention had a large effect on exercise behaviour, and attitude had a large effect on intention. The effect of attitude was twice that of subjective norm. Similar findings were reported by Hagger and colleagues (Hagger, Chatzisarantis and Biddle 2002) with correlations of 0.35 between attitude and behaviour, 0.60 between attitude and intention, and 0.51 between intention and behaviour.

Godin and Shephard (1986a) tested the predictive utility of Kenyon's model against the TRA. In terms of predicting intention to be physically active and actual past exercise behaviour, the TRA attitude component was superior to the subdomains of Kenyon's model, thus supporting our earlier statements about the need to measure specific attitudinal factors to achieve a stronger prediction of behaviour. In a further test of the theory, Godin and Shephard (1986b) studied twelve to fourteen year old Canadian children. They found that boys were more active than girls and that boys had a greater intention to exercise, and higher scores on the attitudinal and normative components of the TRA, although these declined in both boys and girls across the three cohorts studied. Overall, the TRA was only partially supported in its ability to predict exercise intentions. The attitude component was found to be a better predictor of intention than the normative component and is illustrative, in this respect, of many other exercise TRA studies.

The Theory of Reasoned Action: conclusion and critique

The TRA has received support in exercise contexts, and Godin suggests that 'when attitude is measured within a proper theoretical framework, it seems an important determinant of exercise behavior' (Godin 1994: 122). The TRA qualifies as one such 'proper theoretical framework'. Based on the evidence presented, the TRA attitudinal component appears to be influential in predicting intentions to be physical active and intentions predict behaviour to a certain extent. From a practical standpoint this suggests that interventions that attempt to alter beliefs and affective perceptions of the outcomes of physical activity may be useful.

Although the normative component of the TRA has not been a strong predictor of intentions in physical activity studies, it has sometimes contributed in a small way. Interventions that are possible include public health campaigns that persuade the public that exercise is 'normal' and not just for the young, fit and 'sporty'. Unfortunately, the evidence from the Allied Dunbar National Fitness Survey shows that personal beliefs that they are 'not the sporty type' are strong barriers to physical activity, particularly for women. However, subjective norms, such as group norms influenced through the role of the exercise leader, may play an important motivational role for those already possessing positive attitudes (Smith and Biddle 1999). More work is needed on social modelling effects in physical activity.

The TRA has not been without its critics. For example, the following points highlight issues for consideration:

- the TRA is a unidirectional model and fails to offer the possibility that variables in the model can act in a reciprocal manner
- the model relies solely on cognitions and omits other potentially important determinants of action, such as environmental influences
- the TRA predicts behaviour from measures of behavioural intention taken at one point in time. Similar attitudinal models of behaviour (Bentler and Speckart 1981; Triandis 1977) take into account prior behaviour. In the exercise context, 'habitual' physical activity is often the goal of public health initiatives and therefore research may usefully investigate the role of past behaviour in addition to other TRA variables, and this might include 'conscious' processing of the pros and cons of physical activity (as one might expect in a theory of *reasoned* action), as well as the less conscious modes of processing, such as the routine of walking to work when one does not posses a car or have public transport available. In other words, little or no conscious decision-making is required. As it stands, the TRA may only predict new behaviours rather than habitual ones. The distinction between activity adoption and maintenance is important. However, the role of past behaviour is a difficult one to judge at times. It can appear rather obvious, and even unhelpful if we wish to identify behavioural determinants, to state that past behaviour is the best predictor of current or intended behaviour. However, it does suggest that prior activity habits are important (Buckworth and Dishman 2002)
- the distinction between intentions and expectations may be important (Olson and Zanna 1993). We could decide (intention) to exercise but realise that it is rather too difficult

(expectation). This is similar to Kendzierski's (1990) distinction between exercise decision-making and exercise implementation

- the TRA was developed to account for behaviours that are under volitional control (Ajzen 1988). Consequently, the theory may not predict behaviours where other factors may be influential. In the case of physical activity, there may be a number of behavioural barriers preventing the behaviour being totally volitional (for example, responsibilities to others, job, distance from facilities, etc.). A revised TRA – the 'Theory of Planned behaviour' (TPB; see later in this chapter) – is an attempt to account for behaviour under 'incomplete' volitional control

- insufficient attention has been paid to the measurement of behaviour within the TRA. Without an accurate measure of the behaviour, the principle of correspondence cannot be applied satisfactorily. This casts some doubt on several studies, such as when assessment relies on unvalidated self-reports or uses inappropriate 'objective' measures, such as pedometers for people who get their physical activity predominantly through cycling or swimming

- the TRA allows the investigation of the interrelationships between attitudes, subjective norms, intentions and a single behaviour. It does not account for alternative behaviours. For example, although many people intend to be more physically active, few see this through to action in a sustained way (Department of Health 2004b). This could be due to physical activity being of lower priority than other behaviours, and so just does not get to the top of the 'things to do'

- intention should predict behaviour quite well when both intention and behaviour are measured in close proximity or, in the case of measurement taking place some time apart, the prediction will be affected by how intentions change during this time interval (Ajzen and Fishbein 1980). This is the issue of 'intentional stability' and is one that has largely been ignored in physical activity research. Recent evidence suggests that while attitude–intention links are stable over time (at least over six weeks), behaviour–intention relationships weaken over time (Chatzisarantis *et al.* 2005)

- finally, there appears to be a potential discrepancy between the inconsistent role of subjective norms in using the TRA and the belief that social support is a determinant of physical activity (Dishman and Sallis 1994) (see Box 3.1). Although social support may not be exactly the same as social influence/subjective norm (Taylor, Baranowski and Sallis 1994), the similarities are such that we should expect the social normative component of the TRA to be more closely linked to exercise behaviour than has typically been the case. Two explanations are possible. First, we may not be assessing subjective norms appropriately in TRA studies and this may be forcing respondents to misinterpret the meaning behind the statements. A second possibility is that some people may be reluctant to admit that they require motivation from others and certainly do not want to admit that they wish 'to comply' with these people (for example, adolescents with parents).

In summary, the TRA has been at the forefront of re-establishing attitude research as a powerful force in social psychology and both health and exercise psychology have been quick to utilise such an approach. The TRA has proved to be a viable unifying theoretical framework that has been successful in furthering our understanding of exercise intentions and behaviours. It has also been instrumental in moving research on physical activity correlates from being largely atheoretical to theoretical.

Box 3.1 Social norms assessed through questionnaire and interview

It is interesting to note that the statistical information on the role of subjective (social) norms in the TRA and TPB discussed in the main text suggests that subjective norms do not really matter much in physical activity, or at least are less important than attitudes. But is this really the case? Our own personal experiences suggest a different story. This confusion could be the result of the way we are measuring subjective and social norms in questionnaires. Professor Andy Smith, a leading physical activity specialist in the UK, conducted some interviews with participants of an exercise class he had supervised for initially inactive adults. For example, an older member of the class close to retirement said that 'I used to walk a lot, but my friends have scattered and I am less active now'. Another remarked on the support from her spouse: 'I enjoyed myself (on the programme) and having my husband with me helped my motivation'. The following comments from programme members also suggest that social norms/support are important:

- 'good to be with like-minded people'
- 'the course is socially important'
- 'enjoyed the course and social occasion'
- 'enjoyed the social opportunity'.

Social aspects are important but TRA/TPB studies tend to show stronger effects for attitudes. This may be a reflection of the truth or show that we are not assessing the most important elements of social norms and support. This also highlights the importance for both qualitative and quantitative methods of research.

The Theory of Planned Behaviour

The TRA has provided a model that has been successful in predicting behaviour and intentions for actions that are primarily volitional and controllable. However, in the case of physical activity volitional control is likely to be 'incomplete' (Ajzen 1988), although Godin (1993) suggests that different types of physical activity may differ from each other in this respect.

Ajzen's theorising and research (Ajzen 1985, 1988, 1996; Ajzen and Madden 1986; Schifter and Ajzen 1985) suggests that the TRA is insufficient for behaviours where volitional control is incomplete; in other words, where resources and skills are required (Eagly and Chaiken 1993). Consequently, Ajzen proposed an extension of the TRA for such behaviours and called this the Theory of Planned Behaviour (TPB). The TPB is the same as the TRA but with the additional variable of 'perceived behavioural control', as illustrated in Figure 3.3. Perceived behavioural control is defined by Ajzen as 'the perceived ease or difficulty of performing the behaviour' (Ajzen 1988: 132) and is assumed 'to reflect past experience as well as anticipated impediments and obstacles' (Azjen 1988: 132). Figure 3.3 links perceived control with both intentions and behaviour. This suggests that the variable has a motivational effect on intentions, such that individuals wishing to be physically active, but with little or no chance of doing so (because of largely insurmountable behavioural barriers at the time), are unlikely to do so regardless of their attitudes towards activity or the social factors operating. This overcomes one of the problems of the TRA alluded to earlier when a distinction was made between intentions and expectations.

For Ajzen (1991), the construct of perceived behavioural control refers to general perceptions of control. He overtly compared it with Bandura's (1977) construct of self-efficacy that captures judgements of how well one can execute volitional behaviours required to produce important outcomes. The construct of PBC is also underpinned by a set of control beliefs and the perceived power of these beliefs (Ajzen and Fishbein 1980). Control beliefs refer to the perceived presence of factors that may facilitate or impede performance of behaviour and perceived power refers to the perceived impact that facilitative or inhibiting factors may have on performance of behaviour (Ajzen 1991). In the same way that an expectancy–value model is used to form indirect antecedents of attitudes and subjective norm, an indirect measure of PBC can be formed from each control belief multiplied by its corresponding perceived power rating (Ajzen 1991).

The inclusion of perceived behavioural control in the TPB is important because it reveals the personal and environmental factors that affect behaviour (Ajzen 1985). To the extent that PBC influences intentions and behaviour, the researcher can evaluate which behaviours are under the volitional control of the individual and the degree to which the behaviour is impeded by personal and/or environmental factors. Ajzen (1991) hypothesised that when control over the behaviour was problematic, perceived behavioural control would exert two types of effects within the TPB. First, PBC would influence intentions alongside attitudes and subjective norms. This additive effect reflects the *motivational* influence of perceived control on decisions to exercise. Second, perceived behavioural control may predict behaviour directly, especially when perceptions of behavioural control are realistic. This direct effect reflects the actual, real constraints or barriers for the behaviour. In this case PBC is a proxy measure of *actual* control over the behaviour (Ajzen 1991).

Ajzen (1988) argues that perceived behavioural control will accurately predict behaviour under circumstances only when perceived control closely approximates actual control (hence the use of broken line in Figure 3.3). For example, whereas some people may have a strong perception of control over their body weight, the reality might be different since there are biological factors likely to affect weight gain and loss that are beyond personal control. In such situations one would not expect perceived control to be a strong predictor of weight change, although it is possible for it to predict to a lesser degree. Similarly, one would expect better predictions of exercise *behaviour* (for example, frequency of exercise) from perceived control compared with exercise *performance* (for example, a fitness test score) since the latter is less controllable due to factors such as heredity, practice and the test environment.

Evidence from the Theory of Planned Behaviour

The TPB is appropriate for use in the study of physical activity, particularly as it is a behaviour that has many barriers, thus it is only partly under volitional control. The testing of the TPB in the area of physical activity is now extensive (Hagger, Chatzisarantis and Biddle 2002).

Most studies in this area are relatively small, yet Wankel and Mummery (1993) managed to integrate TPB items into the large population survey 'The Campbell Survey of Well-Being'. This involved over 4,000 Canadians who had previously participated in the 1981 Canada Fitness Survey. Although the survey allowed for a test of the TPB, space limitations in the survey did not allow for a strict operationalisation of the TPB variables. However, despite this, the study provides the first population-based assessment of attitudes using the framework of the TPB.

The data set was large enough to allow for analyses to include four age groups for both males and females, and retain suitable sample sizes. In predicting physical activity intention, Wankel and Mummery (1993) found that across the different age and gender groups, variance in intentions accounted for by attitudes, social norm/support and perceived behavioural control ranged from 25–35 per cent. For the total sample, 31 per cent of the variance in intentions was explained by the three TPB variables. This is a reasonable approximation of estimates from other studies. Godin (1993) claimed that about 30 per cent of the variance in intention is explained by the attitude and social norm components and that anything between 4–20 per cent extra variance is accounted for by perceived behavioural control. Wankel and Mummery's data, therefore, are broadly compatible with this which, given the large population sample used, coupled with the problems of operationalising the variables precisely in line with the TPB, is encouraging for the TPB itself.

A comprehensive test of the TPB was conducted by Hagger and colleagues (Hagger, Chatzisarantis and Biddle 2002). They meta-analysed seventy-two studies that allowed calculations of the relationships proposed in either the TRA or TPB. In addition to reporting correlations between variables, they did three things:

1   by using the correlation matrix, they tested the TRA and TPB through path analysis
2   they tested the additional variance accounted for by adding variables to the TRA. This was done by first adding PBC (hence testing the TPB), then self-efficacy and finally past behaviour
3   they tested three moderator variables: age, attitude–intention strength, and the time between the assessment of past behaviour and present behaviour.

Results supported the TPB (see Figure 3.4). Intention was the only direct predictor of behaviour, intention was predicted more strongly by attitudes than subjective norms (the latter showing a small contribution), and PBC was associated with behaviour through intention. Self-efficacy (a more internal aspect of PBC) added to the prediction of both intentions and behaviour, while past behaviour was associated with all TPB variables. Of most importance was the finding that by adding past behaviour to the model, the strength of other paths was reduced, suggesting that studies that do not assess past behaviour may be obtaining artificially high correlations.

Nevertheless, the relationship between attitude and intentions remained even when past behaviour was included. Hagger *et al.* concluded:

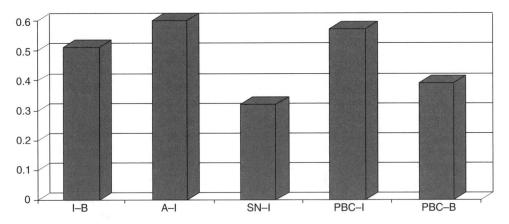

Figure 3.4 Correlations (corrected for sampling and measurement error) between TRA/TPB variables
from data reported by Hagger *et al.* (2002)

Key
B: behaviour; I: intention; A: attitude; SN: subjective norm; PBC: perceived behavioural control

while past behaviour had a significant and direct influence on intention, attitude, PBC, and self-efficacy, these cognitions are also necessary for translating past decisions about behavioural involvement into action. This is consistent with the notion that involvement in volitional behaviours such as regular physical activity involves both conscious and automatic influences.

(Hagger *et al.* 2002: 23)

Hagger *et al.*'s analysis also showed that intentions are more strongly associated with behaviour in older participants, possibly because of their greater experience. Young people may also have additional controls, such as parental influence, precluding full translating of intentions. In addition, results showed that the time between assessment of past behaviour and current behaviour did not affect the strength of relationships.

The Theory of Planned Behaviour: conclusion and critique

Many of the criticisms of the TRA already discussed can be applied to the TPB, with the exception of the point concerning volition since the inclusion of perceived behavioural control accounts for this. However, as Godin (1993) has suggested, it is unclear which physical activities are perceived to be volitionally controlled and which are not. It seems reasonable to suggest that walking will be seen by most people to be quite controllable, yet activities requiring facilities and high costs are likely to be seen to be much less controllable. This needs to be taken into account in future studies as we seek to predict participation in both structured and unstructured physical activities. However, Ajzen warns that

at first glance, the problem of behavioral control may appear to apply to a limited range of actions only. Closer scrutiny reveals, however, that even very mundane activities, which can usually be executed (or not executed) at will, are sometimes subject to the influence of factors beyond one's control.

(Ajzen 1988: 127)

One problem with the TPB is the lack of consistency in defining and assessing perceived behavioural control. Ajzen (1991) defines perceived behavioural control in terms of both perceived resources and opportunities as well as perceived power to overcome obstacles, thus the construct represents both control beliefs and perceived power. Studies incorporating self-efficacy and PBC often find that they make independent contributions to the prediction of intentions or behaviour. For example, Terry and O'Leary (1995) found items reflecting self-efficacy and PBC to be distinct. Moreover, they found that self-efficacy predicted intentions to be physically active, but not activity itself, whereas PBC predicted physical activity but not intention. PBC seems to include beliefs built on past experience as well as external barriers whereas self-efficacy refers to beliefs concerning whether the individual feels that they can perform a behaviour, so-called agent–means connections (Skinner 1995, 1996), without necessarily distinguishing types of constraints. Self-efficacy is more akin to internal control (Hagger, Chatzisarantis and Biddle 2002).

Reasons for the success and popularity of the TPB can be attributed to its efficacy in accounting for variance in intention and behaviour, its relative parsimony and its flexibility. Furthermore, the original constructs of the TPB have been shown to mediate the direct effect of other constructs on intentions and behaviour, suggesting that the belief systems that underpin the directly measured theory constructs are able to account for the effects of other variables that have previously accounted for unique variance in behaviour (Conner and Abraham 2001). However, researchers have also indicated that the theory does not account for all of the variance in intention and behaviour, nor does it mediate the effects of certain 'external variables' (Rhodes, Bowie and Hergenrather 2003), personality and belief-based constructs on intentions and behaviour (Bagozzi and Kimmel 1995; Conner and Abraham 2001; Conner and Armitage 1998; Rhodes, Courneya and Jones 2002). Paradoxically, this 'weakness' has become the theory's greatest strength. Ajzen (1991) states that the theory should be viewed as a flexible framework into which other variables can be incorporated provided they make a meaningful and unique contribution to the prediction of intentions and there is a theoretical reason for the inclusion of such variables.

The theory has demonstrated considerable flexibility and has been adopted by researchers as a general framework to investigate the effect of a number of additional social cognitive constructs on intention and behaviour (Conner and Armitage 1998). To the extent that such constructs have a unique effect on intention or behaviour and are not mediated by the core theory variables of attitude, subjective norm and PBC the researcher has evidence to support the inclusion of that construct within the theory. A number of constructs have been found to have a unique effect on intentions and/or behaviour in this regard, including antici-pated affect and anticipated regret (Sheeran, Norman and Orbell 1999), self-schemas (Sheeran and Orbell 2000), self-efficacy (Sparks, Guthrie and Shepherd 1997), descriptive norms (Sheeran, Norman and Orbell 1999), desires (Perugini and Bagozzi 2001), and self-identity (Chatzisarantis *et al.* in press; Sparks and Guthrie 1998).

Key point: There is no doubt that the Theory of Planned Behaviour has been successful in devel-oping our understanding of attitudes and physical activity.

Implementation intentions

One reason why the theories of reasoned action and planned behaviour do not fully explain the processes by which intentions are translated into action is that people often fail to carry out their intentions (Gollwitzer 1999; Orbell 2000; Orbell, Hodgkins and Sheeran 1997; Sheeran, Norman and Orbell 1999). Alternatively, individuals' execution of their intentions may be interrupted because other competing behaviours gain priority over the original intended behav-iour (Aarts, Verplanken and Van Knippenberg 1998). Social cognitive theories like the TRA and TPB do not address these difficulties associated with the translation or enactment of inten-tions, and as a result may not fully explain the intention–behaviour relationship.

One approach that has been put forward to resolve the inadequacies of the intention–behaviour relationship in the TPB is *implementation intentions* (Gollwitzer 1999). These are self-regulatory strategies, or goals and plans, that involve specifying when, how, and where performance of behaviour will take place. Implementation intentions were devel-oped from concerns about the intention–behaviour gap.

Experimental paradigms using implementation intention strategies require research par-ticipants to specify explicitly *when, where* and *how* they will engage in an intended behaviour to achieve their behavioural goals (Orbell 2000). According to Gollwitzer (1999), implementation intentions help people move from a motivational phase to a volitional phase ensuring that intentions are converted into action (see the HAPA model later and in Chapter 6). Research has indicated that forming implementation intentions decreases the probability of people failing to initiate their goal-directed intentions at the point of initiation (Orbell 2000; Orbell, Hodgkins and Sheeran 1997; Sheeran, Norman and Orbell 1999). This is because planning when and where to initiate a behaviour strengthens the mental association between representations of situations and representations of actions. Research has also shown that increased accessibility of situational representations in memory increases the probability of action opportunities getting noticed, and of action initiation occurring given that the mere perception of action opportunities can automatically trigger a behavioural response (Orbell, Hodgkins and Sheeran 1997; Sheeran, Norman and Orbell 1999). Importantly, implementation intentions increase behavioural engagement through these post-decisional, automatic mechanisms, and not by concomitant increases in motivation or intention (Orbell, Hodgkins and Sheeran 1997).

Recent research has evaluated the effectiveness of interventions that combine motivational techniques with volitional techniques, such as implementation intentions, in influencing the performance of social and exercise behaviour (Koestner *et al.* 2002; Prestwich, Lawton and Conner 2003; Rivis and Sheeran 2003; West *et al.* 2002). The rationale behind this combined approach is that motivational strategies focus on increasing intention levels but do not facilitate the enactment of intentions, while volitional strategies, such as implementation intentions, increase the probability that these strong intentions will be converted into action without changing intentions. Research has supported the use of these combined techniques in increasing exercise behaviour. For example, Prestwich *et al.* (2003) demonstrated that an intervention that had a combination of a rational decision-making strategy, or decisional balance sheet (weighing up the pros and cons), and implementation intentions was more effective in promoting physical activity behaviour than either of the strategies alone. These results support the existence of two distinct phases of motivation: a *motivational or pre-decisional* phase, during which people decide whether or not to perform a behaviour, and a *volitional, post-decisional* or implemental phase during which people plan when and where they will convert their intentions into behaviour (Gollwitzer 1999). As a consequence interventions that combine motivational and volitional techniques are likely to be most effective in promoting physical activity behaviour. We provide more information on interventions and guidelines for practitioners in Part IV.

Alternative attitude models for the study of physical activity

In addition to the widely cited theories of reasoned action and planned behaviour, other models of attitude have been proposed. We provide a brief review of the HAPA model and Rogers' protection motivation theory.

The Health Action Process Approach

The Health Action Process Approach (HAPA) (Schwarzer 1992, 2001) is a model that explicitly integrates continuous and stage assumptions, and could be seen as a *hybrid model* rather than an attitude/belief-based model per se (Biddle *et al.* 2007). The HAPA integrates motivational (prediction of intention) and behaviour-enabling (implemental) models, such as the inclusion of post-decisional aspects of implementation intentions.

The HAPA makes a distinction between a motivation phase and a volition/post-decision phase of health behaviour change. The basic idea is that individuals experience a shift in mindset when moving from the first phase (motivational) to the second (volitional). The moment when people commit themselves to an intention to exercise they enter the volitional phase. Here, a division into two sub-phases appears to be meaningful where people can be labelled as either intenders or actors. First, they intend to act but they remain inactive. Second, they have initiated the intended action. Thus, three phases or stages can be distinguished as shown in Figure 3.5. In (a) the *non-intentional stage,* a behavioural intention is being developed which is similar to the contemplation stage in the transtheoretical model (see Chapter 6). Afterwards, individuals enter (b) the *intentional stage,* where the person has already formed an intention but still remains inactive (or at least not active at the recommended level), while the exercise behaviour is being planned and prepared. If these plans are translated into action, individuals reside in (c) the *action stage.* They are then physically active at the recommended or criterion level.

In the *non-intentional stage,* an intention has to be developed. Risk perception may enable the undecided person to form an intention. Furthermore, it is a prerequisite for a contemplation process and further elaboration of thoughts about consequences and capacities. Risk perception operates at a stage-specific level and therefore its effect on intention is represented by a dashed line in Figure 3.5; in the intentional stage, risk perception has no effect (Lippke, Ziegelmann and Schwarzer 2005). The belief in one's capabilities to perform a desired action (self-efficacy) is necessary. That is, perceived self-efficacy promotes intention formation and behaviour implementation in all stage groups (Lippke, Ziegelmann and Schwarzer 2005) and the arrow is therefore drawn as a solid line, not dashed, in Figure 3.5.

After a decision has been made, the *intentional stage* is entered. The individual has a high intention but is not performing the behaviour. The intention has to be transformed into detailed plans on how to perform the behaviour. These state when, where and how the goal behaviour will be initiated (Lippke, Ziegelmann and Schwarzer 2004); thereby cognitive links between concrete opportunities and the intended behaviour will be built (see Box 3.2) Risk perception has no further influence while outcome-expectancies remain important. Self-efficacy is also important in the planning and initiation process, especially if barriers

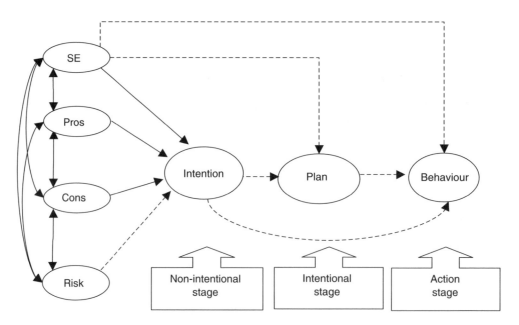

Figure 3.5 The Health Action Process Approach

Box 3.2 Using implementation intentions in field settings

Implementation intentions can be administered as a paper and pencil exercise. Here is an example for physical activity.

> You are more likely to achieve your goal of actively commuting to work on three days of the week if you decide in advance when, where (route) and how this is to be achieved, and then stick to your plan. Decide now and write in the spaces below:
> *When*: when will you be actively commuting? Which days?
> *Where*: which route will you take?
> *How*: will you walk all of the way or part of the way? Will you cycle?

Mental simulation exercises can also be used. These can be both 'process' and 'outcome' simulations.
   Process simulation example:

> In this exercise you are asked to imagine yourself working towards your goal of actively commuting to work three days a week. Imagine how you would actually commute to work using physical activity. See yourself in action! Picture it in your mind! Imagine the changes you could make to implement this behaviour. Picture the effort you will make to have this happen.

Outcome simulation example:

> In this exercise you are asked to imagine yourself having achieved your goal of actively commuting to work three days a week. Imagine how you feel. It is important that you see yourself having been successful in actively commuting for the past weeks. You have worked hard at this goal and now you have managed it. See yourself at this point of success and look back on the effort you put in to get there.

---

occur. Self-efficacy keeps intentions high and the plans flexible to compensate for setbacks and stay on track.

If exercise has been started, the individual enters the *action stage*. To enhance maintenance, self-regulatory skills are important. Effort has to be invested, situations for implementation of the new behaviour have to be identified, and distractions resisted. The behaviour will mainly be directed by self-efficacy (Schwarzer 2001) because it regulates effort and persistence in the face of barriers and setbacks. Behaviour has to be maintained, and relapses have to be managed by different strategies.

Due to individuals having first to set a goal which then may be translated into plans and behaviour, this process is stage-specific; only persons in intentional and action stages are more likely to make plans and subsequently perform the goal behaviour (dashed lines in Figure 3.5) (Lippke, Ziegelmann and Schwarzer 2005). Also the influence of self-efficacy on post-decisional processes, such as planning and behaviour, depends on whether one has decided to change (here it is crucial to believe in one's own competencies) or not (here only intention formation can be supported by self-efficacy). The HAPA also includes other aspects such as situational barriers and resources (Schwarzer 1992, 2001), but not much work has been done on these aspects to date.

Protection Motivation Theory

A model that has some similarities with the Health Belief Model, as well as with the TRA/TPB, is that of Rogers' 'Protection Motivation Theory' (PMT) (Rogers 1983). This too is a cognitive model based on expectancy-value principles and was originally developed as an explanation for the effects of 'fear appeals' in health behaviour change. Some have argued that 'health threats' might be a better term as the model is really one of health decision-making (Wurtele and Maddux 1987). Health behaviour intentions ('protection motivation') are predicted from the cognitive appraisal mechanisms shown in Figure 3.6 (Boer and Seydel 1996).

Support has been found for the model (Rippetoe and Rogers 1987). Similarly, Prentice-Dunn and Rogers (1986) contrast the PMT with the HBM and suggest that the PMT has some distinct advantages. They say that the PMT has more of an organisational framework and is not open to the criticism of merely being a catalogue of variables. Second, the division of cognitive appraisals into threat and coping categories helps to clarify how people think about health decision-making. Third, PMT includes self-efficacy, a variable found to be a powerful mediator of behaviour change in other studies.

Only a few studies have directly tested PMT in an exercise context, although other studies provide evidence indirectly (see Godin 1994). Stanley and Maddux (1986) tested PMT alongside self-efficacy theory in the prediction of exercise behaviour of American undergraduate students. Using an experimental design, they found that manipulations of perceived response efficacy (outcome expectancy) and self-efficacy through written persuasive communications successfully predicted intentions to exercise.

Wurtele and Maddux (1987) asked 160 sedentary undergraduate women to read persuasive appeals for increasing their exercise. The appeals were varied along the four dimensions of severity, vulnerability, response efficacy and self-efficacy. Consistent with Bandura's (1977) theory of self-efficacy, PMT includes two types of efficacy. 'Response efficacy' refers to the belief that a response will produce the desired outcome whereas 'self-efficacy'

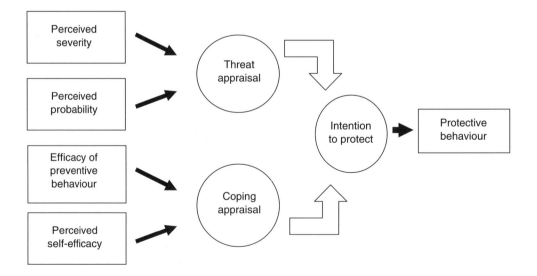

Figure 3.6 A simplified version of Protection Motivation Theory

refers to the belief in one's ability to initiate and maintain the desired behaviour (see Prentice-Dunn and Rogers 1986). Results showed that only vulnerability and self-efficacy predicted intentions to exercise, which in turn were predictive of self-reported exercise. Those with high self-efficacy also had strong intentions to exercise even though they were not exposed to the vulnerability enhancing or response-efficacy enhancing conditions in the study. This confirms the important role of self-efficacy in behaviour change. It was also found that the threat appeals were ineffective in changing exercise intentions.

Fruin, Pratt and Owen (1991) studied Australian adolescents and their beliefs about cardiovascular disease risk and the role of exercise. Response efficacy, response costs and self-efficacy were manipulated in an experimental design such that students received short essays with either 'high' (positive) or 'low' (negative) information on the variable in question (for example, response costs). Results revealed that students in the high self-efficacy condition reported stronger intentions to exercise, and those in the low response efficacy condition reported greater feelings of hopelessness and fatalism. Again, efficacy beliefs have been shown to be important in exercise contexts.

West and colleagues provided a longitudinal test of PMT alongside the use of implementation intentions (West *et al.* 2002). While increases in threat, coping appraisal and intention were brought about through an intervention, exercise behaviour was unchanged. However, enhancement of the PMT-based intervention was achieved by the introduction of a condition that enhanced implementation intentions.

Consistent with West *et al.* (2002), Godin (1994) concluded that 'in general, messages conveying a persuasive threat seem effective in enhancing participants' intention to change their behaviors, but they are less effective in inducing and sustaining changes in behaviour'. However, he then goes on to say that PMT 'has limited usefulness for the study of exercise behavior' (Godin 1994: 117). This conclusion may be premature, certainly when combined with other interventions.

Although one may not be comfortable with physical activity motivation based on fear or health threats, and also noting that the results of PMT research are more favourable towards the role of self-efficacy than health threats per se, research so far suggests that PMT sheds light on some important constructs and processes in physical activity decision-making.

Chapter summary and conclusions

Most people would agree that an important area for the understanding of physical activity is attitudes. However, as with motivation, such an all-embracing construct cannot explain all that we do, but it remains central to the psychology of physical activity determinants.

In this chapter, therefore, we have:

- defined attitude and components of the attitude construct
- summarised the approach adopted through the theories of reasoned action and planned behaviour, the two most commonly used theories in physical activity attitude research
- described other approaches to the study of attitudes, including the Health Belief Model, Protection Motivation Theory and the Health Action Process Approach.

In summary, therefore, we conclude that:

- the early physical activity attitude research was mainly descriptive and assessed only the target of physical activity and not the action, context or time elements of attitude thought to be critical in linking attitude with behaviour. This approach, therefore, has limited utility in predicting participation in physical activity although it may be of use in eliciting descriptive information in population surveys

- the TRA has consistently predicted exercise intentions and behaviour across diverse settings and samples; attitude accounts for about 30–40 per cent of the variance in intentions, but subjective norm is only weakly associated with intentions

- the TPB appears to add to the predictive utility of the TRA in physical activity; perceived behavioural control has been shown to account for 36 per cent of the variance in intentions

- both TRA and TPB models are limited by their focus on conscious decision-making through cognitive processes; they are essentially static and uni-dimensional approaches, and the prediction of physical activity from intentions may depend on the proximity of measurement of these two variables

- the TRA and TPB have, however, been the most successful approaches in exercise psychology, linking attitudes and related variables to intentions and participation; intentions share about 30 per cent of the variance in physical activity assessment.

- the Health Belief Model has been shown to be a reasonably effective integrating social psychological framework for understanding health decision-making, although meta-analytic results suggest small amounts of variance in health behaviours are accounted for by the major dimensions of the HBM

- the utility of the HBM in physical activity settings has not been demonstrated, probably due to the inappropriate emphasis of the HBM on illness-avoidance. However, it may be useful for service providers to evaluate why some people do not accept the opportunity to attend a GP-referral appointment for cardiac rehabilitation class

- the Health Action Process Approach allows for a distinction between a motivation phase and a volition/post-decision phase of health behaviour change and is a 'hybrid' model combining aspects of intention–behaviour links (continuous) and stage-based models

- Protection Motivation Theory may be useful in predicting exercise intentions, but current data are more supportive of the role of efficacy beliefs rather than health threats themselves

- translating intentions into behaviour is a key challenge. Implementation intentions are self-regulatory strategies that involve the formation of specific plans that specify when, how and where performance of behaviour will take place. To this end, implementation intentions are important in distinguishing between two distinct phases of motivation: a motivational or pre-decisional phase, during which people decide whether or not to perform a behaviour, and a volitional, post-decisional or implemental phase during which people plan when and where they will convert their intentions into behaviour. Interventions that combine motivational and volitional techniques are likely to be most effective in promoting physical activity behaviour

- attitudes are important determinants of physical activity, although social norms less so. Intentions and behaviour can be predicted from attitudes if appropriate social psychological theories and procedures are applied. To this end, and until data suggest otherwise, the TRA or TPB is recommended for this purpose, and in particular the TPB.

4 Motivation through feelings of control

Everything's under control!

> In my letters to my children, I regularly urged them to exercise.
>
> (Nelson Mandela, *Long walk to freedom*, 1994)

Purpose of the chapter

The purpose of this chapter is to extend the motivational analysis of physical activity by considering the notion of feelings of 'control'. Specifically, we mainly review concepts of intrinsic motivation and autonomy, and in addition consider locus of control and attributions. We have the following objectives for the chapter:

- to consider a framework for the understanding of perceptions of control
- to appreciate the potential of perceptions of control, expectancies and value as determinants of physical activity
- to develop an understanding of intrinsic motivational processes, specifically in terms of Cognitive Evaluation Theory and perceptions of autonomy (Self-Determination Theory)
- to consider the role of rewards and reinforcement in affecting intrinsic motivation and behaviour
- to understand the principles of the construct of locus of control, including the extent to which it can be applied to physical activity
- to consider the basic principles of attribution theory and perceptions of control and their application to health and physical activity
- to understand the role of beliefs concerning athletic ability in motivation.

Introduction

Expectancy-value theories make the assumption that people's behaviour is guided logically by the anticipated consequences of their behaviour (expectancies) and the value or importance they attach to such outcomes. Whether we actually make such logical decisions is, of course, debatable, but such theories have demonstrated explanatory power (Biddle, 1999). However, as Weiner (1992) proposes, perhaps such theories assume humans to be too logical and rational. Developments from these perspectives, therefore, have also been proposed and the chapter that follows will deal with theories of motivation that draw on competency-based approaches.

Recognition of the importance of perceptions of control in physical activity and health

The research and popular literature contains numerous references to the fact that changes in exercise and health behaviours are thought to be associated with the need to 'take control' or 'take charge' of personal lifestyles. The information that many of the modern diseases linked with premature mortality are 'lifestyle-related' (Powell 1988) has the implicit message that we, as individuals, are at least partly responsible for our health and well-being, thus implying the need for personal control and change. For example, in describing their 'wellness' approach to exercise and fitness, Patton *et al.* state that 'wellness-oriented health/fitness programs have a philosophical base similar to that of humanistic psychology and humanistic education, which recognise self-responsibility as being integral to genuine self-growth' (Patton *et al.* 1986: 26). Similarly, Weiner says that in spite of evidence linking obesity with biological and genetic factors 'fatness tends to be perceived as controllable, and people are considered responsible for being overweight' (Weiner 1985: 75). Moreover, failure to initiate or maintain physical activity is often attributed to a lack of 'will power'.

It should also be recognised, however, that there are potential problems with health messages that consistently encourage personal control as the only way of changing behaviour. This approach is often associated with the 'health fascist' label adopted in the 1980s. Some have argued that a greater emphasis should be placed on social and environmental determinants of health, and some accuse those who overemphasise the need for personal control of adopting the 'victim blaming approach'. Feelings of guilt can develop when problems arise that are out of one's control (for example disease related to environmental pollution), whereas others might blame the victim for a lack of motivation. Similarly, a great deal of good can be achieved by giving control to others, such as doctors, in some circumstances.

A framework for the study of 'control'

Psychological constructs centred on 'control' are numerous, such as self-efficacy, intrinsic motivation, locus of control, and attributions (Biddle 1999). In attempting to integrate and make sense of apparently disparate constructs, we draw on Skinner's (1995, 1996) theorising. In particular we will outline her agent–means–ends analysis and her 'competence system' model.

Skinner's model and different belief systems

Skinner (1995, 1996) makes the point that one way to conceptualise the vast array of control constructs is to analyse them in relation to their place within the tripartite model of agent, means, and ends. This is illustrated in Figure 4.1.

Agent–means connections involve expectations that the agent (self) has the means to produce a response or behaviour (but not necessarily an outcome). This involves capacity beliefs – beliefs concerning whether the individual has the ability to produce the appropriate behaviour. For example, if effort is deemed important to be able to cycle to work, then positive capacity beliefs must involve the belief that 'I can put in the effort when cycling to work'. Self-efficacy research has adopted this approach and has become a major force in motivational research in exercise and sport psychology. This will be discussed in the next chapter. Similarly, perceived competence approaches adopt the agent–means approach and explain why perceptions of competence and confidence are good predictors of actual behaviour.

Box 4.1 The politics of personal control and victim blaming

All governments face the dilemma of taking responsibility for certain actions, or stating that the responsibility lies with 'the people'. The former approach could lead to popularity if resources and energy follow, but the government also faces the possibility of large costs and possibly the accusation of 'central control' and 'nannying'. 'Giving' responsibility to the people may free some resources but it also leaves the government open to criticism on the grounds of cutting costs or shirking responsibility. Who'd be a politician?

Of course, health care falls perfectly into this dilemma and illustrates the problem of responsibility, or what we have discussed in psychology as the issue of personal control. Broadly speaking, right-wing policies support the supremacy of personal choice. Left-wing policies would include more central control as a counter to the view that disadvantaged groups in society have no 'real' choice.

The UK government's *Health of the Nation* document (Department of Health 1993b) was a policy statement of a Conservative (right-wing) government of the time and makes many references to personal choice and responsibilities, and some have accused it of being 'victim blaming'. For example, Marks (1994) outlines what he perceives to be 'fatal flaws' in the *Health of the Nation* document. These include:

- it assumes that behaviour is determined without reference to economic and social influences
- victims of preventable diseases are seen as irresponsible and unworthy of care.

This is similar to Weiner's (1995) analysis of responsibility and blame. The subsequent policies of the UK Labour government led by Tony Blair focused more on reducing social inequalities as one way of improving health. This places less emphasis on individuals, partly by emphasising 'choice', and stresses environmental and social constraints that need to be overcome by governments and policies.

The study of perceived control in psychology, therefore, clearly is not divorced from personal philosophy and politics.

Means–ends connections involve beliefs about the link between potential causes and outcomes. This involves strategy beliefs – beliefs concerning the necessary availability of behaviours (means) to produce the desired outcomes. For example, if trying hard is necessary to cycle to work, a strategy belief is 'I need to try hard to cycle to work', thus contrasting with the capacity belief 'I can try hard ...'.

As Skinner put it, 'connections between people and outcomes prescribe the prototypical definitions of control' (Skinner 1995: 554), hence this connection involves control beliefs. These involve the belief by the agent that a desirable outcome is within their capability: 'I can be successful at cycling to work if I want to'. This has to involve both capacity *and* strategy beliefs.

Intrinsic motivation, perceptions of control and autonomy, and physical activity

It is clear from everyday experiences that we prefer, or are more motivated by, situations where some choice, control and 'self-determination' exist. Conversely, we usually prefer not to be controlled and pressured too much. These constructs underpin the link between perceptions of control and motivated behaviour and are central to intrinsic motivation.

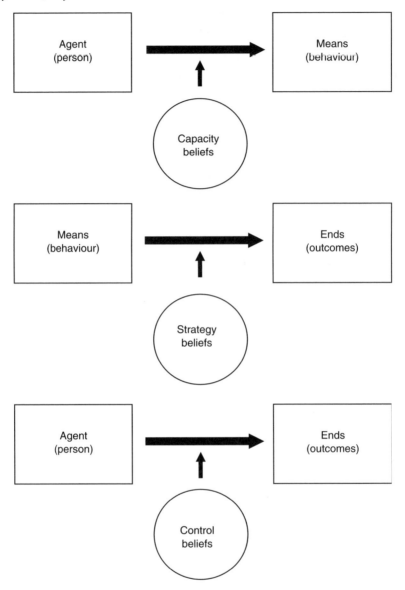

Figure 4.1 (a, b, c) An agent–means–ends analysis and different types of beliefs mediating such links
(adapted from Skinner 1995, 1996)

Intrinsic and extrinsic motivation are well-known constructs in psychology and, although
often under different names, in everyday situations too. Certainly those involved in promoting physical activity for health believe that intrinsic motivation is key to sustaining
involvement. Intrinsic motivation is motivation to do something for its own sake in the
absence of external (extrinsic) rewards. Often this involves fun, enjoyment and satisfaction,
such as recreational activities and hobbies. The enjoyment is in the activity itself rather than
any extrinsic reward such as money, prizes or prestige from others, and participation is free

of constraints and pressure. Such intrinsically pursued activities are referred to as 'autotelic' (self-directing) by Csikszentmihalyi (1975). Such a notion is useful for the present discussion because it suggests that intrinsically motivated behaviour is linked to feelings of self-control or self-determination, or what we shall call 'autonomy' (Deci and Ryan 1985).

Extrinsic motivation, on the other hand, refers to motivation directed by rewards, money, pressure or other external factors. This suggests that if these rewards or external pressures were removed, motivation would decline in the absence of any intrinsic interest. Later, we shall introduce motivational constructs that shed extra light on a continuum of motivation, including motivational processes 'between' pure intrinsic and extrinsic motivation.

The development of intrinsic motivation theories

Deci and Ryan (1985, 1991) suggest that four approaches to the study of intrinsic motivation can be identified in the literature. These are free choice, interest, challenge and 'needs'. Studying intrinsic motivation through the assessment of free choice allows for behaviour to be estimated. In the absence of extrinsic rewards, those intrinsically motivated will be those who choose to participate in their own time (free choice). Intrinsically motivated behaviour is also performed out of interest and curiosity, as well as challenge. Finally, Deci and Ryan outline the important role of psychological needs identified over time through constructs such as 'effectance', 'personal causation', and 'competence' and 'self-determination'.

It is generally acknowledged that the initiation of the shift towards the study of a cognitive perspective on motivational needs was White's (1959) paper on 'effectance motivation'. White suggested that humans have a basic need to interact effectively with their environment. He reviewed a wide range of studies and argued convincingly that operant theories could not account for behaviours such as mastery attempts, curiosity, exploration and play. For all these, and other similar activities, there seems to be no apparent external reward except for the activity itself, and such activities have been termed intrinsically motivating. White argued that successfully mastering such tasks led to feelings of efficacy which, in turn, intrinsically motivated future behaviour.

An alternative approach was taken by deCharms (1968). He argued that self-determination is a basic human need and consequently individuals will be optimally and intrinsically motivated when they perceive themselves to be the 'origin' of, or in control of, their own behaviour. DeCharms (1968) used Heider's concept of perceived locus of causality (PLOC) to describe individuals' sense of autonomy or self-determination. PLOC refers to the perception people have about the reasons they engage in a particular behaviour. People with an internal PLOC feel initiators or 'origins' of their behaviour. On the other hand, people feeling that their actions are initiated by some external force are said to have an external PLOC. External and internal PLOC are not mutually exclusive and they represent opposite ends of a continuum. According to deCharms, people are more likely to be optimally and intrinsically motivated when they have an internal PLOC.

Deci and Ryan (1985) propose that three key psychological needs are related to intrinsically motivated behaviour. These are the needs for competence, autonomy and social relatedness. Competence refers to strivings to control outcomes and to experience mastery and effectance. Humans seek to understand how to produce desired outcomes. Autonomy is related to self-determination. It is similar to deCharms' notion of being the 'origin' rather than the 'pawn', and to have feelings of perceived control and to feel actions emanate from the self. Finally, relatedness refers to strivings to relate to, and care for, others; to feel that others can relate to oneself; 'to feel a satisfying and coherent involvement with the social world more generally' (Deci and Ryan 1991: 245).

Deci and Ryan state that 'these three psychological needs ... help to explain a substantial amount of variance in human behavior and experience' (Deci and Ryan 1991: 245). People seek to satisfy these needs, but of more importance from the point of view of enhancing intrinsic motivation is that they predict the circumstances in which intrinsically motivated behaviour can be promoted. We will return to this later. First, let us consider a perspective on intrinsic and extrinsic motivation that has captured some attention in sport and exercise research.

> Key point: Humans want to satisfy their needs for competence, autonomy (self-determination) and social relatedness. Motivation can be enhanced by creating environments that seek to boost all three needs.

Cognitive Evaluation Theory

The relationship between intrinsic and extrinsic motivation was, at one time, thought to be quite simple – 'more' motivation would result from adding extrinsic to existing intrinsic motivation! This appeared logical given the evidence demonstrating that reinforcements (that is, extrinsic rewards) will increase the probability of the rewarded behaviour reoccurring. However, a number of studies and observations, mainly with children, started to question whether intrinsic motivation was actually undermined by the use of extrinsic rewards. This was done through 'cognitive evaluation theory' (CET).

CET (Deci 1975; Deci and Ryan 1985) reconciled the two conceptions of White and deCharms by postulating that variations in individuals' feelings of competence and perceptions of autonomy will produce variations in intrinsic motivation. Providing individuals with rewards for their participation in an already interesting activity often led to a decrease in intrinsic motivation. Deci (1975) theorised that this was due to a shift in PLOC. Thus, individuals who had an internal PLOC for performing an activity shifted their locus of causality to a more external orientation when they received a reward, and consequently their intrinsic motivation decreased.

Lepper, Greene and Nisbett (1973) tested the relationship between intrinsic motivation and extrinsic rewards with pre-school children. Baseline data on intrinsic interest were collected. Intrinsic motivation was operationally defined as the amount of time spent playing with brightly coloured 'magic marker' highlighting pens during a break in the school day. The children were then assigned randomly to one of three groups:

- 'expected reward condition': the children agreed to play with the pens and expected a reward for doing so (a certificate with seal and ribbon)
- 'unexpected reward condition': the children agreed to play with the pens and but were not told anything about receiving a reward (although did receive one afterwards)
- 'no reward condition': these children neither expected nor received a reward for playing with the pens.

The children then participated in the experimental manipulation and were tested individually in a separate room in one of the three conditions. They were later observed, on another occasion, unobtrusively by the use of a one-way mirror. The pens were available in a classroom alongside a variety of other play equipment. The amount of time, expressed as a percentage of free-choice time, spent playing with the pens for each of the three groups showed that the expected reward group played for a significantly smaller amount of time than the other two groups.

A similar experiment was conducted by Lepper and Greene (1975) with children of the same age as in the previous study. This time they used two reward conditions: expected reward and unexpected reward. In addition, the researchers had three surveillance conditions. Some children were told that while they were playing their performance would be monitored by a video camera most of the time (high surveillance), occasionally (low surveillance) or not at all (no surveillance). Up to three weeks after the experimental manipulation, the children were unobtrusively observed playing. The results showed that intrinsic motivation was lower under surveillance and expected reward conditions.

These two studies supported earlier work by Deci (see Deci and Ryan 1985) who found that people paid to work on intrinsically motivating tasks spent less time on the tasks when given an opportunity to do so in their free time. Collectively, the results of these studies suggest what has been termed an 'overjustification effect'. By rewarding people for participating in an intrinsically interesting task, subsequent involvement in the task is reduced when the reward is no longer available.

The overjustification effect is based on the premise that the behaviour would have occurred anyway, without the need for extrinsic rewards. However, with the use of expected rewards a shift in perceptions occurs from intrinsic to extrinsic. The task is pursued for reasons of obtaining the reward rather than for intrinsic value. Therefore, the reward 'overjustifies' the behaviour and, in the event of the reward no longer being offered, the individual shows reduced intrinsic motivation.

The studies by Lepper and his co-workers, however, demonstrated that it was not the rewards per se that were the problem, but whether the rewards were expected or not. This suggests, therefore, that rewards need not be detrimental to intrinsic motivation in all situations. This led to the formulation of cognitive evaluation theory which states that rewards are likely to serve two main functions:

- *Information function* If the reward provides information about the individuals' competence then it is quite likely that intrinsic motivation can be enhanced with appropriate rewards.
- *Controlling function* If the rewards are seen to be controlling behaviour (that is, the goal is to obtain the reward rather than participate for intrinsic reasons), then withdrawal of the reward is likely to lead to subsequent deterioration in intrinsic motivation.

Attribution theory provides the framework for this analysis since the controlling function of rewards suggests that attributions for participation will be externally focused. This will likely reduce positive emotions under conditions of success and lead to perceptions of lack of control in situations of failure (Weiner 1992). While the informational function of rewards can be positive due to the recognition of competence, this will, of course, only be true for those who experience success. Regular use of rewards for successful outcomes to individuals in groups (for example, at school) could equally de-motivate unsuccessful people as they have their incompetence reinforced. This is referred to by Deci and Ryan (1985) as the 'amotivating' function of rewards and is conceptually related to the concept of helplessness. Figure 4.2 summarises these possibilities.

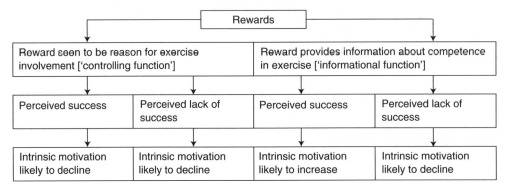

Figure 4.2 Possible links between rewards, structures and intrinsic motivation in exercise settings

It is important to note that informational events are those events that are perceived to convey feedback about one's competence within the context of autonomy. Events where positive feedback occurs under pressure may be less powerful in influencing intrinsic motivation.

In summarising CET, Deci and Ryan (1985) present three propositions:

> *Proposition 1.* External events relevant to the initiation and regulation of behaviour will affect a person's intrinsic motivation to the extent that they influence the perceived locus of causality for that behaviour. Events that promote a more external locus of causality will undermine intrinsic motivation, whereas those that promote a more internal perceived locus of causality will enhance intrinsic motivation.
>
> (Deci and Ryan 1985: 62)

Deci and Ryan say that events that lead to an external locus of causality undermine intrinsic motivation because they deny people 'self-determination' – that is they control people's behaviour. On the other hand, internal locus of causality may enhance intrinsic motivation by facilitating feelings of self-determination, thus creating greater autonomy.

> *Proposition 2.* External events will affect a person's intrinsic motivation for an optimally challenging activity to the extent that they influence the person's perceived competence, within the context of some self-determination. Events that promote greater perceived competence will enhance intrinsic motivation, whereas those that diminish perceived competence will decrease intrinsic motivation.
>
> (Deci and Ryan 1985: 63)

As Proposition 2 suggests, intrinsic motivation is not just about feelings of control but also about perceived competence. The two right-hand routes in Figure 4.2 relate to competence perceptions.

> *Proposition 3.* Events relevant to the initiation and regulation of behaviour have three potential aspects, each with a functional significance. The informational aspect facilitates an internal perceived locus of causality and perceived competence, thus enhancing intrinsic motivation. The controlling aspect facilitates an external perceived locus of causality, thus undermining intrinsic motivation and promoting extrinsic compliance or defiance. The amotivating aspect facilitates perceived incompetence, thus undermining

intrinsic motivation and promoting amotivation. The relative salience of these three aspects to a person determines the functional significance of the event.

(Deci and Ryan 1985: 64)

Deci and Ryan (1985) conclude that, generally speaking, choice and positive feedback are perceived as informational, while rewards, deadlines and surveillance tend to be controlling. Negative feedback is seen to undermine motivation and is therefore referred to as 'amotivating'.

COGNITIVE EVALUATION THEORY IN PHYSICAL ACTIVITY

Since exercise and some forms of physical activity often require persistence, effort, time management, self-regulatory skills and many other things related to motivation, it is relevant to consider the role of intrinsic motivation and self-determination in exercise psychology. Research has mainly focused on competitive sport, although some studies are related to general intrinsic motivation processes, physical fitness or exercise (Chatzisarantis and Biddle 1998; Chatzisarantis, Biddle and Meek 1997; Goudas, Biddle and Fox 1994a; Markland 1999; Mullan and Markland 1997; Mullan, Markland and Ingledew 1997; Vallerand and Fortier 1998; Vallerand and Losier 1999).

Whitehead and Corbin (1991) tested Proposition 2 from CET in the context of fitness testing with children. Studying 12–13 year olds on an agility run test, they sought to test whether changes in perceived competence would vary with changes in intrinsic motivation. They used the Intrinsic Motivation Inventory (IMI) to assess four dimensions of intrinsic motivation: interest/enjoyment, competence, effort/importance and pressure/tension.

After completing the agility run course, two groups of children were given bogus feedback, stating that they were either in the top or bottom 20 per cent for their age. A third group was given no feedback. Clear support for CET was found with the low feedback group (low competence) showing less intrinsic motivation than those receiving the more positive feedback. Intrinsic motivation scores were shown to be influenced by perceptions of competence.

An early study of exercise motivation (Thompson and Wankel 1980) provided some evidence for the role of perceived choice and control in exercise. This study investigated the influence of activity choice on adherence and future exercise intentions. Adult women who enrolled at a health club were asked to list their activity preferences. They were then matched on the basis of these preferences and then randomly assigned to either a 'choice' or 'no choice' group. The choice group were told that their exercise programme was based solely on the choices they had made, whereas the no-choice group were told that their programme was based on a standard format for exercise rather than their own preferences. In reality both groups received activities they had initially selected. The experimental manipulation was in terms of *perceived* choice only. The results showed that the choice group had a significantly better attendance record after six weeks, suggesting that perceived choice is an important factor in exercise motivation. This is consistent with an intrinsic motivation perspective.

COGNITIVE EVALUATION THEORY: A REAPPRAISAL WITH META-ANALYSIS

Although CET has met with general approval in the domain of physical activity, some researchers have attempted clarification of the relationships between rewards and intrinsic motivation. The first of three meta-analyses addressing these issues was reported by Rummel and Feinberg (1988). They included studies that tested the relationship between

Box 4.2 The dos and don'ts of intrinsic motivation for promoting physical activity

Exercise motivation expert Dr Jim Whitehead, from the University of North Dakota, has provided some useful practical guidelines for translating the theory of intrinsic motivation into practical exercise promotion (Whitehead 1993). He suggests some *dos* and *don'ts*.

Do

- emphasise individual mastery
- promote perceptions of choice
- promote the intrinsic fun and excitement of exercise
- promote a sense of purpose by teaching the value of physical activity to health, optimal function and quality of life.

Don't

- overemphasise peer comparisons of performance
- undermine an intrinsic focus by misusing extrinsic rewards
- turn exercise into a chore or a bore
- create amotivation by spreading fitness misinformation.

We fully support these proposals. Indeed on one occasion when Stuart was leading a course on the teaching of health-related exercise for physical education teachers, he suggested that lessons should be made more motivating. One proposal was to use music, either as a beat to follow or just a pleasant and motivating background creating a good climate. However, one teacher said that his head teacher did not allow music in lessons because the lessons might become too much fun! There ended the lesson on intrinsic motivation!

extrinsic rewards and intrinsic motivation and where the reward was conveyed in such a way as to make it 'controlling'. A very large range was found, although only five of the eighty-eight effect sizes contradicted CET. The overall mean effect size was –0.33 (see Table 4.1). It was concluded that rewards do have a moderate detrimental effect on intrinsic motivation and CET was supported.

A small meta-analysis was conducted by Wiersma (1992) on studies in industrial and organisational settings. Only twenty studies were analysed, with those on children and verbal rewards excluded. Analyses were performed separately for free time involvement in a task and for actual performance. The results are shown in Table 4.1 and show that when free time measures of intrinsic motivation are used, rewards have a detrimental effect, but when performance is assessed, rewards have a positive effect. Wiersma concluded that the results show the importance of how intrinsic motivation is operationalised and that performance measures may be combining both intrinsic and extrinsic motivation. For free time measures, at least, CET was supported.

Cameron and Pierce (1994) conducted a comprehensive meta-analysis of studies investigating the relationships between rewards, reinforcements and intrinsic motivation across various domains of behaviour, including physical activity. Four main measures of intrinsic motivation were analysed: free time on a task, attitude (for example self-reported task interest, enjoyment, etc.), willingness to volunteer for a task in the future, and performance. They found that intrinsic motivation did not follow the expected trend predicted by CET for any of

Table 4.1 Results from three meta-analyses on rewards and intrinsic motivation

Study	Measure of intrinsic motivation	Effect size
Rummel and Feinberg (1988)	Various	−0.329[a]
Wiersma (1992)	a) Free time	a) −0.50
	b) Performance	b) 0.34
Cameron and Pierce (1994)	a) Free time overall	a) −0.04
	b) Free time: verbal praise	b) 0.38
	c) Free time: tangible reward	c) −0.22
	d) Attitude overall	d) 0. 14
	e) Attitude: verbal praise	e) 0.30
	f) Attitude: tangible reward	f) 0.05
	g) Performance	g) −0.0004
	h) Willingness to volunteer	h) 0.05

Note
a Sign is reversed from Rummel and Feinberg's paper to enable comparison with other studies.

the measures of intrinsic motivation (see Table 4.1). However, when they looked at the type of reward being offered, they found that those rewarded with verbal praise or positive feedback had higher intrinsic motivation in comparison with those not rewarded. This trend was reversed for tangible rewards when time on task was the measure of intrinsic motivation, but the effect was small.

From this analysis, a central thesis of CET remains unresolved and that is the role of perception of the reward being offered. The discrepancies in intrinsic motivation after the use of rewards are explained through CET by reference to the way that people construe the function of the reward. However, Cameron and Pierce admit that they did not study this. 'Because the present analysis did not evaluate subjects' perceptions about the causes of their behavior, it is impossible to determine whether overjustification explains the results' (Cameron and Pierce 1994: 397).

From the three meta-analyses, therefore, CET is largely supported. The literature in sport and exercise also appears to be supportive although clearly there are issues still to be developed (Vallerand and Fortier 1998). One way forward might be to progress beyond the distinction of intrinsic and extrinsic and, instead, look at a continuum of self-directed behaviour ranging between intrinsic and extrinsic poles and the extent to which people feel self-directed or controlled.

Key point: Use rewards for enhancing feelings of competence rather than a bribe.

Moving towards self-determination

CET involves the processing of information concerning reward structures. Extending this perspective, and including the psychological needs of competence, autonomy and relatedness, Deci and Ryan (1985, 1991) have proposed their 'self-determination theory' (SDT) approach to intrinsic motivation. The nature of motivated behaviour, according to Deci and Ryan, is based on striving to satisfy these three basic needs. This, they say, leads to a process of 'internalisation' – internalising behaviours not initially intrinsically motivating.

Deci and Ryan (1985) have linked the internalisation concept to that of extrinsic and intrinsic motivation. In contrast to their earlier formulations in which they regarded these two motivational types as mutually exclusive, they proposed that they form a continuum where different types of extrinsically regulated behaviour can be located. Although not all theorists depict the continuum in the same way (Fortier *et al.* 1995; Pelletier *et al.* 1995), Deci and Ryan refer to the continuum as one representing 'the degree to which the regulation of a nonintrinsically motivated behavior has been internalized' (Deci and Ryan 1991: 254). Although we have represented intrinsic motivation at one end of the continuum in Figure 4.3, it is the differentiation between external and integrated regulation – the four forms of extrinsic motivation – that are important in understanding the shift from earlier conceptions of a dichotomous variable to one of a continuum.

Types of extrinsic and intrinsic motivation

The four main types of extrinsic motivation are external, introjected, identified and integrated regulation, as shown in Figure 4.3. External regulation might be illustrated by the feeling 'OK, I'll exercise if I really must'. This is an example of where behaviour is controlled by rewards and threats and may be relevant in the case of, say, coercion of patients by medical personnel where physical activity is prescribed for the reduction of health risk factors.

Introjected regulation might be when one says 'I feel guilty if I don't exercise'. This is more internal in the sense that the individual internalises the reasons for acting, but it is not truly self-determined. The individual is acting out of avoidance of negative feelings, such as guilt, or to seek approval from others for their performance or behaviour. The term introjection has been used a great deal in different areas of psychology over the years and refers to someone 'taking in' a value but, at the same time, not really identifying with it; it is not accepted as one's own. As Ryan, Connell and Grolnick suggest, 'in introjected regulation the external regulation has been "taken in" in the form of intrapsychic, self-approval based contingencies' (Ryan, Connell and Grolnick 1992: 174). Gestalt theorists have referred to introjects as being 'swallowed but not digested'. It is an 'internally controlling' form of behavioural regulation illustrated by thoughts such as 'I *have* to ...' or 'I *ought* to ...'. Vallerand describes introjected regulation as saying it is 'as if individuals replace the external source of control by an internal one and start imposing pressure on themselves to ensure that the behavior will be emitted' (Vallerand 1997: 13–14). This is likely to be quite common in exercise; people often state they feel guilty when missing exercise sessions.

Identified regulation reflects feelings such as 'I *want to* exercise to get fit/lose weight'. This is further towards the self-determined end of the motivation continuum where action is motivated by an appreciation of valued outcomes of participation, such as disease prevention or fitness improvement. This is positively correlated with future intentions and in physical

	Extrinsic motivation				
Amotivation • Capacity–ability beliefs • Strategy beliefs • Capacity–effort beliefs • Helplessness beliefs	External regulation	Introjected regulation	Identified regulation	Integrated regulation	Intrinsic motivation • To know • To accomplish • To experience stimulation
	− ◄— Self-determination —► +				

Figure 4.3 A continuum of self-determination in terms of different types of motivation

activity can be the most strongly endorsed reason for exercising (Chatzisarantis and Biddle 1998). Whitehead (1993) has called this stage the 'threshold of autonomy'. It is behaviour acted out of choice where the behaviour is highly valued and important to the individual. It is illustrated by feelings of 'I want to ...' rather than the 'ought' feelings of introjection. The values associated with the behaviour are now 'swallowed and digested'.

Integrated regulation is illustrated by Whitehead (1993) through the phrase 'I exercise because it is important to me and it symbolises who and what I am'. Integrated regulation is the most self-determined extrinsic form of behavioural regulation and the behaviour is volitional 'because of its utility or importance for one's personal goals' (Deci *et al.* 1994: 121). However, the behaviour is still extrinsically motivated because it may be an instrumental action, done to achieve personal goals rather than for the pure joy of the activity itself.

In contrast to these forms of extrinsic motivation, intrinsic motivation is shown through feelings of enjoyment: 'I exercise because I enjoy it'. The individual participates for fun and for the activity itself. Clearly moving towards intrinsically, or integrated, motivated forms of behavioural regulation are advised for stronger levels of intention and sustained involvement in physical activity because they are likely to involve greater feelings of personal investment, autonomy and self-identity.

Ryan and Connell propose 'that the constructs described in internalisation theories can be related to several distinct classes of *reasons* for acting that in turn have a lawful internal ordering. That is, these classes of reasons can be meaningfully placed along a continuum of autonomy, or of self-causality' (Ryan and Connell 1989: 750). They suggest that the continuum should be able to be demonstrated through a simplex-like or ordered correlation structure where variables are ordered 'such that those deemed more similar correlate more highly than those that are hypothetically more discrepant' (Ryan and Connell 1989: 750). We have shown this in the context of children's motivational orientations towards school physical education lessons (Goudas, Biddle and Fox 1994a) as well through meta-analysis (Chatzisarantis *et al.* 2003) (see Figure 4.4). Similarly, by weighting each subscale, an overall 'Relative Autonomy

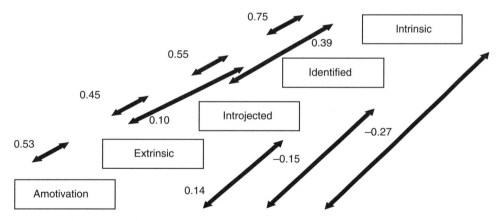

Figure 4.4 Correlations between SDT constructs calculated from a meta-analysis of studies concerning physical activity (Chatzisarantis, *et al.* 2003)

Notes
Amot: amotivation; Extr: extrinsic; Intro: introjected; Iden: identified; Intr: intrinsic. Correlations are for different numbers of studies for each coefficient, ranging from 8 to 17. All coefficients are correlations corrected for measurement and sampling error. Intrinsic motivation scores are represented by the subscale of 'intrinsic motivation to experience stimulation'

Index' (RAI) can be computed, with higher scores indicating higher internality. Figure 4.4 shows that constructs close to each other on the continuum correlate quite highly (0.45 to 0.75), while those distal from other constructs are associated more weakly and sometimes in a negative way (–0.27 to 0.39).

In addition, and as shown in Figure 4.4, there is a state of 'amotivation'. This is where the individual has little or no motivation to attempt the behaviour. Whitehead (1993) describes the move from amotivation to external regulation as crossing the 'threshold of motivation'. Amotivation refers to the relative absence of motivation where a lack of contingency between actions and outcomes is perceived and reasons for continuing involvement cannot be found (Vallerand and Fortier 1998). Vallerand (1997) has likened amotivation to a feeling of learned helplessness. Amotivation may be an important construct in physical activity and exercise. Many adults report feelings of physical inadequacy that prevents participation in physical activity. They display amotivation. There is concern that too few young people are active enough for health gains and further work is required in identifying correlates of physical activity motivation/amotivation. Vallerand and Fortier suggest that the study of amotivation 'may prove helpful in predicting lack of persistence in sport and physical activity' (Vallerand and Fortier 1998: 85).

The use of SDT for studying intrinsic motivation in physical activity is now growing (Chatzisarantis *et al.* 2003; Hagger and Chatzisarantis 2005). For example, in our meta-analysis of the self-determination continuum (Chatzisarantis *et al.* 2003), we found moderately strong correlations between more self-determined forms of motivation and measures of intention and competence (see Figure 4.5).

These results suggest that the construct of autonomy is an important one in the prediction of physical activity. Indeed, and despite the proposals of Deci and Ryan (1985), it is possible to

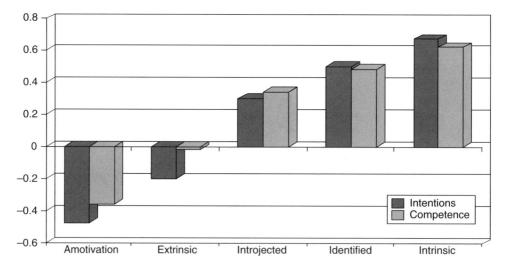

Figure 4.5 Correlations between SDT constructs and intentions and competence calculated from a meta-analysis of studies concerning physical activity (Chatzisarantis *et al.* 2003)

Notes

Amot: amotivation; Extr: extrinsic; Intro: introjected; Iden: identified; Intr: intrinsic. Correlations are for different numbers of studies for each coefficient, ranging from 5 to 8. All coefficients are correlations corrected for measurement and sampling error. Intrinsic motivation scores are represented by the subscale of 'intrinsic motivation to experience stimulation' argue that perceptions of autonomy are the forgotten elements of intrinsic motivation, because most researchers seem to rely more on explanations associated with perceptions of competence. Perceptions of competence are important, but there are many behaviours in health and elsewhere where feelings associated with autonomy may be equally or more important. Individuals who have successfully lost weight often report greater feelings of 'control' over themselves and their lives. Similarly, exercisers may feel 'good' about themselves through the mechanisms of autonomy rather than competence. There are many joggers out there who have minimal levels of jogging competence but feel good about the efforts we make to stay active.

This analysis must also recognise the 'double-edged' sword of autonomy. The SDT continuum from external to internal motivational influences means that some behaviours will be motivated, at least in the short term, by guilt and frustration – not recommended forms of long-term motivation. Pressures vary along this continuum and health behaviours, such as weight control, are often motivated by external influences. The key must be to find ways of moving towards the self-determined end of the continuum. In this way, intentions are more likely to be translated into behaviour (see Figure 4.5).

Skinner has stated 'constructs related to autonomy are outside the proper domain of control' (Skinner 1996: 557). This reflects Deci and Ryan's (1985) distinction between a need for competence *and* a need for autonomy. In addition, Deci and Ryan have stated that autonomy concerns freedom in initiating behaviours whereas control is concerned with perceiving a contingency between action and outcome. In this regard, autonomy is agent–means (competence) and control is agent–ends (competence and contingency) (see Figure 4.1). But where does this leave self-determination in terms of perceived control? Although the continuum uses language similar to that of control – intrinsic, external – it is essentially about *reasons for acting* or what have been termed behavioural regulations. These vary by degrees of self-determination (autonomy), but not necessarily control or competence. Deci says that in his own work with Rich Ryan he has 'proposed that intentional (that is, motivated, personally caused) behaviours differ in the extent to which they are self-determined versus controlled' (Deci 1992: 168). He goes on to say that 'there is a great advantage to specifying different regulatory processes (or motivational orientations); namely, it provides a motivational means of explaining different qualitative aspects of human functioning' (Deci 1992: 168).

As Deci and Ryan state, 'the need for self-determination is an important motivator that is involved with intrinsic motivation and is closely intertwined with the need for competence ... It is important to emphasize that it is not the need for competence alone that underlies intrinsic motivation; it is the need for self-determined competence' (Deci and Ryan 1985: 31–2). In other words, intrinsically motivated states must involve competence and autonomy. To use the example of slaves, they have perfect competence in rowing the ship but no autonomy; they are likely to have no intrinsic motivation. Given freedom of choice, in all likelihood they would not choose to row the boat. The study by Chatzisarantis *et al.* (1997) demonstrated this point by showing that the correlation between intentions and physical activity was high only when intentions were seen as autonomous.

Competence and autonomy, therefore, are part of the wider picture of control, but we should be aware of the differences between the major constructs involved. If intrinsically motivated behaviour, or behaviour regulated by integrated means, is what we strive for in our exercise participants, children, etc., we need both competence and autonomy. Each is 'necessary but not sufficient' since controlling competence or autonomous incompetence will not lead to self-determination. But with integrated regulation of behaviour almost certainly comes heightened feelings of competence and control. Internalised reasons for acting become experienced as self-regulated.

These analyses demonstrate the potential importance of self-perceptions of autonomy in motivated behaviour. It seems to make sense that perceptions associated with self-determined effort will enhance motivation.

Key point: Always seek to move towards more self-determined forms of motivation.

A hierarchical model of intrinsic and extrinsic motivation

Vallerand (1997) organises the constructs of intrinsic and extrinsic motivation into a hierarchical model, as shown in Figure 4.6. Essentially, intrinsic and extrinsic motivation, as well as amotivation, feature at global, contextual and situational levels. At each of these levels, there are antecedents (such as global, contextual or situational factors, and needs for autonomy, competence and relatedness), as well as affective, cognitive and behavioural consequences. The global level refers to a general motivational orientation to which people typically subscribe. The contextual level of the model refers to domains of life, such as education, work, leisure and interpersonal. Finally, the situational level is concerned with situation-specific motivation.

This model is useful for conceptualising the different processes in intrinsic and extrinsic motivation and should help understanding of these constructs in physical activity. For example, patients entering a GP-referral exercise scheme will bring with them their global motivational orientation, yet the activity counsellor or exercise leader is in a position to influence situational cues to alter situation-specific motivation. Indeed, Deci and Ryan (1991) suggest that moving individuals to self-determined forms of motivation is more

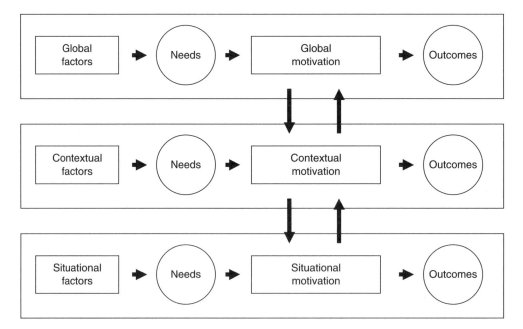

Figure 4.6 A hierarchical model of intrinsic and extrinsic motivation proposed by Vallerand (1997)

likely by altering situational or contextual factors. These include providing a meaningful rationale for the behaviour, acknowledging the individual's perspective, and conveying choice rather than control. In exercise, therefore, the exercise leader might explain why certain exercises are 'good' and others 'bad' and what effect they might have. Empathy with how exercisers feel concerning incompetence, inadequacy, exertion, etc. will also help. Finally, the leader will allow some choice of activities, pace, difficulty, etc.

Further implications for participation in physical activity

It is generally accepted that intrinsic motivation is a desirable quality for continued involvement in physical activities. However, the complex interrelationship between intrinsic motivation, perceptions of control and autonomy, and extrinsic rewards remains to be fully tested in exercise settings. Early summary evidence on adherence (Dishman, Sallis and Orenstein 1985) suggested that adults adopt exercise for reasons of health but are more likely to continue participation because of the more intrinsic feelings of well-being and enjoyment. Large population surveys also show that intrinsic reasons, such as 'feeling better', are important to both active and inactive people, although to varying degrees (Canada Fitness Survey 1983b). This suggests that adults may have an intrinsic orientation to physical activity, whether they are active or not. No doubt the more extrinsic influences of wanting to look 'good' in front of others, or participating to please others, will also be important factors for some people.

Exercise leaders and health promoters should be aware, given our previous discussion, of the interrelationship between rewards and intrinsic motivation. For example, the use of reward systems in health clubs has been a common strategy, though no systematic evaluation of their effectiveness has been reported. While the short-term influence on adherence may be positive, the research reported in this chapter suggests that those wishing to promote greater exercise participation must be cautious in their use of extrinsic rewards, particularly for those already high in intrinsic motivation. Rewarding competence may be appropriate, and it may also be better to reward and reinforce good behaviours rather than performance. In other words, encourage the process of activity by reinforcing frequency and participation, rather than solely reinforcing the product of, say, high fitness scores or the use of comparative reward structures. The rewarding of participation is more likely to lead to feelings of autonomy.

Locus of control

An old construct in psychology is that of 'locus of control' (LOC). It stems from a social learning theory approach to personality (Rotter 1954) where general beliefs are thought to develop from expectations based on prior reinforcements and the value attached to such reinforcements, and hence is an expectancy-value approach to motivation. Locus of control of reinforcements refers to the extent to which people perceive that reinforcements are within their own control, are controlled by others or are due to chance. In Rotter's seminal monograph on LOC he says 'it seems likely that, depending on the individual's history of reinforcement, individuals would differ in the degree to which they attributed reinforcements to their own actions' (Rotter 1966: 2). This led Rotter to formalise the construct of LOC and suggest that a generalised belief existed for internal versus external control of reinforcement. Rotter (1966) defined 'internals' and 'externals' as follows:

Box 4.3 Reconciling theory and practice: the youth fitness incentive schemes conundrum

If you talk with coaches and teachers they nearly always will tell you that badges and other extrinsic reward systems 'work' for children. But haven't you read about cognitive evaluation theory I ask them?! This area often creates a potential clash between the theory and what the practitioners say. Who's right?

The issue of motivating children to become and remain physically active has attracted the attention of physical and health educators, yet there is still relatively little evidence on the motivation of children and youth in the exercise settings beyond the arena of volunteer competitive sport. Despite this it is commonplace in schools and within some national agencies to operate extrinsic reward systems for the promotion of children's sporting and fitness behaviours. There has been much debate about the type of award scheme to implement for physical fitness (Corbin, Whitehead and Lovejoy 1988; Whitehead, Pemberton and Corbin 1990).

Some physical educators have suggested that children should be rewarded for participation in exercise (what Corbin *et al.* (1988) call 'process awards'), rather than superior performance against others. Not only could performance-based awards produce spurious results in terms of implications for health ('I'm fitter than X therefore I don't need to exercise'), but it is also likely to lead to a more external perceived locus of causality. Of course, rewarding exercise behaviour is also open to the negative aspects of rewards as much as 'performance awards' are, but, as with all reward schemes, the key must lie in their use as information on competence by providing positive feedback. As Corbin *et al.* concluded, 'in the absence of research to document various award schemes designed to motivate fitness and regular exercise among youth, we would be wise to apply the best theoretical evidence available' (Corbin *et al.* 1988: 213).

> If the person perceives that the event (the reinforcement) is contingent upon his/her own behaviour or his/her own relatively permanent characteristics, we have termed this a belief in internal control.
>
> (Rotter 1966: 1)

> When a reinforcement is perceived ... as following some action of his/her own but not being entirely contingent upon his/her action, then ... it is typically perceived as the result of luck, chance, fate, as under the control of powerful others, or as unpredictable ... When the event is interpreted in this way, ... we have labelled this a belief in external control.
>
> (Rotter 1966: 1)

In the same monograph Rotter presented psychometric evidence for the measurement of LOC with his internal–external (I–E) scale. This was a measure of 'individual differences in a generalised belief for internal or external control of reinforcement' (Rotter 1966: 1–2). The twenty-nine-item scale yields one score of LOC (high score indicating high externality) thus suggesting that LOC is a unidimensional construct. This has been challenged by a number of researchers. It should be noted, however, that Rotter stated that his I–E scale was a measure of *generalised* expectancy and therefore was likely to have a relatively low behavioural prediction but across a wide variety of situations. It was also likely to have greater predictive powers in novel or ambiguous situations since in specific well-known contexts more specific expectancies will be used (see discussion on self-efficacy in Chapter 5).

Two developments in LOC research that have a bearing on physical activity are the multidimensional nature of LOC and the behavioural specificity of measuring instruments.

Multidimensional LOC

In terms of multidimensionality, a number of researchers have suggested that the unidimensional I–E split is insufficient (Palenzuela 1988), although not all agree on the exact nature of the multidimensionality. Nevertheless, there is some agreement that at least the external pole of LOC should be divided into 'chance' and 'powerful others' since those believing that their life is 'unordered' ('controlled' by chance) would be different from those believing in events being controlled by powerful.

Specificity of measurement

Since Rotter's I–E scale was developed as a generalised measure, it was inevitable that researchers would predict that more situation-specific measures of LOC would allow for better prediction of specific behaviours. One of the most widely used of such measures is the Multidimensional Health Locus of Control Scale (MHLC) (Wallston, Wallston and DeVellis 1978) which yields scores on internal, chance and powerful others sub-scales. The MHLC, however, has had mixed success in predicting health behaviours, largely because of the wide range of possible behaviours it encompasses. It is also orientated towards illness and therefore may have little relationship with more overt health-enhancing behaviours such as exercise, although Dishman and Steinhardt (1990) did find the internal subscale of the MHLC scale to be predictive of habitual 'free-living' physical activity, but not of exercise. Despite the equivocal nature of findings, early reviews of the literature (Strickland 1978; Wallston and Wallston 1978) concluded that there was evidence for a link between health LOC and specific health behaviours.

Research on physical activity and LOC

Research investigating the link between perceived control, as measured by LOC scales, and participation in physical activity and exercise has taken three routes. First, some researchers have tried to identify links between generalised LOC and exercise, some have used health LOC and others have used exercise- and fitness-specific measures. Results collectively provide weak support for LOC in predicting fitness and exercise behaviours, although the extent that this could be a reflection of the inadequacies of the fitness or LOC measures remains to be seen. At best, studies suggest that some group differences may exist between exercisers and non-exercisers at a cross-sectional level on LOC. However, one cannot ascertain whether such differences developed as a result of involvement or whether they were influential in initial decisions to become active. Health LOC does not strongly predict, or relate to, exercise behaviour although some association has been found in some studies.

Such an equivocal conclusion has prompted researchers to ask why such is the case. Three main possibilities exist. First, the theory could be wrong or not applicable to exercise; second, the measuring tools are not sensitive or appropriate enough to demonstrate a relationship between LOC and exercise participation; and third, fitness/exercise 'externals' are rare people thus making it difficult from a research perspective to demonstrate relationships or discriminate between groups. Given the theoretical predictions of LOC research, and the extensive testing of the theoretical constructs involved, one could still propose that a relationship should exist. Most of the studies where no relationship has been found suggest that the LOC measures have not been specific enough to exercise and fitness behaviours, and this includes health LOC. Not all people will perceive exercise as a health-promoting behaviour anyway.

Calls for greater specificity in measurement have been met with several studies that have addressed this issue in exercise and physical fitness.

Several researchers have attempted to develop exercise or fitness LOC scales (Noland and Feldman 1984; Whitehead and Corbin 1988). However, measures have failed to provide evidence that a LOC measure that is specific to exercise is a better predictor than other LOC measures. Indeed, one could safely argue that they do not predict exercise behaviours at all well. No substantive work has been published on this issue in the past decade.

Summary comments on locus of control

The research on LOC has originated from the construct as outlined by Rotter (1966). Subsequent developments have included the use of multidimensional and situation-specific instruments. However, the overall conclusion one can reach about the relationship of LOC (however measured) and participation in exercise or fitness activities is largely weak or inconclusive and appears to have changed little in the past few years – a time when rapid development has occurred in other areas of exercise psychology.

Skinner's (1995, 1996) analysis also sheds light on the nature of LOC. We can conceptualise LOC as a set of beliefs preceding action and outcome, thus we would expect LOC to have a strong impact on behaviour. However, LOC is a construct that fits on the 'means–ends' side of Skinner's model shown in Figure 4.1. This suggests if LOC is primarily involving means–ends relations, and hence strategy beliefs, it is concerned with thoughts about what is *required* for success (contingency) rather than beliefs about whether one actually possesses such requirements (competence). This may weaken the predictive power of LOC on behaviour (Biddle 1999).

In conclusion, the often-stated belief that one needs 'control' over behaviour in order to lead active or healthy lives has not been supported by the LOC literature. This is probably due to a combination of weak methodology, inadequate instrumentation, the role it plays in contingency rather than competence beliefs, and the likelihood that LOC is only a small part of the explanation of exercise and physical activity behaviours anyway.

> Key point: The construct of locus of control remains popular but has not been a strong predictor of physical activity participation.

Attributions and physical activity

The role attributions may play in perceived control of exercise behaviours is potentially important although, as yet, research focusing specifically on exercise is sparse. Nevertheless, any discussion on control and expectancy-value theories of motivation relevant to exercise would be incomplete without some consideration of attributional processes. Similarly, attributions are considered important mediators of some other health behaviours (Adler and Matthews 1994; Stroebe and Stroebe 1995).

Attributions are the perceived causes and reasons people give for an outcome or behaviour and, because the focus is often on the perceived causality of behaviour, the term 'causal attributions' is sometimes used. Although the study of attributions has been applied to many settings, it is in achievement contexts that a great deal of research has been accumulated, particularly concerning academic achievement (see Weiner 1986, 1992), but also in sport (Biddle, Hanrahan and Sellars 2001).

One of the most widely known approaches to attributions is that proposed by Weiner (1986, 1992, 1995). Although originally working in the field of educational achievement, Weiner's theory of achievement motivation and emotion has application to a broader range of issues.

The main attribution elements used in Weiner's research were ability, effort, task difficulty and luck. The classification model used for categorising such elements into the dimensions of locus of control (later renamed locus of causality) and stability is well known. The locus of causality dimension classifies attributions as they relate to the individual (internal) or reside outside of the individual (external). The stability dimension refers to the classification of attributions in relation to their temporal stability, with some attributions being transient (unstable) and others relatively permanent (stable) over time.

Weiner (1979) later modified this model to include a 'controllability' dimension. The locus of control dimension then became locus of causality to reflect better the distinction between this and the 'new' dimension. The controllability dimension classifies attributions in terms of whether they are controllable or uncontrollable. For example, effort is often seen to be internal yet unstable whereas ability (at least in the 'natural ability' sense) is internal but stable. One could argue, therefore, that effort is controllable whereas ability is not. This kind of argument led to the creation of the extra dimension.

Weiner has argued that the attribution dimensions are related to the consequences that attributions may have for motivation, cognition and emotion. For example, making attributions to stable factors is likely to lead to expectations that similar results will occur again in the future, whereas unstable attributions provide less clear-cut information about expectations. Similarly, attributions to internal factors are thought to heighten emotional feelings whereas external attributions may be related to a lessening of emotion. This has subsequently been refined such that locus of causality is thought to be related to feelings of self-esteem and pride whereas the controllability dimension is thought to be related to social emotions, such as guilt and pity. For example, attributing the completion of a half-marathon to well-planned training (internal) could increase the feeling of pride associated with the run. If, however, the run was not completed due to a lack of personal effort (controllable), guilt may ensue or, in the case of someone trying hard but failing due to a perceived lack of ability (uncontrollable), others may feel pity for the individual (Weiner 1995).

One area of attribution research and perceptions of control that may be important in the study of exercise is that of learned helplessness. Again, the relationship with exercise is speculative due to a lack of research, although evidence in educational and clinical psychology does exist (Abramson, Seligman and Teasdale 1978; Peterson and Seligman 1984).

Abramson *et al.* (1978) suggested that uncontrollable failure, when attributed to personal inadequacy (internal, stable attributions), and generalised to other situations ('global' attribution), would generate feelings of helplessness. As a result of such proposals, attribution 'retraining' methods were suggested in an effort to change maladaptive attributions for failure (Forsterling 1988).

Learned helplessness hypotheses retain a great deal of intuitive appeal although there is much disagreement as to the exact mechanisms underpinning such phenomena. Research based on this might be a fruitful avenue for investigating those who drop out from, or do not initiate, an exercise programme and could be investigated alongside similar constructs such as amotivation. Studies could look at the cognitions of adults quitting, or failing to initiate activity programmes, and compare them with their more active counterparts. Developments should also include investigations of attributions at the point of dropout, or over time for those who never participate. Longitudinal studies are required which investigate the development of cognitions in childhood and their relationships, if any, with participation patterns in adulthood.

Attribution research in health

The general notion of perceived control in health has a long history, although it is more recent to see formal attribution paradigms being applied. Several researchers have investigated the causal beliefs attached to chronic illness (asking the 'why me?' question), and attributions have been found to have important roles in the understanding of health behaviour change (Schoeneman and Curry 1990), dietary and smoking behaviours (Eiser and van der Pligt 1988; Hospers, Kok and Strecher 1990; Schoeneman *et al.* 1988a; Schoeneman *et al.* 1988b), and persuasion to attend screening (Rothman *et al.* 1993).

Lewis and Daltroy (1990), in their short review of attributions and health behaviour, propose six possible applications of attributional principles to health education. These have some relevance to exercise promotion.

The six applications are:

- development of therapeutic relationships: eliciting attributions can assist in the development of empathy between patient and carer, or between other relationships in health settings
- creation of correct attributions: assistance in developing informed judgements about one's health status may be important for psychosocial adjustment, particularly where illness is concerned
- alteration of incorrect attributions: attributional change may be functional, either through misattribution alteration or through changes made in the dimensional structure of the attributions formed
- alteration of the focus of the attribution: sometimes the attributional focus may need to be shifted away from one area (for example uncontrollable illness) to another. This may act as a coping mechanism or assist in personal adjustment
- attribution of characteristics of the individual: health educators, and other health professionals, can use attributional statements in reference to the individual client or patient. These might motivate behaviours if the statements give certain cues to the individual, such as how good a person they are or how capable they are
- maintenance of perceived personal effectiveness: making the right attributions will have an influence on perceived competence and efficacy for the maintenance of their health behaviours.

Clearly there is some potential in the application of attributions to health behaviours, particularly as they relate to perceptions of control and subsequent motivation.

Attribution research in physical activity

Knapp (1988) suggests that attributional factors may be important in behavioural change strategies in exercise, but little research currently exists to verify this. McAuley and colleagues have studied attributions in exercise employing Weiner's (1986) theory of achievement attributions and emotions. McAuley, Poag, Gleason and Wraith (1990) studied a small group of middle-aged men and women who had previously dropped out of a structured exercise programme. Using the Causal Dimension Scale II (CDSII) (McAuley, Duncan and Russell 1992), study participants generally reported internal, unstable and personally controllable attributions for ceasing participation in the programme. Results also showed that attributions for dropping out were associated, in a small way, to feelings of shame, guilt, displeasure and frustration.

McAuley (1991) investigated attributions, self-efficacy and emotion midway through a five-month exercise programme for previously sedentary middle-aged adults. Analyses showed that attributing their exercise progress to internal, stable and personally controllable factors was associated with feelings of positive emotion, as was exercise efficacy. However, Vlachopoulos, Biddle and Fox (1996) found that attributions had a negligible effect on exercise-induced feeling states for children involved in track running. However, Vlachopoulos and Biddle (1997), when studying children's overall feelings about physical education, did find that personally controllable attributions augmented positive affect and minimised negative affect, regardless of levels of perceived ability.

Attributional thinking, placed within Skinner's (1995, 1996) model is primarily about interpretation of outcomes, the consequences of which may impact on future beliefs and actions. Attributions, therefore, are more distant from (future) actions and outcomes than most beliefs such as LOC. This may explain the difficulty researchers have had in demonstrating strong relationships between attributions and behaviour in physical activity. Only prospective studies can test this, and these are sparse. It also assumes that little will change between making the attributions and subsequent behaviour, yet we have not tested the longevity or consistency of attributions over time. To make matters worse, we have nearly always assessed attributions immediately after performance. Attributional processing reflects means–ends connections (Skinner 1995) and these involve strategy, not capacity, beliefs. Accordingly, attributional thinking looks to identify causes of outcomes (for example, ability, effort and luck) rather than appraising whether the individual has access to these causes (for example effort). In reality, one could argue that true attributional thinking, while primarily being about identification of causes, is also a response to questions such as 'why did *I* fail at this task?' thus necessitating control beliefs (that is, strategy and capacity beliefs). If so, attributions are more central to control beliefs and will also involve agent–ends connections. True perceptions of control, through control beliefs, require a combination of competence and contingency. Attributions, but not LOC, include both. Attributional processing is likely to involve both means–ends (contingency) and agent–ends (competence).

Further study is required to tease out the relative importance of these beliefs. Given that effort and ability are central constructs both to the beliefs in Skinner's model and within attribution theories, continued linkage in research seems prudent, yet few have taken up this suggestion since we said this in the first edition of this book in 2001. Certainly the evidence points to the utility of addressing attributions people make in physical activity and health settings. Attributions remain an important component of motivational theories using the perspective of perceived control.

Key point: Attributions are important statements and beliefs made in everyday life and may impact on our motivation to be physically active.

Perceptions of the incremental nature of ability

An interesting development in the study of control, goals and attributions has been Dweck's theorising concerning the perceived stability of ability (Dweck 1999; Dweck, Chiu and Hong 1995; Dweck and Leggett 1988). Initially in the domain of intelligence, and more recently extended to include views of morality and stereotyping, Dweck and colleagues have proposed that two clusters of beliefs underpin people's judgements and actions (Dweck

1992, 1996; Dweck, Chiu and Hong 1995; Dweck and Leggett 1988; Levy, Stroessner and Dweck 1998; Mueller and Dweck 1998). These beliefs centre on the way people view the malleability of attributes, such as intelligence. Those subscribing to the view that a particular attribute is fixed and relatively stable hold an 'entity' view or 'entity theory'. Conversely, those seeing the attribute as changeable and open to development hold an 'incremental' view or theory.

Research has shown that those holding an entity view are more likely to have negative reactions, such as helplessness, when faced with achievement setbacks (Dweck and Leggett 1988). Entity theorists are more likely to endorse performance (ego) goals whereas incremental theorists have been shown to endorse learning (task) goals.

There has been little attention given to implicit beliefs in the physical activity domain (Sarrazin *et al.* 1996). This is despite similar notions in prior research, such as ability and effort beliefs in attribution research, or beliefs concerning the causes of success in goal orientations research.

In a small-scale experiment, Kasimatis, Miller and Macussen (1996) told some students that athletic coordination was mostly learned, to create an incremental condition, and told others that coordination was genetically determined (entity condition). After initial success, participants were subjected to a difficult exercise task through video. Results showed that in the face of such difficulty, more positive responses were found for those in the incremental condition. Specifically, such participants reported higher motivation and self-efficacy and less negative affect. However, the implicit beliefs held by the students were not assessed. The nature and extent of entity and incremental beliefs in this sample, therefore, as well as the longevity of such effects, are not known.

We developed a scale for young people to assess entity and incremental beliefs in physical activity (Biddle *et al.* 2003a). Example items are shown in Table 4.2. We reported three studies of over 3,000 children and youth aged 11–19 years and found support for a multidimensional measuring scale that was suitable across age and gender groups. Analyses supported factors of entity and incremental beliefs being underpinned by beliefs that athletic ability is stable and a gift (entity) and open to improvement and being developed through learning (incremental). Incremental (negative) and entity (positive) beliefs predicted self-reported amotivation towards physical education and sport, while a further study provided evidence that enjoyment of physical activity in youth was positively associated with incremental beliefs. Evidence for cross-cultural validity also exists (Wang *et al.* 2005).

The physical activity research reviewed so far suggests that relationships do exist, albeit small at times, between implicit beliefs and goal orientations, as well as other motivational indicators. This could prove to be a useful development in the study of attributional thinking

Table 4.2 Example items from the 'Conceptions of the Nature of Athletic Ability Questionnaire – 2 (CNAAQ-2) (Biddle *et al.* 2003; Wang *et al.* 2005). All items are scored on five-point scales ranging from 'strongly disagree' to 'strongly agree'

Construct assessed	*Example item*
Incremental: learning	To be successful in sport you need to learn techniques and skills, and practise them regularly.
Incremental: improvement	If you put enough effort into it, you will *always* get better at sport.
Entity: stable	We have a certain level of ability in sport and we cannot really do much to change that level.
Entity: gift	To be good at sport you need to be naturally gifted.

in exercise. If sedentary individuals feel that exercising 'ability' is fixed and cannot be developed, they are less likely to try. This is supported by the ADNFS data reported in the previous chapter where over 40 per cent of women reported that feelings that they were 'not the sporty type' presented a significant barrier to physical activity.

> Key point: Believing that we can change our capacity to do things, like being physically active, may be important in creating positive motivation.

Chapter summary and conclusion

The popular health/fitness literature constantly makes reference to the concept of 'control' over lifestyle, fitness and health. This suggests that there is belief that the individual can 'control' their physical activity and, to some extent, their health. While this can be contested, perceptions of control can be important indicators of motivation and mental health. The evidence presented here has been accumulated from one main area – intrinsic motivation – as well as other sources derived from expectancy-value and control theories of motivation: locus of control, attribution-related theories and perceptions of the nature of physical ability. In the chapter, we have:

- reviewed the evidence in physical activity and other settings concerning the role of rewards and reinforcements on intrinsic motivation
- reviewed recent developments in intrinsic motivation theory concerning the role of a continuum of autonomy and self-determination
- reviewed the evidence concerning locus of control in physical activity
- reviewed the principles of attribution theory, and beliefs concerning ability, and provided evidence in the health and physical activity domains.

Having reviewed the evidence, we conclude:

- that Cognitive Evaluation Theory remains a viable theory for the study of motivational processes in physical activity
- that Self-Determination Theory is an important perspective for the study of motivation in physical activity and is likely to increase our understanding of motivation in the future, in particular the different types of extrinsic motivation that might exist in physical activity
- that current research findings are not supportive of locus of control being a strong determinant of physical activity and exercise. However, this could be due to numerous problems with the way that much of this research has been carried out. In particular, most studies violate the original assumptions of locus of control theory and measuring instruments have not been fully tested or have been inappropriately applied
- that despite limited evidence in the physical activity domain beyond competitive sport, the tenets of attribution theory are applicable to health and exercise and could provide an important perspective for understanding cognitive, affective and behavioural aspects of most health domains
- that beliefs concerning the stability of 'athletic ability' may be important motivational factors in physical activity.

5   Motivation through feelings of competence and confidence

I think I can, I think I can, I know I can ...

I did manage to influence some of my more sedentary colleagues. Exercise was unusual for African men of my age and generation. After a while even Walter (Sisulu) began to take a few turns around the courtyard in the morning. I know that some of my younger comrades looked at me and said to themselves 'If that old man can do it, why can't I?' They, too, began to exercise.

(Nelson Mandela, *Long walk to freedom*, 1994)

Purpose of the chapter

We continue our review of motivation for physical activity through reviewing the study of self-perceptions of competence and confidence. Specifically, in this chapter we aim to:

- move from general to specific self-perception theories relevant to the study of exercise
- review how people perceive competence in the physical domain, including general notions of competence, how we assess competence, and different definitions of competence
- outline achievement goal perspectives and related theories as viable ways to study motivation in exercise
- briefly discuss the role of self-schemata in exercise
- review self-efficacy theory and present a comprehensive overview of research findings, methods and issues
- present some alternative views on confidence relevant to the study of physical activity.

So far, we have discussed a number of issues associated with motivation for physical activity. Dominant theories where self-perception has been a central feature in the literature on physical activity are theories based on the constructs of self-efficacy, self-perceptions of worth and competence motivation, and, more recently, perceptions of success and definitions of achievement goals.

From general to specific self-perceptions

Contemporary self-esteem theory proposes that our global view of ourselves ('global self-esteem') is underpinned by perceptions of specific domains of our lives, such as social, academic and physical domains (Shavelson, Hubner and Stanton 1976). Based on this approach, Ken Fox has developed an operational measure of physical self-perceptions whereby psychometrically sound scales assess the higher-order construct of 'physical self-worth' (PSW) and its self-perception subdomains of sport competence, perceived strength, physical condition, and attractive body (Fox 1997a; Fox and Corbin 1989). This hierarchy is shown in Figure 5.1.

It is proposed that everyday events are likely to affect more specific perceptions of self, such as the belief that one can run one mile, which, if reinforced over time, may eventually contribute to enhanced self-perceptions of physical condition or even physical self-worth. As such, self-perceptions can be viewed in terms of being more 'domain general'; that is they operate at the level of general self-perceptions of competence and worth, such as PSW. We carry these around with us at a general level of abstraction and are unlikely to be modified by short-term or trivial experiences. Nevertheless, they could be important psychological constructs guiding general motivated behaviour. Self-perceptions can also be viewed in more specific terms, such as specific competency perceptions – 'can I finish this run?'; 'I have just walked two miles for the first time'.

In line with this analysis, we can identify common theoretical threads running through the literature on physical activity and exercise psychology. At the domain-general level are theories of competence and self-perceptions that, while not exactly trait-like, are generalisable across specific situations within the physical domain. These approaches include competence motivation, exercise self-schemata and goal orientations. At the level of situation-specific perceptions, the dominant approach has been Bandura's 'self-efficacy theory' (1977, 1986, 1997). These approaches form the content of the present chapter.

Domain-general approaches to physical activity motivation

In this section we discuss competence motivation theory, exercise self-schemata and recent perspectives on achievement goals and definitions of competence that are higher-order social–cognitive constructs of motivation and self-perception.

Self-perceptions and competence motivation theory

Attempts at explaining human behaviour through an individual's desire to seek situations where they can display competence is not new in psychology. A comprehensive interpretation of competence motivation has been made by American developmental psychologist Susan Harter (Harter 1978; Harter and Connell 1984). She conceptualised competence as

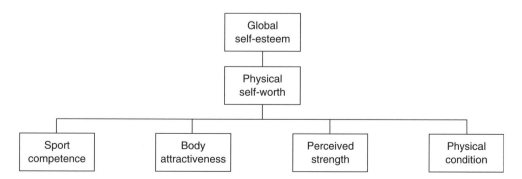

Figure 5.1 Physical self-perception hierarchy proposed by Fox (1990)

multidimensional by specifying domains of competence perceptions, such as scholastic and athletic competence. These domains are likely to become more differentiated with age (see Table 5.1). Second, she related self-perceptions of competence to motivational orientations and perceptions of control. Finally, she developed measuring instruments for the assessment of domains of competence and self-perceptions of adequacy.

Harter's theory suggests that individuals are motivated where their competence can be demonstrated, particularly if they also feel intrinsically oriented in that area and see them-selves as having a perception of personal control. Successful mastery attempts under such conditions are associated with positive emotion and low anxiety. Harter's theory predicts that those high in perceived physical competence would be more likely to participate in physical activity. An over-reliance on perceptions of competence through achievement set-tings may make this approach less relevant to the recreational/health-related context we are mainly concerned with in this book, but nevertheless, the strength and attraction of Harter's theory centre on the development of psychometrically sound and developmentally based instruments for the testing of her model.

The hierarchical model of physical self-worth proposed by Fox (1997a) presents another view of competence perceptions and motivation. The so-called 'self-enhancement' model of self-esteem is where positive self-perceptions play a motivational role in behaviour. For example, if I feel competent in the exercise domain it is more likely that I will want to demonstrate that competence, and hence be motivated to exercise. Indeed, the reverse (lack of motivation through perceptions of incompetence) is likely to be a major determinant of current sedentary habits of adults in industrialised countries. In addition, with exercise being a health behaviour, other motivations will be relevant. Not all exercisers participate to show competence; indeed some probably have relatively low perceptions of competence but are driven by motives of appearance, health, psychological well-being, etc. The picture is a com-plex one. Nevertheless, it is widely accepted that people have a need to maintain or enhance their self-esteem, thus they seek out situations where this is possible. We don't *freely* choose many (any?) behaviours where we demonstrate our incompetence!

Table 5.1 Competence perception/adequacy subdomains as represented in measures by Harter and colleagues

Children <8[a]	Children[b]	Students[c]	Adults[d]
Cognitive competence	Scholastic competence	Creativity	Sociability
Physical competence	Social acceptance	Intellectual ability	Job competence
Peer acceptance	Athletic competence	Scholastic competence	Nurturance
Maternal acceptance	Physical appearance	Job competence	Athletic abilities
	Behavioural conduct	Athletic competence	Physical appearance
		Appearance	Adequate provider
		Romantic relationships	Morality
		Social acceptance	Household management
		Close friendships	Intimate relationships
		Parent relationships	Intelligence
		Humour	Sense of humour
		Morality	

Notes
a Harter and Pike (1983)
b Harter (1985)
c Neeman and Harter (1986)
d Messer and Harter (1986)

Scales have been developed to assess specific physical self-perceptions. These have included the Physical Self-Perception Profile (PSPP) for adults (Fox and Corbin 1989) and children (Whitehead 1995), and the Physical Self-Description Questionnaire (PSDQ) (Marsh *et al.* 1994). However, few authors have challenged the way that competence perceptions have been assessed. Is 'competence' referred to in social comparative terms (for example 'are you better than kids your age?')? Contemporary literature on goal orientations supports the view that people can construe ability, competence and success in different ways, as we discuss later. In reference to his PSPP, Fox (1990) states quite clearly that he uses three orientations in assessing perceived competence. For the sport competence subscale, he assesses perceptions of sport/athletic *ability* (for example '[some people] feel that they are really good at just about every sport'), ability to *learn* sport skills (for example '[some people] always seem to be among the quickest when it comes to learning new sports skills'), and *confidence* in the sports environment (for example '[some people] are among the most confident when it comes to taking part in sports activities'). Even here, though, comparative elements inevitably creep in, such as with reference to 'among the most confident', even though the subject of the statement is mastery (participation) oriented. It would appear, therefore, that more account needs to be taken of the different ways people have of defining competence and success.

Differential definitions of competence and success: goal perspectives theory

Early research in sport and exercise psychology followed the theoretical perspectives associated with 'need for achievement' and expectancy-value theories of Murray, Atkinson and McClelland (see Weiner 1992). However, a major change of direction in the study of achievement motivation and perceptions of ability and competence can be traced to the work of Maehr and Nicholls (1980). They influenced the thinking of many people interested in achievement-related constructs and behaviour, and in particular in education. Such an approach was readily adopted by those in sport psychology, and maintains its relevance to physical activity mainly through the understanding of participation in sport and physical activity by children.

Maehr and Nicholls argued that:

> success and failure are not concrete events. They are psychological states consequent on perception of reaching or not reaching goals ... It follows that, if there is cultural variation in the personal qualities that are seen to be desirable, success and failure will be viewed differently in different cultures.
>
> (Maehr and Nicholls 1980: 228)

Maehr and Nicholls defined three types of achievement motivation: ability-orientated motivation, task-orientated motivation and social approval-orientated motivation. Ability-orientated motivation is when 'the goal of the behavior is to maximize the subjective probability of attributing high ability to oneself' (Maehr and Nicholls 1980: 237). This has been modified in sport psychology to refer to 'ego' goal orientations where success is defined as the demonstration of superiority over others (Duda 2001).

According to Maehr and Nicholls in task-orientated motivation 'the primary goal is to produce an adequate product or to solve a problem for its own sake rather than to demonstrate ability' (Maehr and Nicholls 1980: 239). This is the 'task' goal orientation.

The third goal – social approval-orientated motivation – has been investigated less than the other two goals. This dimension of achievement motivation was defined by Maehr and Nicholls in terms of demonstration of 'conformity to norms or virtuous intent rather than superior talent' (Maehr and Nicholls 1980: 241–2).

Nicholls (1989) has argued that the two main orientations here – task and ego – are based on how people construe competence. In a task perspective, ability and effort are less clearly differentiated and hence is referred to as the 'less differentiated conception of ability'. Cues used to assess competence are effort and task completion and hence are self-referenced. The 'more differentiated conception of ability' (ego orientation) is where competence is judged relative to others, and ability and effort are differentiated as causes of outcomes. This means that an externally referenced view is adopted. Nicholls (1989) also argues that these conceptions of ability give rise to corresponding goals in achievement settings, and these are the task and ego goals referred to. Further, it has been suggested that individuals will be predisposed to task or ego orientations.

> Key point: People define success in different ways and this will have implications for their motivation.

GOAL ORIENTATIONS AND LINKS WITH MOTIVATION

Two interrelated areas of goals and competence perceptions have now been studied in the context of physical activity and shed light on important motivational processes in the physical domain. These are:

- the relationships between individual differences in goal orientations and motivational constructs such as intrinsic motivation and perceptions of ability
- underlying belief structures and goals.

There is now consistent evidence that the adoption of a task goal in physical activity settings can be motivationally adaptive (Biddle *et al.* 2003b). However, ratings of task and ego goal orientations are usually found to be uncorrelated. Hence, goal 'profiles' can be studied whereby combinations of task and ego are accounted for. In other words, some people will be 'low' in both task and ego, some 'high' in task but 'low' in ego, or any other combination. We have found that children low in both task and ego goal orientations have lower perceived sport ability than other groups. Similarly, this group is often over-represented by girls, whereas for the high task/high ego group boys strongly outnumbered girls. One reason for this gender bias could be associated with socialisation and personal identity. It could be argued that it is more important for boys in our society to demonstrate 'competence', however construed, in physical activity settings.

Whereas Fox *et al.* (1994) found that the high task/high ego and high task/low ego groups were similar in their motivational responses when asked about sport in general, in a study of motivational responses following a specific physical fitness task, we found that children in the high task/low ego group had the most motivationally adaptive profile (Goudas, Biddle and Fox 1994b). In addition, a similar study showed that the high task/high ego and high task/low ego groups showed the best motivational profile, depending on the variables assessed (Vlachopoulos and Biddle 1996). Similarly, in a large sample of British children aged 12–15 years, we found that the most 'motivated' groups displayed high levels of task orientation, either alone or with a high ego orientation (Wang and Biddle 2001) (see Figure 5.2). It appears, therefore, that a high task orientation is positive, either singly or in combination with a high ego orientation.

We conducted a systematic review of the correlates of task and ego goal orientations in physical activity (Biddle *et al.* 2003b). Calculations showed associations of varying magnitude between a task orientation and:

- beliefs that effort produces success (positive association: +)
- motives of skill development and team membership (+)
- beliefs that the purpose of sport and physical education is for mastery, fitness and self-esteem (+)
- perceptions of competence (+)
- positive affect (+)
- negative affect (negative association: –)
- parental task orientation (+)
- various measures or markers of behaviour (+).

Associations of varying magnitude were found between an ego orientation and:

- beliefs that ability produces success (+)
- motives of status/recognition and competition (+)
- beliefs that the purpose of sport and physical education is for social status and being a good citizen (+)

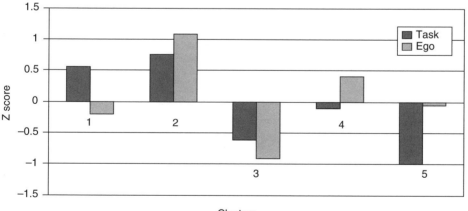

Figure 5.2 Task and ego goal orientation scores, expressed in Z scores, for 5 clusters, showing clusters 1 and 2 with high task orientation (Wang and Biddle 2001)

Notes
Clusters 1 and 2 displayed the most positive motivational profiles on other variables. The least motivated groups were clusters 3 and 5. Z scores are standardised scores with mean = 0 and SD = 1, hence scores above 0 are higher than the overall average, and those below 0 are below average. Typically, scores deviating at least +/- 0.5 are considered 'significant'

- perceptions of competence (+)
- parental ego orientation (+).

These associations suggest that a task orientation is motivationally positive.

The discussion so far has centred mainly on 'domain-general' theories of motivation, that is to say the theories that operate at a higher and more abstract level of generality. In addition, contemporary research has reflected a desire to study more state-specific conceptions of cognition and motivation. Such constructs are liable to be more open to influence, at least in the short term, and hence may have more practical appeal to practitioners attempting to change physical activity and health behaviours.

State-specific theories of motivation for physical activity

The social–cognitive perspectives currently favoured in the exercise psychology literature have drawn extensively on self-efficacy theory and this approach has had a large impact in both exercise (McAuley 1992; McAuley and Courneya 1993b) and health (Stroebe and Stroebe 1995).

Motivation and confidence: self-efficacy theory

Confidence has been identified at the anecdotal and empirical level as an important construct in exercise motivation. Statements associated with self-perceptions of confidence are commonplace in studies on exercise and sport. For example, in the Allied Dunbar National Fitness Survey for England (Sports Council and Health Education Authority 1992), emotional, motivational and time barriers were identified as factors preventing people being more physically active (see Chapter 2). All are likely to be associated, in one way or another, with feelings of confidence to initiate or maintain activity.

Physical self-efficacy is seen as a central construct in Sonstroem and Morgan's (1989) exercise and self-esteem model (Figure 5.3). Using the notion of a hierarchy, Sonstroem and

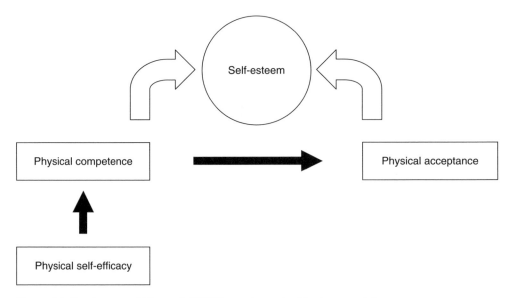

Figure 5.3 Sonstroem and Morgan's (1989) exercise and self-esteem model

Morgan place efficacy as a lower-order 'specific' construct in the model that represents the 'lowest generality level of the competence dimension. Self-conceptions at this level should be the most accurate and the most readily influenced by environmental interactions' (Sonstroem and Morgan 1989: 333). This concurs with Bandura's notions of self-efficacy. Sonstroem and Morgan's model proposes that physical self-efficacy is the first cognitive link between higher order psychological constructs and actual behaviours. The assumption is that behavioural outcomes influence self-efficacy, and onwards to self-esteem. This reflects a 'psychological consequences' approach to self-efficacy. However, self-efficacy theory also supports the reciprocal nature of the relationship between efficacy perceptions and behaviour by stating that the behaviour will not be undertaken unless efficacy perceptions are sufficient. This is dealing with the motivational role of self-efficacy and will be the approach adopted here.

BASIC TENETS OF SELF-EFFICACY THEORY IN PHYSICAL ACTIVITY AND EXERCISE

The need for studying the theories and mechanisms of confidence should be self-evident. However, there are a number of issues that need addressing. It is not known whether there are different types of confidence in exercise, such as the confidence to initiate exercise in the first place or the confidence that exercise will bring about desired results, such as weight loss or gains in fitness. The role of state versus trait factors is unclear, although contemporary approaches to the study of self-confidence suggest that situational cues are likely to dominate over and above any trait confidence factors. Also, the permanence of confidence in particular situations, or across different groups (for example age, gender, class, ethnicity) is rarely studied. This all suggests that self-confidence, despite a great deal of interest in this area of psychological research, and the intuitive logic and appeal of the topic, requires further study before application can be made in some fields.

The shift from reliance on stable personality traits as predictors of behaviour to a more social–cognitive approach has led to the development of a number of theoretical perspectives on self-confidence. These approaches range from efficacy expectations (Bandura 1997) to performance expectations (Corbin 1984), perceptions of competence (Harter 1978) and cognition–emotion relationships with likely behavioural consequences (for example learned helplessness: Abramson *et al.* 1978).

This diversity of approaches has been mirrored in the physical activity literature with studies on self-efficacy theory, performance expectancies, trait and state sport confidence, and movement confidence (Feltz , 1988, 1992; McAuley 1992; Vealey 1986).

Self-efficacy theory (SET) originated in clinical settings but it has subsequently been tested in a variety of physical activity and health contexts, such as sport (Feltz 1992), weight loss (Weinberg *et al.* 1984), exercise (Ewart 1989; McAuley and Blissmer 2000) and with other health-related behaviours (Schwarzer 1992; Strecher *et al.* 1986). Schwarzer, for example, states that 'self-efficacy has proven to be a very powerful behavioural determinant in many studies, and its inclusion in theories of health behaviour, therefore, is warranted' (Schwarzer 1992: 223).

Bandura defines perceived self-efficacy as

> people's judgements of their capabilities to organise and execute courses of action required to attain designated types of performances. It is concerned not with the skills one has but with judgements of what one can do with whatever skills one possesses.
>
> (Bandura 1986: 391)

The key phrase here is 'capabilities to organise and execute courses of action' since Bandura has always differentiated between efficacy expectations and outcome expectations. By this it is meant that beliefs related to the ability to carry out a particular behaviour are *efficacy* expectations whereas beliefs as to whether the behaviour will produce a particular result are *outcome* expectations. For example, efficacy expectations might be the belief that one can successfully adhere to a programme of brisk walking five times each week for thirty minutes each. However, outcome expectations might refer to whether one believes that such activity will produce the weight loss that was desired at the beginning. This is similar to Skinner's model discussed in Chapter 4 whereby capacity beliefs are required to produce the behaviour whereas strategy beliefs are needed to believe that the behaviour will produce the desired outcomes.

Although Bandura's SET refers to the two expectancies as being different, they are both part of the self-confidence concept in physical activity. People are likely to be concerned about both types of expectancy and both require study in exercise psychology research. For example, it is important to know whether efficacy expectations are influential in the adoption of exercise programmes, yet it is also likely that outcome expectations will affect the maintenance of such programmes and the reinforcement necessary for continued involvement. Studies apparently testing SET, however, do not always make it clear whether they are investigating efficacy or outcome judgements.

Key point: Self-efficacy is key to the adoption of many behaviours.

Sources of efficacy information Four main sources of information for self-efficacy beliefs have been identified by Bandura (1986, 1997). These are:

- prior success and performance attainment
- imitation and modelling
- verbal and social persuasion
- judgements of physiological states.

Performance attainment This is thought to be the most powerful of efficacy sources because it is based on personal experience of success and failure. However, the appraisal of such events through the use of attributions is likely to influence expectations of future success. Bandura states that 'successes raise efficacy appraisals; repeated failures lower them, especially if the failures occur early in the course of events and do not reflect a lack of effort or adverse external circumstances' (Bandura 1986: 399). Attribution theory predicts that internal and stable causes of failure, such as lack of ability, are more likely to lead to debilitating and demotivating cognitions and negative emotions than factors which appear more changeable, such as lack of effort or poor strategy.

The study of attributional variables in relation to perceptions of self-efficacy in exercise contexts has been sparse. McAuley (1991) integrates the two theories by studying previously sedentary middle-aged adults midway through a five-month exercise programme. As predicted by theory, efficacious exercisers reported more personally controllable attributions for their exercise progress. In addition, self-efficacy, as well as attributions, predicted exercise emotion.

Imitation and modelling Self-efficacy may also be developed through imitation and model-ling processes. Observing others succeed or fail could affect subsequent efficacy beliefs, particularly if the individual has little or no prior experience to draw on. Bandura (1986) suggests that social comparison information is important in self-efficacy beliefs. For exam-ple, confidence may be associated with certain self-presentational processes, such as social physique anxiety (Leary 1992; Leary, Tchividjian and Kraxberger 1994), and public exercise behaviours, such as street jogging, public swimming or exercise classes are likely to evoke strong self-presentation influences and could be a major source of motivational variation.

Bandura suggests that the social comparison element of vicarious experience is important since in some situations it is not always possible to gauge your success without some kind of reference point, such as another person's score: 'Because most performances are evaluated in terms of social criteria, social comparative information figures prominently in self-effi-cacy appraisals' (Bandura 1986: 400).

Another issue concerning vicarious processes in self-efficacy is the use of certain types of individuals in promoting exercise to non-exercisers or certain groups, such as the obese. It is common in the mass media to use elite sport models, or models displaying high levels of fitness or physique/figure development. Bandura contends that vicarious influences such as modelling are more likely to have an influence when the individual has some empathy with the model being observed. On the other hand, anecdotal evidence suggests that elite models are 'interesting' and 'motivational'. We are no closer to understanding this issue and it needs resolving to make effective use of models in physical activity promotion. Indeed, in our own research, we found that older patients referred into an exercise programme by their family doctor were more confident when exercising with similar individuals. They also reported feeling uncomfortable when around young 'vigorous' exercisers (Biddle, Fox and Edmunds 1994; Fox *et al.* 1997).

Verbal and social persuasion Depending on the source of such efficacy information, per-suasion from others is likely to influence perceptions of self-efficacy. However, it is thought to be a relatively weak source in comparison with the two already mentioned and has not been studied in any systematic way in exercise research. The success of persuasion is also dependent on the realistic nature of the information. Given the potential for regular contact between exerciser and instructor in supervised programmes, verbal persuasion is likely to be a source of self-efficacy worthy of note in some situations.

Judgements of physiological states The original theorising on self-efficacy was based on experiences in clinical settings, and in particular the modification of reactions to aversive events, such as phobias (Bandura 1977). In such situations it was found that self-efficacy was related to how one appraised internal physiological states such as heart rate. Bandura says that 'treatments that eliminate emotional arousal to subjective threats heighten per-ceived self-efficacy with corresponding improvements in performance' (Bandura 1986: 401). The use of such somatic feedback can be a positive influence on self-efficacy, however the evidence in sport has been inconsistent (Feltz 1992) and hardly studied at all, to our knowledge, in exercise, although teaching people how to monitor physiological signs may provide for the possibility of enhancing efficacy perceptions. It seems that studies need to address the links between the concepts of self-efficacy, effort perceptions and the capabilities people have for self-monitoring physical exertion during exercise. This is par-ticularly important for people apprehensive about exertion, such as in rehabilitation contexts.

Box 5.1 Applying self-efficacy theory to the promotion of physical activity

Self-efficacy theory gives clear intervention possibilities through each of its four sources of efficacy information. For promoting health-related activity, the following guidelines are proposed:

Performance attainment In recreational activity it is likely to be less important to participants whether they succeed in an objective way (that is, win the game). However, efficacy expectations for the adoption of physical activity are likely to be enhanced by prior experience in similar situations. Regrettably many people's experiences of physical activity stem from a narrow range of competitive games at school. Coakley and White (1992), for example, provided evidence from an English study that showed that negative perceptions of school physical education (PE) could be related to post-school participation. They attempted to identify the factors on which young people based their decisions about participation in leisure time sport and recreation. They found that involvement in sport reflected factors beyond those associated with competitive sport itself. One factor deemed important by these people was the experience they had had in school PE and sport. Lack of participation was related to negative memories of PE, with boredom, lack of choice, negative evaluation from peers and feelings of stupidity and incompetence being the most commonly cited factors. Girls were more likely to associate physical education experiences with discomfort and embarrassment and this seemed to affect their orientation to leisure time. Such experiences, according to SET, are likely to alter efficacy expectations in those activities experienced in school PE. These may then generalise, to differing degrees depending on the activities, to other physical activity modes.

A similar analysis is possible for school leavers who have experienced courses in health and fitness activities. Their self-efficacy for initiating their own activity programme is likely to be influenced by their experiences at school. The traditional images of 'drill' and 'exercise as punishment' have almost certainly been negative influences on activity patterns in leisure time. Interventions, therefore, must come in the form of enjoyable and reinforcing physical activity where individual perceptions of mastery and intrinsic motivation are enhanced.

Vicarious experience It could be argued that early experience in exercise, and the success of those around you, will influence self-efficacy expectations and, hence, physical activity patterns. Seeing people of similar build and physical ability 'succeed' in activity is likely to have positive effects. However, such effects have a greater probability of occurrence when 'success' is perceived in individualistic mastery-oriented terms (that is in a self-improvement 'task orientation'). Constant comparison with others (an ego-orientation) is more likely to lead to disappointment and potential dropout.

Social and verbal persuasion Although this usually refers to persuasion from others, self-talk has sometimes been found to be an effective strategy for enhancing self-efficacy, although the results have been mixed. In terms of exercise, it is likely that self-talk and personal perceptions of the costs and benefits of exercise will play a role in physical activity adoption or maintenance.

Judgements of physiological states This is probably more important in avoidance behaviours although a relaxed approach to physical activity may enhance the mental health benefits. A greater awareness of physiological symptoms of effort and pain could also be beneficial in maintaining a programme at an appropriate level. High levels of anxiety, such as social physique anxiety, may hinder participation.

Craig Ewart summarised the application of the sources of self-efficacy in the context of promoting exercise in a rehabilitation situation by saying that:

the most effective way to encourage patients to adopt exercise activities for which they lack self-efficacy is to expose them to the recommended activity in gradually increasing doses (performance), arrange for them to see others similar to themselves performing the activity (modelling); have respected health care providers offer encouragement by providing reassurance and emphasizing the patient's accomplishments (persuasion), and arrange the setting of the activity so as to induce a relaxed but 'upbeat' mood (arousal; physiological state).

(Ewart 1989: 684; words in brackets added)

Key point: The enhancement of self-efficacy is based on positive experiences as well as watching others who are similar to you succeed. A non-threatening atmosphere and encouragement will also help.

Measurement of self-efficacy Self-efficacy will vary along the dimensions of magnitude, strength and generality (Bandura 1986):

- magnitude of self-efficacy refers to the ordering of tasks by difficulty, such as feeling that one is capable of sustaining a walking programme but not one for running half marathons
- strength refers to the assessment of one's capabilities for performing a particular task. For example, people are able to rate subjectively their likelihood of maintaining a programme of walking to work every other day
- generality of self-efficacy refers to the extent to which efficacy expectations from one situation generalise to other situations, such as efficacy gained through a walking programme generalising to the lifting of weights in a body conditioning programme (Ewart *et al.* 1983).

Each of these measures of efficacy perceptions should be made, if conforming to Bandura's theory. Rarely is this actually the case. While all studies measure strength of self-efficacy, fewer measure magnitude and generality. The operational measures of self-efficacy, therefore, in physical activity settings appear to be limited.

Self-efficacy in physical activity and exercise: research findings

Self-efficacy is a popular topic of study within the physical activity domain. In addition to the number of studies increasing, there has also been a trend to study non-patient populations in an effort to counterbalance the early bias towards patient groups.

RESEARCH WITH PATIENTS

Ewart and co-workers conducted a number of the early studies on self-efficacy and exercise and they shed light on some important issues (see Ewart 1989). Ewart *et al.* (1983) studied self-efficacy in the context of treadmill running with post-myocardial infarction (MI) patients. Before and after treadmill exercise, assessment of self-efficacy to take part in walking, running, stair climbing, sexual intercourse, lifting and general exertion (but not all at once!) was made. The improvements in self-efficacy are illustrated in Figure 5.4.

These results show that positive changes in self-efficacy took place following treadmill exercise, and that this was greatest for running, suggesting that efficacy effects do generalise but appear to have stronger effects on similar exercise modes. When counselling also took place it was found that efficacy perceptions for sexual intercourse, lifting and general exertion significantly increased above the level attained after treadmill running. This was not true for the other activities indicating that generalisability of self-efficacy is enhanced for dissimilar activities when additional intervention is given.

Ewart *et al.* (1986) investigated the specificity of self-efficacy perceptions of men with coronary heart disease (CHD). Circuit weight training was used and self-efficacy ratings taken prior to a variety of physical fitness tests were shown to correlate more strongly with test results for activities specific to the self-efficacy judgements. For example, efficacy ratings for the performance of lifting activities were significantly correlated with the arm strength test but not with the aerobic endurance treadmill test. Conversely, self-efficacy ratings of jogging were significantly correlated with the aerobic endurance test but not with tests of arm, grip or leg strength.

The studies discussed so far have focused on those with known medical symptoms, such as documented CHD. The extent that such studies can be generalised to other people remains problematic. Given that self-efficacy is a social–cognitive variable open to environmental and perceptual intervention, it might be unwise to generalise from these studies. For example, Ewart (1989) suggests that post-coronary patients are often limited more by fear of exertion than their actual medical condition. This is quite different from individuals free of disease symptoms. Studies on medical patients in exercise rehabilitation suggest that:

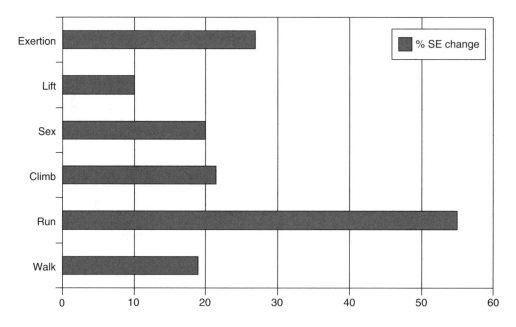

Figure 5.4 Increases in self-efficacy after treadmill running for post-MI men (data from Ewart *et al.* 1983)

- self-efficacy judgements can generalise but will be strongest for activities similar to the activity experienced
- self-efficacy in 'dissimilar' activities can be enhanced through counselling
- self-efficacy better predicts changes in exercise behaviour than generalised expectancies of locus of control.

RESEARCH WITH NON-PATIENT GROUPS

Many research papers have been published on self-efficacy for exercise and physical activity in non-patient groups. Large adult community samples have shown self-efficacy to predict walking (Hofstetter *et al.* 1991) and exercise change over time (Sallis *et al.* 1992). Self-efficacy has also discriminated adherers from dropouts in an exercise weight loss programme (Rodgers and Brawley 1993), has predicted positive affect after exercise (Bozoian, Rejeski and McAuley 1994), and has negatively correlated with psychobiological markers of negative affect (Rudolph and McAuley 1995).

McAuley's work on exercise self-efficacy has been influential (McAuley 1992; McAuley and Courneya 1993b; McAuley and Mihalko 1998). McAuley and Blissmer (2000) summarise evidence on self-efficacy and physical activity in respect of self-efficacy (SE) being a determinant and an outcome of physical activity (see Figure 5.5).

McAuley and colleagues have studied self-efficacy responses of older adults, a population previously underrepresented in the exercise psychology literature. Several studies by McAuley and co-workers focus on a group of previously sedentary 45–64 year olds. These studies have shown that for older adults, exercise self-efficacy:

- can be increased through intervention
- will predict participation, particularly in the early stages of an exercise programme
- declines after a period of inactivity.

McAuley and Blissmer (2000) conclude that while the relationship between self-efficacy and physical activity is well documented, it is also complex. For example, self-efficacy

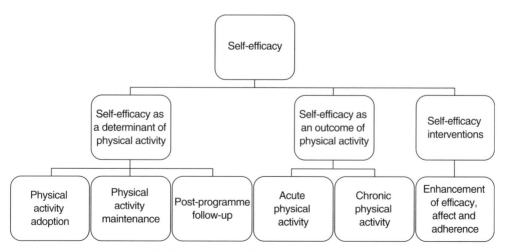

Figure 5.5 A summary of self-efficacy and physical activity, adapted from McAuley and Blissmer (2000)

beliefs are likely to be more influential in conditions that are challenging in comparison with circumstances that are more 'habitual' and requiring of less effort. For this reason, the promotion of habitual physical activity through, say, walking to work, could involve only minimal amounts of self-efficacy, thus holding much promise for behaviour change.

In summary, the studies investigating self-efficacy in non-patient exercise groups show a consistent relationship between self-efficacy and participation in physical activity, as well as relationships with other important factors, such as post-exercise emotion.

> Key point: Self-efficacy is one of the most consistent correlates of physical activity.

Methodological issues in self-efficacy research

It has been argued that self-efficacy needs to be assessed in relation to specific behaviours if increased magnitude of behavioural prediction is required (Bandura 1997; McAuley 1992). Generalised perceptions of confidence are not the same as perceptions of efficacy. Nevertheless, we need more studies on the generalisability of self-efficacy across physical activity settings. Similar to the attitude–behaviour correspondence issue in social psychology (see Chapter 3), the utility of self-efficacy is likely to be greater when measures correspond closely to the behaviour in question, such as cycling three times per week, rather than using a general reference such as 'exercise'.

This issue is not always addressed in the measurement of 'self-efficacy'. For this reason, one must question the assumptions underpinning Ryckman *et al.*'s (1982) Physical Self-Efficacy Scale. Their rationale for developing such a scale was based on the need for measuring self-efficacy for exercise in preference to more global measures of self-concept. However, they too have only assessed generalised perceptions of physical ability and 'self-presentation confidence', and not self-efficacy as defined by Bandura. Indeed, secondary analysis of four previously published data sets shows that the scale assesses physical self-esteem rather than self-efficacy and that the scale was a weaker predictor of behavioural outcomes than in a task-specific measure of self-efficacy (Hu, McAuley and Elavsky 2005).

In addition, Sherer *et al.* (1982) report the development of what they call 'the Self-Efficacy Scale'. However, inspection of the test items and rationale for test construction suggests that their inventory is more akin to a general self-motivation scale and does not approximate Bandura's conceptualisation of self-efficacy. Sallis *et al.* (1988) have developed scales for the assessment of self-efficacy for diet and exercise behaviours. For exercise they derived factors labelled 'resisting relapse' and 'making time for exercise'. Data showed that the two subscales correlated 0.32–0.40 with self-reported vigorous physical activity.

Box 5.2 I'm not the sporty type – but so what?

The Allied Dunbar National Fitness Survey in England, as we discussed in Chapter 2, showed that many adults, and in particular women, felt that they were not active because they were 'not the sporty type'. This reflects a lack of self-efficacy to adopt a physically active lifestyle. It is unfortunate that they link 'sport' with being active more generally. We need to promote physical activity in such a way that it does not conjure up images of vigorous exercise and sport.

The second methodological issue to be considered concerns the behaviours associated with efficacy perceptions. Assessing self-efficacy in any meaningful way requires the behaviour to be associated with effort, potential barriers and behavioural self-regulation. In other words, habitual behaviours, such as tooth brushing, are likely to be unrelated to feelings of efficacy whereas physical exercise may be highly associated with efficacy beliefs since exercise requires planning, effort and often considerable barriers. This is probably why self-efficacy emerges as one of the most consistent predictors of physical activity behaviours, particularly when physical activity includes elements of vigorous exercise. The extent to which less effortful forms of physical activity require self-efficacy remains to be seen.

Other approaches to the study of confidence and physical activity

Although SET has dominated the literature linking confidence perceptions and exercise, other perspectives and approaches have been adopted and shed some interesting light on related issues.

PERFORMANCE ESTIMATION

Bandura (1997) clearly differentiates between efficacy and outcome expectations. However, earlier on it was stated that both types of expectancy are likely to be important in physical activity settings. Using a similar construct to outcome expectations, Corbin and his co-workers have investigated the issue of self-confidence in exercise from the view point of performance estimations (see Corbin 1984). This research programme was based on theorising by Lenney (1977) in the area of women and achievement behaviour. Lenney suggested that while evidence pointed to underachievement by females in some achievement contexts, this was not invariably so and pointed out that female self-confidence was dependent on 'situational vulnerability'. This was determined by three main factors:

- *the sex-typed nature of the task:* confidence is likely to be low in situations where the task is perceived as 'inappropriate'. That is to say a role conflict may be apparent such as in performing tasks sex-typed as 'masculine'. An example would be women in the context of a weight training class where some might lack self-confidence.
- *social evaluation:* Lenney (1977) has suggested that females will underestimate their ability when they are being evaluated or compared, such as in competition
- *feedback:* it has been proposed that females achieve better levels of performance when given objective and accurate feedback.

These factors point to important variables in the physical activity environment and, while originating from the study of women in achievement contexts, could also apply to men in some situations, such as activities sex-typed as 'female' or 'feminine' (for example dance; aerobics). However, given the predominantly masculine stereotyping of many physical activities, particularly sports, the emphasis has been placed on research into female self-confidence (Corbin 1984).

Self-presentational processes

Physical appearance, gestures and movement, public self-consciousness, weight, appearance and physique anxiety, and modesty are all constructs listed in the contents page of Leary's

(1995) book, *Self-presentation*. Clearly, there is great potential for using such constructs in furthering our understanding of physical activity and perceptions of confidence.

Self-presentational concerns may affect physical activity choice, such as when one perceives the activity to be incompatible with one's image, such as in aerobic dance or lifting weights, or where anxiety is felt in displaying low levels of physical competence. As Leary says 'people are unlikely to devote themselves to activities that convey impressions that are inconsistent with their roles, others' values, or social norms' (Leary 1992: 342).

Hart, Leary and Rejeski (1989), for example, have studied the construct of 'social physique anxiety'. Specifically, they propose that people high in such anxiety, in comparison with those not anxious,

> are likely to avoid situations in which their physique is under scrutiny of others (for example swimming in public) ... avoid activities that accentuate their physiques (including aerobic activities that might be beneficial to them) ... and attempt to improve their physiques through a variety of means, some of which may be harmful (for example, fasting).
>
> (Hart, Leary and Rejeski 1989: 96)

The ADNFS data showed that concerns about lack of sports competence were major barriers to participation in physical activity (Sports Council and Health Education Authority 1992). How generalisable such feelings are remains to be seen. For some individuals, feelings of 'not being the sporty type' may generalise across many different physical activities, whereas for others they may only affect one or two specific activities. Indeed, most physical activities such as sports occur in such public settings that self-presentational issues are hard to ignore. Coupled with this is the widespread social acceptance and admiration of physical expertise. This means that social anxiety in physical activity contexts is likely to be common. People are more likely to experience social anxiety when they are motivated to make desirable impressions on others but have low feelings of self-efficacy in being able to so (Leary 1995).

Chapter summary and conclusions

In this chapter, we have attempted to review and synthesise some of the major theoretical approaches in exercise motivation that have focused on self-perceptions of efficacy and competence. Specifically, we have:

- moved from 'domain-general' approaches, including physical self-perceptions, competence motivation and goal orientations, to more state-specific conceptions of competence, such as through self-efficacy theory
- reviewed how people perceive competence in the physical domain, including general notions of competence, how we have assessed competence and the different definitions of competence
- outlined how task and ego achievement goals are viable ways of studying motivation in physical activity
- reviewed self-efficacy theory and presented a comprehensive overview of research findings, methods and issues
- presented some alternative views on confidence relevant to the study of physical activity, including self-presentational concerns.

From our review of the literature, we conclude:

- that participation in physical activity is associated with perceptions of competence, in whatever form competence is operationalised. However, more specific perceptions of competence/efficacy are likely to be better predictors of specific behaviours than gener-alised beliefs in competence
- defining 'competence' is not easy and there may be a bias towards social comparative definitions of competence
- goal perspectives theory proposes that people can define competence and success in different ways, the main ones being ego and task orientations. Research is consistent in showing the motivational benefits of a task orientation, either singly or in combination with an ego orientation
- research using self-efficacy with patient groups demonstrates that exercise self-efficacy can be developed; self-efficacy judgements can generalise but will be strongest for activities similar to the activity experienced; self-efficacy in 'dissimilar' activities can be enhanced through counselling; self-efficacy better predicts changes in exercise behaviour than generalised expectancies
- research with non-patient groups has shown that exercise self-efficacy can be increased through intervention, will predict participation, particularly in the early stages of an exercise programme, will decline after a period of inactivity, and is associated with pos-itive exercise emotion
- self-presentational processes offer additional understanding to physical activity confi-dence and anxiety.

6 Stage-based and other models of physical activity

Moving from thinking to doing

Welcome or not, change is unavoidable.

(Prochaska, Norcross and DiClemente 1994)

Purpose of the chapter

The purpose of this chapter is to consider models that have been constructed as a way of better understanding health behaviours, including physical activity. In particular, we focus on stage-based approaches and specifically the popular 'transtheoretical model'. Other frameworks are also considered. Specifically, in this chapter we aim to:

- outline the popular 'transtheoretical model' approach to physical activity decision-making, including contemporary research findings and the constructs of self-efficacy, pros and cons, and processes of change
- discuss the 'natural history' model of exercise proposed by Sallis and Hovell (1990) and suggest which determinants might be important at the different phases of the model
- outline the relapse prevention model and data from physical activity research
- describe the lifespan interaction model and show how it provides a good global framework for the study of the complex factors associated with participation in exercise and physical activity.

A great deal has been said in recent years on the likely determinants of physical activity. Much of this has centred on psychological and social psychological issues. One way to make sense of this diversity is to use a framework for theories, such as the one we have proposed in Figure S2.2. This has been used to structure Part II of this book. The theories and approaches discussed so far are what could be termed 'linear' approaches like the Theory of Planned Behaviour. Essentially, they operate as continuous and unidirectional models in which specified relationships exist in the prediction of physical activity behaviour. The current chapter deals with models and 'theories' that can best be described as 'stage-based' models of physical activity behaviour. Stage models assume discontinuity between qualitatively different stages. The best-known such model is the transtheoretical model (TTM), sometimes referred to as the 'stages of change' framework.

Several researchers have proposed a stage approach to advance understanding of how people move into or out of participation in exercise or physical activity. First, the TTM will be discussed, followed by Sallis and Hovell's (1990) 'natural history model of exercise'.

This allows for an analysis of possible determinants at different stages of physical activity involvement. A 'hybrid' of continuous and stage models – the health action process approach (HAPA) (Schwarzer 1992, 2001) is also presented briefly, although this has been discussed more fully in Chapter 3. Finally, Dishman's (1990) heuristic model of physical activity (the lifespan interaction model) will be outlined.

The Transtheoretical Model

Research into the nature of behaviour change in smokers and those presenting themselves for psychotherapy has suggested that recovery from problem behaviours, or successful behaviour change, involves movement through a series of stages (Prochaska, DiClemente and Norcross 1992; Prochaska, Norcross and DiClemente 1994; Prochaska and Velicer 1997; Prochaska *et al.* 1994). Literature using the TTM in physical activity is now diverse, including descriptive studies (Marcus, B. H. *et al.* 1992a; Mullan and Markland 1997), interventions (Mutrie *et al.* 2002b), narrative overviews (Prochaska and Marcus 1994), focused reviews (Nigg 2005), a meta-analysis (Marshall and Biddle 2001) and practical guidelines (Marcus and Forsyth 2003).

Even those attempting self-change, as well as those in therapy, seem to move through 'stages of change'. This approach is currently popular in psychotherapy and also in other areas of health, including physical activity behaviour change. The term transtheoretical model, a term used to describe the wider framework that encompasses both the 'when' (stages) and the 'how' of behaviour change, including the processes of change and moderators of change such as decisional balance and self-efficacy. We review the evidence on the TTM and physical activity in this chapter and then make application to interventions in Chapter 12.

Stages of change

Table 6.1 outlines the defining features of the key stages. Typically, studies in physical activity assess precontemplation, contemplation, preparation, action and maintenance stages. Precontemplation includes people who are not currently physically active (at the level specified) and have no intention of doing so in the near future. Those in the contemplation stage include those not currently physically active but who have an intention to start in the near

Table 6.1 Defining stages of the Transtheoretical Model

Stage	Meeting criterion level of physical activity?	Current behaviour	Intention to meet criterion level of physical activity?
Precontemplation	✗	Little or no physical activity	✗
Contemplation	✗	Little or no physical activity	✔
Preparation	✗	Small changes in physical activity	✔
Action	✔	Physically active for less than 6 months	✔
Maintenance	✔	Physically active for more than 6 months	✔

future. Those in preparation are individuals who are 'currently exercising some, but not regularly' (Marcus and Owen 1992: 6), or, as Prochaska and Marcus (1994) suggest, these people are intending to take action in the next month or so. The action stage represents people who are currently active, but have only recently started. As such, Prochaska and Marcus (1994) suggest that it is an unstable stage during which individuals are at high risk of relapse. Finally, the maintenance stage includes those who are currently physically active and have been for some time, usually at least six months.

Other 'stages' sometimes considered include 'termination' and 'relapse'. Termination has not been used in physical activity research but does feature in other TTM research, such as on smoking and alcohol abuse. Prochaska and Marcus define this stage as the point at which people have 'no temptation to engage in the old behaviour and 100 per cent self-efficacy in all previously tempting situations' (Prochaska and Marcus 1994: 163). Relapse has not been tested much in physical activity research but is consistent with Sallis and Hovell's (1990) model, discussed later. While data are available from smoking and alcohol research on the risk of relapse from the maintenance phase, little data are available in physical activity. However, Marcus and Simkin (1994) suggest that maybe 15 per cent fall into the category of being 'relapsers' (that is, regressive movement back to either contemplation or precontemplation).

Attempts to estimate the prevalence within each stage are fraught with difficulties because such efforts will be reliant on how the behavioural criterion is defined. For example, one would expect more people will be in the maintenance group if the criterion measure of physical activity is moderate activity for thirty minutes on three days each week in comparison with the internationally accepted target of at least five days (150 minutes) per week. However, estimates from our meta-analysis (Marshall and Biddle 2001) shown in Figure 6.1 suggest that even this is inconsistent, leading to the conclusion that sampling in TTM studies may be biased. This is supported by the data showing that for studies that actively recruited participants, far more were in the precontemplation stage (25 per cent) than when passive methods

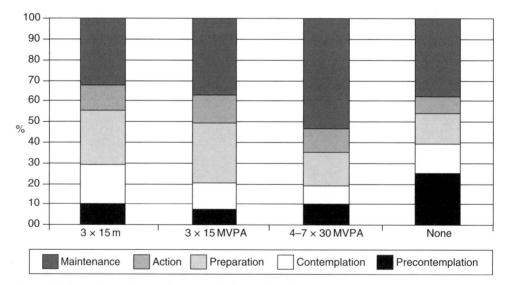

Figure 6.1 Prevalence estimates for stages of change by different levels of physical activity and exercise (data from Marshall and Biddle 2001)

Note
MVPA: moderate to vigorous physical activity

were used (8 per cent). We did estimate the stage distributions for our total sample of 68,580 derived from sixty-eight samples, as well as for four countries. These are shown in Figure 6.2.

The stages outlined suggest a steady linear progression from one stage to the next. However, certainly in the area of addictive behaviours, where most of the research using the TTM approach has been carried out, a linear pattern has given way to the belief that change is cyclical, as suggested in Figure 6.3. In the context of physical activity, Marcus and Simkin

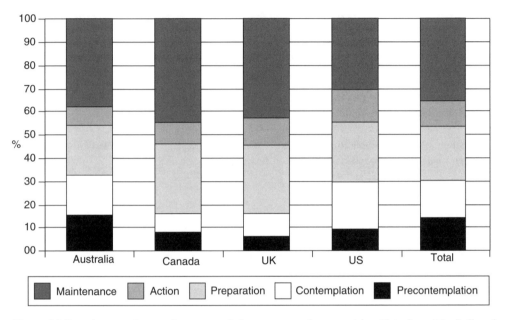

Figure 6.2 Prevalence estimates for stages of change across four countries (data from Marshall and Biddle 2001)

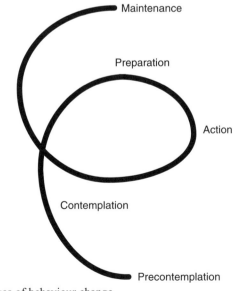

Figure 6.3 Cyclical stages of behaviour change

(1994) suggest that several attempts at change are likely before maintenance is reached. Indeed, Prochaska *et al.* (1992) say that for many the process of 'cycling' back and forth through the stages may help strengthen behaviour change in the long run as people learn from their mistakes and relapses. However, as they succinctly put it, 'much more research is needed to better distinguish those who benefit from recycling from those who end up spinning their wheels' (Prochaska *et al.* 1992: 1105).

More recently, stage models of health behaviour have received more critical appraisal. For example, Weinstein, Rothman and Sutton (1998) present what they see as defining features of stage theories. These are:

- a classification system for defining stages
- an ordering of stages
- common barriers to change facing people in the same stage
- different barriers to change facing people in different stages.

They suggest that cross-sectional comparisons across stages have limited value in testing whether a true stage process is followed in health behaviour change.

Processes of change

The stages of change discussed so far refer to the temporal patterning of behaviour change. By also identifying *processes* of change we are able to better understand why and how this temporal shift might take place. Processes of change, therefore, are important for interventions – for moving people between stages. This is discussed more fully in Chapter 11. For now, we outline the proposed processes of change and report on our summary meta-analytic data.

Processes of change are defined by Marcus *et al.* as 'the cognitive, affective, and behavioral strategies and techniques people use as they progress through the different stages of change over time' (Marcus, B. H. *et al.* 1992b: 425). Table 6.2 describes ten processes of change. Five of these processes are described as cognitive or 'thinking' strategies and the other five as behavioural or 'doing' strategies. The results of our meta-analysis showed that individuals use all ten processes of change when trying to modify their physical activity behaviour. Cognitive processes tended to peak during the action stage and behavioural processes in the maintenance stage. However, the pattern of change for behavioural processes differed from that described in narrative reviews (Prochaska and Marcus 1994; Reed 1999).

Box 6.1 Where have all the ~~flowers~~ precontemplators gone?

Most of the research in exercise psychology is based on the premise that too few people are active enough for health. This suggests that many people are contemplators or precontemplators. However, many research studies sample already active people. This makes it difficult to truly understand the key group of precontemplators. For example, only 13 per cent of Australians were classified as precontemplators, and 10 per cent as contemplators for 'exercise' in a large 'representative' survey by Booth *et al.* (1993), yet it is highly unlikely that so few really are inactive.

Where can we study precontemplators? This is a challenge for researchers. Advice from market researchers may be helpful, as well as seeking locations where such people may be located and willing to participate.

Behavioural processes have been hypothesised to increase in a linear fashion up to the stage of action and then level off during maintenance. However, the meta-analytic evidence showed that precontemplation to contemplation and preparation to action are characterised by sharper increases in behavioural process use compared with other transitions.

Nine of the ten processes followed similar patterns of change across the stages and this is important because it argues against the presence of a stage-by-process interaction whereby some processes are thought to be more important or likely at certain stages. The distinction between the higher-order cognitive and behavioural processes, therefore, may not apply in the physical activity domain.

Few studies are available that make process-specific predictions at each stage of change. It has been suggested that consciousness raising is particularly important when moving from precontemplation to contemplation, and our meta-analysis supported this.

Decisional balance

One strategy that can assist people to make successful behaviour change is to weigh up the advantages of change ('pros') against the disadvantages or costs ('cons'). This 'decisional balance' exercise is one that has been at the core of the TTM. Examples of items in a decisional balance questionnaire for exercise are shown in Table 6.3. Research has shown that at the early stages of behaviour change cons outweigh pros. Those in preparation may have more equality between the pros and cons, whereas those who are in maintenance will perceive more pros than cons. This suggests that influencing perceptions of pros and cons may assist in behaviour change and that reaching the stage of action may be dependent on having pros outweigh cons. This is illustrated by the 'cross-over' point shown in Figure 6.4 where the change from one stage to another is shown.

Table 6.2 Processes of change applied to physical activity (Marcus and Forsyth 2003)

Process	Description
Cognitive/thinking processes	
Increasing knowledge	Increasing information about oneself and physical activity
Being aware of risks	Understanding the risks of inactivity and sedentary living
Caring about consequences to others	Recognising how inactivity might affect others, such as family and co-workers
Increasing healthy alternatives	Increasing awareness of alternative ways of being physically active
Understanding the benefits	Increasing awareness of the benefits of physical activity
Behavioural/doing strategies	
Substituting alternatives	Seeking ways of being physically active when encountering barriers of time, etc.
Enlisting social support	Seeking support from others for your physical activity efforts
Rewarding yourself	Praising and rewarding yourself, in a healthy way, for making successful efforts in physical activity
Committing yourself	Making plans and commitments for physical activity
Reminding yourself	Establishing reminders and prompts for physical activity, such as diary time slots and making equipment easily available

Table 6.3 Example items assessing decisional balance ('pros' and 'cons') for exercise (Marcus and Owen 1992). A five-point Likert scale is used to score responses (not at all important = 1 to extremely important = 5)

1	I would be healthier if I exercised regularly
2	I would feel better about myself if I exercised regularly
3	Other people would respect me more if I exercised regularly
4	My family and friends would get to spend less time with me if I exercised regularly
5	I would feel that I was wasting my time if I exercised regularly
6	I would probably be sore and uncomfortable if I exercised regularly

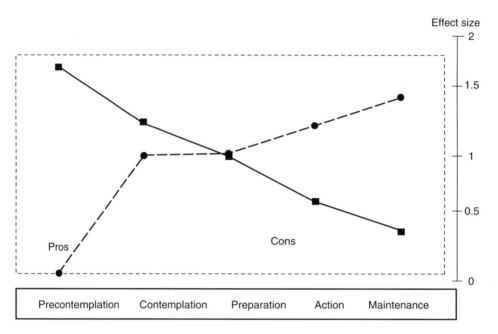

Figure 6.4 Changes or differences in pros and cons across stages (data from Marshall and Biddle 2001)

Self-efficacy

Evidence has shown consistently that increasing self-efficacy is associated with greater exercise readiness – that is, a more 'advanced' stage (Marcus and Owen 1992; Marshall and Biddle 2001; Prochaska and Marcus 1994). Results from our meta-analysis showed that self-efficacy increased with each stage of change, as proposed by the TTM. However, although the pattern of increase appears to be linear on Figure 6.5, the pattern of effects were moderate (precontemplation to contemplation), small-to-moderate (contemplation to preparation), moderate (preparation to action), and moderate-to-large (action to maintenance) (see Figure 6.5), suggesting some non-linearity, contrary to predictions.

Key point: The transtheoretical model involves both the 'when' and 'how' of behaviour change.

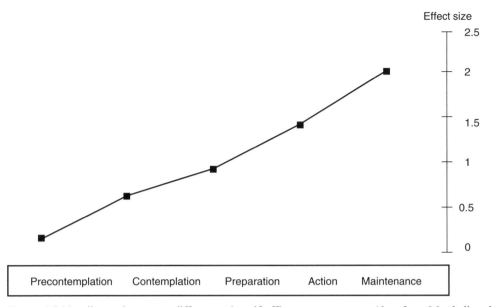

Figure 6.5 Non-linear changes or differences in self-efficacy across stages (data from Marshall and Biddle 2001)

Conclusions and critique of the transtheoretical model

There is no doubt that a dynamic approach to understanding physical activity that includes different stages of 'readiness' is an appropriate framework to understand behaviour and behaviour change. The success of the TTM in other health settings also lends confidence to its application to physical activity. Similarly, Marcus and co-workers, as well as other researchers, have shown the utility of the TTM in physical activity across several countries and in adults of differing ages. With processes of change also proposed, the likelihood of TTM being applied successfully in intervention trials is increased. Indeed, many interventions have used the TTM as their theoretical framework (Cox *et al.* 2003; Dunn *et al.* 1999).

The majority of studies investigating the TTM in physical activity (Marshall and Biddle 2001) and other health behaviour contexts (Sutton 2000) are cross-sectional. This presents difficulties in establishing causal relationships between constructs and stages. Moreover, many studies using such a design provide support for what Weinstein and colleagues (1998) have called 'pseudo-stage' models where there is a linear pattern of 'change' or 'difference' in a cross-sectional design, between variables rather than having an a priori assumption of discontinuity whereby a variable is predicted to act differently at different stages (Sutton 2000). Data from our meta-analysis are more supportive of a pseudo-stage model. For example, physical activity differences between stages followed essentially a linear pattern, with only a hint of discontinuity. In Figure 6.5, self-efficacy has a hint of discontinuity but some might describe the pattern as essentially linear across the stages. Similarly, in a study we conducted on the extent and determinants of promoting physical activity for patients by mental health professionals (Faulkner and Biddle 2001b), we assessed mean score differences in variables from the Theory of Planned Behaviour between three stages: no promotion of physical activity, irregular promotion and regular promotion. Results supported a pseudo-stage model rather than a true stage model because the differences across the three groups for each variable were essentially linear. Future studies on the TTM and physical activity need to test for the discontinuity of variables across stages and establish whether the variable is an antecedent or consequence of stage transition (Sutton 2000).

Non-linear patterns and support for stage assumptions have also been found. Lippke and Plotnikoff (2005), for example, reported the strongest support for discontinuity patterns for perceptions of vulnerability (subjective chances of contracting a disease if one is not physically active). Individuals in the precontemplation stage felt least vulnerable, those in contemplation and action reported the highest vulnerability, and individuals in preparation and maintenance had reduced vulnerability. The higher level of vulnerability in the contemplation stage, in comparison with precontemplation, is in accordance with the stage definition. Individuals in precontemplation are either unaware of the risk behaviour (such as being not physically active enough) or subjectively reduce their vulnerability due to an incorrect optimistic mindset. In contemplation, persons become aware of their risk. However, if they plan to start performing the behaviour in question in the near future, or if they are already performing some behaviour, their vulnerability estimation now becomes relevant and they may express feelings of vulnerability. Individuals in action are likely to be more realistic and those in maintenance are actually reducing their vulnerability because of their behaviour.

A study by Gorely and Bruce (2000) has also located differences within a stage. This might suggest that future research needs to address not only the distinction between stages, but the possible existence of subgroups within stages. Specifically, Gorely and Bruce found that three subgroups of contemplators existed: early and mid contemplators, and those in 'pre-preparation'. Self-efficacy was progressively higher as the sub-stage became more 'advanced', and there were subgroup differences in pros (lowest in pre-preparation) and cons (lowest in early contemplation). Although these subgroup differences may appear to confirm predictions, analysis of the whole sample using cluster analysis did confirm three distinct clusters, as labelled. The authors of the study argued that further work on subgroups within stages is warranted because of the potential practical utility of such findings.

Based on the findings from our present meta-analytic study (Marshall and Biddle 2001), three general conclusions were offered. First, the majority of study designs are cross-sectional, which limits their utility. Cross-sectional studies provide the weakest evidence of true stage theories. More conclusive evidence would come from experimental studies of stage-matched and mismatched interventions. Studies that simply stage participants or examine cross-sectional differences between core constructs of the TTM are now of limited use because, it could be argued, we now have sufficient data to confirm that stage membership is associated with different levels of physical activity, self-efficacy, pros and cons, and processes of change. Future study should examine the moderators and mediators of stage transition.

Second, the growing number of studies that incorporate TTM concepts means that there is an increasing need to standardise and improve the reliability of measurement. Researchers may wish to consider using a consistent response format for staging participants.

Third, the role of processes of change for physical activity behaviour remains unclear. The presence of higher-order constructs is not apparent in applications of the model to physical activity, and stage-by-process interactions are not evident. Because the ten processes emerged from change systems used in psychotherapy to treat addictions, their relevance or importance in the physical activity domain is uncertain. If processes of change are used in interventions, it would be prudent to select on the basis of logic and pilot testing, particularly given that it is clearly impractical to use all processes at all stages (Marcus and Forsyth 2003).

A natural history model of exercise

Early studies investigating differences between 'adherers' and 'dropouts' (see Chapter 2) gave the mistaken impression that physical activity participation was an 'all or none' phenomenon (Sonstroem 1988) rather than a process open to considerable change over time. As suggested by the TTM, people move between stages of contemplation, decision-making and behavioural involvement, and even then maybe not in any linear fashion.

In reviewing the determinants of exercise, Sallis and Hovell (1990) produced a 'natural history' model that has considerable utility in understanding the process of involvement in physical activity and exercise. Their model is shown in Figure 6.6 and depicts the three important transition phases:

- sedentary behaviour to exercise adoption
- exercise adoption to maintenance or dropout
- dropout to resumption of exercise.

We still know relatively little about the exercise adoption process, and hardly anything about exercise resumption. Most research on determinants has investigated maintenance and dropout. However, even this model oversimplifies things, as Sallis and Hovell (1990) recognised. The following additional factors should be taken into account when considering the natural history model:

- There are degrees of being physically active, or 'exercising'. When is someone 'sedentary' for example? We have argued that most definitions of 'sedentary behaviour' are inadequate because they are based on 'activity absence' rather than good measures of actual sedentary behaviours (Biddle and Gorely 2005; Marshall *et al.* 2004). For the sake of clarity, the natural history model assumes that exercise is a dichotomous rather than a continuous variable. The notion of sporadic activity, and its determinants, is a challenge for future research.

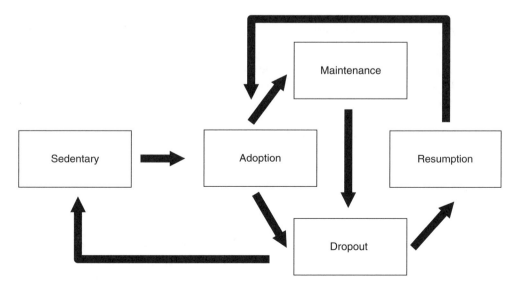

Figure 6.6 Sallis and Hovell's (1990) natural history model of exercise

- The model is simply a useful device for focusing on the dynamic process of exercise. There are many other factors to be considered for a full picture of determinants across the lifespan. For example, we need to consider developmental/lifespan stages, socio-demographic characteristics and actual activity differences. All are likely to operate slightly differently across the phases described here. There are potentially hundreds of permutations of determinants on the basis of categorising determinants into major categories (for example social and environment, attitude, etc.), developmental periods and stages of the natural history model.
- The model is unlikely to be applicable to children as it refers primarily to structured exercise. Children are more likely to involve themselves in sporadic physical activity, through play and personal transportation, as well as structured activities (for example sport). In addition, strong influences will be social norms and parents rather than independent decision-making on the part of the child. The model will become increasingly relevant as young people progress through adolescence.

Determinants may differ across phases of physical activity

'Those who study determinants of exercise behaviour must carefully define which transition they are studying, because the determinants are likely to be different at each transition point' (Sallis and Hovell 1990: 310). Given the extensive discussion on possible determinants that has already taken place in the preceding chapters, this section will consider the factors that could be most influential at each of the phases, or transitions, in the natural history model. For the sake of clarity, we shall describe the model in terms of phases as follows and as shown in Figure 6.6:

- Phase 1: moving from being sedentary to adopting physical activity and exercise
- Phase 2: maintaining involvement in physical activity and exercise
- Phases 3 and 4: ceasing involvement in physical activity and exercise
- Phase 5: resuming physical activity and exercise after previously ceasing participation.

Starting physical activity and exercise

Sallis and Hovell were pessimistic about this phase of their model. They concluded that 'we understand almost nothing about why some people start exercising' (Sallis and Hovell 1990: 313). Most studies, even if they claim to study the adoption process, usually have self-selected or narrow samples, such as CHD patients. Sallis's own work (Sallis *et al.* 1986) is one of the few population-based studies of exercise adoption, but by his own admission the study of determinants lacked a theoretical focus. Their work did show, however, that self-efficacy, knowledge and attitudes were generally associated with the adoption of vigorous and moderate exercise. Logic also dictates that much of the material reviewed in the previous chapters on attitudes and self-efficacy appears to be appropriate for understanding the adoption process. Similarly, research on the TTM in physical activity has shown that self-efficacy levels of contemplators are usually lower than for those in the action or maintenance stages, and that those not yet exercising have more negative beliefs about exercise.

The natural history model deals with exercise and it is not known how appropriate such a model is for habitual physical activity, such as walking or stair climbing. However, it is these habitual activities that may hold the key to moving people from being sedentary to active. The behavioural barriers associated with structured exercise may be much greater than those of habitual physical activity, yet at this point we are not able to demonstrate whether encouraging habitual physical activity will be any more successful than providing structured exercise programmes.

Box 6.2 Does becoming more habitually active predispose people to taking up structured exercise?

I (SJHB) was working as a consultant many years ago with friend and colleague Dr Andy Smith. Andy and I had been asked by the leisure department of a local district council to conduct field research on why three of their leisure/sport centres were struggling to attract customers. We felt that a good way to move forward would be for us to have a one-day informal meeting/discussion with the three centre heads and the director of leisure for the district council.

Half way through the day, Andy raised the issue of centre staff expecting people to come to the centre. He suggested 'why not go out into the community and take your product to them'? This could be done, for example, by initiating work site schemes, or community physical activity plans, like 'cycling to work' days. This, we suggested, might then encourage people to be more physically active which, in turn, might help them take the step into structured exercise at the leisure centres.

To be honest, we don't have any data to guide us on this. We were advising this strategy on the basis of wanting to encourage greater physical activity, but whether it would create more clients in the leisure (sports) centres was not possible to say. Some have argued that it would take clients away if they could exercise elsewhere. One of the reasons why people take structured exercise these days is that everyday situations no longer give us enough activity. This is a conundrum that we are not yet able to solve. Would promoting greater habitual physical activity also increase the number of people using sport/exercise facilities?

As stated, data on adoption of exercise are sparse. Nevertheless, it seems reasonable to propose that enabling factors of beliefs, attitudes, self-efficacy, social support and the perception of few barriers will be a step in the right direction for exercise adoption. Certainly these are consistent with strategies proposed for moving precontemplators to contemplation and preparation (Prochaska, Norcross and DiClemente 1994). Indeed, a review of physical activity adoption studies (Dunn 1996) suggested that increasing self-efficacy and realistic outcome expectations might be helpful.

Maintaining physical acti vity and exercise

We are on much firmer ground when proposing determinants of the maintenance phase of exercise and we have already discussed many of these issues at length in this book. In addition to the factors identified for adoption, two important issues need to be considered as far as psychological determinants are concerned. First is the issue of psychological reinforcement from exercise, and second is the issue of self-regulation.

The reinforcement associated with exercise has also been raised by Sallis and Hovell (1990). They proposed a closer look at learning theories and the role of reinforcement and punishment in exercise. Population studies have shown that many people do not find the effort of physical activity at all pleasant (Sports Council and Health Education Authority 1992) whereas some individuals have reported high levels of enjoyment, with a few even reporting some measure of dependence or 'addiction' to exercise (Polivy 1994).

What appears to be emerging, therefore, is the important role of psychological outcomes from exercise. Typically, the so-called 'mental health' benefits of exercise have largely been studied from the point of view of outcomes (this is reviewed in more detail in Chapters 8–10). From the view of determinants of exercise maintenance, however, we should also consider the mental health outcomes as *reinforcers* of subsequent exercise. Although Sallis and Hovell suggest that 'the punishment of vigorous exercise remains immediate and salient, while the reinforcers of improved health or weight loss are greatly delayed and silent' (Sallis and Hovell 1990: 320), it is possible to suggest that the mood-enhancing and 'feel better' effects of exercise can also be perceived in the short term. The key is to structure exercise experiences such that the probability of perceiving exercise as rewarding is increased. We suggest the 'physiological' message of 'vigorous' and prolonged exercise, which for so long has been standard, has not served us well.

Early reviews on exercise and physical activity determinants support the point we are making. Dishman, Sallis and Orenstein (1985: 166) said that 'feelings related to well-being and enjoyment seem more important to maintaining activity than concerns about health'. Similarly, most reviews on children and physical activity stress the importance of enjoyment and development of perceptions of competence as a means of encouraging physical activity (De Bourdeauhuij 1998).

Recently, Ekkekakis and colleagues have shown that psychological reactions to acute bouts of exercise will depend on the intensity of exercise (Biddle and Ekkekakis 2005; Ekkekakis 2003; Ekkekakis and Petruzzello 1999). This will be discussed in more detail in Chapter 8, but it is worth noting that in the context of exercise reinforcement that evidence does exist for the influence of exercise intensity on feelings of pleasure and displeasure, and by inference therefore, on exercise adherence. Ekkekakis (2003) has proposed that 'moderate' intensity is associated with pleasure, whereas 'severe' intensity of exercise is associated with 'displeasure'. In between, in the range of what he calls 'heavy' exercise, there is great intra-individual variability, with feelings of pleasure and displeasure reported.

The maintenance of exercise is also likely to be enhanced through the operation of self-regulatory strategies and skills. Evidence from the Transtheoretical Model suggests that those in the action and maintenance phases are more likely to have arrived at a positive 'balance' of exercise 'pros' (benefits) and 'cons' (costs) (Prochaska 1994) and this process of decision-balance is itself a conscious exercise in self-regulation. Similarly, some adherence studies showed the importance of 'self-motivation' in distinguishing adherers and dropouts (Dishman and Gettman 1980). Self-motivation includes elements of self-regulation such as goal-setting and self-monitoring. Goal-setting itself has often been found to be effective as a short-term behaviour change strategy (Atkins *et al.* 1984), as has self-monitoring (Juneau *et al.* 1987). Further discussion on individual behaviour change interventions for exercise can be found in Chapter 11.

Ceasing physical activity and exercise

The study of exercise 'dropout' has been controversial, mainly because early studies were not able to identify if those ceasing participation in a structured programme had quit altogether or had merely gone elsewhere to exercise. The word 'dropout', therefore, was difficult to define. The cessation of exercise may also be dependent on a variety of lifecycle influences. For example, Mihalik *et al.* (1989) found that in a study of adults aged eighteen to over fifty years, it was those in the 29–36 year old range who most 'contracted' their physical activity and sport involvement. This is suggestive of key life events, such as marriage, having children and job changes, being influential in physical activity levels.

The message that 'healthy' exercise has to be 'vigorous' has already been questioned from a behavioural and affective point of view (Biddle and Ekkekakis 2005; Ekkekakis 2003). In addition, the promotion of vigorous exercise in structured classes, while enjoyable and appropriate for some, has been implicated in dropout (Buckworth and Dishman 2002; Dishman and Buckworth 1996).

Resuming physical activity and exercise

In discussing the determinants of resumption of exercise after dropout Sallis and Hovell (1990) are quite clear:

> this phase of the natural history of exercise has been completely neglected by both theoreticians and empirical investigators. The extent to which dropouts resume exercise later has never been studied, to our knowledge. Thus, there are no studies on the determinants of resumption of exercise. Research on these issues is desperately needed with both participants in specialised programs and with the general population.
>
> (Sallis and Howell 1990: 315)

Sallis and Hovell's comment has sparked interest in the resumption process but little data have emerged and we are left to speculate about possibilities, one of which is the process of relapse studied in other health fields.

Marlatt (1985) has proposed a 'relapse prevention' model for the explanation of poor adherence to abstaining from various addictions and negative health behaviours, such as excessive alcohol and nicotine consumption. Marlatt defines relapse as 'a breakdown or set back in a person's attempt to change or modify any target behavior' (Marlatt 1985: 3).

Although this definition, as well as the relapse prevention model, provides a starting point for the analysis of exercise resumption, it may not be wholly suitable. Knapp (1988), for example, notes that the behaviours addressed in addiction relapse are high frequency, undesired behaviours yet exercise is low frequency and desired. Nevertheless, it provides us

---

Box 6.3 Establishing guidelines for the promotion of physical activity: scientific 'proof' or common sense?

In 1993, I (SJHB) took part in the 'Moving On' conference in England set up to establish guidelines for physical activity promotion in England as part of the government's *Health of the Nation* strategy. After several days of scientific evidence and discussion, one key message agreed was that adults should be encouraged to reach the 'target' of thirty minutes of moderate activity on most days of the week. Discussion ensued as to whether the thirty minutes could be achieved in two blocks rather than all at once. The 'scientific' evidence seemed to point to thirty minutes being optimal, and not enough evidence, at the time, appeared in defence of the two times fifteen minutes message. But I refused to accept this! I spoke up and said to Steven Blair, the Chair, that I couldn't really accept that under the thirty minute principle, I would be classified as not having reached the target. At that time, my daily walk to work was twenty-two minutes there (it was uphill!), and twenty minutes back! Steven agreed to write to the Prime Minister and ask for special dispensation for me! More importantly, we agreed that it would be nonsense to 'not count' such activity. Consequently, the current message is thirty minutes, in bouts of at least fifteen minutes. A victory for common sense over 'science' in my opinion!

with a workable model in which to identify possible determinants of exercise resumption. Marlatt's model, modified for possible application to exercise, is illustrated in Figure 6.7.

The starting point is identified in Figure 6.7 as the high-risk situation of ceasing to exercise. This risk situation is the threat to self-control that could produce 'relapse' back to physical inactivity. For those with addiction problems, Marlatt (1985) has identified interpersonal conflict, negative emotional states and social pressure as the three primary high-risk situations. Certainly the latter two have been identified as predictors of (in)activity. Whether these situations lead to relapse will be dependent on the adequacy of the individual's coping skills and responses. A high-risk situation for lack of exercise might be extra work pressures, thus producing a perception of reduced time for exercise. The probability of relapse from this is associated with the adequacy of coping response, such as time management skills, as well as self-efficacy towards exercise. A lack of coping response may lead to decreased efficacy and an expectation of less exercise taking place. In the case of drug use, this has been identified as a time when the pleasurable effects of the drug are highlighted. In the case of exercise, this is when rest from physical exertion might be seen as pleasurable. The 'abstinence violation effect' could lead on from this and is where the individual displays feelings of guilt and self-blame, depending on the attributions made for the relapse. For example, attributions reflecting negative personal characteristics and feelings of helplessness and lack of control will increase the probability of a sustained relapse.

Although the model presented is speculative as far as physical activity is concerned, relapse prevention has been successfully applied in physical activity research. King and Frederiksen (1984) demonstrated its success, alongside social support, for a small group of previously sedentary college women attempting increases and maintenance in the frequency of jogging.

Belisle *et al.* (1987) tested Marlatt's relapse prevention model in an experimental design with adult exercisers. In comparison with a standard control group receiving a regular exercise programme, those in the experimental condition also received health education through elements of the relapse prevention model. These included information on overcoming critical situations, awareness of the abstinence violation effect and principles of habit maintenance.

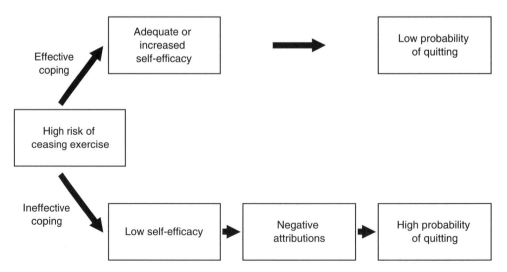

Figure 6.7 Relapse prevention model applied to exercise

Small but consistent effects in favour of the experimental group were noted across three studies. Similarly, positive coping responses were found by Stetson *et al.* (2005) to reduce the likelihood of an exercise 'slip' in high-risk situations. They concluded that 'exposure to high-risk situations per se does not precipitate slips and relapse; rather, it is the manner in which individuals cope with the situations that impacts outcome' (Stetson *et al.* 2005: 33).

The relapse model is consistent with other physical activity determinants research in having a central role for self-efficacy. Also, attributions for relapse or dropout may be important factors in determining the strength of the motivational deficit associated with relapse and the ability that people feel they can cope in high-risk situations.

> Key point: Determinants or correlates will differ across different phases or stages of involvement in physical activity.

Can we prioritise determinants across phases of the natural history of exercise?

Having made the general point concerning the role of different determinants across the phases of exercise, is it possible to put them into any priority or pattern? We have attempted this before (see Biddle 1992) but admitted that it was for heuristic value and was in need of verification. It is not really possible to be any more optimistic today, but we still believe that an effort to identify, however crudely, the key determinants for adoption, maintenance, dropout and resumption should be attempted. Our effort is shown in Table 6.4.

A hybrid model: the health action process approach

The health action process approach (HAPA) (Schwarzer 1992, 2001) is a model that explicitly integrates linear and stage assumptions, and is thereby a *hybrid model*. At the same time, the HAPA integrates motivational (prediction of intention) and behaviour-enabling models. The former include predictions of intention while the latter include post-decisional facets such as implementation intentions. This has been discussed in more detail in Chapter 3.

A lifespan interaction model

So far we have considered 'process' and hybrid models of physical activity and exercise. The TTM tackles physical activity from the point of view of stages in individual decision-making; thus it is a dynamic model operating primarily from an ideographic approach. Sallis and Hovell's (1990) natural history model is a way of viewing the dynamic process of exercise participation that could be applied to the study of determinants at a nomothetic level. In our final model, we discuss a global overview of physical activity and exercise behaviours through the 'lifespan interaction model' proposed by Dishman and Dunn (1988) and refined by Dishman (1990). The model is shown in Figure 6.8.

Rather than explaining the process of exercise and physical activity involvement, the model provides a useful global framework for understanding the multifactorial nature of physical activity and the factors that require investigation. The left segment of the model highlights three broad categories of determinants: psychological, biobehavioural and social environmental. The middle segment concerns the characteristics of physical activity, such as

Table 6.4 Possible determinants of exercise across different stages and phases of exercise and physical activity

Stages[a]	Pre	Con	Prep action maintenance	Relapse	
Phases[b]	Adoption		Maintenance	Dropout	Resumption
Factors/determinants					
Attitudes	**		*	*	**
Social norms	**		**	*	**
Self-efficacy/ control/competence	***		***	***	***
Personality/ self-motivation	*		**	**	*
Environmental	**		**	*	**
Biological	*		**	***	*
Mental health outcomes	*		***	***	**
Self-regulatory skills	**		***	***	***
Attributions	*		*	**	***
Determinants categories					
Environmental	**		**	*	**
Social	**		**	*	**
Cognitive	**		**	***	**
Physiological	*		**	***	*

* Some influence possible ** Expected influence *** Likely strong influence

Notes
a Stages: according to the transtheoretical model; pre = precontemplation; con = contemplation; prep = preparation
b Phases: according to Sallis and Hovell's (1990) 'Natural History' model

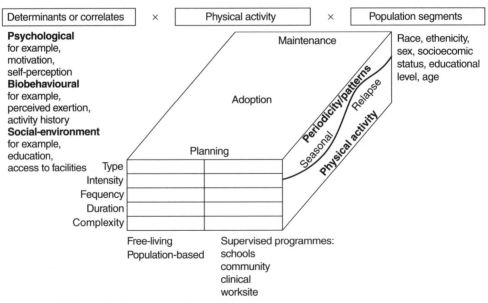

Figure 6.8 Dishman's lifespan interaction model

phases of involvement, type or frequency, settings, etc. The right segment highlights different population groups that may have characteristics or specific issues that interact with the other factors in the model.

The three categories of determinants are very broad and this book has really addressed primarily psychological determinants. However, the model is right to highlight other factors. Sallis and Hovell (1990) use the categories of environmental, social, cognitive, physiological and 'other personal' factors. Whatever the classification system used, it is important to recognise that determinants are multifactorial. However, the extent to which we are able to test such complex models is debatable. Taking the categories proposed by Sallis and Hovell, and their distinction between 'distal' and 'proximal' determinants, and then superimposing this onto a model including adoption, maintenance, dropout and resumption, we have a very complex system indeed! Nevertheless, this is what Dishman (1990) is really trying to highlight – the complexity of the exercise/physical activity process and thereby warning against oversimplified conclusions about why people do or do not exercise or be involved in physical activity. For this reason, the lifespan interaction model serves a useful unifying function.

Chapter summary and conclusions

The research and theorising on the psychological determinants of exercise and physical activity is becoming increasingly complex. Theories have been borrowed, adapted and developed from other branches of the psychological and behavioural sciences and, as such, there is a need not only to review the contribution of these theories to the understanding of physical activity behaviour, as we have done elsewhere in this book, but also to consider more dynamic, process-oriented approaches to behaviour.

In this chapter, we have:

- reviewed and critiqued the Transtheoretical Model of behaviour change applied to physical activity. Specifically, we reviewed evidence concerning the role of self-efficacy, pros and cons (decisional balance) and processes of change
- outlined a 'natural history' model of exercise and discussed determinants appropriate for different phases of the model, including relapse
- described a lifespan interaction model of exercise and physical activity as a useful guiding framework for understanding the complexities of exercise and physical activity determinants.

In summary, therefore, we conclude:

- the TTM provides an important advance on static linear models of exercise and physical activity determinants by hypothesising both the 'how' and 'when' of behaviour change. Measures of stages and processes of change are now available and require validation across more diverse samples
- TTM research needs to advance beyond description of predictable cross-sectional differences between stages
- meta-analytic evidence broadly supports the model, although the classification of processes of change into two higher-order categories is questioned
- a natural history model of exercise is a useful framework for identifying key stages in exercise behaviour

- more needs to be known about which determinants are important at each of the phases of the model
- relapse prevention may depend more on coping strategies than high-risk situations per se
- the hybrid HAPA model allows for the distinction between non-intentional, intentional and action stages of behaviour.
- the lifespan interaction model provides a valuable overarching model for the identification of the complex interactions determining exercise and physical activity involvement.

7 Social and environmental correlates of physical activity

People to see and places to go

Golf is a good walk spoiled.

(Mark Twain)

Twain's idea about golf is rubbish, because it's sociable and in an attractive outdoor environment.

(Stuart Biddle)

Twain obviously did not have the benefit of a good golfing companion or teacher who provided the correct motivational environment for him to enjoy both the golf and the walk.

(Nanette Mutrie)

Purpose of the chapter

The purpose of this chapter is to discuss concepts associated with the social and environmental correlates of physical activity. Specifically, in this chapter we aim to:

- cover important issues associated with social environments in exercise
- discuss exercise leadership issues and models
- discuss the importance of group climate in the development of exercise motivation
- consider the role of social and family support in the encouragement of physical activity
- look at present and possible future research dealing with exercise group settings, and specifically group cohesion and collective efficacy
- summarise the key environmental factors thought to be associated with physical activity, including environmental aesthetics and transport.

The field of 'exercise psychology' has been dominated by an individualistic approach to physical activity behaviour and behaviour change. Recently, a broader perspective has been advocated such that social and environmental factors are also considered in the quest to understand and change physical activity behaviour. Psychologists and sociologists approach physical activity from different ideologies and perspectives. While psychologists tend to emphasise the role of the individual in changing behaviour and being responsible for one's health-related behaviours, those closer to sociology tend to see the key influences stemming from wider social structures. McElroy (2002) argued that given that the problem of physical inactivity is so pervasive in contemporary market economies, then the problem is seen to be one of 'society' rather than just the individual. Therefore she suggested 'that significant improvements in physical activity for so many ... requires us to look beyond individuals to the factors in society' (McElroy 2002: 17). The World Health Organization, in its global strategy for diet and physical activity, also note that inactivity cannot be considered simply as a problem for individuals. The strategy stated that increasing physical activity is a societal, not just an individual problem, and demands a population-based, multi-sectoral, multi-disciplinary, and culturally relevant approach. This is consistent with the ecological approach outlined in Chapter 1.

While we can devote only a small amount of text to this important topic, given the focus on psychological factors of physical activity, the current chapter does provide an overview of social and environmental correlates of physical activity, thus allowing for a better understanding of the factors associated with, or influencing, activity (Sallis and Owen 1999, 2002). Of course, one could argue that while social factors are inevitably important, some social influences will merely be 'distal' factors affecting individual behaviour whereas psychological factors are likely to be more 'proximal' (immediate) in their influence. Nevertheless, it is clear that social correlates of physical activity are important constructs to understand. More recently, investigators and policy-makers have developed an increased interest in the physical environment and how this might influence participation in physical activity. The changes are largely self-evident with more cars, greater urbanisation, perceived danger and lack of play space likely decreasing physical activity while more structured activity facilities, pedestrian-only zones in urban areas, new paths for walking or cycling could all contribute to increases in physical activity.

Social correlates of physical activity

In reviews of the correlates of physical activity in both young people (Biddle *et al.* 2005; Sallis, Prochaska and Taylor 2000) and adults (Trost *et al.* 2002), various social variables have been found to be associated with physical activity. In this chapter, key correlates will be reviewed, including gender, socio-economic status, the family and social support. We then summarise the evidence concerning the social setting of the exercise group, specifically addressing group leadership, the group climate, as well as group cohesion and collective efficacy. However, few physical activity studies have addressed social correlates from a clear theoretical perspective. While some studies have been based on notions of social or family support, or collective efficacy, the theories covered by Bartholomew *et al.* (2001), such as theories of social networks, are largely absent. In addition, theories of wider social change, such as through organisations, have also been ignored in the physical activity literature.

Gender and socio-economic status

There are consistent positive trends for leisure-time physical activity in adults to be associated with male gender, higher levels of education and socio-economic status, and white ethnicity (Trost *et al.* 2002). Similar findings are evident in young people (Sallis, Prochaska and Taylor 2000). Gender differences are highly reproducible and one of the most consistent findings in the literature. Promoting physical activity in girls seems a particular challenge although trials with adults suggest that more women than men show interest in taking part (Mutrie *et al.* 2002). One explanation for the gender difference is that boys and girls are socialised at an early age to believe that physically demanding pursuits are more 'male' oriented, particularly some sports. It is also possible that reward structures in sport and physical activity will be different between males and females (Wold and Hendry 1998). Interestingly, when adolescent girls are attracted to play sport, their overall physical activity levels equate to those of boys (Vilhjalmsson and Kristjansdottir 2003).

The finding that higher levels of SES are associated with higher levels of physical activity may be related to the economic and social access to various activities, such as clubs, facilities or physical activities requiring transport. It is interesting to note that time-use data show a decline in discretionary free time for American children between 1981 and 1997, with declines in general playing, but an increase in structured activities, such as sport (Sturm 2005). Age-group trends, however, are not entirely consistent, as shown in Figure 7.1, although the decline in playing is evident for the younger children. This suggests that structured activities will be needed to replace some of the lost physical activity that would have occurred in free-play settings. Whether this explains differences in activity across SES remains to be seen, but it is a plausible explanation.

Key point: Socio-economic status may play an important role in physical activity participation but is likely to differ across activities.

There is a great deal of interest in social issues in physical activity because of the high priority the current UK government is putting on 'social exclusion' (Collins 2003, 2004). Collins (2004) refers to social exclusion as a process, characterised by a lack of access to democracy, welfare, the labour market, and family and community. There are social gradients in many

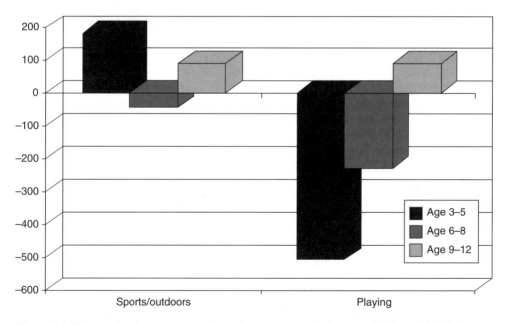

Figure 7.1 Changes in time, expressed as minutes per week, between 1981 and 1997, spent on activities for three age groups (data reported in Sturm (2005))

health-related conditions and behaviours and, as Collins states, 'there is widespread social inequity in exercise' (Collins 2004: 730). One explanation for this is through the social reproduction of inequality. There is support for the view that people 'learn to think and act in correspondence with what is recognized as valuable within their social class' (Wold and Hendry 1998: 122). This can be through parental influence as well as through social systems, such as education. Wold and Hendry suggest that the physical activities of the higher social classes tend to 'track' better into adulthood whereas activities of lower social classes 'tend to be more associated with youth itself and thus to be abandoned on entry into adulthood' (Wold and Hendry 1998: 122).

Family influences on physical activity

Family-related variables, such as parental support or family modelling, are frequently reported as correlates of physical activity (Trost *et al.* 2002). For example, in our systematic review of correlates of physical activity in adolescent girls, elements of family and parental support had small-to-moderate associations with physical activity, whereas Sallis *et al.* (2000) found evidence for adolescents' physical activity to be associated with direct parental help, parental support, support from significant others and sibling physical activity, although no consistent associations were located for pre-adolescent children. Inconsistencies such as this may require us to look beyond purely social factors and investigate the social-environmental constraints and prompts on physical activity, such as busy roads and availability of home-based equipment (Cavill and Biddle 2003). A summary of family-related variables is provided in Table 7.1.

Further work is required, however, to tease out the differential influence of adults at different stages in childhood. For example, when do teachers influence children more than parents, if at all? What, if any, are the gender effects between children and adult modelling? The literature is not clear on these issues. When do parents have less influence than peers? Until we have a better understanding, it may be best to support a commonsense approach, such as that of the Centers for Disease Control and Prevention (1997) who recommend that parents and guardians are included in physical activity instruction and programmes and are encouraged to support their children's participation.

Although evidence supports the potential influence of parents and families on young people's physical activity, the relationship could also work in reverse through children constraining adult activity. For example, Brown and Trost (2003) found that certain family-related life events over a four-year period were associated with a greater likelihood of being physically inactive for young women. Specifically, their analysis of the Australian Longitudinal Study of Women's Health showed that the risk of inactivity was increased if the women became married and had children, with the risks being escalated by 50–230 per cent. Interviews with twelve mothers of young children suggested that reasons for such inactivity centre on a struggle for time, pressure and expectation that they will be caring for their children, and a lack of partner support (Miller and Brown 2005). Similarly, McElroy (2002) highlights that changing structures and responsibilities of families in contemporary society means less time for child rearing and support of elderly relatives, and this may reduce physical activity in families.

Key point: There is still much to learn about how and why families might influence physical activity levels of its members.

Table 7.1 A summary of family variables and their association with physical activity (PA). Data from reviews by Biddle *et al.* (2005), Trost *et al.* (2002), and Sallis *et al.* (2000)

Review	Population studied	Family construct	Association with physical activity
Sallis *et al.* (2000)	Children aged 4–12	Parent PA	Indeterminate
		Parent PA with child	Indeterminate
		Benefits of PA perceived by parent	None (based on 2 studies)
		Parent barriers to PA	None (based on 2 studies)
		Parental encouragement (persuasion)	None
		Parent transports child	None
		Parent pay fees for PA	None
	Youth aged 13–18	Parental PA and modelling	None
		Sibling PA	Clearly positive
		Direct parental help in PA	Positive
		Parental support	Positive
Biddle *et al.* (2005)	Adolescent girls	Family and parental support	Positive (small-to-moderate association)
		Mother's PA	Indeterminate
		Father's PA	Positive (small-to-moderate association)
Trost *et al.* (2002)	Adults	Past family influences	None
		Social support from spouse/family	Clearly positive

Box 7.1 A negative exercise environment: exercise as punishment (last one in – ten press-ups!)

Those of you who have taught exercise classes, and certainly those who have taught children, will likely have used exercise as punishment, or, if you prefer, for motivation! Go on, admit it – we have in the past but don't now!

For years, in places like the military and schools, exercise has been used as an aversive experience and yet, at the same time, we hear all about the good qualities of exercise and the need to encourage it! What a contradiction! It is likely that if members of the public were asked what they thought of 'cross-country running' or 'press-ups' at school they would give quite negative replies. It seems to make perfect sense to us, as psychologists and exercise promoters, that if we wish to encourage exercise we need to make the exercise experience as positive and reinforcing as possible. This means never allowing the association between exercise and pain/punishment to be established. Whether this strategy is appropriate for competitive sports could be debated. For example, the harsh regime depicted in the film 'Coach Carter', in which the coach, played by Samuel L. Jackson, doled out highly demanding shuttle running ('suicides') as punishment, eventually 'paid off', but it would be a mistake to extrapolate from that to physical activity and public health.

If you need to punish someone, but believe in the benefits of exercise, try something other than exercise. It makes good psychological sense.

The stability and 'tracking' of physical activity from childhood

If the influence of the family is generally positive, one might expect such social influences to have lasting effects. Although the assumption that behaviours learned in childhood and adolescence will transfer ('track') into adulthood seems reasonable, evidence to substantiate it is mixed. Many factors in the transition from childhood into adolescence and then into adulthood are likely to affect the levels and patterns of physical activity and changes in the adult life cycle itself will affect the extent that adults are active.

The Surgeon General's Report in the United States (Department of Health and Human Services and Centers for Disease Control and Prevention 1996) states that childhood and adolescence are 'pivotal times' for adults as well as youth. The report subscribes to the view that maintaining physical activity habits in youth helps prevents sedentary behaviour in adults. Similarly, the British Heart Foundation (2000) says that 'physically active children are more likely to be active adults', while Mulvihill, Rivers and Aggleton believe that 'since patterns of behaviour are established in childhood and during adolescence, young people who do not engage in adequate levels of physical activity are unlikely to do so in adulthood' (Mulvihill, Rivers and Aggleton 2000: 1). Moreover, one often-stated objective for school physical education programmes is the development of healthy habits for adulthood, including physical activity.

Evidence from the Allied Dunbar National Fitness Survey (ADNFS) in England provides some support for the view, at least indirectly, that early participation is associated with a greater likelihood of involvement later in life (Sports Council and Health Education Authority 1992). Through interview, participants were requested to recall the moderate-to-vigorous physical activity they took part in at the ages of sixteen, twenty-four and thirty-four years. The results showed:

- that those currently over fifty-five years of age were much less active at age thirty-four than those currently younger than fifty-five years. This suggests that younger adults today are more active than their older counterparts
- 'adult participation in sport and recreation in later years was strongly associated with behaviour at an earlier age' (Sports Council and Health Education Authority 1992: 64). This was supported by data showing that 25 per cent of those very active between the ages of fourteen and ninteen years were active currently, whereas only 2 per cent currently active were inactive in the past during those teenage years. In addition, about 30 per cent of the adults in the survey remained in the same activity category across the three time periods studied.

Data from Sweden also supports the view that activity in childhood is a predictor of activity in adulthood. Engstrom (1991) followed 2,000 Swedish youths from fifteen to thirty years of age. Using the fairly liberal definition of 'activity' as weekly involvement in activity of the intensity of jogging, he found a steep decline in activity between the ages of fifteen and twenty years, with some levelling after that. To test for tracking effects from childhood to adulthood, Engstrom used three conditions as indicators of early (aged fifteen years) activity involvement. These were:

- at least four hours per week of sports or physical activities at age fifteen years
- being a member of a sports club at fifteen years of age
- having a high grade in physical education in the eighth grade (in Sweden).

An index of 'psychological readiness' at the age of thirty was then calculated from 'attitude towards keep-fit activities and self-esteem concerning the body and sports capabilities' (Engstrom 1991: 478). Unfortunately, no further details on these measures were given. The results of Engstrom's (1991) analysis are shown in Figure 7.2. This shows a clear relationship between the number of conditions fulfilled for activity involvement at fifteen years of age and high psychological readiness at age thirty. For example, for women fulfilling all three of the criteria at fifteen years, 52 per cent had a high psychological readiness at thirty years, whereas for those not fulfilling any of the criteria, only 17 per cent had a readiness.

These data are supported by a clear relationship between psychological readiness at age thirty years and actual involvement in physical activity for both men and women. Engstrom (1991) also analysed environmental circumstances and involvement in physical activity. The following four conditions were used to assess environmental circumstances:

- physically active mate/spouse
- most friends are physically active
- no children
- academic education.

Again, there was a clear relationship between the number of environmental conditions fulfilled at the age of thirty years, and current activity involvement. For example, for men not fulfilling any of the criteria, only 16 per cent were currently active, whereas for men fulfilling all four criteria, 80 per cent were active. This begs the question whether it is the environmental support or the psychological readiness that predicts activity since both correlated highly with physical activity. To answer this, Engstrom (1991) created four groups: low readiness/negative environment; high readiness/negative environment; low readiness/positive

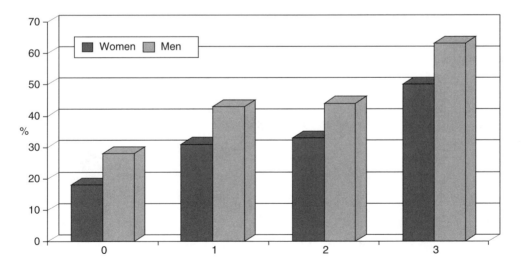

Figure 7.2 Percentage of individuals with high psychological readiness for physical activity at the age of 30 years according to indicators of sport experience at 15 years (data from Engstrom 1991)

Note
The number of conditions on the horizontal axis refer to the practice of sport at least 4 hours/week at the age of 15 years, member of a sports club at 15, and a high grade in PE at school

environment; high readiness/positive environment. The high/positive group showed very high activity levels in comparison with the low/negative group, as expected. However, of more interest was the finding that those with a positive environment, but low readiness, were more active than those with high readiness but a negative environment, suggesting a dominant role for environmental circumstances.

Engstrom (1991) provided an interesting perspective on the issue of physical activity tracking. Although his short conference paper did not allow full analysis of his methods, his results do lend clear support to the view that 'early experience with physical activity during childhood and adolescence ... is of importance for the practice of keep-fit activities in adulthood' (Engstrom 1991: 480–1). However, the criterion measure of activity was weak.

The most comprehensive review on physical activity tracking was conducted by Malina (1996). He concluded that the magnitude of tracking during adolescence and into adulthood is 'low to moderate'. Riddoch (1998), drawing on similar studies to Malina (1996), arrived at the same conclusion and highlighted that the correlations for tracking are particularly weak when self-report measures are used. Telama *et al.* (2005), reporting twenty-one years of follow-up data from the 'Cardiovascular Risk in Young Finns' longitudinal study, showed correlations between measures of physical activity for nine, twelve, fifteen, eighteen and twenty-one year follow-ups (see Figure 7.3). These declined with time, as expected, and generally were low-to-moderate in strength, although some association was still evident after twenty-one years. Moreover, the same data set showed that high participation in organised sport as a youth was associated with a five to six times greater likelihood of activity in adults compared with those with little sport involvement (Telama *et al.* 2006).

One of the few studies using more 'objective' measures of activity in tracking was reported by Pate *et al.* (1996). Using heart rate measures, they reported three year correlations for activity levels that were quite high ($r = 0.57$–0.66). However, this study investigated 3–4 year olds over a three-year period. This is a time when relatively little change in environmental, social and psychological factors is expected. Stability of behaviour, therefore, is likely.

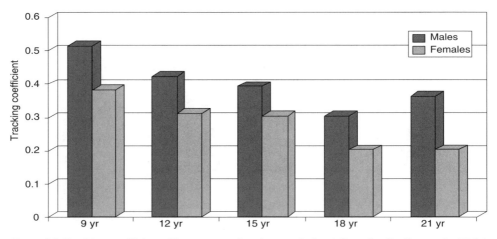

Figure 7.3 Tracking coefficients (Spearman rank order correlations) from the Cardiovascular Risk in Young Finns Study (Telama *et al.* 2005)

Notes
Data are average coefficients across 4–6 cohorts within each tracking interval. The intervals are up to 2001 from 1992 (9 years), 1989 (12 years), 1986 (15 years), 1983 (18 years), and 1980 (21 years)

Since Riddoch's (1998) review, Pate *et al.* (1999) have reported tracking data for rural, predominantly African-American ten year olds over three years using self-report measures. Stability was low-to-moderate for vigorous physical activity ($r = 0.36$), moderate-to-vigorous physical activity (0.24), estimated after-school energy expenditure (0.41), and TV watching (0.41). This may support the view of some that inactivity (sedentary behaviours) could track better than physical activity (Biddle, Gorely and Stensel 2004).

Evidence from reviews and primary studies on the stability of physical activity across key life stages can be summarised as follows:

- the statistical relationship between physical activity in adulthood and activity in childhood or adolescence is low-to-moderate
- slightly stronger effects can be found for the nature of early life experiences in physical activity as precursors of adult physical activity, but still these effects appear small
- the small effects identified may be real or the result of other factors, such as motor competence or early maturation, with children experiencing early success less likely to quit later on
- research into tracking must account for the quality of childhood experiences in physical activity as well as the changes in activity levels during childhood, adolescence and adulthood (Cavill and Biddle 2003).

The role of the family is unknown in long-term, tracking studies. However, it is expected that where tracking does occur, early family influence will be in evidence, although the strength of such influence is not known.

> Key point: The assumption that active children make active adults is an oversimplification of the issue. Tracking is generally small to moderate and will be influenced by many factors.

Social support

In health psychology, social support has been studied and found to be beneficial for various aspects of health and well-being, such as stress control (Stroebe and Stroebe 1995). However, from the point of view of the correlates of physical activity, we are defining social support in motivational terms in respect of the social influence of people on the physical activity patterns of others. Sheridan and Radmacher, for example, define social support as 'the resources provided to us through our interactions with other people' (Sheridan and Radmacher 1992: 156).

Social support is usually seen in terms of emotional, informational and material support (Stroebe and Stroebe 1995; Taylor, Baranowski and Sallis 1994), and Table 7.2 shows the

Table 7.2 Types of social support and examples from physical activity and exercise

Type of social support	Example
Emotional support	Empathy from others in your attempt to be physically active. You feel that they 'are on your side'.
Informational support	Information and advice is given by others concerning exercise, such as details of a local running event.
Material (instrumental) support	Direct help, such as driving children to a sports centre or buying them a bicycle for transportation to school.

possible role of each in physical activity. Similarly, the measurement of social support in physical activity and exercise has been suggested as being multidimensional. Sallis and colleagues (1987) developed the 'Social Support and Exercise Survey' assessing three subscales. The item stem was 'During the past three months, my family (or members of my household) or friends ...'. Each item was responded to twice, once for family and once for friends. The three subscales are:

- family participation: example item – '... exercised with me'
- family rewards and punishment: example item – '... complained about the time I spent exercising'
- friend participation: example item – '... talked about how much they liked to exercise'.

The scale structure was supported by Treiber *et al.* (1991). They also showed that the relationship between social support and exercise in young adults differed across race, gender, type of support and type of physical activity, suggesting that social support in physical activity may be more complex than first thought.

Social support can be associated with physical activity in adults and youth. Trost *et al.*'s (2002) review showed a clear positive effect on physical activity for social support from friends/peers and family/spouse. In addition, they reported evidence for the influence of one's GP (family physician), but not for social support from staff/instructor. For children aged 4–12 years, Sallis *et al.* (2000) found no effect for 'peer influence' or 'subjective norm'. For adolescents, they reported a clearly positive association for support from significant others, no associations with peer modelling or teacher support/modelling, and an indeterminate association with subjective norms/social influence. Similarly, we found an indeterminate association for peer involvement/support in adolescent girls (Biddle *et al.* 2005).

Social support could sometimes inhibit or restrict physical activity. Many parents are concerned about the safety of their children and, as such, actively prevent them from taking some forms of physical activity, such as cycling on busy roads and walking or playing in certain areas. The latter is often associated with a perception of risk of physical attack (the fear of so-called 'stranger danger'). In both cases, motorised transport is likely to be used instead of physical activity, such as travelling to school. For understandable reasons, therefore, the social influence of parents could also be detrimental to children's physical activity.

Box 7.2 Physical activity: moving from 'fitness freak' to 'Norman Normal'

It is unfortunate that the media sometimes portray regular exercisers as 'fitness freaks'. This creates the image that exercise is not normal. We need to create, instead, a culture where the physically active option, if available, is taken. It is likely that the more people we observe being active, and particularly people who look 'normal' and 'like us', the more likely it is we too will follow, or at least accept that this is 'normal' behaviour. Let's dispense with the 'fitness freak' label and embrace the exerciser who is 'Norman Normal'!

Social environments and physical activity

A great deal of structured exercise takes place in a social context, such as an exercise class. Consequently, the role of social-environmental factors may be important in furthering our understanding of exercise determinants. Indeed, as already discussed, self-presentational factors have been shown to influence individual perceptions of the exercise stimulus. Also, commonsense notions in fitness classes will support the important role of the exercise environment, including the class leader and the group climate. At the moment in the UK there is substantial investment in leisure provision via the private sector (Department of Culture, Media and Sport 2002). This has created an industry that employs graduates and others who are trained through specialist courses, such as those offered by the YMCA. It is surprising that given the potential for the exercise leader and the style of the class to influence adherence (and therefore continued membership to the facilities) that attention has not been given to these topics in specialist training courses.

Exercise leadership

Surprisingly little has been written about the role of the exercise leader yet for this type of exercise setting the leader could be the single most influential factor for adherence. The growth of 'personal trainers' is support for the motivational role of an exercise leader but there is virtually no evidence for their effectiveness.

Weber and Wertheim (1989) investigated the influence of staff attention on the adherence patterns of new recruits to a community gymnasium in Australia. The fifty-five women, on arrival at the exercise facility, were randomly allocated to one of three groups: control, self-monitoring of gym attendance, and self-monitoring plus extra staff attention. Over a twelve-week period it was found that attendance was highest for the self-monitoring group and lowest for the control group. However, the attendance of the self-monitoring plus staff attention group, although slightly better than the control, was not significantly superior. The intervention based on the exercise leader, therefore, was not successful over and above that of self-monitoring. It may be that trying to identify one set of successful leadership behaviours in health-related exercise will prove as unfruitful as in other contexts, including sport, due to the complex interaction between personal and environmental factors. Nevertheless, exercise leaders will almost certainly be important individuals in helping exercisers maintain participation.

Some recent work we have been doing with exercise provided in a clinical setting highlights the importance of the exercise leader as part of the success of the exercise intervention. In a focus group study, we explored the experiences of women undergoing treatment for breast cancer who had taken part in a supervised group exercise trial (Emslie *et al.* 2007). We found that setting up classes solely for women with breast cancer, led by an expert facilitator, helped to reduce gender-related barriers to physical activity, such as difficulties in prioritising exercise over caring roles and worries about changed appearance. Respondents stressed the importance of exercising with other women who had breast cancer and valued the expert leadership from the specifically trained teachers. These teachers were highly praised for their expertise and ability to adjust the pace and the exercises according to the composition of the class. This experience of the trained leader was different to that which could be found in standard exercise, which participants also had tried. For example one participant said,

> To go along to a class at your local sports centre in no way would measure up to what's offered by Anna (exercise leader) ... it is tailored to your needs and you don't have to explain yourself. And that's really important, because you don't want to be explaining yourself all the time! You just want to be relaxed.
>
> (Emslie *et al.* 2007)

It may be that research on the role of the exercise leader in clinical populations will provide new information on the importance of the leader for continued support and motivation.

In contrast to the paucity of information concerning exercise leaders, a great deal has been said on the role of leadership in sport settings (Chelladurai 1993). After initial and somewhat unsuccessful attempts to identify leadership 'types' through personality profiling, leadership research in sport has supported two main approaches. First, there is the 'situational' approach, advocated by Smith and Smoll, whereby they propose a set of 'universal' behaviours associated with good coaching (Carron and Hausenblas 1998; Smith and Smoll 1996; Smith, Smoll and Curtis 1979). These characteristics can be modified with training and are observable through the 'Coaching Behavior Assessment System' (CBAS). The CBAS involves observers noting the 'reactive' and 'spontaneous' behaviours of coaches, usually in youth sport settings.

The second approach to sport leadership has been an interactional and multidimensional one proposed by Chelladurai (1993). His model is based on the premise that there are antecedents of leader behaviour, such as situational, leader and group member characteristics, different dimensions of leader behaviour, such as required, actual and preferred behaviours, and finally, there are consequences of these interactions for behaviour and satisfaction. The model is shown in Figure 7.4.

The important point about Chelladurai's model is that it allows for different aspects of leadership to be considered. Not only is the actual behaviour of the leader included, but so is the behaviour required of the situation, and the behaviour preferred by the group members.

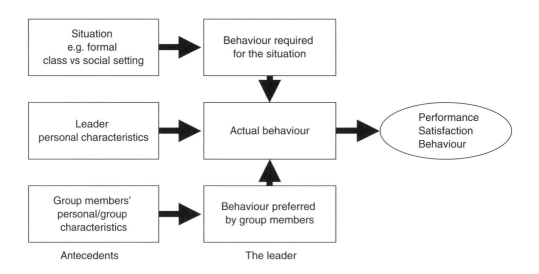

Figure 7.4 Modified version of Chelladurai's multidimensional model of leadership

The application of leadership theory from sport to exercise is long overdue. Chelladurai's model may be a suitable start and the importance of exercise leadership is clear to see and should feature in future exercise psychology studies (Carron, Hausenblas and Estabrooks 1999). For example, Martin and Lutes (2000) showed that exercise participants taught by a leader using an 'enriched' leadership style had lower levels of social anxiety in the class than those taught by a leadership adopting a 'bland' style.

Group climate and exercise motivation

Closely related to the issue of leadership is that of the climate, or atmosphere, created within the exercise group. In Chapter 5 we discussed the role of individual perceptions of success – 'achievement goal orientations' – and showed how they were related to motivation. A similar line of research has evolved concerning individual perceptions of the group climate. This work started in classroom environments (Ames and Archer 1988) and has now been extended to include sport and physical education settings (Biddle *et al.* 1995; Duda and Whitehead 1998; Ntoumanis and Biddle 1999; Papaioannou 1995; Papaioannou and Goudas 1999), but little has been said about wider physical activity contexts for adults.

Individual achievement goals have referred to mastery/task and ego/comparative elements. Perceptions of the 'motivational climate' can be categorised as 'mastery' or 'performance'. A mastery climate is one in which the group members perceive that the dominant ethos is one of self-improvement, where mistakes are viewed as part of learning, and praise may be given for high effort regardless of the actual outcome. A 'performance' climate, however, is one where group members are often compared with each other, where praise will usually only be given for normatively superior performance, and where anxiety is often felt about making mistakes.

Biddle *et al.* (1995) and Papaioannou (1994) have worked on the development of psychometric scales for the measurement of class climate in school physical education (PE). Papaioannou (1994) was the first to assess PE class goals by developing the 'Learning and Performance Orientations in PE Classes Questionnaire' (LAPOPECQ) from data on over 1,700 Greek school students. The questionnaire comprised the two higher-order constructs of learning (mastery) and performance and were underpinned by subscales assessing: (a) learning: 'teacher-initiated learning orientation'; 'students' learning orientation', and (b) performance: 'students' competitive orientation'; 'students' worries about mistakes'; 'outcome orientation without effort'. We modified this slightly to construct a questionnaire comprising four mastery and two performance subscales (Biddle *et al.* 1995; Goudas and Biddle 1994). The mastery subscales were: 'class mastery orientation', 'teachers' promotion of mastery orientation', 'student perception of choice' and 'teacher support'. The performance subscales were 'class performance orientation' and 'worries about mistakes'.

Ames and Archer (1988), in a classroom study, found that students' perceptions of class mastery goals were positively related to attitudes towards their class, a preference for challenging tasks and to the use of effective learning strategies. Conversely, perceptions of a performance climate were associated with maladaptive motivational patterns, such as attributing failure to lack of ability. Intrinsic motivation was found to be correlated with mastery climate perceptions in a study of British (Goudas and Biddle 1994) and Greek (Papaioannou 1994) physical education classes. Similarly, analysis of two PE activities for the same group of children showed that perceptions of a mastery class climate were good predictors of intrinsic interest and future intentions to participate (Biddle *et al.* 1995).

In an intervention study, we manipulated the teaching style offered to a class of girls being taught track and field athletics (Goudas *et al.* 1995). It was found that motivation was consistently higher in the classes taught with a style that included more student choice – itself a dimension of a mastery climate. Interventions to change the climate of groups and classes, therefore, should be possible for exercise research.

A meta-analysis of climate studies across all physical activity settings quantified the links between climates and positive psychological outcomes (such as satisfaction, intrinsic motivation and positive emotion) and negative psychological outcomes (such as anxiety and boredom) (Ntoumanis and Biddle 1999). The overall effects from fourteen studies involving over 4,000 participants showed a large effect for mastery climate on positive outcomes, a moderate effect for performance climate on negative outcomes, and small-to-medium effects for performance climate on positive outcomes and mastery climate on negative outcomes (see Figure 7.5).

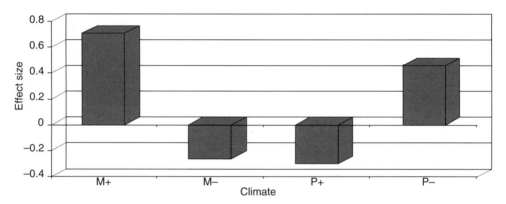

Figure 7.5 Effect sizes from a meta-analysis of motivational climate in physical activity showing relationships between mastery (M) and performance (P) climates and positive (+) and negative (–) psychological outcomes (Ntoumanis and Biddle, 1999)

Note
Correlations have been corrected for measurement and sampling error. Key: M: mastery climate; P: performance climate; +: positive psychological outcomes (e.g. enjoyment); –: negative psychological outcomes (e.g. anxiety)

Box 7.3 Creating the right environment for GP referral exercise patients

In the UK, there has been a tremendous increase in the number of 'GP-referral' exercise schemes (GP: 'general practitioner' – family doctor). Some time ago now, one of us (SJHB), along with colleagues Ken Fox and Laurel Edmunds (Fox *et al.* 1997), conducted a review of GP-referral exercise schemes throughout England. In addition to telephone and mailed survey data, we conducted eleven case study visits throughout the country.

One of the factors that clearly had been addressed in some community sports/leisure centres was the need to create the 'right' environment for a group of people not used to using such facilities. One centre manager was very aware of this and had changed the lighting and the music in the fitness room to accommodate this new client group. They even enlarged the cycle seats to accommodate a new type of physique!

This case study was illustrative of facility managers becoming aware of the need to create a (motivational) climate that was suitable for a specific group. Further interviews with the patients themselves confirmed the importance of this and of the need to change the 'young/sporty' image of the facilities if older patient groups were to be accommodated properly.

In summary, the lead given by researchers investigating group climates in educational and sport settings provides a good platform for exercise researchers. Although group exercise settings are not necessarily the best ways of promoting mass participation in exercise across the community, they provide an important setting for exercise for many people. Indeed, creating the correct motivational climate that fosters task motivation may be one of the most important skills that teachers and coaches can provide. In discussing the possibilities for studying exercise motivational climate, Ntoumanis and Biddle say:

> When using or developing scales for this area of research, elements unique to the exercise context should be included, such as items relating to the perception of social norms associated with fitness or body appearance. For example, it would be relevant to know whether instructors in exercise classes stress individual improvement in fitness or whether they promote interpersonal comparison.
>
> (Ntoumanis and Biddle 1999: 662)

Group cohesion and group efficacy in exercise

Franklin (1988) has proposed that a lack of group spirit is likely to predispose people to drop out of group exercise programmes. Carron, Hausenblas and Estabrook state their case in stronger terms: 'the need for interpersonal attachment is a fundamental human motive – a fact that has important implications for promoting adherence in exercise and physical activity' (Carron, Hausenblas and Estabrook 1999: 4). It appears that strategies designed to increase adherence should include the encouragement of group participation.

Exercise group cohesion

The study of group dynamics, cohesion and individual adherence to group activities, such as exercise, is an important line of research if we are interested in structured exercise contexts. Although group cohesion is a very old topic in psychology, it has not been studied much in the field of exercise.

Cohesion is defined as the forces attracting members to remain in a group as well as forces preventing group disruption (Carron and Hausenblas 1998). Two areas of investigation have dominated the research on group cohesion in sport: the measurement of group cohesion, and the relationship between cohesion and performance. Group cohesion is nearly always considered important in sport yet whether it is important for exercise, where group performance is rarely a desired outcome, remains to be seen. However, it is likely that some aspects of cohesion, such as group attraction, could influence adherence patterns.

Carron, Widmeyer and Brawley (1988) continued their research programme on group cohesion in sport (Carron and Hausenblas 1998; Carron, Hausenblas and Estabrooks 1999; Widmeyer, Brawley and Carron 1985; Widmeyer, Carron, and Brawley 1993) by investigating cohesion and adherence in fitness and recreation contexts. Carron, Widmeyer and Brawley (1988) looked at fitness class adherers and non-adherers as well as elite sport adherers and non-adherers. These four groups were assessed using the Group Environment Questionnaire (GEQ; Widmeyer, Brawley and Carron 1985). The GEQ is a self-report instrument yielding scores on four subscales: individual attraction to the group – task (ATG–T); individual attraction to the group – social (ATG–S); group integration – task (GI–T); and group integration – social (GI–S). Slight modification was made to the GEQ to allow it to be administered to the fitness groups since the original scale was written for sport groups. Analysis of the fitness group scores showed that two of the GEQ variables significantly discriminated adherers from non-adherers. Specifically, adherers had higher scores on both ATG subscales, showing that dropouts were less personally attracted to the group's task and to the group as a social unit.

In a meta-analysis by Carron, Hausenblas and Mack (1996), small-to-moderate effects were found between social influence variables and exercise behaviours. Key findings from the meta-analysis showed:

- moderate effects on exercise adherence for the variables of task cohesion, the exercise class leader, and social support from important others and family
- intention to exercise and exercise affect were positively associated with family and significant others
- support from family members was stronger when involving exercise prescription from a health professional in comparison with other exercise programmes.

A meta-analysis by Burke *et al.* (2006) showed that exercise groups where team-building strategies were used to enhance cohesion had superior adherence when compared with standard exercise groups.

Our work with group exercise opportunities for women undergoing treatment for breast cancer also highlights how important the group itself might be for continued exercise motivation. Women from our focus group study emphasised the importance of exercising with women in similar circumstances time and time again; indeed phrases such as 'the same boat', 'the same position' or 'people that are the same as you' were used in every discussion with respondents from the exercise group (Emslie *et al.* 2007). Women valued the empathy they received from others, and described moving from feeling isolated to feeling accepted. Friendships formed amongst women in the exercise groups. Indeed, respondents who had taken part in the pilot project over three years ago had remained friends and still sometimes exercised together. Again the clinical setting may offer exercise psychologists opportunities to study important aspects of exercise motivation such as group processes.

Considerably more work is required, however, in understanding the nature and extent of social psychological variables of the group and exercise adherence. The following issues require attention:

- The type of exercise may be crucial. Studies on diverse activities such as distance running, weight training, and aerobic 'step' classes may reveal different results. Exercise groups for those with clinical conditions for whom exercise has been recommended as part of treatment may reveal other important issues.
- The type of participant and the exercise leader are important ingredients in this research. Although it is usual to encourage sedentary people to take part in exercise with a partner or in groups, much more needs to be known before specific advice about the nature of such group factors and exercise adherence can be made. For example, it is now common for exercise classes to consist of more than fifty people. We know little about the motivational effects of being in such a large group, the concomitant lack of individualised instruction and attention, or whether these are unimportant given enjoyable exercises and motivating music. Alternatively, the anonymity of exercising in a large group may be perceived as a positive feature for some people due to reduced self-presentational pressures, yet the degree of social loafing in large groups is likely to be quite high. Group size, therefore, requires further investigation.

- Although a group environment may be perceived positively in the short term, longer-term adherence to exercise may suffer if individual behavioural skills are not taught or learned, particularly if the exercise group ceases after a period of time. Typically, exercise prescriptions in supervised settings work on ten to twelve week schedules.
- The GEQ was developed from a conceptual model of sport group cohesion. Half of the GEQ is concerned with aspects of the group task. The extent to which exercise groups perceive themselves to have a 'task' is debatable. Further work is required on group cohesion measurement in exercise.

Carron, Hausenblas and Estabrook (1999) proposed some principles for promoting group adherence in exercise, including:

- distinctiveness: feelings of group distinctiveness, such as wearing group T-shirts or logos, can increase feelings of cohesion
- group norms: cohesion can increase by having group members share common expectations
- interaction and communication: cohesion and interaction between members of the group are positively correlated.

Exercise group efficacy

The literature on the determinants of individual participation in exercise and physical activity is quite clear in identifying self-efficacy as a consistent and important determinant (see Chapter 5). However, the concept of group, or collective, efficacy has been proposed for the study of group motivation. For example, Bandura says 'people do not live their lives in social isolation. Many of the challenges and difficulties they face reflect group problems requiring sustained collective effort to produce any significant change' (Bandura 1986: 449). Bandura suggests that collective efficacy will influence group motivation by affecting what people do, how much effort is exerted and their motivation in adverse circumstances, such as group failure. Interestingly, Bandura does not see self-efficacy as divorced from collective efficacy, but rather collective efficacy is rooted in self-efficacy; 'inveterate self-doubters are not easily forged into a collective efficacious force' (Bandura 1986: 449).

As with group cohesion, one can see the relevance of collective efficacy for sport groups (George and Feltz 1995). However, whether some exercise groups require collective efficacy is likely to be variable. There is evidence, nonetheless, for collective efficacy to be associated with exercise performance. Specifically, Bray (2004) tested the muscular endurance performance of students acting in groups of three. Collective efficacy positively predicted performance on a second trial, even after accounting for performance at the first trial. It appears that perceptions of group confidence – collective efficacy – might assist in more demanding exercise tasks.

Key point: Social environments are a neglected area of study in exercise psychology. Exercise motivation can be enhanced through the application of knowledge on leadership and groups.

Environmental correlates of physical activity

The ecological model for understanding and increasing physical activity suggests that there are many environments that will influence people's ability to be active (see Chapter 1). In this section we discuss influences at the level of the physical environment in which people live. As Sallis and Owen point out, when we discuss the term environment, within the context of ecological models of behaviour, it simply means the space outside the person (Sallis and Owen 2002). Given this definition, environment is therefore a hugely important topic to consider as an influence on physical activity behaviour.

Environmental influences have now been recognised in many health fields. For example, environments that promote sedentary behaviour, while at the same time making it easy to buy food with high fat values, have been labelled 'obesogenic' (Egger and Swinburn 1997). We will soon need a similar term just for the activity element of this description: we suggest 'slothogenic'!

Considerations of how the environment might influence activity could include: seasonal variation in the amount of daylight and pleasant weather for being active (for some, unpleasant is cold and wet and for others it is hot and humid); easy access to facilities or places to be active; and the design of housing developments or characteristics of neighbourhoods that promote or inhibit walking and cycling as means of transport. However, there has been less research on these important influences than there has been on interpersonal or intrapersonal determinants of physical activity.

Systematic reviews of environmental influences on physical activity

Humpel and colleagues have provided an excellent systematic review on the environmental factors that might influence physical activity for adults (Humpel, Owen and Leslie 2002). They identified nineteen studies that examined the relationship between attributes of the physical environment and physical activity behaviour and found five groupings of findings relating to accessibility of facilities, opportunities for activity, weather, safety and aesthetics. The pattern of results suggested significant associations with physical activity for ease of access to facilities, having places nearby to be active and perceived positive aesthetics of the local area (such as enjoyable scenery). However, weather and safety did not show a pattern of significant associations.

Sallis *et al.* (2000), in their systematic review of correlates of physical activity for young people, reported consistent associations between physical activity and programme/facility access and time outdoors for children, and 'opportunities to exercise' for adolescents. In our own systematic review of correlates of physical activity for adolescent girls (Biddle *et al.* 2005), eighteen environmental variables were located. However, each was studied only once or twice, thus precluding firm conclusions to be drawn. More needs to be known about the role of environmental variables in adolescent girls' physical activity participation. A large-scale ($n = 17{,}766$) population data set for boys and girls from Gordon-Larson, McMurray and Popkin (2000) suggests that higher levels of physical activity are associated with use of a community recreation centre and lower levels of crime.

Relative influence of psychosocial and environmental variables

The literature is currently not able to provide enough information about the relative influence of environmental and psychosocial variables. For example, in an Australian study it was shown that, at least for walking, physical environmental variables were equally important as the psychosocial determinants (Pikora *et al.* 2003). However, in a European study it was found that the variance explained by environmental factors in determining what predicted achievement of the recommended minimum levels of activity was lower (1 per cent to 8 per cent) than that explained by psychosocial factors (maximum 42 per cent) (De Bourdeaudhuij *et al.* 2005). We recognise that environments interact with individual choices and it would be naive to suggest that 'if you build it they will come'. Putting bike lanes into busy streets is likely to have little influence on cycling unless there are simultaneous information opportunities for cyclist and drivers, and unless cars are penalised if they use the bike lane. However, Owen and colleagues point out that if the environmental influences strongly constrain or facilitate behaviours they are likely to predominate over the psychosocial determinants. In certain settings, therefore, the environment may be the most dominant influence while in others the psychosocial variables may dominate (Owen *et al.* 2004). Owen *et al.* have also tried to blend together the psychosocial and environmental influences into a 'behaviour settings' approach to understanding these varying influences (Owen *et al.* 2000). Such behaviour settings include those in a community context (for example, public recreational space or sports facilities), indoor and outdoor spaces at home, the workplace, educational settings and transport. In each setting there are different choices to be made between active or sedentary pursuits. For example, in the transport setting a person can make a choice to commute actively some or all of the way to work or to use a car or public transport and be more sedentary.

In a recent North American nationally representative survey ($n = 2,181$), researchers summed responses to various questions to create environmental, transportation, social and time barrier variables (Zlot *et al.* 2006). Logistic regression was then used to find out if these variables had a significant association with physical activity levels. Not surprisingly, it was found that people who reported low levels of these barriers were more likely to meet the recommended physical activity levels compared with those people who reported medium or high levels of these barriers. However, of importance to the present discussion on the relative influence of environmental and psychosocial variables, it was found that transportation, social capital and time barriers independently contributed to the low levels of physical activity. Thus, while we cannot say with certainty how much of influence the environment has, it is clear that some aspects, such as transport and social capital, have an important role to play in determining activity levels and more large-scale survey research is needed to verify these findings.

Key point: The environment, including access to active opportunities, the weather, perceived safety and aesthetics of a locale, has potential to influence activity levels. Not enough is known yet about the relative influence of environmental variables in comparison with psychosocial variables in determining activity levels.

Environmental aesthetics

The notion of how we perceive the aesthetics of our local environment has been examined by several researchers. A great deal of this work has been done in Australia where Neville Owen has been influential in highlighting the need for research. Walking has been shown to be influenced by how people perceive various aspects of their environment. In a cross-sectional survey of over 3,000 Australians, both men and women who perceived their locale as less environmentally pleasing or less convenient were less likely than those with more favourable perceptions to have walked in the past two weeks (Troiano, Macera and Ballard-Barbash 2001). For women in particular, having no company or a pet to walk also meant they were less likely to walk. Again the researchers call for interventions that focus on the changeable aspects of these perceptions to determine if physical activity can be influenced. Giles-Corti and colleagues found that using public open space for walking was more likely when people found it attractive as well as convenient (Giles-Corti *et al.* 2005). Having convenient facilities is not always perceived as something that promotes activity or is associated with health. Using health survey data from almost 14,000 UK residents, Cummins and colleagues found that there were six attributes of neighbourhoods that were related to self-reported poor health (Cummins *et al.* 2005): poor physical quality residential environment, left-wing political climate, low political engagement, high unemployment, lower access to private transport and lower transport wealth. However, self-rated health was not significantly associated with five other neighbourhood measures, one of which was access to public recreation facilities.

The connection between attractiveness of locale and physical activity has also been questioned. In another Australian study, a geographic information system (GIS) approach (see Box 7.4) was used to measure aspects of the local geography, such as distance to footpaths, along with a telephone interview about environmental perceptions and physical activity of over 1,000 residents from the town of Rockhampton (Duncan and Mummery 2005). The researchers found that in terms of predicting the likelihood of obtaining sufficient levels of physical activity, proximity to parkland had an influence, but that when people did not agree that their neighbourhood was clean and tidy they were more likely to achieve sufficient activity. Such a counter-intuitive finding could be explained by those who are more active having more opportunities to view the neighbourhood. The likelihood of engaging in recreational walking was also explored and again a slightly counter-intuitive finding emerged, with those who did not agree that local footpaths were in good condition being more likely to engage in recreational walking. Again, perhaps active people may be more aware of the footpaths. The number of counter-intuitive findings in these cross-sectional studies certainly highlights the need for further research and reminds us to resist the temptation to conclude that it is obvious how the environment influences activity!

Box 7.4 Geographic information systems (GIS)

Underpinning at least half of the present chapter is the proposition that our behaviours will be influenced by the environment in which we live. As far as physical activity is concerned, the physical environment can encourage or discourage activity. One challenge for researchers is how to measure the physical attributes of the environment. In the past, prior to modern computer systems and software, manual mapping techniques were used to calculate distances and environmental features. Clearly these are laborious and time-consuming tasks. More recently, computer-based systems have been developed to analyse information contained on maps. Such geographic information systems (GIS) allow for greater objectivity in measuring the built environment (Forsyth *et al.* 2006). Although GIS has been commonly used in urban geography and transport research, it is only quite recently that physical activity researchers have used such tools. Variables of interest might include urban land use, street connectivity and distances (Porter *et al.* 2004).

Transport as an environmental influence

There are various health issues that result from transport. Currently, there are great concerns about pollution that is created from transport that could have a negative impact on respiratory disorders. However, there is also noise pollution, road accidents and reduction in safe walking and cycling to be considered. On the other hand, transport can enhance access to various services and leisure opportunities. In many countries it has been recognised that transportation planning must involve how to increase walking and cycling and therefore transport policies can have a direct influence on physical activity levels. In Chapter 13 we review the evidence for promoting active commuting as a means to increase physical activity, but here we want to show the key considerations of how transport policy might influence physical activity.

There are various aspects of transport that could have a potential influence. These include the provision of public transport that is integrated with physical activity opportunities, such as signage and cycle storage, the accessibility of public transport, the provision of car parking, street design that includes separate pedestrian or cycle paths, and safety issues. A recent systematic review by Heath and colleagues (2006) showed that studies addressing issues of urban design and land-use policies were associated with greater levels of physical activity.

As many cities are facing a transportation crisis in which cars are causing congestion, it is important that the physical activity agenda is considered when plans are made to reduce such congestion. For example, London now has a congestion charge for private vehicles entering a designated inner-city zone, and electronic metering operates at the point when cars enter the city centre in Singapore. However, transport planners have probably not considered the physical activity consequences of their plans sufficiently with injury prevention being the main concern (Morrison, Pettricrew and Thomson 2003). At present there is little available evidence on how such plans will influence activity. Ogilvie and colleagues have pointed out the difficulties that researchers face in trying to evaluate the physical activity consequences of congestion charging or increasing urban motorways (Ogilvie *et al.* 2004). These include the need to have sufficient advance notice of such plans to allow baseline measures to be taken, the definition of the population who may be influenced, finding a control group for comparison and the lack of precision in self-reported measures of physical activity. They suggest a longitudinal quasi-experimental design as a solution. Thus, while transport-related physical activity could be increased by transport policies, at present we do not have an evidence base to help determine how best this could be achieved.

The research agenda

The number of investigations in the area of physical activity and the physical environment has been growing and reviews conducted in the near future are likely to find more studies, with more discerning variables, such as the intensity and mode of activity, and more precise measurements of the variables. For example, a data collection tool that allows measurement of how neighbourhoods can promote active living has been developed and validated (Gauvin *et al.* 2005). In addition, the 'walkability' of a neighbourhood is now a term that is commonplace for those trying to influence planning (Ewing *et al.* 2006; Greenberg and Renne 2005; Moundon *et al.* 2006). Using pooled data from several surveys, Ewing *et al.* (2003) showed that 'urban sprawl' had a small but significant effect on physical activity in that more sprawling locales, in which aspects of the community are further apart, had lower levels of activity in comparison with less sprawling locales.

Owen *et al.* (2004) have offered a research agenda that would help us further understand the environmental influences on walking. The agenda includes the development of tools that provide valid and reliable measures of environmental attributes, determining if the associations seen in cross-sectional data have a causal pathway, and developing theoretical models that take account of environmental and other determinants.

The key development in this field will be the evaluation of interventions that seek to change aspects of the environment that have been found from cross-sectional studies to link to physical activity. We will discuss these interventions in Chapter 13. If behaviour change follows environmental change then there is a strong case for policies to promote the development of environments that promote activity. Such policies will influence building regulations, transport planning, green space provision, urban street design, access laws and many more regulations which might currently dissuade activity, such as the perception that streets are unsafe and the ubiquitous 'no ball games' signs (Lawlor *et al.* 2003)!

An American study showed strong support from the public for such policy changes. In a cross-sectional telephone survey of almost 2,000 randomly selected adults (Brownson *et al.* 2001), having pavements (sidewalks), enjoyable scenery, heavy traffic and hills were all positively associated with physical activity. The authors suggested that the counter-intuitive findings regarding traffic and hills may relate to urban areas and scenic activity areas respectively. However, the important additional information from this study was strong support from the respondents for health policy changes that would create funding for changing the environment to influence physical activity.

A conceptual framework

Pikora and colleagues have developed a framework for taking forward research into environmental influences on physical activity, particularly walking and cycling (Pikora *et al.* 2003). They used published literature and a Delphi study, which gains opinions from selected experts, to develop the framework. This has four environmental features that should be taken into account: functional, safety, aesthetic and destination considerations. They also listed the hypothesised factors that contribute to each of these features of the environment and offered a data collection tool. This work should add considerably to the knowledge base on environmental influences (see Table 7.3).

Table 7.3 Physical environmental factors that might influence walking (Pikora *et al.* 2003)

Environmental feature	Elements	Items and examples
Functional	Walking surface	Path type, surface type, maintenance, continuity
	Streets	Width
	Traffic	Volume, speed, traffic control devices
	Permeability	Street design, intersection design and distance, other access points
Safety	Personal	Lighting, surveillance
	Traffic	Crossings, verge width
Aesthetic	Streetscape	Trees, garden maintenance, cleanliness, pollution, parks
	Views	Sights, architecture
Destination	Facilities	Parks, shops

This area is set to flourish. In 2004 Jim Sallis (USA), Ilse De Bourdeaudhuij (Belgium) and Neville Owen (Australia) collaborated in launching the International Physical Activity and the Environment Network (IPEN) The network aims to:

- increase communication and collaboration between researchers investigating environmental correlates of physical activity
- stimulate research in physical activity and the environment
- recommend common methods and measures
- support researchers through sharing of information, feedback, letters of support, etc.
- bring together data from multiple countries for joint analyses
- aid in the publication of data through papers, special journal issues, symposia, etc.

IPEN is clearly hoping to make a big impact in the world of physical activity research. Information is available at www.ipenproject.org.

Chapter summary and conclusions

This chapter has considered a range of issues associated with social and environmental correlates of physical activity. Specifically, in this chapter we have:

- reviewed the evidence for associations between social variables and participation in physical activity
- assessed the nature and extent of family influence on physical activity, including whether physical activity is stable over time
- shown how leadership and group climate need to be considered in exercise motivation theory and practice
- considered the issue of social influence in physical activity
- discussed the potential of studying group cohesion and efficacy in furthering our understanding of exercise groups
- summarised likely associations between physical activity and the environment
- discussed the relative influence of environmental and psychosocial variables on activity levels
- summarised what is known about the role of environmental aesthetics
- considered the role of motorised and active transport in the wider agenda of the physical environment and activity
- discussed a possible research agenda and conceptual framework in the field of the physical environment and physical activity.

In summary, therefore, we conclude:

- a number of social factors are related to participation in physical activity by adolescents and adults
- sibling physical activity, parental support and father's physical activity are associated with physical activity in adolescents
- social support from spouse and family are associated with physical activity in adults

- insufficient evidence is available to conclude anything about the most appropriate way of studying exercise leadership, but research in sport settings suggests that Chelladurai's multidimensional model of leadership has many characteristics that might be appropriate for future research in exercise
- extrapolating from studies in sport and physical education, mainly with children, the development of a mastery motivational climate in exercise classes and groups appears to be desirable for motivational and other positive psychological outcomes
- research on group cohesion has shown that exercise group dropouts have lower perceptions of cohesion than those who stay. However, the direct applicability of a conceptual model of group cohesion developed for sport requires further testing in wider physical activity and exercise settings
- the notion of collective efficacy in exercise groups is largely untested, although initial data are promising in showing positive effects for collective efficacy on exercise performance
- significant associations with physical activity have been found for ease of access to facilities, having places nearby to be active, and perceived positive aesthetics of the local area
- studies addressing issues of urban design and land-use policies show that such factors can be associated with greater levels of physical activity
- four key environmental features that should be taken into account in physical activity research are functional, safety, aesthetic and destination considerations.

Part III

Physical activity

A feel-good effect?

8 Psychological well-being

Does physical activity make us feel good?

Running and worrying don't mix.

(Glasser 1976)

Exercise dissipates tension, and tension is the enemy of serenity.

(Mandela 1994)

Purpose of the chapter

The purpose of this chapter is to review the evidence on the relationship between participation in physical activity and psychological well-being (PWB). Specifically, we review the areas of mood and affect, including enjoyment, self-esteem, cognitive functioning, personality and adjustment, and sleep. Specifically, in this chapter we aim to:

- highlight the concept of health-related quality of life and how it is typically measured
- review the evidence linking physical activity and exercise with measures of mood and affect
- highlight the definitional problems associated with the construct of enjoyment in exercise and present four approaches to the study of enjoyment in physical activity
- comment on the psychological effects of depriving people of exercise
- provide evidence on factors moderating the relationship between exercise and mood/affect
- summarise the evidence linking physical activity with the development and enhancement of self-esteem and physical self-perceptions
- comment on studies investigating the links between exercise and cognitive functioning, and exercise and personality/psychological adjustment
- briefly highlight results from meta-analyses on the effects of exercise on sleep
- discuss how physical activity and exercise may provide benefits for women experiencing menstruation, pregnancy or menopause.

A case was made in Chapter 1 for the diverse health benefits of a physically active lifestyle. However, although there is plenty of anecdotal support for the view that physical activity has positive effects on psychological well-being, the emphasis is often placed more firmly on the physical outcomes. Nevertheless, the publication of health-related documents in England by the British government in the 1990s (Department of Health 1993b) marked a significant change in approach in health care and promotion in England and placed greater emphasis on aspects of well-being. For example, in the overall aims of the government's Health of the Nation initiative were the desire for 'adding years to life' – reduce premature mortality and improve life expectancy – and 'adding life to years', that is improving the quality of life.

Similarly, the influential Surgeon General's Report on physical activity and health in the United States (Department of Health and Human Services 1996) recognised the importance of physical activity for well-being as well as disease prevention. More recently, the UK government's Chief Medical Officer's report on physical activity and health (Department of Health 2004a) recognised the positive effects that physical activity can have on various elements of psychological well-being in children and adults.

The promotion of health through physical activity, therefore, now incorporates the recognition of the importance of psychological well-being. This chapter reviews the evidence on the links between physical activity and psychological well-being. There is also the possibility that physical activity could have negative consequences on mental health and well-being, for example in promoting unhealthy exercise or eating habits. Such issues will be dealt with in Chapter 10 when we address the issue of exercise dependence.

Evidence for this chapter has been drawn from an extensive literature. Narrative and meta-analytic reviews, epidemiological surveys and controlled trials are reviewed in an effort to reach conclusions from varied approaches. In addition, we will discuss a range of topics associated with psychological well-being, including:

- health-related quality of life
- emotion and mood
- enjoyment
- exercise deprivation
- self-esteem
- personality and psychological adjustment
- exercise and sleep
- specific issues for women

Health-related quality of life

Rejeski, Brawley and Shumaker (1996) suggest that it is typical for health-related quality of life (HRQL) to be defined in terms of participants' perceptions of function. They outline six types of HRQL measures:

- *global indices of HRQL:* these might include general life satisfaction or self-esteem
- *physical function:* perceptions of function; physical self-perceptions; health-related perceptions
- *physical symptoms:* fatigue; energy; sleep
- *emotional function:* depression; anxiety; mood; affect; emotion
- *social function:* social dependency; family/work roles
- *cognitive function:* memory; attention; problem-solving.

Rejeski, Brawley and Shumaker (1996) state that the US National Institutes of Health mandate researchers to include measures of HRQL in most clinical trials. However, HRQL measures are usually viewed simply in terms of physical function and this is a narrow view. There are many HRQL instruments and these include affective measures. Some (Muldoon *et al.* 1998) suggest a simple division of HRQL into functional measures and those assessing quality of life.

Key HRQL measures include the SF-36, the Nottingham Health Profile (Hunt, McEwan and McKenna 1986) and the EuroQol (Buxton, O'Hanlon and Rushby 1990, 1992). The SF-36 is the best known measure and is a thirty-six-item questionnaire designed to assess eight health dimensions covering functional status, well-being and overall evaluation of health (Dixon *et al.* 1994). The SF-36 (also known as the SF-36 Health Survey and the Rand 36-item Health Survey) has an anglicised version for use in the UK as well as a short form (SF-12). The SF-36 assesses the following dimensions of well-being: physical functioning, social functioning, role limitations due to physical problems, mental health, energy/vitality, pain, and general health perception. It also has one item assessing perceptions of recent changes in health (Bowling 1997).

Although the use of SF-36 is quite extensive, evidence for its validity is mixed. Dixon *et al.* (1994) concluded that the SF-36 is not designed for specific patient groups, is not directly based on lay views and has little evidence that it detects change.

One global dimension of HRQL is perceptions of life satisfaction. This might be particularly important for older adults as they experience physical and mental decline. McAuley and colleagues have conducted extensive research on HRQL outcomes in older adults involved in physical activity interventions. In a five-year follow-up, Elavsky *et al.* (2005) showed that positive self-efficacy, physical self-worth and affect resulting from enhanced levels of physical activity predicted life satisfaction after one year. Moreover, self-efficacy, physical self-worth and affect showed good stability over four years and again predicted life satisfaction. The authors concluded that enhanced life satisfaction associated with physical activity is mediated by enhanced feelings of self-efficacy, physical self-worth and affect.

Rejeski, Brawley and Shumaker (1996) provide a comprehensive review of HRQL and physical activity and offer the following conclusions:

- HRQL test batteries should include general and condition- or population-specific measures
- the degree of change observed in HRQL through physical activity will depend on baseline levels
- the degree of impact of physical activity on HRQL will depend on both the physiological stimulus as well as social and behavioural characteristics of the treatment or intervention
- people vary in the extent to which they value certain health-related outcomes from physical activity; hence this will affect HRQL perceptions of those in intervention studies.

HRQL, therefore, includes an affective dimension that requires further consideration, such as through measures of mood, self-esteem, anxiety, and depression.

Affective outcomes of physical activity

The affective reactions associated with exercise have a potentially important role in physical activity and health promotion. If we believe that physical activity is a positive health behaviour to be encouraged and promoted, how people feel during and after activity may be critical in determining whether they maintain their involvement. This means that the discussion in earlier chapters concerning motivation and adherence cannot be divorced from aspects of psychological well-being. Affect may have motivational properties for an important health-related behaviour. In addition, positive affect is an important health outcome in its own right.

Defining affect, emotion and mood

The terms 'affect', 'emotion' and 'mood' are closely related and often perceived to be synonymous concepts that require more careful clarification and definition. These are necessarily difficult concepts to define, and demarcations are not always clear, but an effort to summarise them is shown in Table 8.1.

'Affect' is the generic 'valenced' (good/bad) response that is a broader construct than emotion. It is a basic human response with Russell and Barrett referring to 'core affect' as 'the most elementary consciously accessible affective feelings' (Russell and Barrett 1999: 806). Affect can be studied from the viewpoint of neuro-anatomy and biology (Buckworth and Dishman 2002), psychological and cognitive (Russell 2003), or a mixture of the two (Ekkekakis 2003; Ekkekakis, Hall and Petruzzello 2004).

Mood or 'mood states' are commonly targeted in physical activity studies (Berger and Motl 2001; Buckworth and Dishman 2002). Mood can be seen as a global set of affective (feeling) states we experience on a day-to-day basis and may last hours, days, weeks or even months (Oatley and Jenkins 1996). Mood can be conceptualised in terms of distinct mood states, such as vigour and depression, but these, as mood states, are not a reaction to a specified event but more likely stemming from generic feelings. The origin of mood states is more difficult to specify, such as 'feeling down' for no obvious reason, hence they tend to be 'diffuse' and relatively low in intensity.

Emotion is normally defined in terms of specific feeling states generated in reaction to certain events or appraisals. They are likely to last for minutes or hours, but not longer (Oatley and Jenkins 1996) and can be intense. Given that a cognitive appraisal takes place for an emotional reaction to be elicited, physical activity studies do not always assess true emotional outcomes. Most physical activity studies are testing the affective states, or changes, resulting from single or multiple bouts of activity and may not test cognitive appraisals of specific events. Sometimes, emotions are assessed, such as feelings of efficacy following successful negotiation of a new exercise programme. Regrettably, the distinction between mood and emotion in physical activity research studies is often not

Table 8.1 Defining features of affect, emotion and mood

Construct	Defining features	Intensity and time	Cognitive mediation	Example
Affect	Basic and generic valenced (pleasant/ unpleasant) responses	Varied	A cognitive appraisal might be involved when affect is a component of emotion or mood, but is not necessary (see text). Affect can occur independently	Energetic or tired
Emotion	Affective states resulting from an appraisal of specific events	Usually high intensity; short duration	Cognitive appraisal of a specific eliciting event	Proud or ashamed
Mood	Diffuse affective states not resulting from specific events but more likely associated with general views at a point in time	Lower intensity; can be prolonged	Cognitive appraisal of larger issues or events in the distant past or future	Irritable or jovial

made clear. For example, the meta-analysis by Arent, Landers and Etnier (2000) concerning the effects of exercise on 'mood' in older adults was really a review of positive and negative affect rather than 'mood' per se.

It is important to note that affect can also be a component of moods and emotions. For example, pride will feel pleasant and depression will feel unpleasant. Readers are referred to Beedie, Terry and Lane (2005), Buckworth and Dishman (2002), Ekkekakis and Petruzzello (2000), Oatley and Jenkins (1996) and Vallerand and Blanchard (2000) for further discussion on definitional issues.

> Key point: Defining the key terms of affect, mood and emotion is not easy, but we should provide working definitions in research projects and not assume they are one and the same.

Measurement issues

In psychology, there is a debate concerning the nature of affective states, including emotion (Cacioppo, Gardner and Berntson 1999; Diener 1999; Green, Salovey and Truax 1999; Russell and Barrett 1999; Watson *et al.* 1999). Some prefer to define affective states in terms of discrete emotional reactions, such as pleasure and fear (Clore, Ortony and Foss 1987; Lazarus 1991; Weiner 1995). This is the 'categorical' approach to measurement of affect. Others suggest that affect is best defined in terms of their common properties, or dimensions, such as positive and negative affect (Watson, Clark and Tellegen 1988) – the 'dimensional' approach. Lazarus (1991), however, argues that the distinct qualities of emotional reactions are lost, or blurred, when reduced to a few affective dimensions. He argues that each emotion is unique because it is created by a different appraisal of the perceived significance of an event. However, it is also logical to see emotions clustered according to common categories. Watson, Clark and Tellegen (1988) have derived two major factors from an analysis of emotions – positive affect and negative affect. The former refers to feelings such as alert and active, whereas negative affect refers to unpleasant affective states such as anger and fear.

Russell has also advocated a dimensional approach to the study of affect (Russell 1980). In his 'circumplex' model, he suggests that emotion can best be defined in terms of the two dimensions of valence (that is, pleasant–unpleasant) and arousal (that is, high–low). This gives rise to emotions being classified into four quadrants, as shown in Figure 8.1.

Ekkekakis and Petruzzello (2000) argue that the decision on whether categorical or dimensional approaches should be used depends on the nature of the research question. For studies wishing to test the affective responses to exercise in the context of exercise adherence, dimensional measures of affective valence (good/bad) are likely to be appropriate, particularly when the current state of knowledge is such that hypotheses concerning specific affective states or emotions are not always possible. This is because reinforcement of exercise adherence is likely to relate to generic feelings of good or bad. Nor do we know much about mediating variables that might be causing the affective responses, hence it is logical to assess along affective dimensions. However, if we wish to test the effects of specific environments (for example exercising in classes), or contexts (for example trying a new activity), then assessing discrete emotions might be applicable, such as anxiety or self-efficacy.

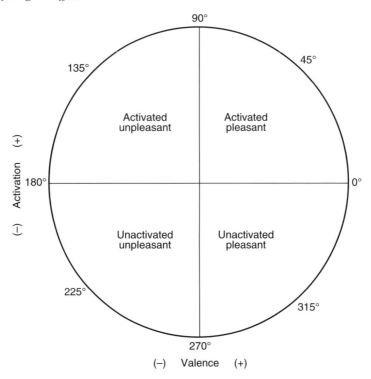

Figure 8.1 The circumplex model of affect proposed by Russell (1980)

Measures of affect, emotion and mood in physical activity

Dimensional measures of affect in physical activity have typically used the circumplex model (Figure 8.1). In addition to the advantages of this approach that have already been discussed, because this method involves simple assessment scales of arousal/activation and valence, multiple measures can be taken in single exercise bouts. This allows for the assessment of affect before, during and after exercise. Typically studies have failed to describe the affective states during exercise and may be making erroneous conclusions based on only having measures before and after exercise.

Many studies have used Hardy and Rejeski's (1989) 'Feeling Scale' to assess affective valence. This scale requires the participant to rate their feeling on an eleven-point scale anchored by 'very good' (+5) and 'very bad' (−5). Activation/arousal can be measured using the Felt Arousal Scale (Svebak and Murgatroyd 1985) – a six-point scale anchored by 'low arousal' (0) and 'high arousal' (6). Using the circumplex, affective states can be plotted, as shown in Figure 8.2. This example shows that a fifteen-minute treadmill walk at a self-chosen pace results in an activated pleasant state during and immediately after its completion. A ten-minute seated recovery period leads to a low-activation pleasant state. A treadmill test, lasting on average just over eleven minutes, during which the speed and grade are gradually increased until the point of volitional exhaustion, leads to an activated *unpleasant* state. A subsequent cool-down and ten-minute seated recovery period bring about a return to a low-activation pleasant state. The ventilatory threshold (indicated by 'VT'), which is a marker of the transition from aerobic to anaerobic metabolism, appears to be the turning point toward displeasure during the treadmill test. This is discussed in more detail later, but does question

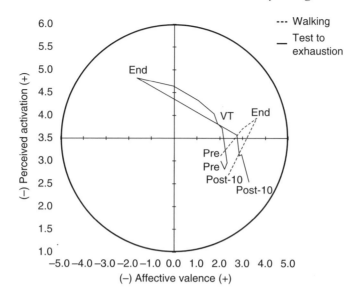

Figure 8.2 Affective responses to two bouts of physical activity, plotted in circumplex space, where the horizontal dimension represents self-rated affective valence, ranging from displeasure to pleasure, and the vertical dimension represents perceived activation

Notes
'Pre' indicates the beginning of each activity, 'End' indicates its end and 'Post-10' indicates 10 minutes after the end. Plotted with data from Ekkekakis *et al.* (2000) and Hall *et al.* (2002). VT: ventilatory threshold

the common assumption that exercise is always associated with positive affect. There are likely to be situations, possibly related to higher intensity exercise, where affective valence becomes negative (Ekkekakis 2003; Hall, Ekkekakis and Petruzzello 2002).

The majority of studies in physical activity and affect have adopted the categorical approach to measurement. Where generic measures of mood have been used, typically the Profile of Mood States (POMS) (McNair, Lorr and Droppleman 1971) has been the instrument of choice (Berger and Motl 2001). However, McDonald and Hodgdon (1991) also located exercise studies using the Multiple Affect Adjective Check List (MAACL) (Zuckerman and Lubin 1965), assessing only anxiety, depression and hostility. The POMS assesses five negative moods and only one positive mood (vigour), although the bipolar form of the POMS (Lorr and McNair 1984; Lorr, Shi and Youniss 1989) allows the assessment of both positive and negative poles for each construct. The subscales in the bipolar version are energetic–tired, elation–depression, confident–unsure, composed–anxious, agreeable–hostile and clearheaded–confused. However, a large sample size is required to produce sufficient statistical power to detect changes. For this reason, the bipolar version of POMS may not be the most suitable or sensitive instrument for physical activity studies. The POMS can also be varied, however, according to the instructions, such as how participants feel 'right now' or 'over the past few weeks', depending on the research question.

In addition to more generic measures of mood and affect, some researchers have developed scales for the assessment of 'exercise-related' affect or 'feeling states'. Both types of measures used in physical activity research are summarised in Table 8.2, showing dimensional and categorical measures.

Table 8.2 A summary of categorical and dimensional measures of mood and affect commonly used in physical activity research

Instrument	Reference	Measures	Comments
Dimensional measures			
BFS (Befindlichkeitsskalen)	Abele and Brehm (1993)	Forty-item scale devised in German to assess two-dimensional model of mood: activation (high/low) and evaluation (positive/negative). eight subscales: • activation (high/positive) • elation (high/positive) • calmness (low/positive) • contemplativeness (low/positive) • excitation (high/negative) • anger (high/negative) • fatigue (low/negative) • depression (low/negative)	• extensive German research supporting validity of scale in sport and exercise settings • state scale
PANAS (positive and negative affect schedule)	Watson, Clark and Tellegen (1988)	Two ten-item affect scales assessing: • positive affect: e.g. excited, enthusiastic, inspired • negative affect: e.g. distressed, hostile, irritable.	• good psychometric properties • assesses only two general dimensions • time instructions can be varied • can be a state or trait scale • general scale not specific to physical activity
FS (feeling scale)	Hardy and Rejeski (1989)	• single-item scale assessing hedonic tone (pleasure–displeasure)	• developed for exercise research • state scale • eleven-point scale ranging from −5 to +5
Categorical measures			
POMS (profile of mood states)	McNair, Lorr and Droppleman (1971)	Sixty-five-item scale assessing: • tension • depression • anger • vigour • fatigue • confusion	• only one positive subscale • used extensively in PA research • short and bipolar forms available • time instructions can be varied • can be a state or trait scale • general scale not specific to physical activity

continued

Table 8.2 continued

Instrument	Reference	Measures	Comments
MAACL (multiple affect adjective check list)	Zuckerman and Lubin (1965)	• scale comprises 132 adjectives • assesses anxiety, depression and hostility	• time instructions can be varied • can be a state or trait scale • general scale not specific to physical activity • some doubts expressed about psychometric properties (see McDonald and Hodgdon 1991)
EFI (exercise feeling inventory)	Gauvin and Rejeski (1993)	Twelve-item adjective scale assessing four dimensions: • engagement • tranquillity • revitalisation • physical exhaustion	• developed for exercise research • sound psychometric properties • positive state scale
SEES (subjective exercise experiences scale)	McAuley and Courneya (1994)	Twelve-item adjective scale assessing three dimensions: • positive well-being • psychological distress • fatigue	• developed for exercise research • sound psychometric properties • state scale

In reaction to their dissatisfaction with global measures, such as the PANAS, Gauvin and Rejeski (1993) developed the Exercise-induced Feeling Inventory (EFI) in an effort to capture four distinct feeling states in exercise: revitalisation, tranquillity, positive engagement and physical exhaustion. Psychometric support has been reported for adults (Gauvin and Rejeski 1993) and children (Vlachopoulos, Biddle and Fox 1996), although the conceptual underpinnings of such 'exercise-specific' measures have been criticised (Ekkekakis and Petruzzello 2001a, 2001b):

> A measure of affect tailored to tap only those affective states believed to be relevant to exercise leads to some considerable logical problems. An important problem stems from the fact that most studies investigating the exercise–affect relationship involve assessments of affect under non-exercise conditions, such as before exercise ... how meaningful would any comparisons be between exercise and all the non-exercise conditions where this measure is likely to be employed?
>
> (Ekkekakis and Petruzzello 2001a: 7)

In a similar vein to Gauvin and Rejeski (1993), McAuley and Courneya (1994) developed the Subjective Exercise Experiences Scale (SEES) comprising three factors of positive well-being, psychological distress, and fatigue. This has some support (Markland, Emberton and Tallon 1997) although, again, it has been criticised in relation to its conceptual underpinnings similar to the EFI (Ekkekakis and Petruzzello 2001b).

Key point: How you measure affective responses to exercise will depend on the research question.

Evidence for relationships between physical activity and affect

There are a very large number of studies investigating the relationship between exercise and affective states. Conclusions are drawn from both acute (single bout) exercise studies and studies involving a programme of physical activity over time (chronic exercise studies). Moreover, we can draw on evidence from narrative and meta-analytic reviews, large-scale population surveys and experimental trials.

Narrative and meta-analytic reviews

From the numerous narrative reviews available, there is cautious support for the proposition that exercise is associated with enhanced affect and mood (Biddle 2000). The caution comes from the relatively weak research designs utilised. For example, the comprehensive review by Leith (1994) showed that experimental evidence was less convincing than for pre-experimental or quasi-experimental studies. Leith demonstrated that the percentage of studies finding positive mood effects drops from 100 per cent of pre-experimental studies to 79 per cent of quasi-experimental, to 62.5 per cent of true experimental studies. These cautiously positive conclusions are enhanced, however, by the fact that the reviews span several countries and populations, such as those in the workplace, women and people with disabilities. Also, diverse methods and measuring instruments are used yet yield similar findings. In addition, hardly any studies report negative mood effects.

McDonald and Hodgdon (1991) conducted a meta-analysis of exercise and mood research. They delimited their review to aerobic fitness training studies and found that researchers used mainly the uni-polar POMS or MAACL. Results showed a clear relationship between exercise and vigour and a lack of negative mood and this corresponds to the typical 'iceberg profile' (see Figure 8.3) reported in other settings (Berger and Motl 2001). McDonald and Hodgdon concluded that 'aerobic fitness training produces some positive change in mood ... at least on a short-term basis' (1991: 98).

A meta-analysis summarising the effects of exercise on positive and negative affect in older adults (Arent, Landers and Etnier 2000) also showed beneficial effects. Selected results are shown in Figure 8.4. Positive effects were found for experimental over control

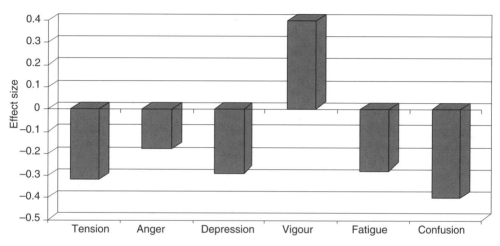

Figure 8.3 Effect sizes from McDonald and Hodgdon's (1991) meta-analysis of aerobic fitness training and mood states

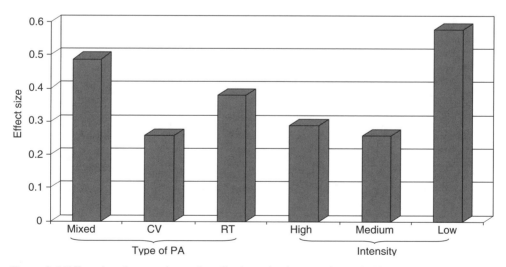

Figure 8.4 Effect sizes for experimental studies investigating exercise and affective ('mood') states in older adults (Arent, Landers and Etnier 2000)

Note
CV = Cardiovascular exercise; RT = Resistance training

groups for all forms of physical activity, but particularly mixed modes, and greater effects were noted for lower intensities of physical activity.

Population surveys

Although often suffering from methodological shortcomings, population (epidemiological) surveys have the advantage over some other studies in so far as they usually have large samples, are representative of the population, and hence allow good generalisability of findings. Five such studies from Britain are summarised in Table 8.3 and show clear positive relationships between physical activity and psychological well-being. Confidence in these results is enhanced by noting that the surveys cover both adolescents and adults, use clinical, non-clinical, quantitative and qualitative assessments, and cover a total sample of over 23,000. However, as noted by Thirlaway and Benton (1996), not all groups seem to benefit from physical activity. In addition, one cannot conclude that these effects are uniquely related to physical activity. Although the Allied Dunbar National Fitness Survey (ADNFS) (Sports Council and Health Education Authority 1992) demonstrated that the same trend was evident for those in poor as well as good health, large-scale surveys offer few clues on the cause of psychological well-being.

Nevertheless, the British studies are comparable to Stephens' (1988) secondary analysis of four North American surveys. Across several measures, and with over 55,000 adults, there was a clear association between PA and psychological well-being. For example, positive affect was associated with PA for both men and women in the two age groups under and over 40 years. Stephens provided the following clear conclusion:

> the inescapable conclusion of this study is that the level of physical activity is positively associated with good mental health in the household populations of the United States and Canada, when mental health is defined as positive mood, general well-being, and relatively infrequent symptoms of anxiety and depression. This relationship is independent of the effects of education and physical health status, and is stronger for women and those age 40 years and over than for men and those age under 40. The robustness of this conclusion derives from the varied sources of evidence: four population samples in two countries over a 10-year period, four different methods of operationalizing physical activity and six different mental health scales.
>
> (Stephens 1988: 41–2)

Evidence from population surveys, therefore, supports a relationship between physical activity and affect. The nature of such surveys means that we can only conclude that participation in exercise, or the quantity of physical activity taken, is associated with psychological well-being over time. Acute effects of activity cannot be studied in this way. Similarly, whether this relationship can be said to be causal remains to be seen. In this regard, evidence from experimental trials is required.

Experimental trials

Studies investigating the effects of exercise on affect and mood through controlled experimental trials have increased over recent years and many show that the intensity of exercise is important in determining the effects on affect. Three studies by Steptoe and his colleagues in London (Moses *et al.* 1989; Steptoe and Bolton 1988; Steptoe and Cox 1988)

Table 8.3 Summary of findings from British population surveys investigating the relationship between physical activity and psychological well-being

Study	Survey design and scope	Results and conclusions
Hendry, Shucksmith and Cross (1989)	Postal and supervised survey of 5,862 14–20 year olds in Scotland. Assessment with General Health Questionnaire and sports participation	• GHQ (mental health) scores improved as participation in sport increased for both boys and girls. • competitive sports 'types' had better mental health than non-competitive 'types'
Sports Council and Health Education Authority (1992)	Allied Dunbar National Fitness Survey (ADNFS) for England of 16–74 year olds (N = 4,316). One section of interview assessed perceived well-being	• small but consistent trend showing relationship between PA and well-being. Same trend evident for those in poorest health, reducing the chance that only those who are 'well' choose to exercise • association between PA and well-being stronger for those fifty-five years and over • trends evident for all age groups and both sexes
Thirlaway and Benton (1996)	National Health and Lifestyle Survey data. Representative British sample (N = 6,200). Assessed on PA and General Health Questionnaire. (Unpublished survey data reported in book chapter.)	• higher PA associated with better mental health in women over thirty years and men over fifty years • no relationship for those under thirty years of age
Steptoe and Butler (1996)	Investigation of the association between emotional well-being and regular sport/vigorous PA in sixteen year olds (N = 5,061). Data from 1986 follow-up to 1970 British Cohort Study	• greater sport/vigorous PA was positively associated with emotional well-being independent of gender, SES or health status • participation in non-vigorous activity was associated with high psychological and somatic symptoms on Malaise Inventory
Gordon and Grant (1997)	1,634 teenagers from Scotland (aged 13.5–14.5 years). Qualitative method used with open-ended questionnaire responses to 'how do you feel today?'	• about one-quarter reported that sport made them feel happy and good about themselves • large gender differences

showed that moderate, but not high intensity exercise, has mood-enhancing effects. Similarly, Parfitt, Markland and Holmes (1994) show that 'feeling states' in exercise are significantly worse at a higher intensity for less active individuals, and Boutcher, McAuley and Courneya (1997) found that greater positive affect was reported after aerobic treadmill exercise for trained runners in comparison with matched untrained participants. This suggests that training status may account for post-exercise affective responses. Hardy and Rejeski (1989) reported more negative moods after higher intensity exercise than after less intense activity. Such findings led Leith to recommend that 'moderate-intensity exercise appears to have the best potential to impact on participant mood states' (Leith 1994: 146).

Raglin (1997) suggested that high-intensity activity may delay rather than eliminate post-exercise anxiety reductions. The increases in negative mood after high-intensity exercise reported in Steptoe's research may be due to the higher exertion required, but studies have shown that positive mood is still enhanced some time later. The temporal nature of changes in mood after different intensities of exercise, therefore, seems to be important and argues in favour of assessment using a dimensional approach.

Ekkekakis and colleagues have conducted a series of studies investigating the links between exercise, affect and the intensity of exercise (Ekkekakis, Hall and Petruzzello 2004; Ekkekakis *et al.* 2000; Hall, Ekkekakis and Petruzzello 2002; Van Landuyt *et al.* 2000). Using a measure of affective valence, they have assessed affective states before, during and after exercise of varying intensities. For example, when assessing affective valence before, during and after treadmill running to exhaustion, Ekkekakis, Hall and Petruzzello (2004) found that feelings of pleasure showed a clear decline after reaching the ventilatory threshold (VT; a marker of the transition from aerobic to anaerobic metabolism). This suggests that the VT may be a useful marker for self-monitoring of exercise intensity with a view to maximising positive affect and adherence.

An 'inverted-U' relationship between exercise intensity and affect is often assumed to exist. This is where low levels of exercise intensity are thought to be insufficient to elicit much affective change, whereas exercise that is too severe will be ineffective or simply aversive, thus leaving 'moderate' intensity exercise as the optimal dose for affective benefits (Biddle and Ekkekakis 2005). The data concerning changes during exercise, and the role of the ventilatory threshold identified by Ekkekakis and colleagues, supports an alternative, more complex, dose–response model, as shown in Table 8.4 (Biddle and Ekkekakis 2005; Ekkekakis 2003). This is based on five phenomena identified by Ekkekakis (2003):

- 'There are positive affective responses during and for a short time following bouts of physical activity of mild intensity and short duration' (Ekkekakis 2003: 217). For example, fifteen-minute self-paced walks have been shown to produce improved affective valence (Ekkekakis *et al.* 2000), contrary to the inverted-U proposal.
- 'Affective responses during moderately vigorous exercise are characterised by marked intra-individual variability, with some individuals reporting positive and some reporting negative changes' (Ekkekakis 2003: 219). Intra-individual variability has rarely been considered in the literature on exercise and affect yet the data show that Ekkekakis's proposition is correct (Van Landuyt *et al.* 2000). For example, Ekkekakis, Hall and Petruzzello (2005) summarise data from five studies showing the variability of responses as a function of exercise intensity. These data are shown in Figure 8.5 and illustrate very clearly that studies one and two (self-paced ten- and fifteen-minute walking) produced a highly positive change in affect for over 70 per cent of the participants. Study 3 was thirty minutes of cycling at 60 per cent of maximal oxygen consumption and showed much

Table 8.4 Affective responses to varying levels of exercise intensity, proposed by Ekkekakis and colleagues (Biddle and Ekkekakis 2005; Ekkekakis 2003)

Intensity range	Affective reaction to exercise	Variability of response	Influencing factors
Moderate	Pleasure	Homogeneous	Cognitive factors play small role
Heavy	Pleasure or displeasure	Variable	Cognitive factors play a major role
Severe	Displeasure	Homogeneous	Interoceptive factors play a major role

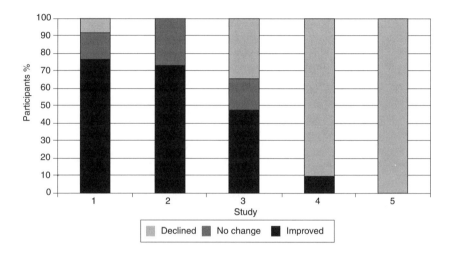

Figure 8.5 Intra-individual variability in affective responses to different exercise stimuli. Data from five studies reported in Ekkekakis *et al.* (2005)

Notes:
Study 1: 10–min self-paced walk. Study 2: 15–min self-paced walk. Study 3: 30 minutes of cycling at 60% of maximal oxygen consumption. Study 4: Incremental treadmill running to exhaustion. Study 5: Cycling to exhaustion under conditions of dehydration

more variable responses. Conversely, the negative responses in studies 4 and 5 were almost universal. These studies involved exercising to exhaustion.

• 'Responses immediately following moderately vigorous exercise are almost uniformly positive, regardless of whether the responses during exercise were positive or negative' (Ekkekakis 2003: 221). This is the so-called 'rebound' effect, the robustness of which Ekkekakis describes as 'remarkable' (Ekkekakis 2003: 221).

• 'Affective responses during strenuous exercise unify into a negative trend as the intensity of exercise approaches each individual's functional limits' (Ekkekakis 2003: 222). The ventilatory threshold has been suggested as one biological marker for when this shift occurs. As shown in Table 8.4, this level of intensity will mean that the link between affective valence and interoceptive factors will strengthen, often shown by increases in measures such as heart rate, rating of perceived exertion (RPE) and blood lactate.

- 'There is a homogeneous positive shift in affective valence immediately following strenuous exercise' (Ekkekakis 2003: 224). This is also a rebound effect similar to that observed after moderately vigorous exercise.

Key point: Evidence points to beneficial affective changes with exercise, but this relationship is influenced by the intensity of exercise.

Enjoyment and physical activity

If physical activity is associated with psychological well-being, it seems obvious that an element of enjoyment of physical activity must also be present. Enjoyment is an important element of motivation, particularly when physical effort might be required, like in exercise classes. Despite all of this, enjoyment has remained an illusive concept for many years. Despite some research into the topic, even now there is disagreement about how enjoyment should be conceptualised (Kimiecik and Harris 1996; Wankel 1997). Kimiecik and Harris (1996) adopted Csikzentmihalyi's approach and defined enjoyment in terms of 'flow' (see next section). They suggest that enjoyment is not positive affect but an optimal psychological state. In other words, 'enjoyment is a psychological state that leads to ... positive feelings states' (Kimiecik and Harris 1996: 256). They also suggest that enjoyment is 'not an affective product of the experience, but a psychological process that is the experience' (Kimiecik and Harris 1996: 257).

At least four approaches to enjoyment can be identified that have relevance to physical activity, although not all are consistent with Kimiecik and Harris's definition:

- Csikzentmihalyi's 'flow' model
- intrinsic motivational processes
- Scanlan's study of sport enjoyment
- exercise-related affective states.

Enjoyment and flow

Csikzentmihalyi (1975) studied why people invested huge amounts of time and energy in tasks appearing to yield limited external rewards. Such activities were described as 'autotelic' (meaning 'self-goal' or 'self-purpose'). In asking people involved in a range of activities, including rock climbers, composers, chess players, dancers and basketball players, why they enjoyed their chosen activity, 'intrinsic' factors were clearly evident. For example, the highest ranked reasons were 'enjoyment of the experience and use of skills' and 'the activity itself – the pattern, the action, the world it provides'. The least favoured reason was 'prestige/regard/glamour'.

One of Csikzentmihalyi's (1975) conclusions was that motivation seemed highest when the difficulty of the task (challenge) was matched by the personal abilities and skills of the individual. This matching led to a state of 'flow', or supreme enjoyment and engagement in the task. A mismatch can lead to either boredom (low challenge relative to skills) or anxiety (high challenge relative to skills). This is shown in Figure 8.6.

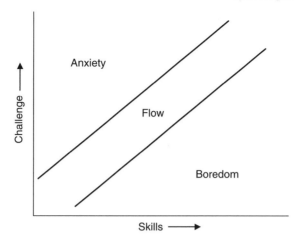

Figure 8.6 Csikzentmihalyi's model of 'flow'

Kimiecik and Stein (1992) draw on Csikzentmihalyi's work to propose six dimensions of flow in sport. Application to wider exercise settings is still scant (Karageorghis, Vlachopoulos and Terry 2000). The six dimensions are:

*   matching of action and awareness: this occurs when the matching of skills with the challenge produces feelings that the action itself is spontaneous and automatic, and awareness of oneself does not differ from awareness of the activity
*   clear goals and unambiguous feedback
*   concentration on the task at hand
*   the paradox of control: flow is associated with feelings of control and, at the same time, feelings that reflect a lack of worry concerning the loss of control
*   the loss of self-consciousness: less conscious awareness of one's actions
*   transformation of time: flow is often associated with loss of awareness of time; time is 'distorted by the experience' (Kimiecik and Stein 1992: 148).

Enjoyment and intrinsic motivation

The development of intrinsic motivation is a key consideration for many promoting physical activity and has already been discussed in Chapter 4. High intrinsic motivation includes high effort, feelings of enjoyment, competence and autonomy (self-determination), and low levels of pressure and anxiety (Deci and Ryan 1985). Intrinsic motivation, enjoyment and flow are clearly interrelated. Csikzentmihalyi (1975) spoke of 'autotelic' activities being the ones where flow was most likely, and Deci and Ryan (1985) speak about the 'self-determination' of behaviour through intrinsic motivation.

Scanlan's sport enjoyment model

Scanlan first proposed a preliminary model of sport enjoyment for children (Scanlan and Lewthwaite 1986) after studying 9–14 year old American boys. Sport enjoyment was defined as 'an individual's positive affective response to his or her competitive sport experience which reflects feelings and/or perceptions such as pleasure, liking, and experiencing fun' (1986: 32). They proposed a model of sport enjoyment centred on the two continua of intrinsic–extrinsic and achievement–non-achievement with predictors of enjoyment in each quadrant being:

- *intrinsic–achievement:* personal perceptions of mastery and competence
- *intrinsic–non-achievement:* physical movement sensations and excitement
- *extrinsic–achievement:* perceptions of competence derived from others (for example social approval)
- *extrinsic–non-achievement:* non-performance related, such as affiliation.

Exercise-related affective states

Earlier, we suggested that a circumplex model of affect can be represented by the activation and evaluation dimensions of affect (see Figure 8.1). Positive feelings, accompanied by high activation, could be associated with enjoyment during physical activity. Similarly, the positive engagement subscale of the Exercise-Induced Feeling Inventory (Gauvin and Rejeski 1993) is closely associated with enjoyment. However, while enjoyment is a key to motivation, its nature and measurement is still in need of development and refinement. The only specific scale purporting to assess physical activity enjoyment is Kendzierski and DeCarlo's (1991) eighteen-item Physical Activity Enjoyment Scale (PACES), and this may be overlong for some studies wishing to assess many other constructs. Example items are shown in Table 8.5.

A study by Karageorghis, Vlachopoulos and Terry (2000) linked exercise affect and flow. A cross-sectional survey of over 1,200 adult participants (83 per cent were women) from aerobic dance exercise classes in London health clubs showed that higher self-reported flow from exercise was associated with higher feelings of 'positive engagement', 'revitalisation' and 'tranquility', supporting the notion that the different constructs addressing enjoyment that we have summarised in this chapter will be closely related.

Key point: Empirical evidence and intuition tell us that enjoyment is important for exercise motivation. However, the contruct of enjoyment has been poorly understood.

Exercise deprivation

The literature on exercise deprivation also lends some support to the notion that physical activity is associated with psychological well-being. Exercise deprivation occurs when regular exercisers are forced (often for experimental purposes) to give up their usual pattern of exercise. Studying the psychological consequences of such deprivation provides an interesting way

Table 8.5 Example items from the twenty-item Physical Activity Enjoyment Scale (PACES) (Kendzierski and DeCarlo 1991). All items are rated on a seven-point scale anchored by statements, such as those shown. The instructions state 'please rate how you feel *at the moment* about the physical activity you have been doing'

Item	Anchor 1 (score 1 or 7)	Anchor 2 (score 7 or 1)
1	I enjoy it (score = 7)	I hate it (score = 1)
9	It's very pleasant (score = 7)	It's very unpleasant (score = 1)
15	It's not all stimulating (score = 1)	It's very stimulating (score = 7)

of looking at the benefits of exercise and an insight into why some people continue in regular activities. It may also assist in our understanding of the mechanisms of psychological benefits from exercise.

Researchers have asked regular exercisers to stop exercise for a period of days, weeks (Morris *et al.* 1990) or months (Baekeland 1970) and have found that deprivation caused a 'feel worse' effect which disappeared once exercise was reinstated. However, despite the appeal of this paradigm, the difficulty of recruiting those who are willing to give up their exercise routines for research purposes has prevented there being a substantial literature in this area. A review by Szabo (1995) suggests that findings from survey, cross-sectional and experimental studies show that interruption to the normal exercise pattern of an habitual exerciser will have a negative impact on psychological well-being. This negative impact is most frequently expressed as a series of 'withdrawal' symptoms such as guilt, irritability, tension and depression.

This literature provides us with two possible ways of understanding psychological outcomes and physical activity. First, it is suggested that some regular exercisers experience withdrawal on deprivation of their usual exercise because this deprives them of regular enjoyable experiences, such as mood enhancement, social interaction and the joy of movement (Pierce 1994). Alternatively, and perhaps even simultaneously, some exercisers need the increase in arousal level that exercise brings in order to avoid negative feelings from low sympathetic arousal such as lethargy and sluggishness (Pierce 1994). Thus, the benefit of exercise can be seen as a way to maintain good feelings and avoid bad feelings associated with inactivity.

Physical activity and self-esteem

Self-esteem is often seen to be the single most important measure of psychological well-being. Indeed, enhanced self-esteem resulting from physical activity is often claimed by those promoting exercise and sport participation, and is a common rationale for the teaching of physical education for children. This is illustrated by Sonstroem's conclusion from his review of the effects of exercise on self-esteem:

> the consistently positive results ... suggest a basis for the belief in the salutary effects of physical training programs. It is concluded that exercise programs are associated with significant increases in the self-esteem scores of participants. These score increases are particularly pronounced in subjects initially low in self-esteem. ... These conclusions refer to exercise programs rather than fitness increases, and to increases in self-esteem scores rather than in self-esteem per se.
>
> (Sonstroem 1984: 138)

Self-esteem refers to the value placed on aspects of the self, such as academic and social domains. It is an extension of the construct of self-concept, which merely describes aspects of the self, although many researchers prefer to use the terms interchangeably. Self-esteem, therefore, attaches a value to such descriptors. Until recently, the measurement of self-esteem was a factor preventing substantial progress being made in understanding the potential links between physical activity and self-esteem. Often researchers have employed a global measure of self-esteem rather than a multidimensional one. It has been shown that self-esteem is a global construct underpinned by a multidimensional and hierarchical structure. Global self-esteem is composed of differentiated perceptions of the self, such as physical, social and academic self-perceptions. These, in turn, are underpinned by increasingly transient perceptions of worth and competence, such as sport ability or physical appearance for the physical subdomain of global self-esteem (Fox 1998, 1997b; Fox and Corbin 1989). Figure 5.1 on page 101 shows Fox's physical self-perception model based on this approach.

Two approaches to self-esteem and exercise can be identified. First, there is the 'motivational approach' or 'personal development hypothesis' (Sonstroem 1997a, 1997b) whereby self-esteem acts as a motivational *determinant* of physical activity (see Figure 8.7a). Here individuals high in self-esteem, or more specifically in physical self-worth and related physical self-perceptions, are more likely to approach physical activity contexts since this is an area where competence and self-worth can be maintained or enhanced.

In addition, there is the 'skill (personal) development' hypothesis (Sonstroem 1997a, 1997b). This proposes that self-esteem can be changed through experience, either positive or negative, through development in skills, task mastery, success etc (see Figure 8.7b). This refers to self-esteem as an *outcome* of involvement in, say, physical activity, in contrast to the motivational emphasis of the self-enhancement hypothesis. The skill development hypothesis underpins many physical education programmes for children. Of course, in reality, the two approaches are not mutually exclusive as initial involvement in physical activity, which may be externally motivated, may lead to enhanced self-perceptions of esteem and worth which, in turn, become motivators of subsequent activity (Biddle 1997).

Measurement of self-esteem in the physical domain

Such theoretical advances have led to advances in psychometric assessment. Fox and Corbin (1989) developed the Physical Self-Perception Profile (PSPP) (Fox 1998). This is a measure of physical self-worth and four subdomains of this construct: sport competence, body attrac-

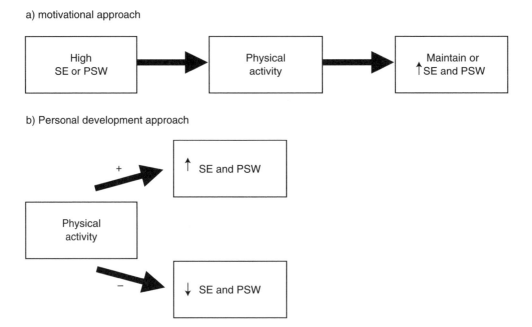

Figure 8.7 'Motivational' and 'self-enhancement' approaches to self-esteem

tiveness, perceived strength and physical condition. These factors were derived initially from research on an American student population but seem to hold well with younger populations (Hagger *et al.* 2003; Newman *et al.* 2003; Whitehead 1995).

What the PSPP, and other similar instruments, such as Marsh's 'Physical Self-Description Questionnaire' (PSDQ) (Marsh *et al.* 1994), should allow is the investigation of how exercise might affect differential aspects of self-perceptions, and how these might impact on self-esteem. For example, participation in exercise may increase positive feelings about physical condition that may, in turn, affect physical self-worth and self-esteem. These relationships are thought to be more likely if the domain in question is seen to be important to the individual (Fox 1998). However, Marsh and Sonstroem (1995) raise the issue of the function and specificity of importance ratings. For example, someone who perceives themselves to have low body attractiveness, but attaches high importance to attractiveness, may act in a similar way to another individual who has strong positive self-perceptions of their attractiveness and also high importance for the domain. The first person could be motivated for improvement (for example, weight loss) whereas the second seems to demonstrate the effect of competence on behaviour – they are motivated because they are competent or look good in the aerobics context. In other words, 'although self-concept researchers have often asked subjects to rate the importance of different self-concept domains, they may need to ask why a particular domain is important or in what situations it is important' (Marsh and Sonstroem 1995: 101).

Reviews of the literature

Doan and Scherman (1987) analysed the relationship between various personality measures, including self-esteem/concept and exercise. Of eleven pre-experimental studies, seven showed a positive effect and four no effect; for quasi-experimental studies, five were positive and three showed no change, while of the ten experimental studies, five were positive and five showed no change. No study reported a negative effect for exercise on self-esteem.

A review by Fox (2000) identified thirty-six randomised controlled trials (RCTs) in the literature since 1970, with nine being unpublished postgraduate theses. Positive changes in physical self-perceptions or general self-esteem were found in 76 per cent of all RCTs. It was concluded that exercise can be used to promote positive physical self-perceptions, but the mechanisms underpinning such changes are not clear.

Results from meta-analyses

Based on the proposals offered through the hierarchical and multidimensional model, as well as other reviews of the literature, it is accepted that physical activity can enhance either physical self-worth or self-esteem, or both. However, the strength of effect remains an important issue to identify. There are three meta-analytic reviews concerning physical activity and self-esteem, with two focused on adults (McDonald and Hodgdon 1991; Spence, McGannon and Poon 2005) and one on children (Gruber 1986).

McDonald and Hodgdon (1991) investigated the link between aerobic fitness training and 'self-concept'. This term included most standard measures of self-perceptions, including self-esteem, but also measures of body image. This weakens the ability of the study to isolate effects for more global measures of self-esteem. McDonald and Hodgdon reported an overall ES of 0.56 ($n = 41$), showing that fitness training is associated with improved ratings of the 'self'.

McDonald and Hodgdon (1991) included self-related measures from personality tests to form their 'self-esteem cluster'. This involved all measures from the 'self-concept' studies above, plus the self-sufficiency (scale Q2) and insecurity (scale O) subscales from the 16PF. The ES was a 'moderate' 0.35 for the cluster.

Spence, McGannon and Poon (2005) meta-analysed 113 studies, including seventy-one that were unpublished. The overall effect size was 0.23, showing a small effect for physical activity on self-esteem in adults. There were no significant differences on the basis of exercise-related variables (intensity, frequency, duration, mode and length of programme), and neither did groups differing in initial levels of fitness or self-esteem show differential effects. The overall effect size was also independent of sample variables, including age, gender and health status and measurement variables (for example, publication status, scale used and study quality). However, a larger effect was shown for those who improved their physical fitness over those who did not, and for the type of exercise programme used. Specifically, the largest effects were noted for 'lifestyle' programmes (those including other activities alongside exercise, such as nutrition advice and relaxation). Those for skills training, such in sports, were ineffective in changing self-esteem. Results are shown in Figure 8.8.

Spence and colleagues concluded that while there is an effect for exercise on self-esteem in adults, the overall effect appears to be smaller than previously thought, and smaller than that reported by McDonald and Hodgdon (1991). However, Spence *et al.* found that larger effects were observed for studies where participants improved their physical fitness, and this is more akin to the studies included in the meta-analysis by McDonald and Hodgdon. For example, an experimental study by Asci (2003), in which participants were randomly assigned to an exercise (three aerobic training sessions per week for ten weeks) or control (no exercise) group, showed increases in self-esteem from baseline (pre-test) only in the experimental group, and at two time points (mid-point of the intervention and at the conclusion). These trends are shown in Figure 8.9.

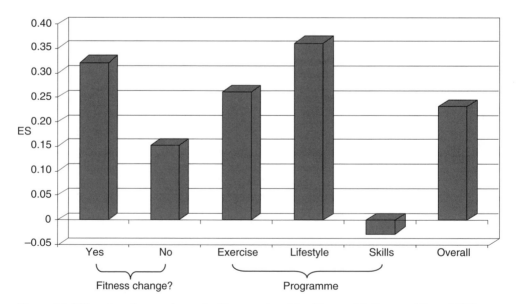

Figure 8.8 Effect sizes for exercise and self-esteem in adults (Spence, McGann and Poon 2005)

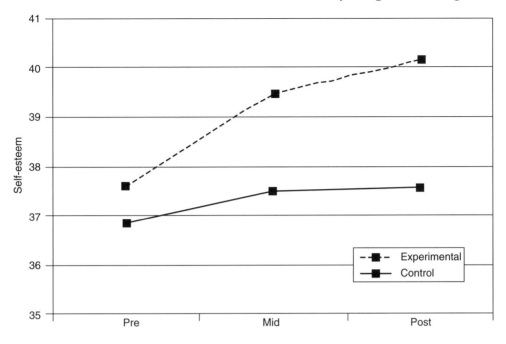

Figure 8.9 Aerobic exercise increased self-esteem (Asci 2003)

In a meta-analysis of play and physical education programmes for children, Gruber (1986) calculated an overall ES of 0.41 for self-esteem from twenty-seven studies. Sixty-one per cent of the studies produced positive effects on self-esteem. These results support a positive effect for physical activity on the self-esteem of youngsters. However, an average ES of only 0.12 was reported from three randomised controlled trials (RCT) for youth reviewed by Calfas and Taylor (1994).

Key point: The belief that exercise improves self-esteem is too simplistic. Exercise can enhance self-esteem, and this is likely due to changes in physical self-perceptions.

Self-esteem: summary

Exercise is related to small but significant positive changes in self-esteem, although more information will be obtained about the nature of such changes through domain-specific measures of self-perceptions. However, several issues in the literature now appear in need of revision, at least based on Spence, McGannon and Poon (2005) meta-analysis. For example, Sonstroem (1997a) claims that increases in physical fitness are not related to changes in self-esteem, yet Spence *et al.* found larger effects for those improving their fitness. Second, Sonstroem claimed that positive changes in self-esteem are more likely for those with low self-esteem, yet Spence and colleagues found this not to be the case.

Physical activity and cognitive functioning

> I found that I worked better and thought more clearly when I was in good physical condition.
>
> (Mandela 1994)

Subjective reports from runners (Mutrie and Knill-Jones 1986) suggest that over half of those questioned perceived that after running they can think more clearly. This would suggest that running, and maybe other forms of activity, can have a positive effect on some form of cognitive functioning. The term cognitive functioning embraces a wide variety of tasks ranging from simple reaction time to complex information processing.

Kirkendall (1986) concluded that a modest positive relationship existed between motor performance and intellectual performance in children and that this relationship was strongest in the early stages of development. Intervention techniques for learning-disabled children have also been investigated but a meta-analysis of 180 studies (Kavale and Mattson 1983) showed no positive effect on academic, cognitive or perceptual motor performance from perceptual–motor training on children whose average IQ was eighty-eight at the age of eight years. In an experimental study, MacMahon and Gross (1987) found no effect on academic performance for a group of boys with learning disabilities who were given a twenty-week vigorous aerobic exercise programme. A more recent narrative review of the use of exercise with learning disabled children (Bluechardt, Wiener and Shephard 1995) also concluded that exercise programmes had not been successful in improving motor performance. Claims that exercise for children helps them perform better academically have been used in support of daily physical education programmes (Dwyer *et al.* 1983; Pollatschek and O'Hagan 1989), although a review by Shephard led him to conclude that 'daily programs of physical education should not be introduced with the expectation that they will lead to major gains in academic performance' (Shephard 1997: 123).

The literature on physical activity and cognitive development in children shows the strongest links in the early, pre-school years. Research in perceptual–motor development has suggested that the early development of psychomotor function and neuromuscular control could assist academic learning in young children. Increases in cerebral blood flow have been documented after physical activity, and this could assist in cognitive functioning. Similarly, activity will increase blood flow in the prefrontal somatosensory and primary motor cortices of the brain (Williams 1986). However, despite these plausible mechanisms, the studies of cognitive change in children exposed to physical activity interventions have been poorly controlled and open to severe methodological criticism.

At different times there has been significant interest in the relationship between physical activity and cognitive performance/academic achievement in young people. A recent meta-analysis (Sibley and Etnier 2003) attempted to reconcile a conflicting and apparently inconclusive body of literature (Mutrie and Parfitt 1998). From a meta-analysis of forty-four studies, Sibley and Etnier concluded that there is a significant positive relationship (ES = 0.32) between physical activity and cognitive functioning in children aged 4–18 years. Moderator analyses showed that the relationship holds for all participants, including healthy participants, those with mental impairments, and those with physical disabilities, as well as all ages. Moreover, there were no differences across types of activity (for example, resistance/circuit training, PE programmes and aerobic exercise). These findings were qualified by the authors because of lack of control for confounding variables which limit the ability to attribute changes in cognitive performance to manipulations of physical activity, the relatively small number of peer-reviewed true experimental designs ($n = 9$) and measurement issues, particularly of the dependent measure of cognitive functioning. Despite this qualification, Sibley and Etnier concluded that physical activity will not harm cognitive performance or academic achievement and may be related to enhancement.

Tomporowski and Ellis (1986) reviewed literature on the effects of exercise on cognitive processing and concluded that there was conflicting evidence. The explanation for this seems to lie in the experimental designs used. There is a need for studies to rule out the effects of different fitness levels (rather than just the effects of exercise) by having participants work at relative rather than absolute work loads, and it may be that differing intensities and duration of exercise will have differing effects. Two key issues can be addressed – the effect on cognition during exercise and the post-exercise effect. Finally, the tests used to measure cognitive functioning must be free from influences of prior experience and learning.

Boutcher (2000) reviewed fourteen experimental studies on physical activity and cognitive functioning in older adults and found that only five showed positive effects after aerobic training. Etnier *et al.* (1997) conducted a meta-analysis of 134 studies and reported a mean overall ES of 0.25 – a relatively small, though significant, effect. The effect was small for acute (ES = 0.16) and chronic (ES = 0.33) designs, but larger for cross-sectional (ES = 0.53) and mixed designs (ES = 0.54) In addition, more threats to the internal validity of both acute and chronic exercise studies yielded larger effect sizes.

Inconsistent findings may be moderated by the type of cognitive functioning being assessed. Colcombe and Kramer (2003) provided four types of cognitive functioning measures in their meta-analysis of the effects of fitness on cognitive functioning in older adults. These are:

- speed tasks, such as reaction time
- visuospatial tasks
- controlled processing tasks, such as tasks involving controlled and effortful processing of information but which, through learning, become more automatic
- executive control tasks, such as coordination and working memory where mediation by the central executor is required, and they do not become automatic over time.

In their meta-analysis of RCTs involving older adults, an overall effect size for experimental participants was 0.48 (calculated from the mean of pre and post intervention scores). Interestingly, the largest effect was for executive control tasks (ES = 0.68), although gains were seen in other categories: controlled processing (ES = 0.46), visuospatial (ES = 0.43), and speed (ES = 0.27). These findings support the role of exercise and physical fitness in enhancing cognitive functioning in older adults, but suggest that effects will be moderated by the type of cognitive task assessed.

Physical activity, personality and adjustment

The question every sport and exercise psychologist has confronted is 'does physical activity affect personality?'. Indeed, it is still commonly accepted that playing sport, at least for children and youth, is inherently 'good' and associated with 'character development'. Similarly, companies are willing to pay for their staff to attend outdoor activity centres in the belief that such activities assist in the development of leadership skills, positive group dynamics, etc. However, while this topic has occupied the minds of psychologists for many years, it has also been one of the most controversial and there are many factors likely to mediate any effects of physical activity on personality.

Box 8.1 Can physical activity reduce anti-social behaviour?

Governments make much of sport, exercise and physical activity as a 'social good', including the belief that involvement can help with the social ills of society such as crime and anti-social behaviour. Can it? Politicians often argue that sport is a viable way of creating positive moral and social behaviour (Biddle and Gorley 2005). While professional and spectator sport, in particular, can also be associated with undesirable behaviours, most people involved in sport believe that positive behavioural outcomes are possible and should be sought (Chang *et al.* 2004). Mutrie and Parfitt reviewed eight papers investigating sport involvement for young people and delinquency. They concluded that 'there is equivocal evidence about the relationship between involvement in sport and anti-social behaviour' (Mutrie and Parfitt 1998: 61). Similarly, Coalter's review concluded that 'because of a widespread lack of robust, cumulative, and comparative research data it is very difficult to be precise about the relationship between sports participation and reduced anti-social behaviour and crime' (Coalter 2005: 205). He goes on to conclude 'taking the balance of probabilities:

* the most effective use of sport to address systematically anti-social behaviour and criminal behaviour is in combination with programs that seek to address wider personal and social development
* sports' salience can be used to attract young people to integrated programs that offer formal programs in personal development, health awareness, and employment training
* leadership is perhaps the most important element in determining the positive impact of a program
* locally recruited leaders and a bottom-up approach maximize the chances of success'.

(Coalter 2005: 205–6)

Given that this area is replete with anecdotal evidence and potentially biased claims, it is important to seek some kind of scientific consensus. Three reviews of the field provide guidance. First, McDonald and Hodgdon (1991) report a meta-analysis of aerobic fitness training and trait personality measures; second, Doan and Scherman (1987) review studies of exercise and personality; finally, Leith and Taylor (1990) provide a review of exercise and psychological well-being, including personality and self-perceptions.

McDonald and Hodgdon (1991) found nine different personality inventories used in studies of aerobic fitness training, but only three had a sufficient number of studies to analyse quantitatively. These were the 16PF (Cattell, Eber and Tatsuoka 1970), the Eysenck Personality Inventory (EPI) (Eysenck and Eysenck 1963), and the Minnesota Multiphasic Personality Inventory (MMPI) (Hathaway and McKinley 1943). No significant effects were found for aerobic fitness training on extraversion or neuroticism subscales of the EPI, but increased scores on the 16PF were found for intelligence (ES = 0.38) and self-sufficiency (ES = 0.30), and reduced scores for insecurity (ES = –0.18) and tension (ES = –0.38). Such results are consistent with other areas reviewed in this book, such as cognitive functioning (intelligence), anxiety (tension), and mood and psychological well-being (insecurity and self-sufficiency).

Studies using the MMPI mainly involved clinical groups so generalising to other populations is not possible. However, six of the ten clinical scales in the MMPI showed favourable changes. In addition, McDonald and Hodgdon's 'adjustment cluster' of hypochondriasis (–), social introversion (–), intelligence (+), schizophrenia (–) and hysteria (–) yielded an overall ES of 0.33, suggesting a small positive effect for aerobic fitness training on personality and adjustment.

Doan and Scherman (1987) listed sixteen 'personality' studies in their review and found that six of eight pre-experimental studies showed positive effects, but only three of six quasi-experimental studies and one of two experimental studies showed positive effects. None showed negative effects. This area, however, is plagued with measurement and definitional problems and caution is advised in interpreting these data.

Finally, Leith and Taylor (1990) used the same approach as Doan and Scherman (1987) and analysed results of studies according to whether they were pre-experimental, quasi-experimental or experimental. Of three pre-experimental studies investigating personality, all showed 'positive' effects for exercise, with two also demonstrating improvements in fitness. All of these studies used the 16PF to assess personality. Of the forty-six quasi-experimental studies, only one was considered to assess personality. This showed a positive effect for exercise and fitness was also improved. Of the twenty-six experimental studies Leith and Taylor reviewed, only one referred to 'psychological adjustment' and none were classified as studying personality. The study of psychological adjustment showed no change in fitness and no change in psychosocial adjustment. In conclusion, positive associations between exercise and personality and adjustment have been found.

Exercise and sleep

There is anecdotal evidence and a commonsense belief that exercise can improve quality of sleep. In addition, a number of reviews suggest that sleep can be positively affected by exercise (Horne 1981; O'Connor and Youngstedt 1995). In addition, two meta-analyses have been conducted. Kubitz *et al.* (1996) found that acute exercise yielded significant effect sizes for a number of sleep variables. The ESs showed that individuals who exercised fell asleep faster, and slept longer and deeper than those not exercising. The meta-analysis by Youngstedt, O'Connor and Dishman (1997) confirmed these findings, with the exception of sleep onset latency. For chronic exercise, Kubitz *et al.* (1996) found that fitter individuals fell asleep faster, and slept deeper and longer than less fit individuals. ESs were small to moderate for both acute and chronic exercise.

Physical activity and psychological well-being in women

Our objective in this section is to review the evidence for the role of exercise psychology on topics relating to women's reproductive functions: menstruation, menopause and pregnancy. Throughout the book we have always tried to include discussion of both men and women whenever data allowed and to point out instances of gender inequality. In this next section we address some particular topics that are specific to women's reproductive function. These topics will relate to how exercise psychology can play a role for these specific times in women's lives either by providing evidence for psychological benefit or by addressing specific issues concerning adherence. First, we discuss what is known about psychological benefits of exercise in relation to menstruation. Then we address the topic of psychological responses to exercise during and after pregnancy, including the topic of post-natal depression. Finally, we discuss the growing literature on exercise and menopausal status.

Exercise, menstruation and mood

Exercise as a treatment for menstrual cycle symptomatology is not a new idea. It has been advocated in the lay literature for some time now but such recommendations have lacked theoretical rationale and empirical support. Only two intervention studies have been carried out, one to assess the effects of exercise on dysmenorrhoea (Israel, Sutton and O'Brien 1985) and the other to assess the effects on premenstrual syndrome (Prior and Vigna 1987). The results of both studies are suggestive of positive effects of exercise in alleviating premenstrual syndrome or dysmenorrhoea, although neither study measured psychological states.

Data from cross-sectional studies indicate strong associations between physical exercise and positive psychological states during the menstrual cycle. Choi and Salmon (1995) prospectively monitored women who exercised at different levels for a whole month. The women, who had regular menstrual cycles, completed a specially devised mood adjective checklist on a daily basis. There were three groups: thirty-three high exercisers (those who regularly exercised more than three times a week), thirty-six low exercisers (those who exercised less than three times a week) and thirty-none sedentary women. The results showed that not only were positive mood and negative mood related to cycle phase in all groups, high exercisers experienced the most positive moods and the least negative moods throughout the cycle. In addition, a significant interaction showed that not only did the high exercisers feel better emotionally than the other two groups over the whole cycle, they did not experience a decline in positive mood from mid-cycle to the premenstrual phase. A similar trend was seen in negative mood although this only approached statistical significance. Similar results did not emerge for the menstrual phase of the cycle. This may reflect different mechanisms that lower mood premenstrually and menstrually. For example, acute pain that is often present while menstruating, but not premenstrually, suggests one obvious way in which the sources of distress and discomfort may be different. Furthermore, it is not clear how self-perceptions influence either the reporting of menstrual discomfort or the role of exercise in alleviating discomfort. Cultural influences passed from mother to daughter may lead to the view for some women that menstruation is a time of incapacity; participation in exercise runs counter to this view and may therefore operate to influence feelings of strength rather than incapacity. This viewpoint is reflected in the current advertising trend for sanitary products to be associated with women who lead physically active lives.

Choi and Salmon (1995) suggest that their findings indicate possible protection from premenstrual deterioration in mood in women who routinely take high levels of exercise. This is, of course, a tentative suggestion because of the cross-sectional design of the study. The association may be the result of more severe premenstrual symptoms, or a perception of incapacity during menstruation, leading to some women being sedentary. Equally, those women with fewer symptoms premenstrually may be more inclined to be active. There is a clear need for further experimental research to follow up the promising results from the cross-sectional data. However, the possibility of a mood-enhancing effect from exercise may have important implications for women who do suffer negative moods at certain points of the menstrual cycle.

Key point: Physical activity may have a role in promoting positive moods at key points in the menstrual cycle.

Exercise and pregnancy

The topic of physical activity and childbirth has engaged the interest of physicians for a very long time. This interest was initially medical with commentary relating to ease of childbirth and health of the baby. For example, Eccles (1982, cited in Rankin, Hillan and Mutrie 2000) notes that in Tudor times in England obstetricians observed that rich women had more difficult births than working-class women and speculated that this was because of sedentary living for the more privileged classes. During the seventeenth and eighteenth centuries pregnant women were encouraged to exercise, with certain limitations and within the acceptable culture of the times, such as use of a spinning wheel and outdoor walking in low-heeled shoes (Rankin, Hillan and Mutrie 2000). However, during the Victorian era, pregnant women, especially those from the middle and upper classes, were discouraged from activity and pregnancy was seen as 'confinement' with much reduced social interactions. In the early twentieth century, when medical records began to show an association between physical work, typically in lower-class women, and lighter birthweight, and therefore easier labour, exercise was advocated as a pre-requisite of a healthy pregnancy (Rankin, Hillan and Mutrie 2000). Nowadays exercise programmes are often advocated both before and after pregnancy to help prepare women for the physical and emotional demands of childbirth and the transition to parenthood. Such classes also provide specialist advice as to what is or is not appropriate activity since the knowledge in this area has increased in recent years (Rankin 2002).

An emerging area of importance concerns the role of exercise in psychological well-being and physical self-perceptions during pregnancy. In comparison with the literature available on the physiological issues of exercise during pregnancy (Lokey *et al.* 1991), there is very little literature on the psychological issues. The transition to parenthood can be seen as a developmental crisis and there are emotional as well as social changes during pregnancy. The pregnant woman may feel that she is perceived of only as a 'pregnancy' and that her own identity becomes submerged (Alder 1994). In addition, a woman's perception of her pregnancy will be influenced by both peer and cultural pressures. Strang and Sullivan (1985) reported that pregnancy resulted in negative changes in body image for many women. Wallace *et al.* (1986) conducted a cross-sectional study of pregnant women who were participants in aerobic exercise compared with pregnant women who were sedentary and found that the exercising women had higher self-esteem scores and lower discomfort scores than the sedentary women. Hall and Kaufmann (1987) reported that pregnant women who had exercised during pregnancy retrospectively had improved self-image, reduced tension and decreased discomfort during the time of participation. In a prospective study, Slavin *et al.* (1988) found that exercise allowed women to feel more in control of their bodies and helped them maintain a positive self-image during pregnancy. These authors suggest that one of the most consistent benefits of exercise during pregnancy is psychological, because it allows women to feel control over their bodies at a time when many bodily changes that occur are biologically driven. However, there is a lack of well-designed studies in which exercise 'treatment' was randomly assigned to women and with adequate numbers to allow robust statistical analysis. One study that managed a more controlled design was completed in Scotland by a practising midwife with knowledge of exercise science. Rankin (2002) randomly assigned 157 women to receive either normal antenatal care or normal care plus antenatal exercise. Forty-eight women assigned to the control group and fifty assigned to the exercise intervention completed the three assessments at early pregnancy, late pregnancy and after pregnancy. Many psychological variables were measured alongside variables related to physical health, childbirth and labour. The pattern of results for the psychological variables was remarkably consistent with the control group experiencing a deterioration of positive aspects over the course of the pregnancy and the exercise group showing a maintenance of early pregnancy levels of the same variables. An example of one of these variables, namely perceptions of coping assets, is shown in Figure 8.10. Rankin also noted that there were no detrimental effects of

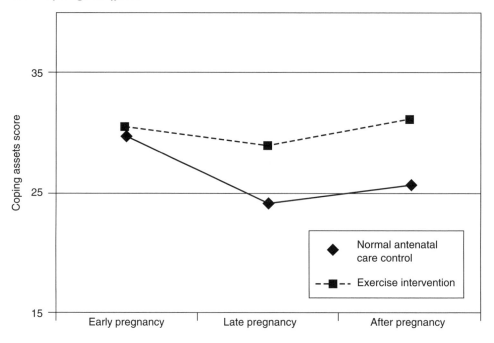

Figure 8.10 Mean scores for perceptions of coping assets over the course of pregnancy (Rankin 2002)

the exercise programme on length of labour or on indices of the newborn baby's health. Thus, the overwhelming conclusion from this study was that adding exercise to routine antenatal care prevented the decline in women's perceptions of well-being that is normally seen through the course of pregnancy. Although more research is needed, this study created changes in local provision of antenatal exercise classes and training for leaders of such classes. For further details see Rankin (2002).

A further new area of development in terms of exercise psychology and women's reproductive function concerns the topic of post-natal depression. You will read in Chapter 9 that, in our judgement, there is good evidence that exercise can both prevent and treat depression. It would therefore seem obvious that we should study the role of exercise in both prevention and treatment of post-natal depression. In 2001 we reported that there had been no specific studies in this area but it is pleasing to note that this is changing. What has also changed is the knowledge about the extent of this particular kind of depression. A meta-analysis measuring the incidence of post-natal depression around the world suggests that around 13 per cent of all women giving birth might develop this problem (O'Hara and Swain 1996). This kind of depression is potentially more problematic than experiencing depression at other times because the mother and baby each have very special needs at this time and depression will make this transition time even more difficult, perhaps even resulting in future mental health problems for the child. Standard treatment for depression, that includes either medication or therapy, may be inappropriate at this time because of issues of feeding the baby and the need for timely intervention since this sort of depression may have a short time course. Exercise may be particularly good as an alternative since it is a self-help strategy, could involve socialisation, therefore diminishing isolation as a problem, and literally help women 'get out of the house'. However, it is also clear that exercise can pose challenges at this time. Sometimes women are still recovering from childbirth and may not feel ready to exercise or they may not want to or cannot leave the baby because of feeding or caring needs. Thus, we need studies that address the feasibility of exercise in terms of location, mode, frequency, intensity and duration. One innovative idea has been to introduce exercise for post-partum women in the guise of pram pushing. A survey of the perceived benefits and barriers associated with pram walking for 450 new mothers in Australia found a high percentage believed that such activity could increase both physical and mental health even to the extent of relieving post natal depression (Currie and Develin 2002). To date, only one study could be found that has actually used pram pushing as an intervention. Armstrong and Edwards (2004), using a randomised controlled design with an exercise and social comparison group, found a significant decrease in depression scores for the exercise group. This is clearly a mode of activity that deserves further attention from exercise psychologists and it is good to know that a pilot study is under way in Birmingham in the UK (A. Daley personal communication).

Key point: Physical activity may help pregnant women maintain pre-pregnancy levels of psychological well-being and should be explored as a means to prevent and treat post-natal depression.

Exercise and the menopause

The psychosocial challenges of the transitional years during which women gradually lose their reproductive function (medically termed the climacteric, but more commonly known as the menopause) are many. These include coming to terms with the end of reproductive years, changing roles in the family as children mature and leave home, potential increase in health problems of parents, self and partner, and opportunities for dedicating more time to career and self-development. Many women report that the climacteric is a positive time of change and an opportunity to experience more independence (Musgrave and Menell 1980). However, some women may experience a certain amount of physical and psychological distress during the climacteric. Vasomotor symptoms, such as nocturnal sweating and hot flushes, are the most commonly reported physical symptoms and are related to hormonal changes (Hunter, Battersby and Whitehead 1986). There is also evidence of non-clinical psychological symptoms with loss of self-confidence, and increased depression and anxiety being the most frequently reported (Barlow *et al.* 1989; Hunter and Whitehead 1989). There are equivocal findings regarding sexual function. It has been suggested that loss of self-esteem is the most general climacteric symptom and several factors combine to reduce a woman's sense of self-esteem during the climacteric. These factors are low socio-economic status, negative attitude towards the menopause and its consequences, limited social network, poor marital relationships and stressful life events.

In the latter part of the twentieth century, hormone replacement therapy (HRT) was heralded as a panacea for women who were suffering from menopausal symptoms with the apparent promise that such therapy might prevent osteoporosis, reduce risk of cardiovascular disease and make women look and feel younger. But the early promise of HRT was questioned once some large trials began reporting a lack of association with prevention of cardiovascular disease (Writing Group for the Women's Health Initiative Investigators

2002). There have also been reports of adverse side effects when taking HRT, including an increased risk of breast cancer (Hope, Wager and Rees 1998; Million Women Study Collaborators 2003). Now in the early part of the twenty-first century, medical opinion would seem to be that HRT should only be prescribed in the smallest dose and for the shortest possible time (UK Committee for Safety and Medicine 2003). This means that women and clinicians are looking for alternatives to HRT and exercise may come into this frame. Indeed, with substantial evidence for effectiveness for the role of exercise in reduction of cardiovascular risk, for prevention and treatment of osteoporosis, for enhanced mood and psychological well-being (Department of Health 2004a), it would certainly seem that exercise has a lot to offer and that women facing menopause, surrounded by literature of what they should and should not do in terms of supplements, HRT, diet and nutrition, might take our advice – if there is one thing that they should do it is to keep moving! Gannon noted in 1988 this potential for the use of exercise to alleviate some of the symptoms commonly reported by women during the climacteric (Gannon 1988). Since then there have been five large-scale surveys, covering between them over 100,000 women, that have added some substance to this notion by establishing a strong relationship between higher frequency of reporting vasomotor symptoms of menopause and lower levels of activity (Daley *et al.* 2007). For example, in one study only 5 per cent of women who were highly active reported severe vasomotor symptoms whereas 14–16 per cent of those who had little or no weekly activity reported these symptoms (Ivarsson, Spetz and Hammar 1998). In a large UK survey ($n = 2,399$), Daley *et al.* (2007) found that that active women reported better health-related quality of life scores than inactive women suggesting a positive association between health-related quality of life and participation in regular exercise for menopausal women. Not all surveys have found this association. Surveys showing no association between physical activity and menopausal symptoms have all been rather small-scale, most involving fewer than 100 women, in comparison with the studies that do show this relationship. Thus the weight of the observational evidence is supportive and it should also be noted that there have been no instances of studies that have found detrimental effects on menopausal symptoms related to physical activity.

However, there is still very little experimental research to support the suggestion that women could benefit by increasing activity during the menopause. Bachman *et al.* (1985) randomly assigned post-menopausal women to either an exercise group ($n = 12$) or a control group ($n = 10$) and noted improvements in fitness and psychological well-being, with no change in sexual vitality, after thirteen weeks of exercise. Crammer, Neiman and Lee (1991) found similar results from a ten-week exercise programme for premenopausal women. In this study, the women were randomly assigned to either a walking programme or to a sedentary control group. The exercise group showed improvements in cardiovascular function and psychological well-being but no change in percentage body fat after the ten-week programme.

No other experimental studies on women during the climacteric years could be found in searching the literature. However, Harris, Rohaly and Dailey (1993) provided qualitative data on why middle-aged, menopausal women exercise. They identified five primary motives for exercise from their analysis of interview data:

1   personal power/control – 'I really like being in shape ... there's a certain element of personal power that's involved in it'; 'I feel fairly good about myself, and confident in the things that I can do'
2   reclaiming the body – 'When I look in the mirror, I want to see a fit body'; 'Exercise has probably enabled me to look better in my clothes and feel better about myself'

3   well-being – 'It relieves me of a lot of tension'; 'I think the main reward in exercising is just feeling good. I know how much better I feel when I exercise regularly'
4   enjoyment – 'I really love the walk'; 'I enjoy having fun'
5   adjusting to the years – 'This is the way I want to grow old – active and thin'; 'I guess I want to be independent. I want to feel stronger'; '(As I get older I want to) look the way I want to look and feel about myself the way I want to feel'.

Although the women in this study were not asked directly about their menopausal symptoms, it is evident from the examples of responses that their high self-esteem, happiness and satisfaction with the process of ageing are being attributed to physical exercise. These qualitative data provide information not attainable by traditional experimental designs. We recommend that further qualitative studies are undertaken which help us understand why some women exercise throughout their lives and why others stop. For example, use of the life history approach suggested by Sparkes (1997) may prove fruitful.

Further evidence on the association between exercise and menopausal status is available from cross-sectional studies. In one such study of women attending a hospital clinic for menopausal symptoms, thirty-eight were interviewed as they waited for their appointments (Mutrie and Choi 1993). They also completed a questionnaire on exercise habits, the Climacteric Symptoms Scale (Greene 1991) and the Physical Self-Perception Profile (PSPP) (Fox and Corbin 1989). On the basis of their responses the group were divided into those who were exercising for health or leisure purposes for at least sixty minutes per week ($n = 17$) and those who were sedentary ($n = 21$). The exercisers reported a higher estimation of their physical self-worth and physical condition than the non-exercisers and a trend to have less anxiety than the non-exercisers. This suggests that either those women who exercise have positive psychological advantages over non-exercisers or that more positive psychological dispositions allow women to exercise. The next generation of research must disentangle the cause and effect relationship, but it does appear from previous research that exercise can cause positive changes. Since this was a clinical sample, and remembering that it has been suggested that a reduction in self-esteem is the most general symptom of the climacteric, then exercise could be used as an adjunctive and or alternative treatment for this population of women.

Together, the studies suggest that exercise may be a useful self-help and clinical treatment for menopausal symptoms and may be particularly important in promoting positive changes in body image and physical self-perceptions. Future experimental research must establish the effectiveness of such a treatment. Daley and colleagues are currently conducting a systematic review of the evidence with a view to providing guidelines for clinicians dealing with this issue (Daley *et al.* under review).

Key point: Physical activity may be beneficial for women who are experiencing menopause.

Is 'fit' a feminist issue?

Although the preceding sections suggest that exercise can be very positive for women facing the various challenges of reproductive function, elsewhere we have noted that promotion of physical activity for women presents exercise psychologists with certain dilemmas (Mutrie and

Choi 2000). Just as there was a rebellion from feminist thinkers about the constant pressure on women to become thinner, which is best represented in the classic text *Fat is a feminist issue* (Orbach 1978), there is a viewpoint that promoting increased exercise for women represents their 'continued oppression through the sexualisation of physical activity' (Theberge 1987: 389). Even in challenging the cultural assumptions of the menopause Germain Greer has more to say against exercise than in favour of it. In Greer's view, 'face-lifts, mammoplasty, buttock-lifting, aerobic dancing ...' are all means by which the patriarchal beauty industry has exploited menopausal women (Greer 1992: 128). One dilemma for exercise psychologists is to decide whether or not it matters that one main reason for women to exercise is the pursuit of the body beautiful. If this more 'extrinsic' motivation gets women to initiate activity and that initial experience results in a shift towards more intrinsic motivation, we might expect long-term adherence and thus all the health benefits would follow (see Chapter 4). That would be ideal. However, we know that it is more likely that women will not achieve body toning and weight loss goals in the kind of classes that promise the perfect body (does your local exercise centre offer a class along the lines of 'bums, thighs and tums'?), and that their motivation therefore decreases because the unrealistic goals have not been met and they therefore stop exercising. So readers have to decide for themselves if this is a dilemma, but those promoting getting women started into exercise and physical activity by the goal of weight loss must work very hard to try to move motivations towards the intrinsic end of the spectrum.

Our second dilemma relates to perceptions of what some kinds of activity might do to body shape. Many women feel that the increased strength that exercise might provide would make them feel uncomfortable rather than 'empowered' and do not want to do some activities because of that. Anecdotal reports from personal trainers and exercise leaders suggest that many women do not want to do strength training in case they get 'big muscles'. Of course, strength training is particularly important for postmenopausal women to help promote bone health and to help prevent falls. This is a cultural perception that is difficult to overcome but must always be challenged otherwise some women will lose out on the benefits of maintaining or gaining strength. It is very unlikely that even perfect adherence to strength training guidelines for health could result in 'big muscles'. The dilemma for applying exercise psychology in these circumstances is the difficulty of promoting activities that may go against the cultural 'norm' and therefore be unlikely to be adhered to. More creative solutions are required! The reader is referred to Precilla Choi's excellent text for further review and discussion of these topics as they relate to women's involvement in physical activity and exercise (Choi 2000).

Key point: 'Fit' is a feminist issue and exercise psychologists must explore how to promote motivations for exercise that will help women remain active throughout the life course.

Physical activity and psychological well-being: mechanisms

This chapter suggests that physical activity is associated with numerous dimensions of psychological well-being. However, we also need to know *why* and *how* such effects occur. This necessitates a brief discussion on the mechanisms of such links.

Mechanisms explaining the effects of exercise on psychological well-being have not been clearly identified. Several proposed mechanisms are plausible, including biochemical, physiological and psychological (Biddle and Mutrie 1991; Boutcher 1993; Morgan 1997).

Possible biochemical and physiological mechanisms include:

- changes associated with an increase in core body temperature with exercise – the thermogenic hypothesis (Koltyn 1997)
- increase in endorphin production following exercise – the endorphin hypothesis (Hoffmann 1997)
- changes in central serotonergic systems from exercise – the serotonin hypothesis (Chaouloff 1997)
- the effects of exercise on neurotransmitters, such as the norepinephrine/noradrenaline hypothesis (Dishman 1997)
- the 'feel-better' effect from physical activity may result from changes in physical self-worth and self-esteem from mastering new tasks, having a greater sense of personal control, or from time away from negative or more stressful aspects of our lives.

In an elegant analysis of possible mechanisms and their interaction with exercise experience, Boutcher (1993) proposes that for those just starting exercise (that is, in the 'adoption phase'), greater emphasis should be placed on psychological mechanisms since the exerciser had not adapted, physiologically, to the exercise stimulus. In the maintenance phase, Boutcher suggests that both psychological and physiological mechanisms are likely to be important, and in the final habituation phase, he suggests that emphasis should be placed on physiological mechanisms and the influence of behavioural conditioning. These ideas are appealing since they integrate the context and experience of physical activity with possible mechanisms.

Researchers looking at the psychological outcomes of physical activity are strongly advised to attempt to refine our understanding of mechanisms. Possible explanations for why physical activity might influence mental health and well-being are likely to work in a synergistic way in which people may feel better, perceive an increased sense of control, notice less tension in muscles, sleep better, use less effort in daily tasks and have higher levels of circulating neurotransmitters. Perhaps it is this 'gestalt' which provides the effect rather than one mechanism explaining one outcome. This discussion on potential mechanisms will be expanded at the end of Chapter 10.

Chapter summary and conclusions

The relationship between physical activity and psychological well-being is one of the oldest areas of study in philosophy and psychology. It is not surprising, therefore, that evidence is both voluminous and controversial. Much of the debate stems from weak research designs and low statistical power in many studies, thus creating doubt about the true effects of exercise on psychological well-being. However, nearly all areas studied show positive effects for exercise across diverse methods of investigation, including meta-analyses, population surveys and experimental trials, and virtually none show negative effects.

In this chapter, we have:

- reviewed the evidence on physical activity and various indices of psychological well-being, including mood and affect, self-esteem, enjoyment, cognitive functioning, personality, sleep and well-being in women when considering reproductive health
- used meta-analyses, population surveys and experimental trials, where available, to reach a research consensus
- summarised the likely mechanisms linking physical activity with psychological well-being.

In summary, therefore, we conclude:

- exercise and physical activity participation is consistently associated with positive mood and affect
- quantified trends show that aerobic exercise has small-to-moderate positive effects on vigour, and small-to-moderate negative effects for fatigue, confusion, depression, anger and tension
- experimental trials support the effect of moderate exercise on psychological well-being
- exercise is related to positive changes in self-esteem and related physical self-perceptions
- exercise can have a positive effect on personality and psychological adjustment
- small effects suggest that individuals who exercise fall asleep faster, and sleep longer and deeper than those not exercising
- exercise can have positive benefits for women's experiences of menstruation, pregnancy and menopause.

9 The relationship between physical activity and anxiety and depression

Can physical activity beat the blues and help with your nerves?

Buckworth and Dishman pointed out that as long ago as 1899 William James said that 'our muscular vigor will ... always be needed to furnish the background of sanity, and cheerfulness to life, to give moral elasticity to our dispositions, to round off the wiry edge of our fretfulness, and make us good-humoured' (Buckworth and Dishman 2002: 91). Maybe now we are ready to listen to this message!

Chapter objectives

The purpose of this chapter is to focus on how physical activity relates to two of the most common mental health issues: anxiety and depression.

Specifically, in this chapter we aim to:

- define anxiety and depression for clinical and non-clinical populations
- introduce and define the topic of mental illness
- discuss the lack of acknowledgement of the role of physical activity in prevention and treatment of mental illness
- discuss the evidence base and mention the problems of cross-sectional data
- review and summarise the evidence linking exercise with non-clinical states of anxiety
- summarise the evidence about exercise and clinical anxiety disorders
- review and summarise the findings about exercise and non-clinical depression
- provide an in-depth review of the literature on physical activity and exercise on clinical depression
- provide a critique of whether or not the evidence shows a causal relationship between exercise and depression
- offer directions for future researchers in this area.

Introduction: the continuum from normal to clinical in defining anxiety and depression

There is a continuum in defining anxiety and depression that ranges from feelings which are short-lived and do not interfere much with our lives to long-lasting symptoms that suggest a clinical diagnosis of a mental illness. We have therefore planned this chapter to cover the literature that suggests physical activity and exercise may have a role to play in prevention and treatment at both ends of this continuum. We will offer technical definitions of anxiety and depression at an appropriate point but here we want to ensure that readers understand the spectrum that we are considering. At one end of the spectrum, where feelings of anxiety or depression are short-lived, we consider that physical activity may be able to minimise the duration of these events and encourage more positive moods. We consider this to be the promotion of good mental health. At this end of the spectrum people do not generally seek or need help for the alleviation of such feelings and so physical activity can be seen as a self-help strategy. At the other end of the spectrum, where feelings of anxiety and depression last for a long time and interfere with normal functioning at work or at home, professional help is often sought. Here we are dealing with mental illness and we consider that physical activity and exercise may have a role in both prevention and treatment.

Defining mental illness

Mental illness has various definitions and is commonly studied under the heading of abnormal psychology. Other terms include psychiatric disorders, psychological disorders and mental disorders. Mental disorder had been defined by the American Psychiatric Association (1994) as:

> a clinically significant behavioral or psychological syndrome or pattern that occurs in an individual and that is associated with present distress (for example, a painful symptom) or disability (that is, impairment in one or more important areas of functioning) or with a significantly increased risk of suffering death, pain, disability, or an important loss of freedom. In addition, this syndrome or pattern must not be merely an expectable and culturally sanctioned response to a particular event, for example, the death of a loved one.
>
> (American Psychiatric Association 1994: xxi)

In the area of public health, UK government initiatives currently prioritise mental health as an area of concern. A recent policy paper (Department of Health 2004b) stated that improving mental health was an overarching health priority because mental well-being is crucial to good physical health and to making healthy choices; because stress is the commonest reported cause of sickness and a major cause of incapacity; and because mental ill health can lead to suicide.

Mental health is linked to physical health problems

In addition to the importance of mental health in its own right, it has now been recognized that negative emotions, particularly depression, as well as personality and socio-economic status, may have a negative impact on the functioning of various organs and therefore increase the risk of chronic disease (for example coronary heart disease) (Trigo, Silva and Rocha 2005). The levels of depression that are noted in studies that show significant relationships between depressive symptoms and risk of cardiovascular disease and mortality are often not at a clinical level and this makes it more important to investigate 'sub-clinical' levels and understand how these lower levels might influence overall health (Wassertheil-Smoller *et al.* 2004). Of particular interest to the physical activity debate is the proposal that there is a Type D (distressed) personality that is characterised by negative emotions and an inhibition to expressing these emotions. This personality type has been strongly associated with increased risk of cardiovascular disease (Sher 2005). Clearly physical activity has a well-established role in the prevention of cardiovascular disease, but the rationale has been based on physiological benefits. The proposal that mental health problems, and depression in particular, may be new markers that put people at risk of cardiovascular diseases is still being debated (Shimbo *et al.* 2005).

Another new and timely area of interest is the idea that childhood depression may increase the risk of adult weight increase and obesity (Hasler *et al.* 2005). Given that childhood depression is treatable and given the worldwide concern about obesity levels, this association needs further study. These connections between negative emotion and various diseases suggest an increased role for activity since it may provide a means of improving positive emotions in those who are at risk of disease because of poor mental health.

Classifying mental illness

Classifying the various types of mental illness is commonly done with reference to either the Diagnostic and Statistical Manual of Mental Disorders (DSM), of which version IV is the most recent (American Psychiatric Association 1994), or the International Classification of Diseases–10 (ICD–10) (World Health Organization 1993) which classifies (and gives a numerical code to) all diseases including mental and behavioural disorders. These classification systems allow both clinicians and researchers to have a common language concerning the various disorders and a known method of diagnosis, although experience and expert training in psychiatry or psychology is required to undertake any diagnosis. DSM–IV has five axes on which the classification of mental illness is made. The first two list all possible disorders and the remaining three allow the diagnosis to characterise physical health, the extent of stressful life circumstances and the overall degree of functioning. Table 9.1 shows the five axes. The ICD–10 (1993) chapter on mental and behavioural disorders contains classifications as specified by codes F00–F99 which are shown in Table 9.2.

Table 9.1 Five axes from DSM-IV for classifying mental illness

Axis	Description
I. Clinical disorders	In this axis each major disorder is described and criteria listed. The headings include depressed mood, anxiety, unexplained physical symptoms, cognitive disturbance, problematic substance abuse, sleep disturbance, sexual dysfunction, abnormal eating, psychotic symptoms, psychosocial problems and other mental disorders such as manic symptoms.
II. Personality disorders	In this axis dysfunctional personality traits are described and disorders usually first diagnosed in infancy, childhood or adolescence such as academic skills disorders or impaired social interaction.
III. General medical conditions	This axis is often the starting point of diagnosis since symptoms may be related to a recognised disorder. For example depressed mood may be related to hypothyroidism and that is a different diagnosis than depressed mood with no related medical condition.
IV. Psychosocial and environmental problems	In this axis family, educational, housing, economic and legal problems are assessed.
V. Global assessment of functioning	The global assessment of functioning has a 100-point scale (GAF) which allows assessment of psychological, social and occupational functioning. The GAF scale ranges from 'persistent danger of severely hurting self or others' which would get a score of 1–10, to 'serious symptoms or any serious impairment in social, occupational, or school functioning' which would score 41–50 and to 'superior functioning in a wide range of activity' which would score 91–100.

Table 9.2 ICD–10 codes for mental and behavioural disorders

Numerical code	Description
F00–F09	Organic, including symptomatic, mental disorders (e.g. dementia)
F10–F19	Mental and behavioural disorders due to psychoactive substance use (e.g. dependence syndrome)
F20–F29	Schizophrenia, schizotypal and delusion disorders (e.g. paranoid schizophrenia)
F30–F39	Mood (affective) disorders (e.g. depression)
F40–F48	Neurotic, stress-related and somatoform disorders (e.g. phobias)
F50–F59	Behavioural syndromes associated with physiological disturbances and physical factors (e.g. eating disorders)
F60–F69	Disorders of adult personality and behaviour (e.g. kleptomania)
F70–F79	Mental retardation (e.g. mild mental retardation)
F80–F89	Disorders of psychological development (e.g. developmental disorders of speech and language)
F90–F98	Behavioural and emotional disorders with onset usually occurring in childhood and adolescence (e.g. hyperkinetic disorders)
F99	Unspecified mental disorder

Treatment

Settings for treatment of psychological disorders include general practice, hospitals, specialist clinics (or resource centres), private therapy and informal settings. When people do not seek help for feelings of anxiety and depression they may discuss these feelings informally within family or friendship groups or they may try to cope with such feelings by themselves. When people do seek out treatment the first port of call may be the GP, in which case some form of medication may be offered. Analyses of Department of Health data suggested that between 1991 and the year 2003 the number of prescriptions made in England for antidepressant medication increased more than three-fold from nine to twenty-eight million (Department of Health 2005). This alarming trend can be seen in Figure 9.1.

In extreme cases more invasive procedures such as electroconvulsive therapy or psychosurgery (such as prefrontal lobotomy) are performed. Some people may be offered counselling style therapies that include focusing on the way the person is thinking or feeling and acknowledging their social circumstances. The range of trained professionals who might undertake this therapy include psychiatrists, clinical psychologists, counselling psychologists, hypnotherapists and social workers. Within this area there are many approaches ranging from psychoanalysis (which perhaps is the lay person's impression of therapy involving a couch and a person taking notes), to client-centred and cognitive–behavioural approaches. Sometimes the whole family may be involved in the therapeutic process.

Of interest to us is the role of physical activity in the prevention and treatment of psychological disorders. Physical activity could be seen as part of a treatment programme that might assist with enhancing moods and self-esteem, encouraging socialising and improving physical health. In thinking about how physical activity might prevent psychological disorders, it is possible that it provides a means by which one's sense of self develops, promotes more positive moods, allows competencies to develop, provides opportunities for socialisation and promotes physical health and fitness.

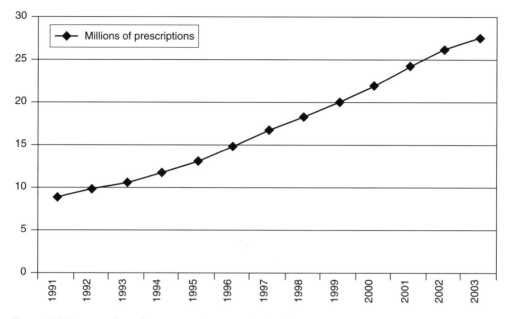

Figure 9.1 Increases in antidepressant drug prescriptions in England 1991–2003 (source: Department of Health statistics)

Key point: There is a range of levels of anxiety and depression that might be classed as normal at one level and clinical at another. Clear definitions exist for the clinical end of this spectrum.

Prevalence of mental illness

Mental illness is not a trivial topic that only affects a small number of people. Around the world, mental illness presents a serious public health concern. It accounted for almost 11 per cent of the global burden of disease in 1990 and this is expected to rise to 15 per cent by 2020, which would make it the leading disease burden if this estimate is correct (Murray and Lopez 1997). In both 1996 and 2000, the WHO global burden of disease studies ranked depression as the fourth leading cause of disease burden in global terms by using estimates that take account of both mortality and disability (DALYs – disability adjusted life years) (Uston *et al.* 2004). The WHO study of the year 2000 estimated that depression caused the largest amount of non-fatal burden. The prevalence of mental illness in the UK is 230 per 1,000 referrals to primary care services and data from social trends analysis in the year 2000 showed that one in six adults living in the UK reported some kind of neurotic disorder such as depression, anxiety or a phobia, in the week prior to the interview (Office of National Statistics 2005).

The prevalence of mental illness is clearly a concern for public health. In the UK, the Office for Population Census and Surveys (OPCS) published a survey on the prevalence of psychiatric morbidity (Meltzer *et al.* 1995). This survey used the Clinical Interview Schedule (CIS) to classify neurotic disorders, functional psychosis, and alcohol and drug dependence. The survey was representative of adults aged 16–64 years in Great Britain and involved over 10,000 interviews. It was concluded that 160 per 1,000 adults had suffered a neurotic disorder in the week prior to interview, with the most common disorder being mixed anxiety and depression. Neurotic disorders were more common amongst women than men. There was a much smaller incidence of functional psychosis, such as schizophrenia, with a prevalence rate of four per 1,000 noted. Alcohol and drug dependence had prevalence rates of forty-four and twenty-two per 1,000 respectively, but young adults aged between 16–24 years had much higher incidences for both alcohol dependency (176 per 1,000) and drug dependency (111 per 1,000), making alcohol dependence a problem for one in six young adults. Overall about 14 per cent of the population scored twelve or above on the CIS, thus indicating mental illness. Table 9.3 shows the prevalence of common cardiovascular conditions in Scotland as reported in the 1995 Scottish Health Survey (Dong and Erins 1997). It can be seen from this table that none of the common cardiovascular conditions are as prevalent as mental illness. Thus mental illness is not a trivial issue affecting small proportions of the population. Rather, it is as common as high blood pressure and much more common than heart attacks and strokes. In addition, the survey statistics just described only relate to adults aged 16–64 years. The prevalence of mental health problems among children in the UK is estimated at up to 20 per cent with 7–10 per cent having moderate to severe problems which prevent normal functioning (Kurtz 1992). Although 3.4 per 1,000 require in-patient psychiatric care, those with mild to moderate symptoms also place a heavy burden on health services.

Depression is the most prevalent disorder with 5–10 per cent of the population estimated to be affected by clinical depression (Weismann and Klerman 1992). The 1995 Health Survey for England showed that 20 per cent of women and 14 per cent of men have at some time suffered mental illness (Prescott-Clarke and Primatesta 1998). The treatment of mental illness requires 17 per cent of all health care expenditure and mental and behavioural disorders now account for more incapacity benefit claims than musculoskeletal problems such as low back pain (Henderson, Glozier and Elliot 2005). Taken together this evidence suggests a large and expensive burden in health care resources in the treatment of mental illness and depression in particular. This clearly makes mental health a major public health issue.

Key point: Mental health is a public health concern and physical activity may assist in prevention and treatment.

Table 9.3 Prevalence of common cardiovascular conditions in Scotland (Dong and Erins 1997)

Condition	Percentage of men reporting condition	Percentage of women reporting condition
Angina	3.1	2.5
Heart attack	2.4	1.1
Stroke	1.0	0.5
Hypertension	13.3	13.9
Diabetes	1.5	1.5
Heart murmur	2.1	3.2

I am a forty-eight year old woman with a history of depression. In my youth, I tried self-medicating what I thought of as 'moodiness', with a variety of drugs. These included popular street drugs such as marijuana, amphetamines, barbiturates and alcohol. Through the rather hazy, but fun years of the late seventies, I didn't sense a problem because the use of these sorts of drugs was socially acceptable at that time.

Later, as I became sober and clean as result of luck, maturity, and circumstance, it became apparent that more was afoot than mood swings. The eighties were the years that there was a huge popular movement toward seeking help with Alcoholics Anonymous, and other twelve-step meetings, that examined sobriety. It was inside this structure that I identified my extensive family history of depression, and my own personal version of a Wild Ride came to halt.

By the late eighties, I was taking Prozac as treatment for my, by then diagnosed, Dysthymia. With great results. As time went by, the effectiveness waned (a now known aspect of Prozac). Over the last decade my doctor and I have tinkered with and switched types of antidepressants, as well as dosages according to effectiveness, tolerable side effects, etc. For the last four years I have been quite stabilized on a moderate dosage of Effexor (Venlafaxine HCL), a newer generation of psycho-therapeutic medicine.

I have been often slow to see the obvious, and as recently as six months ago, I started walking daily, sometimes five days a week, for a half an hour. This was inspired by my decision to help my heart, get a bit more fit, and possibly shed a pound or two. Although my work is physically demanding, it is not aerobic, as I own and operate a home cleaning business.

After just a few weeks of walking, I started feeling better, not entirely in the ways I'd expected. My sleep habits became easier to regulate, and weren't nearly as erratic as in the past. I didn't ruminate as much before bed, went to sleep easier and awoke refreshed. My energy levels doubled, almost immediately. Coffee wasn't absolutely necessary (although still pretty desirable) to get me going in the morning. Primarily what stunned me was how the state of my mental health improved. Here's what I mean by mental health.

Depression has a way of creating an internal voice that is a bit like the Winnie Pooh character, Eeyore. Inside your head resides a voice that is driven, humorless, full of paranoia and defeat. antidepressants had given me back my birthright to a certain extent; i.e. I didn't wish life would just end all the time. But the level of my optimism, and my ability not just to deal with what came my way graciously, but to meet it with creativity, humour and authority, doubled when I exercised regularly.

Walking became difficult as winter arrived. This past October, I purchased a fold-away treadmill, and became determined to keep up the routine of walking in my home. Walking in the outdoors is a moving meditation, but treadmills are dead boring. So I watch television or listen to music, until I can return outdoors and see animals and flowers, as I walk.

It is common knowledge that exercise equals better health. However the benefits of exercise to mental health is not commonly discussed or written about. There are media campaigns to educate our sedentary, obese culture about the benefits of exercise. However, only physical benefits are highlighted in these campaigns, such as weight loss, heart disease prevention, and other 'body' benefits.

There is a simultaneous drive to educate the public about the hazards of depression, with millions suffering its crippling effects, including suicide, but the aspects of exercise, as they relate to improved mental health, are not brought into the discussion.

It is now obvious to me that my brain's serotonin levels are enhanced by regular exercise. I'm certainly appreciative of the recent advances Western medicine has made in the areas of psycho-therapeutic medications, but I believe that that exercise may well be an invaluable factor for many people suffering from depression, and should be advocated by the mental health profession.

Donna

Lack of acknowledgement from mental health professionals of the role of physical activity and exercise

Over the past twenty years the literature in the area of physical activity, exercise and mental health has been growing. The evidence, however, has not persuaded mental health agencies, such as the American Psychiatric Association, to endorse the role of exercise in treating mental illness such as depression. In the UK, an overview of depression and its treatment did not mention the value of exercise at all (Hale 1997). This is in contrast to coronary artery disease in which inactivity is now recognised as a primary risk factor (Pate *et al.* 1995). Perhaps the evidence for the role of exercise in treating and preventing mental illness is not yet convincing. Maybe the mental health literature is suffering from a dualist tendency to treat the mind (mental health) and body (physical health) as separate issues, thereby failing to recognise the mental outcomes of a physical treatment such as exercise (Beesley and Mutrie 1997; Faulkner and Biddle 2001a). Rejeski and Thompson are more optimistic in suggesting that we are moving away from dualism: 'The mind–body distinction has slowly, but noticeably yielded to the concept of biopsychosocial interactions – the position that the body, the mind, and the social context of human existence are reciprocally interdependent on one another' (Rejeski and Thompson 1993: 7). If we are indeed moving away from dualism then perhaps we would expect those who treat mental health problems to promote exercise as part of treatment. However, McEntee and Halgin (1996) reported that while many psychotherapists believe in the therapeutic value of exercise, very few (around 10 per cent) recommend exercise to their clients. From their survey of 110 practising psychotherapists, McEntee and Halgin concluded that one of the major reasons for this reluctance to discuss exercise was that it was perceived as inappropriate in so far that exercise was perceived as being very directive and perhaps dealt with better by physicians or physical recreation specialists. 'Many therapists simply do not see their work as pertaining to the body, and they believe that most clients come to therapy to discuss psychological ailments, not physical or exercise-related ones' (McEntee and Halgin 1996: 55). These are similar views to those expressed by leaders of British clinical psychology training programmes (Faulkner and Biddle 2001a). It would therefore seem that there is much work to be done to convince those who deliver mental health services to focus on the links between mind and body and to look more positively on the role of exercise in mental health issues.

On a more positive note, there is some evidence that this reluctance to consider the 'body' in the treatment of mental health may be shifting. In the UK, the National Health Service has produced a website to enable patients to understand what they are experiencing and to offer self-help strategies. In describing the prevention of depression the web site suggests that exercise could help and in the treatment section it is suggested that increasing physical activity levels might be something to consider (www.nhsdirect.nhs.uk). In addition recent leaflets about depression from the Royal College of Psychiatrists in the UK suggest that exercise is a good self-help strategy for depression.

Another aspect of the treatment of mental illness, that suggests that it is worthwhile to pursue the possibility of the use of exercise, is that of patient choice. In the UK, drugs continue to be the most frequently used treatment for depression although psychotherapy and ECT are also used (Hale 1997). Patients often report that they do not want drugs (Scott 1996). Consequently, exercise is a reasonable option with few negative side effects and could be cost-effective in comparison with other non-drug options such as psychotherapy. Studies on the cost-effectiveness and cost–benefit of exercise versus drugs or other therapies must be undertaken so that the potential economic advantages of exercise can be measured. Perhaps the economic arguments will be the most powerful in persuading mental health professionals to include exercise as a treatment option.

Reviewing the evidence base

Evidence has been drawn from an extensive literature. Narrative and meta-analytic reviews, epidemiological surveys and controlled trials are reviewed in an effort to reach conclusions from varied approaches. The review will cover general health and well-being from population surveys and then will deal separately with anxiety and depression since these are the most common mental health issues. In each case the spectrum from clinical to non-clinical will be covered.

Population surveys of general well-being

In this section we will review large-scale, cross-sectional population surveys that have included measures of mental health and physical activity. Surveys that have specifically mentioned depression or anxiety, particularly if a clinical definition was used, will be reviewed later in the chapter. Prospective studies, with more than one time point, are also reviewed later under separate headings of anxiety and depression.

In the Scottish Health Survey of 1995 (Dong and Erens 1997), physical activity was assessed by self-report and covered activity at home, at work, and sports and exercise. The responses were then classified into six levels from nought (sedentary) to five (vigorous activity at least three times per week) and are similar to the criteria adopted in the English National Fitness Survey (Sports Council and Health Education Authority 1992). Table 9.4 shows the classifications.

The Scottish survey reported a relationship between levels of physical activity and psychological well-being, as measured by the General Health Questionnaire (GHQ) (Goldberg *et al.* 1970). For both men and women the percentage with a GHQ score over four (indicating mental health problems) was lowest in activity level five and highest in activity level nought.

There may be an issue of whether or not both men and women benefit from the psychological benefits of activity. Data from a national health and lifestyle survey in the UK showed that men who exercise ninety-two minutes or more a day were less likely to report common mood and anxiety states than men who exercised less than this (Bhui and Fletcher 2000). However, these authors found no such relationship for women. We will return to this topic later.

The Copenhagen Heart Health Study has already provided valuable epidemiological data that supports the notion that physical activity is associated with lowered risk for cardiovascular disease. The same study has now begun to explore the data held about physical activity and psychological well-being (Schnohr *et al.* 2005). The data are from 12,028 randomly selected men and women aged 20–79 years. The results show that with increasing physical

Table 9.4 Classifications of six levels of activity used in the Scottish Health Survey (Dong and Erins 1997)

Level	Criterion
5	Three or more occasions of vigorous activity per week
4	Three or more occasions of a mixture of vigorous and moderate activity per week
3	Three or more occasions of moderate activity per week
2	More than one, less than three occasions of moderate or vigorous activity per week
1	One occasion of moderate or vigorous activity per week or less
0	No occasions of moderate or vigorous activity per week

activity in leisure time, there was a decrease in high level of stress and life dissatisfaction, (odds ratio (OR) = 0.30). Moderate levels of activity (two to four hours walking per week) showed the most pronounced difference in comparison with those who had low levels of activity. Adjustments in the analysis were made for sex, age, body mass index, smoking, alcohol consumption, education and income.

Taken together these descriptive data certainly indicate an association at a population level between activity and good mental health. There are some issues that clearly require further evidence and debate, such as potential gender differences and the amount and intensity of activity required to confer benefit. These issues are also apparent in the surveys that have more specific data on anxiety and depression which we will discuss later in the chapter.

Adolescents and children

Steptoe and Butler (1996) reported data from a cohort of 5,061 adolescents. They noted that 'greater participation in vigorous sports and activities was associated with lower risk of emotional distress, independently of sex, social class, illness during the previous year, and use of hospital services' (Steptoe and Butler 1996: 1791). More recently, Allison *et al.* (2005) analysed data from 2,104 Canadian adolescents that showed a significant negative relationship between physical activity (undertaken at a vigorous level usually through sport) and problems with social functioning. In this data set the expected negative relationship between physical activity and depression/anxiety was in the predicted direction but did not reach significance when age, gender and socio-economic status were included in the analysis.

In a US cross-sectional study of 1,870 Hispanic and non-Hispanic white adolescents, in which participation in physical education and in physical activity was measured as well as indices of sadness and suicidal thoughts, it was found that higher attendance in physical education class was inversely related to feelings of sadness (odds ratio (OR), 0.80 (95 per cent confidence interval (CI), 0.68–0.94)); participation in more total physical activity sessions per week was associated with a lower risk of considering and planning suicide (OR, 0.72 (95 per cent CI, 0.65–0.79) and OR, 0.65 (95 per cent CI, 0.48–0.87) respectively) (Brosnahan *et al.* 2004). This potential link of high levels of physical activity to lower risk of considering and planning suicide is very important since there is a high rate of suicide amongst young men in particular (Office of National Statistics 2005).

Very few studies have focused on young children and so a report of a study of 933 children aged between eight and twelve years is a welcome addition given the rates of childhood depression that we have already noted. Here, Tomson *et al.* (2003) asked parents or teachers to classify children as active or inactive, asked information about playing sports outside of school, and categorised children depending on whether or not they met guidelines for health-related fitness. These variables were then related to depressive symptoms. The results showed that for each of these measures of activity, those who were inactive had a significantly greater risk (range of relative risk (RR) 1.3–4.0) of reporting depressive symptoms in comparison with their active peers.

Taken together, these population studies of adolescents and children show a positive relationship between various measures of physical activity, including sport, physical education and more general activity, and measures of psychological well-being. Most of these studies are recent additions to the literature and show the growing epidemiological interest in physical activity and its relationship to mental health.

Problems of cross-sectional data

These cross-sectional data are open to the criticism that the relationship is created because those people who are reporting symptoms of poor mental health are inactive (lethargy is a common symptom of mild depression for example) rather than inactivity causing the poor mental health. The correlational nature of such cross-sectional data does not allow causal connections to be made. However, such data are still very important in providing evidence of associations and particular issues that can then be explored either experimentally or in prospective longitudinal designs. Such issues include possible gender differences and the amount or intensity of activity required to confer benefit. Prospective studies are required that track populations over time and can therefore provide good evidence for the relationship between activity levels and the onset of mental illness. Steptoe and Butler (1996) suggested that this could be done with British data from a cohort study initiated in 1970 which they have already used to show a positive association between sport participation and emotional well-being for the cohort during adolescence. Such studies have appeared in relation to depression and will be reported later in the chapter but to date there have been no longitudinal data sets that track good mental health and physical activity over time.

Exercise and non-clinical anxiety

Most people have feelings of worry from time to time and may say that they feel anxious. Such feelings are normal reactions to circumstances life presents us with, such as preparing for exams or realising there is not as much in our bank account as we thought. However, if such feelings persist over time and begin to interfere with work or personal and family relationships, these feelings may be classified as generalised anxiety disorder (GAD). This would require a medical (clinical) diagnosis. Related anxiety topics are panic attacks, phobias (persistent, excessive or irrational fear of things such as flying, spiders or being out in open spaces), or post-traumatic stress disorder. So there is no one thing that can be clearly labelled as 'clinical anxiety'. GAD is common with about one in twenty adults getting an anxiety disorder in their life-time. It is more common in women than men and it is often present with another mental illness such as depression or panic disorder (NHS Direct 2006). In the following section of this chapter the relationship between physical activity/exercise and anxiety at a non-clinical level will be reviewed first, followed by a review of the literature on the clinical end of the spectrum. The study of the proposed anxiety-reducing effects, sometimes called anxiolytic effects, of exercise has a long history in sport and exercise psychology and has remained an area of considerable interest to researchers. Anxiety is defined in terms of both state (transitory) and trait (enduring) characteristics, and sometimes with reference to both cognitive (worry) and somatic (bodily tension) elements. In addition, exercise researchers have been interested in the psychophysiological stress reactions of participants differing in fitness levels.

Although many mood and affect studies include measures of tension and anxiety (such as those using the POMS (see table 8.2)), it is clearer conceptually to deal with anxiety as a separate construct, partly because of the volume of such research. Most studies of exercise and anxiety have assessed state anxiety using either the state scale of the State-Trait Anxiety Inventory (STAI) (Spielberger, Gorsuch and Lushene 1970), POMS tension subscale (McNair, Lorr and Droppleman 1971) or the MAACL anxiety subscale (Zuckerman and Lubin 1965). When trait anxiety has been assessed, studies have used almost exclusively the trait scale of the STAI.

Meta-analytic findings

The results from four meta-analyses (Long and van Stavel 1995; McDonald and Hodgdon 1991; Petruzzello *et al.* 1991; Schlicht 1994) help in reviewing the effects of exercise on anxiety. Schlicht (1994) located twenty-two samples between 1980 and 1990 and found a small and non-significant effect size of –0.15, thus concluding that exercise had little effect of anxiety. However, Petruzzello (1995) criticised this paper strongly by pointing out that Schlicht had under-represented the field by not locating all of the studies (Schlicht 1995). Although Schlicht (1994) analysed twenty-two samples from twenty studies, Petruzzello *et al.*'s (1991) meta-analysis used fifty for Schlicht's time period, and 104 overall. Consequently, Schlicht was unable to conduct moderator analyses and his meta-analysis lacked statistical power (see Schlicht 1995). Table 9.5 summarises results from four meta-analyses.

Petruzzello *et al.* (1991) have conducted one of the most comprehensive meta-analyses of the field. We review their findings alongside the more focused meta-analyses of McDonald and Hodgdon (1991) and Long and van Stavel (1995). Petruzzello *et al.* (1991) analysed data from 124 studies that examined the effect of exercise on anxiety. They included studies published between 1960 and 1989 that investigated state anxiety, trait anxiety and psychophysiological indicators of anxiety. Published and unpublished studies were included, as well as studies varying in methodological design. By coding such variables, the effect for methodological adequacy could be tested.

Table 9.5 Summary results from four meta-analyses on exercise and anxiety

Study	Outcome variables	Activity/fitness measure	N of effect sizes	Mean effect size
McDonald and Hodgdon (1991)	State anxiety	Aerobic fitness training	13	–0.28[a]
	Trait anxiety	Aerobic fitness training	20	–0.25[a]
Petruzzello *et al.* (1991)	State anxiety	Exercise	207	–0.24[a]
	Trait anxiety	Exercise	62	–0.34[a]
	Psycho-physiological indicators	Exercise	138	–0.56[a]
Schlicht (1994)	State and trait anxiety	Exercise	22	–0.15[b]
Long and van Stavel (1995)	Within-group pre-post studies	Exercise training	26	–0.45[a]
	Contrast group studies	Exercise training	50	–0.36[a]

Notes
a Effect size significantly different from zero
b Estimation of population effect size using the Hunter and Schmidt correlation effect sizes (Hunter and Schmidt 1990): effect size of 0.1 = small, 0.3 = moderate, 0.5 = large (Cohen, 1988)

McDonald and Hodgdon (1991) restricted their meta-analysis to studies investigating the effects of aerobic fitness training on psychological outcomes in adults, one of which was anxiety. This yielded thirty-six effect sizes from twenty-two studies. No date limitation was reported in their search procedures. However, they did not consider unpublished studies, abstracts and dissertations and included only studies using standardised anxiety measures, as well as fitness measures, and pre- and post-test measures. Finally, Long and van Stavel (1995) restricted their meta-analysis to adults involved in quasi-experimental or experimental training studies using standardised anxiety measures. Clinical studies (psychiatric and Type A) were omitted leaving forty studies and seventy-six effect sizes.

The main findings from these meta-analyses are summarised in Table 9.5 and show that exercise has a significant small-to-moderate effect on anxiety. Petruzzello *et al.* (1991) found that for state anxiety studies using no-treatment control groups and motivational control groups both showed a significant ES, but this was larger for studies utilising a pre-post within-subjects design. McDonald and Hodgdon (1991) found that survey studies produced a lower ES than experimental studies. These findings suggest that the internal validity of the study may not necessarily influence effect sizes but anxiety change can occur when motivational factors are controlled. In addition, Petruzzello *et al.* found that exercise was as effective as other anxiety-reducing treatments. This finding may be particularly important given the low cost of exercise.

Aerobic exercise showed greater effects than non-aerobic exercise, but caution must be expressed concerning this result since only thirteen effect sizes were used to calculate the effects of non-aerobic exercise by Petruzzello *et al.* (1991). They found no differences between types of aerobic exercise, a finding supported by McDonald and Hodgdon (1991).

Interestingly, the length of the exercise session might be related to anxiety. Petruzzello *et al.* (1991) showed superior effects for exercise lasting twenty to thirty minutes in comparison with sessions less than this. However, when the effect sizes in the nought to twenty-minute category that were calculated from comparisons with other anxiety-reducing treatments were eliminated, the ES increased from –0.04 to –0.22, and was not significantly different from the –0.41 for the twenty-one to thirty-minute duration.

When reviewing exercise and affect, we suggested that higher-intensity exercise may not produce such positive effects as more moderate exercise. However, for state anxiety, Petruzzello *et al.* (1991) found that effect sizes for the intensity of exercise were homogeneous. For psychophysiological indices of anxiety, though, the meta-analysis showed the highest effect size for 40–59 per cent of HR_{max} or VO_{2max} (ES = –1.06; n = 13) and this was significantly different from 70–79 per cent intensity (ES = –0.41; n = 24). All four intensity categories, though, including 80 per cent and above, showed effect sizes significantly different from zero. These results suggest that moderate-intensity exercise may be particularly beneficial for anxiety reduction, but other higher intensities can be also.

Key point: Exercise has a small to moderate effect on reducing non-clinical levels of anxiety.

Population surveys

The extensive secondary data analysis of physical activity and mental health reported by Stephens (1988) includes evidence on anxiety. Data on over 10,000 adults in Canada showed that reporting symptoms of anxiety was less likely in more active individuals. This held for men of all ages, and for women over 40 years of age, but not for younger women.

There are very few populations surveys in which anxiety is categorised separately from mental health but at a non-clinical level. In the UK we have examined cross-sectional relationships between physical activity and mental health as measured by the HADS (Zigmond and Snaith 1983) anxiety and depression scores in a sample of 1,742 participants from the third wave of the Twenty07 Study: Health in the Community (Mutrie and Hannah 2007). Respondents reported their levels of physical activity at work, in the home, and in leisure time, and the intensity of activity was also determined. Physical activity was related to depression scores but not to anxiety scores. There was no relationship between work physical activity and depression score. Among women, depression score increased with each additional episode of vigorous home activity. In both sexes, depression score decreased with each additional episode of vigorous leisure activity and for men the decrease in depression score with moderate leisure activity was reversed if too much moderate activity was undertaken. Thus, we concluded that not all settings confer the same mental health benefits for activity even if these settings provide adequate frequency, intensity and duration for other health benefits. This study also questions whether or not a relationship does exist between activity and anxiety.

Experimental trials

In a review of exercise and anxiety, Leith (1994) identified twenty experimental studies. Of these, fourteen (70 per cent) showed reduced anxiety from exercise, with the rest showing no change. None showed increased anxiety from exercise. A series of experimental trials in the UK by Steptoe and his colleagues provides a useful framework for drawing conclusions concerning experimental work on exercise and anxiety.

Steptoe and Cox (1988) studied the psychological responses of thirty-two female medical students to both high (cycle ergometry exercise of 50 rpm against 2 kg/100 W) and low (0.5 kg/25 W) exercise intensities. For the anxiety–tension subscale scores from the POMS, they found a significant level × time interaction. This showed a significant increase in anxiety from pre- to post-test for the high-intensity condition and a non-significant decrease for low-intensity exercise.

Moses *et al.* (1989), testing sedentary adults across high-intensity, moderate-intensity, attention–placebo and waiting list conditions, also found evidence for anxiety reduction in the moderate- but not high-intensity group. In fact, those exercising at a higher intensity reported increases in anxiety from pre- to post-test. Moderate intensity exercise undertaken by low-active anxious adults in the study by Steptoe *et al.* (1993) was also associated with anxiety reduction whereas an attention–placebo condition showed no change.

These studies illustrate that exercise is associated with anxiety reduction under experimental conditions. However, Steptoe's data are particularly striking as they suggest that it is moderate- rather high-intensity exercise than produces anxiety reduction during exercise, although anxiety has also been shown to reduce in the post-exercise recovery period. This is consistent with the discussion in Chapter 8 concerning the dual-mode model proposed by Ekkekakis (2003).

Exercise and stress reactivity

Studies have investigated physiological reactivity to psychosocial stressors. A typical experimental design is for participants to be assigned to 'low' and 'high' aerobic fitness groups on the basis of laboratory tests of aerobic fitness and then to be assessed on their physiological reactivity (for example, blood pressure) to a stressor such as cold water immersion. Crews and Landers (1987) conducted a meta-analysis of thirty-four such studies and reported a mean ES of –0.48, showing a moderate effect for fitness on stress reactivity with fitter individuals showing less reactivity. Stronger effects were shown after acute exercise rather than chronic involvement in exercise. The majority of studies used blood pressure and heart rate as dependent measures, but these may be confounded with the independent variable of fitness measurement.

A national review and research consensus process in England on physical activity and psychological well-being (Biddle, Fox and Boutcher 2000) also considered reactivity to stress. After considering the evidence, Taylor (2000) concluded that 'single sessions of moderate exercise can reduce short-term physiological reactivity to and enhance recovery from brief psycho-social stressors'.

While the reviews by Crews and Landers (1987) and Taylor (2000) provide useful data on exercise and stress reactivity, this field has a number of methodological concerns. For example, there are only a few experimental studies and many studies are correlational. The influence of fitness, independent of physical activity history, has yet to be determined, and all studies employ short-term stressors. In addition, Taylor suggested that we need to know more about the effects of exercise on naturally occurring stressors. If exercise does affect stress reactivity, further knowledge is needed on the underlying mechanisms of such effects.

Factors moderating the relationship between exercise and anxiety

Moderators of the relationship between exercise and anxiety have been alluded to in the results of the meta-analyses and other studies. In summary, exercise-induced anxiety reduction is evident across all ages and both genders. Where differences have been identified, these have not been consistently observed across studies. Data are lacking on differences between groups varying by ethnicity, SES and education.

Clinical anxiety disorders

There is evidence of the anxiety-reducing effects of exercise from several meta-analytic reviews which we discussed earlier in the chapter (Long and van Stavel 1995; McDonald and Hodgdon, 1991; Petruzzello *et al.* 1991). However, almost none of the studies included in these reviews involved clinically diagnosed anxiety disorders. Taylor (2000) notes that for studies of acute exercise the majority of study participants were college students and that for chronic exercise only three studies (out of twenty-seven reviewed) focused on groups with an anxiety disorder. Presenting symptoms for a person with a clinical level of anxiety might include fear, worry and inappropriate thoughts or actions. Diagnosis might include phobias (such as agoraphobia), panic attacks, obsessive–compulsive disorder, stress disorders (such as post-traumatic stress) and generalised anxiety. The ICD-10 (WHO 1993) section on neurotic, stress-related and somatoform disorders (codes F40–F48) covers phobias, anxiety disorders, obsessive–compulsive disorders, reactions to severe stress, dissociative disorders (that is, lack of integration of past and present) and somatoform dysfunctions, such as unexplained pain. Anxiety itself is therefore an inadequate heading but one which is commonly used in the literature. DSM–IV provides criteria for all of these conditions. An example of the diagnostic criteria for generalised anxiety disorder is:

- excessive anxiety and worry, for more days than not, that are out of proportion to the likelihood or impact of feared events
- the worry is pervasive and difficult to control
- the worry is associated with symptoms of motor tension (for example, trembling, muscle tension), autonomic hypersensitivity (for example, dry mouth, palpitations), or hyperarousal (for example, exaggerated startle response, insomnia)
- the anxiety, worry or physical symptoms cause clinically significant distress or impairment in social, occupational or other important areas of functioning
- the condition has lasted for at least six months.

Populations surveys

Very few population surveys actually measure anxiety disorders. A large cross-sectional analysis of 8,098 US adults, conducted as part of the national co-mormidity survey, is one of the few studies that have measured a range of anxiety disorders and the relationship with physical activity (Goodwin 2003). The results showed a significant association between regular physical activity and lower prevalence of current major depression (OR = 0.75 (0.6, 0.94)), panic attacks (OR = 0.73 (0.56, 0.96)), social phobia (OR = 0.65 (0.53, 0.8)), specific phobia (OR = 0.78 (0.63, 0.97)) and agoraphobia (OR = 0.64 (0.43, 0.94)) after adjusting for differences in sociodemographic characteristics, self-reported physical disorders and comorbid mental disorders. This study also showed evidence of a dose–response effect with those reporting the highest physical activity also reporting the lowest prevalence of mental disorders.

In a cross-sectional study of community-dwelling women aged seventy years and over (*n* = 278; mean age = 74.6 years), it was found that physically active women were half as likely to be anxious when compared with their physically inactive counterparts (OR = 0.5, 95 per cent CI = 0.3–0.8) (Cassidy *et al.* 2004).

Both anxiety and depression were measured in a Scandinavian study of 20,207 men using the HADS scale (Thorsen *et al.* 2005). The prevalence of HADS-defined depression and anxiety was lower among those who were physically active than in those who were physically inactive. However, when multivariate analysis was used to confirm these associations, with adjustments for various confounding variables, then only the link with depression remained significant (adjusted odds ratio = 0.58; 95 per cent CI (0.51, 0.65)). These findings are similar to those we have found in Glasgow and reported earlier in this chapter (Mutrie and Hannah 2007). In the Glasgow study we did not limit the analysis to those who were defined as depressed or anxious using the HADS criteria. Both sets of data cast doubt on whether a relationship exists between activity and anxiety. With so few studies that have reported on population levels of clinically defined anxiety a clear conclusion on this topic is not possible.

Key studies

Only four physical activity studies could be found in which participants had clinically diagnosed anxiety disorders. The first is a study by Orwin (1981), in which eight patients diagnosed as agoraphobic were treated with a running programme. Patients were asked to run to situations that they found fearful, such as supermarkets. Such places normally create feelings of anxiety for those with agoraphobia, but these patients were taught to attribute increased respiration and heart rate to the running and not to their phobic response. Orwin (1981) reported that all eight patients recovered from such repeated exposure after running and had similar success with situational phobias. Here the running seemed to be operating as a method of desensitising patients to the onset of anxiety symptoms by attributing bodily changes to the demands of the exercise. However, no other studies in which phobic patients have been treated this way have been reported. Of course, Orwin's studies were pre-experimental with no control group, thus providing little evidence that exercise could be used as a treatment for phobias.

A series of Norwegian studies have tried to unravel some of the issues in the use of exercise for treating anxiety disorders. Martinsen, Sandvik and Kolbjornsud (1989) included patients with agoraphobia in an exploratory study of the value of exercise for ninety-two non-psychotic patients who had various different psychiatric diagnoses. Exercise involved an eight-week programme which was an adjunct to other treatment. There was no control group. Results showed short-term gains for those diagnosed with agoraphobia with panic disorder but these were not maintained at the one-year follow-up. At the end of the programme fitness improvement and symptom reductions were significant. However, without a control group it is not clear if the symptom reductions were part of the normal course of recovery or accelerated by the exercise.

Martinsen, Hoffart and Solberg (1989a) undertook a further study of exercise in the treatment of anxiety disorders. The anxiety disorder was diagnosed by clinical interview (using DSM–III criteria) and patients ($n = 79$) in a Norwegian psychiatric hospital were participants. The patients were randomly assigned to aerobic exercise (jogging or walking) or non-aerobic exercise (strength and flexibility training). Both training programmes lasted about sixty minutes for three times each week for eight weeks. Both groups decreased anxiety as rated by therapists blind to treatment conditions, but only the aerobic exercise group increased maximum oxygen consumption. These results are identical to those reported for the depressed patients by the same authors (Martinsen, Hoffart and Solberg 1989b). The results suggest a beneficial effect of both aerobic and non-aerobic exercise on anxiety disorder. The fact that aerobic fitness improvement was not required to produce the beneficial effects suggests that the explanatory mechanisms are more likely to be psychological than physiological. However, one major drawback of this design is the lack of a control group. The exercise was alongside other treatment but did involve work with specialist instructors. The psychological effect of gaining extra attention and support from these instructors was therefore not controlled.

Another Norwegian study examined the effects of different intensities of aerobic exercise on anxiety disorders (Sexton, Maere and Dahl 1989). Participants were in-patients ($n = 52$) in a three to four week programme in a psychiatric hospital and were diagnosed by DSM–III criteria as having non-psychotic anxiety disorders. Patients were randomly assigned to moderate (walking) or vigorous activity (jogging) and had supervised exercise (thirty minutes four to five times each week) for the duration of their programme. They were expected to continue the activity unsupervised for a total of eight weeks and were also followed up at six months. Both intensities of exercise showed reductions in anxiety symptoms at eight weeks and six months. Fitness gains were greater for the jogging group at eight weeks but the difference between groups had disappeared by six months. Aerobic gain did not correlate with reduction in anxiety. More joggers than walkers dropped out of the programme leading the authors to recommend the moderate rather than vigorous activity for other therapy programmes. Despite several good design features this study did not have a non-exercising control group required to show that the exercise had an effect over and above the normal treatment effect of the psychiatric programme.

There has also been a suggestion that exercise is contraindicated for those suffering from anxiety neurosis. Pitts and McLure (1967) proposed that exercise could lead to the onset of anxiety symptoms in such patients, due to increases in lactate levels in the bloodstream. This hypothesis was refuted by Morgan (1979), but the evidence for the refutation came from studies on non-clinical participants. For some reason, perhaps an ethical one, the Pitts–McLure hypothesis has not been properly tested in a well-designed study involving patients with clinical anxiety. However, O'Connor *et al.* conducted a review of all studies where participants were diagnosed with a panic disorder and noted that only five panic attacks had occurred in 444 exercise bouts performed by 420 panic disorder patients (O'Connor, Smith and Morgan 2000). They concluded that the weight of the published evidence shows that acute physical activity does not provoke panic attacks in panic disorder patients and thus refuted the Pitts–McLure hypothesis.

From these studies we can conclude that there is a suggestion that both aerobic and non-aerobic exercise can help reduce clinical anxiety symptoms. Moderate-intensity exercise seems best for adherence and higher levels of intensity do not necessarily improve the outcome. However, since none of the studies included a non-exercising control group it is difficult to conclude that there is a causal link.

> Key point: There is too little evidence to make firm conclusions about the role of exercise in the prevention or treatment of anxiety disorders.

Clinical anxiety disorders: conclusions

Population studies do not provide a convincing conclusion that physical activity is associated with reduced risk of clinically defined anxiety. Experimental studies do not provide much more evidence. Very little is known about how exercise affects clinical anxiety disorders in comparison with what is known about depression (see next part of chapter). This may partly be due to the number of diagnoses at the clinical level which could include symptoms of anxiety. A further difficulty in the area of anxiety disorders is separating anxiety from depression. Sometimes the symptoms of these two conditions present together and are diagnosed as mixed anxiety and depression. In their exploratory study, Martinsen, Sandvik and Kolbjornsud (1989) found that patients with a single rather than a mixed diagnosis had better outcomes from exercise. From the studies reported, it is only possible to conclude that there is a potential association between exercise and reduction in symptoms. Further studies, which incorporate control groups and provide a specific definition of the anxiety disorder, are needed to expand the knowledge in this important area of mental health. On the other hand, there is no evidence that exercise might induce further anxiety or panic in participants who have anxiety disorders.

Anxiety: summary

Based on the evidence reviewed, the following summary statements can be made. Concerning non-clinical anxiety:

* meta-analytic findings suggest that exercise is associated with a significant small-to-moderate reduction in non-clinical anxiety. This holds for acute and chronic exercise, state and trait anxiety, psychophysiological indices of anxiety and groups differing by gender and age
* evidence concerning the different effects for aerobic and non-aerobic exercise is unclear
* experimental studies support an anxiety-reducing effect for exercise, mainly for moderate exercise during activity, but for both moderate- and high-intensity exercise post-activity

- large-scale epidemiological surveys offer mixed support for anxiety-reducing effects for exercise but there are few surveys that have anxiety data
- physiological reactivity to psychosocial stressors appears to be reduced for those high in aerobic fitness.

Concerning anxiety disorders:

- very little is known about how physical activity and exercise relate to clinical anxiety conditions at a population level
- experimental studies are not yet convincing enough to suggest a causal link between activity and reduction of clinical anxiety
- there is no evidence that exercise might induce panic or anxiety in participants with anxiety disorders.

Exercise and non-clinical depression

Definitions of depression range from episodes of unhappiness that affect most people from time to time, to persistent low mood and inability to find enjoyment. In addition, depression may be secondary to other medical conditions, such as alcohol addiction and is often associated with chronic diseases such as Type 2 diabetes, HIV and cardiac disease. Most cases of depression are treated in general practice but more severe cases are referred to psychiatric services.

We often talk about being 'depressed' or 'fed up' or getting the 'blues'. If these feelings are experienced for a short period of time, when nothing seems to be going right for us, they are not classified as an illness. Most people who have these feelings recover as circumstances change and do not seek help. Clinical depression might be diagnosed if such feelings interfere with daily life and persist over a long period of time (weeks and months). For someone suffering from bipolar depression they will experience extremes of depression and euphoria in a cyclical way. Seasonal Affective Disorder (SAD) is a type of depression or mood disorder that comes on as the daylight hours shorten in winter. This is a very common problem with up to one in eight people in the UK experiencing milder symptoms of winter 'blues' and around one in fifty people being diagnosed with SAD (NHS Direct 2006).

Depression is one of the most common psychiatric problems. An estimated 20 per cent of patients in primary care have some degree of depressive symptomology (Paykel and Priest 1992). In addition, from analysis of American employee health insurance data, depression is the most common complaint in the workplace with a higher prevalence in women than men (Anspaugh, Hunter and Dignan 1996). It has been estimated that clinically defined depression affects 5–10 per cent of the population of most developed countries (Weismann and Klerman 1992).

The relationship between exercise and depression for those with clinical levels of depression is reviewed later in the chapter. Here we investigate such a relationship for non-clinical populations, that is, those with mild-to-moderate symptoms and not classified as having clinical levels of depression.

McDonald and Hodgdon (1991) identified five measures of depression in their meta-analysis of aerobic training studies. These were the BDI, the Centre for Epidemiological Studies Depression Scale (CES–D) (Radloff 1977), Lubin's (1965) Depression Adjective Check List (DACL), the Symptom Check List 90 (SCL–90) (Derogatis, Lipman and Covi 1973), and Zung's (1965) Self-Rating Depression Scale (SDS). In addition, the POMS depression subscale has been used (see Leith 1994) although McDonald and Hodgdon used this as part of their analysis of mood rather than depression per se.

Meta-analytic findings

Two meta-analyses have been conducted that include both non-clinical and clinical levels of depression. McDonald and Hodgdon (1991) have meta-analysed depression as an outcome variable for their study of aerobic fitness training. In addition, North, McCullagh and Tran (1990) reported a meta-analysis of eighty studies yielding 290 effect sizes on exercise and depression. The main results from these two meta-analyses are summarised in Table 9.6.

Table 9.6 Summary results from two meta-analyses on exercise and depression

Study	Outcome variables	Activity/fitness measure	N of effect sizes	Mean effect size[a]
North, McCullagh and Tran (1990)	Depression	Exercise	290	−0.53
	Depression	Exercise programmes	226	−0.59
	Depression	Follow-up	38	−0.50
	Depression	Single exercise sessions	26	−0.31
	Depression	Exercise for initially non-depressed	143	−0.59
	Depression	Exercise for initially depressed	120	−0.53
	Depression	Weight training	7	−1.78
	Depression	Various aerobic	54	−0.67
	Depression	Walk and/or jog	89	−0.55
	Depression	Aerobic class	13	−0.56
	Depression	Jogging	66	−0.48
McDonald and Hodgdon (1991)	Depression	Aerobic fitness training	17	−0.97
	Depression 'cluster'[b]	Aerobic fitness training	Mean of 7 combined ESs	−0.55
	SDS	Aerobic fitness training	7	−0.66[c]
	BDI[d]	Aerobic fitness training	5	−1.22[c]
	DACL[d]	Aerobic fitness training	3	−1.54[c]
	CES-D	Aerobic fitness training	2	−0.73[c]
	SCL-90	Aerobic fitness training	1	−1.02

Notes

a All effect sizes are significantly different from zero unless stated (or with ES $n = 1$);

b Cluster comprised: depression scores from the MAACL (Multiple Affect Adjective Checklist), POMS, MMPI (Minnesota Multiphasic Personality Inventory) and other 'mixed tests'; POMS confusion scale; POMS vigour scale (reversed); POMS fatigue scale.

c No significance levels reported.

d Both BDI (Beck Depression Inventory) and DACL (Depression Adjective Checklist) were used in one study together.

North, McCullagh and Tran (1990) conclude that both acute and chronic exercise are associated with depression reduction and that this is also the case in follow-up, and the effect sizes are mainly moderate in strength. Similarly, McDonald and Hodgdon's (1991) more focused review showed that aerobic fitness training studies also provided evidence for a moderate effect of exercise on depression. In addition, when logical clusters of effect sizes were calculated, the depression cluster was found to have a higher ES than for anxiety, self-esteem and psychological adjustment (McDonald and Hodgdon 1991).

Although these meta-analyses probably constitute the best evidence in this area to date, there are a number of issues that should caution over-confidence. Many of these are argued well by Dunn and Dishman (1991) and Dishman (1995). For example, some studies in the meta-analyses may have included individuals suffering from depression with a primary anxiety component. Dunn and Dishman argue this point on the basis of evidence showing a large number of people meeting DSM–II–R criteria for agoraphobia and panic attacks also suffer from depression or have a history of depression. In these cases, exercise may reduce state anxiety and elevate mood that could then produce changes in depression. North *et al.*'s meta-analysis is also questioned on the basis of non-uniformity in defining depression, as well as the discrepancy between the results of the meta-analysis and other studies.

Population surveys

The large-scale survey analysis reported by Stephens (1988), and discussed earlier, provides evidence concerning physical activity and depression assessed with the CES-D. Results from over 3,000 North American adults from the first National Health and Nutrition Examination Survey (NHANES–I) showed that depression was highest for those reporting 'little/no exercise' in comparison with those classified in the 'moderate' and 'much' exercise categories (see Figure 9.2). Interestingly, this difference suggests that moderate exercise may be sufficient for antidepressant effects and that additional activity yields no additional benefit.

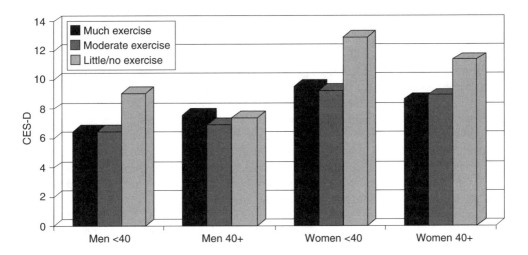

Figure 9.2 Relationship between physical activity and depression assessed with the CES-D (Stephens 1988)

More recent evidence from a national cohort study (n = 9,333) of young women in Australia showed that lower exercise status was one aspect of lifestyle that was significantly associated with reporting of depressive symptoms (France, Lee and Powers 2004). Other data from Australia (Cassidy *et al.* 2004) showed that activity levels were also important for older women. For women aged 70 years and over (n = 278; mean age = 74.6 years), those who were physically active were half as likely to be depressed (BDI score greater than or equal to 10 thus only mild depression) when compared with their physically inactive counterparts (OR = 0.5, 95 per cent, CI = 0.3–0.8 adjusted for marital status and smoking) (Cassidy *et al.* 2004). Thus, the evidence is consistent for there being a negative relationship between activity and depression at a non-clinical level for women.

Measurement of feelings of anxiety and depression in these surveys may be capturing simply transient mood or general well-being. Measures of physical activity are weak, often using single item self-report measures assessed in a cross-sectional rather than prospective design. Thus findings about the relationship between activity levels and non-clinical levels of depression must be treated with caution.

Factors moderating the relationship between exercise and non-clinical depression

The results reported so far suggest that exercise is associated with reduced depression. However, the evidence is not strong in indicating clear differences between groups, such as men and women or across different ages. Evidence could not be located in groups differing by SES or ethnicity, although some studies have controlled for these factors and still located anti-depressant effects for exercise, such as Farmer *et al.* (1988) for SES. It remains plausible that the greatest effects are likely to be seen in those who are most depressed. However, there are two problems with this idea. At the most extreme end of depression immediate help is required to avoid potential suicide. In most clinical trials researchers are ethically bound to report those extreme scores and refer the person in question to those who can provide immediate help. It is unlikely that exercise alone can provide this immediate short-term solution. At the other end of the spectrum there are many people with levels of depression that do not meet clinical thresholds but nevertheless they find themselves perhaps seeking help in order to improve how they feel. It may be that such sub-threshold levels of depression have equal or even greater costs to health services since the presenting symptoms are unclear and not easy to diagnose or treat (Judd, Schettler and Akiskal 2002). It has been suggested that increasing levels of physical activity may be particularly helpful to this group (Brown and Shirley 2005). In public health terms the greatest effects might be for those with sub-threshold levels of depression or those with mild and moderate levels because, in simple terms, there are more of them.

In attempting to locate moderators for exercise and depression, it is important to recognise a number of factors identified by O'Connor, Aenchbacher and Dishman (1993) in their review of exercise and depression in the elderly. For example, they highlight that age is confounded by health status. Factors likely to lead to depression, such as poor health status, will be disproportionately represented in elderly groups. This means that any correlations between physical activity and depression in the elderly could be explained by many factors often not controlled for.

O'Connor, Aenchbacher and Dishman (1993) suggest that depression is more difficult to assess in the elderly and that age may by confounded by inactivity. The latter point concerns cohort effects for activity, such as evidence showing that the social acceptability of exercise is less in older adults than in their younger counterparts. Therefore, age per se may not be the factor accounting for age differences in physical activity in the elderly. Finally, the assessment of physical activity is particularly problematic in the elderly. Combining the issues identified by O'Connor, Aenchbacher and Dishman (1993) highlights the potentially problematic area of locating moderators of the relationship between exercise and depression, at least in this age group.

In looking for moderators what we are attempting is to identify how confident we are in concluding that exercise or physical activity *cause* a reduction in depression. To this end, some researchers have suggested that we adopt criteria used in epidemiological research for this purpose (Dishman 1995; Mutrie 2000). This is used to judge the results of clinical studies in the next section of the chapter.

> Key point: It may be that many people who have mild to moderate depression, or even sub-clinical levels of depression, could benefit from increased activity.

Non-clinical depression: summary

Based on the evidence reviewed, the following summary statements can be made concerning exercise and non-clinical depression:

- meta-analytic findings suggest that exercise is associated with a significant moderate reduction in depression. This holds for acute and chronic exercise, different exercise modalities and groups differing by gender and age
- large-scale epidemiological surveys support the claim that a physically active lifestyle is associated with lower levels of depression.

Clinical levels of depression

Defining clinical depression

One issue that has plagued our understanding of the relationship between physical activity and depression is the lack of agreement amongst researchers concerning the criteria defining depression. Many previous reviews have included cases of 'depression' that would not reach clinically defined criteria and may be better defined as transitory negative affect. In this section of the chapter only clinically defined depression will be discussed. For clinically defined depression, patients will have sought help for their symptoms and a diagnosis made using standard instruments or interviews. The DSM–IV criteria for a major depressive disorder are summarised in Table 9.7.

The most common questionnaire used for assessment, especially in exercise studies, is the Beck Depression Inventory (BDI) (Beck *et al.* 1961). This has now been updated to include the DSM–IV criteria and is called the BDI–II. Moderate depression on the BDI is defined as a score of sixteen or above. However, many exercise studies have included people with scores lower than sixteen at baseline. This is considered as a transitory or normal score and such studies are not included in this part of the chapter. In respect of clinical interview, diagnosis of depression is made using criteria listed in the DSM–IV (American Psychiatric Association 1994), or the ICD–10 (World Health Organization 1993). In research studies, the Research Diagnostic Criteria are often used (Spitzer, Endicott and Robins 1978). Depression can also occur with other chronic diseases and mental disorders and such cases will be included in this section of the chapter, but all will have met the criteria for clinical depression.

Table 9.7 Summary of DSM–IV criteria for major depressive episode

Category	Criteria
A	At least five of the following symptoms have been present during the same two-week period, nearly every day, and represent a change from previous functioning. At least one of the symptoms must be either (1) depressed mood or (2) loss of interest or pleasure
A(1)	Depressed mood (or alternatively can be irritable mood in children and adolescents)
A(2)	Markedly diminished interest or pleasure in all, or almost all, activities
A(3)	Significant weight loss or weight gain when not dieting
A(4)	Insomnia or hypersomnia
A(5)	Psychomotor agitation or retardation
A(6)	Fatigue or loss of energy
A(7)	Feelings of worthlessness or excessive or inappropriate guilt
A(8)	Diminished ability to think or concentrate
A(9)	Recurrent thoughts of death, recurrent suicidal ideation without a specific plan, or a suicidal attempt or a specific plan for committing suicide
B	Symptoms are not better accounted for by a mood disorder due to a general medical condition, a substance-induced mood disorder, or bereavement (normal reaction to death of a loved one)
C	Symptoms are not better accounted for by a psychotic disorder (e.g. schizo-affective disorder)

Populations studies – prevention of depression

We owe a great debt to the work of William Morgan who pioneered much of the initial research investigating the role of exercise and mental health (Morgan 1968, 1969, 1970a, 1985, 1994, 1997; Morgan and Goldston 1987; Morgan and O'Connor 1988). It was perhaps his early findings showing that fitness levels, for both male (Morgan 1968, 1969) and female (Morgan 1970b) psychiatric patients were lower than non-hospitalised controls which led to experimental work in using exercise as part of a treatment regime for such patients. Martinsen and colleagues (Martinsen, Strand, Paulson and Kaggestad 1989) replicated these findings with Norwegian psychiatric patients near time of admission. Morgan (1970a) also showed that patients admitted to a psychiatric hospital, but discharged after a short period of time (on average sixty-one days), had higher levels of muscular endurance on admission than patients with similar initial levels of depression who remained in hospital for longer (at least one year). Such cross-sectional data raised intriguing questions about whether lack of exercise can cause depression or whether depression causes lack of exercise, and whether increasing fitness levels could influence recovery. There were also questions about how much heredity and motivation play a part in the results of fitness tests obtained in these studies. However, some of these early questions have now been answered. In the next section, the review of epidemiological evidence suggests that depression is indeed associated with low activity/fitness and that those who maintain activity are less likely to develop depression.

There are several cross-sectional studies that show a negative relationship between physical activity and depression. A good example of one such study was conducted by Weyerer (1992) who showed that in a community sample from Bavaria ($n = 1,536$), the physically inactive were over three times more likely to have depression than those who were regularly active. All people in this study were interviewed by a research psychiatrist and 8.3 per cent were identified as depressed using a clinical scale. There was some evidence for a dose–response relationship with those reporting only occasional physical activity being 1.55 times more likely to have depression compared with those who were regularly physically active, although this was not statistically significant.

However, cross-sectional studies, as mentioned earlier in the chapter, cannot help us disentangle cause and effect. Since lethargy and inactivity are common symptoms of depression it is as equally likely that the depression causes low activity, as it is that high levels of activity reduce depression scores. What is required to clarify the direction of these associations is data that are collected over time so that changes in activity or depression can be tracked. Thus the strongest epidemiological evidence comes from prospective studies that have followed cohorts over time. These studies are listed in Tables 9.8 and 9.9. In all of these studies depression was clinically defined (at least at a mild to moderate level) and in one study depression was diagnosed by psychiatric interview (Weyerer 1992). Statistical adjustments for potential confounding variables, such as age and socio-economic background, were also made.

In Table 9.8, eight prospective studies show that a low level of activity at some preceding date (minimum two years, maximum around thirty years) is associated with clinically defined depression at a later date. All have good design features in that physical activity was adequately measured and depression clinically defined. Ages in the cohort studied ranged from adolescents to those over sixty-five years. These studies suggest that inactivity *precedes* depression and thus the possibility that the association found in cross-sectional data is just as likely to be caused by those who are depressed being inactive can be refuted. It is important to reiterate that other possible variables, such as physical health status, were accounted for since people may well be inactive because they are disabled or prevented from taking part in activity because of a medical condition. One study showed that including or excluding those who were unable to walk did not attenuate the relationship (Strawbridge *et al.* 2002). However, there are other reasons, such as lack of social skills or socio-economic status, which could also predict both inactivity and depression that may not have been fully accounted for.

On the other hand, Table 9.9 shows three prospective studies that did not show a protective effect from physical activity. These studies do not always have good measures of activity. For example, the Kritz–Silverstein study used a yes/no single-item response question about whether respondents engaged in regular strenuous exercise and another single-item yes/no response about whether respondents did this at least three times per week. This way of assessing physical activity may be a limitation and may explain why there is no predictive relationship; relatively few of these older adults were doing this level of activity at either time point. Authors of other studies in Table 9.9 that used only a vigorous or strenuous definition of physical activity (for example, Cooper-Patrick *et al.* (1997) only counted exercising 'to a sweat') argue that such measurements are valid because they show predicted associations with cardiovascular risk markers. Mental health outcomes may have a different relationship to physical activity and by not also measuring more moderate levels of activity, such as walking, that are related to lifestyle activity rather than pursued for health and fitness reasons, these researchers may be creating the risk of a type 2 statistical error in their results; perhaps they are missing a possible protective effect of moderate activity on depression? This seems a real possibility because Mobily *et al.* (1996) used daily walking as their measure of physical activity and found a significant protective effect for this on depression scores for older adults. There is, of course, a possible publication bias at play here both for experimental and epidemiological studies in which it may be easier to get statistically significant results published in comparison with those studies which have results that do not show statistical significance. Thus the impression that there are more positive results than non-significant results could be explained by publication bias, but it should be noted that there have been no studies that have reported statistically significant negative effects on exercise in

Table 9.8 Prospective longitudinal studies that include measures of physical activity and depression at two time points that show a protective effect from physical activity

Authors and geographical location	Participants	Design	Measures	Results
Farmer *et al.* (1988) USA	1,497 respondents to the National Health and Nutrition Examination Survey follow up study (NHANES)	Prospective longitudinal 8-year follow-up	Center for Epidemiological Studies Depression Scale	Women who had engaged in little or no recreational activity were twice as likely to develop depression at follow-up as those who had engaged in 'much' or 'moderate' activity (95% CI = 1.1–3.2). There was no significant association over the same time period for men or for non-recreational activity in a usual day for either women or men. For men who were depressed at baseline, inactivity was a strong predictor of continued depression at the eight-year follow-up
Camacho *et al.* (1991) USA	8,023 in systematic sample from community	9- and 18 year-follow-up after baseline in 1965	Frequency of commonly reported physical activity resulting in a physical activity index ranging from 0 (no activity) to 14 (high active with strenuous activity). Depression measured by standard instrument used in Human Population Laboratory studies	In the first wave of follow-up (1974), the relative risk (RR) of developing depression was significantly greater for both men and women who were low active in 1965 (RR 1.8 for men, 1.7 for women) compared with those who were high active. Some evidence of dose–response relationship. The second wave of follow-up (1983) suggests that decreasing activity levels over time increases the risk of subsequent depression (OR = 2.02) although the odds ratio was not significant once the model was fully adjusted (OR = 1.61)
Paffenbarger, Lee and Leung (1994) USA	10,201 Harvard alumni (men only)	23–27-year follow-up	Rich data on all types and intensities of physical activity – self-reported. Physician diagnosed depression	Men who engaged in 3 or more hours of sport activity per week at baseline had a 27% reduction in the risk of developing depression at follow-up compared with those who played for less than one hour per week. Statistical evidence of dose–response relationship

Continued

Table 9.8 continued

Authors and geographical location	Participants	Design	Measures	Results
Mobily *et al.* (1996) USA	2,084 rural dwelling older adults (aged 65 or older)	3-year follow-up	Physical activity measured by self-reported walking. Modified CES-D used to measure depression	In the cohort reporting more depressive symptoms at baseline, those that walked daily were a third less likely to report more depressive symptoms at follow-up (OR 0.38)
Strawbridge *et al.* (2002) USA	1,947 community dwelling adults (age 50–94)	Baseline 1994 and follow-up 1999	DSM criteria used to define depression. Physical activity measured on an 8 point scale	Physical activity was protective of incident depression at five-year follow-up (OR 0.83). Excluding disabled participants, who may be depressed but unable to be active, did not attenuate results
van Gool *et al.* (2003) Netherlands	1,280 community dwelling late middle aged and older people	6-year follow-up	CES-D scale	155 people became depressed from baseline to follow-up and this was associated with changing from an active to a sedentary lifestyle (RR 1.62) and significantly associated to a decrease in minutes of physical activity
Motl *et al.* (2004) USA	4,594 adolescents	Data collection at three time points over 2 school years	Self-reported physical activity outside of school and CES-D	A decrease (of 1 SD unit) in the frequency of leisure-time physical activity over 2 years was inversely related to an increase in depressive symptoms (of 0.25 SD unit). The significance of the relationship remained after controlling for all available confounding factors such as sex, socio-economic status and attitudes towards health
Bernaards *et al.* (2006) Netherlands	1,747 workers from 34 companies	Prospective longitudinal with 3-year follow up	Dutch version of Center for Epidemiologic Studies Depression scale. Those scoring 6 and above defined as depressed	For workers with a sedentary job, strenuous leisure time physical activity (1–2 times per week) was significantly associated with a reduced risk of future depression and emotional exhaustion. Higher frequencies (3 times per week) did not show this relationship

Table 9.9 Prospective longitudinal studies that include measures of physical activity and depression at two time points not showing a protective effect from physical activity

Authors and geographical location	Participants	Design	Measures	Results
Weyerer (1992) Germany	1,536 community dwelling adults	Cross-sectional and prospective (5 year follow-up)	All people in this study were interviewed by a research psychiatrist and 8.3% were identified as depressed using a clinical scale	Cross-sectional data showed that those reporting only occasional physical activity were 1.55 times more likely to have depression than those who were regularly physically active, although this was not statistically significant. Low physical activity was not a predictor of depression at a 5-year follow-up
Cooper-Patrick et al. (1997) USA	973 physicians (men only)	Prospective study. Baseline taken during medical school and follow-up happens every 5 years. In this study baseline was 1978 and follow-up 1993	Self-reported physical activity (frequency of exercising 'to a sweat') and self-reported clinical depression	There was no evidence for increased risk of depression for those reported exercising 'to a sweat' compared with those who did not or for those who became inactive over the follow-up period (15 years)
Kritz-Silverstein (2001) USA	Adults aged 50–89 in 1984–7 (932 men 1,097 women) and followed up 1992–5 (404 men and 540 women)	Cross-sectional and prospective (12 year follow-up)	BDI Physical activity graded low medium high by yes/no responses to 2 questions about strenuous physical activity at leisure or work	Cross-sectional data showed that physical activity significantly related to lower depression scores. No evidence of predictive effect of low activity on follow-up depression scores

which depression scores have increased with increasing activity levels. All of these issues suggest that a judgement about what the weight of the evidence shows is required and a full discussion of this will be made later in the chapter.

> Key point: Higher levels of physical activity are consistently related to lower levels of depression in population surveys. The question remains about which comes first. This may be more easy to answer about depression than it was about anxiety.

A good example of one of the prospective studies is described in detail below to show the design features. Camacho *et al.* (1991) found an association between inactivity and incidence of depression in a large population from Alameda County in California. Baseline data were collected in 1965 and followed up in 1974 and 1983. Physical activity was categorised as low, medium or high. In the first wave of follow-up (1974), the relative risk (RR) of developing depression was significantly greater for both men and women who were low active in 1965 (RR 1.8 for men, 1.7 for women) compared with those who were high active. There is some evidence for a dose–response relationship with those who were moderately active in 1965 showing lower risk of developing depression than those who were low active (see Figure 9.3).

In the second follow-up in 1983, four categories of activity status were created. These categories are shown in Table 9.10 and are defined as follows:

1 those were low active in 1965 and remained low in 1974 (low/low)
2 those who had been low active in 1965 but had increased activity level in 1974 (low/high)
3 those who had been high active in 1965 and decreased activity by 1974 (high/low)
4 those who had been high active at both times points (high/high).

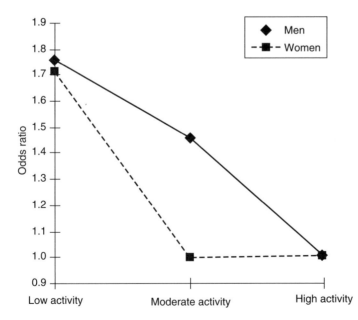

Figure 9.3 Relative risk of developing depression at follow-up from different levels of baseline physical activity (Camacho *et al.* 1991)

Table 9.10 Changes in physical activity status and subsequent depression (Camacho *et al.* 1991)

Activity status 1965/1974	Odds ratio for developing depression in 1983	Confidence interval for odds ratio
1. low/low	1.22	0.62–2.38
2. low/high	1.11	0.52–2.21
3. high/low	1.61	0.80–3.22
4. high/high	1.00	reference group

Those who were inactive in 1965 but had increased activity in 1974 were at no greater risk of developing depression in 1983 than those who had been active at both time points (the reference group for computing the odds ratio). This suggests that physical activity may have a protective effect. None of the odds ratios computed for risk of depression in 1983 showed a significant difference between the four activity categories. The largest odds ratio, however, was for those who had relapsed from activity in 1965 to inactivity in 1974. They were 1.6 times more likely to develop depression in 1983 than those who had maintained activity, but it must be remembered that this did not reach significance. The authors note, however, that this odds ratio was relatively unaffected by adjustments for age, sex, physical health, socio-economic status, social support, life events, anomie, smoking status, relative weight, 1965 level of depression and alcohol consumption. This led the authors to believe it is a robust finding. Given that only 137 people were in this category, it is perhaps not surprising that the odds ratio did not reach significance. However, the evidence from the 1974 follow-up did provide statistically significant evidence that low activity preceded the reported depression.

In summary, cross-sectional data are supportive of a negative association between activity level and depression. However, epidemiological studies that go beyond cross-sectional data and report depression and activity levels at two different time points are more equivocal. These studies are presented in summary form in Tables 9.8 and 9.9. As can be seen in Table 9.8, the weight of the evidence is supportive of a protective effect but there are three studies that do not show this effect. Research difficulties in this area, which may play a part in the lack of consistent findings, include the measurement of both physical activity and depression, the interval of time between baseline and follow-up, and the age and socio-economic status of the cohort.

Key point: The weight of evidence from prospective population surveys suggests that physical activity has a protective effect in terms of clinical levels of depression.

The work of Andrea Dunn and her colleagues at the Cooper Institute for Aerobics Research in Dallas, Texas has added considerably to the knowledge base and to the conceptual issues required to conduct experimental trials in the area of clinical depression and physical activity. In a seminal paper, Dunn *et al.* (2001) reviewed all available evidence about the relationship between physical activity and anxiety and depression with the aim of determining if there was a dose–response relationship. There are several reasons that make this such an important contribution to the literature. First, they used DSM–IV criteria to define depression and anxiety. They also focused on sub-types of anxiety and depression that bio- logically could be related to physical activity status. For example, they excluded phobias and other disorders that seemed unlikely to respond to exercise therapy. Finally, they used stan- dard drug therapy and psychotherapy criteria for successful treatment. These include response (often defined as 50 per cent reduction in symptoms), remission, prevention of relapse, recovery and prevention of recurrence. After detailed review of nine cross-sectional, nine prospective studies and eighteen experimental studies they concluded that 'There is lit- tle evidence for dose–response effects, although this is largely because of a lack of studies rather than a lack of evidence. A dose–response relation does, however, remain plausible' (Dunn *et al.* 2001: S587).

Hopefully, there will be more prospective epidemiological data that will help us form a picture of the time course of the onset of depression in relation to inactivity and allow for fur- ther exploration of variables predicting inactivity and depression. In particular, longitudinal studies are required to elucidate the possible benefits and risks of involvement in physical activity for youth on adult psychological functioning. Steptoe and Butler (1996) suggested that this could be done with British data from a cohort study initiated in 1970 that they have already used to show a positive association between sport participation and emotional well- being for the cohort during adolescence. A final point to note is that there is no evidence to suggest that increasing physical activity or exercise increases the risk of depression.

Physical activity as a treatment for depression

In this section, results from two meta-analyses will be presented and discussed. The outcome of meta-analytic reviews are subject to the quality of the input. Dishman (1995) suggests that averaging together results from studies with different designs and different methods of measuring the variables of interest is not helpful and concludes that there are too few studies with similar features to warrant confidence in the results of meta-analyses in this area. The issue of whether depression has been clinically defined is particularly important. In fact, very few studies included in North, McCullagh and Tran (1990) or McDonald and Hodgdon's (1991) meta-analyses on depression had clinically diagnosed individuals. We have therefore decided only to review meta-analyses that have only included studies with clinically defined depression.

Craft and Landers (1998) meta-analysis included thirty studies, many of which were unpublished dissertations. The average effect size was calculated at –0.72. Further analysis of the moderating variables showed that the effect sizes for mode of exercise (aerobic versus non-aerobic) did not differ, nor was there a difference between exercise treatment and psy- chotherapeutic or behavioural interventions. However, there was a greater effect size for those initially classified as moderate-to-severe in depression compared with those classified as mild-to-moderate. The results of this meta-analysis are therefore very encouraging.

Lawlor and Hopker (2001) limited their review to randomised control trials (RCT) and included fourteen studies. The mean ES for exercise compared with no treatment was –1.1 (95 per cent CI –1.5 to –0.6). Cognitive therapy had a similar ES but there are not sufficient studies to compare exercise to medication. The mean difference between exercise and con- trol groups in BDI score was –7.3 (95 per cent CI –10 to –4.6). Effectiveness has been shown by the ES in these meta-analyses but the clinical significance of this level of change in the BDI was questioned by Lawlor and Hopker who concluded that, 'The effectiveness of exercise in reducing symptoms of depression cannot be determined because of lack of good quality research on clinical populations with adequate follow up' (2001: 1).

However, we believe that this conclusion was a very negative interpretation of the evidence for the following reasons. First, the effect sizes found are similar to those for other treatments of depression such as cognitive–behavioural therapy and the seven-point mean reduction on the BDI score could be clinically significant. Second, while it is true that more evidence is needed from well-designed studies, Lawlor and Hopker restricted their meta-analysis to fourteen randomised controlled trials, some of which have very good design features and some of which lack areas such as blinding of assignment to researchers. However, overall the standard of design is not so very different from that in other areas of psychology and the results should not be dismissed for poor design. Third, almost all of the studies they used had clinical definitions of depression and thus represent a solid body of research on clinical populations. We agree with the conclusion that more research is needed, especially with longer follow-up, but these results suggest to us a need for practitioners to consider seriously the role of exercise in the treatment of depression.

Nevertheless, even with a well-conducted meta-analysis in this area it is not possible to account for various influences, such as the length of time required to see an effect emerge, since there are still too few studies to allow comparisons. It seems best, therefore, to also look at individual studies in detail rather than relying solely on conclusions from meta-analyses.

Key studies

Most narrative reviews (Biddle and Mutrie 1991; Byrne and Byrne 1993; Gleser and Mendelberg 1990; Martinsen 1989; Morgan 1994) of the topic of exercise and depression make cautious positive conclusions but note the methodological limitations of studies and this criticism has been echoed many times (Dishman 1995). However, with the exception of Martinsen (1989, 1993, 1994), Craft and Landers (1998) and Lawlor and Hopker (2001), reviews to date have included non-clinical depression. Morgan (1994) noted that one of the most reliable findings in this area is that exercise will not decrease depression in those who are not depressed in the first place. It would seem appropriate, therefore, to examine all studies in which exercise has been used to treat those with clinical depression and to limit the discussion to studies having the best design features. All studies from 1970 that could be located by standard search methods, that appeared in a peer-reviewed journal, incorporating random assignment of participants to groups, and including a clinically defined measure of depression were reviewed. This process excluded some well-designed studies, such as that of McCann and Holmes (1984), because depression levels were below sixteen on the BDI and there was no clinical interview to confirm the diagnosis. The fourteen key studies identified are summarised in Table 9.11.

Conclusions from key studies

Table 9.11 shows fourteen randomised controlled trials that have been published in peer-reviewed journals. Two of them have follow-ups which are separate publications. All studies have good design features, and similar results have been found from studies conducted in the USA, Europe and India, thus both internal and external validity are high. All show positive effects for exercise, with some of these effects being similar to that achieved by psychotherapy and some being equivalent to that achieved by drug therapy. Positive effects from exercise were noted in short time frames (four to eight weeks). Longer-term effects showed that exercise had advantages over medication at six months in that those who had continued to exercise reported less use of medication and fewer of them were classified as depressed by clinical interview.

Table 9.11 Published randomised controlled studies of exercise treatment for clinically defined depression

Authors and geographical location	Participants and clinical assessment	Design (all RCT)	Treatment groups	Measures	Results (statistically significant at 0.05)
Greist et al. (1979) USA	n = 28 (15 women), RDC criteria for depression	10 weeks of treatment, 1- and 3-month follow-up	1) 10 sessions of time-limited psychotherapy; 2) time-unlimited psychotherapy; 3) running with a leader 3 × 30–45 mins/week	SCL	The running treatment was as effective as the two psychotherapy treatments
Klein et al. (1985) USA	n = 74 (53 women), mean age 30 years, recruited via media, RDC criteria for depression	12 weeks of treatment and 1-, 3- and 9-month follow-up	1) running with a leader, 2 × 45 mins/week; 2) group meditation, 2 hours/week; 3) group therapy, 2 hours/week	SCL and psychiatric interview	The running treatment was as effective as the other two treatments
Martinsen et al. (1985) Norway	n = 43, mean age 40 years, hospitalised depressives; clinical assessment by DSM-III	9 weeks of treatment	1) exercise group, aerobic training, 50–70% max. V_{O_2}, 1 hour, 3/week; 2) control group, occupational therapy, 1 hour, 3/week	BDI; predicted max. V_{O_2}	The exercise group decreased depression scores and increased fitness more than the control group
Doyne et al. (1987) USA	n = 40 (all women) recruited through mass media; mean age 29 years; clinical assessment by RDC	8 weeks of treatment; 1, 7, 12-month follow-up	1) aerobic group (running), 4/week; 2) non-aerobic group (weight-lifting); 4/week; 3) waiting list control group	BDI; HRSD; cardiovascular fitness (METS) from sub-maximal test	Both exercise conditions reduced depression more than waiting list control. Levels of depression remained lower than baseline to 1-year follow-up
Fremont and Craighead (1987) USA	n = 49, recruitment via advertisement, BDI scores of 16 and above	10 weeks of treatment and 2-month follow-up	1) cognitive therapy 1 hour/week; 2) running with a leader, 3 × 20mins/week; 3) both cognitive therapy and running	BDI	All three groups improved. Improvements maintained at 2-month follow-up
Martinsen, Hoffart and Solberg (1989b) Norway	n = 99 (63 women), mean age 41 years, hospitalised depressives, RDC classification	8 weeks of treatment	1) aerobic training, 3 × 1 hour/week; 2) strength and flexibility training, 3 × 1 hour/week	Montgomery–Asberg rating scale, predicted V_{O_2} max.	Both groups decreased depression scores. Only the aerobic group made gains on max. V_{O_2}

Continued overleaf

Table 9.11 continued

Authors and geographical location	Participants and clinical assessment	Design (all RCT)	Treatment groups	Measures	Results (statistically significant at 0.05)
Veale et al. (1992) trial 1 UK	$n = 83$ (53 women) mean age 36 years, clinical assessment by CIS	12 weeks of treatment	1) standard treatment; 2) aerobic exercise (3/week running) adjunctive to standard treatment	CIS, BDI, predicted V_{O_2} max.	Exercise group reduced depressive symptoms (CIS) and trait anxiety more than standard group despite incomplete adherence by some S's
Veale et al. (1992) trial 2 UK	$n = 41$; clinical assessment by CIS	12 weeks of treatment	each group received standard treatment and either: 1) aerobic exercise (3/week); or 2) non-aerobic exercise (stretching, yoga) (3/week)	CIS, BDI, predicted V_{O_2} max.	Both exercise groups showed similar changes to that seen in study 1 above. No differences between groups on any measures
Bosscher (1993) Netherlands	$n = 24$ (12 women), mean age 34 years, hospitalised depressives, RDC classification, SDS >40	8 weeks of treatment	1) standard movement therapy of mixed games and exercises, 50 mins. 3/week; 2) running 45 mins. 3/week	SDS	Only the running group showed significant decreases in depression although scores still above entry level criteria. No fitness measures taken
Singh, Clements and Fiatarone (1997) USA and Singh, Clements and Singh (2001)	$n = 32$ (20 women), mean age 71 years, clinical assessment by DSM-IV criteria	10 weeks of supervised treatment with follow-up at 20 weeks and 26 months	1) progressive resistance training (PRT) 3/week; 2) attention – control group meeting 2/week	BDI, HRSD, SF-36, strength (1 repetition max.)	At 10 weeks, all depression measures, strength, SF-36 subscales of bodily pain, vitality, social functioning and role emotional showed significantly greater improvements in PRT group than controls. BDI scores at 20 weeks and 26 months significantly reduced in exercisers compared to controls. 33% exercisers and 0% controls still weight lifting at 26 months
Janakiramaiah et al. (2000) India	$n = 45$ inpatients with melancholia	4 weeks	1) Sudarshan Kriya Yoga (SKY); 2) modified electroconvulsive therapy (ECT); 3) imipramine (IMN)	HRSD, BDI	All three groups decreased depression over time. Remission rates were 67%, 93% and 73% for groups 1–3 respectively

Continued

Table 9.11 continued

Authors and geographical location	Participants and clinical assessment	Design (all RCT)	Treatment groups	Measures	Results (statistically significant at 0.05)
Blumenthal *et al.* (1999) and Babyak *et al.* (2000) USA	*n* = 156 (113 women), mean age 57 years, clinical assessment by DSM-IV criteria. Recruited via media and local physicians	16 weeks of treatment and follow-up 6 months later	1) aerobic exercise 3/week supervised; 2) antidepressant medication; 3) a combination of 1 and 2	HRSD, BDI, peak aerobic capacity (Balke protocol)	All 3 groups reduced depression scores at 16 weeks and maintained the reduction at 6 months. Both exercise groups increased aerobic fitness. Faster response to medication alone. At 6 months, fewer in exercise group classified as depressed, had relapsed or used medication
Mather *et al.* (2002) UK	Older adults (aged over 53 years) with poorly responsive depressive disorder. Clinical interview with ICD-10 classification	10 weeks of treatment and follow-up at 34 weeks	1) exercise classes; 2) health education talks	HRSD	A significantly higher proportion of the group assigned to exercise classes (55% versus 33%) experienced greater than 30% decline in HRSD scores at 10 weeks
(Singh *et al.* 2005) USA	Older adults aged over 60 years (*n* = 60)	8 weeks	1) High intensity (80% max) progressive resistance training (PRT) 3 days per week; 2) Low intensity (20% max) PRT 3 days per week; 3) Standard care by GP	HRSD, response rate and various quality of life indices including sleep.	High-intensity PRT was more effective than low-intensity PRT or GP care. A 50% reduction in HRSD score was achieved in 61% of the high-intensity, 29% of the low-intensity, and 21% of the GP care group (p = 0.03).
Dunn *et al.* (2005) USA	*n* = 80 (75% women), age range 20–45, assessment by SCID. Recruited via a depression and anxiety programme in a medical centre	12 weeks of supervised exercise in laboratory setting. Public health dose of exercise defined as 17.5 kcal/kg/week	1) placebo exercise control (stretching); 2) 7kcal/kg/week achieved in 3 days' aerobic exercise; 3) 7 kcal/kg/week achieved in 5 days' aerobic exercise; 4) 17.5 kcal/kg/week achieved in 3 days' aerobic exercise (public health dose); 5) 17.5 kcal/kg/week achieved in 5 days' aerobic exercise (public health dose)	HRSD, response and remission rates	The public health dose of exercise was more effective in reducing depression scores to a clinically acceptable level than the lower dose or the control condition. Frequency was not important

Continued overleaf

Table 9.11 continued

Key to abbreviations

RDC	(Research Diagnostic Criteria) (Spitzer, Endicott and Robins 1978)
DSM-III or IV	(Diagnostic and Statistical Manual of Mental Disorders) (Association 1980, 1994)
SCL	(Symptom Checklist) (Derogatis, Lipman and Covi 1973)
BDI	(Beck Depression Inventory) (Beck *et al.* 1961)
HRSD	(Hamilton Rating Scale) (Hamilton 1960)
POMS	(Profile of Mood States) (McNair, Lorr and Droppleman 1971)
CIS	(Clinical Interview Schedule) (Goldberg *et al.* 1970)
SDS	(Zung Depression Scale) (Zung, Richards and Short 1965)
SF-36	(Medical Outcomes Survey Short Form) (Ware *et al.* 1993)
CES	Center for Epidemiological Studies Depression Scale

This should be viewed as substantive evidence of the role of exercise in the treatment of depression. Since Lawlor and Hopker completed their systematic review and meta-analysis in 2001 new studies with more sophisticated designs have been added to the literature (and some studies included by Lawlor and Hopker have not been included here because they were not published in peer reviewed journals). New themes include the comparison of exercise and drug therapy, the use of progressive resistance training as an exercise mode and more studies focusing on older adults. There remains, as with our commentary on the available literature in the previous edition of this book in 2001, a serious gap in the literature concerning the use of exercise as a treatment for depression in children and adolescents. The studies in Table 9.11 span ages from over twenty-five to over seventy, but not under twenty-five years. Only one study on the use of exercise as an adjunctive treatment in clinically diagnosed mental illness in children was found (Brown *et al.* 1992), but it was excluded from the table of key studies because it did not reach the design criteria.

Gaps in the literature

Only two studies in Table 9.11 compared the effects of exercise treatment with drug treatment. This seems surprising given that drugs are the most common treatment for depression in the UK, and it is also surprising that so few studies have been conducted in the UK. The next step for researchers in this area is to compare drug therapy with exercise therapy in a realistic setting such as primary care. A trial of this nature is currently under way in Bristol in the UK and the results should again add to the knowledge in this important area. A trial of exercise for depression on adolescents and children is also required. Although seven of the studies have now reported follow-ups, we still do not know much about adherence levels to exercise especially in the follow-up phases. Finally, many patients do not wish to take medication and exercise is a potential alternative for them (Scott 1996), but no studies have examined the issue of exercise as an element of patient choice. There is also a continuing debate about how well this evidence matches up to the criteria that might be required to show a causal connection between activity levels and depression and this will be tackled later in the chapter. There is still a long research agenda on this topic!

Examples of studies with good design features

Two studies will now be discussed in more detail since they show good design features. The studies by Blumenthal *et al.* (1999) and Dunn and colleagues (2005) have taken this area of work forward considerably. Blumenthal compared exercise to standard drug therapy or a combination of both treatments over a sixteen-week period and found that all three groups reported significant reductions in depression (see Figure 9.4). In a follow-up study of the same participants, Babyack *et al.* (2000) reported some advantages for exercise over a six month period including smaller percentages of those in the original exercise intervention being classified as depressed or using medication. This landmark study was the first to show that exercise by itself had similar outcomes to standard antidepressant medication.

Dunn *et al.* (2005) conducted a very tightly controlled study which aimed to answer some of the questions concerning dose–response. In particular, this study compared frequency of exercise (three or five days per week) and total energy expenditure per week (7 kcal/kg/week 'low dose' versus 17.5 kcal/kg/week 'public health dose') in a twelve-week protocol. Four aerobic exercise conditions allowed these comparisons; two groups exercised on three days a week – one expended 7 kcal/kg/week and the other 17 kcal/kg/week; two other groups exercised on five days a week but expended the same totals of either 7 or 17.5 kcal/kg/week.

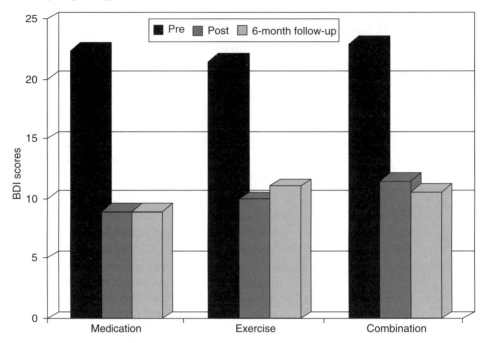

Figure 9.4 BDI scores pre and post 16 weeks of treatment (from Blumenthal *et al.* 1999) and 6-month follow up (Babyak *et al.* 2000)

Participants were randomly assigned to one of these four groups or to a placebo exercise condition which involved stretching exercises on three days of the week. Results showed that the public health dose reduced depression scores more than the lower dose but that frequency did not matter (see Figure 9.5). All the exercise was completed in sessions which were supervised but in which the participants were isolated from other exercisers. Thus the effect of exercising in a group cannot be one of the possible explanations of these results. This is the first trial that has been well enough controlled to rule out a number of previous possible explanations and shows that exercise at a dose recommended for public health (the equivalent of thirty minutes on most days of the week) can be a stand-alone treatment for mild and moderate depression. So far these authors have not yet reported any follow-up data but hopefully this will be forthcoming.

It is clearly difficult to conduct studies with good design features in this area. Dunn *et al.*'s study is one of the few that overcome some of the most common limitations and challenges to researchers in this area. Below are limitations and challenges noted along with a comment about the Dunn *et al.* study:

- achieving a large enough sample to ensure statistical power (could the findings of 'no difference' between some conditions be a type 2 statistical error?): Dunn *et al.*'s study did achieve sufficient statistical power for between-group comparison.
- equalising time in contact with professionals in the different treatment conditions: Dunn *et al.* achieved this and show a benefit for a public health dose of exercise in comparison with other conditions that had equal time in contacts
- conducting 'double-blind' studies. The gold standard within RCTs, in which the effect of a drug is being tested, is that both the researcher and the client/patient is blind to what

drug treatment they have been given. In exercise studies this is not possible to achieve because the patient will certainly know, in a way that is different from receiving an unmarked tablet, that they are exercising. While every effort should be made to keep studies single-blind (that is, the researcher taking outcome measures should not know the group assignment), it remains a challenge to achieve this. Clients and patients often reveal their assignment to researchers who are otherwise blind to assignment in conversation, such as 'I really enjoyed that weight training'

- avoiding resentful demoralisation in a no-treatment group or a group given the 'routine' or placebo condition as opposed to the 'new' treatment. Dunn *et al.* acknowledge that the placebo control group had a bigger dropout after randomisation than the exercise conditions and 'resentful demoralisation' remains a challenge for researchers to overcome
- controlling for the effects of the positive characteristics of an exercise leader or the social effect of a group. Dunn *et al.* equalised the leadership effect and negated the social effect. However, they still found an effect for exercise. Nevertheless, the social aspect of group exercise may add further benefits and group versus individual exercise should now be compared
- conducting long-term follow-up. Blumenthal achieved six months and hopefully Dunn *et al.* will follow up participants in their study
- finding adequate measures of the variables of interest including total energy expenditure. Dunn *et al.* measured total energy expenditure and not just self-reported physical activity.

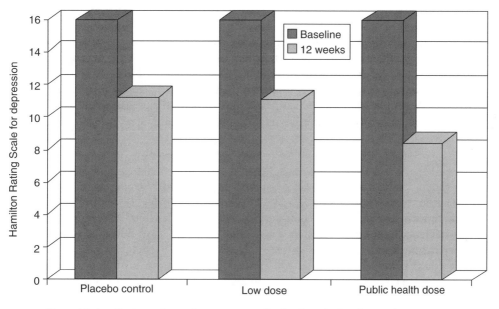

The public health dose of exercise was more effective in reducing depression scores to a clinically acceptable level than the lower dose or the control condition. Frequency of exercise (3 or 5 days/week) was not important.

Figure 9.5 Exercise treatment for depression: efficacy and dose–response (Dunn *et al.* 2005)

Evaluating the evidence for the antidepressant effect of exercise

It is still difficult to conclude that there is a causal link between exercise and reduction in depression because there are many peripheral issues (such as the effect of an exercise leader or a class effect) associated with most of the successful programmes. Also there are relatively few experimental studies in comparison with areas such as the physiological benefits of exercise. Nevertheless, given the addition of epidemiological data to the discussion, it may be appropriate to use Hill's (1965) classic criteria for deciding whether there is a causal link between observed illness (in this case depression) and some environmental condition (in this case exercise status). Hill suggested eight criteria that can be used to help scientists and practitioners decide if a causal interpretation of evidence can be made. These eight criteria will be used to draw conclusions concerning any antidepressant effect of exercise. The eight criteria are:

- strength of association
- consistency of evidence
- specificity of effect
- temporal sequencing
- dose–response relationship
- biological plausibility
- coherence
- experimental evidence.

Strength of association

Meta-analytic studies show an effect size between -0.53 and -1.1 for exercise on depression. Epidemiological studies suggest a relative risk of around 1.7 for the inactive reporting depression at a later date. This evidence is not quite as strong as that for exercise and coronary heart disease, where a range of relative risk of between 1.5 to 2.5 for the inactive has been reported (Pate *et al.* 1995). Nevertheless, the strength of association between exercise and depression is clear to see and is moderate-to-large in magnitude.

Consistency

Hill's second criterion is consistency – the question of whether or not the association between exercise and depression has been shown in different places, with different people, at different times and in different circumstances. If we look at Table 9.11 we can see that experimental evidence has been found in the USA, UK and elsewhere in Europe. The same is true of the epidemiological evidence shown in Tables 9.8 and 9.9. Men and women have been studied, adults of middle and older ages groups have been included, the data span three decades, and the circumstances include community, hospitals and primary care settings. So it does seem that the findings are consistent.

Specificity

Specificity refers to whether or not other associations exist between the environmental conditions and disease. Hill argues that if specificity can be claimed (that is, limiting the conditions to the disease, such as smoking and lung cancer) that this strengthens the argument for causation. In exercise studies specificity does not exist. Depression is not the only disease linked to inactivity, nor is inactivity the only environmental condition associated to depression. Furthermore, depression itself has multiple causes (Kaplan *et al.* 1987). However, Hill also argued that if specificity is not present other criteria may supply extra evidence.

Temporal sequence

In order to conclude that there is a causal link between inactivity and depression we must demonstrate that inactivity precedes the onset of depression. Early cross-sectional studies could not provide an answer to this question because it was equally likely that depression preceded inactivity. However, there are now eight prospective populations studies showing that the inactive are more likely to develop depression (Table 9.8) while three such studies failed to show this protective effect (Table 9.9). Thus the weight of the evidence supports the notion of the temporal sequence being appropriate which strengthens the causation argument.

Dose–response relationship

Hill's fifth criterion is evidence for a dose–response curve or biological gradient. Several of the prospective epidemiological studies have shown a dose–response gradient, with the least active at baseline being most at risk of developing depression at follow-up, while the most active had the lowest risk. In terms of experimental studies, although both aerobic and non-aerobic exercise have produced an antidepressant effect, almost all the aerobic exercise has been based on moderate intensity (60–75 per cent) levels with a typical prescription of three times per week for twenty to sixty minutes. Dunn *et al.*'s (2005) experimental study has provided evidence that, at least for aerobic exercise, the public health dose (equivalent to thirty minutes on most days of the week) produced an antidepressant effect whereas a smaller dose did not. Thus, while there are a variety of 'doses' that have not yet been tested, there is evidence for a dose–response relationship which again adds to the evidence for a causal connection.

Plausibility

The sixth criterion is biological plausibility. Here we are looking for the explanation of the observed association. There is agreement that the underlying mechanisms of the effects of exercise on mental illness are not yet known (Biddle and Mutrie 1991; Morgan 1997; Morgan and Goldston 1987; Plante 1993). Several possible mechanisms, including biochemical changes, such as increased levels of endorphins, and psychological changes, such as an increased sense of mastery, have been proposed (La Forge 1995; Petruzzello *et al.* 1991). The studies showing an antidepressant effect for non-aerobic exercise suggest that improvement in aerobic fitness is not a key issue. However, objective measures of all possible fitness parameters (aerobic, strength, flexibility and body composition) should be included in studies to provide evidence that the exercise programme has had the desired fitness effect and to shed light on potential mechanisms.

The fact that we do not know which mechanism operates should not prevent us saying they remain 'plausible'. Dishman (1995), in his excellent review of this topic, concludes that our lack of knowledge about the biological plausibility of the association between exercise and mental health is a major shortcoming. This may contribute to the lack of acceptance of the role of exercise by psychiatrists (Hale 1997). However, Hill reminds us that we should not demand too much of this criterion because 'what is biologically plausible depends upon the biological knowledge of the day' (Hill 1965: 298). Determining the mechanisms for the psychological effects of exercise in general and for depression in particular is perhaps the greatest challenge to exercise scientists trying to illuminate the relationship between exercise and mental health. It is clear that the answer to this complex question will not be found in exercise laboratories alone. We must collaborate with colleagues in neuroscience and psychological medicine to expand our knowledge. A longer discussion of potential mechanisms can be found in Chapter 10.

Coherence

The possible mechanisms should not conflict with what is understood to be the natural history and biology of mental illness. This is Hill's criterion of coherence. While, as with many other aspects of these criteria, the evidence is far from complete, two examples might show coherence. More women than men report depression and women report less activity than men. Also the prevalence of depression increases with age and so does the prevalence of inactivity. Development of animal models to study inactivity and depression, and the use of exercise to combat depression, will provide further evidence for coherence.

Experimental evidence

Perhaps the best evidence comes under Hill's criterion of experimental evidence. This has already been discussed in the conclusions from the key studies represented in Table 9.11. The experimental evidence supports a causal link between exercise programmes and depression reduction.

In reviewing the evidence using Hill's (1965) criteria it can be seen that the only criterion not satisfied is that of specificity. Other criteria, such as plausibility and coherence, have only modest evidence, but there is no evidence for specificity. However, when all of this evidence is taken together we think it is reasonable to conclude that there is supportive evidence for a causal link between inactivity and depression. There are those who might say that the evidence is still insufficient and therefore we should not recommend the use of exercise in the treatment of depression or consider inactivity to be a factor in the onset of depression. However, as Hill reminded us,

> All scientific work is incomplete – whether it be observational or experimental. All scientific work is liable to be upset or modified by advancing knowledge. That does not confer upon us a freedom to ignore the knowledge we already have, or postpone the action that it appears to demand at a given time.
>
> (Hill 1965: 12)

The potential benefit of advocating the use of exercise as part of treatment for depression far outweighs the potential risk that no effect will occur. There are very few possible negative side effects (for example, injury, exercise dependence) and there have been no negative outcomes reported in the literature. In addition, there are potential physical health benefits such as an increase in fitness, weight reduction and decreased coronary artery disease risks. Therefore, physical activity and exercise should be advocated as part of the treatment for clinically defined depression.

Other reviewers are less positive about this causal connection. For example, Landers and Arent (2001) said that 'It is premature ... to state with certainty that exercise causes reductions in depression' and O'Neal *et al.* stated that 'there is insufficient evidence to fully describe the relationship between exercise and depression' (O'Neal, Dunn and Martinsen 2000). In 2001, Dunn *et al.* said 'At this point the evidence is suggestive but not convincing' (Dunn, Trivedi and O'Neal 2001). We have always argued that the evidence as it stands could be viewed in a glass half empty or a glass half full kind of way. We favour the half-full view and believe that there really is a causal connection to be made.

While we would not want to overstate the evidence we do wonder what the risk of looking at the evidence in a glass half full and optimistic way really is. Some people might say that the evidence is not causal and that there are only associations or even a placebo effect. Such a response is difficult for researchers to refute without further evidence but should not stop people advocating the use of exercise for depression. Others might take the view that this will not work for everyone. Of course this is true and it is also true of many treatments in medicine. But exercise has an advantage here because it really is a 'win–win' scenario. Providing that people do increase their physical activity levels, then there are numerous health benefits that can be accrued even if it does not help with depression. There are very few treatments that can boast this kind of promise. Then there are those who are sceptical because we do not know exactly why exercise might have this positive effect on depression. Just because we do not know how a treatment works should not really stop us using it. For example, one treatment for depression that is still used for extreme cases in the UK is electro convulsive therapy (ECT). This is still advocated even though it is not known how it works. Furthermore, there have been no negative effects reported from the use of exercise for depression which cannot be said for most of the antidepressant medications, the literature accompanying which usually clearly states the risk of negative side effects.

The fact that the knowledge base is incomplete and that the evidence for a causal connection between inactivity and depression is not universally accepted should not stop mental health practitioners of all kinds from advocating that their patients and clients should become more physically active. At best this may help them feel less depressed and at worst this could have a positive health impact on other aspects of their lives – what is there to lose? For example, it has been shown that those who experience bipolar disorder have increased risk of mortality from cardiovascular causes and pulmonary embolism, and increased risk of morbidity from obesity and Type 2 diabetes, in comparison with the general population (Morriss and Mohammed 2005). In addition, such patients often have low exercise levels, so even if by exercising they do not improve the bipolar disorder (it is recognised that there may well be genetic factors that make it unlikely that exercise could be a stand-alone treatment for this disorder), they may decrease their overall health risks – exercise is a win–win scenario if used correctly.

Summary: clinical depression

The evidence concerning the relationship between physical activity and clinical depression shows:

- cross-sectional population surveys support an association between higher levels of physical activity and lower levels of depression
- the weight of evidence shows that prospective studies suggest a protective effect from activity on the development of depression, but not all studies show this
- meta-analytic findings show a large effect size from studies that have used exercise as a treatment for depression
- the weight of the evidence suggests that there is a causal connection between physical activity/exercise and depression.

Future research directions

We offer the following directions for future work:

- use population studies to show connections with physical activity and mental health – physical activity must be adequately measured
- feasibility and pilot studies are required with specific categories of anxiety disorder to determine if physical activity and exercise could be useful adjuncts to treatment
- studies that explore the relationship between physical activity and mental health for children and adolescents are required
- further studies on comparisons of exercise treatment and standard drug treatments are required in the area of depression
- multi-disciplinary research is required to determine the mechanisms by which exercise can produce the 'feel-better' or antidepressant effects

Chapter summary

In summary, for the whole chapter, the major conclusions are:

- meta-analytic findings suggest that exercise is associated with a significant small-to-moderate reduction in non-clinical anxiety
- experimental studies support an anxiety-reducing effect for non-clinical anxiety
- large-scale epidemiological surveys offer mixed support for anxiety-reducing effects for exercise but there are few surveys that have anxiety data
- physiological reactivity to psychosocial stressors appears to be reduced for those high in aerobic fitness
- very little is known about how physical activity and exercise relate to clinical anxiety conditions at a population level
- experimental studies are not yet convincing enough to suggest a causal link between activity and reduction of clinical anxiety
- there is no evidence that exercise might induce panic or anxiety in participants with anxiety disorders
- meta-analytic findings suggest that exercise is associated with a significant moderate reduction in non-clinical depression
- large-scale epidemiological surveys support the claim that a physically active lifestyle is associated with lower levels of non-clinical depression
- the weight of evidence shows that prospective studies suggest a protective effect from activity on the development of clinical levels of depression
- meta-analytic findings show a large effect size from studies that have used exercise as a treatment for clinically defined depression
- the weight of the evidence suggests that there is a causal connection between physical activity/exercise and depression reduction.

10 The psychology of exercise for clinical populations

Exercise can be good for you even when you are ill

Exercise was invented and used to clean the body when it was too full of harmful things.

Christobal Mendez, 1500–1561

(Berryman 2000)

Chapter objectives

This chapter aims to review the role of physical activity and exercise in the treatment of a variety of clinical populations. Anxiety and depression have been excluded from this chapter because they are comprehensively reviewed in Chapter 9, but other mental illnesses, such as schizophrenia and substance abuse are included. We use the American College of Sports Medicine's (ACSM) classification of disease and disability as a framework and examples of psychological issues for specific conditions from each category have been given. Specifically, this chapter will:

- highlight the psychological issues associated with exercise for clinical populations
- discuss the role of exercise psychology in a clinical team
- use the American College of Sports Medicine's framework for classifying disease and disability
- provide examples of psychological issues for each category in the ACSM framework, including:

  - cardiovascular and pulmonary diseases
  - metabolic diseases
  - immunological and haematological disorders
  - orthopaedic diseases and disabilities
  - neuromuscular disorders
  - cognitive, emotional and sensory disorders

- summarise what we know in this area of exercise psychology
- offer a guide to good practice
- provide recommendations for conducting research in exercise psychology with clinical populations.

Clinical populations can be defined as those people who have sought help for a particular medical condition, who are under medical observation or who have been diagnosed by a relevant clinical specialist. Structured or supervised exercise has been promoted for a host of medical conditions for some time. Bouchard, Shephard and Stephens (1994) listed twenty-four medical conditions for which exercise has a potential therapeutic role. Research on the efficacy of exercise for these clinical groups grew out of the knowledge that had been accumulated on the prevention and treatment of cardiovascular disease through exercise and activity (Pate *et al.* 1995). Initial interest in the role of exercise for clinical populations came from physicians and exercise physiologists who used exercise tests as part of a medical diagnosis or who sought physical improvements and decreased morbidity and mortality for their patients. More recently it has been recognised that longevity is perhaps not the key issue for exercise with these patient groups, and that quality of life and the ability to function in everyday activities are more salient issues. The American College of Sports Medicine (ACSM) has produced a comprehensive text on managing exercise programmes for clinical populations to assist the increasing number of exercise specialists in this area (American College of Sports Medicine 1997a). Moore (1997), in the introductory chapter of this text, summarised the short history of the rationale for exercise programmes with clinical populations as follows:

> in the 1980s, research and clinical applications for exercise expanded to populations with a variety of chronic diseases and disabilities, for whom exercise is perhaps more fundamentally related to quality of life rather than quantity of life. Perhaps the greatest potential benefit of exercise is its ability to preserve functional capacity, freedom and independence.
>
> (Moore 1997: 3)

There are two issues to be considered in discussing the psychological aspects of exercise for clinical populations. First, exercise clearly has a contribution to make to enhancing quality of life for clinical populations. Quality of life could be considered as a broad heading under which various physical and psychological outcomes from exercise programmes could be placed. Quality of life can be measured by life conditions such as employment status and, more commonly by subjective appraisals. Such appraisals can be made using standard 'quality of life' tools such as the SF–36 (Jenkinson *et al.* 1999) or the EuroQol (Brooks 1996), but they can also be made qualitatively because what is important to each person in terms of their perception of their own quality of life will vary. Felce (1997) provided a model of quality of life which integrated objective and subjective indicators and individual values across a broad range of life domains. These domains include six areas in which quality of life issues emerge: physical, material, social, productive, emotional and civic well-being (Felce 1997). It is clear that exercise has the potential to influence both objective and subjective indicators in this framework. The framework should assist exercise psychologists to assess the relationship between exercise and quality of life by various techniques such as standard questionnaires, qualitative interviews and, providing they are appropriately trained, by the use of tests of physical function.

Second, if exercise is to be beneficial to patients we must be able to keep them involved in activity over the longest time possible and thus psychologists clearly have a role to play. The process of keeping people involved in beneficial activity has been under-researched in comparison with the medical outcomes from such activities. In order to promote exercise adherence for patients who have a defined medical condition, an understanding of the psychological factors which affect adherence, along with an understanding of the particular challenges to exercise which the various medical conditions create, is required. The prescribed exercise treatment may present problems because patients are not confident of their physical abilities or the medical conditions themselves may present difficulties for the intending exerciser.

Key point: It is important to apply principles of exercise psychology to clinical populations because quality of life is an important outcome from exercise and long-term adherence is beneficial to these patient groups.

The focus of this chapter will be the assessment of quality of life, using the broadest definition of this phrase, and the psychology of starting and maintaining exercise for these patient groups. Guidelines for good practice and for researching psychological outcomes and adherence are also provided.

Working with clinical populations

It is likely that exercise specialists working with clinical populations will be part of a team of clinicians and paramedical staff such as physiotherapists. In many situations the physiotherapists are seen as the exercise specialist and so this chapter may apply not only to exercise specialists but also to physiotherapists. Exercise is one part of a multi-treatment package designed to help the patient. It is clear that such exercise specialists need an understanding of the physiological demands of exercise and the adaptations and limitations that various conditions will impose. Such specialists may be in charge of exercise testing for diagnostic or exercise prescription purposes. Thus a solid background in exercise physiology is required. However, it is clear that knowledge of exercise psychology is also very important. Exercise psychology will provide an understanding of the psycho-social issues that will affect test results (for example, anxiety may affect exercise treadmill tests involving voluntary termination) and the ability to undertake the prescription of exercise (for example, the patient may not believe exercise will help and is thus unlikely to adhere to the programme). In addition there are beneficial psychological outcomes from exercise participation which may play an important motivational role (Fox 1997b); when people perceive benefit then it is more likely that they will continue to be active. Some hospitals now employ exercise therapists who work alongside physiotherapists providing appropriate exercise prescriptions. Some specialists groups, such as the British Association of Cardiac Rehabilitation (BACR), provide training courses for exercise specialists working in cardiac rehabilitation and this training includes exercise psychology. The British Association of Sport and Exercise Sciences (BASES) provides an accreditation and supervised experience system to ensure quality control in the area of physical activity and health. Many local authorities offer specialist classes for those with low back pain, or those suffering from osteoporosis or who are undertaking cardiac rehabilitation in a community setting. The leaders of such classes must be specialists in the particular kind of exercise that may be most beneficial, the contraindications that such conditions present and also on how to help people maintain activity beyond the class. It would seem that this is an expanding field of application.

It is likely that the prevailing ethos in clinical settings is one that adheres to a medical model that focuses more on diagnosis and prescription of treatment than on the person. This model would normally lead to the same exercise prescription being offered for all patients, such as group classes in cardiac rehabilitation. However, with regard to exercise adherence, a person-centred approach should be considered. This implies that the same exercise prescription is not suitable for all people. Instead the exercise prescription must be tailored to each person's circumstances and provide them with control over their exercise rather than maintaining control within the hospital setting. The long-term goal must be independent exercisers and not exercisers who are dependent on hospital supervision or even specialised classes. This idea fits very well with the current 'Active Living' recommendations for increasing activity; this suggests that sedentary people should aim to accumulate around thirty minutes of moderate intensity activity, such as walking, most days of the week (Pate *et al.* 1995).

> Key point: The long-term goal for exercise specialists working with patient populations is to assist them in becoming independent exercisers.

Loughlan and Mutrie (1995) have advocated a consultation approach which uses a variety of cognitive–behavioural techniques to maximise adherence to recommendations and we have tested these in a variety of clinical populations including Type 2 diabetics and cardiac rehabilitation. It is likely that patients are not active and therefore a consultation approach may be more appealing to them. This approach includes:

• understanding the person's exercise and activity history
• allowing them to say what they feel are the benefits and drawbacks of increasing activity levels
• helping them see ways to overcome stated barriers to activity
• looking for ways to assist motivation like finding an exercise 'buddy'
• getting support from family and friends
• helping them set realistic short- and long-term goals concerning their activity levels
• discussing with them relapse prevention strategies.

This approach will be further explained in Chapter 11 but applications to Type 2 diabetic patients, to cardiac rehabilitation and to group exercise opportunities for women undergoing treatment for breast cancer will be discussed in this chapter.

Categories of clinical populations

The framework suggested by ACSM (1997a), which is shown in Table 10.1, classifies forty separate medical conditions into six categories of disease or disability. This framework has been adapted for use in this chapter. Within each category we have selected at least one and often several of the sub-categories to provide more detailed discussion. These sub-category examples will focus on the known physical and psychological benefits of exercise, special challenges for adherence, and what is known about motivations and barriers. The inclusion of certain conditions within each category was based on current literature searches using adherence (and associated words) or psychological benefits as key terms and our own work in these areas. We are not intending to provide a comprehensive review of each of the conditions within each of the categories. Instead we have selected relevant examples and this may have resulted in omissions of areas that do have lessons for exercise psychology.

Table 10.1 The American College of Sports Medicine's classification of diseases and disabilities (American College of Sports Medicine 1997a)

Major category of disease/disability	Sub-categories
1 Cardiovascular and pulmonary diseases	Myocardial infarction
	Coronary artery bypass grafting angioplasty
	Angina and silent ischaemia
	Pacemakers and implantable cardioverter defibrillators
	Valvular heart diseases
	Congestive heart failure
	Cardiac transplant
	Hypertension
	Peripheral arterial disease
	Aneurysms and marfan syndrome
	Pulmonary disease
	Cystic fibrosis
2 Metabolic diseases	Renal failure
	Diabetes
	Hyperlipidaemia
	Obesity
	Frailty
3 Immunological/Haematological disorders	Cancer
	Anaemia
	Bleeding disorders
	Acquired immune deficiency syndrome
	Organ transplant
	Chronic fatigue syndrome
4 Orthopaedic diseases and disabilities	Arthritis
	Low back pain syndrome
	Osteoporosis
5 Neuromuscular disorders	Stroke and head injury
	Spinal cord injury
	Muscular dystrophy
	Epilepsy
	Multiple sclerosis
	Polio and post-polio syndrome
	Amyotrophic lateral sclerosis
	Cerebral palsy
	Parkinson's disease
6 Cognitive, emotional and sensory disorders	Mental retardation
	Alzheimer's disease
	Mental illness
	Deaf and hard of hearing
	Visual impairment

Cardiovascular and pulmonary diseases

Chronic obstructive pulmonary disorders (COPD)

COPD includes asthma, chronic bronchitis and emphysema (Higgins 1989). As much as 10 per cent of the world's population suffer from asthma and the incidence of asthma is increasing, particularly for children. In the UK, asthma is the most frequent medical reason for children being absent from school and for repeated visits to their GP (Holgate 1993). There is often a spiral of inactivity from COPD sufferers since one main symptom is dyspnoea (the sensation of breathlessness). When dyspnoea is experienced activity levels are likely to drop and this leads to further 'deconditioning', meaning that activity may feel more difficult and non-adherence is therefore more likely. Pulmonary rehabilitation programmes based on exercise have a short but reasonably successful history (Lacasse *et al.* 1996). Adherence to exercise programmes for people with COPD has been studied (Atkins *et al.* 1984) and the results have enhanced knowledge on the effectiveness of various adherence strategies. These studies show that cognitive behaviour modification strategies will work with this patient group, with simple techniques such as goal-setting increasing the number of minutes walked in an eleven-week programme almost four times as much as the control group.

Exercise programmes also confer psychological benefits in terms of increased quality of life and decreased depression and anxiety (Singh *et al.* 1997). It would appear that part of the explanation of such benefits lies in the social interaction which exercise classes provide and the reassurance that other people of a similar age and with the same illness can cope and improve their exercise capacity. It has also been noted that such rehabilitation programmes can benefit the patient's family by providing them with reassurance that other families cope with breathlessness and that exercise is to be encouraged (Petty 1993). Special challenges for COPD patients and exercise include the issue that for some asthmatics exercise is a double-edged sword. On the one hand it can improve overall functional capacity and reduce breathlessness but, on the other hand, it can also induce an asthmatic attack (Belman 1989). Exercise programmes must be tailored to avoid breathlessness and there may be the need to overcome a belief from such patients and their families that they should not exercise. Special advice on how and when to use medication in conjunction with exercise is usually required (Gordon 1993b).

Cardiac rehabilitation

Exercise-based cardiac rehabilitation programmes were widespread in the USA in the 1980s (Naughton 1985) but their introduction in the UK was relatively slow by comparison (Gloag 1985), despite the greater percentage of the UK population who will suffer a myocardial infarction (MI) (Tunstall-Pedoe and Smith 1986). The reasons for such caution in the UK are unclear. Perhaps the reason is as simple as finding the extra cost of mounting these programmes within an already stretched National Health Service budget. Perhaps the reason is the more complex point that medical consultants review success in medical treatment of MI in terms of decreased mortality and the early evidence for that via exercise was equivocal (Naughton 1985). Meta-analysis with varying inclusion criteria have concluded that MI patients who had a cardiac rehabilitation programme that included exercise have between 20 per cent and 27 per cent reduction in mortality compared with controls (Jolliffe *et al.* 2000; O'Conner *et al.* 1989; Oldridge *et al.* 1988).

Given the need to heal infarcted heart tissue and improve the efficiency of the cardiovascular system, it is not surprising to note that most research on the effect of exercise during cardiac rehabilitation has focused on physiological and cardiovascular parameters (Dugmore 1992). Oldridge *et al.* (1988) suggested that improvements in psychological well-being and quality of life may be more beneficial than changes in exercise tolerance.

Anxiety and depression are perhaps the most frequently measured psychological outcomes. Milani, Lavie and Cassidy (1996) estimated that 20 per cent of cardiac patients exhibit symptoms of depression four to six weeks after a cardiac event. There has been more work on psychological outcomes for this group of patients than any other clinical group. Kugler, Seelbach and Kruskemper (1994) completed a meta-analysis of fifteen studies that had investigated anxiety and/or depression as outcomes of exercise-based cardiac rehabilitation programmes. These authors found low to moderate effect sizes (ES) for anxiety (ES = 0.31) and depression (ES = 0.46) as a result of exercise-based cardiac rehabilitation. These effects are perhaps underestimates of the true effects of exercise on anxiety and depression because not all the participants in the studies reported will have symptoms of anxiety or depression. Thus there appear to be both physiological and psychological benefits associated with exercise in cardiac rehabilitation.

The field of exercise adherence has benefited from the research conducted in cardiac rehabilitation settings and the findings suggest that we need to learn about how to maintain long-term adherence. Oldridge, Donner and Buck (1983) report that 40–50 per cent of Canadian patients drop out of cardiac rehabilitation programmes six to twelve months after referral. In the UK, Pell *et al.* (1996) reported a 58 per cent completion rate for Glasgow hospital-based rehabilitation programmes. Quaglietti and Froelicher (1994) noted that adherence declines over time with only 30–55 per cent of patients continuing to exercise four years after the initial cardiac event. Finally, and most pessimistically, Prosser, Carson and Phillips (1985) established that only 12 per cent of patients were doing regular exercise six to nine years after a short hospital-based programme.

An example of a study that highlights the issue of long-term adherence was completed by Rovario, Holmes and Holmsten (1984). They randomly assigned cardiac patients to either a three times per week supervised exercise programme (n = 27) or a routine care programme which included exercise advice but no supervised sessions (n = 19). After three months of supervised training and at a follow-up four months later, patients in exercise-based rehabilitation had improved more than those in routine care on measures of cardiovascular functioning, self-perceptions and psychosocial functioning, including reduced employment-related stress, more frequent sexual activity and increased household activities. However, when these patients were followed up six years later (Holmes 1993), the advantages for the original exercise-based groups had disappeared. The authors suggested that the explanation lay in the increased level of activity in the routine care group and the decreased level in the group who initially had supervised exercise. This issue raises the question of how the exercise classes within a hospital setting might achieve the long-term goal of creating independent exercisers who can find ways of continuing exercise after the initial supervision. Hospital-based programmes have been classified as Phase III cardiac rehabilitation programmes and programmes that continue in the community beyond Phase III are known as Phase IV programmes. There is an urgent need to investigate how Phase IV programmes can maximise adherence to regular activity for those who have received cardiac rehabilitation in a hospital setting.

There is a concern, therefore, that many patients do not get the benefits from exercise programmes because they do not complete it. There have been some excellent studies of the factors associated with such dropout (Oldridge, Donner and Buck 1983) and there is a general conclusion that individual factors and factors related to the programme itself provide reasons for dropout (see Chapter 2). Given the concern over adherence levels in cardiac rehabilitation it is surprising that very few studies have sought patient viewpoints on the content of the programme. In the UK, Campbell *et al.* (1994) interviewed twenty-nine patients who had recently suffered a myocardial infarction. Patients frequently suggested exercise as a desirable element for the cardiac rehabilitation programme, but it was also clearly noted that the hospital was not the best location. Programmes in more local centres with supervision were requested. It was also noted by a majority of patients that bad weather was off-putting for walking programmes and other imaginative alternatives must be considered such as walking round large DIY stores or shopping centres.

A variety of exercise programmes have been tried including hospital-based and home-based, aerobic and strength-based programmes and differing exercise intensities. Home-based programmes that encourage walking seem to have the best chance of long-term adherence. Moving from Phase III (hospital-based) to Phase IV (community-based) is a particularly challenging time for exercise adherence. Hughes *et al.* (2002b) showed that providing patients with an exercise counselling session at the end of Phase III was more effective than providing exercise information alone in increasing physical activity levels in the short term. Hughes *et al.* (2007) developed this research and, using a well-controlled design in which seventy Phase III patients were randomised to receive standard care or standard care plus exercise counselling, found that the group receiving counselling increased self-reported physical activity over twelve months. Both groups showed decreases in indices of cardiorespiratory function over this time but the group receiving exercise counselling showed less decline (Hughes *et al.* 2002a; 2007). Thus counselling patients towards physical activity is beneficial investment. The literature in this area has recently been summarised by Hughes and Mutrie (2006).

Key point: Maintaining regular activity after supervised hospital-based programmes is difficult for cardiac rehabilitation patients and requires urgent attention from exercise psychology research.

For managers of cardiac rehabilitation programmes, Quaglietti and Froelicher offer the following suggestions:

> reduce the waiting time, provide expert supervision, tailor the exercise to avoid physical discomfort and frustration, use variable activities including games, incorporate social events, recall absent patients, involve the patient's family or spouse in the program, and involve the patient in monitoring his or her progress.
>
> (Quaglietti and Froelicher 1994: 599)

Special challenges for this patient group include fear of another MI, and the possible interaction of exercise with commonly prescribed drugs such as beta-blockers. Beta-blockers will attenuate heart-rate response and thus exercise intensity is best introduced to the patient via ratings of perceived exertion. Perhaps because of the fear of a further MI there is a concern that patients become dependent on the hospital environment and it is a challenge to assist patients to become independent exercisers and to sustain this. The British Association of Cardiac Rehabilitation is addressing the problem directly by providing training for exercise leaders and physiotherapists in Phase IV (community-based) cardiac rehabilitation. The issues of exercise psychology and long-term adherence are addressed in this training.

Metabolic diseases

Perhaps the most prevalent of metabolic disorders is obesity (see Chapter 1). Reviews suggest that physical activity is a critical behaviour in reducing the risks of obesity (Blair and Brodny 1999; Prentice and Jebb 1995). However, obesity itself is not often viewed as a disease and will not be reviewed here. There is, however, global concern for increasing rates of obesity and readers are referred to the report of a consensus conference held on the topic of how much activity is required to prevent the development of obesity or to prevent weight regain for those who have been obese (Saris *et al.* 2003). As this consensus report shows, the challenge for exercise psychology in assisting obese individuals to become active is considerable since they require two or three times more activity than that required for health. In this section diabetes has been chosen as the most frequent metabolic disease.

> Key point: Treating obesity and preventing weight gain through physical activity requires two or three times more activity (for example, up to ninety minutes) than the amount of activity required for health. This is a challenge for participants and exercise psychologists.

Diabetes

Both Type 1 (insulin-dependent, IDDM) and Type 2 (non-insulin-dependent, NIDDM) diabetics are usually advised to exercise as part of their treatment along with medication, modification of diet and monitoring of glucose levels (Wing *et al.* 1986) (see Chapter 1). A joint position statement by ACSM and the American Diabetes Association (American College of Sports Medicine 1997b) provides anyone involved with either Type 1 or 2 diabetic patients with a comprehensive set of guidelines concerning exercise. In this position statement benefits to cardiovascular, peripheral arterial and metabolic systems from exercise are described and preparing the diabetic patient for exercise is discussed. Interestingly, from the point of view of exercise adherence, no reference is made to maintenance of exercise or psychological outcomes. The psychological effects of facing a lifetime of dealing with diabetes, and the consequent emotional and social adjustments are very well documented by health psychologists, as is the need for patient education about treatment (Dunn 1993). Given the wealth of literature on these psychological issues in diabetes, and the standard recommendation that exercise should be part of treatment, it is surprising that neither the psychological benefits of exercise for diabetics nor patient education in appropriate exercise have received much attention from researchers. Literature searches suggest that no experimental work has been carried out on the psychological effects of exercise on IDDM or NIDDM. Two articles based on anecdotal evidence suggest that there are psychological effects of exercise for diabetics such as sense of control and a reduction in stress (Norstrom 1988; Vasterling, Sementilli and Burish 1988). A two-year observational study showed positive associations between physical activity and psychological well-being in Type 2 diabetics (Stewart *et al.* 1994). It is possible that central to these reported benefits is a changing view of the physical self from one which is compromised by the need to monitor food intake and blood sugar levels to one coping with exercise and feeling improvements in physical condition. Berg suggested that:

> The psychological effects of exercise may be just as important as the more readily measured physical and physiological effects. The realisation that participation in physical activity, including vigorous sport, can be engaged in safely and even beneficially may do much to create a positive feeling about life. Physically active diabetics may even be encouraged to maintain a higher degree of control of their condition so that they can maintain a vigorous lifestyle.

(Berg 1986: 428)

Some recent work (Swift *et al.* 1995) has shown that among NIDDM patients who regularly participated in exercise, over half selected diabetes control as the main reason for starting and continuing with exercise. Barriers to exercise included physical discomfort from exercise, fear of reactions from low blood sugar, being too overweight to exercise, and lack of family support. A large-scale survey (n = 1,030) of IDDM patients' motivations and barriers to exercise (Marsden 1996) suggested that fear of a hypoglycaemic event was not seen as a major barrier. Instead, and similar to non-diabetic populations, time constraints were listed as the major barrier. Motivations to exercise were to avoid future diabetic complications and to improve physical health.

Marsden's work also revealed that less than a third of IDDM patients took regular exercise, but that at least another third are contemplating starting or are doing some exercise on an irregular basis. This work highlights the need for exercise education to be part of diabetic patient care. There is also a clear need for further professional training for the medical team because the majority of patients in Marsden's survey had not received advice about exercise from their hospital clinic (Marsden and Kirk 2005). Ary *et al.* (1986) showed that only 20 per cent of Type 2 patients received any specific advice about how to exercise despite the fact that the majority of patients were told that they ought to exercise. A study of knowledge and attitude towards exercise amongst children with IDDM also underlines the need for education for patients and professionals. Rickabaugh and Saltarelli (1999) found some serious gaps in knowledge about IDDM and exercise amongst children and their parents and physical education (PE) teachers. They recommended that PE teachers in particular needed pre-service training on the management of exercise for IDDM.

The need to take into account individual motivations and barriers and the lack of advice regarding exercise for this patient group, suggests that both IDDM and NDDM patients need similar exercise counselling (Loughlan and Mutrie 1995) to that recommended for non-clinical populations (see Chapter 11). Two pilot studies have confirmed that, for both Type 1 and Type 2 patients, an exercise consultation increased physical activity more than exercise information from the British Diabetic Association's exercise leaflet. Hasler *et al.* (1997) showed that the exercise consultation was effective for Type 1 patients in increasing activity over a three-week period. A similar design, used with Type 2 diabetics attending a routine appointment, showed that the exercise consultation increased physical activity levels more than the standard leaflet over a five-week period (Kirk *et al.* 2000). Kirk then conducted a well-designed controlled trial with seventy inactive Type 2 diabetics who were randomly assigned to receive routine care or routine care plus physical activity counselling. Figure 10.1 shows the participant flow through this trial. Physical activity counselling, conducted using the transtheoretical model as a framework, increased both self-reported and objectively recorded physical activity over twelve months (Kirk *et al.* 2004b) (see Figure 10.2). These increases were effective in improving glycaemic control and reducing cardiovascular risk factors in the counselling group in comparison with the control group (Kirk *et al.* 2004a). These results are illustrated in Figures 10.3 and 10.4.

Marsden and Kirk have provided excellent practical guides for undertaking exercise consultations and constructing exercise programmes for diabetic patients (Marsden and Kirk 2005, Kirk *et al.* 2007). The special challenge to Type 1 diabetics is to balance insulin control, glucose and exercise bouts. Patients need adequate knowledge of how to do this including the knowledge that exercise should not be undertaken with high levels (>250 mg/dl) of blood glucose. Blood glucose monitoring should therefore be encouraged before and after exercise. Type 2 patients may have different challenges that include being overweight and perhaps less motivated to deal with their condition. The special challenge in

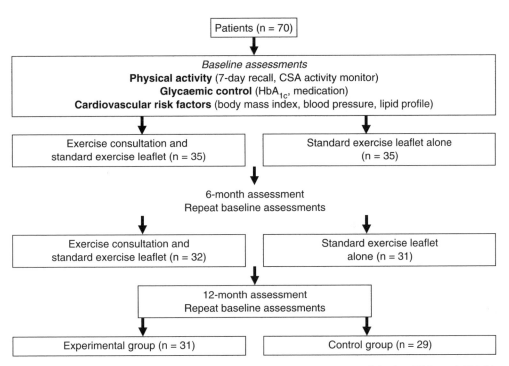

Figure 10.1 Flow of participants through physical activity trial for Type 2 diabetics (Kirk *et al.* 2004b)

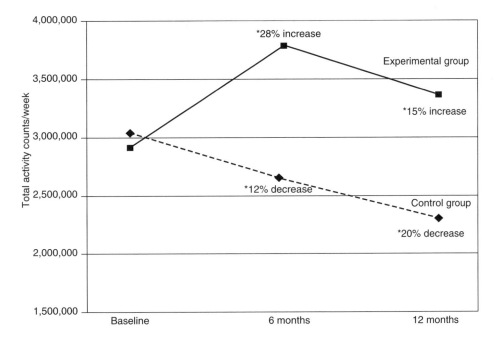

Figure 10.2 Increases in objectively measured physical activity following physical activity counselling (Kirk *et al.* 2004b)

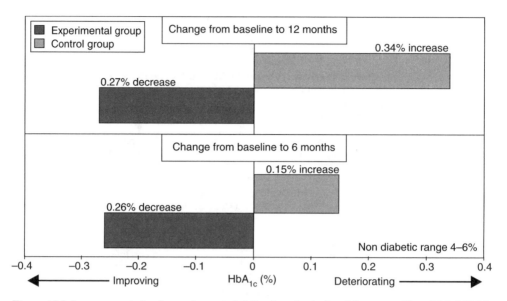

Figure 10.3 Improvements in glycaemic control following physical activity counselling (Kirk 2004a)

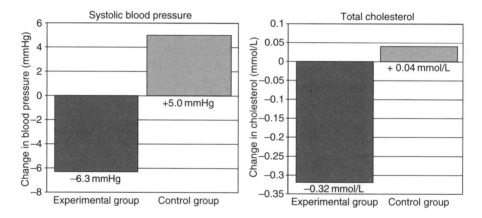

Figure 10.4 Improvements in cardiovascular risk factors following physical activity counselling (Kirk 2004a)

Notes
Between groups difference for change in systolic BP (baseline to 6 months) and change in total cholesterol (baseline to 12 months)

working with overweight individuals is to find activities which do not increase the stress on joints and which avoid potential embarrassment. Swimming might seem like an obvious non-weight bearing activity, but swimsuits and public swimming pools may be too threatening for many obese people. The active living message, and walking in particular, may prove more realistic for this patient group.

Immunological and haematological disorders

Cancer

It has long been recognised that coping with the diagnosis and treatment of cancer may require assistance in the form of psychological interventions (Anderson 1992). It is also recognised that exercise as part of treatment has the potential to improve both physical (for example, fatigue, nausea, weight change) and psychological functioning, although it was originally thought that exercise was unlikely to have positive effects on the cancer itself (see Chapter 1). Simon (1990) concludes his discussion of an excellent review of exercise immunity, cancer and infection by Calabrese by stating:

> There is little systematic information dealing with the role of exercise in the functional or psychological rehabilitation of cancer patients. There is little reason to expect that exercise training will help induce remissions in these patients, but there is good reason to expect that exercise may improve their quality of life.
>
> (Simon 1990: 586)

Since 1990 there has been considerable increase in the knowledge about how physical activity and exercise may be of benefit to cancer patients. During cancer treatment and rehabilitation, 'rest is best' was the traditional approach and, similar to the early days of cardiac rehabilitation, cancer patients were generally advised to avoid exercise. However, there are several important reasons why cancer patients should be active. Low levels of physical activity in cancer patients result in further deconditioning and symptoms of fatigue, loss of functional capacity and reductions in quality of life (Courneya and Friedenreich 1999; Lucia, Earnest and Perez 2003; Stricker *et al.* 2004). Inactive cancer patients may also be at higher risk of secondary tumours (Demark-Wahnefried *et al.* 2000) and a recent study of breast cancer survivors has indicated a 50 per cent risk reduction in mortality among those who are regularly active when compared with inactive patients (Holmes *et al.* 2005). Now it seems that exercise can indeed have an effect on remission of cancer. Furthermore physical activity levels tend to reduce after cancer diagnosis and remain low after treatment is completed (Blanchard *et al.* 2003; Friedenrich and Courneya 1996). From this low baseline there is great scope for exercise interventions to improve the health and well-being of cancer patients. A recent systematic review of thirty-three controlled trials showed moderate support for physical activity improving physical function, and no evidence of any adverse effects, but there were insufficient studies of good quality to make clear conclusions about quality of life outcomes (Stevinson, Lawlor and Fox 2004).

Kerry Courneya and his colleagues in Canada have had a major impact on our knowledge of exercise psychology in relation to cancer. He has contributed to several reviews that indicate the beneficial role (physical, psychological and immunological) that exercise can play for cancer patients and survivors (Courneya 2003; Courneya, Mackey and McKenzie 2002; Fairey *et al.* 2002; Schmitz *et al.* 2005). He has also made a considerable contribution to our understanding of adherence for exercise in cancer patients (Courneya *et al.* 2004;

Karvinen *et al.* 2005; Rogers *et al.* 2006) and shown the importance of the views of cancer care specialists on the role of exercise (Jones *et al.* 2004). Improving quality of life for patients and survivors has been a constant theme in Courneya's work and a good summary of this contribution can be found in a recent book chapter (Courneya 2005).

In the UK there are now several exercise psychology projects related to cancer. In Bristol, Ken Fox and colleagues have been investigating the provision of exercise opportunities for cancer patients within the NHS and found that less than 10 per cent of hospitals included exercise in rehabilitation programmes. Despite this nurses who were surveyed reported willingness to include exercise but cited lack of expertise and resources as barriers (Stevinson and Fox 2004). The same authors have presented a feasibility study on how to put exercise into cancer care in the UK (Stevinson and Fox 2006).

In Sheffield Amanda Daley and her colleagues are investigating whether or not aerobic exercise is the key to improvements in quality of life for breast cancer patients who had finished their treatment for at least one year (Daley *et al.* 2004, 2007) and also if exercise promotes improvements in immunological variables (Saxton *et al.* 2005).

In Glasgow we have been studying the effects of group exercise opportunities, taking place in community facilities, on various functional and psychological parameters of women who are undergoing cancer therapy. In our pilot study, which involved twenty-two women randomised to receive exercise classes in additional to usual care or usual care alone, we found significant improvements after twelve weeks in quality of life, minutes of weekly activity and meters completed in a twelve-minute walk test for the exercise group in comparison with usual care (Campbell *et al.* 2005). These results can be seen in Figure 10.5. We have now completed a larger study (n = 200) funded by Cancer Research UK and our results suggest that women who are undergoing treatment for breast cancer, who received exercise in the form of supervised classes for twelve weeks, had significant improvements in both functional and psychological variables in comparison with women receiving usual care (Mutrie *et al.* 2007).

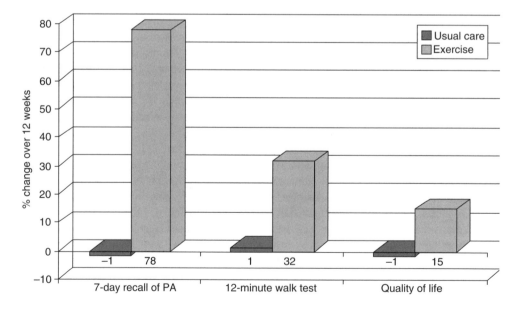

Figure 10.5 Pilot study – exercise as rehabilitation during breast cancer treatment (n=22) (data from Campbell *et al.* 2005)

We will soon have results from follow-up studies of these women that we are conducting annually. Our exercise programmes had the aim of developing independent exercisers and we incorporated elements of individual counselling into each exercise class. We are therefore interested to determine if adherence levels were improved as a result of using a group format to teach cognitive and behavioural skills that have been shown to help individuals increase activity levels.

Clear objectives for future research with exercise and cancer patients are to investigate the role of exercise on patients with different cancers, explore the feasibility of different types of exercise, including home-based and non-supervised programmes, to further understand motivations and barriers, and to estimate adherence rates at various stages of the disease including treatment and long-term follow-up.

Special challenges for exercise prescription with cancer patients include exercising whilst recovering from intensive treatment such as chemotherapy, muscle weakness and perhaps embarrassment in public facilities because of hair loss due to treatment or fear of what people might think of a mastectomy scar.

HIV/AIDS

There is increasing interest in the use of exercise as part of a treatment schedule for people who have contracted Human Immunodeficiency Virus (HIV) (Lawless, Jackson and Greenleave 1995; Rigsby *et al.* 1992). These initial studies focused on the immune system response to exercise and they found that there were no adverse effects (Birk 1996). Indeed, LaPerriere *et al.* (1991) suggested that physical training can increase CD4 cell counts (the helper cells which are important in immune response) by around 50 cells per cubic millimetre, which is comparable to the effect of certain AIDS drugs, but with none of the side effects. Other researchers have not been able to find the association with CD4 cell counts but have noted an inverse relationship between viral load and physical activity (Dudgeon *et al.* 2004).

The advent of antiretroviral therapy for HIV presents patients with more hope that their illness will not progress to AIDS or be fatal but they still face the challenge of living with a chronic disease. HIV infection and its treatment is associated with unfavourable alterations in body composition and fat distribution, and these alterations may increase the risk for cardiovascular and metabolic complications, as well as reduce functional independence and lower self-esteem. Thus another interest in this condition is whether or not exercise can decrease the risk of these alterations to body composition resulting from treatment. A review of evidence suggested that exercise training, particularly aerobic training, can help reduce total body and visceral fat, as well as normalising lipid profiles in HIV-infected patients, but that the effects of resistance training were less clear (Malita *et al.* 2005). Metformin has been used as a medication to help with these body composition alterations (this drug is often used in treatments of metabolic disorders). In a randomised controlled trial of exercise in combination with metformin, in comparison with metformin alone, there were significant improvements in cardiovascular and biochemical parameters for HIV-infected patients who had the exercise added to treatment (Driscoll *et al.* 2004).

Other studies show the potential for exercise to have positive psychological effects for the HIV population, including increased ability to cope with HIV positive status (LaPerriere *et al.* 1990), increased perception of well-being (Lox, McAuley and Tucker 1995) and improved quality of life (Stringer *et al.* 1998). In a descriptive study of sixty-eight HIV-positive Hispanics in Puerto Rico it was found that physically active participants had higher life satisfaction scores and healthier body composition compared with those who were inactive

(Ramirez-Marrero *et al.* 2004). Recent systematic reviews have found a total of ten studies and the authors concluded that performing constant or interval aerobic exercise, or a combination of constant aerobic exercise and progressive resistive exercise, for at least twenty minutes, at least three times per week for four weeks, appears to be safe and may lead to significant reductions in depressive symptoms as well as potentially clinically important improvements in cardiopulmonary fitness (Nixon *et al.* 2005; O'Brien *et al.* 2004). These reviews acknowledge that studies often have small sample sizes and high attrition rates and that few participants have been followed up for any length of time. Perhaps this is another area, like schizophrenia, in which qualitative research is needed to determine more about how patients with HIV experience exercise and what the perceived motivations and barriers to participation are.

Clearly, there are some special concerns for adherence to exercise for this population since 75 per cent dropped out of one twenty-four-week study of the effects of exercise on HIV (McArthur, Levine and Berk 1993). However, a study which compared the effects of high and moderate intensity aerobic training with a control group, had more optimistic adherence results. Stringer *et al.* (1998) reported a study in which thirty-four individuals with HIV+ were enrolled and 77 per cent completed the six-week programme. In addition, the authors reported 91 per cent adherence to the two exercise regimes that included three session of cycle ergometry per week for six weeks. There was no discussion from the authors of these excellent adherence results about how the programme compared with previous exercise programmes with this population. This was unfortunate since future researchers have no guidance about how to structure an exercise programme to maximise adherence. Clearly a six-week programme is much less of an adherence challenge than the twenty-four-week programme of McArthur, Levine and Berk (1993). Nevertheless, to get good adherence at twenty-four weeks, there must be good adherence earlier and we clearly need to know more about the time course, modalities and intensities of activity which provide the best adherence.

HIV positive patients may have limitations to their exercise such as reduced aerobic capacity, but Stringer (1999) noted that the majority of these patients are deconditioned and that aerobic capacity can be returned to normal with appropriate exercise programmes. Special challenges in working with such individuals include obtaining ethical approval for studies which involve laboratory testing, protection of confidentiality, public prejudice against this group if exercise is conducted in public facilities, poor muscle mass and muscle weakness.

Orthopaedic diseases and disabilities

Arthritis

Sharratt and Sharratt (1994) present an excellent summary of the role of exercise in both rheumatoid arthritis (inflammation of the membrane surrounding the joint) and osteoarthritis (degeneration of cartilage within the joint). It would seem that in this particular disease there is a consensus that exercise can enhance the quality of life by maintaining range of movement and functional capacities connected with daily living (Stenstrom 1994). From a review of systematic reviews, it was concluded that exercise therapy was effective for patients with both acute and chronic knee osteoarthritis and hip osteoarthritis, but there was not enough evidence in these reviews to conclude anything about rheumatoid arthritis (Smidt *et al.* 2005). Other reviewers have found positive benefits for exercise with rheumatoid arthritis in terms of improved aerobic capacity, muscle strength, functional ability and psychological well-being, but call for further work on what kind of exercise mode and intensity is suitable at the various stages of this disease (de Jong and Vlieland 2005). Tai Chi may be a particularly enjoyable mode of exercise for this patient group and may result in increased range of movement (Han *et al.* 2004).

It is clear that good adherence to exercise will maximise the benefits of activity for these patients (van Gool *et al.* 2005) but there is still a paucity of research that can contribute to our understanding of how to promote exercise to this patient group to maximise long-term adherence (Manigandan *et al.* 2004). It has been suggested that supervised classes are as effective as treatments provided on a one-to-one basis but that adherence to home pro-grammes is poorer (Kettunen and Kujala 2004).

In one of the few studies addressing motivations and barriers for this patient group, Neuberger *et al.* (1994) surveyed 100 patients with either rheumatoid or osteoarthritis to determine perceptions about exercise. They established that perceiving benefits from exer-cise was a significant predictor of exercise participation; those with less formal education and a longer duration of arthritis perceived fewer benefits from exercise. In addition, those who exercised in their youth reported more benefits of exercise.

The major challenge for arthritis sufferers who are exercising is the issue of joint pain and the type of activity that should be undertaken. Exercise should take place at the time of day at which inflammation is at its lowest and non-weight-bearing activities such as swimming and cycling are particularly recommended. If inflammation or increased pain occurs as a result of exercise, then the exercise may have to be adjusted so that the affected joint is not so stressed. Gordon (1993a) has written a very good guide to exercise for those suffering from arthritis which deals directly with the issue of pain and is essential reading for anyone constructing exercise opportunities for this patient group.

Osteoporosis

Osteoporosis is the condition in which there is a decrease in absolute amount of bone, ren-dering the skeleton susceptible to breakage and fractures (see Chapter 1). Osteoporosis can affect both males and females because there is a gradual decline in bone density with age. However, the loss of bone mass accelerates for women when ovarian function decreases dur-ing and after menopause. Thus postmenopausal women are more susceptible to osteoporosis than any other segment of the population (Kanis *et al.* 1990). In addition, osteoporosis suf-ferers often have to contend with pain, disability, depression and decreased confidence in their physical abilities (Rickli and McManus 1990; Vaughn 1976).

A variety of treatments have been tested but none are without controversy. Hormone replacement therapy (HRT) slows down the process of bone loss (Gannon 1988) but if treatment ceases, this effect will be sustained for only up to three years (Lindsay *et al.* 1976). There is also considerable debate about the desirability of taking HRT and so other treatment options have been considered. Several reviews have suggested that physical activity can enhance bone density and therefore should be considered as part of the treat-ment for osteoporosis (Gannon 1988; Marcus, R. *et al.* 1992). Clinical trials suggest that appropriate weight-bearing activity can enhance bone density by around 4 per cent which is similar to improvements noted from drug therapies (Chow, Harrison and Notarius 1987; Kemmler *et al.* 2004; Simkin, Ayalon and Leichter 1987; Smith, Smith and Gilligan 1990; Yamazaki *et al.* 2004).

Kriska *et al.* (1986) have noted that adherence to exercise programmes has been the major problem in most studies evaluating the effect of exercise on bone, but very few studies have attempted to study adherence issues. Wallace, Boxall and Riddick (2004) found that women were more willing to change their diet than increase their exercise and so there is much work for exercise psychologists to do in this area! Mitchell, Grant and Aitchison (1998) reported very high adherence to a twelve-week class-based programme of exercise for osteoporotic women. On average, the sixteen exercisers in this study attended 87 per cent of the target of twenty-four classes. In a larger study of 135 women who attended a special education session on exercise it was found that two variables predicted adherence to exercise over eighteen months (Mayoux-Benhamou *et al.* 2005). The variables were contraindication for hormone replacement therapy and low physical function scores from a quality of life questionnaire. In fact only a minority of the women (18 per cent) in this study adhered to a home-based exercise programme after eighteen months again showing the need for further studies of how to max-imise adherence for this group of patients.

Very little is known about exercise behaviour over a longer period of time for this patient group. This includes motivations and barriers, how patients view activity and the benefits it may provide, or what strategies the medical professions might adopt to increase or maintain adherence for a period of time which would allow bone measurements to alter as a result of exercise (that is, nine to twelve months). One study on this issue used a postal questionnaire to a local branch of the National Osteoporosis Society to establish current activity patterns and attitudes towards activity (Paton 1993). A response rate of 55 per cent was achieved (seventy-four out of 140) but no follow-up of non-respondents was possible because the society required that responses be anonymous. Thus the results may not be representative of the larger group of osteoporotic patients. All of the respondents had been diagnosed as osteoporotic for at least five years. 26 per cent of this group were sedentary and of the 74 per cent who reported that they were physically active more than half were participating in three exercise bouts each week. The most popular activity was walking. The three most commonly noted motivations for exercise were 'to feel better physically', 'to prevent further osteoporosis' and 'to feel better mentally'. The three most commonly perceived barriers to exercise were 'no facilities nearby', 'no knowledge of how to exercise' and 'not fit enough'. It is interesting to note that only 24 per cent of these respondents reported that they had been advised to begin exercise on diagnosis of the con-dition. Clearly, further studies on this population are required to enhance the understanding of motivation to exercise, but based on these results it would seem that exercise is perceived to have benefits and that barriers could be overcome through educa-tion on how to undertake exercise.

Special challenges for this population exist, including:

- finding enjoyable weight-bearing activity that will influence bone density
- the need for both aerobic and strength-enhancing components in the exercise programme
- overcoming fear of falling or worsening the condition by undertaking exercise
- decreased mobility and low fitness levels
- the need to modify programmes depending on limitations imposed by the disease.

Chronic low back pain

Managing chronic low back pain (that is, pain that is almost always present in the lower spine) is a serious problem for health services (see Chapter 1). In the UK, low back pain as a reason for being absent from work has increased by 104 per cent in the last decade (Klaber Moffet *et al.* 1995) and is the most common reason for attendance at out-patient physiother-apy clinics (Jette *et al.* 1994). There appears to be no consensus as to the most effective treatment (Waddell 1992) although both general and isokinetic exercise (Timm 1991) have been suggested as being effective.

There is some agreement that exercise has a very important role to play in the management of chronic low back pain. In a systematic review of sixty-one randomized controlled trials (6,390 participants) of the use of exercise with acute, subacute and chronic low back pain, it was found that exercise therapy was effective at decreasing pain and improving function. For those cases of subacute low back pain there was some evidence that a graded activity programme improves absenteeism outcomes. For acute low back pain, it was concluded that exercise therapy is as effective as either no treatment or other conservative treatments (Hayden *et al.* 2005). A futher review by the same authors noted that individually designed and supervised programmes, including stretching or strengthening, may improve pain and function but that strategies were needed to encourage adherence (Hayden, van Tulder and Tomlinson 2005). There is also a lot of interest, and a number of new exercise classes, based on the notion that improving the strength of the muscles that provide postural control (core stability) will help prevent or treat low back pain (Hodges 2003).

In the UK a definitive trial was conducted to determine the effect of adding exercise classes, spinal manipulation, or manipulation followed by exercise to 'best care' in general practice for patients consulting with back pain. Over 1,300 patients were recruited from over 180 general practices. The results showed that relative to 'best care' in general practice, manipulation followed by exercise had the best effect and that exercise alone only had modest short-term benefits (UK Beam Trial Team 2004). Thus exercise seems to be an important element of primary care treatment of low back pain.

Frost *et al.* (1995) showed that a four-week supervised fitness programme was more effective than a home-based programme in reducing perceived disability and pain and in increasing self-efficacy for daily living tasks. The difference in perceived disability between the two groups was maintained at a six-month follow-up. These authors suggested that the changes in self-efficacy may be due to endorphins released during exercise decreasing pain perception or increasing feelings of well-being, although the two groups did not differ in psychological change as measured by the General Health Questionnaire. Klaber Moffat *et al.* (1999) showed that back pain classes, which teach patients how to move safely and exercise, were more effective than traditional general practitioner management in reducing perceived disability and pain for up to twelve months. In addition, the patients who received the back pain classes had fewer days off work and used fewer health care resources thus making the back pain classes cost-effective. What is becoming evident in this area of research is that the patient's psychological state (including pain perception, depression and self-efficacy) may be very important in determining recovery. In this sense the psychological outcomes of exercise programmes designed to manage low back pain may be just as important as the physiological responses such as increased strength, flexibility or aerobic performance.

Frost *et al.* (1995) described a teaching style used by the physiotherapist conducting the fitness programme. This incorporated psychological principles such as increasing self-efficacy for exercise, and reinforced positive physical self-perceptions (for example, 'I am a regular exerciser') rather than negative perceptions (for example, 'I am a disabled patient'). This suggestion emphasises the important role of exercise psychology in exercise programmes designed to manage low back pain. It is important to note that this teaching approach produced very high (87 per cent) adherence levels over four weeks. However, it is presumably easier to attend for a short duration, and the authors do not report adherence to exercise in the six-month follow-up results. No other adherence statistics for exercise as part of back pain management could be found.

Special challenges for this group include overcoming the fear that movement will cause further injury. Perhaps what is required in the early stages is not an exercise programme but a movement education programme. Once patients realise that movement does not necessarily involve pain then gentle exercise can begin. There is also the challenge of finding enjoyable and interesting low-impact activities.

> Key point: Exercise psychology could help construct a movement education programme for those suffering from back pain that increases patients' confidence that they can move in a pain-free way.

Neuromuscular disorders

Two examples of the psychological aspects of exercise in the treatment of neuromuscular disorders have been chosen. The first is stroke and brain injury. The pathophysiology of stroke and brain injuries is often similar and so they have been linked together in this brief review. However, there are certain dissimilarities as well, not least of which is the variety of causes of brain injury (for example, car accidents) and therefore brain damage. In assessing the risks associated with exercise for those with brain injury, physical, psychological (such as aggressiveness) and behavioural (such as disruptive behaviour) issues all have to be considered (Vitale *et al.* 1995). In a review of the benefits of aerobic exercise after stroke, Potempa *et al.* (1996) concluded that enhanced motor unit recruitment, improved functional capacity, reduced cardiovascular risk and increased confidence in physical activity were all potential benefits for this patient group. Exercise has become a recommended aspect of treatment after brain injury for a variety of reasons including increasing cognitive function, increasing blood perfusion to certain areas of the brain, influencing neurotransmission and decreasing fatigue. However, most of the information about the effects of exercise come from quasi-experimental designs because of the low numbers of patients at any one time, but these studies show that twelve to sixteen weeks of training are required to show effects (Jankowski and Sullivan 1990; Wollman *et al.* 1994). Grealy, Johnson and Rushton (1999) showed that a single session of exercise, which also involved engagement in a virtual reality environment, significantly improved movement and reaction times. These authors reported that over four weeks the exercise and virtual reality training improved verbal and visual learning in comparison with scores on these tests for participants in a control group with similar injuries. Enriching the environment in this way may have added advantages for other clinical populations and is worthy of investigation.

Special challenges for these patients include the mode of exercise. Very often the exercise will have to be conducted on a piece of stationary equipment, such as a cycle ergometer, because of other movement limitations. Even then special precautions may have to be taken to ensure patient safety and comfort such as a chest brace or handlebar adjustments. Poor concentration may also be a problem and exercise may have to be accumulated in short bouts.

The second example of a neuromuscular disorder is Parkinson's disease. The main features of this disease are tremor and rigidity in muscles, poor gait and posture, and hypokinesia. For most patients, physical activity reduces during the course of this disease but increasing physical activity and exercise has the potential of improving motor function and impacting on how these patients feel about themselves. Specific stretching and strengthening exercise can have an impact on the physical features of this disease but exercise may also have an effect on the neurotransmission problems that are the root cause of the disease. Later in this chapter, possible mechanisms for the psychological benefits of exercise will be explored Dopamine release occurs during exercise and this may be one way in which psychological benefits occur. In Parkinson's disease, there is a loss of dopamine production and so there is added potential for exercise to be beneficial. One study has shown decreased mortality for Parkinsonian patients who were regularly exercising over a four-year period (Kuroda *et al.* 1992).

A handful of studies have attempted to show the effects of intervening with a form of exercise on motor ability but none have measured how patients perceive this treatment. Interventions have ranged from passive mobilisation conducted by physiotherapists, to sports training such as karate (Palmer *et al.* 1986). The results have been equivocal and the study designs, because of the preliminary nature of this work, have not been strong. Banks (1989) showed that home-based physiotherapy could improve activities of daily living but there was no control group for comparison. On the other hand, Gibberd *et al.* (1981) concluded that physiotherapy for these patients did not improve functional capacity, but the programme of exercise was not standardised. One randomised controlled trial (RCT) has been reported on the effects of an intensive physical rehabilitation programme (Comella *et al.* 1994). This study showed positive effects for the intensive programme on daily activities and motor function, but these effects had been lost after six months. Adherence to intensive programmes without supervision is clearly a problem. Reuter *et al.* (1999) provided training in motor coordination and muscle function in gymnasia and swimming pools, which they describe as 'sports training', to sixteen Parkinsonian patients. They found that there were significant improvements in motor abilities, subjective well-being and cognitive function at the end of the fourteen-week training period. These improvements had not been lost six weeks after the training had finished. However, this was a one-group pre–post design and it is therefore not clear if the subjective improvements are related to group membership and extra time from therapists. The value to the patients was clear since they refused to be without the sports training for more than six weeks. There is clearly a need for more RCTs and qualitative investigations in this area.

Special considerations include knowledge of how to construct an exercise programme that will focus on the particular motor problems faced by these patients, and altered heart rate and blood pressure responses.

Cognitive, emotional and sensory disorders

Mental illness is listed in this final section of the ACSM's categorisation of disease and disability. There has been a great deal of research into the benefits of exercise in mental illness and two of the most common mental illnesses (anxiety and depression) have been covered separately in Chapter 9. In this section we begin by reviewing other mental illness such as schizophrenia and alcohol and drug abuse and explore how physical activity may play a role in providing mental health benefits even where there is little chance that the activity will cure the illness. We have also included a section on the issue of exercise dependence which parallels dependence on other substances such as drugs or alcohol. We then review the cognitive and sensory disorders and what is known about exercise and physical activity.

Schizophrenia

Schizophrenia is a psychotic illness affecting a small proportion of the population, but is the most common serious mental illness and, as such, places a disproportionately heavy burden on resources in psychiatric care (Faulkner 2005). It is characterised by thought disturbance such as delusions, speech disturbance, difficulties in interpersonal functioning, inappropriate behaviours and emotional responses, and is most commonly treated with antipsychotic medication. A brief description of the DSM–IV criteria for schizophrenia is as follows:

- a disturbance that lasts for at least six months and includes at least one month of active-phase symptoms (for example, delusions, hallucinations, disorganised speech, grossly disorganised or catatonic behaviour, negative symptoms)
- there must be significant impairment in one or more major areas of functioning (for example, work, interpersonal relationships) for most of the time since the onset of the disturbance, and the functioning must be significantly lower than that prior to the onset of the disorder.

Treatment for schizophrenia typically involves drugs that have an antipsychotic effect although there is much debate about the effectiveness of these drugs and there is also concern about compliance. Some patients may have access to psychosocial interventions in addition to the drug therapy while others may be hospitalised (Faulkner 2005).

There is a potential role for exercise in the treatment of schizophrenia and there is a growing literature on this topic. The role for activity may involve improvements in physical and mental health functioning, but it is clear that physical activity is very unlikely to be a stand-alone treatment for this disorder. Instead, physical activity may have a very important adjunctive role in the treatment of schizophrenia.

Early studies were typically descriptive but provided the suggestion that physical activity might be an important consideration. Chamove (1986) noted that physical activity and fitness levels are known to be low in schizophrenic patients especially those in psychiatric hospitals. We now know that such low activity levels will make these patients at risk for cardiovascular and metabolic diseases, depression and obesity and so, for prevention of risk, increasing physical activity levels will be very important. Early studies of the effect of increasing activity for such patients had positive outcomes but these studies tended to be pre-experimental. Some of the positive effects for increased activity noted in a study of forty schizophrenic patients were:

- less psychotic features
- less movement disorder
- improved mood
- more social interest and competence (Chamove 1986).

Patients seemed to understand these benefits themselves. For example, Falloon and Talbot (1981) reported that as many as 78 per cent have used exercise as a way of reducing hallucinations. Pelham and Campagna (1991) reported three single-subject case studies which incorporated quantitative information from standard fitness tests, Beck Depression Inventory and Mental Health Inventory scores with qualitative information from interviews. The results showed physiological and psychological benefits and information was also gathered on long-term exercise adherence. The article concluded with a useful set of guidelines on exercise programmes for schizophrenic patients.

The same researchers (Pelham *et al.* 1993) also reported an experimental design which showed that psychiatric patients (diagnosed with schizophrenia or major affective disorder) who undertook a twelve-week aerobic exercise programme decreased depression scores and increased aerobic fitness. The control group undertaking non-aerobic exercise did not show these improvements. This does not support Martinsen's findings that both aerobic and non-aerobic exercise decreased depression scores for a group of hospitalised depressed patients (Martinsen 1990a, 1990b). However, only five individuals were assigned to each group in the Pelham *et al.* (1993) study and the statistical conclusions may therefore not be valid. In addition, it may be that schizophrenic patients respond differently from other psychiatric patients to exercise or it may be that initially low fitness levels influenced the results. Furthermore, Pelham *et al.* (1993) seemed to focus on depression as the major dependent variable which is only one aspect of schizophrenia.

In reviewing the very limited evidence for the use of exercise in the treatment of psychoses such as schizophrenia, Plante concluded that 'the current research results suggest that exercise may assist these patients with mood and self-esteem factors much more than with thought disturbances associated with psychotic symptomatology' (Plante 1993: 367). Similarly, Faulkner and Biddle (1999) concluded from a review of eight pre-experimental, three quasi-experimental and one experimental study that 'the existing research does not allow firm conclusions ... as to the psychological benefits of exercise for individuals with schizophrenia. It does, however, support the potential efficacy of exercise in alleviating negative symptoms of schizophrenia and as a coping strategy for the positive symptoms' (Faulkner and Biddle 1999: 453).

Guy Faulkner and collaborators have made some very important contributions to the literature on this topic. For example, Faulkner and Sparkes (1999) have reported a qualitative study of exercise as therapy for schizophrenia. Three patients who began a ten-week exercise programme implemented in their hostel setting were studied through an ethnographic approach. Two of the three patients perceived the exercise programme to be very beneficial, while the third patient ceased participation after seven weeks. One main theme which emerged from the analysis was the role of exercise in encouraging patients out of their 'internal world' and into the 'social world', such as a swimming pool or a walking route. Another theme was that exercise helped the secondary symptoms of depression and low self-esteem, helped control auditory hallucinations and promoted better sleep patterns and general behaviour. The authors recommended that care plans for schizophrenic patients should include exercise, but comment on how difficult that is to achieve. In the hostel where the exercise programme was carried out the staff were very enthusiastic about the way in which exercise had helped patients and noted deterioration when the programme stopped. Despite this there were no plans to ensure that the exercise programme would become a routine element of treatment. The lack of standard randomised controlled trial data on the physical and mental benefits of exercise for schizophrenic patients may be one reason for the reluctance to spend money on exercise as parts of treatment packages. However, in this area it will be very difficult to find sufficient participants to conduct such a study and the environment of a hostel or hospital setting is not conducive to random assignment to groups without contamination or resentment. Thus, a qualitative approach is appropriate and the evidence from such studies indicates that there are many potential benefits for exercise programmes to be put in place.

An Australian study has provided further qualitative data on this topic (Fogarty and Happell 2005). Six residents of a community care unit in Melbourne took part in an exercise programme for three months. A focus group interview was conducted with the participants and various staff involved. Here four themes emerged from the focus group discussions: participants had enjoyed the graduated and individualised programme; the benefit of increased physical fitness; the benefit of the group approach; and the intention of participants to continue the programme. This was also the case in Faulkner's study reported above but he noted that the programme had not been sustained. The evidence is beginning to build and it is hoped that policy for treatment may include the opportunity for schizophrenic patients to exercise. However, longer-term evaluation of whether or not such programmes can be sustained, and therefore be of benefit to patients, beyond the realms of research projects, are now called for.

Future studies in this area must also evaluate exercise programmes in a variety of ways (for example, physical and mental health benefits, cost-effectiveness, patient and staff perception of benefit). In addition, they need to include the issue of how to negotiate with administrators, psychiatrists and those in charge of care, in hospitals, hostels or in the community, about the inclusion of exercise in the management and treatment of schizophrenic patients. A recent guide to how to design and adapt physical activity programmes for psychiatric patients and provide them as part of normal treatment has also been provided (Richardson *et al.* 2005).

In a recent review of the available evidence Faulkner calls for a distinction of the effects of physical activity on the positive symptoms of schizophrenia (such as dillusions and thought disorders) and the negative symptoms (such as low mood, apathy and social withdrawal) in future studies (Faulkner 2005). As studies progress in this area we may also see discussion about the most appropriate mode and dosage of activity which will parallel discussions in the much more developed field of physical activity and depression (see Chapter 9).

> Key point: Schizophrenic patients report benefit from exercise and further research on this patient group should explore what kind of exercise and what dose of exercise is best.

Alcohol and drug dependence

The topic of dependence on alcohol and drugs falls into all of the commonly used classifications of mental illness. Using ICD–10 (World Health Organization 1993), a diagnosis of dependence is made through noting various dependence syndromes. These features are noted in Table 10.2. If three or more of these features are present then a diagnosis of dependence is made.

Table 10.2 ICD–10 classification of dependence syndrome (World Health Organization 1993)

Classification	Dependence syndrome
Compulsion	Desire/compulsion to take the substance
Impaired control	Difficulty in controlling behaviour in regard to onset, termination and level of substance taking
Withdrawal	Physiological withdrawal state occurs when substance withdrawn
Relief use	Substance used to avoid or relieve withdrawal symptoms
Tolerance	Increased amount of substance required to achieve effect similar to lower dose previously
Salience	Increased amounts of time spent in obtaining or taking substance or recovering from its effects Persistence despite awareness of harmful response

Even if a clinical diagnosis is not made, levels of alcohol and drug use below this level are still a concern to health, to health care cost and to social order. There is particular concern about the increasing incidence of both alcohol and drug use amongst young people since a variety of health problems may follow but also because of the possible social disorder that may result (Sutherland and Shepherd 2001).

ALCOHOL DEPENDENCE

Alcohol dependence is a common problem and one that is growing in prevalence. In 1992 a national survey showed that 24 per cent of men and 7 per cent of women were drinking at levels above the recommendations for safe limits (HMSO 1992). A decade later these figures had risen to 44 per cent of men and 30 per cent of women exceeding recommended levels (Office of National Statistics 2004) indicating a large percentage of the population who are at risk of becoming dependent and whose health may suffer as a result of high levels of alcohol consumption.

The topic of appropriate treatment for alcohol abuse has received much discussion with no one method showing distinct advantages (Heather, Roberston and Davies 1985). Rehabilitation from an addictive behaviour involves establishing self-control strategies and finding coping strategies for the emotions involved with withdrawal and continued abstinence (Marlatt and Gordon 1985). Three stages of treatment have been recognised as follows: stage 1: detoxification, emergency treatment and screening; stage 2: rehabilitation including primary and extended care; stage 3: relapse prevention and care required for maintenance (Institute of Medicine 1990).

In considering why physical activity or exercise might be included as part of any stage of treatment, as with other topics in this chapter, there are both physical and mental health reasons for inclusion. Self-esteem is often very low as the problem drinker faces the need for treatment and realises the physical and mental damage that alcohol may have caused (Beck, Weissman and Kovacs 1976). It is intriguing to note that one of the earliest documented pieces of research in exercise psychology was in the area of alcohol rehabilitation (Cowles 1898) although several decades passed before the research was replicated. Cowles' conclusion provides a challenge to current researchers to provide experimental evidence of the declared benefits of exercise:

> The benefits accruing to the patients from the well-directed use of exercise and baths is indicated by the following observed symptoms: increase in weight, greater firmness of muscles, better colour of skin, larger lung capacity, more regular and stronger action of the heart, clearer action of the mind, brighter and more expressive eye, improved carriage, quicker responses of nerves, and through them of muscle and limb to stimuli. All this has become so evident to them that only a very few are unwilling to attend the classes and many speak freely of the great benefits derived.
>
> (Cowles 1898: 108)

Problem drinkers often have low levels of cardiorespiratory fitness and muscle strength and appropriate programmes of exercise have been shown to be effective in improving these physical parameters (Donaghy, Ralston and Mutrie 1991; Tsukue and Shohoji 1981). Since regular exercise has been associated with improved mental health, decreased levels of depression and anxiety and increased self-esteem, and these are commonly reported problems in alcohol rehabilitation, the use of exercise as part of the treatment for alcohol rehabilitation has been piloted in several locations (Donaghy, Ralston and Mutrie 1991; Frankel and Murphy 1974; Gary and Guthrie 1972; Murphy, Pagano and Marlatt 1986; Palmer, Vacc and Epstein 1988; Sinyor *et al.* 1982). In these studies the exercise programmes can be considered to be lifestyle interventions providing the problem drinker with the skills to undertake a positive health promoting behaviour (exercise), simultaneously providing self-control strategies, coping strategies and an alternative to drinking (Marlatt and Gordon 1985; Murphy *et al.* 1986).

Donaghy and Mutrie (1998) reported a randomised controlled trial in which 117 problem drinkers were assigned to either a three-week supervised exercise programme (followed by a twelve-week home-based programme), or a placebo group. The latter received a stretching programme for three weeks and advice to continue exercising for the next twelve weeks. The exercise group improved scores on physical self-worth and perceptions of strength and physical condition at one and two months after entry to the programme. The between-groups difference in physical self-perceptions was not evident at five months, but this may be due to drop off in exercise adherence (Donaghy and Mutrie 1997). Evidence exists, therefore, that a structured exercise programme added to a three-week treatment programme can help problem drinkers improve their perception of physical self-worth. Adherence to exercise was a problem with 26 per cent having left the treatment programme (not just the exercise) at the end of three weeks and by the second month follow-up a further 30 per cent had dropped out. Activity levels were sustained for the exercise groups for eight to twelve weeks following the three-week programme but had dropped to the level of the control group by five months.

Donaghy and Ussher (2005) have recently summarised the available evidence on this topic and conclude that the support for the physical benefits of an exercise programme as part of alcohol rehabilitation, such as improved aerobic fitness and strength, is strong. However, the evidence for mental health benefits and for any effect on improving abstinence from alcohol is weaker (Donaghy and Ussher 2005). Special challenges for this population include low starting levels of fitness and muscle weakness, relapse to drinking with consequent effects on exercise behaviour, social isolation and lack of support. There is clearly a need for help, such as telephone contact or regular meetings, to sustain activity levels initiated in treatment programmes for this patient group. There is also a need to integrate the exercise into other treatments such as discussion groups, self-help groups or forms of cognitive behavioural therapy. Reinforcing the value of exercise and encouraging adherence could be topics for group leaders and therapists in these other forms of treatment.

> Key point: Evidence suggests that problem drinkers can benefit from exercise programmes in terms of physical outcomes. However, evidence for mental health benefits or any advantage to reducing alcohol intake is weaker.

DRUG DEPENDENCE

Illegal drugs are used for recreational purposes worldwide. Substance misuse in which a dependence has become apparent is a growing problem and is one of the most prevalent psychiatric disorders in modern society. Opiates, tranquillisers and crack cocaine are the three most common types of drug that create problems of dependence for users in the UK.

Treatment for drug dependence can take place in primary care or in specialist drug treatment services and often involves prescribing substitute drugs such as methadone. The Department of Health (1999) suggested the following aims for the treatment of drug misuse:

- assist the patient to remain healthy, until, with appropriate care and support, he or she can achieve a drug-free life
- reduce the use of illicit or non-prescribed drugs by the individual
- deal with problems related to drug misuse
- reduce the dangers associated with drug misuse, particularly the risk of HIV, hepatitis B and C, and other blood-borne infections from injecting paraphernalia
- reduce the duration of episodes of drug misuse
- reduce the chance of future relapse from drug misuse
- reduce the need for criminal activity to finance drug misuse
- reduce the risk of prescribed drugs being diverted onto the illegal drug market.

(Department of Health 1999: 9)

It is clear from these treatment aims that physical activity could not be a panacea but that it could have a possible role such as improving physical health, providing a diversion from drugs, providing an alternative social network and possibly helping prevent relapse. However, evidence for the use of exercise in drug rehabilitation programmes is very hard to find. A recent review found six published studies published between 1991 and 2002 (Donaghy and Ussher 2005). Five of the studies were from North America and one from China. Only two of these studies had control groups showing, as with schizophrenia, the difficulty of finding adequate numbers in most treatment settings to mount a randomised trial. Overall there is promising evidence from these studies that including an exercise programme for those in drug rehabilitation has the potential to increase abstinence and reduce withdrawal symptoms and positively influence fitness levels and self-esteem. The only evidence from the UK appears to come from unpublished dissertations (Adamson 1991; Hyman 1987; Murdoch 1988). The problems faced in drug rehabilitation are similar to those in alcohol rehabilitation; high levels of anxiety and depression are often reported as well as low self-esteem (Banks and Waller 1988) and thus it might be assumed that exercise could have the same potentially therapeutic effect. One unique problem for drug rehabilitation is the variety of drugs and their effects both during addiction and withdrawal. In addition, drug misuse often involves the use of many drugs by the same person (Arif and Westermeyer 1988). It may be that this variety of responses makes the standard 'clinical' trial experiment untenable, because there is likely to be a large variation in the dependent variables but only small numbers of participants available because of the nature of the treatment programmes. In addition, these are often residential. Qualitative methodology may therefore be the best way to gather information in this area.

A recent study conducted in Scotland attempted a multiple baseline design of clients attending a special exercise programme organised by the Community Drug Team in Greenock (Smith 2006). Qualitative data were also collected from clients and service providers. Twenty-one participants, who were all misusing more than one substance, attended some or all of a ten-week exercise programme. Baseline measures were taken on a minimum of three occasions to establish whether or not a stable condition was present and then clients began the exercise programme. The main change over time was improvements in the distance walked in six minutes and indication of self-perceived physical health benefits. However, adherence was so varied that it was difficult to conclude the exercise programme was related to these outcomes. Thus even a multiple baseline design proved difficult to enact in this setting. It was also noted that the clients already had high levels of everyday activity because they walked to most places for transport. Thus it may be important to consider strengthening and stretching exercise in programmes to emphasise aspects of fitness other than aerobic training. Indeed one of the most interesting studies reviewed by Donaghy and

Ussher (2005) involved a Chinese martial art form and perhaps an activity such as Tai Chi would be appropriate to consider. The qualitative results in the Scottish study were interesting with clients attending the group perceiving a number of benefits such as something to look forward to, something that helped them feel fitter and something that improved mental health. The following quote from one user shows some of this effect:

> Well, it didnae [did not] cost any money to feel good an' stuff. So, em, feeling good, about feeling good without taking drugs, made you feel good anyway!

Staff members also felt that the programme was worthwhile although it was acknowledged that there are many barriers to overcome for those in drug rehabilitation to attend regular exercise classes (Smith 2006). This study has provided some new evidence for the role of exercise in a drug rehabilitation programme in the UK but it is clear that it is still very difficult to mount a service for clients and even more difficult to evaluate it. The qualitative approach remains the best research methodology in this setting.

Exercise programmes for those attempting to withdraw from drugs have a particular challenge in overcoming adverse withdrawal effects from drugs. Such patients are liable to forget appointments for exercise, and the withdrawal effects may prevent exercise completely on some days or an inability to leave the house to go to an exercise facility. Keeping in regular contact with these patients is very helpful to them. Perhaps home-based exercise, such as through an exercise videotape, could provide some support through difficult phases, but regular phone calls and visits may also be required.

TOBACCO DEPENDENCE

A more recent question regarding the role of exercise in drug dependence relates to whether or not physical activity can play a role in helping people who are trying to give up cigarette smoking. Of course tobacco use is not normally considered as a clinical problem. Nevertheless people do seek help to attempt to quit. Ussher has conducted most of the studies on this topic in the UK and has employed rigorous research methods. Ussher and Taylor have recently provided a summary of the literature on the role of physical activity in coping with withdrawal from tobacco (Taylor and Ussher 2005). Their extremely thorough review of the growing literature in this area suggests that it is too early to make firm conclusions about exercise and smoking cessation. The strongest findings relate to single sessions of exercise at a low to moderate level of intensity (such as walking) helping people with withdrawal symptoms and nicotine cravings. Given the substantial evidence on the health benefits of quitting smoking and the known difficulty of overcoming dependence on tobacco, this new approach of using exercise must be encouraged and further research carried out. Even if exercise does not help in a direct way, the positive health benefits of increasing activity must be considered as evidence enough that exercise should be an important adjunct to any attempts to quit.

EXERCISE DEPENDENCE

In the previous sections and chapters there has been more evidence of psychologically beneficial effects of physical activity or exercise than detrimental effects. Anyone who has had negative experiences of being ridiculed for lack of skill by schoolmates may tell a different story. Novice exercisers who judge themselves failures because they give up their exercise plan may also have trouble accepting that exercise is good for mental health. There is an acknowledged 'dark side' to physical activity in which self-esteem may be damaged or physique anxiety created as a result of poor experiences (Brewer 1993), but much less literature exists on that topic than the beneficial effects. Recent evidence has suggested that some people can approach exercise in a way that many would see as mentally unhealthy. Some can become dependent on, or addicted to, exercise and will exhibit very high levels of activity on a daily or twice-daily basis. There is often informal discussion amongst various professionals about the risk of creating people who are dependent on exercise when using exercise as part of treatment. This is particularly true in working with other dependencies such as alcohol or drug use in which it is easy to suggest that the clients are swapping one dependency for another. The term exercise dependence was first used by Veale (1987) to describe a state in which exercise has become a compulsive behaviour. Previous literature describing this phenomenon was hampered by lack of an agreed definition. For example, the term obligatory exercise has been used and a questionnaire exists to measure this trait (Thompson and Pasman 1991). Davis, Brewer and Ratusny (1993) note that lack of agreement on terminology and measurement has plagued this area of research. Veale (1987) provided a set of diagnostic criteria to help researchers and clinicians describe this kind of exercise behaviour in a consistent manner. Veale used his knowledge of dependence syndrome which was shown in Table 10.2 and developed these specific exercise criteria from them. These are shown in Table 10.3. In addition, he distinguished between primary exercise dependence and exercise dependence that is secondary to eating disorders.

Exercise dependence is characterised by:

- a frequency of at least one exercise session per day
- a stereotypical daily or weekly pattern of exercise
- recognition of exercise being compulsive and of withdrawal symptoms if there is an interruption to the normal routine
- reinstatement of the normal pattern within one or two days of a stoppage.

Table 10.3 Diagnostic criteria for exercise dependence (Veale 1987)

Criteria
A Narrowing of repertoire leading to a stereotyped pattern of exercise with a regular schedule once or more daily
B Salience with the individual giving increasing priority over other activities to maintain the pattern of exercise
C Increased tolerance to the amount of exercise performed over the years
D Withdrawal symptoms related to a disorder of mood following the cessation of the exercise schedule
E Relief or avoidance of withdrawal symptoms by further exercise
F Subjective awareness of the compulsion to exercise
G Rapid re-instatement of the previous pattern of exercise and withdrawal symptoms after a period of abstinence

Associated features
H Either the individual continues to exercise despite a serious physical disorder known to be caused, aggravated or prolonged by exercise and is advised as such by a health professional, or the individual has arguments or difficulties with his/her partner, family, friends, or occupation
I Self-inflicted loss of weight by dieting as a means towards improving performance

The problems that exercise dependence can create range from tiredness and chronic injury to relationship problems and eating disorders (Veale and Le Fevre 1988). However, the prevalence for this problem is not known and there is no universal agreement on these criteria. Szabo (2000) suggests that it is very rare. Other authors who have reviewed the topic, but used other terms such as obligatory exercise, call for better assessment of the extent of the problem (Draeger, Yates and Crowell 2005). Hausenblas and Downs (2002a) recently completed a systematic review of the literature on exercise dependence and found seventy-seven studies on the topic. However, their review could not provide clear conclusions because of the lack of good experimental designs, lack of definition of terms and poor measures.

Key point: Dependence is a potentially serious negative consequence of exercise. However, the prevalence of this problem is not known.

There is clearly a need for a validated questionnaire to measure exercise dependence. Davis, Brewer and Ratusny (1993) have provided some evidence for the validity of the Commitment to Exercise Scale which is related to, but not based on, Veale's concept of exercise dependence. Szabo (2000) has conducted a review of research into this field, but of the seventeen studies he cites not one of them is actually measuring exercise dependence. Measures used included questionnaires on commitment to running, self-perceived addiction to running, negative addiction, obligatory running, and in-depth qualitative interviews and case studies. Thus it is difficult to draw conclusions about the extent of the problem. Hausenblas and Downs, who also conducted the systematic review mentioned earlier, have provided preliminary data on an exercise dependence scale which is based on the recognised clinical criteria for dependence (Hausenblas and Downs 2002b) and this should move the field forward again.

Exercise dependence may well present at a mental health clinic, sports injury clinic or be associated with eating disorders. Given that a very small percentage of the population exercises at a sufficient level to obtain fitness effects (that is at least twenty minutes of continuous aerobic activity three times/week), it is likely that only a very small percentage of the overall population could be diagnosed as exercise dependent and so it is not a public health problem. Nevertheless, the media seem interested in this more 'sensational' aspect of exercise and give it greater coverage than sometimes it deserves.

Furthermore, it is difficult to say how harmful exercise dependence really is to an individual. If the person continues to exercise against medical advice then the risk of chronic injury is clear. It may also be economically harmful to neglect work responsibilities in favour of exercise. Damage to personal and social relationships may be psychologically harmful. It is clear in these cases that the exercise dependent individual needs to regain a balance in terms of their need to exercise and other important life issues. If exercise professionals notice someone who appears to be dependent then some information on seeking appropriate advice or following some self-help strategies should be made available. As with other kinds of behaviour change, raising awareness of the issue is a first step. Box 10. 1 offers a format for use in creating a poster in gyms and sports injuries clinics to raise awareness and offer avenues of advice.

Box 10.1 An example of a poster format for raising awareness and offering self-help strategies for potential exercise dependents (Veale 1987; Zaitz 1989)

1 Do you think exercise is compulsive for you?
2 Is exercise the most important priority in your life?
3 Is your exercise pattern very routine and rigid? Could people 'set their watches' by your exercise patterns?
4 Are you doing more exercise this year than you did last year to gain that feel good effect?
5 Do you exercise against medical advice or when injured?
6 Do you get irritable and intolerant when you miss exercise and quickly get back to your exercise routine if you are forced to change it?
7 Have you ever considered that you were risking your job, your personal life or your health by overdoing your exercise?
8 Have you ever tried to lose weight just to make your exercise performance better?

If you answered YES to most of these questions, or if you are worried about becoming dependent on exercise, please speak to a member of staff or follow these self-help strategies:

*   use cross-training to avoid over-use injuries; remember aerobic fitness, strength and flexibility are all important aspects of fitness
*   schedule a reasonable rest period between two bouts of exercise to prevent mental and physical fatigue
*   schedule one complete rest day each week and notice how energetic you feel the next day
*   exercise your mind by getting involved in mental and social activities that can lower anxiety and lift self-esteem
*   try to learn a stress management technique such as relaxation, yoga, tai chi or meditation

Someone who is exercise dependent may manage to prevent physical, personal or financial harm, but may still acknowledge a compulsion to exercise. Is this harmful, or is it what Glasser (1976) describes as 'positive addiction'? Veale (1995), the author of the suggested diagnostic criteria, admits that he has, in his professional capacity as a psychiatrist, interviewed very few people who could be diagnosed as having primary exercise dependence. Many people who may have the characteristics of dependence are probably functioning quite well and have no need to seek help. Iannos and Tiggemann (1997) found no evidence of personality dysfunction in a cross-sectional study examining various personality characteristics of high-level exercisers (more than eleven hours of exercise per week) compared with moderate- and low-level exercisers. They concluded that these high levels of activity may be psychologically beneficial to these exercisers since it could help maintain feelings of self-esteem and personal control.

Exercise dependence secondary to eating disorders Veale (1995) pointed out that cases of secondary exercise dependence are more frequently encountered than cases of primary exercise dependence. Secondary dependence is when a person uses excessive exercise as part of another disorder, such as an eating disorder or a body dysmorphic disorder. He recommended studies that attempt to determine whether or not primary exercise dependence exists independently of eating disorders. Davis *et al.* (1998) suggested that around 80 per cent of patients with anorexia nervosa have exercised extensively, thus indicating the extent of secondary exercise dependence. There is also a suggestion that high levels of exercise may trigger eating disorders, although there is considerable controversy in the literature. For example, Brehm and Steffan (1998) showed in a cross-sectional study that adolescents who were categorised as obligatory exercisers were more likely to have a drive for thinness (a major element in defining eating disorders) than adolescents who did exercise but were not classified as obligatory exercisers. The authors concluded that obligatory exercise could trigger eating disorders. Iannos and Tiggemann (1997) showed that for women who exercised more than eleven hours per week there was a high level of eating disordered behaviour. This association was not evident for the men in the study who exercised at equally high levels, which suggests that there may be different motivations for men and women who are exercise dependent. On the other hand, Szabo (2000) reviewed sixteen studies which have explored the association between eating disorders and exercise and noted that the conclusions are equivocal and that some of the discrepancies in findings related to the definitions of exercise used. This again outlines the need for standardised ways of measuring exercise dependence.

Exercise dependence secondary to eating disorders may not always be negative. Some treatment programmes may require cessation of exercise, but given that there may be some psychological gain from exercise in such conditions, it could be that modified exercise could be used as part of the treatment. For example, the caloric expenditure of an exercise session could be modified. Non-aerobic activities, such as strength training or flexibility training, will typically use fewer calories than aerobic activities undertaken for the same period of time and may help prevent the loss of lean tissue. Thus the psychological benefit may be retained for less caloric expenditure if strength and flexibility training was substituted for some aerobic activity. Alternatively, lower-intensity activity, such as walking rather than running, for the same amount of time could save calories, but provide a positive aspect to treatment. Exercise itself could be used as a reward (a pleasurable experience) in a programme in which eating patterns are being modified. There is at least one example of a randomised trial in which exercise was used as a positive aspect of treating eating disorders. Levine, Marcus and Moulton (1996) successfully used a walking programme to help control binge eating in obese women.

Exercise dependence secondary to muscle dysmorphia A much newer aspect of secondary exercise dependence relates to the newly named problem of muscle dysmorphia. Pope and colleagues have been the main researchers investigating this topic which was originally named 'reverse anorexia' (Phillips, Osullivan and Pope 1997; Pope *et al.* 1997; Pope, Katz and Hudson 1993). The distinguishing feature of this disorder, which is considered as a special case of body dysmorphic disorder, is the perception of lack of muscularity even when those concerned (mostly men) do have well-developed musculature (Choi, Pope and Olivardia 2002). Associated features include fear of public scrutiny of body such as in swimming pools or changing rooms, and a lifestyle in which training correctly and eating correctly to enhance muscularity is the most important issue. Having muscle dysmorphic disorder is the primary problem but the secondary issue is the dependence on exercise (typically strength training using weights). It is unclear if this compulsion to eat correctly is perhaps related to eating disorders as well. It is also clear that there may be a degree of social physique anxiety related to this condition and several researchers have shown a high prevalence of steroid and other drug abuse taken with the aim of increasing muscularity (Kanayama *et al.* 2001). Pope and colleagues have reported high levels (as high as 46 per cent) of steroid use among both male (Olivardia, Pope and Hudson 2000) and females (Pope *et al.* 1997) identified as having muscle dysmorphic disorder. Pope has also compared quality of life scores for those identified as having body dysmorphic disorder and those with the more specific muscle dysmorphic disorder and found that the muscle dysmorphic group had lower scores and also reported more suicide attempts. This study also established that the disorder is different from the more general diagnosis of body dysmorphic disorder (Pope *et al.* in press). Clearly muscle dysmorphia could damage both physical and mental health.

There is little discussion in the literature about the prevalence of this particular disorder or about the treatment and there is no agreed diagnostic criteria. Smith has developed and validated a scale to measure exercise dependence in body builders which should help this area move forward (Smith and Hale 2004, 2005). It remains to be seen if there is primary dependence on strength training exercise that is distinguishable from secondary dependence as a result of muscle dysmorphia. There is plenty of scope for qualitative, quantitative and psychometric research on this new topic within exercise psychology.

Are athletes doing high volumes of training exercise dependent? One particularly difficult area in the definition of exercise dependence is whether or not competitive athletes in training would be defined as dependent. At first glance many athletes would fulfil the criteria in Table 10.3, but their 'dependence' is almost a requirement of the pursuit of their primary goal which is the enhancement of performance. Perhaps the major concerns for athletes are the associated features H and I in Table 10.3 that can clearly lead to physical and mental harm over time. Weight loss that may appear similar to an eating disorder is a secondary condition in both exercise dependence and in sports in which 'leaness' is an advantage (for example, distance running), or in which weight control for competition categories is required (for example, judo, weightlifting), or in which muscularity is required (for example body building). A research study recently attempted to find if competitive body builders were more likely than recreational weight trainers to be muscle dysmorphic and concluded that there was no evidence for this (Pickett *et al.* 2005).

Coaches, exercise leaders and athletes must be aware of possible risks to long-term eating patterns which could be created by pressure to be a certain weight (Dummer *et al.* 1987), although the prevalence of eating disorders in these sports is not well described. In addition, Morgan (1994) reminded us that overtraining can have detrimental mental health effects such as mood disturbances and depression. Coaches and sports scientists should therefore be aware of the harmful effects of exercise dependence and overtraining and be ready to counsel and assist athletes who appear to be displaying such features, or mood disturbances over prolonged periods of time.

Why does exercise dependence occur? It is not clear why primary exercise dependence occurs. It has been shown that such extreme exercise behaviour in men is associated with an obsessive–compulsive personality trait (Davis, Brewer and Ratusny 1993) and that exercise dependent people are literally 'running away' from other, perhaps undiagnosed, problems. Szabo (2000) suggests that the literature points to self-esteem being negatively related and anxiety positively related to exercise dependence. It has also been proposed that a person who is exercise dependent has become addicted to the feelings associated with increased endorphin or adrenaline production as a result of exercise (Pierce 1994) but these speculations remain difficult to demonstrate empirically. Another physiologically based explanation has been termed the 'sympathetic arousal hypothesis' (Thompson and Blanton 1987). Regular exercise may cause decreased sympathetic arousal at rest that feels like lethargy to the individual. Dependence may occur because such an individual seeks out further bouts of activity to help achieve a preferred state of arousal. Beh, Mathers and Holden (1996) offered some support for this notion. They measured EEG in dependent and non-dependent exercisers and found that those classified as dependent had higher alpha frequencies than those non-dependent. The authors interpreted this as suggesting that dependent exercisers have higher levels of tonic arousal. This runs counter to the idea that sympathetic arousal is depressed as a result of exercise but is consistent with the notion of a preferred arousal level.

Other suggestions about why exercise dependence occurs include the possibility that exercise is an analogue for anorexia nervosa, although this has been heavily criticised and no supportive evidence has been produced (Biddle and Mutrie 1991). However, Davis, Brewer and Ratusny (1993) did show an association between excessive exercising and weight preoccupation in both men and women and while this finding may not show an analogue to more serious eating disorders, it certainly suggests a link. Furthermore, we know that exercise dependence is very often present with eating disorders, but what we do not know is whether primary exercise dependence occurs for the same reasons that eating disorders occur. Davis *et al.* (1998) have suggested, from quasi-experimental studies on anorectic patients, that those with higher levels of obsessive–compulsive symptomatology also have higher levels of excessive exercising. This finding led these authors to conclude that excessive exercising may exacerbate obsessive symptomatology when an eating disorder has developed. This particular connection provides some clinical evidence for an animal model of anorexia nervosa which shows that when experimental animals are deprived of food and have free access to a running wheel, they will reduce food intake and increase physical activity (Epling and Pierce 1988). This appears counter to self-preservation (as does excessive exercise and self-imposed starvation in humans), but can perhaps be explained by the similar effect which exercise and starvation have on increased 5–HT (serotonin) synthesis and turnover. The hypothesis for the biological link between the need to reduce food intake and increase exercise, as explained by Davis *et al.,* is that 'activity-induced 5–HT stimulation or turnover leads to reduced food intake and body weight which in turn provides a further stimulus for physical activity' (Davies *et al.* 1998: 193).

Further investigation of this intriguing biological mechanism may help explain exercise dependence and provide a new theory as to why it is seen so often in those with eating disorders. Techniques involved in these studies may also shed light on the positive psychological outcomes noted from physical activity such as a mood-enhancing effect or an antidepressant effect.

There is also discussion in the literature on secondary exercise dependence (both in eating disorders and in muscle dysmorphia) being connected to increased pressure from society and the media to have a particular physical shape (Leit, Gray and Pope 2002). The media pressure on women to be thin is one example of this but a newer example is the media pressure on men to look muscular. In 1999 Pope demonstrated how the notion of the ideal male shape has changed over the years by measuring the features of action toys for boys such as Action Man (Pope *et al.* 1999). The research showed that current dimensions of chest muscularity exceeded that present in the world's largest body builders. These studies show that society may be producing pressures that lead both men and women to be overly concerned about body image and this may result, in extreme cases, in eating disorders or muscle dysmorphic disorder both of which are associated with excessive amounts of physical activity.

EXERCISE DEPENDENCE: CONCLUSIONS

All health professionals should be aware of the characteristics of exercise dependence. Although the public health risk is negligible, an individual who is exercise dependent may be at risk of mental or physical ill health. All professionals who are likely to come in contact with such individuals should raise awareness of the issue and offer avenues for seeking help. Those treating eating disorders will be aware of the use of exercise in these conditions but might also consider how exercise could play a positive role in the treatment of eating disorders. Coaches must be aware that there is a risk of triggering eating disorders by demanding a particular body weight or shape. Such issues need to be carefully handled to avoid long-term harm. Finally, further research is required to understand the prevalence and characteristics of those who are exercise dependent. In particular a measurement scale, which could be validated against the diagnostic criteria, is required.

COGNITION

Cognition is also an area that has attracted considerable research interest from exercise scientists, but the application of this interest to individuals with clinical problems has been restricted to those with stroke or brain injury, as reported above. Etnier *et al.* (1997) conducted a meta-analysis of all the available studies (n = 134) that had examined the influence of fitness and exercise on cognitive function and found an overall effect size of 0.25. This suggests that exercise improves cognitive function by a small, but significant, amount. They noted that this effect was smaller with increasing experimental rigour and larger when longer term programmes were examined. They investigated a wide range of moderator variables including normal or impaired mental fitness that could be considered as a clinical condition. However, mental fitness did not have a significant impact on the effect size noted above, which suggests no added advantage to this potential clinical group. Impaired mental fitness may not equate to a clinical condition and so it is probably better to conclude that there are potential cognitive gains for 'clinical' individuals, such as those with brain injury, as discussed above.

Also in this final category are hearing and visual impairments and in both these conditions potential benefits to the patient's self-image, confidence and social skills are noted along with more physical benefits such as balance and fitness (American College of Sports Medicine 1997a). However, there is almost nothing in the published research literature that can help us with creating and sustaining adherence to exercise for these patients. Similarly, although Alzheimer's disease and mental retardation are listed in this category, again there is very little research to guide us about the potential benefits of exercise for these populations or any special considerations in relation to exercise adherence. There is an obvious need for further research here.

Guidelines for practice

- Medical teams in clinical settings should encourage regular activity for most patient groups. There are few conditions in which some benefit for increasing activity cannot be found and there are few conditions in which exercise would be contraindicated.
- Medical teams should undertake training in the basic principles of exercise psychology.
- Use continuing professional development (such as the British Association of Cardiac Rehabilitation courses) to keep staff up-to-date in specialist areas.
- Where physical activity/exercise is advocated as part of treatment (for example, cardiac rehabilitation or diabetes), the goal should be to create independent exercisers. Supervised exercise should be restricted to initial phases.
- Where physical activity/exercise has been recommended, records of activity levels should be recorded at all clinic appointments.

- Use Quaglietti and Froelicher's (1994) suggestions for improving adherence in cardiac rehabilitation as a guide for all clinical settings in which exercise is recommended:

  > reduce the waiting time, provide expert supervision, tailor the exercise to avoid physical discomfort and frustration, use variable activities including games, incorporate social event, recall absent patients, involve the patient's family or spouse in the program, and involve the patient in monitoring his or her progress.
  >
  > (Quaglietti and Froelicher 1994: 599)

Recommendations for research with clinical populations

- There is plenty of scope for research in the areas of adherence to exercise and psychological outcomes from exercise for most clinical populations.
- Researchers should try to form links with medical teams dealing with specific conditions.
- Qualitative research may often provide a starting point for such research because many of the situations do not lend themselves to standard clinical trials.
- Explore a variety of programmes such as home-, community- and hospital-based or combinations of these. While close supervision may be required in the early stages, the long-term goal is independent exercise for these populations.
- Both researchers and practitioners should operate with a model of behaviour change to guide them.
- Activity must be recorded before and after any exercise programme or intervention. Self-reported activity is a start point (see for example Craig *et al.* 2003), but objective data such as that provided by accelerometers or pedometers should also be considered. It is often important to know both how much activity the person is doing and how (for example by exercise classes, walking or gardening) they are doing it.
- Report the uptake for any exercise programme from the potential client population.
- Investigate motivations and barriers to exercise in each patient group as a whole and also for those who have taken up the offer or completed an exercise programme.
- Record and report (via a register or via contact) adherence at regular intervals (for example, weekly class register or monthly phone calls for home-based programmes). Report adherence to exercise prescription as a percentage of target in as many ways as possible, for example, minutes of activity per week, number of sessions completed, full weeks of exercise. If this is self-report data, provide corroboration via class registers, friends and relatives, pedometers, etc. Once this is done various outcomes, including motivations and barriers, can be described for high and low adherers.
- Report dropout rate. This will involve reporting those who dropped out before commencing and those who did not complete different stages. A definition of non-completion is required and completion of less than a half of the required programme is suggested as a working definition. Provide a between-groups analysis of dropout rate so that potential causes can be investigated. Make every effort to contact dropouts to establish reasons for not continuing.
- Ideally include qualitative and quantitative analysis on motivations and barriers for high, low or no adherence.
- Describe the exercise programme and the amount of supervision and encouragement given.
- Aim to provide adherence information at six months but a longer follow-up is even better.
- Include relevant psychological outcomes in all intervention studies.

- Include the issue of the potential mechanisms of psychological benefit.
- Use standardised questionnaires that have known validity and reliability.
- If possible provide qualitative information from health professionals and medical staff of their view of role of exercise for any given patient group.

Why does exercise make us feel good? A discussion of possible mechanisms

There is considerable agreement that the underlying mechanisms related to the positive effects from exercise on mental health are not yet known (Biddle and Mutrie 1991; Morgan 1997; Morgan and Goldston 1987; Plante 1993; Landers and Alderman 2007). Several possible mechanisms, including biochemical changes (for example, increased levels of endorphins) and psychological changes (for example, increased sense of mastery), have been proposed (Petruzzello *et al.* 1991). We have discussed these ideas briefly in Chapters 8 and 9 but here we offer a longer discussion. Psychosomatic principles have suggested for a long time that what we think and feel will have an impact on our physical functioning. What we appear to be searching for is a parallel to understanding psychosomatic processes since the body's activity affecting how we feel can easily be classed as 'somatopsychic' (Harris 1973). Somatopsychic principles suggest that what happens in the body will have an effect on how we think, feel and behave. This body–mind relationship is challenging to a number of disciplines such as philosophy, psychology and neuroscience. What is intriguing to scholars who place importance on physical activity is that the relationship is usually studied from mind to body and, in Western thought at least, the mind is given the lead role in most discussions – hence mind–body and psychosomatic. The importance of the mind over the body is suggestive of what philosophers have described as 'dualism' or a belief that the mind and body are separate with different functions. However, evolution has ensured that we have skilful bodies engineered for movement and we believe that our search for the somatopsychic processes, which will provide an answer to why physical activity might help people feel better, must at least equate the importance of body and mind. Buckworth and Dishman (2002) suggested that understanding the interconnection of body and mind (or brain) is one of the basic concepts of exercise psychology. They stated that, ' There is extensive empirical evidence that changes in the brain, including the expression of genes, produce changes in behaviour and that changes in behaviour in turn produce changes in the brain' and 'Thus, an understanding of exercise psychology would be incomplete without an examination of neurobiological systems' (Buckworth and Dishman 2002: 18). One good overview of the potential neurobiological systems that may be operating when people report that exercise makes them feel better or less depressed has been provided by La Forge (1995).

> Key point: Physical activity and exercise affect how we think and feel – this is known as the somatopsychic process.

La Forge (1995) has provided one of the best reviews of the possible mechanisms because he started from a standpoint of integrating the possible mechanisms rather than describing them as separate processes. This integration occurs via neural connections and to accept La Forge's model one has to accept the philosophical position that all emotions have a neurological explanation. Table 10.4 shows the mechanisms La Forge has integrated. This table

Table 10.4 Mechanisms for exercise-associated mood changes reviewed by La Forge (1995)

Name of hypothesis	Indicative reference	Major principles	Comments
Opponent-process theory	Solomon (1980)	Processes which oppose the heightened state of arousal brought about by exercise seek to return the body's systems to homeostasis. These opponent processes get stronger through training and thus may cause relaxation and anxiety reduction post exercise in trained individuals	Very difficult to obtain empirical evidence as many processes could potentially oppose. Thus hypothetically linked to all the other processes mentioned
Opioids	Schwarz and Kindermann (1992)	Opioids (e.g. endorphins, enkephalins, dynorphins) are associated with increased mood and decreased pain sensations. Exercise increases plasma levels of opioids and thus opioids could therefore be responsible for post-exercise mood enhancement. This system is linked to the cardiovascular, respiratory, reproductive and immune systems	It is not clear if the plasma levels reflect the central nervous system levels of opioids and research investigating the exercise and mood link has been equivocal
Monoamines	Chaouloff (1997)	Monoamines (dopamine, norepinephrine, epinephrine, serotonin) are involved in depression and anxiety. Much antidepressant medication is aimed at increasing the amounts of these amines. Exercise may also stimulate production	Most of the exercise research is animal based but since medications have extensive human research it is a very plausible hypothesis
Neocortical activation	Kubitz and Landers (1993)	Incoming signals from muscles, etc. during movement stimulate areas of the cortex responsible for mood. In addition exercise may cause a shift to right hemisphere processing. Links to the concept of exercising to find 'optimal' levels of arousal	Methods have been inconsistent and often no mood or anxiety measure taken. Associating mood states with activity in specific brain regions is not an exact science at present but the technology to assess this is advancing quickly
Thermogenic changes	Petruzzello et al. (1991)	Increased core temperature decreases muscle tension and has been hypothesised to reduce anxiety. Certain types of exercise will increase core temperature	Very little support for this hypothesis has emerged from the literature. Given the body's ability to maintain core temperature against hostile environments this does seem an unlikely explanation but the process of maintaining temperature may link to the opioids or to cortical activity
Hypothalamic–pituitary–adrenal (HPA) axis changes	Peronnet and Szabo (1993)	The HPA axis is the framework for mind–body communication; it plays a role in depression, eating disorders and stress response. Stress hormones are released by this axis in response to physical (exercise) and mental stress. High levels of stress hormones are associated with negative moods. Training decreases the amount of stress hormone release, but overtraining increases it	The mechanisms which elicit responses by the HPA axis to exercise stress and to psychosocial stress are probably different and need to be better understood before this hypothesis can be advanced

provides a brief summary and commentary on these hypotheses. He also points out that all of the mechanisms in the table overlap in terms of structure and function and in terms of neuro-anatomic pathways. The integrated model he proposes accepts this overlap and suggests that it is the integration that must be studied rather than the isolated mechanisms. However, and paradoxically, this seems only to be achievable by researchers focusing on each part, and then bringing their research together. This leads to the call for interdisciplinary research and the need to employ the latest imaging technologies to enhance understanding of what happens in the exerciser's brain.

What is particularly appealing in this integrated model is that, in terms of mental illness, exercise can be seen to play the same role as some antidepressant drugs but at the same time it could have more widespread, and potentially beneficial, effects. La Forge's model also deals with two of the most prominent models of depression namely, the monoamine hypothesis and the HPA axis model, and thus is particularly important for those who are trying to understand why exercise could operate as an antidepressant. Readers who wish to understand these mechanisms in more depth are directed to the work of Rod Dishman (see Buckworth and Dishman 2002).

However, some of the more widespread effects that we have discussed elsewhere in this book are not yet accounted for in this model. For example perhaps exercise makes us feel good because we change our perception of our physical selves and increase our sense of self-worth? Or perhaps exercise can help people recover from depression because it gets them out of the house and reduces feelings of isolation? If exercise is done in a group setting there is the chance that interacting with others in the group or the attention and feedback from the group leader may make us feel better. One of the most important omissions from the La Forge model is how exercise can provide a sense of mastery and control. For example, one theory of depression suggests that depression is a result of feeling that there is no action that can be taken to alleviate a problem. This feeling of helplessness is learned over a period of time and from a variety of situations, and results in the person having an external locus of control (Abramson, Seligman and Teasdale 1978; Peterson, Maier and Seligman 1993; Seligman 1975). It has been suggested that exercise can play a role in helping the person who is suffering in this way to gain control in one area of life, namely the physical self. In addition, if the exercise is programmed correctly, the sense of achievement and progression from week to week builds on this sense of control and may even provide a sense of mastery (Greist *et al.* 1981). Self-esteem enhancement has therefore featured as a potential explanation for how exercise can alleviate depression and anxiety (Ossip-Klein *et al.* 1989). La Forge's integrated model, as it stands, does not account for the neurobiology of achievement or self-esteem enhancement, or psychosocial explanations of the feel-good effect ... but it could. New technologies will soon be able to show which areas of the brain are activated when we sense achievement and such pathways will undoubtedly link to those already identified by La Forge. A way forward in this area might be to use the hierarchical model of physical self-worth (Fox, 1997a, 1997b; Fox and Corbin 1989) to explore how exercise may alter feelings of self-worth for those suffering from mental illness and then finally to map the areas of the brain responsible for the perceptions of these changes. We are not so very far away from this technology now. For example Brad Hatfield, in his keynote lecture to the 11th World Congress in Sport Psychology, explained advances in cognitive neuroscience that will provide better understanding of what is happening in the brain during successful sport performances (Hatfield 2005). Such advances include improvement measurements of brain activity. These techniques could also be applied to exercise to help us understand 'successful' exercise experience, for example an experience that makes the exerciser 'feel good'.

At the same congress Dr Arne Dietrich explained the transient hypofrontality hypothesis which he has developed from his work with brain imaging (Dietrich 2005). This hypothesis suggests that people may feel less depressed or anxious after exercise because the central nervous system has to cope with the very high demand to process the signals from movement and this allows less capacity to process neural activity related to anxiety and depression. Does this hypothesis provide the neurobiology of exercise causing a 'distraction' from negative emotions? Dietrich has also suggested that endocannabinoids could provide a new explanation of the psychological benefits of exercise and dismisses the more common opioid hypothesis as oversimplistic (Dietrich 2005). These new ideas suggest that new technology which will allow improved understanding of the brain during movement will help us understand why exercise can make us feel better. This is an exciting area of research and the next decade of work should shed light on what remains a very plausible concept that exercise can influence the brain and this can make us 'feel good'.

The final comment on this model is that it also has to account for the apparent pleasure in inactivity which the vast majority of the population experience. Can we have learned that homeostasis (staying still and inactive) is more pleasurable than all the built-in connections which seem to reward activity? In evolutionary terms it is easy to see that activity needed to be rewarded, but perhaps the rewards are only available once we get past a certain level of conditioning (readiness to be active for survival) and prior to that our responses to activity are suggestive of pain and punishment (safer to be still) rather than reward and pleasure. For deconditioned people it is more pleasurable to maintain inactivity. Ekkekakis, Hall and Petruzzello (2005) has recently provided a framework for understanding how we feel when we have been exercising from an evolutionary perspective (see Chapter 8 for further discussion of this work). The dual-mode model that he suggested proposes that at moderate levels of intensity (below the lactate threshold) activity will be found to be pleasurable, but at higher levels of intensity only some people will find pleasure and others will not. What will determine our sense of pleasure from exercise at higher levels are cognitive factors such as our personality, previous experience, goals that we have set and the level of confidence that we can complete the exercise. This dual-mode model is in contrast to the general acceptance that there is a dose–response curve associated with benefits of physical activity. It may be that affective responses do not operate that way.

For health professionals keen to get more of the population active the slow and gradual approach towards activity at a moderate level is essential if we are to gain the feelings of pleasure which are potentially available for activity and avoid evoking displeasure and pain. This means that the old training adage of 'no pain no gain' has no place in the promotion of physical activity for health. As Biddle and Ekkekakis suggested, a revision of prescriptions for exercise based on percentages of heart rate maximum or other measures of physiological capacity must be considered. They stated that 'more effort should be directed at understanding the self-selection of physical activity intensity. Some evidence exists to suggest that individuals will intuitively adjust their pace to optimize pleasure' (Biddle and Ekkekakis 2005: 494).

There is still much to learn about why exercise provides the feel-better effect but the integrated model is a starting point on which both theories of motivation to exercise and explanations of psychological effects from exercise can be built. La Forge provided this sensible guide to future practice:

> The mechanism is likely an extraordinary synergy of biological transactions, including genetic, environmental, and acute and adaptive neurobiological processes. Inevitably,

the final answers will emerge from a similar synergy of researchers and theoreticians from exercise science, cognitive science and neurobiology.

(La Forge 1995: 28)

This synergy of researchers is not always easy to achieve in the current academic climate in which resources follow demarcated research groups, but it is an ideal worth pursuing for those with a passion to find out exactly why exercise may help us feel better.

Chapter summary and conclusions

This chapter has:

- considered the role of physical activity and exercise in the treatment of a variety of clinical populations
- used the American College of Sports Medicine's classification of disease and disability
- provided examples of psychological issues for specific conditions from each category
- discussed possible mechanisms that could explain why physical activity has psychological benefits.

We conclude:

- patients in almost all categories of disease and disability could benefit from exercise. There are few contraindications
- knowledge about adherence and psychological outcomes is incomplete. The area of cardiac rehabilitation offers the most information on adherence
- good short-term adherence (four to twelve weeks) can be achieved from supervised programmes of exercise. However, for some populations, such as those in drug rehabilitation or those with HIV positive status, even short-term adherence may need special support systems
- long-term adherence (12 months–4 years) is poor and not well documented. The best information comes from follow-up of those in cardiac rehabilitation which suggests that 30–55 per cent are still exercising after four years
- home-based walking programmes seem to offer the best hope for long-term adherence but other modalities must be explored
- very little is known about the level of exercise in clinical populations. For example, only one-third of Type 1 diabetics are regular exercisers despite the fact that exercise is well recognised as part of diabetic treatment
- dropout from exercise programmes is associated with factors to do with the programme and factors to do with the person and his/her circumstances
- motivations for exercise are clearly to do with improved health
- barriers to exercise are similar to those for non-clinical populations (for example, lack of time) but also include issues to do with the particular disease state (for example, fear of another MI or fear of worsening osteoporosis) which could be overcome through appropriate patient education
- cognitive–behavioural strategies can be effective and the use of a counselling approach should be encouraged in all clinical settings.

- psychological outcomes are often mentioned anecdotally but are rarely measured in exercise programmes or interventions. The potential psychological benefits range from increasing a person's sense of confidence, control and self-esteem, improving mood, increasing social opportunities, improving cognitive function and improving quality of life
- there is a need for raising awareness in some medical teams concerning the role of exercise, the potential psychological benefits and the need to assist patients with adherence to exercise
- exercise dependence is a potentially harmful outcome from exercise but the prevalence is not known. Exercise dependence secondary to eating disorders or muscle dysmorphia may be more common than primary exercise dependence
- there is no clear consensus about the mechanisms that could explain the psychological benefits experienced from physical activity. New technology may offer greater understanding of this topic in the near future.

Part IV

Physical activity

What works in helping people be more active?

11 Intervention strategies aimed at groups and individuals

'Talking the talk and walking the walk'

The drama of behaviour change and resistance to it plays itself out across the full spectrum of daily life.

(Rollnick, Mason and Butler 1999)

Chapter objectives

The purpose of this chapter is to give examples of interventions aimed at groups and individuals that are designed to increase physical activity.

Specifically, in this chapter we will:

- provide a framework for discussing interventions aimed at increasing physical activity levels
- summarise recent reviews that cover individual and group approaches
- give examples of studies that have used a group setting to promote physical activity
- give examples of studies that have used individuals as the focus for promoting physical activity
- discuss the use of pedometers as a tool to promote physical activity
- describe the process of physical activity consultation and show results of studies using this approach
- show how the primary care setting can be used to increase physical activity
- discuss limitations to the evidence base regarding groups and individuals
- draw conclusions about current research knowledge in this area
- make recommendations for researchers and practitioners.

A framework for discussion

The ecological model of behaviour change that we presented in chapter 7 provides a framework for discussion of what we know about intervening to promote changes in physical activity behaviour. In this chapter we will focus on the interpersonal and intrapersonal aspects of that framework (Sallis and Owen 2002a). However, we will not deal with clinical populations who may receive these interventions here. They have already been mentioned in Chapter 10. Interventions that operate at other levels of this model are discussed in Chapters 7 and 12.

Recent reviews of interventions aimed at individuals and groups

Several reviews have been conducted in this area and provide us with guidance for practice. Hillsdon and Thorogood (1996) conducted a systematic review of intervention strategies for the promotion of physical activity and found that, at least in 1996, there was not one single UK trial which fitted their review criteria. Their conclusions suggested that individual interventions that do not require attendance at a facility, such as walking, are likely to be most successful and that regular follow-up improves adherence.

Kahn *et al.* (2002) produced a recent systematic review of interventions to promote physical activity along with an evidence-based set of recommendations (Fielding *et al.* 2002). The systematic review was commissioned by the US Task Force on Community Preventive Services as an element in the Guide to Community Preventive Services. Information about the Guide to Community Services and its importance for Public Health can be found at www.thecommunityguide.org/. The methods used to construct this systematic review are described in Briss *et al.* (2000) and involve extensive and rigorous procedures which include the appointment of a review team, the development of a conceptual framework for the review, the systematic searching, retrieval and review of relevant evidence, and summarising the strength of the body of evidence using standard techniques. The body of evidence is then designated as strong, sufficient or insufficient. These techniques are similar to those used by Cochrane reviews (www.cochrane.org).

The Kahn *et al.* (2002) systematic review used changes in physical activity behaviour and aerobic capacity as measures of effectiveness and the conceptual framework divided the possible interventions into three areas: those that provided information, those that used behavioural skills and social support and those that focused on environmental or policy changes. They considered 253 candidate studies but rejected 159 that did not match the criteria for the review. The diverse measures used in these studies could not be transformed into the same scale and it was therefore not possible for Kahn *et al.* (2002) to provide a single quantitative summary of effect size. As a result various effect sizes are presented so that a general direction of effect can be judged. These effect sizes are presented as median net changes with inter-quartile ranges (IQR). The conclusions that are particularly relevant to interventions that target individual adult behaviour change by behavioural and social interventions can be summarised as follows:

- There was insufficient evidence that family-based social support interventions effectively increased physical activity. This topic will be discussed further later on in this chapter.
- There was strong evidence that strengthening local support networks through buddy systems, walking groups and exercise contacts increased physical activity. The review of interventions that increased physical activity through improved social support in the community considered nine papers. These studies typically involved recruiting groups of people to support each other via phone calls, discussion groups considering strategies to overcome barriers, and buddying systems. The effect sizes from five interventions showed median net increases in time spent being physically active of 44.2 per cent (IQR of 19.9 per cent to 45.6 per cent). The evidence showed median net increases in frequency of exercise of 19.6 per cent (IQR of 14.6 per cent to 57.6 per cent) and median net increases in aerobic capacity of 4.7 per cent (IQR 3.3 per cent to 6.1 per cent). Highly structured and less formal support appeared to be equally effective. One study showed that more frequent support improved effectiveness. These interventions were effective across a range of countries and settings.

- There was strong evidence that personalised health behaviour-change programmes, tailored to an individual's specific stage of behaviour or interest, were effective in increasing physical activity. Activities such as goal setting, social support schemes, self-reward schemes, relapse prevention and active living approaches to physical activity promotion were viewed as particularly effective. The review of personalised behaviour change interventions considered eighteen studies. These studies were all based on a theoretical behavioural approach (for example transtheoretical model or health belief model) and all included goal setting and self-monitoring, self-reward/reinforcement, social support building, strategies for behavioural maintenance and relapse prevention techniques. The interventions were delivered in groups, by mail, telephone or through other specific media. In terms of effectiveness, the available evidence showed a median net increase of 35.4 per cent in time spent in physical activity (IQR of 16.7 per cent to 83.3 per cent), a median increase in maximum oxygen uptake of 6.3 per cent (IQR 5.1 per cent to 9.85) and showed median increase of 64.3 per cent in energy expenditure (IQR of 31.2 per cent to 85.5 per cent). The review concluded that the interventions were applicable to a wide range of settings and groups with the caveat that interventions must be adapted to the target population.

A more recent review comes from the Health Development Agency in the UK (Hillsdon *et al.* 2003). This 'review of reviews' summarises the evidence from sixteen systematic reviews and meta-analyses of interventions that promote physical activity for adults. Table 11.1 provides a summary of the findings of the review. As can be seen from the table there are plenty of gaps in the evidence, but the current evidence suggests that short-term change is feasible, that use of a behaviour change theory will help, referring to an exercise specialist will help and walking may be the best mode of activity to promote.

> Key point: Systematic reviews suggest that short-term changes in physical activity are achievable but that long-term change is difficult to achieve.

Interventions that focus on groups

Project Active

In the USA, Project Active (Dunn *et al.* 1998, 1997, 1999) aimed to establish if an active living approach to promoting physical activity could be as effective as a traditional fitness-oriented approach. The project used the TTM as a basis for the interventions aimed to change sedentary behaviour. The project recruited 116 men and 119 women (mean age forty-six years) by press and other media in Dallas, Texas. The participants were randomly assigned to one of two groups. One group was labelled 'Structured Exercise' and followed ACSM guidelines for cardiorespiratory fitness via a traditional gym-based approach at the Cooper Aerobics Centre. Participants in this group were supervised for six months and then paid a fee to remain a 'member' of the aerobics centre. The second group was labelled 'Lifestyle Counselling' and followed the 'Active Living' guidelines. When they met they did not exercise but had group discussions designed to assist adoption and maintenance of active living. At first the meetings were weekly (first four months); these then tapered to bi-weekly from four to six months, monthly from six to twelve months, bi-monthly from twelve to eighteen months, and finally tri-monthly from eighteen to twenty-four months.

Table 11.1 Summary of evidence from 'review of reviews' (Hillsdon *et al.* 2003)

In health care settings

- Brief advice from a health care professional can lead to modest short-term (less than 12 weeks) increases in PA
- Referral to an exercise specialist can lead to longer-term change (up to 8 months)
- Walking is the most frequent mode of PA recommended

In community settings

- Short- and medium-term change in PA feasible
- Interventions based on behaviour change theory best
- Moderate-intensity (walking) and non-facility-based interventions are best
- Contact with an exercise specialist can help sustain change

---

Workplace settings

- No consistent evidence

Gaps in the evidence

- Black and ethnic minority groups (no evidence available)
- Policy interventions (no evidence available)
- Changing the built environment (no evidence available)

At six months, 85 per cent of the Structured group and 78 per cent of the Lifestyle group were achieving the minimum Active Living criteria. Both groups had improved cardiorespiratory fitness (although the Structured group improved more than the Lifestyle group). In addition, both groups had reduced total cholesterol, total cholesterol/HDL–C ratio, diastolic BP and percentage body fat. There was a 15 per cent reduction in CHD risk overall (17 per cent Structured, 12 per cent Lifestyle).

By twenty-four months both groups increased total energy expenditure (TEE) and cardiorespiratory fitness from baseline and had similar decreases from six months. These results are illustrated in Figures 11.1 and 11.2. Twenty per cent of the participants were still on or above the active living recommendations. There was a dose–response relationship with those doing the most consistent activity (maintaining minimum guidelines for 70 per cent of the twenty-four weeks) showing the best fitness and TEE responses. In addition, both groups decreased BP and percentage body fat while body weight remained unchanged. The authors drew the conclusion that the lifestyle approach was as effective as a traditional fitness approach in improving activity, fitness, BP and body composition and declare this to be good news for those who could not tolerate or maintain the 'fitness' approach. However, there are aspects of this project limiting both the internal and external validity of the results.

Key point: 'Project Active' was the first study to show that promoting active living had similar fitness effects to promoting more traditional structured exercise.

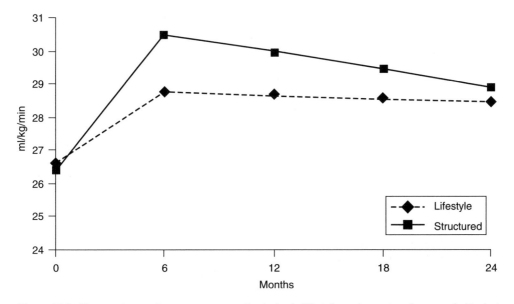

Figure 11.1 Changes in maximum oxygen uptake in both lifestyle and structured groups in Project Active (data from Dunn *et al.* 1999)

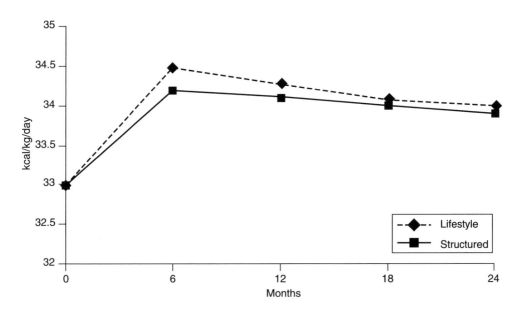

Figure 11.2 Changes in total energy expenditure in both lifestyle and structured groups in Project Active (data from Dunn *et al.* 1999)

It could be said that this is not a true randomised controlled trial since there is no control group. The lack of a control group raises the issue of whether or not anyone motivated to sign up for such a project would have made similar changes over twenty-four months even if they had not received either of the interventions. Given the wealth of evidence suggesting that long-term exercise is difficult to achieve, this is possible but unlikely. The changes which were recorded were modest (for example less than 2 per cent body fat loss and less than 2 ml/kg/min improvement in aerobic fitness) and only 20 per cent of participants were still achieving the active living recommendations at twenty-four months. On the one hand it could be argued that if this kind of change could be achieved across the population substantial health gains could also be achieved. On the other hand it could be argued that this was an expensive method of achieving minimal changes in activity levels, which also may be difficult to generalise to other locations. It is hard to imagine any local health promotion agency being able to sustain the regularity of meetings required for the lifestyle counselling group (twenty hours in the first six months) with a population who do not have the motivation for being involved in a research project. In addition, Project Active recruited a population of participants who were well educated and likely to be interested in healthy lifestyles. Is it possible that the same techniques could be successful with a more representative population?

Overall, the findings support the concept of the Active Living approach and this was the first piece of research demonstrating long-term outcomes. This means that health promoters can be more confident in suggesting that the Active Living approach can produce fitness and health benefits. In addition, a cost-effectiveness analysis showed that at six months the cost of the Active Living approach was $46 per person while the Structured Excercise approach cost $190 per person (Sevick *et al.* 2000). Thus the Active Living approach has the strong advantage of being cheaper to deliver. However, we need further research that tests cheaper and more readily applicable means of changing physical activity behaviour if we are to achieve changes across all socio-economic groups.

The SWEAT trial

The SWEAT ('Sedentary Women Exercise Adherence') trial (Cox *et al.* 2003; McTiernan *et al.* 2003) used the TTM as the theoretical basis for an intervention testing the effectiveness of supervised versus home-based exercise for middle- and older-aged sedentary women. Four intervention arms were tested: centre-based moderate exercise, centre-based vigorous exercise, home-based moderate exercise and home-based vigorous exercise. The centre-based groups attended supervised exercise sessions three times per week while the home-based groups attended training sessions for the first five weeks and then exercised at home three times per week after that. All participants exercised from home after six months. Written materials were produced that matched stages of change. At baseline, all were in contemplation or preparation stages and were given information on the processes of change that were deemed appropriate (that is, experiential processes). These became more behavioural as the trial progressed into the six, twelve and eighteen month phases. Results showed that the centre-based intervention was slightly more successful for energy expenditure at six and twelve months, but by eighteen months it was the same as home-based. For adherence, the centre-based intervention was successful at 6 months but no differences between conditions were evident at twelve and eighteen months.

The effectiveness of interventions such as group-based or gym-based programmes may be attributed to the social support element inherent in such contexts. In addition, many approaches to behaviour change stress the role of social support, including the TTM via some of the processes of change, and interventions based on the theory of planned behaviour whereby changes to subjective norms are targeted. Details of these theories of behaviour change have already been provided in earlier chapters.

Social support interventions

Regarding social support interventions, Kahn *et al.* (2002) located nine studies and concluded that the typical intervention of this type involved the recruitment of people into voluntary groups in which companionship and support were provided for attaining physical activity-related goals. Examples include telephone support and discussion groups. Their overall conclusion was that there is 'strong evidence that social support interventions ... are effective in increasing levels of physical activity, as measured by an increase in the percentage of people engaging in physical activity, energy expenditure, or other measure of physical activity' (Kahn *et al.* 2002: 85). This evidence was applicable to a wide range of settings and populations. However, although no barriers to implementation were identified, economic effectiveness could not be assessed.

One interpersonal setting that is often thought to have potential for physical activity behaviour change is that of the family. Although this is often targeted at children (Sallis 1998), it also has potential to influence adults, such as spouses and partners without children (Kahn *et al.* 2002). Studies in this category identified by Kahn *et al.* included family-based educational interventions (for example, goal-setting) and a family component of a school-based intervention (for example, take-home materials). From eleven studies, Kahn *et al.* concluded that, due to inconsistency across studies, there was 'insufficient evidence to assess the effectiveness of family-based social support interventions' (2002: 84).

Key point: Families have the potential to influence activity levels of all generations but there is currently limited evidence about the effectiveness of interventions that target families.

Kahn *et al.* (2002) also reviewed what they called 'individually adapted' programmes, such as those already discussed in the section on the TTM in Chapter 6. The interventions were often delivered by people in group settings or through other outlets such as by phone or mail. Reviewing eighteen such studies they concluded that there was strong evidence for effectiveness and good applicability across diverse settings and populations. They located some evidence for economic effectiveness, but warned that successful interventions of this type require careful planning, well-trained staff and adequate resources.

The topics of motivational climate and exercise leadership clearly have an impact on whether or not group activity influences adherence. Both topics are therefore very pertinent to this discussion and the reader is referred to Chapter 7 for further information.

Promoting physical activity to individuals

Promoting physical activity in university students

University students are often in a transitional stage between school and work and at a stage in life where lifestyle behaviours are under their own control. Sports have always been a feature of student life but typically only a minority of students – those who already feel competent in the arena of competitive sport take part. There are still substantial numbers of students who are not regularly active. Encouraging physical activity, especially to those who enter university without a love of sports, could be considered as a transferable skill that higher education can provide. Transferable skills are considered to be those learned in one location (in this case higher education) that can be transferred to other areas such as employment or in this case lifestyle. Indeed, we have shown that being active is a transferable skill since students who were active during their studies were able to continue their physical activity after graduation despite new demands of work and lack of facilities (Carney, Mutrie and McNeish 2000). To explore how to get inactive students into physical activity, and provide them with a potential transferable skill, Woods, Mutrie and Scott (2002) used a postal intervention based on the stage of change model, targeted to sedentary undergraduate students (Woods, Mutrie and Scott 2002). The design of this study involved almost 3,000 first-year students at a large city university. Baseline information was collected from these students while they waited in line to register at the university. The baseline information included current stage of change for physical activity and exercise, participation pattern for physical education in the last two years of schooling, and intentions towards activity in the next six months. Those who were categorised as precontemplators or contemplators (n = 459) were then randomly assigned to an experimental or control group. The experimental group was sent, by post, stage-matched materials that were designed to encourage participation in Active Living or in the university's structured exercise programmes. Follow-ups were conducted at seven and nineteen months on all students. The design of this study is shown in Figure 11.3.

The baseline results showed that 46 per cent of the student population was not achieving the current minimum physical activity targets. Thirty-five per cent had not taken part in PE during their final two years at school. There was a significant positive association between taking part in PE at school and current activity. Those who had participated in PE were more likely to be in the regularly active stages of change and to intend to exercise in the future. This association is shown in Figure 11.4. This shows the potentially important part that schools can play in promoting attendance at PE that clearly relates to continued involvement in activity beyond the years of schooling.

> Key point: A large percentage of university students do not achieve minimum levels of physical activity but students are more likely to be active if they had attended PE classes in their final years of schooling.

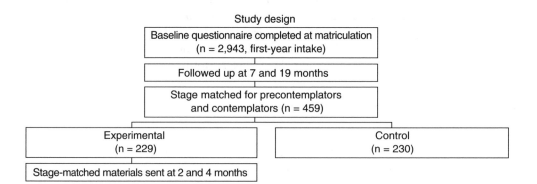

Figure 11.3 Study design for a postal intervention targeted at precontemplating and contemplating students (Woods, Mutrie and Scott 2002)

Stage of change and physical education

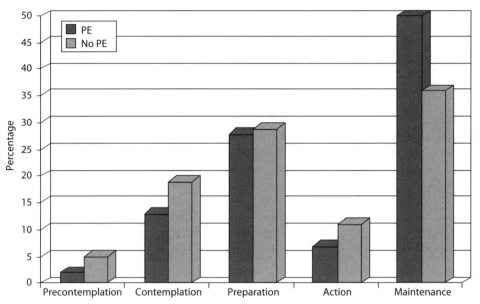

Those who had participated in PE during their final two years in school were more likely to be in active categories of SOC (PE χ^2 (4, N = 2,853) = 79.86, p < 0.001) and to intend to exercise in the future (PE χ^2 (4, N = 2,857) = 93.58, p< 0.001)

Figure 11.4 Percentage of students at each stage of exercise behaviour change who had participated in physical education (PE) during the final two years of schooling (Woods, Mutrie and Scott 2002)

At seven months, more of the experimental group (80 per cent) than the control group (68 per cent) had increased stage of change and, at nineteen months, more of the experimental group (42 per cent) than the control group (27 per cent) were in action and maintenance stages of exercise behaviour. The most frequently used processes of behaviour change, for those who improved their stage of change over time, were self-re-evaluation, self-liberation and reward management (see Chapter 6 for explanation of these processes of behaviour change). These results suggest that using postal, self-instruction material is a cheap way of encouraging the least active students into an active lifestyle as they arrive at university and that the effect can last into their second year at university.

Some of the most interesting material from this research came from qualitative data. Nine focus groups were carried out to explore the perceptions of these students about physical activity during their initial years at university. Several important findings emerged from both a content analysis and a group dynamics analysis. The results revealed how young adults talk about their past and current experiences of physical activity, how these experiences influenced current levels of participation, and what might help them to be active in the future. Themes to emerge from the data included the importance of social determinants (for example, the role of significant others) and self-empowerment (for example, belief in your ability to be part of an exercise culture) in physical activity adoption and maintenance. The following excerpt from the transcription of the focus group discussions shows the importance of social support in overcoming feelings of incompetence in certain activities:

I suppose it was recently we started exercising again because I thought people will laugh at me and I didn't do anything till this year again because it was just I thought will people laugh at me I'm not any good at this, why should I bother I've not been good at it before. The only thing that I enjoyed was swimming. I'm still a bit overweight. I recently lost a lot of weight and I wouldn't have gone in a pool in a swimming costume or anything. It's friends that encouraged me to go back and I'm so glad I did because I really enjoy it now but not beforehand.

The data also supported the staging of individuals though the stage of change questionnaire, as individuals could be categorised into different levels of activity and inactivity due to their comments in the interviews. These corresponded favourably to their self-selected stage of change in a questionnaire. Focus group participants viewed the intervention materials as quite useful, but they concluded that the materials should be more realistic to young adults. For example, they felt that the statistics on levels of inactivity should refer only to young adults and preferably to those at the university. Future research into the production of intervention materials in physical activity should examine the effect of stage matching, but also make the intervention age- or population-specific.

Using pedometers as motivational tools

Pedometers are currently being widely employed as a means to promote walking. For example the 'Walk the way to health' initiative (see www.whi.org.uk/) reported that pedometers (known as Step-O-Meters in the campaign) have real potential to motivate and also to raise awareness of how little walking people actually do. However, the informal surveys of users of the pedometers that has been carried out showed that during the first week of wearing the Step-O-Meter, people tended to do about 30 per cent more activity but that activity dropped once they were in the habit of wearing it. There is clearly a need to study the motivational effects of pedometer use and, because people like them, they do indeed have potential to influence walking behaviour.

Pedometers are not new inventions. For many years they have been used as objective measurement tools for walking and hillwalkers have used them to assist with accurate navigation. What is new is that they have been mass-produced with electronic displays and are now marketed as part of the fitness and health industry. Recent studies have also shown that the modern pedometers can accurately and reliably count steps (Crouter *et al.* 2003; Tudor-Locke *et al.* 2002). Modern pedometers are cheap to manufacture and they have been used by some of the big food companies as free gifts to show association with healthy living. In various parts of the world the notion that 10,000 steps a day are required for health has been promoted. For example, a large-scale community campaign in the town of Rockhampton in Australia employed widespread media advertising, harnessed support from health services and attempted policy and environmental change to engage the public in a '10,000 steps' campaign. Evaluations of such complex community interventions are not straightforward but results suggest that there was a 1 per cent increase in the proportion of Rockhampton residents who were sufficiently active for health benefit as a result of this campaign (Brown *et al.* 2006). Residents in a comparison town showed a 7 per cent decline in activity over the same time period, suggesting that there may be secular trend for decreased activity and that the campaign may have halted this decline in Rockhampton. However, there is very little evidence that 10,000 steps is the correct message or that pedometers can actually motivate people to walk more. Some studies are now emerging to address these issues.

Key point: Pedometers are cheap and accurate tools for measuring step counts but can they motivate people to walk more?

In terms of the number steps to be achieved, a systematic review of thirty-two studies (Tudor-Locke and Myers 2001) showed that the 10,000 step goal may be too low for children and too high for sedentary individuals and individuals with chronic illness. It is also clear that 10,000 steps equates to more than the public health recommendation of thirty minutes walking (Le Masurier, Sidman and Corbin 2003). Tudor-Locke and Myers (2001) concluded that thirty minutes of walking actually equates to 3,100–4,000 steps. Attempting and subsequently failing to achieve the 10,000 steps goal may lead to reduced motivation to continue a walking programme. Therefore walking programmes should use personalized step-goals of adding approximately 3,000–4,000 steps to normal everyday step-counts. This requires that researchers and practitioners assess baseline step-count levels (perhaps over the course of the previous week) in order to provide individual goals. The most recent research has begun to focus on aligning step-count targets with public health recommendations. Jordan and colleagues (Jordan *et al.* 2005) suggested that the current public health recommendation of weekly energy expenditure can be met by engaging in three to four moderately intense walking sessions per week, with each session averaging about 5,500 steps. There remains a need for further research to quantify the active living message in terms of step requirement.

In terms of pedometers having a motivational effect, studies have shown that the presence of a pedometer alone (Rooney *et al.* 2003), or feedback from a pedometer can increase walking steps (Stovitz *et al.* 2005). However, these studies lacked rigorous control and it is not clear if the pedometer itself caused the changes that have been noted. Other studies have shown less positive results. For example, Eastep *et al.* (2004) randomly assigned twenty-six participants who had enrolled in '*walking for fitness*' classes to a condition in which they wore a pedometer open for three weeks or a condition in which they wore a sealed pedometer for three weeks. Neither group increased their walking behaviour significantly over time. This contradicts the findings of Rooney *et al.* (2003) that pedometer presence alone is enough to increase walking behaviour. The evidence base for pedometers increasing physical activity is weak at this point and the National Institute for Health and Clinical Excellence (NICE) has recently recommended that there was insufficient evidence to recommend the use of pedometers (National Institute for Health and Clinical Excellence 2006). Clearly there is a need to increase this evidence base since the public are now well aware of pedometers and practitioners are willing to try using them to promote activity (Eakin *et al.* 2004a). There are very few physical activity promotions that have both public and practitioner support and so we have begun a series of studies that look at how pedometers might influence physical activity levels.

In order to investigate whether or not pedometers could add to the motivational effect of being set goals to increase walking we enrolled fifty participants to a 'walk for health' project (Mutrie *et al.* 2004). They were randomly assigned to a four-week walking programme with goals based on pedometer step-counts or a similar programme with goals based on minutes. The step-counts we used can be seen in Table 11.2. Step-counts, questionnaire responses based on the transtheoretical model (TTM) and self-reported seven-day recall of physical activity were obtained at baseline, and at week 4. We then followed up these same participants twelve months later. In the short term we found that both groups significantly increased step-counts from baseline to week 4. However, in the longer term both groups sig-

Table 11.2 Goals set in minutes and in step-counts for a four-week walking programme (Mutrie *et al.* 2004)

	Graduated weekly goals	
Week	Goals set in step counts from levels established at baseline	Goals set in minutes of walking from levels measured at baseline
1	1,500 extra steps at least three days of the week	15 extra minutes at least three days of the week
2	1,500 extra steps at least five days of the week	15 extra minutes at least five days of the week
3	3,000 extra steps at least three days of the week	30 extra minutes at least three days of the week
4	3,000 extra steps at least five days of the week	30 extra minutes at least five days of the week

nificantly decreased step-counts after the four week point and twelve months later the step-counts had returned to baseline levels. We concluded that goals set in minutes may be as effective as goals set in steps using a pedometer in the short term. In the long term additional support may be required to sustain increases in walking as only two of the participants were still using their pedometer at this point. These results are illustrated in Figure 11.5.

To continue this line of research we conducted a similar study but included a waiting list control condition for the first four weeks and incorporated supportive email messages to half of the participants over the course of the twelve-month follow-up period (Baker and Mutrie 2005). In this project we enrolled sixty-one participants who were then randomly assigned to: a pedometer intervention (PI) group (n = 21) that followed a four-week walking programme based in steps using a pedometer; a minutes intervention (MI) group that followed a four-week walking programme based in minutes and wore a sealed pedometer for baseline and final seven days only; a control (C) group that walked at normal levels for four weeks and wore a sealed pedometer for baseline and final seven days only. All participants were randomly assigned at eight months either to receive continuous email support based around the processes of exercise behaviour change or receive no support. Participants were followed up

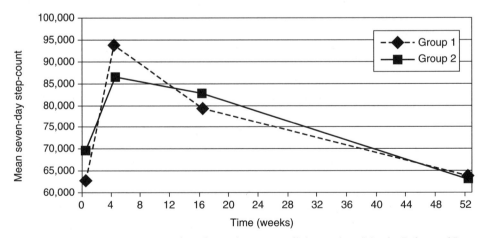

Figure 11.5 Mean step-count comparison for each group at all time-points (Mutrie, Baker and Lowry under review)

at twelve months and wore sealed pedometer for seven days to record step counts. The PI participants significantly increased step-counts (by 21,039 steps per week or roughly 3,000 steps per day) from baseline to week 4 (p<0.01) MI and C participants recorded no significant change baseline to week 4. PI participants subsequently significantly decreased step-counts (by 12,595 per week) at follow-up. MI and C participants recorded no significant change from week 4 to week 52. There was no significant difference in the change in step-counts for those who had received the supportive email messages compared with those who had not. We concluded that this study supported the notion that pedometers can provide a short-term motivational effect, but that this effect is not evident in the long term. We also concluded that sustaining these initial increases requires more than email support.

As we mention elsewhere in this book, sustaining changes in physical activity levels remains a challenge to exercise science and will require input from behavioural programmes (such as those that use pedometers), as well as input from environmental programmes that are beginning to show the determinants of walking in neighbourhoods. We believe that both behavioural and environmental research will be required to solve the problem of how to increase the level of activity in the population. The next wave of pedometer research must continue to use robust designs, incorporate objective measurement of physical activity other than walking that might be prompted by walking projects, include measures of how the environment facilitates or hinders walking and continue to follow up participants for as long as the research funding will allow!

Using a physical activity consultation/counselling[1] approach for increasing physical activity

The TTM assumes that individuals move through stages of decision-making and behaviour change. Sometimes this happens spontaneously or through 'self-help' procedures. In addition, health professionals can assist people to move to a more advanced stage through appropriate methods of advice and counselling. One approach that is receiving a great deal of interest in health behaviour change is that of 'motivational interviewing' (MI). While it is not specifically associated with the TTM, it has many parallels and applications (Rollnick, Mason and Butler 1999).

MI is a 'client-centred counselling style for eliciting behaviour change by helping clients to explore and resolve ambivalence' (Rollnick and Miller 1995: 326). Ambivalence is the conflict clients experience when considering the costs and benefits of taking action. For example, in considering the adoption of physical activity, a sedentary person may express the view that 'exercise will be good for helping me lose weight', but also believe that 'exercise is time consuming and hard work' (see Breckon (2002) for an application of MI to exercise).

Rollnick and Miller (1995) outline what they see as the spirit of MI and offer seven key points:

- motivation for behaviour change needs to come from the client rather than be imposed by the counsellor
- articulation and resolution of ambivalence must come from the client rather than the counsellor
- the counsellor is directive in helping the client identify, examine and resolve ambivalence
- direct persuasion is not an effective method for resolving ambivalence
- the counselling style is often one of quiet elicitation and opposite to direct persuasion

and aggressive confrontation

- the readiness of the client for change is not seen in terms of personality characteristics but rather a 'fluctuating product of interpersonal interaction' (Rollnick and Miller 1995: 327). For example, resistance to change, in MI, is a sign that the counsellor needs to modify their strategies
- the client–counsellor relationship is one of partnership.

Rollnick, Mason and Butler (1999) suggest that behaviour change counselling needs to centre on the three key issues of:

- importance: Why should I change? Is it worthwhile?
- confidence: Can I change? How will I cope if ...?
- readiness: Should I do it now? What about other issues?

Readiness is likely to be strongly associated with the importance attached to change and the confidence (self-efficacy) one has to make changes. This is a very promising approach that should be applied to physical activity research using robust randomised and controlled designs in order to determine efficacy of this behaviour change approach. In the meantime, all involved in physical activity counselling should develop these skills. As Rollnick suggested, 'Enhancing motivation and encouraging change is a complex task that demands skilful consulting and practitioners might benefit from refining their existing skills, particularly in the use of a guiding style' (Rollnick *et al.* 2005: 963).

> Key point: Motivational interviewing is a counselling style that holds much promise for changing physical activity levels.

Physical activity consultation in fitness centres

Many local authority and private leisure centres offer fitness testing/assessment for members as a way of encouraging attendance. However, there has been surprisingly little evidence to support the notion that fitness assessment could be motivating for long-term exercise. Computerised fitness assessments are now commercially available, and this has become a popular service to members of facilities. In contrast, a more person-centred approach has also become popular, such as one based on the concept of motivational interviewing, pioneered by Miller and Rollnick (1991). Loughlan and Mutrie (1995) offered guidelines about using a person-centred exercise consultation approach to increasing activity levels. These guidelines were based on the available knowledge of what assists people in making exercise behaviour change. The person doing the consultation must have excellent communication and reflective listening skills, and empathy for the people who are seeking help. Exercise consultants must also have good knowledge about physical activity for general and clinical populations, including the current activity recommendations and any contraindications for particular groups. Finally, exercise consultants must understand the various theories of behaviour change and the various factors that will influence whether or not a person will succeed in becoming more active. The steps in a typical physical activity consultation session are shown in Table 11.3.

Table 11.3 Steps in a typical physical activity counselling session

Step	What it involves
Step 1: determine physical activity history	Discuss the reasons that the person has for wanting to increase activity. Take note of when the person was last active, the kinds of activities they might like now and a measure of recent physical activity, e.g. 7-day recall.
Step 2: discuss decision balance	Ask the person to consider what the 'pros' and 'cons' of increasing activity are for them. If there are more cons than pros ask them to consider how to minimise some of the cons.
Step 3: ensure social support	Determine with the person what kind of support they might need and who can provide it.
Step 4: negotiate goals	Help the person set realistic and time-phased goals for gradually increasing activity up to a level they have determined, e.g. in 4 weeks time I would like to be walking for 30 minutes more on at least 3 days of the week. Write these goals down.
Step 5: discuss relapse prevention	If there is time or if the counselling session is with someone who is already active then discussion on how to prevent relapse from regular activity should take place.
Step 6: provide information on local opportunities	All information on relevant local activities, such as walking paths, swimming pools and classes should be on hand to supplement discussion as required.

A similar model of physical activity counselling has been described by Laitakari and Asikainen (1998). They advocate a more detailed assessment procedure that includes quality of life, health status, health practice and living environment. Such details may be helpful but they may also take more time. A trade-off between details and time may be required. Laitakari and Asikainen have not yet reported on the efficacy of their approach but results will be helpful in determining if a longer consultation is effective. The consultation approach described by Loughlan and Mutrie (1995) has now been tested in several settings and we will provide examples of these settings in the next section. Another example has been shown in Chapter 10 in the section concerning Type 2 diabetes (see Kirk *et al.* in press for further details).

Loughlan and Mutrie (1997) randomly assigned 179 National Health Service employees to receive a fitness assessment, an exercise consultation or an information booklet. The participants were all in the contemplation or preparation stage of exercise behaviour change. Using a seven-day recall of physical activity questionnaire (Lowther *et al.* 1999) all three groups were found to increase activity levels at four weeks, three months and six months post-intervention. There was evidence that on-going support was needed to maintain initial increases in physical activity. It was suggested that exercise consultation showed trends to sustain activity more than the fitness assessment or information. It would seem that when people are ready to change even simple and cheap interventions such as information could provide a short-term stimulus to change.

A further study on the same theme was undertaken over twelve months to assess the longer-term effectiveness of the consultation process. Lowther, Mutrie and Scott (1999) compared the effectiveness of fitness assessment and exercise consultation in increasing activity levels in a community setting. Almost 400 people responded to a local mailshot offering them the chance to participate in a physical activity project. Respondents chose whether they wanted a fitness assessment or an exercise consultation and then were randomly assigned to experimental or control groups. The control groups received information about physical activity and the experimental groups received either an exercise consultation or a fitness assessment with a three-month follow-up. The study design is summarised in Figure 11.6. The measures included stage and processes of change and a seven-day recall of physical activity.

The results showed that, for those who were not regularly active at baseline, by three months all groups had significantly increased physical activity. This supports our earlier findings that information alone can assist people in making a short-term change in activity levels (Loughlan and Mutrie 1997). At six months, both experimental groups had maintained the initial increases in physical activity but both control groups relapsed back to their baseline levels. This finding suggests that support is required to maintain activity since both experimental groups received a second assessment or consultation after three months. At twelve months only the exercise consultation experimental group reported significantly more physical activity than at baseline. This supports the view that the cognitive–behavioural skills, which are the focus of the consultation process, may have the best long-term effects in increasing physical activity for individuals. Lowther has also reported on the processes of change that are associated with increased activity (Lowther *et al.* 2007)

> Key point: Physical activity counselling offers a method of helping individuals change their physical activity levels. Counsellors must develop appropriate counselling skills as well as knowledge about physical activity.

This study also provided excellent information on the kind of person who might chose an exercise consultation. Figure 11.7 shows that significantly more of the people who chose an exercise consultation were classified in pre-contemplation, contemplation or preparation stages than in action and maintenance stages. This was not true for fitness assessment, which attracted equal numbers of active versus inactive people. In addition, older rather than younger adults were more likely to choose exercise consultation in preference to fitness assessment (Lowther, Mutrie and Scott 1999). Thus, offering an exercise consultation service from a leisure centre may attract different segments of the population in comparison

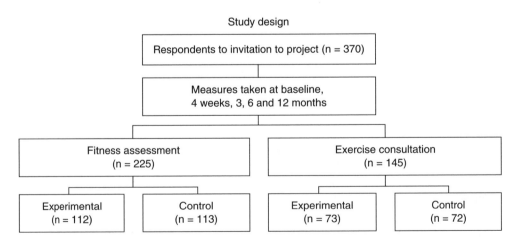

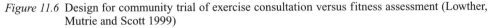

Figure 11.6 Design for community trial of exercise consultation versus fitness assessment (Lowther, Mutrie and Scott 1999)

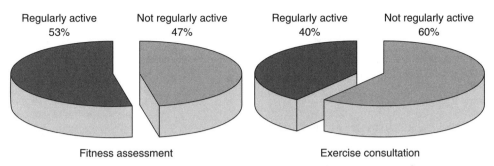

Regularly active   Not regularly active   Regularly active   Not regularly active
53%   47%   40%   60%

Fitness assessment   Exercise consultation

Exercise consultations attracted significantly more not regularly active participants ($\chi^2 = 5.03$, $p<0.05$)

Figure 11.7 Percentage of the participants who opted for exercise consultation by physical activity
status (Lowther, Mutrie and Scott 1999)

with the standard opportunity to have a fitness assessment. For example, Bailey and Biddle
(1988) found that only 17.3 per cent of men and 14.4 per cent of women who volunteered for
a fitness test at the Health Fair of the 1986 National Garden Festival in England were found
to be below average on age-related fitness norms. In addition, of the 3,000 individuals
analysed in this study (from a total of 13,373 who completed a fitness test), only 21 per cent
of women and 18 per cent of men were over forty-five years of age. These data reflect the
bias towards the young and fit individual being attracted to such an activity and lend further
support to the potential efficacy of exercise consultation in attracting a wider population.

Further discussion on how physical activity counselling can influence behaviour change
in clinical populations is included in Chapter 10.

There are many other ways that individuals can be reached. We have already described
the use of the print media, and email prompts. However, web-based approaches and other
information technology advances such as text messaging or messages to personal organisers
have also been tried. To date there has not been a review of the effectiveness of these more
technological media. One immediate concern is that the more technological the approach,
the less likely it will be to reach those in the most disadvantaged groups in society.

Promoting physical activity in primary health care settings

The primary health care (PHC) setting has become popular for the testing of physical activity interventions. There are several good reasons why PHC should address physical activity
promotion more than it has done in the past. These include the following:

- PHC has become increasingly oriented towards prevention, therefore physical activity
  can more easily be promoted alongside other health behaviours, such as smoking cessation and dietary modification.
- the PHC team has regular contact with large numbers of people who could benefit from
  increases in physical activity. It is estimated in England that 90 per cent of a PHC practice
  population visit their surgery within a three-year period, and about 70 per cent annually.
- GPs (family physicians) are thought to be particularly influential in changing attitudes
  and behaviours since they are often viewed as credible sources of information.

Primary care, therefore, seems an appropriate setting in which to test the effectiveness of individually oriented counselling approaches.

> Key point: The primary care setting offers the opportunity to counsel people who are not achieving the minimum levels of physical activity and help them become more active.

IS THE GP WELL PLACED TO PROMOTE PHYSICAL ACTIVITY?

Despite the proliferation of GP referral schemes, little systematic evaluation has taken place across the many PHC interventions in physical activity. However, some researchers have suggested that the GP is well placed to provide advice about physical activity although some may lack knowledge about physical activity and how to promote it (Gould *et al.* 1995). A survey of 161 GPs in Finland showed that they rated further training for themselves in exercise counselling less important than ten other health behaviours (Miilunpalo 1991).

Reed, Jensen and Gorenflo (1991) attempted to identify factors associated with GPs in the USA who encouraged more than 50 per cent of their patients to exercise. The higher rates of patient encouragement were given by more experienced GPs (more than ten years in practice), by GPs who estimated that greater than 10 per cent of their patients had a personal exercise programme, participated in an exercise programme of their own and had a method of patient follow-up. The extent to which PHC personnel are active themselves may be an important precursor to getting interventions started (Fox *et al.* 1997), although evidence on whether these individuals are good role models is not particularly encouraging (Pender *et al.* 1994).

EFFECTIVENESS OF INTERVENTIONS

Evidence from reviews Three major reviews of interventions aimed at PHC or related settings are now available. Riddoch, Puig-Ribera and Cooper (1998) located twenty-five papers from the UK. They concluded that 'the majority of studies report some form of improvement in either physical activity or related measures. However, the size of the effect is generally small, and there is no real consistency across studies' (Riddoch, Puig-Ribera and Cooper 1998: 25). Similar conclusions were drawn by Riddoch *et al.* from an analysis of non-UK studies.

Although not restricted to primary health care, Simons-Morton *et al.,* in their review of interventions in health care settings, concluded that 'interventions in health care settings can increase physical activity for both primary and secondary prevention. Long-term effects are more likely with continuing intervention and multiple intervention components such as supervised exercise, provision of equipment, and behavioral approaches' (Simons-Morton *et al.* 1998: 413).

A more recent systematic review of evidence for the effectiveness of clinician counselling to promote physical activity (Eden *et al.* 2002) found nine trials that met the inclusion criteria. The review reports that two studies showed statistically significant improvements in physical activity attributed to physician counselling and three further studies showed an effect if the advice was given under certain conditions such as with a written prescription or a written goal. There was an interesting gender difference noted in one study where women but not men increased activity levels following counselling and phone call support. However, the review concludes that the available evidence about whether or not clinicians in primary care settings can promote increased physical activity in their patients is inconclusive. One of the criteria for this systematic review was that the clinician had to perform some component of the intervention. This may limit how these findings could be generalised to schemes in which other members of the primary care practice team, or those outside that team, play the lead role in either referral or delivery of counselling. Most UK schemes, for example, are run by local authority service staff.

Key studies Reliable data on the effectiveness of PHC interventions to change physical activity behaviours and health outcomes are sparse. Tai, Gould and Iliffe (1997) suggested that, although the benefits of increasing activity have been well documented, the feasibility of providing interventions based in primary care has not been well tested. Their paper focused primarily on older people and provided a helpful analysis of how to design and evaluate interventions aimed at increasing physical activity. They recommended that a series of feasibility studies are needed to refine recruitment strategies and that continuing professional development is required for GPs about the health benefits of exercise before full-scale testing of exercise promotion within primary care is undertaken.

Swinburn *et al.* (1998) showed that giving patients written advice about increasing activity was more effective than verbal advice. The same authors (Swinburn *et al.* 1997) conducted qualitative research with the GPs involved in their study and established that GPs were positive about the notion of prescribing exercise and that training and resource materials, including patient follow-up, were considered important aspects of a successful programme.

There have only been a handful of studies that have attempted to determine the effectiveness of primary care based schemes in increasing physical activity or providing health benefits. In the UK, three randomised controlled trials of methods of promoting activity in primary care have produced different conclusions. A controlled trial was undertaken in a well-publicised scheme in the south of England by Taylor, Doust and Webborn (1998). They targeted GP patients with at least one coronary heart disease risk factor. 142 patients were randomly assigned to attend a ten-week exercise programme at a local leisure centre or to be in a control group. At eight weeks and at sixteen weeks the intervention group reported more vigorous activity than the control group but by the final thirty-seven-week follow-up activity levels had returned to baseline. However, the control group had no significant changes over the course of the study. In addition, more of the intervention group (61 per cent) than the control group (23 per cent) reported that they were in the action or maintenance stages of exercise behaviour change at the final follow-up. Thus there is evidence from this study that short-term changes in activity are possible from leisure centre-based GP referral schemes but that long-term change is difficult to achieve.

The second study was conducted in Newcastle (England) and produced different, but questionnable, conclusions. Harland *et al.* (1999) ran an ambitious and well-designed study aimed at determining if different motivational strategies produced different adherence to exercise over twelve months. Participants were patients attending their GP's clinic who were randomly assigned to one of four groups:

- a control group (who received a fitness assessment, activity information and advice)
- a brief motivational interview group
- a group who received financial incentives as well as a motivational interview
- a group who received more intensive interviewing.

However, despite the good research design (good numbers of participants all randomly assigned to groups with twelve-month follow-up) there were methodological flaws which resulted in negative conclusions being drawn by the authors despite what appears to be positive data. The authors wanted to know whether there was a difference between the various interventions and controls in changes in physical activity score from twelve weeks to one year. At one year there were no statistical differences between the four groups in terms of the percentage of participants who were physically active. The British Medical Journal (BMJ) issue in which the article was published put the headline in the 'today in the BMJ' section of the journal 'exercise prescription is a waste of scarce resources'. This, of course, is a very serious accusation and may have influenced budget controllers to think again about existing or potential exercise referral schemes. However, we think that Harland *et al.* asked the wrong question of the data. Instead of looking at differences between groups, a better question would have been to ask whether any group had increased their activity at one year compared with baseline. According to the data the authors present in table 2 of their paper, the percentage of participants who had increased physical activity scores at one year compared with the baseline ranged from 23 per cent in the control group to 31 per cent in Intervention Group 3. If these are significant changes from baseline then the conclusion might have been that even the control condition can have a substantial impact in increasing physical activity over one year. Further economic analysis might then determine that the control group (which seemed to include the basis of many intervention techniques such as assessment, feedback and the provision of information) was the most cost-effective intervention. The authors' conclusion that brief interventions are of questionable effectiveness is wrong since none of their interventions or even the control condition could be described as brief. The previous section of this chapter shows that much briefer interventions and even information alone can positively influence physical activity levels. We also think that the outcome measures asked the wrong questions since they were based on an outdated questionnaire. This focused on fitness rather than active living. A better option would have been to determine if participants had achieved the current targets for sedentary individuals of accumulating thirty minutes of moderate activity on most days of the week.

The authors also claimed that the research was based on the stage of change model. However, they did not report how interventions were tailored to stages, any details of pre- or post-intervention stages, effectiveness of interventions by stage, or of the other crucial elements of this model described earlier in this chapter and in Chapter 6, such as the processes of change and self-efficacy measures.

These flaws mean that the key messages from this paper are very misleading and that the conclusions drawn are not based on the evidence. Such misinterpretation could severely limit future research and service developments. Clearly, there is a need for further trials of methods of promoting physical activity in the primary care setting in the UK.

The third UK randomised controlled trial cast further doubt on whether or not primary care can successfully promote physical activity. Hillsdon *et al.* (2002) conducted a large-scale RCT in primary care with a no-treatment control group being compared with an intervention group that received a brief negotiation interview aimed at increasing physical activity or a group that received direct advice about physical activity. Using an intention to treat analysis there was no difference between the groups at twelve months in terms of physical activity. Thus the authors conclude that 'The most effective way of increasing physical activity in primary care has yet to be determined' (Hillsdon *et al.* 2002: 814).

Key point: Current evidence suggests that the most effective way of increasing physical activity in the primary care setting has not yet been developed.

In the USA there have been two large-scale trials of promoting activity in primary care. Both of these have been informed by small-scale trials of training physicians to counsel patients to increase physical activity, for example Marcus *et al.* (1997), and many of the same authors are involved in the two larger-scale trials. The first was Project PACE (Physician-based Assessment and Counselling for Exercise) which used the transtheoretical model to design short interventions that were delivered by family physicians (Patrick *et al.* 1994). The project intervention consists of providing brief (three to five minute) counselling with each patient. The counselling focuses on benefits and barriers to increasing activity, self-efficacy and gaining social support for increasing activity. The strategies differ depending on the stage of exercise behaviour of each patient and in this sense the intervention is described as stage-matched. Physicians themselves find the PACE tools acceptable (Long *et al.* 1996) and a randomised controlled trial showed that the PACE interventions did increase physical activity, particularly walking (Calfas *et al.* 1996). In addition, Calfas *et al.* (1997) have shown that the intervention does influence the processes of change. This suggests that there is a good theoretical structure to the intervention tools although further refinements would enhance validity.

The second USA trial (activity counselling trial – ACT) has not yet reported the final results but the design is worth describing. ACT is a large-scale (over 800 participants) and long-term (twenty-four month) trial of two different models of primary care activity counselling versus standard care (King *et al.* 1998). Again, the elements of the transtheoretical model were used in the design of this project along with additional cognitive–behavioural techniques known to assist behaviour change. The standard care model involves physician advice with limited written materials, and the two other models both utilise that same basic start point but add to it. The first model is described as staff assistance and added to the standard care by providing an educational video and a short counselling session that results in short-term activity goals. Follow-up supportive materials are provided via twenty-four newsletters. The second model is described as staff counselling and used all the materials and interventions of the staff assistance model but adds to that more personal contact in the form of telephone support, one-to-one counselling and behaviour change classes.

Programmes of health behaviour change that include physical activity There are also lessons to be learned from studies in primary care which have focused on improving healthy behaviour in general and not just physical activity. For example, Steptoe *et al.* (1999) reported on a large-scale (over 800 participants) trial of the use of behaviourally oriented counselling for primary care patients at increased risk of coronary heart disease. The intervention group received counselling from the practice nurse who had been trained in an approach based on the stage of change model. At both four and twelve months the intervention group, in comparison with the control group, had a favourable reduction in cigarette smoking, reduction in fat intake and increased physical activity. Biomedical outcomes, such as body mass index, diastolic blood pressure and total serum cholesterol concentrations, were not influenced by the intervention. This study demonstrated that physical activity, and other health behaviours, can be influenced by a counselling approach in the primary care setting. On the other hand, it also demonstrated the difficulty of translating such behaviour into biologically significant change.

There may, of course, be other outcomes of equal importance not measured by such studies. For example, participants who have made successful changes in health behaviours may feel an increase in self-esteem or quality of life, which, in the longer term, may influence adherence to healthy living and make a difference to biological markers. Butler *et al.* (1999) costed training in motivational consulting, similar to the counselling approach used by Steptoe *et al.* (1999), for smoking cessation to be around £70 for each GP and the extra time needed around £14 for each patient.

TRENDS IN PHC PHYSICAL ACTIVITY INTERVENTIONS

Physical activity promotion in PHC has generally not been well documented. In England, the Health Education Authority (HEA) funded a national research project on PHC promotion of physical activity to find out the nature and extent of this type of intervention (see Fox, Biddle, Edmunds, Bowler and Killoran 1997). An initial search revealed 121 schemes, of which 40.5 per cent were labelled 'practice-based'. These involved the management of the patient residing primarily in the PHC setting, such as with the practice nurse or an exercise counsellor/leader. Most schemes were 'leisure centre-based' schemes (59.5 per cent), most of which were in the pilot stage. These schemes involved the GP or other member of the PHC team handing over the management of the patient to a local leisure/sports centre. In addition, fifty-two schemes were planned, suggesting that a large expansion in schemes was likely to follow. This has indeed been the case and the proportion of schemes adopting the leisure-centre model has increased further. In-depth analysis of eleven schemes identified several issues that appeared to be important for this form of intervention.

In the UK, the National Health Service has provided a set of guidelines about how to set up referral schemes in primary care (National Health Service 2001). These guidelines suggest that:

- home and community strategies may prove to be more effective than facility based schemes
- the accumulation of thirty minutes of moderate activity on most days of the week should be recommended
- schemes should be based on a theoretical behaviour model
- training should be provided for referral and intervention staff on techniques of counselling and motivational interviewing
- specialist training for exercise leaders is important.

These guidelines, along with the earlier review by Riddoch, Puig-Ribera and Cooper (1998), emphasised the need for such schemes to be evaluated against more than biological or physical health outcomes and for the methodologies used to be relative to the size, intensity and outcomes expected of the interventions. Riddoch, Puig-Ribera and Cooper (1998) suggested that some of the potential benefit from participation in such schemes might be in relation to mental health or social health outcomes. They indicated that many evaluations have lacked process information about the actual intervention that would allow lessons to be generalised to other similar contexts. The existence of these guidelines, and the proliferation of such schemes, may indicate a stronger belief amongst health professionals of potential holistic health benefits from increasing physical activity in primary care than might be expected given the strength of the existing evidence base.

More recent guidance from the National Institute for Health and Clinical Excellence casts some doubt on the continuation of exercise referral schemes (National Institute for Health and Clinical Excellence 2006). The guidance, issued in March 2006, recommended that there was insufficient evidence about the effectiveness of exercise referral schemes and further suggested that people should only be referred to schemes that are part of a robust evaluation. This may result in premature withdrawal of funding for such schemes before the evidence base has been allowed to grow. However, the same guidance endorses the use of brief interventions by members of a general practice team aimed at increasing physical activity for those who are sedentary. The recommendation was that

> Primary care practitioners should take the opportunity, whenever possible, to identify inactive adults and advise them to aim for thirty minutes of moderate activity on five days of the week (or more). They should use their judgement to determine when this would be inappropriate (for example, because of medical conditions or personal circumstances).
>
> (National Institute for Health and Clinical Excellence 2006: 4)

Thus there remains, in the most recent guidance, a clear role for primary care in physical activity promotion.

WHO CONSULTS WITH THE PATIENT?

The majority of physical activity promotion schemes in PHC in England involve an alliance between the PHC team and leisure centres. The other schemes are essentially PHC practice-based, varying in complexity. Some of the practice-managed schemes centred on one GP who is particularly enthusiastic about promoting physical activity. He or she might have organised other elements in the practice, such as local classes or an in-house clinic, or they may simply increase their consultation periods to emphasise a physically active lifestyle.

Other practice-managed schemes involved GPs referring patients to a practice-based clinic held at fixed times in the week. The clinics were sometimes staffed by a practice nurse or someone employed on a part-time basis as an physical activity leader/counsellor. Patients received assessment, advice and support, often with the opportunity of attending an in-practice class or one held in the community. Alternatively, patients were advised on self-directed behaviour change. A more comprehensive alternative was where patients can be referred, often after in-house assessment and counselling, to community-based facilities and activities. However, the management and monitoring of the patient remained within the practice.

For the leisure-centre managed schemes, GPs referred directly to a local leisure/sports centre where staff supervised all aspects of the intervention, including assessment, programme design and exercise supervision. While such centres have personnel trained in exercise, as well as attractive surroundings and sophisticated exercise equipment, it was also noted that they can be intimidating environments for the inexperienced exerciser. Nevertheless, the research project identified many successful schemes where leisure centre staff changed the environment to suit the patients (Fox, Biddle, Edmunds *et al.* 1997).

Both leisure centre and practice-based schemes have their own advantages and disadvantages, and these are summarised in Table 11.4. However, the best system is likely to be a comprehensive community-linked scheme with the GP referring directly to a physical activity clinic.

Table 11.4 Advantages and disadvantages of different PHC schemes for promoting physical activity

Type of PHC scheme	Advantages	Disadvantages
Practice-managed schemes	Counselling can be made available on site Available to larger percentage of patients Physical activity can be delivered within a 'healthy lifestyle' message Greater flexibility for patients who can be directed to a choice of several outlets in the community Better opportunities for record-keeping	Facilities not often available on site Finding trained personnel may be difficult May not provide sufficient motivational boost to get patients started Difficult to provide support with Patients left too much on their own difficult to create social atmosphere Unless exercise class takes place on site the scheme may be perceived as medical rather than intrinsically worthwhile and enjoyable
Leisure centre managed	Eases the burden of the GP No costs for PHC Facilities readily available on site Trained personnel are usually available Motivation and support for the patient can be high Social benefits for the patient can be high	Sporty image has to be overcome in order to attract patients Physical activity is restricted to discrete exercise sessions rather than lifestyle change Facilities are often only available during slack day-time hours Scheme often has an end-point with limited follow-up Doctors may not be willing to refer patients Currently schemes attract a very small percentage of patients Some schemes could not cope with large numbers of patients

Regardless of how the patient was managed, the schemes given the most positive feedback by patients reflected a common programme philosophy of 'wellness' promotion. Here indicators of programme success emphasised gradual and comfortable changes in lifestyle, the 'process' of involvement in physical activity and exercise rather than the 'product' of physical outcomes, and the social and mental benefits accruing from physical activity.

TRAINING OF PHC PERSONNEL

The PHC resource in England, *Better living, better life* (Department of Health 1993a), in reference to physical activity promotion in PHC, states that 'a general lack of experience of this aspect of health promotion in primary care means that further training will often be advisable'. Similarly, Pender *et al.* (1994) identified further training for doctors and nurses in physical activity expertise and counselling.

The delivery of effective physical activity interventions in PHC is potentially complex since any one scheme might involve a GP, practice nurse, health visitor, physical activity counsellor and exercise leader. Each will bring different expertise to bear and, at the same time, require different expertise to be developed for specific roles within the intervention. For example, the GP may need to be well versed on methods of eliciting physical activity levels of patients through interview methods, but will probably not require 'hands-on' expertise of fitness testing procedures. The reverse could be true for other members of the PHC team. The areas of expertise associated with members of the PHC team are identified in Table 11.5.

The Physician-Based Assessment and Counselling for Exercise (PACE) project in the USA was developed to assist GPs and other PHC professionals, to better counsel patients for physical activity (see Pender *et al.* 1994). The system involves the GP assessing initial activity levels as well as physical and psychological readiness for exercise, the latter being based on the stages of change model already discussed (see Chapter 6). Based on the interaction between these assessments, patients are given one of three protocols:

- protocol 1 'getting out of your chair': designed for those at a low level of readiness and addresses benefits and barriers of moderate level physical activity
- protocol 2 'planning the first step': designed for those contemplating and 'ready' for exercise and involves both behavioural and exercise guidance for the adoption of physical activity
- protocol 3 'keeping the PACE': designed for those already active, this intervention involves reinforcement as well as maintenance and relapse prevention strategies and advice.

Table 11.5 Areas of expertise required in GP-referral exercise schemes (Fox, Biddle, Edmunds *et al.* 1997)

	Personnel		
Knowledge and skills	*General practitioner*	*Activity counsellor*	*Exercise leader*
Knowledge			
Health benefits of physical activity	***	***	***
How much physical activity is enough	***	***	***
National participation patterns	**	*	*
Contraindications of physical activity	***	***	***
Behavioural determinants of physical activity involvement	***	***	***
Barriers to physical activity	***	***	***
Behaviour change strategies	***	***	***
Monitoring progress	***	***	**
Measurement of programme effectiveness	***	**	*
Skills			
Assessment of physical activity	***	***	*
Screening for contraindications	***	***	***
Activity counselling	**	***	*
Implementing behaviour change strategies	**	***	***
Exercise teaching: individuals		*	***
Exercise teaching: groups		*	***
Monitoring programme effectiveness	***	**	**

* Useful
** Desirable
*** Essential

Key point: GPs and other members of the primary care team should receive appropriate training in physical activity counselling.

RECOMMENDATIONS FOR PHYSICAL ACTIVITY PROMOTION IN PHC

There is a need for high quality personnel well versed in a wide variety of physical activity knowledge and skills. This is particularly important given the apparent increase in the number of such schemes across developed countries. A key recommendation for the development of physical activity promotion in PHC, therefore, concerns training. Collaboration between medical and exercise/physical activity professionals is essential.

A second recommendation, and one that stems directly from our experience with the English national project, concerns communication between PHC team members. Two keys lines of communication can be identified:

- GP to physical activity counsellor: GP needs to inform the counsellor of the medical needs of the patient; the counsellor needs to communicate with the GP about suitability of some exercises, possible contraindications and feedback progress being made
- physical activity counsellor to exercise leader: there needs to be a suitable 'fit' between the advice given by the counsellor, such as on behaviour change, and that given by the exercise leader.

The PHC setting will become increasingly important as more GPs and health professionals embrace physical activity. To this end, the US Surgeon General's report (Department of Health and Human Services 1996) encourages health care providers to talk routinely with patients about physical activity and how it can be accommodated in their lifestyles.

Caveats about the evidence for interventions aimed at groups and individuals

Reaching the 'hard to reach'

All reviews of physical activity promotion comment on the lack of evidence for promoting physical activity to black and ethnic minority groups. We may have been guilty of researching the 'easy to reach' and this may be defensible given the short history of exercise psychology. Typically, interventions have under-represented those low in socio-economic status, ethnic minorities and those with disabilities, and these groups abe also likely to be less active than other population groups (Taylor, Baranowski and Young 1998). In a review by Taylor *et al.* 1998, studies of low-income groups overlapped with those of ethnic minorities. Results showed that interventions had limited success with only two of ten studies reporting consistent and positive changes. For people with disabilities, four interventions were located by Taylor *et al* 1998. and included conditions such as low back pain and COPD. Generally, these interventions were successful. However, few interventions were located that targeted other impairment groups, such as those with spinal cord injuries, cerebral palsy, visual impairment or learning disabilities (Messent, Cooke and Long 1999, 2000). It is now time to focus more research effort on the 'hard to reach' segments of the population.

Reaching the whole population

By definition, the impact on public health of individual or small group interventions is likely to be smaller than for community interventions. However, it is important to consider the public health impact of all interventions. For example, Estabrooks and Gyurcsik (2003) argue that less attention has been given to the 'translatability' and public health impact of interventions in comparison with the assessment of the efficacy of an intervention. Efficacy trials typically are well-controlled studies testing whether the intervention affects physical activity levels. Estabrooks and Gyurcsik draw on Glasgow's 'RE-AIM' framework (Glasgow *et al.* 2002; Glasgow, Vogt and Boles 1999):

- Reach
- Efficacy
- Adoption
- Implementation
- Maintenance.

Reach is concerned with the numbers of people taking part in the intervention as well as their participation rate and how representative they are of the population. Efficacy is the effectiveness of the intervention in terms of desired outcomes at the individual level of analysis. Adoption refers to the reach of the intervention at the level of the setting or organisation, such as the number of worksites adopting the intervention and characteristics of the worksites who adopt the intervention. Implementation refers to whether the intervention was delivered as intended, while maintenance is concerned with the extent to which behaviour change is maintained or whether relapse effects are noted. Maintenance can be considered both at the individual level and at the level of the organisation, such as the number of organisations continuing to support the intervention in the long term. The RE-AIM framework provides a wider view for judging intervention effectiveness.

Key point: The RE-AIM principles offer a public health perspective on how to evaluate interventions.

Getting evidence into practice

Blamey and Mutrie (2004) have highlighted the difficulty of getting the available evidence base into practice. Practitioners are faced with the problem that the current evidence base has a number of gaps. These gaps include: knowledge of the economic efficiency of interventions; details of the settings in which interventions may take place; the minimum or optimum length of a programme; the ideal degree of intensity or saturation necessary to guarantee an impact; and the amount of tailoring for particular subgroups that is required (socio-economic, gender or ethnic groups). However, practitioners also face barriers to implementing the evidence that is available. These barriers include difficulties in conducting systematic reviews, disagregating knowledge about physical activity from complex interventions aimed at wider health changes and making local adaptations to existing evidence. On the other hand, practice fails to inform the evidence base because of the lack of an evaluation culture, ethical and pragmatic difficulties in designing interventions at a local level, selecting appropriate outcome measures, poor designs and implementation of evidence. The difficulties of getting evidence into practice are shown in Figure 11.8.

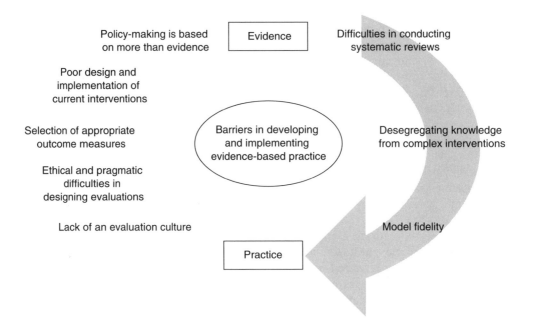

Figure 11.8 The difficulties encountered when trying to translate evidence into practice (Blamey and
          Mutrie 2004)

There are obviously no simple answers to many of the caveats that we have highlighted here
but there is plenty of scope for further research!

Summary and conclusions

In this chapter we have:

- provided a framework for discussing interventions aimed at increasing physical activity
  levels
- summarised recent reviews about how to increase physical activity levels via groups
  and individuals
- given examples of interventions that have focused on groups
- given examples of interventions that have focused on individuals
- discussed the use of pedometers as motivational tools
- examined counselling approaches to increasing physical activity
- outlined the key issues and results concerning the primary care setting and the promotion of physical activity.
- provided caveats about the evidence in this area.

From our analysis, we conclude that:

- it is possible to increase the physical activity levels of sedentary individuals
- short-term (three to twelve weeks) increases in PA are relatively easy to achieve
- long-term change (six to twenty-four months) is hard to achieve.

In addition, we make the following recommendations for researchers:

- there is a clear need for research in the area of support for long-term exercise behaviour change
- more specific relapse prevention strategies for exercise and physical activity must be explored and tested
- there is a need to explore different and new media for delivering the messages such as information technology, video conferencing and telephone contact
- Project Active is a good demonstration of how to promote physical activity and it needs to be repeated in other cultures and with more minimal intervention strategies
- the effect of physical activity counselling with a variety of follow-up options (such as another consultation, telephone support, postal reminders) needs to be tested over the long term
- more work is required in primary care settings to establish how the primary care team can influence physical activity levels
- research must focus on the 'hard to reach'
- researchers and practitioners must work together to get more of the evidence into practice.

We offer the following recommendations for practice:

- promoting physical activity in the community should involve unsupervised activity opportunities as well as supervised classes
- walking offers the simplest and most accessible mode of physical activity for the majority of the sedentary population (See Ogilvie *et al* 2007)
- all promotion should include cognitive–behavioural principles of behaviour change
- primary care teams should consider training of staff in physical activity promotion
- evaluation is central to increasing the available evidence base.

Note

1 We have used the terms consultation and counselling interchangeably in this section. In some cases counselling is the more appropriate term when a particular approach, for example person-centered, is used. In other cases, consultation may be more appropriate because the person providing the consultation has specific knowledge (and not just a good counselling style) to bring to the discussion, such as knowledge of contraindicated exercises.

12 Interventions in organisations and communities
Helping people become more active where they work and live

What is important is the message and the benefits to you of receiving it.

(Sir Winston Churchill)

Chapter objectives

The purpose of this chapter is to consider interventions to increase physical activity in organisations, where we work and study including the school and the workplace, and in communities where we live. We will also consider interventions at governmental level. Specifically, in this chapter we aim to:

- consider physical activity promotion and interventions in schools
- discuss the role of physical education in exercise promotion and to evaluate the evidence on specific interventions to change physical activity levels
- evaluate whether physical activity in childhood predicts participation in adulthood
- consider physical activity promotion and interventions in the workplace
- present a rationale for physical activity promotion in the workplace and associated evidence on its effectiveness
- consider physical activity promotion and interventions in the community
- discuss contemporary social psychological approaches to persuasion and attitude change
- highlight a social marketing approach to physical activity promotion
- discuss recent initiatives from national governments to promote physical activity within broader health policy
- show how an integration is possible between different levels of interventions in physical activity.

In the previous chapter we discussed interventions enabling individuals and groups to become more physically active. However, there is also a need to intervene at a macro level. Clearly, macro and micro (individual) interventions are often complementary since many strategies planned at, say, the community level also need to be translated into individual action at the micro level. In addition to personal and interpersonal approaches to physical activity intervention, King (1991) has identified two levels of macro intervention: organisational/environmental and institutional/legislative. At the organisational/environmental level, King lists schools, worksites, neighbourhoods, community facilities (for example, cycle paths) and organisations, and sites for 'daily living' activity which might include stairways, shopping centres and car parks. For the level of institutional/legislative interventions, King suggests that the main channel for change is through policies, laws and regulations. In addressing the problem of sedentary behaviour in developed nations, King said that an approach was required that

> emphasizes all levels of interventions, including personal and interpersonal strategies that target individuals or small groups, and organizational, environmental, and societal strategies that influence the broader milieu ... Although gains in knowledge have been made, it is clear that to achieve a significant impact on the whole population, strategies that target the environmental and social forces influencing exercise behavior will require far greater attention.
>
> (King 1994: 183)

We shall consider both of the broad categories of intervention outlets identified by King (1991). Specifically, we shall discuss physical activity promotion in schools and the workplace, as well as wider community initiatives. Finally, we consider broader political initiatives on health and physical activity. This plan is in keeping with the ecological model that we have previously described.

Organisations

The importance of promoting physical activity through organisations is now recognised. The advantages of such 'captive audiences' make this an appealing area for intervention. Although there are many organisational settings where physical activity can, and sometimes is, promoted, such as prisons and churches, the three settings in which systematic work can be located are schools, the workplace and primary health care (Department of Health and Human Services 1999).

Schools have at least three obvious benefits for the targeting of physical activity. First, this captures a critical age range at which changes appear most likely to be possible; second, school-wide strategies should enable virtually all members of an age cohort to be targeted; third, a delivery structure, through physical and health education, is already in place.

The workplace, while targeted extensively in North America, has shown inconsistent involvement in physical activity promotion in other countries. Nevertheless, it has been estimated that most adults spend about one quarter of their time at their place of work during their working lives (Department of Health 1993b). Similarly, the workplace has the advantage of targeting large numbers of adults and, at least for larger companies, may have an infrastructure to support health promotion initiatives, such as medical support and sport/exercise facilities.

Interventions in schools

Interest in the potential of schools to promote physical activity has been stated in policy documents in many countries. For example, the American College of Sports Medicine (ACSM) opinion statement on 'Physical Fitness in Children and Youth' stated the following recommendation: 'School physical education programs are an important part of the overall education process and should give increased emphasis to the development and maintenance of lifelong exercise habits and provide instruction about how to attain and maintain appropriate physical fitness' (American College of Sports Medicine 1988: 422). This statement mirrors a concern in Britain and elsewhere in the Western world about the apparent lack of regular physical activity in some groups of children. For example, the review of the National Curriculum in England and Wales, undertaken by Dearing, proposed that 'we must encourage our young people to develop a fit and healthy lifestyle' (Dearing 1994: 45).

There would appear to be a need to look closely at the promotion of physical activity and exercise in schools (Harris and Cale 1997; Salmon *et al.* 2005). This has important implications from the point of view of socialising children into healthy lifestyles. The central part of a school that is identified with the promotion of exercise is that of physical education (PE), although the more generic health promotion activities can, and should, combine across curriculum areas.

> Key point: Schools have a responsibility to teach children about physically active lifestyles and encourage regular activity – but are they doing this as well as they should?

Physical education and exercise promotion

Physical education has taken a much more prominent role in health promotion in recent years and has changed from a narrow medical rationale to one based on a more holistic approach stressing lifetime participation, enjoyment and motivation. However, politicians have also applied pressure to bolster the 'games/sports' lobby, sometimes at the expense of health/fitness activities. It appears, however, that success at international sport has no relationship with physical activity levels of the population (Powell *et al.* 1991). Indeed, the *Healthy People 2000* project in the USA states that one of its objectives is to increase the proportion of PE lessons in which children are active 'preferably engaged in lifetime physical activities'. These activities are defined as those 'that may be readily carried into adulthood because they generally need only one or two people ... Competitive group sports and activities typically played only by young children such as group games are excluded' (Department of Health and Human Services 1991: 102).

Behavioural issues in health/fitness promotion with children

In discussing psychological factors associated with schools and physical activity, we shall consider the effects of PE programmes and special interventions on the enhancement of physical activity levels.

INTERVENTIONS IN PHYSICAL EDUCATION PROGRAMMES

Interventions have mainly been conducted in primary (elementary) schools, although secondary school interventions do exist. Studies vary from extensive increases in time, such as through daily PE interventions, to relatively minor changes in emphasis in existing curriculum time (Almond and Harris 1998; Harris and Cale 1997).

Two large-scale interventions in the USA have been reported – the Sports, Play and Active Recreation for Kids (SPARK) project and the Child and Adolescent Trial for Cardiovascular Health (CATCH) project by McKenzie, Sallis and co-workers (McKenzie *et al.* 1996, 1997; Sallis *et al.* 1997). For example, Sallis *et al.* suggest:

For public health benefit, physical education should promote generalization of physical activity outside of school, because physical activity recommendations cannot be met through physical education alone ... specific programs to promote generalization must be developed and rigorously evaluated.

(Sallis *el al.* 1997: 1328)

Two comprehensive reviews have addressed physical activity interventions in schools (Kahn *et al.* 2002; Stone *et al.* 1998). Kahn *et al.* found thirteen studies suitable for review that addressed the issue of increasing time spent in PE lessons in moderate-to-vigorous activity. Results showed:

- consistent increases in physical activity in lessons when such changes were targeted, such as through modified activities, or changing the length or frequency of PE classes
- positive changes in aerobic fitness and energy expenditure
- interventions are likely to be effective across diverse settings (for example, in different countries and educational system)
- measures of body fat showed some positive, but often inconsistent, effects
- no evidence was found for increasing time in PE harming academic achievement
- no studies assessed economic indicators of the interventions
- barriers to implementation were mainly internal to the school, such as curriculum time pressures.

Overall, Kahn *et al.* concluded 'there is strong evidence that school-based PE is effective in increasing levels of physical activity and improving physical fitness' (2002: 81). An earlier review by Stone *et al.* (1998) concluded that the strongest evidence base was for those in the later years of primary school and for changes to the school environment. Moreover, they found inconsistent evidence for changes in physical activity outside of school. In other words, some interventions designed to increase activity in PE lessons had a positive effect on activity elsewhere, whereas other studies either showed no effect or a decrease in activity.

PROJECT INTERVENTION EXAMPLES: SPARK AND CATCH

The SPARK intervention involved a number of American primary schools in which PE classes were designed to promote and teach high levels of physical activity and movement skills that are enjoyable. Typically lessons were of thirty minutes' duration divided equally between health-related and skill (sport)-related activities. A classroom-based 'self-management' programme was also taught for thirty minutes each week in which students learned self-monitoring, goal-setting, reinforcement, and related skills. Homework and newsletters were designed to stimulate parent–child interaction.

Three groups of lessons were created. Some children were taught the SPARK intervention only by physical education specialists, others by classroom teachers who did not specialise in PE, with the third, control, condition providing 'normal' PE. Overall, 955 students from seven schools provided complete data over a two-year period. Results showed that the amount of PE time was greater in the two experimental conditions compared with the control condition, and that within lessons children were more active in the classes taught by a PE specialist than those led by classroom teachers, with the control group children even less active. These results are shown in Figure 12.1. However, similar differences out of school were not observed although favourable changes in fitness measures were obtained,

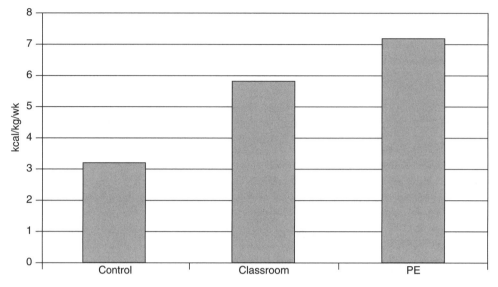

Figure 12.1 Energy expenditure of children taught in two experimental SPARK conditions and a control group condition (data from Sallis *et al.* 1997)

thus showing similar findings to those in Belgium by Pieron *et al.* (1996). Further work is required to see why out-of-school differences were not evident. Sallis *et al.* (1997) suggest several possibilities, including restrictions created by parents on safety grounds, and the lack of independent decision-making available to children of this age.

Further analysis of the SPARK project is reported by McKenzie *et al.* (1997). When a follow-up was conducted eighteen months after termination of the intervention, energy expenditure declined during lessons for those originally taught by PE specialists (see Figure 12.2). This suggests that the type of teacher is important in promoting health-related activity in lessons because the SPARK project has shown that the PE specialist creates more time for this activity, but this declines when other teachers replace them.

The CATCH intervention is described by McKenzie *et al.* (1996). It involved ninety-six primary/elementary schools studied for two years. After baseline assessment of various parameters, schools were randomly assigned to either a 'measurement only' or 'intervention' condition. For the intervention condition, schools were further randomly allocated into either 'school-based intervention' or 'school-based plus family intervention'. The intervention was multi-factorial and, in addition to PE interventions, included interventions on tobacco, food, classroom learning on cardiovascular health, school policy and a home/family component. As far as the PE goals were concerned, interventions were designed to improve existing PE programmes to promote 'children's enjoyment of and participation in moderate-to-vigorous physical activity during PE classes and to provide skills to be used out of school and throughout life' (McKenzie *et al.* 1996: 424). In addition, the PE intervention included curriculum content and materials, teacher training and on-site consultation to teachers.

The results showed that schools in which teachers were trained to deliver the intervention increased the amount of moderate-to-vigorous activity more than control schools. This activity increased by 39 per cent in intervention schools with such schools recording over 50 per cent of lessons in this type of activity. Similarly, intervention children had higher energy expenditure, higher energy expenditure per lesson, and greater overall physical activity levels than those in the control schools.

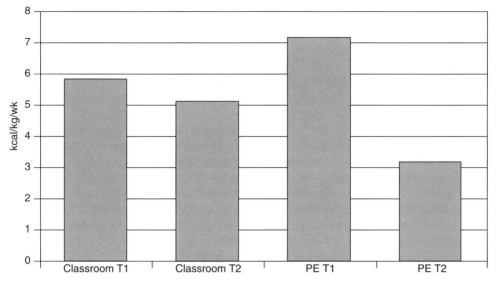

Figure 12.2 Energy expenditure of children taught either by classroom or PE teachers during the SPARK project (data from McKenzie *et al.* 1997)

Notes
T1: data during the intervention; T2: data 18 months after the end of the intervention

McKenzie *et al.* (1996) point out that half of the lessons in the intervention conditions were taught by classroom teachers, not by PE specialists, thus showing that the programme can be effective for both types of teachers. The effectiveness of the CATCH programme was 'accomplished through the implementation of a developmentally appropriate activity-based program and improved instruction and class management' (McKenzie *et al.* 1996: 430). It is noteworthy that such results come from a large multi-site randomised controlled intervention.

SUITABILITY OF PHYSICAL EDUCATION FOR PROMOTING LIFETIME PHYSICAL ACTIVITY

Many have questioned the relevance of current PE curricula for the development of active lifestyles in adulthood. For example, Coakley and White (1992), in a qualitative study using in-depth semi-structured interviews with British adolescents, found that participation in community sport programmes was influenced by past experiences in school physical education classes. In particular, such memories guided future expectations of sport and exercise. Negative memories centred on boredom and lack of choice, feeling stupid and incompetent, and receiving negative evaluation from peers. This parallels theoretical developments in sport and exercise psychology in intrinsic motivation, enjoyment, achievement goal orientations and motivational climate, as we discussed in Part II. For example, the reactions reported by Coakley and White are consistent with the need to promote intrinsic motivation. This is likely to be achieved through promoting high perceptions of autonomy and competence by allowing participants to make choices and have some involvement in decision-making procedures, and allowing for individual interpretations of success for the maximisation of enjoyment. In addition, the class climate may need reappraising so that all pupils are valued for their own efforts. This might help reduce negative peer evaluation and increase intrinsic motivation (Papaioannou and Goudas 1999).

SEDENTARY BEHAVIOUR CHANGE THROUGH SCHOOLS

There are a number of studies that have addressed the issue of physical inactivity (that is, sedentary behaviour) rather than activity itself (Biddle and Gorely 2005; Marshall *et al.* 2004). Some are laboratory based (Epstein and Roemmich 2001) while others have used educational interventions, including the school classroom (Gortmaker *et al.* 1999; Robinson 1999). Kahn *et al.* (2002), in reviewing three studies where reductions in TV viewing and video game playing were targeted, concluded that there was insufficient evidence to suggest that such strategies increased physical activity, thus being consistent with meta-analytic data from Marshall *et al.* (2004). However, Kahn *et al.* did conclude that such interventions 'may lower adiposity' (2002: 83).

Targeted sedentary behaviours can be reduced, but the time will be filled by a mixture of physical activity and substitute sedentary behaviours (Biddle and Gorely 2005). Saelens (2003) concluded from his review of this area that 'given the variability across studies ... conclusions regarding the relationship between sedentary behavior and adiposity in youth are necessarily tentative'.

Cycling and walking to school

Promoting walking or cycling to school has a number of advantages, including a large potential population (children and parents/guardians), reduction in car use, and the creation of healthy habits at an early age, although we still know rather little about this potentially important area of physical activity (Tudor-Locke Ainsworth and Popkin 2001). Estimates show that some 62 per cent of primary-age pupils walk to school compared with 45 per cent for those at secondary school. Moreover, the annual distance walked by children today in the UK has fallen by 28 per cent over the past thirty years (Rowland *et al.* 2003). However, there are very few studies providing guidance on the motivational influences of walking to school, although simply the distance between home and school will be an obvious factor (Biddle, Gorely, Marshall and Cameron 2005).

An analysis by Cleary (1996) showed more pupils walk home from school than to school. The trends for car use are opposite. This is interesting as it suggests that many pupils are within walking distance of school but appear to be driven there in the morning, possibly due to parents delivering their children on the way to work. The increase in employment rates among women over the past few decades may also be a factor here. Finally, traffic volume has been reported as a major deterrent to walking to school (The Pedestrians' Association 1997).

Two studies in the UK suggest that walking to school is associated with greater overall levels of physical activity in both adolescents (Alexander *et al.* 2005) and pre-adolescents (Cooper *et al.* 2003). However, this may be due to either active children preferring to walk, or that the walking itself is sufficient to boost overall levels of physical activity quite significantly. One study with five-year olds showed no effects (Metcalf *et al.* 2004), although this could be due to the high levels of sporadic activity in children of this age.

Walking to school is likely to be strongly influenced by social–environmental, rather than just psychological factors, although the social psychology of the parent may be important. The key social–environmental factors appear to be:

- work patterns of the parents
- convenience of driving children to school prior to going on to work
- proximity of school to home
- degree of parental consent to allow children to travel independently to school.

INFLUENCING THE SCHOOL RUN

It has been recognised that there is a need to inform parents, teachers and children about the issues surrounding transporting children to school on 'the school run'. Such issues include adding to local traffic congestion, increasing numbers of accidents around schools and, of course, decreasing opportunities for children to be active by walking or cycling to school. Trend analyses from a variety of sources suggest that active travel to school has been declining (Dollman, Norton and Norton 2005). On an encouraging note, 84 per cent of local authorities in Britain surveyed by The Pedestrians' Association (1998) reported 'encouraging' walking to school. Initiatives included cycle lanes and traffic calming. Many initiatives have been attempted to solve this problem including providing curriculum resources, employing school travel coordinators, and guidance for local authorities. Travel coordinators are expected to assist in producing a school travel plan. This sets out options for encouraging more walking, cycling and public transport use, and less car use. However, research suggests that such plans are largely ineffective (Rowland *et al.* 2003).

As with many other aspects of this relatively new area of interventions intended to influence transport, there have been very few evaluations that show how effective these interventions are. Merom and colleagues in Australia evaluated a 'walk safely to school day' initiative, and concluded that this provided moderate short-term change in *walking* behaviour (Merom *et al.* 2005). They identified several barriers perceived by parents and concluded that stronger interventions would be required to overcome these barriers and maintain changes.

In Scotland we used a quasi-experimental design to evaluate participation in 'Travelling Green' – a school-based active travel project (McKee *et al.* in press). Participants were two primary school classes (age around nine) and their families who used a set of interactive materials for one school term. An active travel component was integrated into the curriculum and children and their families used travel planning resources at home. The intervention school received these materials first while the control school received them in the next school year. A novel computer map tool was used for children to trace their journeys to school pre and post the intervention. This allowed an accurate assessment of the parts of the journey that were made on foot. Post-intervention, the mean difference in the distance travelled by walking from baseline to follow-up was 602.59 metres for the intervention group compared with 47.42 metres for the control group t (53) = –4.498, p<0.001 (95 per cent CI –802.7 to –307.6 metres). At follow-up, the intervention group travelled less distances to school by car than the control group t (53) = 4.078, p<0.001 (95 per cent CI 432.175 to 1268.82 metres). These results represent evidence that a modal shift can occur from car use to walking by using school-based intervention materials. However, there is an urgent need to evaluate other initiatives that are in place to promote active transport for school children and to minimise the negative health outcomes which surround the 'school run'.

Schools: summary

As far as young people are concerned, whether they are involved in physical education programmes or not, current consensus on physical activity guidelines is apparent. Sallis and Patrick (1994) convened an international consensus conference on physical activity for adolescents, and in England a similar process was undertaken by the Health Education Authority, this time for all young people aged five to eighteen years (Biddle, Sallis and Cavill 1998; Cavill, Biddle and Sallis 2001). The recommendations are given in Table 12.1. Recommendations for both school and community programmes for physical activity for young people are given in Table 12.2.

Table 12.1 Physical activity guidelines for young people

Source	Age group	Guidelines
Sallis and Patrick (1994)	Adolescents	All adolescents should be physically active daily, or nearly every day, as part of play, games, sports, work, transportation, recreation, physical education, or planned exercise, in the context of family, school, and community activities Adolescents should engage in three or more sessions per week of activities that last 20 minutes or more at a time and that require moderate-to-vigorous levels of exertion
Biddle *et al.* (1998)	5–18 year olds	*Primary recommendations* All young people should participate in physical activity of at last moderate intensity for one hour per day Young people who currently do little activity should participate in physical activity of at least moderate intensity for at least half an hour per day *Secondary recommendation* At least twice per week, some of these activities should help to enhance and maintain muscular strength and flexibility, and bone health

Table 12.2 Recommendations for school and community promotion of physical activity for young people (Department of Health and Human Services 1997)

Area	Recommendation
Policy	Establish policies that promote enjoyable, lifelong physical activity
Environment	Provide physical and social environments that encourage and enable safe and enjoyable physical activity
Physical education	Implement PE curricula and instruction that emphasise enjoyable participation in physical activity and that help students adopt and maintain physically active lifestyles
Health education	Implement health education curricula and instruction that help students adopt and maintain physically active lifestyles
Extra-curricula activities	Provide extra-curricula physical activity programmes that meet the needs and interests of all students
Parental involvement	Include parents and guardians in physical activity instruction and in extra-curricular and community physical activity programmes, and encourage them to support their children's participation in enjoyable physical activities
Personnel training	Provide training for education, coaching, recreation, health care, and other school and community personnel that impart the knowledge and skills necessary to effectively promote enjoyable, lifelong physical activity
Health services	Assess physical activity patterns among young people, counsel them about physical activity, refer them to appropriate programmes, and advocate physical activity instruction and programmes
Community programmes	Provide a range of developmentally appropriate community sports and recreation programmes that are attractive to all young people
Evaluation	Regularly evaluate school and community physical activity instruction, programmes and facilities

In reality, physical education, while a very important context for the development of health-related behaviours, cannot be expected to change children's physical activity and fitness a great deal. The current political climate in many Western European and North American countries appears to be favouring 'core' academic skills in the curriculum. This often leads to PE being forced to take a cut of available curriculum time. With the multitude of objectives physical educators have set themselves, fitness and activity change cannot realistically be achieved in the short term. Nevertheless, work must continue to find the best way to promote long-term changes through the infrastructure already in place in schools. Intervention studies, such as SPARK and CATCH, provide some hope in this regard. Other strategies might include health education that complements a health-related PE curriculum, parental education and an expansion of extra-curricula physical activity that caters for more than just competitive sports and those young people who are gifted in such activities (Harris and Cale 1997). Influencing transport to school in favour of active commuting is favourable both from the perspective of physical activity and from the perspective of reducing traffic congestion and accidents.

Interventions in the workplace

An area that has seen considerable expansion in the field of health and fitness promotion is that of worksite fitness and physical activity programmes. Young (1997) reports that for companies with between fifty and ninety-nine employees in the USA, about 33 per cent have worksite programmes, a figure rising to over 80 per cent for companies employing over 750 people. King (1994) suggests that more needs to be done with smaller worksites.

Workplace initiatives are often more extensive than just exercise and fitness programmes and may include other health behaviours, such as non-smoking. This expansion over the past decade or so is particularly evident in North America and Japan, although European initiatives also exist. European workplace initiatives have tended to focus on safety rather then preventive medicine, as seen in the UK's 1974 Health and Safety at Work Act, although with the recognition of the workplace as an important setting for health promotion this is now changing.

We have argued elsewhere (Smith and Biddle 1995) that to understand the cultural difference between European and North American initiatives in workplace health promotion, one needs an understanding of the motivation of the corporation, factory or office involved in the project. Often it can be a case of simple economic self-interest. This motivation has accounted for the rapid growth of fitness campaigns in American corporations. The huge financial cost of private health insurance for American companies provides a powerful motivator for such initiatives. In the UK, the system of National Insurance contributions and the National Health Service has removed the urgency to address such issues. However, concerning the economic criteria for assessment, much of the rationale for worksite interventions in physical activity reflects a cost–benefit analysis (CBA) approach whereby an evaluation of the economic effectiveness of the programme is performed. Other approaches could also be used, such as a cost-effectiveness analysis (CEA) or a cost–utility analysis (CUA). CEA evaluates the effectiveness of the intervention in relation to investment in other resources. CUA considers the effect the programme has on length and quality of life. It is likely that companies interested in developing a wellness programme will go beyond a cost–benefit analysis and look towards a cost-effectiveness analysis whereby competing resources are considered. However, ultimately, a cost–utility analysis may be used whereby the quality of life of the employees may be the prime consideration. This suggests that the motivation and rationale for interventions in the workplace can be quite varied and need not necessarily be economic.

Workplace exercise and health promotion programmes:
rationale and outcomes

Some of the major benefits claimed for programmes are improved corporate image and recruitment, better productivity, lower absenteeism and worker turnover, and reduced medical costs and incidence of industrial injuries. A recent Australian review concluded that more in-depth evaluation strategies and complete descriptions of intervention programmes are required, in order to identify the most effective strategies (Eakin *et al.* 2004b).

Gettman said that 'considering the evidence presented through a wide variety of studies, it is concluded that physical activity is economically beneficial' (Gettman 1996: 4). Opatz, Chenoweth and Kaman (cited in Kaman and Patton (1994), in an evaluation of health promotion in the workplace, concluded that the potential economic impact in the short term was 'moderate' for health care costs, and 'moderate-to-strong' for absenteeism and productivity. Similarly, Warner *et al.* (1988), in a review of twenty-eight articles on exercise in the workplace, suggest that the current evidence is as follows:

- epidemiology – prevalence and health impact: generally quite good information, suggestive of an impact but not definitive
- health effects of behaviour change – prevalence and health impact: generally quite good information, suggestive of an impact but not definitive
- cost information (types, measurements): very little research
- cost–benefit or cost-effectiveness: very little research. However, Shephard concludes that 'in the short term, work-site fitness and health programs appear to yield corporate benefits that more than match program costs, although this view would be strengthened by more controlled experiments' (Shephard 1992: 366).

A recent review from a research team in the Netherlands, who were particularly interested in how physical activity might prevent musculoskeletal injuries concluded that worksite physical activity programmes were needed both to increase the level of physical activity and to reduce the risk of musculoskeletal disorders. For the other outcome measures, the reviewers concluded that there was very limited scientific evidence mainly as a result of the small number of high-quality trials (Proper *et al.* 2003). There is clearly a need for more randomised, controlled trials with good design.

It has been argued that the type of person attracted to a company offering a comprehensive wellness programme will be a high achiever, have a low absenteeism record, and good productivity. This is difficult to quantify although the improved company image that may stem from such an intervention should enhance recruitment prospects. Such factors may, directly or indirectly, increase worker satisfaction.

Subjective reports have indicated favourable changes in productivity with the introduction of a company fitness or wellness programme. However, many of the studies have examined the impact on white collar workers where the measurement of productivity is difficult. In addition, it is problematic to measure productivity of blue collar or shop floor workers since they are unlikely to support a wellness programme with productivity improvements as a key outcome. Kaman and Patton conclude that 'in the absence of standardised, objective measures of productivity, this outcome may remain one with many hopeful claims, but with little substantive data to support them ... Nevertheless, there continues to be a thread of continuity between improved fitness and desirable work behaviors' (Kaman and Patton 1994: 139–140). However, in a review by Shephard (1992), twenty-three of twenty-six studies did actually show increases in productivity, measured in a variety of ways, after intervention.

Similarly, studies on absenteeism and corporate fitness programmes are favourable, and Shephard (1992) reports such a trend in thirty-six of thirty-nine studies. It is possible, however, that a self-selection process is at work here with only the conscientious workers choosing the health/fitness programmes. Also, anecdotal evidence suggests that some workers will volunteer to participate in fitness programmes, if conducted in work time, in order to avoid their work commitments. Indeed, Kaman and Patton (1994) report that absenteeism is actually quite low even in companies that do not offer health promotion programmes.

There is little systematic evidence on the effects of fitness programmes on staff turnover. However, if the previous suggestions concerning recruitment, company image and worker satisfaction are true, one could expect a reduced turnover of staff with such a programme. This, of course, is not always positive as all corporations will want some turnover to maintain a freshness of approach and to generate new ideas. For the health economist, however, there is the conundrum of extra pension costs accruing from prolonged life for the healthy, but now retired, members of the company!

Research in North America suggests that medical costs can be reduced substantially through appropriate health/fitness interventions in the workplace (Shephard 1989, 1992). Kaman and Patton say that 'substantial evidence suggests that exercise program components within work site health promotion programs lower participants' health risks and therefore lower related health care costs' (Kaman and Patton 1994: 135). Similarly, estimates from Britain suggest that over two million people consult their family doctors about back pain in any one year with the peak occurring in the forty-five to sixty-five year old group – often the most valuable to industry. Back pain also accounts for nearly 10 per cent of the days lost through certified incapacity for work (Wells 1985). Health/fitness interventions could reduce this burden on industry and on the individual. Exercise may be an appropriate strategy for some back pain sufferers, although other interventions are also possible, such as posture and lifting education classes, stress management, and ergonomic considerations in the workplace. For example, based on the review by Biering-Sorensen *et al.* (1994), the consensus statement from the 2nd International Consensus Symposium in Toronto stated that 'a reduction of the amount of weight lifted and other ergonomic modifications of the work site can reduce the risk of certain types of occupational low back pain' (Bouchard *et al.* 1994: 51). Also, positive results have been reported from a small number of studies investigating fitness programmes and industrial injuries (Shephard 1989, 1992).

Despite the benefits summarised so far, a meta-analytic review has suggested that work-site interventions have yet to demonstrate improvements in physical activity or fitness (Dishman *et al.* 1998). Forty-five effect sizes were obtained from twenty-six studies (total n over 8,500). The average effect for a worksite intervention was no more than one-quarter of a standard deviation, or increasing success rates from 50 to 56 per cent after the intervention.

Physically active commuting to work

Physically active commuting to work has several advantages as an intervention strategy. First, many adults commute to work on most days of the week, thus providing a huge group of people to target for regular activity. Second, the time allocated to work travel is clearly identifiable in the routine of the typical day and week. Again, this allows for effective intervention. It has been estimated in the UK that only one in ten commuter journeys are on foot

(Transport 2000). Physical activity as a means of commuting to work will be discussed in more detail later in this chapter along with other transport-related initiatives.

Further psychological issues in workplace physical activity programmes

One of the most important issues associated with corporate physical activity and exercise programmes, as well as more general health promotion initiatives, is that of adherence. The investment in staff, facilities and other aspects of the programme may affect only a small percentage of the workforce if there is a high dropout rate.

In a review of the effectiveness of fitness promotion programmes in modifying exercise behaviours, Godin and Shephard (1983) suggested that the workplace offers a convenient and cost-effective environment in which to promote physical fitness. However, they also recognise that changes must occur in society at large before physical activity and fitness promotion in the workplace becomes more successful than the current adherence rates suggest. Shephard's (1985) comments on the establishment of a corporate fitness programme suggest that more emphasis is required on psychological issues if such programmes are to be effective. He concluded:

- only 20 per cent of employees will take up the offer of a regular exercise programme; half will have dropped out within a few months
- physicians (GPs) should be contacted for support of the company programme
- blue collar workers and people at the 'low end' of the white collar organisations need to be targeted
- the most frequently pursued activities (for example, jogging, walking, swimming) require little organisation, equipment and no partner
- the main perceived barrier is lack of time
- a fairly slow rate of progression in exercise programmes should be adopted in order to avoid injury, discomfort, etc.
- graded classes should be provided to accommodate varying ability/fitness levels
- the reasons why employees will want to become active are: looking good, feeling good, making social contacts, and better health.

Interventions that promote active transport

In Chapter 7 we pointed out that one important determinant of everyday activity was the local transport infrastructure. However, transport planners have not normally made considerations of how traffic and transport can influence physical activity levels. More recently, with the need to consider how to reduce traffic congestion and the need to increase activity levels, active transport has been more prominent in plans. Early in the 1990s Vuori and his colleagues in Finland established from four different studies that activity achieved through active commuting could achieve health and fitness outcomes (Vuori, Oja and Paronen 1994). In the decade that has followed initiatives aimed at achieving more people walking or cycling have been put in place around the world, but as we will see few evaluations have been conducted.

Key point: Active commuting offers a regular opportunity to achieve recommended physical activity levels. However, few initiatives that promote active commuting have been evaluated.

Cycling

In several European cities, there has been a systematic development of cycle lanes that were separated from traffic. The city of Copenhagen is a good example. However, older and denser cities may find it difficult to alter streets to allow the ideal scenario of cycling lanes being added. We found that even in a city where cycle lanes were provided, but were not separate from traffic, participants in a project aimed at promoting active travel did not want to cycle and opted more to walk (Mutrie *et al.* 2002). City planners ideally want a modal shift from people using cars, to people using public transport and actively commuting. However, as Ogilvie and colleagues established in a systematic review of twenty-two intervention studies, in which shifting participants to more active means of transport was a goal, there was no evidence that publicity campaigns, engineering measures and other interventions are effective (Ogilvie *et al.* 2004). They did find some evidence that targeted behaviour change programmes could change the behaviour of motivated subgroups and that this may result in short-term improvements in certain measures of health and fitness. The challenge of intervening and evaluating plans to change people's travel behaviour at a population level remains.

London has recently introduced a congestion charging scheme and the London Cycling Campaign reported that, using official transport statistics, there was an overall 31 per cent increase in the number of cyclists entering the charging zone in the first year of charging. The manager of the London Cycling Campaign said:

> Many Londoners have discovered that cycling is not only one of the most quick and convenient ways to travel around London, it's also healthy and great fun. The boom in cycling has been made possible thanks to improved cycle routes, dedicated cycle maps and an increase in accessible cycle parking.
>
> (www.lcc.org.uk/ accessed 17 February 2006)

However, there has not been a published paper on this apparent positive outcome and this may relate to the difficulties evaluators have in gaining in-depth baseline data prior to the establishment of the congestion charging scheme (Ogilvie *et al.* 2004). There is also great potential for congestion charging to encourage more walking but information about whether it has or not done so is difficult to find. However, as with many other areas of physical activity promotion, more evidence is required: recent guidance from the National Institute for Health and Clinical Excellence suggested that there was insufficient evidence to recommend the use of cycling schemes to promote physical activity (National Institute for Health and Clinical Excellence 2006). The guidance suggested that, with the current evidence available, people should only be encouraged to join cycle schemes that are part of a study which is being evaluated. Hopefully this guidance will result in an increase in the number of evaluation studies that are conducted but it could also reduce the number of people that even attempt to change travel patterns to cycle use.

Walking

In Ogilvie *et al.*'s reviews they established that targeted behaviour change programmes could increase active travel in motivated subgroups (Ogilvie *et al.* 2007). One of the few studies in their review that had a randomised control design was the 'walk in to work out' trial that we conducted in Glasgow (Mutrie *et al.* 2002). We provided a group of participants who were recruited from workplaces with a 'walk in to work out' pack, which contained written interactive materials based on the transtheoretical model of behaviour change, local information about distances and routes, and safety information. The control group received the pack six months later. The intervention group was almost twice as likely to increase walking to work as the control group at six months (odds ratio of 1.93, 95 per cent confidence intervals 1.06 to 3.52). These results are illustrated in Figure 12.3. As can be seen in Figure 12.3, the contemplators, that is those who had been considering active commuting at the beginning of the trial, added more minutes per week to their walking than the preparers. Preparers started from a position of already achieving some walking to work and as can be seen the intervention was successful in increasing walking for this group in comparison with the preparers in the control group.

The intervention was not successful at increasing cycling. There were no distance travelled to work, gender or age influences on the results. Twenty-five per cent (95 per cent confidence intervals 17 per cent to 32 per cent) of the intervention group, who received the pack at baseline, were regularly actively commuting at the twelve-month follow-up. These materials have now been updated and reproduced both in Scotland and England and are available to employers who wish to promote active commuting to their workforces.

Campaigns that focus on car-free days or active transport days provide a new way of encouraging active transport. An evaluation of a walk to work day in Australia showed that such a campaign significantly decreased 'car only' use as a mode of transport and that there was an increase in walking combined with public transport (Merom *et al.* 2005). Campaigns such as this, perhaps coupled with materials such as those used in the walk in to work out trial, could help sustain short-term changes in walking.

Key point: Promoting active commuting by walking at least part of the journey may be easier to achieve than promoting cycling.

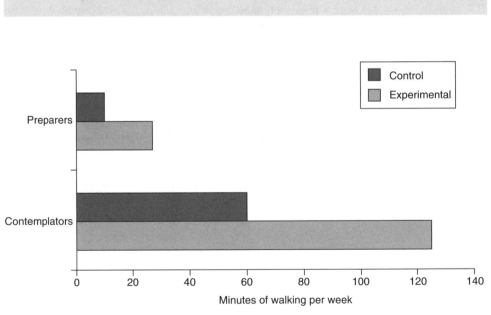

Figure 12.3 Changes in minutes of walking reported in the 'walk in to work out' trial for contemplators and preparers (Mutrie *et al.* 2002)

Walking has been the focus of many studies that have used pedometers as tools for measuring steps or motivating increased walking. We reviewed such studies in Chapter 11 and we have published a recent review on how to promote walking (Ogilvie *et al.* 2007).

The community

So far in this chapter we have considered interventions in organisations or specific settings, such as schools. Although these interventions may have a significant effect on the lifestyle and health of some groups, they are likely to be local and somewhat restricted. For physical activity to have a significant effect on public health, interventions aimed at communities and mass populations must also be used. Unfortunately, there would seem to be an inverse relationship between the size of the target population and the degree of behavioural change achieved.

Evidence from systematic reviews

Kahn *et al.* (2002) produced a systematic review of interventions to promote physical activity along with an evidence-based set of recommendations (Fielding *et al.* 2002). The Kahn *et al.* systematic review used changes in physical activity behaviour and aerobic capacity as measures of effectiveness and the conceptual framework divided the possible interventions into three areas: those that provided information, those that used behavioural skills and social support and those that focused on environmental or policy changes. We have already referred to the results of this review in Chapter 11 where they were concerned with individuals. The conclusions that are relevant to community interventions can be summarised as follows.

There was strong evidence that the use of large-scale, high-visibility, multi-strand community-wide campaigns that used a range of methods was effective in increasing physical activity. The community-wide campaigns reviewed tended to address a range of risk factors, not only physical activity. They had strong communication and education elements and were directed at wide-ranging audiences. They were also likely to involve social support activities across a range of settings. The review considered these activities as a combined package and did not separate out different effect sizes for the different interventions. The review included ten studies with the interventions ranging from six weeks to six months in duration. The median net increase in the proportion of people being active was 4.2 per cent (range –2.9 per cent to 9.4 per cent) and two of the ten studies showed median net increase in energy expenditure of 16.3 per cent (range 7.6 per cent to 21.4 per cent). The studies were conducted in the US or Europe and included both rural and urban areas and all socio-economic groups. Kahn *et al.* (2002) indicated that such interventions are likely to be effective across diverse settings and groups but that interventions should be adapted to specific target populations.

Additional information about community interventions from the Kahn *et al.* review concluded that there was strong evidence that strengthening local support networks through buddy systems, walking groups and exercise contacts increased physical activity. The review of interventions that increased physical activity through improved social support in the community considered nine papers. These studies typically involved recruiting groups of people to support each other via phone calls, discussion groups considering strategies to overcome barriers and buddying systems. The effect sizes from five interventions showed median net increases in time spent being physically active of 44.2 per cent (interquartile range (IQR) of 19.9 per cent to 45.6 per cent). The evidence showed median net increases in frequency of exercise of 19.6 per cent (IQR of 14.6 per cent to 57.6 per cent) and median net increases in aerobic capacity of 4.7 per cent (IQR 3.3 per cent to 6.1 per cent). Highly structured and less formal support appeared to be equally effective. One study showed that more frequent support improved effectiveness. Again these interventions were effective across a range of countries and settings.

Persuasion and the social marketing of physical activity

In Chapter 3 we discussed approaches to exercise promotion based on attitude theories. At the time we were primarily concerned with individual behaviour and determinants of exercise. However, attitude theory is also central to understanding the communication of messages to large numbers of people, such as in community health campaigns. Unfortunately, some campaigns have been based on a simplistic and atheoretical understanding of the nature of attitude and its relationship with behaviour. Many physical activity campaigns have simply listed the potential positive outcomes that may accrue from participation, such as weight loss, improved aerobic fitness and an improved figure/physique. As Fishbein and Ajzen (1975) have demonstrated, these outcome beliefs must be supported by positive behavioural evaluations (values).

Social psychological approaches to persuasion and attitude change

An area of attitude theory relevant to this discussion is that of persuasion. Olson and Zanna say that 'the single largest topic within attitudes literature is persuasion: attitude change resulting from exposure to information from others' (Olson and Zanna 1993: 135). For example, McGuire's (1969) sequence of cognitive responses, or 'chain of persuasion', suggests that for a message to influence behaviour, it must involve the following:

- exposure: the recipient must be exposed to the message
- attention: the message must be attended to
- comprehension: the message must be understood. It is thought that when the message is not clearly understood, attitudes may be more influenced by the credibility of the source, whereas this is thought not to be so important when the message is understood (Olson and Zanna 1993)
- yielding: the message must be persuasive; the recipient is persuaded by the content
- retention: the message must be retained, even in the face of competing messages and influences
- retrieval: the ability to retrieve the message from memory when needing to act
- decision: a decision to act in accord with the message, sometimes in the face of competing messages
- behaviour: acting in accordance with the message.

The approach to attitude change advocated by McGuire (1969) suggests that attitudes are formed and changed as a result of careful thought and consideration of the relevant issues. This is similar to the Ajzen/Fishbein approach already discussed through the theories of reasoned action and planned behaviour (see Chapter 3). Other attitude change theories suggest that the processing of information is not so logical. For example, the 'heuristic–systematic' model, proposed by Chaiken (1980), says that such thoughtful processing of information only occurs when the person is motivated and able to so. Persuasion may occur, however, if the person is unmotivated but this will be temporary and may depend on other factors, such as environmental cues. When motivated, the strength of the argument is thought to determine the degree of persuasion and attitude change is likely to be more permanent.

Similar to the heuristic–systematic approach is the 'elaboration-likelihood' model, proposed by Petty and Cacioppo (1986). They proposed that the 'central' route to attitude change involves an elaboration of the message through conscious thought, as in the heuristic–systematic model. The 'peripheral' route to attitude change and persuasion includes other forms of attitude change that are not related to deliberation or much thought, such as being exposed to the message. The elaboration-likelihood approach advocates that people are motivated to hold 'correct' attitudes. 'Elaboration involves making relevant associations, scrutinising the arguments, inferring their value, and evaluating the overall message' (Fiske and Taylor 1991: 478). Important factors to consider in these approaches to attitude change include:

- the communicator of the message, such as attractiveness and expertise
- the message itself, including difficulty, repetition and 'involvement' with the message or attitude object
- audience involvement; 'the respondent's amount and valence of cognitive response determines the type of effect that occurs. Because cognitive responses demand an actively thinking recipient, audience involvement has influenced each of the effects (communicator and message) discussed so far' (Fiske and Taylor 1991: 487; words in brackets added for clarity).

These approaches to persuasion and attitude change have not been studied in the context of exercise and physical activity, at least not directly through research. However, recently, a 'social marketing' approach to community physical activity promotion has been advocated and this is consistent with some of the notions just discussed.

Social marketing and physical activity

While psychologists, and other behavioural scientists, may be well placed to advise on aspects of communication, attitude change and behaviour, they are not necessarily expert on the 'selling' of the message to appropriate target groups. This is one reason why techniques of successful marketing have been applied to health and other persuasion campaigns (Maibach and Parrott 1995). In an excellent overview of social marketing applied to physical activity, Donovan and Owen define social marketing as 'the applications of the principles and methods of marketing to the achievement of socially desirable goals' (Donovan and Owen 1994: 250). Readers are referred to Donovan and Owen (1994) for a comprehensive overview of this expanding area.

MASS MEDIA AND SOCIAL MARKETING

One important distinction that Donovan and Owen (1994) make is between the use of mass media and the use of social marketing. Although mass media may be used as part of social marketing, it is only a part. Drawing on McGuire's 'chain of persuasion', Donovan and Owen propose that mass media advertising may work best in the early stages of this chain – for example, exposure, attention, comprehension – rather than at the level of behaviour change. This may account for the belief that mass media campaigns are not that successful at producing behaviour change (Redman, Spencer and Sanson-Fisher 1990). Indeed, the

---

Box 12.1 Understanding what the consumer wants

We make the point in the text, when discussing social marketing, that the psychologist may not necessarily be the most expert person for the 'selling' of the community-wide message. A recent story illustrates this.

A small survey was carried out by a local team of health/exercise specialists in a health authority 'district' in England. They wanted to find out the type of health interventions that might be appealing to residents on a fairly deprived housing estate on the edge of a town. The 'classic' replies were expected, such as interventions to stop smoking, start exercising, eat more healthily, etc. Instead, rather more 'basic' answers were given. The priorities for a 'healthy lifestyle' identified by these residents included 'proper lighting in alleyways' and 'keeping dog shit off the pavements'!

The need to match the message to the clients is clear to see.

---

effectiveness of such methods for changing community activity patterns has been questioned. However, Aaro (1991) reports on the favourable outcomes of a combined community and mass media physical activity campaign in Norway. He suggests that the reasons for such success are twofold. First, local action is stimulated by mass media coverage, and, second, mass media brings more attractive and appealing material than traditional 'medical' approaches to health promotion. Both these reasons are consistent with the view just expressed about McGuire's chain of persuasion. Indeed, Aaro suggests that the process of behaviour change needs to be viewed in several ways:

> It is important to point out that behavioural outcomes are not the only criteria of success in mass media campaigns promoting fitness. The change of health-related behaviour can be regarded as a process in which change in the actual behaviour itself is an end product of a number of less visible (perhaps invisible) intermediate changes. Sometimes ... a series of campaigns with no effect on behaviour produces a substantial change in behaviour when the results are summed.
>
> (Aaro 1991: 199)

One assumes he is referring to changes in the early stages of the persuasion 'chain'.

The most extensive review of the impact of mass media on physical activity was conducted by Marcus *et al.* (1998). They located twenty-eight studies satisfying certain criteria, including the use of an experimental or quasi-experimental design. In summary, they concluded:

- recall of messages was high
- little impact was detected on physical activity itself
- interventions using print or telephone were effective in changing behaviour in the short term
- interventions tailored to a target audience were most effective.

Kahn *et al.* (2002) concluded that there was insufficient evidence that mass media campaigns, when used alone, effectively changed physical activity. National agencies tasked with the promotion of physical activity and the need to raise the public's awareness are now faced with a dilemma about whether or not to spend money on mass media campaigns.

Perhaps the aim of a mass media campaign is not behaviour change, which seems hard to achieve, but awareness raising (Cavill and Bauman 2004)? Thinking of the transtheoretical model, discussed in Chapter 6, we could hypothesise that mass media had the role of moving pre-contemplators to contemplation or contemplators to preparation rather than achieving action or maintenance. Two UK evaluations of mass media approaches to promoting physical activity provided some information that might help national organisations decide whether or not to spend money on this approach to physical activity promotion.

In Scotland, a television advert featuring the captain of a Scottish rugby team, now affectionately known as the 'Gavin ad', produced very high levels of awareness of the message that walking was a good form of exercise. Seventy per cent of the participants in the evaluation said that they were aware of the advert one month after it had been televised, but the advert did not produce any changes in behaviour (Wimbush, Macgregor and Fraser 1997). In England, the evaluation of a national campaign 'Active for Life' was done using a cohort of the population which was followed up over three years (Hillsdon *et al.* 2001). The English evaluation showed that six to eight months after the main advertising on television 38 per cent were aware of the campaign. There was a small increase (3.7 per cent) in the percentage of the cohort who knew that thirty minutes of activity was the recommended minimum, but it was not clear that the campaign caused this increase. However, there was no overall increase in physical activity. Evaluating such campaigns is not straightforward since it is very difficult to find control populations not exposed to the campaign with which to compare results. It may well be that campaigns do not show increases but prevent decreases that might otherwise be the secular trend in the population. These evaluations also show that the goal of mass media campaigns is not behaviour change and that a more realistic goal is awareness raising.

> Key point: Mass media campaigns relating to physical activity should have the goal of raising awareness rather than changing behaviour.

MARKET SEGMENTATION

An aspect of social marketing that develops from the broader impact of a mass media approach is that of market segmentation. Promotional messages need to be appropriate for different segments of the market, or target populations. This may differ in regard to the 'four Ps' of what Donovan and Owen (1994) call the 'marketing mix':

- product: range, types, etc.
- price
- promotion
- place: for example, availability.

Successful techniques for the promotion of physical activity begin with a clear statement of the behaviour to be promoted. Fishbein and Ajzen's (1975) concept of the relationship between attitudes, social norm and confidence clearly illustrates the need for a specifically stated 'target behaviour'. The first step in defining the target behaviour is to distinguish between physical activity, exercise and sport. Unfortunately, these terms are often used interchangeably when each calls for a different form of promotion and marketing. From a community perspective, the target behaviour is most likely to be physical activity, such as walking programmes and 'lifestyle' activity. This target behaviour is selected because it is the least behaviourally challenging and is a possible stepping stone for a sedentary population to move on to exercise and sport.

Eadie and Leathar (1988) suggested that social marketing of fitness in the community should observe four main guidelines:

- it should have a positive appeal. Fitness was seen as relatively unimportant to many in their study. Therefore, negative fear appeals are likely to be rejected. Marketing should emphasise the more immediate social and mental benefits
- a greater emphasis on 'universal representation' is required to make fitness and exercise a socially acceptable activity for all and not just for those fit and good at sport
- campaigns must recognise individuality by suggesting a wide range of opportunities for people to choose from
- fitness marketing should highlight the informal nature of participation since many people appear to be put off highly structured and professionalised activities.

Killoran, Cavill, and Walker (1994) have presented promotional messages for physical activity in England based on a segmentation analysis. Four groups were identified:

- sedentary
- irregular moderate activity
- regular moderate activity
- regular vigorous activity.

The exact definitions of each group are not necessary at this stage since it is the concept of market segmentation that we wish to demonstrate. For sedentary individuals the message proposed by Killoran *et al.* was:

> be a little more physically active; anything is better than nothing. Try walking more often, taking it gently to start with, and then gradually increase the amount that you do. Check with your doctor if you're worried about your health, or if you're having problems being more active.
>
> (Killoran, Cavill, and Walker 1994: 151)

For those classified as doing 'irregular moderate activity', the proposed message was:

> work up to being active on five days of the week. Aim for a total of thirty minutes of physical activity on each of these days. Make this total from shorter bouts of ten minutes, if that is easier for you, but build up to these gently. You can do it!
>
> (Killoran, Cavill, and Walker 1994: 151)

For the 'regular moderate' group:

> keep it up at that level. You may want to do some vigorous level activities instead of some of your moderate level ones, or try putting a little more effort into the activities that you do. Step up the pace – gradually.
>
> (Killoran, Cavill, and Walker 1994: 151)

Finally, for the 'regular vigorous' segment: 'keep it up!' (Killoran, Cavill, and Walker . 1994: 151).

Killoran, Cavill, and Walker (1994) identified the sedentary and irregularly active as priority groups for targeting and recognised them as having 'distinct characteristics and promotional needs'. For example, sedentary adults in England tend to be older, overweight and from lower socio-economic backgrounds, as well as having some negative views about physical activity. This approach to segmentation is broadly in agreement with that advocated by Donovan and Owen (1994).

Killoran, Cavill, and Walker (1994) state that the competition for the promotion of physical activity is intense with commercial interests being strong. With the increasing recognition by health and exercise specialists that more moderate forms of physical activity can give significant health benefits, 'the promotion of moderate physical activity will need to establish a specific "niche" to be effective' (Killoran, Cavill, and Walker 1994: 167). To a certain extent, therefore, as this 'moderate' message is assimilated, we are in a position of communicating a message that may require some time to be understood. This is because the public had often previously been told that exercise must be 'vigorous' to be healthy. An analysis of 'message effects' in the elaboration-likelihood model of attitude change suggests that a 'difficult' message can cause attitude change if the message is thought about and involves something deemed important. Comprehending the message will encourage persuasion (Fiske and Taylor 1991) – a challenge for the promotion of the 'new' message of moderate physical activity. Indeed, there is some evidence (Killoran, Cavill, and Walker 1994) that people do not like general messages at all and that they want a clearer 'prescription' for exercise. This may make it more difficult for the marketing of moderate rather than vigorous physical activity.

Another segmentation strategy is that based on the stages of change (SOC) discussed more fully in Chapter 6. In other words, the marketing is based on the stage of readiness of the individual to consider and take up physical activity or exercise. Strategies then draw on appropriate characteristics of people classified within the segments. For example, research has shown that 'contemplators' hold less positive views about exercise and lack confidence to start exercise. Marketing appropriate persuasive messages for this segment should address these issues.

A summary of community intervention projects

A number of community projects have been reported that have included the promotion of physical activity (see Table 12.3). However, all of these are multiple risk factor interventions where physical activity is but one, and sometimes a peripheral health behaviour that is targeted.

The 'ParticipAction' campaign in Canada focused specifically on physical activity and primarily used mass media. Considerable resources were invested and it was suggested that a very high proportion of the Canadian population became aware of the campaign. However, increases in physical activity resulting from the intervention are unclear. Later messages centring on the concept of 'active living' provided a stronger orientation toward more moderate activity. As discussed earlier in the context of market segmentation, this message has not always been understood, particularly as some have seen it as a change from previous messages. King (1994) suggests that the following lessons can be learned from the 'ParticipAction' campaign:

Table 12.3 Examples of community physical activity interventions studies (adapted from King 1994)

Project	Individual outcomes	Organisational outcomes	Target audiences	Behaviour targets	Strategies	Significant changes
North Karelia (Finland)	None specifically targeted	Media events and community organisations involved	General; community organisations; GPs	Multi-risk factor	Mass media; community organisations	Decrease in CVD > controls
Stanford 5 Cities Project (USA)	Knowledge, awareness, participation, energy expenditure, body weight, resting HR	Media events; availability of exercise facilities	General; women; Hispanics; work sites; schools	Multi-risk factor	Mass media; community events; fitness assessment; school and worksite contests; talks; health professional training	Participation in moderate and vigorous PA > controls; resting HR < control
ParticipAction (Canada)	Knowledge and awareness		General	Physical activity; active living	Mass media; community organisation	Awareness and knowledge
Australia National Heart Foundation Campaign	Knowledge, awareness, intentions, self-reported adoption and maintenance	Media events	General	Physical activity	Mass media; professional talks; use of personalities; state contests and events	Awareness increased, especially for women; increase in walking, especially in adults >60 years

- awareness and knowledge can be increased with a well-planned campaign
- changes in physical activity resulting from such awareness changes are not easy to quantify
- more powerful behaviour change may result from focused messages and specific targeting.

At a more general level of analysis, Owen and Dwyer propose the following guidelines for the promotion of exercise in the community:

- '[E]mphasise the role of environmental settings and social supports' (Owen and Dwyer 1988: 343): adoption is likely to be greater with facilities in workplaces, such as showers and child care, exercise facilities, as well as environmental changes that encourage greater physical activity, such as cycle paths.
- '[U]se a judicious combination of media' (Owen and Dwyer 1988: 343): a combination of approaches is advocated, including the coordination of 'community events, classes, media promotions, self-help materials and other methods within the framework of a systematic campaign' (343). This is consistent with the view expressed earlier that mass media campaigns alone may only affect knowledge and awareness, whereas additional promotions and facility access may better promote the behaviour itself.
- '[O]perate simultaneously on a number of different levels, and identify clearly those aspects of the process of behaviour change which are of concern' (Owen and Dwyer 1988: 343): this recognises the concept of market segmentation and the need to target specific groups with appropriate interventions, such as knowledge and confidence for those contemplating exercise and, for example, social support networks for those attempting maintenance.
- '[P]rovide a variety of specific exercise options' (Owen and Dwyer 1988: 343): again, this emphasises the need to target specific groups and provide varied, but appropriate options for each group.
- '[D]evelop and promote exercise options which are intrinsically interesting and appealing' (Owen and Dwyer 1988: 343): consistent with intrinsic motivation theory (see Chapter 4) and the knowledge that people have multiple motives for participation in physical activity (see Chapter 2), it is important to allow people choice and variety, and to emphasise the intrinsic pleasure of exercise rather than promote exercise purely for health. The 'disease prevention' approach will not motivate many people over the long term.
- 'make soundly-based information and instruction readily available' (Owen and Dwyer 1988: 344): while the need for expert exercise instructors is clear, it is also recognised that many people do not find exercise classes attractive and thus seek help in different ways. This necessitates good self-help materials, or a system of advice, such as through primary health care counselling, as discussed earlier. Indeed, an integration of the two 'systems' is possible since one way to personalise the physical activity message to the community is through health professionals becoming more expert at physical activity promotion. For example, in Somerset, a training module for primary health care nurses has been established. The objective of this has been to empower such people to promote physical activity with their client groups. The training course has focused on behaviour change strategies rather than teaching a repertoire of physical movement skills. The nurses and health visitors will go back into their communities and promote physical activity rather than simply teach exercise classes. By the nature of their role, health visitors will come into contact with a large number of sedentary people. They deal with

young mothers, older adults, and single-parent families. These groups would not normally come into contact with an exercise leader but can be advised through their existing relationship with a health professional (Smith and Biddle 1995).

Environmental interventions

Evidence from reviews

We have discussed the evidence for interventions that seek to change the environment around us to promote more active lifestyles in Chapter 7. Kahn *et al.*'s (2002) systematic review of interventions made particular conclusions that focused on environmental and policy changes and these can be summarised as follows.

There was strong evidence that improved access to opportunities and active environments (for example walking or biking trails, local activities in local centres and workplaces, educational counselling, risk screening and workshops), along with educational activities that connected to these opportunities, increased physical activity. This part of the review included ten studies. These included worksite interventions, partnerships to promote increased access, opportunities to use equipment and formal (classes) and informal (active living based) opportunities. Behavioural techniques, training and referrals to GPs were often included. The median effect for increased aerobic capacity was 5.1 per cent (IQR 2.8 per cent to 9.6 per cent) and for increased energy expenditure was 8.2 per cent (IQR –2.5 to 24 per cent). The percentage of people reporting leisure time physical activity showed a median increase of 2.9 per cent (IQR –6 per cent to 8.5 per cent).

During 2006 and 2007, The National Institute for Health and Clinical Excellence (NICE) led a programme of review on the topic of how the environment might influence physical activity and, more importantly, how we might change the environment in order to increase physical activity levels. The scope of this programme of review, which will result in guidance being issued for the NHS and other organisations in the public, community, voluntary and private sectors, is available from the NICE website (www.nice.org.uk).

A synopsis of the reviews was made available on the NICE website in April 2007 for consultation. Reviews focused on evidence of effectiveness and cost-effectiveness in six different areas: transport, urban planning, the built environment, natural environment, policy, and economics (see http://guidance.nice.org.uk/page.aspx?o=420920). This synopsis suggests that changes to the environment may indeed result in increased physical activity levels and that such changes would be cost-effective. The detailed guidance which will follow from this process could have a major effect on physical activity levels in the UK if the various responsible organisations (for example local authorities) follow what is recommended.

Prompting stair walking

A recent review also confirmed what earlier reviews had found about a particular kind of environmental intervention in which stair use is prompted (Foster *et al.* 2006). Kahn *et al.*'s review of interventions had already rated the evidence from stair walking interventions as satisfactory with five studies available to them showing a median increase in stair use was 53.9 per cent (Kahn *et al.* 2002). The more recent review found a larger set of studies (twenty-one) that had examined environmental prompts to use stairs instead of less active choices such as escalator or lift use. These studies have been conducted in transport, workplace and commercial settings.

All studies showed short-term increases in stair use with a variety of prompts such as posters and banners on the staircase itself. Frank Eves and his colleagues have made a systematic study of the kind of message, the position of the prompt, the size of the poster, the number of messages and even the colour of the banners that might work best (see for example Webb and Eves 2005). What is less clear is whether or not this behaviour can be sustained and if there are different effects across different categories of users such as gender, age, weight status, activity status and ethnicity. The reviewers also call for more sophisticated research designs that will have control group comparisons. However, this will be a significant challenge to researchers. Finding a control group in a setting that is very similar to the intervention site will be difficult. Perhaps large companies that have identical architecture for their premises in different towns offer one possibility but that comparison will be difficult to generalise elsewhere. Given the consistent positive findings in this area it is time for research to examine how to increase and sustain stair use. This may require the prompt to change on a regular basis just as adverts do.

We have been involved in two examples of stair walking studies. In the first Blamey, Mutrie and Aitchison (1995) aimed to discover if Scottish commuters would respond to motivational signs encouraging them to 'Stay Healthy, Save Time, Use the Stairs'. The signs were placed in Glasgow city centre underground station where stairs (thirty steps) and escalators were adjacent. The study spanned a sixteen-week period and a total of 22,275 observations were made on Mondays, Wednesdays and Fridays between 8.30 and 10 a.m. during eight of these weeks. The eight observation weeks were split into four stages: a one-week baseline, a three-week period when the sign was present, a two-week period immediately after the sign was removed, and two one-week follow-ups (during the fourth and twelfth weeks after intervention). Observers recorded the number of adults using the escalators and stairs and categorised them by sex. Those carrying luggage or with pushchairs were excluded. A comparison was made between the baseline week stair use and each of the seven subsequent observation weeks. This process was repeated for the total sample as well as for males and females separately.

Stair use during the one-week baseline period was around 8 per cent. This increased to the order of 15–17 per cent during the three weeks that the sign was present. Figure 12.4 shows the overall percentage improvement from baseline compared with each of the subsequent seven weeks. Stair use significantly increased after the signs were in place and continued to increase during the three intervention weeks. A sudden decrease in stair use occurred once the sign was removed. At the twelve-week follow-up stair use remained significantly higher than at baseline. There is, however, an obvious downward trend suggesting a possible eventual return to baseline levels. It was found that females were less likely to use the stairs than males at all times, although the intervention had a similar effect for both females and males.

The results show that a motivational sign positively influenced stair use and in order to determine more about the responses of the commuters to these prompts we also conducted interviews. These were conducted during the time taken to go up the escalator or walk up the stairs – about 45 seconds. Stair users reported saving time and health as the main motivating factors while escalator users cited laziness, and stair climbing taking too much time and effort as the main barriers to stair climbing. In general, males reported higher levels of physical activity and lower perception of the effort required to climb stairs than females. Adults over 50 years of age gave a higher rating of the perception of effort required to climb the stairs.

This study resulted in the Health Education Board for Scotland (now NHS Health Scotland) producing a resource pack to encourage stair use in the workplace. These packs

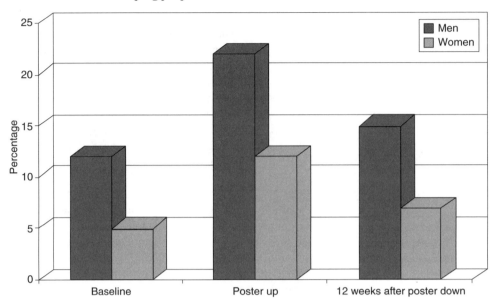

Figure 12.4 Stair-climbing before and after a promotional intervention (data from Blamey *et al.* 1995)

have been updated and include signage about where to find the stairs and a variety of messages that can be used to prompt stair use.

The second study we have been involved in was conducted in a worksite setting and used a prompt that had been tested by members of the public for acceptance (Eves, Webb and Mutrie in press). The prompt focused on the message that as little as seven minutes of stair walking a day might improve health. Very few of the stair walking studies have been conducted in workplace settings and here we found a much smaller effect for the prompt than has been found in transport or commercial settings. This may be because some people have fixed destinations that either make it possible (office on first floor) or improbable (office at top of building) that prompts will influence behaviour or because social opportunities are afforded when travelling together on the lift. However, we did find a greater effect of the prompt for those who were coded (from videotape footage of the stair wells) as overweight. This is important because of the need to find acceptable physical activity interventions for overweight people.

Some people may question whether or not increasing stair use has any implication for public health. There are several ways that its importance can be demonstrated. First epidemiological data suggest that climbing ten to twenty flights per week (Lee and Paffenberger 2000) or just seven minutes per day (Yu *et al.* 2003) has a protective effect. Second, if stair climbing is done as an element of everyday life such as in travel or at work or at home, then it will be extremely regular activity and could contribute to the accumulation of thirty minutes of activity on most days of the week. Third experimental trials have shown that as little as ten minutes stair climbing per day can increase fitness and reduce cardiovascular risk factors (Boreham *et al.* 2005; Boreham, Wallace and Nevill 2000).

We consider that prompting stair walking remains one of the clearest ways that local budgets could be targeted for increasing physical activity – imagine if every elevator or escalator displayed a prompt to use the stairs instead! The evidence that such prompts will be effective is consistent although the issue of sustaining the change remains a problem. However, we also suggest that the next generation of research involves radical changes to the environment with respect to the design and placement of stairs. If stairs were attractive and in a prominent locations and the elevator was less obvious and low in capacity, would stair walking be the norm? – that remains to be tested!

Key point: Prompting people to use the stairs instead of taking a lift or escalator is an intervention that has support from research reviews and could be implemented in many places.

Opportunities to access active environments

There was also a conclusion from the Kahn review (2002) that there was strong evidence that improved access to opportunities and active environments (for example walking or biking trails, local activities in local centres and workplaces, educational counselling, risk screening and workshops), along with educational activities which connected to these opportunities, increased physical activity. This part of the review included eleven studies. These included worksite interventions, partnerships to promote increased access, opportunities to use equipment and formal (classes) and informal (active living based) opportunities. Behavioural techniques, training and referrals to GPs were often included. The median effect for increased aerobic capacity was 5.1 per cent (IQR 2.8 per cent to 9.6 per cent) and for increased energy expenditure was 8.2 per cent (IQR 2.5 per cent to 24 per cent). The percentage of people reporting leisure time physical activity showed a median increase of 22.9 per cent (IQR 6 per cent to 8.5 per cent).

Concluding remarks on interventions in communities

Community-wide interventions pose a dilemma. They are potentially the most effective way of making a significant impact on public health yet they are the most difficult to manage in terms of appropriate targeting of messages to specific groups. An understanding of the social psychology of persuasion and attitude change, therefore, is important in making progress in this field. Recent developments, such as social marketing, may go some way to translating these concepts into actual behaviour change. However, at present, where evaluations of large-scale campaigns or interventions to increase community physical activity have taken place, the results have not been particularly encouraging for changing behaviour, although they are more optimistic for showing changes in awareness and knowledge. In a systematic review of interventions using a randomised controlled design, Hillsdon and Thorogood (1996) concluded:

- physical activity can be increased
- this increase can be maintained for up to two years
- sustainable increases are more likely for walking and exercise not requiring facilities
- follow-up contact enhances participation.

Dishman and Buckworth (1996) also supported the view that low-to-moderate intensity physical activity could be significantly increased through intervention. This was shown by an extensive meta-analytic review. In addition, they showed that interventions were effective using behaviour modification methods, for physical activity in leisure time, and in general community settings. In conclusion, Dishman and Buckworth said

> a conservative interpretation ... is that interventions for increasing physical activity have a moderately large effect ... The analysis of effects weighted by sample size suggests that interventions based on the principles of behavior modification, delivered to healthy people in a community, are associated with large effects, particularly when the interventions are delivered to groups using mediated approaches or when the physical activity is unsupervised, emphasizing leisure physical activity of low intensity, regardless of the duration or frequency of participation.
>
> (Dishman and Buckworth 1996: 712)

Political initiatives and interventions for increasing physical activity

King (1991) identified several levels of physical activity interventions, from individual to legislative. Although physical activity is widely recognised as a key element in health promotion and disease prevention, it is only recently that we have seen political and governmental involvement. The initiatives in the USA, such as the 'Healthy People 2000' project (Department of Health and Human Services 1991), have been discussed by many physical activity researchers (Dishman 1994). However, as King (1994) points out, physical activity is a free-choice behaviour and not a product that can be controlled like cigarettes or certain foods. Indeed, it could be claimed that governments have been rather 'lukewarm' about physical activity until very recently.

One very important reminder to governments around the world about the serious implications of low activity levels was the emergence in 2004, of the WHO global strategy on diet, physical activity and health. Having a global strategy indicated that inactivity is not just a problem for developed countries (World Health Organization 2004). WHO recognised that physical activity levels worldwide were falling as a result of industrialisation, urbanisation and economic development. The strategy calls for WHO member states to develop national strategies, tailored to local cultural needs, that seek to increase the level of physical activity. Scotland now has a strategy in place to increase the level of physical activity in the Scottish population over the next twenty years (Scottish Executive 2002). In England there is best practice guidance, in the form of a Department of Health physical activity action plan (Department of Health 2005), but no agreed 'strategy' at this point in time. These strategies are discussed in more detail in Chapter 1.

Key point: The emergence of a global strategy for increasing physical activity levels should encourage more governments to put appropriate national strategies in place.

Policy interventions

Polices that promote physical activity have been introduced around the world (Bull *et al.* 2004; Lankenau, Solari and Pratt 2004). Some commentators have suggested that such policies on their own will have little impact and that the driving force of the commercial world such as insurance agents, markets and bankers may be needed to ensure change occurs (Rigby, Kumanyika and James 2004). Where policies are in place they have not yet been evaluated but frameworks of how to create and evaluate such policies have been offered (Shephard *et al.* 2004). In 1998 Sallis *et al.* reviewed environmental and policy interventions to promote physical activity (Sallis, Bauman and Pratt 1998). They identified policies related to incentives and resources for activity (or inactivity) such as those relating to available information, car use, stair use, promoting activity at worksites, the entertainment industry and recreation facilities. As we have suggested in earlier sections, these suggestions may have been adopted and put into government policies around the world, but the effectiveness of such policies has yet to be evaluated.

Chapter summary and conclusions

This chapter has considered physical activity interventions at organisational, community and governmental levels. Specifically, we have:

- considered physical activity promotion in schools, and in particular discussed the role of physical education and school-based interventions
- discussed physical activity promotion and interventions in the workplace and reviewed evidence on its effectiveness
- reviewed issues associated with physical activity promotion and interventions in the community, including attitude change, social marketing and mass media
- discussed recent initiatives from national governments to promote physical activity.

In summary, therefore, we conclude:

- that schools are well placed to promote healthy lifestyles, including physical activity, and that physical education has the potential to reach large numbers of children of all backgrounds and abilities
- interventions to increase physical activity in or through schools have met with mixed success or have not been properly evaluated. Two large controlled trials in the USA have shown some effectiveness
- the objectives, content and delivery of health-related exercise in schools are often confused and sometimes PE has failed groups in the promotion of a lifetime of physical activity
- in some countries, the workplace has been identified as an important setting for physical activity and health promotion
- there is evidence for the effectiveness of physical activity interventions in the workplace on absenteeism, productivity and reduced health care costs, but effectiveness in increasing physical activity has not been demonstrated
- the greatest potential public health impact of physical activity promotion is likely to come through community interventions
- social psychological approaches to attitude change and persuasion hold considerable promise in the identification of appropriate strategies for community interventions
- principles of social marketing require further application to exercise and physical activity, and in particular note should be taken of the importance of market segmentation and targeted groups

- governments of developed countries have only recently been involved in legislative initiatives in physical activity and this interest has helped to legitimise physical activity as an important health behaviour
- effective physical activity promotion requires coordination across all levels of interventions as described by the ecological model and endorsed by the WHO global strategy. The ecological model provides guidance on how to achieve this and the principles are shown in Table 12.4.

Table 12.4 Principles of ecological approaches to health behaviour change applied to physical activity (based on Sallis and Owen 2002)

Principle	*Description*	*Examples of application to physical activity*
Multiple dimensions of influence on behaviour	In addition to intra- and inter-personal influences, ecological models include social, cultural, and physical environments as important influences on health behaviours	Social 'acceptance' of physical activity in different cultural groups Inhibitory physical environment for physical activity
Interactions of influences across dimensions	An ecological approach should say how the different types of determinants will interact to influence health behaviours	A research study testing the interaction between intra-personal beliefs concerning walking and use of a pedestrianised city centre
Multiple levels of environmental influences	Ecological models specify levels of influence, such as different types of environment (e.g. urban, climate)	The prevalence of physical activity in places differing in climate and inner-city cycle paths
Environments directly influence behaviours	Ecological models propose that environments directly influence health behaviours as well as indirectly through other factors such as individual beliefs	Physical activity will be directly influenced by local traffic conditions regardless of intra- or inter-personal differences

Part V
Summary and future directions

13 Conclusions and future developments

Bringing it all together

> Changing the level of physical activity in the population is not rocket science ... it is much more complicated than that.
>
> (Anon)

This chapter will highlight key conclusions we have drawn from our review of the psychology of physical activity. We summarise key points from each of the main areas of study – determinants, psychological outcomes and interventions – and then raise important issues for debate over the next few years.

Key points and conclusions

Determinants of physical activity

Descriptive approaches

Concerning largely descriptive approaches to the study of determinants, we conclude:

- despite well-known benefits, only a minority of people in industrialised countries are sufficiently physically active to have a beneficial effect on their health. This necessitates a greater understanding of the determinants (correlates) of involvement in exercise and physical activity, including motivation
- descriptive research on participation motives has tended to reflect motives for children's involvement in sport and adults' involvement in exercise and recreational physical activity. For children and youth common motives are fun, skill development, affiliation, fitness, success and challenge, whereas for adults motives change across stages of the lifecycle. Younger adults are motivated more by challenge, skill development and fitness, whereas older adults are more interested in participation for reasons of health, relaxation and enjoyment
- key barriers are lack of time and, for young people, issues of safety and feelings of incompetence
- correlates of sedentary behaviour in the form of TV viewing can be identified, but they are largely non-modifiable. TV viewing may be better studied alongside other sedentary and active behaviours rather than in isolation.

Comments Descriptive studies of determinants (correlates) are valuable but must lead to better informed interventions or policy. Widening the approach to include different research methods and behaviours (for example, sedentary behaviours) is required.

Theoretical approaches

Concerning more theoretical approaches to the study of determinants, we conclude:

- the theory of reasoned action (TRA) has consistently predicted exercise intentions and behaviour across diverse settings and samples; attitude accounts for about 30–40 per cent of the variance in intentions, but social norm is only weakly associated with intentions
- the theory of planned behaviour (TPB) appears to add to the predictive utility of the TRA in physical activity; perceived behavioural control has been shown to account for 36 per cent of the variance in intentions
- both TRA and TPB models are limited by their focus on conscious decision-making through cognitive processes; they are essentially static and uni-dimensional approaches, and the prediction of physical activity from intentions may depend on the proximity of measurement of these two variables
- the TRA and TPB have, however, been the most successful approaches in exercise psychology linking attitudes and related variables to intentions and participation; intentions share about 30 per cent of the variance in physical activity assessment
- the health belief model (HBM) has been shown to be a reasonably effective integrating social psychological framework for understanding health decision-making, but the HBM in physical activity settings has not been supported
- the health action process approach (HAPA) allows for a distinction between a motivation phase and a volition/post-decision phase of health behaviour change and is a 'hybrid' model combining aspects of intention–behaviour links (continuous) and stage-based models
- translating intentions into behaviour is a key challenge. Implementation intentions are self-regulatory strategies that involve the formation of specific plans that specify when, how and where performance of behaviour will take place and are likely to be effective in promoting physical activity behaviour
- self-determination theory is an important perspective for the study of motivation in physical activity and is likely to increase our understanding of motivation in the future, in particular the different types of extrinsic motivation that might exist in physical activity
- current research findings are not supportive of locus of control being a strong determinant of physical activity and exercise
- participation in physical activity is clearly associated with perceptions of competence. More specific perceptions of competence/efficacy are likely to be better predictors of specific behaviours than generalised beliefs in competence
- goal perspectives theory proposes that people can define competence and success in different ways, the main ones being ego and task orientations. Research is consistent in showing the motivational benefits of a task orientation, either singly or in combination with an ego orientation
- research using self-efficacy with patient groups demonstrates that exercise self-efficacy can be developed; self-efficacy judgements can generalise but will be strongest for activities similar to the activity experienced; self-efficacy in 'dissimilar' activities can

be enhanced through counselling; self-efficacy better predicts changes in exercise behaviour than generalised expectancies
- research with non-patient groups has shown that exercise self-efficacy can be increased through intervention, will predict participation, particularly in the early stages of an exercise programme, will decline after a period of inactivity and is associated with positive exercise emotion
- the transtheoretical model (TTM) of behaviour change provides an important advance on static linear models of exercise and physical activity determinants by hypothesising both the 'how' and 'when' of behaviour change
- meta-analytic evidence broadly supports the model, although the classification of processes of change into two higher-order categories is questioned
- the hybrid HAPA model allows for the distinction between non-intentional, intentional and action stages of behaviour.

Comments Initial scanning of the field suggests that psychological theories and models are too numerous to provide definitive guidelines for behaviour change. However, closer inspection shows that approaches that articulate the important role of intentions, perceptions of competence and beliefs concerning autonomy and control have degrees of overlap and provide important messages for individual and population change. In addition, stage-based and hybrid models provide pragmatic frameworks to apply theoretical principles.

Social and environmental approaches

Concerning more social and environmental approaches to the study of determinants, we conclude:

- sibling physical activity, parental support and father's physical activity are associated with physical activity in adolescents
- social support from spouse and family are associated with physical activity in adults
- extrapolating from studies in sport and physical education, mainly with children, the development of a mastery motivational climate in exercise classes and groups appears to be desirable for motivational and other positive psychological outcomes
- research on group cohesion has shown that exercise group dropouts have lower perceptions of cohesion than those who stay
- there is a positive relationship between exercise behaviour and some social influence variables, such as family support
- significant associations with physical activity have been found for ease of access to facilities, having places nearby to be active, and perceived positive aesthetics of the local area
- studies addressing issues of urban design and land-use policies show that such factors can be associated with greater levels of physical activity
- four key environmental features that should be taken into account in physical activity research are functional, safety, aesthetic and destination considerations.

Comments Identifying social and environmental determinants is complex for the very same reason – social and environmental influences are complex! It is early days in identifying such factors, but evidence does exist that can provide useful guidance for behaviour change.

Psychological outcomes of physical activity

In this book, we have discussed psychological outcomes of physical activity through the topics of heightened psychological well-being, physical activity's role in ameliorating negative psychological states, and a host of mental health and other issues for clinical populations.

Promoting good mental health

Concerning the promotion of good mental health via physical activity we conclude:

- physical activity participation is consistently associated with positive mood and affect
- quantified trends show that aerobic exercise has small-to-moderate positive effects on vigour, and small-to-moderate negative effects for fatigue, confusion, depression, tension and anger.
- experimental trials support the effect of moderate exercise on psychological well-being
- exercise is related to positive changes in self-esteem and related physical self-perceptions
- exercise can have a positive effect on sleep and positive benefits for women's experiences of menstruation, pregnancy and menopause
- meta-analytic findings suggest that exercise is associated with a significant small-to-moderate reduction in non-clinical anxiety
- experimental studies support an anxiety-reducing effect for non-clinical anxiety
- physiological reactivity to stress is reduced for those high in aerobic fitness
- meta-analytic findings suggest that exercise is associated with a significant moderate reduction in non-clinical depression
- large-scale epidemiological surveys support the claim that a physically active lifestyle is associated with lower levels of non-clinical depression
- meta-analytic findings show a large effect size from studies that have used exercise as a treatment for clinically defined depression
- the weight of the evidence suggests that there is a causal connection between physical activity/exercise and depression reduction
- there is no clear consensus about the mechanisms that could explain the psychological benefits experienced from physical activity. New technology may offer greater understanding of this topic in the near future.

Clinical populations

Concerning the study of physical activity in clinical populations, we conclude:

- patients in almost all categories of disease and disability could benefit from exercise
- good short-term adherence (four to twelve weeks) can be achieved from supervised programmes of exercise. However, for some populations, such as those in drug rehabilitation or those with HIV positive status, even short-term adherence may need special support systems
- long-term adherence (twelve months to four years) is poor and not well documented. The best information comes from follow-up of those in cardiac rehabilitation which suggests that 30–55 per cent are still exercising after four years
- very little is known about the level of exercise in clinical populations
- barriers to exercise are similar to those for non-clinical populations (for example, lack of time) but also include issues to do with the particular disease state (for example, fear of

another MI or fear of worsening osteoporosis) which could be overcome through appropriate patient education

- cognitive–behavioural strategies can be effective and the use of a counselling approach should be encouraged in all clinical settings
- psychological outcomes are often mentioned anecdotally but are rarely measured in exercise programmes or interventions for clinical populations
- there is a need for raising awareness in some medical teams concerning the role of exercise, the potential psychological benefits and the need to assist patients with adherence to exercise
- exercise dependence is a potentially harmful outcome from exercise but prevalence rates are not known. Exercise dependence secondary to eating disorders or muscle dysmorphia may be more common than primary exercise dependence.

Comments The topic of psychological well-being and physical activity is not new. However, we are still struggling to convince some health professionals and researchers of the benefits. Often this is the result of weak designs and measurement. Nevertheless, if all of the evidence is assembled, it is clear that physical activity has a major role to play in psychological well-being and general mental health. More innovative and creative research questions and designs are still required, as is the need to study diverse groups, populations and conditions (Faulkner and Taylor 2005).

Interventions to enable physical activity behaviour change

We have addressed behaviour change from the perspectives of individual, group and community levels. We conclude:

- it is possible to increase the physical activity levels of sedentary individuals, with short-term (three to twelve weeks) increases in activity being relatively easy to achieve
- long-term change (six to twenty-four months) is hard to achieve and there is a clear need for research in the area of support for long-term exercise behaviour change
- more specific relapse prevention strategies for exercise and physical activity must be explored and tested and there is a need to explore new media for delivering the messages such as information technology, video conferencing and telephone contact
- the effect of physical activity counselling with a variety of follow-up options (such as another consultation, telephone support, postal reminders) needs to be tested over the long term
- more work is required in primary care settings to establish how the primary care team can influence physical activity levels
- research must focus on the 'hard to reach'
- schools are well placed to promote healthy lifestyles, including physical activity, and physical education has the potential to reach large numbers of children
- interventions to increase physical activity in or through schools have met with mixed success or have not been properly evaluated
- there is evidence for the effectiveness of physical activity interventions in the workplace on absenteeism, productivity and reduced health care costs, but effectiveness in increasing physical activity has not been demonstrated
- the greatest potential public health impact of physical activity promotion is likely to come through community interventions

- social psychological approaches to attitude change and persuasion hold considerable promise in the identification of appropriate strategies for community interventions
- principles of social marketing require further application to physical activity, and note should be taken of the importance of market segmentation and targeted groups
- governments of developed countries have only recently been involved in legislative initiatives in physical activity and this interest has helped to legitimise physical activity as an important health behaviour
- effective physical activity promotion requires coordination across all levels of interventions as described by the ecological model and endorsed by the WHO global strategy.

Comments Interventions to change physical activity are still in their infancy. Successful interventions have been hard to identify, probably due to the wider social, physical and political environment that often reinforces or encourages sedentary living (Swinburn and Egger 2004).

Developing the field of exercise psychology

Throughout this book we have been emphasising the important role that exercise psychologists have in the task of increasing the prevalence of people who are physically active. Particular contributions include investigating the determinants of active and inactive lifestyles, developing assessment tools for psychological outcomes from both acute and chronic involvement in activity, developing appropriate theoretical frameworks for interventions, conducting robust evaluations of interventions, training other professionals in behaviour change strategies, and advising on mental health outcomes from activity. Given that the field is still relatively young and in development, we suggest there are several issues facing 'exercise psychology' that must be considered and resolved to ensure progress. In this final part of the book we will raise some of these topics for debate.

Moving from the theory of the problem to the theory of action

Exercise psychologists must decide what it is they are trying to achieve. Bartholomew and colleagues (2001) posed the question of whether efforts should be focused on creating 'theories of the problem' or 'theories of action'. Theories of the problem are concerned with the formulation of appropriate determinants while theories of action point to methods of behaviour change that fit with the determinants. While both approaches are required perhaps exercise psychologists of the next decade must focus more on the action and less on the problem. Using the theory of planned behaviour as an example (see Chapter 3), it could be argued that the efforts of the last decade have been in relation to understanding the influence of attitudes, subjective norms and perceived behavioural control on intentions to be active. Perhaps the efforts of the next decade should focus more on how intentions relate to behaviour – the so-called 'intention–behaviour' gap. Such research might help us understand why different segments of the population vary in behaviour, how environmental factors influence intention and behaviour, and what strategies we might use to influence intentions and to move intention into actual behaviour.

Moving from behaviour change theories to a wider socio-ecological approach

It is also true to say that in the last decade we have focused mostly on individual behaviour change theories and the field of exercise psychology is only now beginning to focus on the wider socio-ecological approach that we have mentioned throughout the book. While we would support this change in focus we also want to emphasise the need for understanding the *interaction* between individuals and the environments they live and work in. There is ample evidence that the provision of environments that support activity by themselves will not encourage a large percentage of people to be more active. For example, most towns have always had pavements (sidewalks) but the rates of walking have declined. People choose not to use the stairs even when they are easily found. Bike lanes alone will not necessarily encourage more people to cycle. Even in Denmark where there is a very positive cycling environment, with bike lanes separated from traffic, health promoters and city planners had to use a variety of promotional prompts to increase the percentage of the population choosing to cycle. Understanding how the environment interacts with individuals remains another developmental challenge for exercise psychology. Such a challenge must involve working in partnership with other psychologists (such as health and environmental psychologists) and other professionals because exercise psychologists cannot solve this alone!

Filling the gaps in current knowledge

All reviews of physical activity promotion comment on the lack of evidence for promoting physical activity to black and ethnic minority groups. We may have been guilty of researching the 'easy to reach' and this may be defensible given the short history of exercise psychology. It is now time to focus on the 'hard to reach', to learn about the different needs of different segments of the population, such as children, older adults, black and ethnic minorities and clinical populations. In addition, evidence of long-term behaviour change is missing. There is plenty of scope for further research to determine what works for whom and for how long.

Training and supervision

Around the world the training and supervision of *sport* psychologists has been discussed and supported. In many countries, in order to use the term 'sport psychologist' a person must receive a certain level of training and supervision. This has become increasingly important as the role of psychology in producing excellence for sport performers has become accepted. Many Olympic and world championship teams now have their own sport psychologist and it has therefore become important that such individuals are appropriately qualified and trained. In the UK this training has been supplied by the British Association of Sport and Exercise Sciences (BASES), working in collaboration with the British Psychological Society. In other countries, in order to use the term 'psychologist' practitioners must have a state licence. The question is, are we providing the same level of training in exercise psychology as we do in sport psychology? Almost all accreditation processes that exist around the world focus on assuring quality in the delivery of support for sport performers. Very few countries have a similar scheme for the training of exercise psychologists. Some examples do exist, such as the BASES supervised experience process that can be pursued in either exercise or sport psychology (see BASES website www.bases.org.uk). Developing the training and supervisory needs for exercise psychology is another developmental challenge.

Is exercise the correct title?

In creating a title for our book we were careful to use the wider definition of physical activity, and we commented in Chapter 1 that exercise has a more restrictive usage. However, the field is still generally known as exercise psychology. Would physical activity psychology show the wider concern for all types of activity? Would this change align us more with health psychology than sport psychology and would this be a good or bad thing? While psychological principles and theories span a variety of different behaviours, one might argue that health behaviour change unites health and exercise psychologists more than human performance unites sport and exercise psychologists. The title of the field is another developmental challenge for the future of 'exercise' psychology. We hope that the readers of this book will help take our field forward by taking on and solving these challenges that have been posed.

We close by restating what we said in 2001 in our first edition of the book. It seems equally appropriate now:

> All scientific work is incomplete – whether it be observational or experimental. All scientific work is liable to be upset or modified by advancing knowledge. That does not confer upon us a freedom to ignore the knowledge we already have, or postpone the action that it appears to demand at a given time.
>
> (Hill 1965: 12)

We call on all readers to take action now: be active, be a good role model for a physically active lifestyle, and use exercise psychology to help you achieve these behaviours.

References

Aaro, L. E. (1991) Fitness promotion programs in mass media: Norwegian experiences. In P. Oja and R. Telama (eds), *Sport for all* (pp. 193–200). Amsterdam: Elsevier.

Aarts, H., Verplanken, B. and Van Knippenberg, A. (1998) Predicting behavior from actions in the past: Repeated decision making or a matter of habit? *Journal of Applied Social Psychology, 28*(15), 1355–74.

Abele, A. and Brehm, W. (1993) Mood effects of exercise versus sports games: Findings and implications for well-being and health. In S. Maes, H. Leventhal and M. Johnston (eds), *International Review of Health Psychology* (Vol. 2) (pp. 53–80). Chichester: John Wiley.

Abramson, L. Y., Seligman, M. E. P. and Teasdale, J. D. (1978) Learned helplessness in humans: Critique and reformulation. *Journal of Abnormal Psychology, 87,* 49–74.

A.C. Nielson Company (1990) *1990 Nielson report on television.* Northbrook, IL: Nielson Media Research.

Adamson, M. J. (1991) *The role of exercise as an adjunct to the treatment of substance abuse.* Unpublished MEd thesis, University of Glasgow.

Adler, N. and Matthews, K. (1994) Health psychology: Why do some people get sick and some stay well? *Annual Review of Psychology, 45,* 229–59.

Ainsworth, B. E., Montoye, H. J. and Leon, A. S. (1994) Methods of assessing physical activity duing leisure and work. In C. Bouchard, R. J. Shephard and T. Stephens (eds), *Physical activity, fitness, and health* (pp. 145–59). Champaign, IL: Human Kinetics.

Ajzen, I. (1985) From intentions to actions: A theory of planned behavior. In J. Kuhl and J. Beckmann (eds), *Action control: From cognition to behavior* (pp. 11–39). New York: Springer-Verlag.

Ajzen, I. (1988) *Attitudes, personality and behaviour.* Milton Keynes: Open University Press.

Ajzen, I. (1991) The theory of planned behavior. *Organizational Behavior and Human Decision Processes, 50,* 179–211.

Ajzen, I. (1996) The directive influence of attitudes on behavior. In P. M. Gollwitzer and J. A. Bargh (eds), *The psychology of action* (pp. 385–403). New York: The Guilford Press.

Ajzen, I. and Fishbein, M. (1980) *Understanding attitudes and predicting social behaviour.* Englewood Cliffs, NJ: Prentice-Hall.

Ajzen, I. and Madden, T. J. (1986) Prediction of goal-directed behaviour: Attitudes, intentions, and perceived behavioural control. *Journal of Experimental Social Psychology, 22,* 453–74.

Alder, B. (1994) Postnatal sexuality. In P. Y. L. Choi and P. Nicolson (eds), *Female sexuality: Psychology, biology and social context.* London: Harvester Wheatsheaf.

Alexander, L. M., Inchley, J., Todd, J., Currie, D., Cooper, A. R. and Currie, C. (2005) The broader impact of walking to school among adolescents: Seven day accelerometry based study. *British Medical Journal, doi:10.1136/bmj.38567.382731.AE.*

Allison, K. R., Adlaf, E. M., Irving, H. M., Hatch, J. L., Smith, T. F., Dwyer, J. J. M., Goodman, J. (2005) Relationship of vigorous physical activity to psychological distress among adolescents. *Journal of Adolescent Health, 37*(2), 164–66.

Almond, L. and Harris, J. (1998) Interventions to promote health-related physical education. In S. J. H. Biddle, N. Cavill and J. F. Sallis (eds), *Young and Active? Young people and health-enhancing physical activity: Evidence and implications* (pp. 133–49). London: Health Education Authority.

American Academy of Pediatrics (1986) *Television and the family.* Elk Grove Village III: American Academy of Pediatrics.

American College of Sports Medicine (1978) Position statement on the recommended quantity and quality of exercise for developing and maintaining fitness in healthy adults. *Medicine and Science in Sports, 10,* vii–x.

American College of Sports Medicine (1988) Opinion statement on physical fitness in children and youth. *Medicine and Science in Sports and Exercise, 20,* 422–3.

American College of Sports Medicine (1990) Position stand: The recommended quantity and quality of exercise for developing and maintaining cardiorespiratory and muscular fitness in healthy adults. *Medicine and Science in Sports and Exercise, 22,* 265–74.

American College of Sports Medicine (1997a) *ACSM's exercise management for persons with chronic diseases and disabilities.* Champaign, IL: Human Kinetics.

American College of Sports Medicine (1997b) American College of Sports Medicine and American Diabetes Association joint position statement: Diabetes mellitus and exercise. *Medicine and Science in Sports and Exercise, 29*(12), i–vi.

American Psychiatric Association (1994) *Diagnostic and statistical manual of mental disorders-IV.* Washington, DC: APA.

Ames, C. and Archer, J. (1988) Achievement goals in the classroom: Students' learning strategies and motivation strategies. *Journal of Educational Psychology, 80,* 260–7.

Andersen, R. E., Crespo, C. J., Bartlett, S. J., Cheskin, L. J. and Pratt M. (1998) Relationship of physical activity and television watching with body weight and level of fatness among children: Results from the third National Health and Nutrition Examination Survey. *Journal of the American Medical Association, 279*(12), 938–42.

Anderson, B. L. (1992) Psychological interventions for cancer patients to enhance quality of life. *Journal of Consulting and Clinical Psychology, 60,* 552–8.

Andrew, G. M. and Parker J. O. (1979) Factors related to dropout of post myocardial infarction patients from exercise programs. *Medicine and Science in Sports, 11,* 376–8.

Andrew, G. M., Oldridge, N. B., Parker, J. O., Cunningham, D. A., Rechnitzer, P. A., Jones, N. L., Buck, C., Kavanagh, T., Shephard, R. J. and Sutton, J. R. (1981) Reasons for dropout from exercise programs in post-coronary patients. *Medicine and Science in Sports and Exercise, 13,* 164–8.

Anspaugh, D. J., Hunter, S. and Dignan, M. (1996) Risk factors for cardiovascular disease among exercising versus nonexercising women. *American Journal of Health Promotion, 10*(3), 171–4.

Arent, S. M., Landers, D. M. and Etnier, J. L. (2000) The effects of exercise on mood in older adults: A meta-analytic review. *Journal of Aging and Physical Activity, 8,* 407–30.

Arif, A. and Westermeyer, J. (1988) *Manual of drug and alcohol abuse guidelines for teaching in medical and health institutions.* New York: Plenum.

Armstrong, K. and Edwards, H. (2004) The effectiveness of a pram-walking exercise programme in reducing depressive symptomatology for postnatal women. *International Journal of Nursing Practice, 10,* 177–94.

Armstrong, N. and Van Mechelen, W. (1998) Are young people fit and active? In S. J. H. Biddle, J. F. Sallis and N. Cavill (eds), *Young and active? Young people and health-enhancing physical activity: Evidence and implications* (pp. 69–97). London: Health Education Authority.

Ary, D. V., Toobert, D., Wilson, W. and Glasgow, R. E. (1986) Patient perspectives on factors contributing to non adherence to diabetes regimen. *Diabetes Care, 9,* 168–72.

Asci, F. H. (2003) The effects of physical fitness training on trait anxiety and physical self-concept of female university students. *Psychology of Sport and Exercise, 4,* 255–64.

Association, A. P. (1980) *Diagnostic and statistical manual* (3rd edn) Washington, DC: APA.

Association, A. P. (1994) *Diagnostic and statistical manual of mental disorders-IV.* Washington, DC: APA.

Astrand, P.-O. (1994) Physical activity and fitness: Evolutionary perspective and trends for the future. In C. Bouchard, R. J. Shephard and T. Stephens (eds), *Physical activity, fitness, and health* (pp. 98–105). Champaign, IL: Human Kinetics.

Atkins, C. J., Kaplan, R. M., Timms, R. M., Reinsch, S. and Lofback, K. (1984) Behavioral exercise programs in the management of chronic obstructive pulmonary disease. *Journal of Consulting and Clinical Psychology, 52,* 591–603.

Australian College of Paediatrics (1994) The Australian College of Paediatrics: Policy statement – Children's television. *Journal of Paediatric and Child Health, 30,* 6–8.

Babyak, M., Blumenthal, J. A., Herman, S., Khatri, P., Doraiswamy, M., Moore, K., *et al.* (2000) Exercise treatment for major depression: Maintenance of therapeutic benefit at 10 months. *Psychosomatic Medicine, 62,* 633–38.

Bachman, G., Leiblum, S., Sandler, B., Ainsley, W., Narcissioan, R., Sheldon, R. and Nakajima, H. (1985) Correlates of sexual desire in post menopausal women. *Maruritas, 7,* (211–16).

Backhouse, S. H., Bishop, N. C., Biddle, S. J. H. and Williams, C. (2005) Effect of carbohydrate and prolonged exercise on affect and perceived exertion. *Medicine and Science in Sports and Exercise, 37,* 1768–73.

Baekeland, F. (1970) Exercise deprivation: Sleep and psychological reactions. *Archives of General Psychiatry, 22,* 365–9.

Bagozzi, R. P. and Kimmel, S. K. (1995) A comparison of leading theories for the prediction of goal-directed behaviours. *British Journal of Social Psychology, 34,* 437–61.

Bailey, C. and Biddle, S. J. H. (1988) Community health-related physical fitness testing and the National Garden Festival Health Fair at Stoke-on-Trent. *Health Education Journal, 47,* 144–7.

Baker, G., and Mutrie, N. (2005) *Are pedometers useful motivational tools for sedentary adults?* Paper presented at the Walk21-VI Everyday Walking Culture, Zurich, Switzerland.

Bandura, A. (1977) Self-efficacy: Toward a unifying theory of behavioral change. *Psychological Review, 84,* 191–215.

Bandura, A. (1986) *Social foundations of thought and action: A social cognitive theory.* Englewood Cliffs, NJ: Prentice Hall.

Bandura, A. (1997) *Self-efficacy: The exercise of control.* New York: W.H. Freeman.

Banks, A. and Waller, T. A. N. (1988) *Drug misuse: A practical handbook for GPs.* London: Blackwell Scientific Publications.

Banks, M. A. (1989) Physiotherapy benefits patients with Parkinson's disease. *Clinical Rehabilitation, 3,* 11–16.

Barker, D. J. P. and Rose, G. (1990) *Epidemiology in medical practice.* Edinburgh: Churchill Livingstone.

Barlow, D. H., Grosset, K. H., Hart, H. and Hart, D. M. (1989) A study of the experience of Glasgow women in the climacteric years. *British Journal of Obstetrics and Gynaecology, 96,* 1192–7.

Bartholomew, L. K., Parcel, G. S., Kok, G. and Gottlieb, N. H. (2001) *Intervention mapping: Designing theory- and evidence-based health promotion programs.* Mountain View, CA: Mayfield.

Batty, D. and Thune, I. (2000) Editorial: Does physical activity prevent cancer? *British Medical Journal, 321,* 1424–5.

Beck, A. T., Ward, C. H., Mendelsohn, M., Mock, J. and Erbaugh, H. (1961) An inventory for measuring depression. *Archives of General Psychiatry, 4,* 561–71.

Beck, A. T., Weissman, M. and Kovacs, M. (1976) Alcoholism, hopelessness and suicidal behavior. *Journal of Studies on Alcohol, 37,* 66–77.

Becker, M. H., Haefner, D. P., Kasl, S. V., Kirscht, J. P., Maiman, L. A. and Rosenstock, I. M. (1977) Selected psychosocial models and correlates of individual health-related behaviours. *Medical Care, 15 (Supplement),* 27–46.

Beedie, C. J., Terry, P. C. and Lane, A. M. (2005) Distinctions between emotion and mood. *Cognition and Emotion, 19,* 847–78.

Beesley, S. and Mutrie, N. (1997) Exercise is beneficial adjunctive treatment in depression. *British Medical Journal, 315,* 1542.

Beh, H. C., Mathers, S. and Holden, J. (1996) EEG correlates of exercise dependency. *International Journal of Psychophysiology, 23,* 121–8.

Belisle, M., Roskies, E. and Levesque, J.-M. (1987) Improving adherence to physical activity. *Health Psychology, 6,* 159–72.

Bell, A. C., Ge, K. and Popkin, B. M. (2002) The road to obesity or the path to prevention: Motorized transportation and obesity in China. *Obesity Research, 10,* 277–83.

Belman, M. J. (1989) Exercise in chronic pulmonary obstructive disease. In B. A. Franklin, G. Seymour and G. C. Timmis (eds), *Exercise in modern medicine* (pp. 175–91) Baltimore: Williams and Wilkins.

Bentler, P. and Speckart, G. (1981) Attitudes 'cause' behaviours: A structural equation analysis. *Journal of Personality and Social Psychology, 40,* 226–38.

Berg, K. (1986) Metabolic disease: Diabetes mellitus. In V. Seefeldt (ed.), *Physical activity and well-being* (pp. 425–40). Reston, VA: American Alliance for Health, Physical Education, Recreation and Dance.

Berger, B. G. and Motl, R. (2001) Physical activity and quality of life. In R. N. Singer, H. A. Hausenblas and C. M. Janelle (eds), *Handbook of sport psychology* (2nd edn) (pp. 636–71). New York: John Wiley.

Bernaards, C. M., Jans, M. P., van den Heuvel, S. G., Hendriksen, I. J., Houtman, I. L. and Bongers, P. M. (2006) Can strenuous leisure time physical activity prevent psychological complaints in a working population? *Occup Environ Med, 63*(1), 10–16.

Berryman, J. W. (2000) Exercise science and sports medicine: A rich history. *Sports Medicine Bulletin, 35*(1), 8–10.

Bhui, K., and Fletcher, A. (2000) Common mood and anxiety states: Gender differences in the protective effect of physical activity. *Social Psychiatry and Psychiatric Epidemiology, 35*(1), 28–35.

Biddle, S. J. H. (1992) Adherence to physical activity and exercise. In N. Norgan (ed.), Physical activity and health (pp. 170–189) Cambridge: Cambridge University Press.

Biddle, S. J. H. (1995) Exercise motivation across the lifespan. In S. J. H. Biddle (ed.), *European perspectives on exercise and sport psychology* (pp. 5–25). Champaign, IL: Human Kinetics.

Biddle, S. J. H. (1997) Current trends in sport and exercise psychology research. *The Psychologist: Bulletin of the British Psychological Society, 10*(2), 63–9.

Biddle, S. J. H. (1999) Motivation and perceptions of control: Tracing its development and plotting its future in exercise and sport psychology. *Journal of Sport and Exercise Psychology, 21,* 1–23.

Biddle, S. J. H. (2000) Emotion, mood and physical activity. In S. J. H. Biddle, K. R. Fox and S. H. Boutcher (eds), *Physical activity and psychological well-being* (pp. 63–87). London: Routledge.

Biddle, S. J. H. and Ashford, B. (1988) Cognitions and perceptions of health and exercise. *British Journal of Sports Medicine, 22,* 135–40.

Biddle, S. J. H. and Ekkekakis, P. (2005) Physically active lifestyles and well-being. In F. A. Huppert, N. Baylis and B. Kaverne (eds), *The science of well-being* (pp. 141–68). Oxford: Oxford University Press.

Biddle, S. J. H. and Gorely, T. (2005) Couch kids: Myth or reality? *The Psychologist, 18*(5), 276–79.

Biddle, S. J. H. and Mutrie, N. (1991) *Psychology of physical activity and exercise: A health-related perspective.* London: Springer-Verlag.

Biddle, S. J. H. and Mutrie, N. (2001) *Psychology of physical activity: Determinants, well-being and interventions.* London: Routledge.

Biddle, S. J. H. and Nigg, C. R. (2000) Theories of exercise behavior. *International Journal of Sport Psychology, 31,* 290–304.

Biddle, S. J. H., Fox, K. R. and Boutcher, S. H. (eds) (2000) *Physical activity and psychological well-being.* London: Routledge.

Biddle, S. J. H., Fox, K. R. and Edmunds, L. (1994) *Physical activity promotion in primary health care in England.* London: Health Education Authority.

Biddle, S. J. H., Gorely, T. and Stensel, D. J. (2004) Health-enhancing physical activity and sedentary behaviour in children and adolescents. *Journal of Sports Sciences, 22,* 679–701.

Biddle, S. J. H., Hanrahan, S. J. and Sellars, C. N. (2001) Attributions: Past, present, and future. In R. N. Singer, H. A. Hausenblas and C. M. Janelle (eds), *Handbook of sport psychology* (pp. 444–71). New York: Wiley.

Biddle, S. J. H., Sallis, J. F. and Cavill, N. (eds) (1998) *Young and active? Young people and health-enhancing physical activity: Evidence and implications.* London: Health Education Authority.

Biddle, S. J. H., Gorely, T., Marshall, S. J. and Cameron, N. (2005) Weekday motorised and active travel in UK youth: It's where you live not what you do. *Paper presented at Walk21 Satellite Symposium on Transport-related Physical Activity and Health,* Magglingen, Switzerland.

Biddle, S. J. H., Hagger, M. S., Chatzisarantis, N. L. D. and Lippke, S. (2007) Theoretical frameworks in exercise psychology. In G. Tenenbaum and R. C. Eklund (eds), *Handbook of sport psychology* (3rd edn) New York: Wiley.

Biddle, S. J. H., Wang, C. K. J., Chatzisarantis, N. L. D. and Spray, C. M. (2003a) Motivation for physical activity in young people: Entity and incremental beliefs about athletic ability. *Journal of Sports Sciences, 21,* 973–89.

Biddle, S. J. H., Wang, C. K. J., Kavussanu, M. and Spray, C. M. (2003b) Correlates of achievement goal orientations in physical activity: A systematic review of research. *European Journal of Sport Science, 3*(5), www.humankinetics.com/ejss.

Biddle, S. J. H., Whitehead, S. H., O'Donovan, T. M. and Nevill, M. E. (2005) Correlates of participation in physical activity for adolescent girls: A systematic review of recent literature. *Journal of Physical Activity and Health, 2,* 423–34.

Biddle, S. J. H., Cury, F., Goudas, M., Sarrazin, P., Famose, J. P. and Durand, M. (1995) Development of scales to measure perceived physical education class climate: A national project. *British Journal of Educational Psychology, 65,* 341–358.

Biering, F. S., Bendix, T., Jorgensen, K., Manniche, C. and Nielsen, H. (1994) Physical activity, fitness, and back pain. In C. Bouchard, R. J. Shephard and T. Stephens (eds), *Physical activity, fitness, and health* (pp. 724–36). Champaign, IL: Human Kinetics.

Birk, T. J. (1996) HIV and exercise. *Exercise Immunology Review, 2,* 84–95.

Blair, S. N. (1988) Exercise within a healthy lifestyle. In R. K. Dishman (ed.), *Exercise adherence: Its impact on public health* (pp. 75–89). Champaign, IL: Human Kinetics.

Blair, S. N. (1994) Physical activity, fitness, and coronary heart disease. In C. Bouchard, R. J. Shephard and T. Stephens (eds), *Physical activity, fitness and health* (pp. 579–90). Champaign, IL: Human Kinetics.

Blair, S. N. and Brodny, S. (1999) Effects of physical inactivity and obesity on morbidity and mortality: Current evidence and research issues. *Medicine and Science in Sports and Exercise, 31*(11 (Supplement)), S646–S62.

Blair, S. N., Cheng, Y. and Holder, J. S. (2001) Is physical activity or physical fitness more important in defining health benefits? *Medicine and Science in Sports and Exercise, 33*(6), S379–S399.

Blair, S. N., Kohl, H. W. and Goodyear, N. N. (1987) Rates and risks for running and exercise injuries: Studies in three populations. *Research Quarterly for Exercise and Sport, 58,* 221–8.

Blair, S. N., Kohl, H. W., Paffenbarger, R. S., Clark, D. G., Cooper, K. H. and Gibbons, L. W. (1989) Physical fitness and all-cause mortality: A prospective study of healthy men and women. *Journal of the American Medicial Association, 262*(17), 2395–401.

Blamey, A. and Mutrie, N. (2004) Changing the individual to promote health-enhancing physical activity: the difficulties of producing evidence and translating it into practice. *Journal of Sports Sciences, 22*(8), 741–54.

Blamey, A., Mutrie, N. and Aitchison, T. (1995) Health promotion by encouraged use of stairs. *British Medical Journal, 311,* 289–90.

Blanchard, C. M., Cokkinides, V., Courneya, K. S., Nehl, E. J., Stein, K. and Baker, F. (2003) A comparison of physical activity of post-treatment breast cancer survivors and non-cancer controls. *Behavioral Medicine, 28,* 140–9.

Bluechardt, M. H., Wiener, J. and Shephard, R. J. (1995) Exercise programmes in the treatment of children with learning disabilities. *Sports Medicine, 19,* 55–72.

Blumenthal, J. A., Williams, R. S., Wallace, A. G., Williams, R. B. and Needles, T. L. (1982) Physiological and psychological variables predict compliance to prescribed exercise therapy in patients recovering from myocardial infarction. *Psychosomatic Medicine, 44,* 519–27.

Blumenthal, J. A., Babyak, M. A., Moore, K. A., Craighead, W. E., Herman, S., Khatri, P. *et al.* (1999) Effects of exercise training on older patients with major depression. *Archives of Internal Medicine, 159,* 2349–56.

Boer, H. and Seydel, E. R. (1996) Protection motivation theory. In M. Conner and P. Norman (eds), *Predicting health behaviour: Research and practice with social cognition models* (pp. 95–120). Buckingham: Open University Press.

Booth, M. L., Bauman, A., Owen, N. and Gore, C. J. (1997) Physical activity preferences, preferred sources of assistance, and perceived barriers to increased activity among physically inactive Australians. *Preventive Medicine, 26,* 131–7.

Booth, M. L., Macaskill, P., Owen, N., Oldenburg, B., Marcus, B. H. and Bauman, A. (1993) Population prevalence and correlates of stages of change in physical activity. *Health Education Quarterly, 20,* 431–40.

Boreham, C. A. G., Wallace, W. F. M. and Nevill, A. (2000) Training effects of accumulated daily stair-climbing in previously sedentary young women. *Preventive Medicine, 30,* 277–81.

Boreham, C. A. G., Kennedy, R. A., Murphy, M. H., Tully, M., Wallace, W. F. and Young, I. (2005) Training effects of short bouts of stair climbing on cardiorespiratory fitness, blood lipids, and homocysteine in sedentary young women. *British Journal of Sports Medicine, 39*(9), 590–3.

Bosscher, R. J. (1993) Running and mixed physical exercise with depressed psychiatric patients. *International Journal of Sport Psychology, 24,* 170–84.

Bouchard, C. and Despres, J. P. (1995) Physical activity and health: Atherosclerotic, metabolic, and hypertensive diseases. *Research Quarterly for Exercise and Sport, 66,* 268–75.

Bouchard, C. and Shephard, R. J. (1994) Physical activity, fitness, and health: The model and key concepts. In C. Bouchard, R. J. Shephard and T. Stephens (eds), *Physical activity, fitness, and health* (pp. 77–88). Champaign, IL: Human Kinetics.

Bouchard, C., Shephard, R. J. and Stephens, T. (eds) (1994) *Physical activity, fitness and health: International proceedings and consensus statement.* Champaign, IL: Human Kinetics.

Bouchard, C., Shephard, R. J., Stephens, T., Sutton, J. R. and McPerson, B. D. (eds) (1990) *Exercise, fitness and health: A consensus of current knowledge.* Champaign IL: Human Kinetics.

Boutcher, S. H. (1993) Emotion and aerobic exercise. In R. N. Singer, M. Murphey and L. K. Tennant (eds), *Handbook of research on sport psychology* (pp. 799–814). New York: Macmillan.

Boutcher, S. H. (2000) Cognitive performance, fitness, and ageing. In S. J. H. Biddle, K. R. Fox and S. H. Boutcher (eds), *Physical activity and psychological well-being* (pp. 118–29). London: Routledge.

Boutcher, S. H., McAuley, E. and Courneya, K. S. (1997) Positive and negative affective response of trained and untrained subjects during and after aerobic exercise. *Australian Journal of Psychology, 49,* 28–32.

Bowling, A. (1997) *Measuring health: A review of quality of life measurement scales* (2nd edn). Buckingham: Open University Press.

Bozoian, S., Rejeski, W. J. and McAuley, E. (1994) Self-efficacy influences feeling states associated with acute exercise. *Journal of Sport and Exercise Psychology, 16,* 326–33.

Bray, S. R. (2004) Collective efficacy, group goals and group performance of a muscular endurance task. *Small Group Research, 35,* 230–8.

Breckon, J. (2002) Motivational interviewing and exercise preparation. In D. Lavallee and I. Cockerill (eds), *Counselling in sport and exercise contexts* (pp. 48–60). Leicester: Sport and Exercise Psychology Section of the British Psychological Society.

Brehm, B. J. and Steffen, J. J. (1998) Relation between obligatory exercise and eating disorders. *American Journal of Health Behavior, 22*(2), 108–19.

Brewer, B. W. (1993) *The dark side of exercise and mental health.* Paper presented at the VIII World Congress of Sport Psychology, Lisbon.

Briss, P. A., Zaza, S., Pappaioanou, M., Fielding, J., Wright-De Aguero, L., Truman, B. I., Hopkins, D. P., Mullen, P. D., Thompson, R. S., Woolf, S. H., Carande-Kulis, V. G., Anderson, L., Hinman, A. R., McQueen, D. V., Teutsch, S. M. and Harris, J. R. (2000) Developing an evidence-based guide to community preventive services – Methods. *American Journal of Preventive Medicine, 18*(1), 35–43.

British Heart Foundation (2000) *Couch kids: The growing epidemic.* London: The British Heart Foundation.

British Nutrition Foundation (1999) *Obesity: The report of the British Nutrition Foundation Task Force.* Oxford: Blackwell Science.

Brooks, R. (1996) EuroQol: the current state of play. *Health Policy, 37*(1), 53–72.

Brosnahan, J., Steffen, L. M., Lytle, L., Patterson, J. and Boostrom, A. (2004) The relation between physical activity and mental health among Hispanic and non-Hispanic white adolescents. *Arch Pediatr Adolesc Med, 158*(8), 818–23.

Brown, M. A. and Shirley, J. L. (2005) Enhancing women's mood and energy. *Holistic Nursing Practice, 19*(6), 278–84.

Brown, S. W., Welsh, M. C., Labbe, E. E., Vitulli, W. F. and Kulkarni, P. (1992) Aerobic exercise in the psychological treatment of adolescents. *Perceptual and Motor Skills, 74,* 555–60.

Brown, W., Mummery, K. W., Eakin, E. G. and Schofield, G. (2006) 10,000 Steps Rockhampton: Evaluation of a whole community approach to improving population levels of physical activity. *Journal of Physical Activity and Health, 3*(1), 1–15.

Brown, W. J., and Trost, S. G. (2003) Life transitions and changing physical activity patterns in young women. *American Journal of Preventive Medicine, 25*(2), 140–43.

Brownell, K. D. and Rodin, J. (1992) Prevalence of eating disorders in athletes. In K. D. Brownell, J. Rodin and J. H. Wilmore (eds), *Eating, body weight and performance in athletes* (pp. 128–45). Philadelphia: Lea and Febiger.

Brownson, R. C., Baker, E. A., Housemann, R. A., Brennan, L. K. and Bacak, S. J. (2001) Environmental and policy determinants of physical activity in the United States. *American Journal of Public Health, 91*(12), 1995–2003.

Buckworth, J. and Dishman, R. K. (2002) *Exercise psychology.* Champaign, IL: Human Kinetics.

Bull, F. C., Bellew, B., Schoppe, S. and Bauman, A. E. (2004) Developments in national physical activity policy: An international review and recommendations towards better practice. *Journal of Science and Medicine in Sport, 7*(1, Supplement), 93–104.

Burke, S. M., Carron, A. V., Eys, M. A., Ntoumanis, N. and Estabrooks, P. A. (2006) Group versus individual approach? A meta-analysis of the effectiveness of interventions to promote physical activity. *Sport and Exercise Psychology Review, 2*(1), 13–29.

Butler, C. C., Rollnick, S., Cohen, D., Bachmann, M., Russell, I. and Stott, N. (1999) Motivational consulting versus brief advice for smokers in general practice: A randomized trial. *British Journal of General Practice, 49,* 611–16.

Buxton, M. J., O'Hanlon, M. and Rushby, J. (1990) A new facility for the measurement of health-related quality of life. *Health Policy, 16,* 199–208.

Buxton, M. J., O'Hanlon, M. and Rushby, J. (1992) EuroQoL: A reply and reminder. *Health Policy, 20,* 329–32.

Byrne, A. and Byrne, D. G. (1993) The effect of exercise on depression, anxiety and other mood states. *Journal of Psychosomatic Research, 37,* 565–74.

Cacioppo, J. T., Gardner, W. and Berntson, G. G. (1999) The affect system has parallel and integrative processing components: Form follows function. *Journal of Personality and Social Psychology, 76,* 839–55.

Calabrese, L. H. (1990) Exercise, immunity, cancer, and infection. In C. Bouchard, R. J. Shephard, T. Stephens, J. R. Sutton and B. D. McPherson (eds), *Exercise, fitness and health* (pp. 567–79). Champaign, IL: Human Kinetics.

Calfas, K. J. and Taylor, W. C. (1994) Effects of physical activity on psychological variables in adolescents. *Pediatric Exercise Science, 6,* 406–23.

Calfas, K. J., Sallis, J. F., Oldenburg, B. and Ffrench, M. (1997) Mediators of change in physical activity following an intervention in primary care: PACE. *Preventive Medicine, 26,* 297–304.

Calfas, K. J., Long, B., Sallis, J. F., Wooten, W., Pratt, M. and Patrick, K. (1996) A controlled trial of physician counseling to promote the adoption of physical activity. *Preventive Medicine, 25,* 225–33.

Camacho, T. C., Roberts, R. E., Lazarus, N. B., Kaplan, G. A. and Cohen, R. D. (1991) Physical activity and depression: Evidence from the Alameda county study. *American Journal of Epidemiology, 134,* 220–31.

Cameron, J. and Pierce, D. (1994) Reinforcement, reward and intrinsic motivation: A meta-analysis. *Review of Educational Research, 64,* 363–423.

Campbell, A., Mutrie, N., White, F., McGuire, F. and Kearney, N. (2005) A pilot study of a supervised group exercise programme as a rehabilitation treatment for women with breast cancer receiving adjuvant treatment. *European Journal of Oncology Nursing, 9,* 56–63.

Campbell, N., Grimshaw, J., Rawles, J. and Ritchie, L. (1994) Cardiac rehabilitation: The agenda set by post-myocardial infarction patients. *Health Education Journal, 53,* 409–20.

Canada Fitness Survey (1983a) *Canadian youth and physical activity.* Ottawa: Author.

Canada Fitness Survey (1983b) *Fitness and lifestyle in Canada.* Ottawa: Author.

Cantu, R. C. (1982) *Diabetes and Exercise.* Ithaca, NY: Mouvement.

Carney, C., Mutrie, N. and McNeish, S. (2000) The transition from University and its effect on physical activity patterns. *International Journal of Health Promotion and Education 38*(3), 113–18.

Carron, A. V. and Hausenblas, H. A. (1998) *Group dynamics in sport* (2nd edn). Morgantown, WV: Fitness Informaton Technology.

Carron, A. V., Hausenblas, H. A. and Estabrooks, P. A. (1999) Social influence and exercise involvement. In S. J. Bull (ed.), *Adherence issues in sport and exercise* (pp. 1–17). Chichester: Wiley.

Carron, A. V., Hausenblas, H. A. and Mack, D. (1996) Social influence and exercise: A meta-analysis. *Journal of Sport and Exercise Psychology, 18,* 1–16.

Carron, A. V., Widmeyer, W. N. and Brawley, L. R. (1988) Group cohesion and individual adherence to physical activity. *Journal of Sport and Exercise Psychology, 10,* 127–38.

Caspersen, C. J. (1989) Physical activity epidemiology: Concepts, methods, and applications to exercise science. *Exercise and Sport Sciences Reviews, 17,* 423–73.

Caspersen, C. J., Merritt, R. K. and Stephens, T. (1994) International physical activity patterns: A methodological perspective. In R. K. Dishman (ed.), *Advances in exercise adherence* (pp. 73–110). Champaign, IL: Human Kinetics.

Caspersen, C. J., Powell, K. E. and Christenson, G. M. (1985) Physical activity, exercise and physical fitness: Definitions and distinctions for health-related research. *Public Health Reports, 100,* 126–31.

Cassidy, K., Kotynia-English, R., Acres, J., Flicker, L., Lautenschlager, N. T. and Almeida, O. P. (2004) Association between lifestyle factors and mental health measures among community-dwelling older women. *Australian and New Zealand Journal of Psychiatry, 38*(11–12), 940–7.

Cattell, R. B., Eber, H. W. and Tatsuoka, M. M. (1970) *Handbook of the 16PF questionnaire.* Champaign, IL: Institute of Personality and Ability Testing.

Cavill, N. and Bauman, A. (2004) Changing the way people think about health-enhancing physical activity: Do mass media campaigns have a role? *Journal of Sports Sciences, 22*(8), 771–90.

Cavill, N. and Biddle, S. J. H. (2003) The determinants of young people's participation in physical activity, and investigation of tracking of physical activity from youth to adulthood. In A. Giles (ed.), *A lifecourse approach to coronary heart disease prevention: Scientific and policy review* (pp. 179–97). London: TSO (The Stationery Office).

Cavill, N., Biddle, S. J. H. and Sallis, J. F. (2001) Health-enhancing physical activity for young people: Statement of the United Kingdom Expert Consensus Conference. *Pediatric Exercise Science, 13,* 12–25.

Centers for Disease Control and Prevention (1997) Guidelines for school and community programs to promote lifelong physical activity among young people. *Morbidity and Mortality Weekly Report, 46*(RR-6), 1–36.

Chaiken, S. (1980) Heuristic versus systematic information processing and the use of source versus message cues in persuasion. *Journal of Personality and Social Psychology, 39,* 752–66.

Chamove, A. S. (1986) Positive short-term effects of activity on behaviour in chronic schizophrenic patients. *British Journal of Clinical Psychology, 25,* 125–33.

Chaouloff, F. (1997) The serotonin hypothesis. In W. P. Morgan (ed.), *Physical activity and mental health* (pp. 179–98). Washington, DC: Taylor & Francis.

Chatzisarantis, N. L. D. and Biddle, S. J. H. (1998) Functional significance of psychological variables that are included in the theory of planned behaviour: A self-determination theory approach to the study of attitudes, subjective norms, perceptions of control, and intentions. *European Journal of Social Psychology, 28,* 303–22.

Chatzisarantis, N. L. D., Biddle, S. J. H. and Meek, G. A. (1997) A self-determination theory approach to the study of intentions and the intention-behaviour relationship in children's physical activity. *British Journal of Health Psychology, 2,* 343–60.

Chatzisarantis, N. L. D., Hagger, M. S., Biddle, S. J. H. and Smith, B. (2005) The stability of the attitude-intention relationship in the context of physical activity. *Journal of Sports Sciences, 23,* 49–61.

Chatzisarantis, N. L. D., Hagger, M. S., Biddle, S. J. H., Smith, B. and Wang, C. K. J. (2003) A meta-analysis of perceived locus of causality in exercise, sport, and physical education contexts. *Journal of Sport and Exercise Psychology, 25,* 284–306.

Chatzisarantis, N. L. D., Hagger, M. S., Biddle, S. J. H., Karageorghis, C. I., Smith, B. M. and Sage, L. (in press) The influences of perceived autonomy support on physical activity within the theory of planned behavior. *Journal of Sport and Exercise Psychology.* Chelladurai, P. (1993) Leadership. In R. N. Singer, M. Murphey and L. K. Tennant (eds), *Handbook of research on sport psychology* (pp. 647–71). New York: Macmillan.

Choi, P. Y. L. (2000) *Femininity and the physically active woman.* London: Routledge.

Choi, P. Y. L., Pope, H. G. and Olivardia, R. (2002) Muscle dysmorphia: A new syndrome in weightlifters. *British Journal of Sports Medicine, 36*(5), 375–6.

Choi, P. Y. L. and Salmon, P. (1995) Symptom changes across the menstrual cycle in competitive sportswomen, exercisers and sedentary women. *British Journal of Clinical Psychology, 34,* 447–60.

Chow, R., Harrison, J. E. and Notarius, C. (1987) Effect of two randomized exercise programmes on bone mass of healthy postmenopausal women. *British Medical Journal, 295,* 1441–4.

Cleary, J. (1996) *Safe routes to school project: Findings of schools survey.* Bristol: Sustrans.

Clore, G. L., Ortony, A. and Foss, M. A. (1987) The psychological foundations of the affective lexicon. *Journal of Personality and Social Psychology, 53,* 751–66.

Coakley, J. and White, A. (1992) Making decisions: Gender and sport participation among British adolescents. *Sociology of Sport Journal, 9,* 20–35.

Coalter, F. (2005) *Social benefits of sport: An overview to inform the community planning process.* Edinburgh: Sportscotland.

Cohen, J. (1988) *Statistical power analysis for the behavioral sciences.* Hillsdale, NJ: Erlbaum.

Colcombe, S. and Kramer, A. F. (2003) Fitness effects on the cognitive function of older adults: A meta-analytic study. *Psychological Science, 14*(2), 125–30.

Collins, M. (2003) *Sport and social exclusion.* London: Routledge.

Collins, M. (2004) Sport, physical activity and social exclusion. *Journal of Sports Sciences, 22,* 727–40.

Comella, C., Stebbins, G., Toms, N. and Goetz, C. (1994) Physical therapy and Parkinson's disease: A controlled clinical trial. *Neurology, 44,* 376–8.

Conner, M. and Abraham, C. (2001) Conscientiousness and the theory of planned behavior: Toward a more complete model of the antecedents of intentions and behavior. *Personality and Social Psychology Bulletin, 27,* 1547–61.

Conner, M. and Armitage, C. (1998) Extending the theory of planned behavior: A review and avenues for further research. *Journal of Applied Social Psychology, 28*(15), 1429–64.

Conner, M. and Norman, P. (1994) Comparing the health belief model and the theory of planned behaviour in health screening. In D. R. Rutter and L. Quine (eds), *Social psychology and health: European perspectives* (pp. 1–24). Aldershot: Avebury.

Conner, M. and Norman, P. (eds) (1996) *Predicting health behaviour.* Buckingham: Open University Press.

Conner, M. and Sparks, P. (1996) The theory of planned behaviour and health behaviours. In M. Conner and P. Norman (eds), *Predicting health behaviour* (pp. 121–62). Buckingham: Open University Press.

Cooper, A. R., Page, A. S., Foster, L. J. and Qahwaji, D. (2003) Commuting to school: Are children who walk more physically active? *American Journal of Preventive Medicine, 25*(4), 273–6.

Cooper-Patrick, L., Ford, D. E., Mead, L. A., Chang, P. P. and Klag, M. J. (1997) Exercise and depression in midlife: a prospective study. *Am J Public, 87*(4), 670–3.

Corbin, C. B. (1984) Self confidence of females in sports and physical activity. *Clinics in Sports Medicine, 3,* 895–908.

Corbin, C. B., Whitehead, J. R., and Lovejoy, P. (1988) Youth physical fitness awards. *Quest, 40,* 200–18.

Courneya, K. S. (2003) Exercise in cancer survivors: An overview of research. *Medicine and Science In Sports And Exercise, 35*(11), 1846–52.

Courneya, K. S. (2005) Exercise and quality of life in cancer survivors. In G. E. J. Faulkner and A. H. Taylor (eds), *Exercise, health and mental health. Emerging relationships* (pp. 114–34). London: Routledge.

Courneya, K. S. and Friedenreich, C. M. (1999) Physical exercise and quality of life following cancer diagnosis: A literature review. *Annals of Behavioral Medicine, 21*(2), 171–9.

Courneya, K. S., Mackey, J. R. and McKenzie, D. C. (2002) Exercise for breast cancer survivors: Research evidence and clinical guidelines. *Physician and Sportsmedicine, 30*(8), 33–42.

Courneya, K. S., Segal, R. J., Reid, R. D., Jones, L. W., Malone, S. C., Venner, P. M., Parliament, M. B., Scott, C.G., Quinney, H. A. and Wells, G. A. (2004) Predictors of adherence in a randomized controlled trial of exercise in prostate cancer survivors. *Medicine and Science in Sports and Exercise, 36*(5), S230–1.

Cowles, E. (1898) Gymnastics in the treatment of inebriety. *American Physical Education Review, 3,* 107–10.

Cox, K. L., Gorely, T. J., Puddey, I. B., Burke, V. and Beilin, L. J. (2003) Exercise behaviour change in 40–65 year old women: The SWEAT study (Sedentary Women Exercise Adherence Trial). *British Journal of Health Psychology, 8,* 477–95.

Craft, L. L. and Landers, D. M. (1998) The effect of exercise on clinical depression and depression resulting from mental illness: A meta-analysis. *Journal of Sport and Exercise Psychology, 20,* 339–57.

Craig, C. L., Marshall, A. L., Sjostrom, M., Bauman, A. E., Booth, M. L., Ainsworth, B. E., Pratt, M., Ekelund, U., Yngve, A., Sallis, J. F. and Oja, P. (2003) International physical activity questionnaire: 12-country reliability and validity. *Medicine and Science in Sports and Exercise, 35*(8), 1381–95.

Crammer, S. R., Neiman, D. and Lee, J. (1991) The effects of moderate exercise training on psychological well-being and mood state in women. *Journal of Psychosomatic Research, 35,* 437–9.

Crews, D. J. and Landers, D. M. (1987) A meta-analytic review of aerobic fitness and reactivity to psychosocial stressors. *Medicine and Science in Sports and Exercise, 19*(5, Supplement), S114–20.

Crouter, S., Schneider, P., Karabulut, M. and Basset, J. (2003) Validity of 10 electronic pedometers for measuring steps, distance, and energy cost. *Medicine and Science in Sports and Exercise, 35*(8), 1455–60.

Csikszentmihalyi, M. (1975) *Beyond boredom and anxiety.* San Francisco: Jossey-Bass.

Cummins, S., Stafford, M., Macintyre, S., Marmot, M. and Ellaway, A. (2005) Neighbourhood environment and its association with self rated health: Evidence from Scotland and England. *Journal of Epidemiology and Community Health, 59*(3), 207–13.

Currie, J. L. and Develin, E. D. (2002) Stroll your way to well-being: A survey of the perceived benefits, barriers, community support and stigma associated with pram walking groups designed for new mothers, Sydney. *Health Care Women International, 23,* 882–93.

Daley, A., MacArthur, C., Stokes-Lampard, H. and Mutrie, N. (under review) *Cochrane protocol: exercise for the management of women with vasomotor menopausal symptoms (Ref 1211).*

Daley, A. J., Mutrie, N., Crank, H., Coleman, R. and Saxton, J. (2004) Exercise therapy in women who have had breast cancer: Design of the Sheffield women's exercise and well-being project. *Health Education Research, 19*(6), 686–97.

Daley, A., MacArthur, C., Stokes-Lampard, H., McManus, R., Wilson, S. and Mutrie, N. (2007) Exercise participation, body mass index, health-related quality of life in menopausal aged women. *British Journal of General Practice, 57*(535), 130–36.

Daley, A., Crank, H., Saxton, J., Mutrie, N., Coleman, R. and Roalfe, A. (2007) Randomized trial of exercise therapy in women treated for breast cancer. *Journal of Clinical Oncology, 25*(13), 1713–21.

Davis, A. and Jones, L. J. (1996) Children in the urban environment: an issue for the new public health agenda. *Health and Place, 2,* 107–13.

Davis, A. and Jones, L. J. (1997) Whose neighbourhood? Whose quality of life? Developing a new agenda for children's health in urban settings. *Health Education Journal, 56,* 350–63.

Davis, C., Brewer, H. and Ratusny, D. (1993) Behavioral frequency and psychological commitment: Necessary concepts in the study of excessive exercising. *Journal of Behavioral Medicine, 16,* 611–28.

Davis, C., Kaptein, S., Kaplan, A. S., Olmsted, M. P. and Woodside, D. B. (1998) Obsessionality in anorexia nervosa: The moderating influence of exercise. *Psychosomatic Medicine, 60,* 192–7.

de Almeida, M. D. V., Graca, P., Afonso, C., D'Amicis, A., Lappalainen, R. and Damkjaer, S. (1999) Physical activity levels and body weight in a nationally representative sample in the European Union. *Public Health Nutrition, 2*(1a), 105–13.

De Bourdeauhuij, I. (1998) Behavioural factors associated with physical activity in young people. In S. J. H. Biddle, J. F. Sallis and N. Cavill (eds), *Young and active? Young people and health-enhancing physical activity: Evidence and implications* (pp. 98–118). London: Health Education Authority.

De Bourdeaudhuij, I. and Van Oost, P. (1999) A cluster-analytical approach toward physical activity and other health-related behaviors. *Medicine and Science in Sports and Exercise, 31,* 605–12.

De Bourdeaudhuij, I., Teixeira, P. J., Cardon, G. and Deforche, B. (2005) Environmental and psychosocial correlates of physical activity in Portuguese and Belgian adults. *Public Health Nutrition, 8*(7), 886–95.

de Jong, Z. and Vlieland, T. P. (2005) Safety of exercise in patients with rheumatoid arthritis. *Current Opinion in Rheumatology, 17*(2), 177–82.

Dearing, R. (1994) *The National Curriculum and its assessment: Final report.* London: School Curriculum and Assessment Authority.

deCharms, R. (1968) *Personal causation.* New York: Academic Press.

Deci, E. L. (1975) *Intrinsic motivation.* New York: Plenum.

Deci, E. L. (1992) On the nature and functions of motivation theories. *Psychological Science, 3,* 167–71.

Deci, E. L. and Flaste, R. (1995) *Why we do what we do: Understanding self-motivation.* New York: Penguin.

Deci, E. L. and Ryan, R. M. (1985) *Intrinsic motivation and self-determination in human behavior.* New York: Plenum Press.

Deci, E. L. and Ryan, R. M. (1991) A motivational approach to self: Integration in personality. In R. A. Dienstbier (ed.), *Nebraska symposium on motivation: Perspectives on motivation* (Vol. 38) (pp. 237–88). Lincoln, NE: University of Nebraska Press.

Deci, E. L., Eghrari, H., Patrick, B. C. and Leone, D. R. (1994) Facilitating internalisation: The self-determination theory perspective. *Journal of Personality, 62,* 119–42.

Demark-Wahnefried, W., Peterson B., McBride C., Lipkus I. and Clipp, E. (2000) Current health behaviours and readiness to pursue life-style changes among men and women diagnosed with early stage prostate and breast carcinomas. *Cancer, 88,* 674–84.

Department for Culture, Media and Sport (2002) *Game Plan: A strategy for delivering Government's sport and physical activity objectives.* London: Cabinet Office.

Department of Health (1993a) *Better living – better life.* Henley: Knowledge House.

Department of Health (1993b) *The Health of the Nation: A strategy for health for England.* London: HMSO.

Department of Health (1998) *Our healthier nation: A contract for health.* London: The Stationery Office.

Department of Health (1999) *Drug misuse and dependence. Guidelines on clinical management.* Retrieved from http://www.dh.gov.uk/prod_consum_dh/groups/dh_digitalassets/@dh/@en/documents/digitalasset/dh_4078198.pdf

Department of Health (2004a) *At least five a week: Evidence on the impact of physical activity and its relationship to health. A report from the Chief Medical Officer.* London: Author.

Department of Health (2004b) *Choosing health: Making health choices easier.* London: Department of Health.

Department of Health (2005) *Choosing activity: a physical activity action plan.* London: Department of Health.

Department of Health and Human Services (1980) *Promoting health/Preventing disease: Objectives for the nation.* Washington, DC.: US Government Printing Office.

Department of Health and Human Services (1986) *Midcourse review: 1990 physical fitness and exercise objectives.* Washington, DC: US Government Printing Office.

Department of Health and Human Services (1991) *Healthy people 2000: National health promotion and disease prevention objectives* (No. DHHS Pub. No. PHS 91–50212) Washington, DC: US Government Printing Office.

Department of Health and Human Services (1996) *Physical Activity and health: a report of the Surgeon General.* Atlanta: US Department of Health and Human Services, Centers for Disease Control and Prevention, National Center for Chronic Disease Prevention and Health Promotion.

Department of Health and Human Services (1997) Guidelines for school and community programs to promote lifelong physical activity among young people. *Morbidity and Mortality Weekly Report, 46*(March 7), 1–36.

Department of Health and Human Services (1999) *Promoting physical activity: A guide for community action.* Champaign, IL: Human Kinetics.

Department of Health and Human Services (2000) *Health people 2010: Understanding and improving health.* Washington, DC: Author.

Department of Health and Human Services and Centers for Disease Control and Prevention (1996) *Physical Activity and Health: A report of the Surgeon General.* Atlanta, GA: Author.

Derogatis, L. R., Lipman, R. S. and Covi, L. (1973) The SCL-90: An outpatient psychiatric rating scale. *Psychopharmacology Bulletin, 9,* 13–28.

Diabetes Prevention Program Research Group (2002) Reduction in the incidence of Type 2 diabetes with lifestyle intervention or metformin. *New England Journal of Medicine, 346,* 393–403.

Diener, E. (1999) Introduction to the special section on the structure of emotion. *Journal of Personality and Social Psychology, 76,* 803–4.

Dietrich, A. (2005) *The transient hypofrontality hypothesis.* Paper presented at the International Society of Sport Psychology 11th World Congress of Sport Psychology, Sydney, Australia.

DiGiuiseppi, C., Roberts, I., and Li, L. (1997) Influence of changing travel patterns on child death rates from injury: Trend analysis. *British Medical Journal, 314* (http://bmj.com/cgi/content/full/314/7082/710).

Dishman, R. K. (1981) Biologic influences on exercise adherence. *Research Quarterly for Exercise and Sport, 52,* 143–59.

Dishman, R. K. (ed.) (1988) *Exercise adherence: Its impact on public health.* Champaign, IL: Human Kinetics.

Dishman, R. K. (1990) Determinants of participation in physical activity. In C. Bouchard, R. J. Shephard, T. Stephens, J. R. Sutton and B. D. McPherson (eds), *Exercise, fitness, and health* (pp. 75–101). Champaign, IL: Human Kinetics.

Dishman, R. K. (1994) Consensus, problems and prospects. In R. K. Dishman (ed.), *Advances in exercise adherence* (pp. 1–27). Champaign, IL: Human Kinetics.

Dishman, R. K. (1995) Physical activity and public health: Mental health. *Quest, 47,* 362–85.

Dishman, R. K. (1997) The norepinephrine hypothesis. In W. P. Morgan (ed.), *Physical activity and mental health* (pp. 199–212) Washington, DC: Taylor & Francis.

Dishman, R. K. and Buckworth, J. (1996) Increasing physical activity: A quantitative synthesis. *Medicine and Science in Sports and Exercise, 28,* 706–19.

Dishman, R. K. and Dunn, A. L. (1988) Exercise adherence in children and youth: Implications for adulthood. In R. K. Dishman (ed.), *Exercise adherence: Its impact on public health* (pp. 155–200). Champaign, IL: Human Kinetics.

Dishman, R. K. and Gettman, L. (1980) Psychobiologic influences on exercise adherence. *Journal of Sport Psychology, 2,* 295–310.

Dishman, R. K. and Sallis, J. F. (1994) Determinants and interventions for physical activity and exercise. In C. Bouchard, R. J. Shephard and T. Stephens (eds), *Physical activity, fitness, and health* (pp. 203–13). Champaign, IL.: Human Kinetics.

Dishman, R. K. and Steinhardt, M. (1990) Health locus of control predicts free-living, but not supervised physical activity: A test of exercise-specific control and outcome-expectancy hypotheses. *Research Quarterly for Exercise and Sport, 61,* 383–94.

Dishman, R. K., Sallis, J. F. and Orenstein, D. (1985) The determinants of physical activity and exercise. *Public Health Reports, 100,* 158–71.

Dishman, R. K., Washburn, R. A. and Heath, G. W. (2004) *Physical activity epidemiology.* Champaign, IL: Human Kinetics.

Dishman, R. K., Oldenburg, B., O'Neal, H. and Shephard, R. J. (1998) Worksite physical activity interventions. *American Journal of Preventive Medicine, 15,* 344–61.

Dixon, P., Heaton, J., Long, A. and Warburton, A. (1994) Reviewing and applying the SF-36. *Outcomes Briefing, 4,* 3–25.

Doan, R. E. and Scherman, A. (1987) The therapeutic effect of physical fitness on measures of personality: A literature review. *Journal of Counselling and Development, 66,* 28–36.

Doganis, G. and Theodorakis, Y. (1995) The influence of attitude on exercise participation. In S. J. H. Biddle (ed.), *European perspectives on exercise and sport psychology* (pp. 26–49). Champaign, IL: Human Kinetics.

Dollman, J., Norton, K. and Norton, L. (2005) Evidence for secular trends in children's physical activity behaviour. *British Journal of Sports Medicine, 39*(12), 892–7; discussion 897.

Donaghy, M E. and Mutrie, N. (1997) Physical self-perception of problem drinkers on entry to an alcohol rehabilitation programme. *Physiotherapy, 83*(7), 358.

Donaghy, M. E. and Mutrie, N. (1998) A randomized controlled study to investigate the effect of exercise on the physical self-perceptions of problem drinkers. *Physiotherapy, 84*(4), 169.

Donaghy, M. E. and Ussher, M. H. (2005) Exercise interventions in drug and alcohol rehabilitation. In G. E. J. Faulkner and A. H. Taylor (eds), *Exercise, health and mental health. Emerging relationships* (pp. 48–69). London: Routledge.

Donaghy, M. E., Ralston, G. and Mutrie, N. (1991) Exercise as a therapeutic adjunct for problem drinkers. *Journal of Sports Sciences, 9,* 440.

Dong, W. and Erins, B. (1997) *Scottish Health Survey 1995.* Edinburgh: The Stationery Office.

Donovan, R. J. and Owen, N. (1994) Social marketing and population interventions. In R. K. Dishman (ed.), *Advances in Exercise Adherence* (pp. 249–90) Champaign, IL: Human Kinetics.

Doyne, E. J., Ossip-Klein, D. J., Bowman, E., Osborn, K. M., McDougall-Wilson, I. B. and Neimeyer, R. A. (1987) Running versus weightlifting in the treatment of depression. *Journal of Consulting and Clinical Psychology, 55,* 748–54.

Draeger, J., Yates, A. and Crowell, D. (2005) The Obligatory Exerciser: Assessing an overcommitment to exercise. *Physician and Sportsmedicine, 33*(6), 13–16; 21–3.

Driscoll, S. D., Meininger, G. E., Lareau, M. T., Dolan, S. E., Killilea, K. M., Hadigan, C. M., Lloyd-Jones, D. M., Klibanski, A., Frontera, W. R. and Grinspoon, S. K. (2004) Effects of exercise training and metformin on body composition and cardiovascular indices in HIV-infected patients. *AIDS, 18*(3), 465–73.

Duda, J. L. (2001) Achievement goal research in sport: Pushing the boundaries and clarifying some misunderstandings. In G. C. Roberts (ed.), *Advances in motivation in sport and exercise* (pp. 129–82). Champaign, IL: Human Kinetics.

Dida, J. L. and Whitehead, J. (1998) Measurement of goal perspectives in the physical domain. In J. L. Duda (ed.), *Advances in sport and exercise psychology measurement* (pp. 21–48). Morgantown, WV: Fitness Information Technology.

Dudgeon, W. D., Phillips, K. D., Bopp, C. M. and Hand, G. A. (2004) Physiological and psychological effects of exercise interventions in HIV disease. *AIDS Patient Care and Stds, 18*(2), 81–98.

Dugmore, D. (1992) Exercise and heart disease. In K. Williams (ed.), *The community prevention of coronary heart disease* (pp. 43–58). London: HMSO.

Dummer, G., Rosen, L., Heusner, W., Roberts, P. and Counsilman, J. (1987) Pathogenic weight control behaviors of young competitive swimmers. *The Physician and Sportsmedicine, 15*(5), 75–84.

Duncan, M. and Mummery, K. (2005) Psychosocial and environmental factors associated with physical activity among city dwellers in regional Queensland. *Preventive Medicine, 40,* 363–72.

Dunn, A. L. (1996) Getting started: A review of physical activity adoption studies. *British Journal of Sports Medicine, 30,* 193–9.

Dunn, A. L. and Dishman, R. K. (1991) Exercise and the neurobiology of depression. *Exercise and Sport Sciences Reviews, 19,* 41–98.

Dunn, A. L., Trivedi, M. H. and O'Neal, H. A. (2001) Physical activity dose-response effects on outcomes of depression and anxiety. *Medicine and Science in Sports and Exercise, 33*(6, Supplement), S587–97.

Dunn, A. L., Trivedi, M. H., Kampert, J., Clark, C. G. and Chambliss, H. O. (2005) Exercise treatment for depression. Efficacy and dose-response. *American Journal of Preventive Medicine, 28*(1), 1–8.

Dunn, A. L., Garcia, M. E., Marcus, B. H., Kampert, J. B., Kohl, H. W. and Blair, S. N. (1998) Six-month physical activity and fitness changes in Project Active, a randomized trial. *Medicine and Science in Sports and Exercise, 30,* 1076–83.

Dunn, A. L., Marcus, B. H., Kampert, J. B., Garcia, M. E., Kohl, H. W. and Blair, S. N. (1997) Reduction in cardiovascular disease risk factors: six-months results from Project Active. *Preventive Medicine, 26,* 883–92.

Dunn, A. L., Marcus, B. H., Kampert, J. B., Garcia, M. E., Kohl, H. W. and Blair, S. N. (1999) Comparison of lifestyle and structured interventions to increase physical activity and cardiorespiratory fitness: A randomized trial. *Journal of the American Medical Association, 281,* 327–34.

Dunn, S. W. (1993) Psychological aspects of diabetes in adults. In S. Maes, H. Leventhal and M. Johnston (eds), *International Review of Health Psychology* (Vol. 2) (pp. 175–197). London: John Wiley.

Durnin, J. V. G. A. (1992) Physical activity levels past and present. In N. Norgan (ed.), *Physical activity and health* (pp. 20–27). Cambridge: Cambridge University Press.

Dweck, C. (1992) The study of goals in psychology. *Psychological Science, 3,* 165–7.

Dweck, C. (1996) Implicit theories as organizers of goals and behavior. In P. Gollwitzer and J. Bargh (eds), *The psychology of action* (pp. 69–90). New York: Guilford Press.

Dweck, C. (1999) *Self-theories: Their role in motivation, personality, and development.* Philadelphia, PA: Taylor & Francis.

Dweck, C. and Leggett, E. (1988) A social-cognitive approach to motivation and personality. *Psychological Review, 95,* 256–73.

Dweck, C., Chiu, C. Y. and Hong, Y. Y. (1995) Implicit theories and their role in judgments and reactions: A world from two perspectives. *Psychological Inquiry, 6,* 267–85.

Dwyer, T., Coonan, W. E., Leitch, D. R., Hetzel, B. S. and Baghurst, R. A. (1983) An investigation of the effects of daily physical activity on the health of primary school students in South Australia. *International Journal of Epidemiology, 12,* 308–13.

Eadie, D. R. and Leathar, D. S. (1988) *Concepts of fitness and health: An exploratory study.* Edinburgh: Scottish Sports Council.

Eagly, A. H. and Chaiken, S. (1993) *The psychology of attitudes.* Fort Worth, TX: Harcourt Brace Jovanovich College Publishers.

Eakin, E. G., Brown, W. J., Marshall, A. L., Mummery, K. and Larsen, E. (2004a) Physical activity promotion in primary care: Bridging the gap between research and practice. *American Journal of Preventive Medicine, 27,* 297–303.

Eakin, E. G., Brown, W. J., Marshall, A. L., Mummery, K. and Larsen, E. (2004b) Physical activity promotion in primary care: bridging the gap between research and practice. *American Journal of Preventive Medicine, 27*(4), 297–303.

Eastep, E., Beveridge, S., Eisenman, P., Ransdell, L. and Schultz, B. (2004) Does augmented feedback from pedometers increase adults' walking behavior? *Perceptual and Motor Skills, 99,* 392–402.

Eden, K. B., Orleans, C. T., Mulrow, C. D., Pender, N. J. and Teutsch, S. M. (2002) Does counseling by clinicians improve physical activity? A summary of the evidence for the U.S. Preventive Services Task Force. *Annals of Internal Medicine., 137*(3), 208–15.

Egger, G. and Swinburn, B. A. (1997) An 'ecological' approach to the obesity pandemic. *British Medical Journal, 315,* 477–80.

Eiser, J. R. (1986) *Social psychology.* Cambridge: Cambridge University Press.

Eiser, J. R. and van der Pligt, J. (1988) *Attitudes and decisions.* London: Routledge.

Ekkekakis, P. (2003) Pleasure and displeasure from the body: Perspectives from exercise. *Cognition and Emotion, 17,* 213–39.

Ekkekakis, P. and Petruzzello, S. J. (1999) Acute aerobic exercise and affect: Current status, problems and prospects regarding dose-response. *Sports Medicine, 28,* 337–74.

Ekkekakis, P. and Petruzzello, S. J. (2000) Analysis of the affect measurement conundrum in exercise psychology: I. Fundamental issues. *Psychology of Sport and Exercise, 1,* 71–88.

Ekkekakis, P. and Petruzzello, S. J. (2001a) Analysis of the affect measurement conundrum in exercise psychology: II. Conceptual and methodological critique of the exercise-induced feeling inventory. *Psychology of Sport and Exercise, 2,* 1–26.

Ekkekakis, P. and Petruzzello, S. J. (2001b) Analysis of the affect measurement conundrum in exercise psychology: III. Conceptual and methodological critique of the subjective exercise experiences scale. *Psychology of Sport and Exercise, 2,* 205–32.

Ekkekakis, P., Hall, E. E. and Petruzzello, S. J. (2004) Practical markers of the transition from aerobic to anaerobic metabolism during exercise: Rationale and a case for affect-based exercise prescription. *Preventive Medicine, 38,* 149–59.

Ekkekakis, P., Hall, E. E., and Petruzzello, S. J. (2005) Variation and homogeneity in affective responses to physical activity of varying intensities: An alternative perspective on dose-response based on evolutionary considerations. *Journal of Sports Sciences, 23*(5), 477–500.

Ekkekakis, P., Hall, E. E., Van Landuyt, L. M. and Petruzzello, S. J. (2000) Walking in (affective) circles: Can short walks enhance affect? *Journal of Behavioral Medicine, 23,* 245–75.

Elavsky, S., McAuley, E., Motl, R. W., Konopack, J. F., Marquez, D. X., Hu, L. *et al.* (2005) Physical activity enhances long-term quality of life in older adults: Efficacy, esteem, and affective influences. *Annals of Behavioral Medicine, 30*(2), 138–145.

Emslie, C., Whyte, F., Campbell, A., Mutrie, N., Lee, L., Ritchie, D. *et al.* (2007) 'I wouldn't have been interested in just sitting round a table talking about cancer'; exploring the experiences of women with breast cancer in a group exercise trial. *Health Educ. Res.,* cyl159.

Engstrom, L.-M. (1991) Exercise adherence in sport for all from youth to adulthood. In P. Oja and R. Telama (eds), *Sport for all* (pp. 473–83). Amsterdam: Elsevier.

Epling, W. F. and Pierce, W. D. (1988) Activity-based anorexia: A biobehavioral perspective. *International Journal of Eating Disorders, 7,* 475–85.

Epstein, L. H. and Roemmich, J. N. (2001) Reducing sedentary behaviour: Role in modifying physical activity. *Exercise and Sport Sciences Reviews, 29*(3), 103–8.

Estabrooks, P. and Gyurcsik, N. C. (2003) Evaluating the impact of behavioral interventions that target physical activity: Issues of generalizability and public health. *Psychology of Sport and Exercise, 4,* 41–55.

Etnier, J. L., Salazar, W., Landers, D. M., Petruzzello, S. J., Han, M. and Nowell, P. (1997) The influence of physical fitness and exercise upon cognitive functioning: A meta-analysis. *Journal of Sport and Exercise Psychology, 19,* 249–77.

Eves, F., Webb, J. O. and Mutrie, N. (in press) A work place intervention to promote stair climbing: Greater effects in the overweight. *Obesity, 14* (12): 2210–160.

Ewart, C. (1989) Psychological effects of resistive weight training: Implications for cardiac patients. *Medicine and Science in Sports and Exercise, 21,* 683–88.

Ewart, C. E., Stewart, K. J., Gillilan, R. E., and Kelemen, M. H. (1986) Self-efficacy mediates strength gains during circuit weight training in men with coronary artery disease. *Medicine and Science in Sports and Exercise, 18,* 531–40.

Ewart, C. E., Taylor, C. B., Reese, L. B. and DeBusk, R. F. (1983) Effects of early post myocardial infarction exercise testing on self perception and subsequent physical activity. *American Journal of Cardiology, 51,* 1076–80.

Ewing, R., Handy, S., Brownson, R. C., Clemente, O. and Winston, E. (2006) Identifying and measuring urban design qualities related to walkability. *Journal of Physical Activity and Health, 3*(Supplement 1), S223–40.

Ewing, R., Schmid, T., Killingsworth, R., Zlot, A. I. and Raudenbush, S. (2003) Relationship between urban sprawl and physical activity, obesity, and morbidity. *American Journal of Health Promotion, 18,* 47–57.

Eysenck, H. J. and Eysenck, S. (1963) *Manual of the Eysenck Personality Inventory.* San Diego, CA: Educational and Industrial Testing Service.

Fagard, R. H. (2001) Exercise characteristics and the blood pressure response to dynamic physical training. *Medicine and Science in Sports and Exercise, 33*(6, Supplement), S484–92.

Fairey, A. S., Courneya, K. S., Field, C. J. and Mackey, J. R. (2002) Physical exercise and immune system function in cancer survivors: A comprehensive review and future directions. *Cancer, 94*(2), 539–51.

Falloon, I. R. H. and Talbot, R. E. (1981) Persistent auditory hallucinations: Coping mechanisms and implications for management. *Psychological Medicine, 11,* 329–39.

Farmer, M., Locke, B., Moscicki, E., Dannenberg, A., Larson, D. and Radloff, L. (1988) Physical activity and depressive symptoms: The NHANES-I epidemiological follow-up study. *American Journal of Epidemiology, 128,* 1340–51.

Faulkner, G. E. J. (2005) Exercise as an adjunct treatment for schizophrenia. In G. E. J. Faulkner and A. H. Taylor (eds), *Exercise, health and mental health: Emerging relationships* (pp. 27–47). London: Routledge.

Faulkner, G. E. J. and Biddle, S. J. H. (1999) Exercise as an adjunct treatment for schizophrenia: A review of literature. *Journal of Mental Health, 8,* 441–57.

Faulkner, G. E. J. and Biddle, S. J. H. (2001a) Exercise and mental health: It's just not psychology! *Journal of Sports Sciences, 19,* 433–44.

Faulkner, G. E. J. and Biddle, S. J. H. (2001b) Predicting physical activity promotion in health care settings. *American Journal of Health Promotion, 16*(2), 98–106.

Faulkner, G. E. J. and Sparkes, A. (1999) Exercise as therapy for schizophrenia: An ethnographic study. *Journal of Sport and Exercise Psychology, 21,* 52–69.

Faulkner, G. E. J. and Taylor, A. H. (eds) (2005) *Exercise, health and mental health. Emerging relationships.* London: Routledge

Felce, D. (1997) Defining and applying the concept of quality of life. *Journal of Intellectual Disability Research, 41*(Pt 2), 126–35.

Feltz, D. L. (1992) Understanding motivation in sport: A self-efficacy perspective. In G. C. Roberts (ed.), *Motivation in Sport and Exercise* (pp. 93–105). Champaign, IL: Human Kinetics.

Feltz, D. L. (1988) Self-confidence and sports performance. *Exercise and Sport Sciences Reviews, 16,* 423–57.

Fentem, P. H., Bassey, E. J. and Turnbull, N. B. (1988) *The new case of exercise.* London: The Sports Council and Health Education Authority.

Fielding, J. E., Mullen, P. D., Brownson, R. C., Fullilove, M. T., Guerra, F. A., Hinman, A. R., Isham, G. J., Land, G. H., Mahan, C. S., Nolan, P. A., Scrimshaw, S. C., Teutsch, S. M., Thompson, R. S. and Briss, P. A. (2002) Recommendations to increase physical activity in communities. *American Journal of Preventive Medicine, 22*(4), 67–72.

Fishbein, M. and Ajzen, I. (1975) *Belief, attitude, intention and behaviour: An introduction to theory and research.* Reading, Mass: Addison-Wesley.

Fiske, S. T. and Taylor, S. E. (1991) *Social cognition.* New York: McGraw-Hill.

Fletcher, G. F., Blair, S. N., Blumenthal, J., Caspersen, C., Chaitman, B., Epstein, S., Falls, H., Froelicher, S. S., Froelicher, V. F. and Pina, I. L (1992) Statement of exercise: Benefits and recommendations for physical activity programs for all Americans. *Circulation, 86,* 340–4.

Fogarty, M. and Happell, B. (2005) Exploring the benefits of an exercise program for people with schizophrenia: A qualitative study. *Issues in Mental Health Nursing, 26*(3), 341–51.

Forsterling, F. (1988) *Attribution theory in clinical psychology.* Chichester: Wiley.

Forsyth, A., Schmitz, K. H., Oakes, M., Zimmerman, J. and Koepp, J. (2006) Standards for environmental measurement using GIS: Toward a protocol for protocols. *Journal of Physical Activity and Health, 3*(Supplement 1), S241–S57.

Fortier, M. S., Vallerand, R. J., Briere, N. M. and Provencher, P. J. (1995) Competitive and recreational sport structures and gender: A test of their relationship with sport motivation. *International Journal of Sport Psychology, 26,* 24–39.

Foster, C., Hillsdon, M., Cavill, N., Bull, F. C. L., Buxton, K. and Crombie, H. (2006) *Interventions that use the environment to encourage physical activity: Evidence review.* National Institute of Health and Clinical Excellence.

Fox, K. R. (1990) *The physical self-perception profile manual.* DeKalb, IL: Office of Health Promotion, Northern Illinois University.

Fox, K. R. (1997a) The physical self and processes in self-esteem development. In K. R. Fox (ed.), *The physical self: From motivation to well-being* (pp. 111–39). Champaign, IL: Human Kinetics.

Fox, K. R. (ed.) (1997b) *The physical self: From motivation to well-being.* Champaign, IL: Human Kinetics.

Fox, K. R. (1998) Advances in the measurement of the physical self. In J. L. Duda (ed.), *Advances in sport and exercise psychology measurement* (pp. 295–310). Morgantown, WV: Fitness Information Technology.

Fox, K. R. (1999) Aetiology of obesity XI: Physical inactivity. In B. N. Foundation (ed.), *Obesity* (pp. 116–131). Oxford: Blackwell Scientific.

Fox, K. R. (2000) The effects of exercise on self-perceptions and self-esteem. In S. J. H. Biddle, K. R. Fox and S. H. Boutcher (eds), *Physical activity and psychological well-being* (pp. 88–117). London: Routledge.

Fox, K. R and Corbin, C. B. (1989) The Physical Self Perception Profile: Development and preliminary validation. *Journal of Sport and Exercise Psychology, 11,* 408–30.

Fox, K. R., Biddle, S. J. H., Edmunds, L., Bowler, I. and Killoran, A. (1997) Physical activity promotion through primary health care in England. *British Journal of General Practice, 47,* 367–9.

Fox, K. R., Goudas, M., Biddle, S. J. H., Duda, J. L. and Armstrong, N. (1994) Children's task and ego goal profiles in sport. *British Journal of Educational Psychology, 64,* 253–61.

France, C., Lee, C. and Powers, J. (2004) Correlates of depressive symptoms in a representative sample of young Australian women. *Australian Psychologist, 39*(3), 228–37.

Frankel, A. and Murphy, J. (1974) Physical fitness and personality in alcoholism: Canonical analysis of measures before and after treatment. *Quarterly Journal of Studies on Alcohol, 35,* 1271–8.

Franklin, B. (1988) Program factors that influence exercise adherence: Practical adherence skills for the clinical staff. In R. K. Dishman (ed.), *Exercise adherence: Its impact on public health* (pp. 237–58). Champaign, IL: Human Kinetics.

Fremont, J. and Craighead, L. W. (1987). Aerobic exercise and cognitive therapy in the treatment of dyshoric moods. *Cognitive Therapy and Research, 11,* 241–51.

374   *References*

Friedenrich, C. M. and Courneya, K. S. (1996) Exercise as rehabilitation for cancer patients. *Clinical Journal of Sports Medicine, 6,* 237–44.

Frost, H., Klaber-Moffett, J. A., Moser, J. S. and Fairbank, J. C. T. (1995) Randomized controlled trial for evaluation of a fitness programme for patients with chronic low back pain. *British Medical Journal, 310,* 151–4.

Fruin, D., Pratt, C. and Owen, N. (1991) Protection motivation theory and adolescents' perceptions of exercise. *Journal of Applied Social Psychology, 22,* 55–69.

Gannon, L. (1988) The potential role of exercise in the alleviation of menstrual disorders and menopausal symptoms: A theoretical synthesis of recent research. *Women and Health, 14*(2), 105–27.

Gary, V. and Guthrie, D. (1972) The effects of jogging on physical fitness and self-concept in hospitalized alcoholics. *Quarterly Journal of Studies on Alcoholism, 33,* 1073–8.

Gauvin, L. and Rejeski, W. J. (1993) The Exercise-Induced Feeling Inventory: Development and initial validation. *Journal of Sport and Exercise Psychology, 15,* 403–23.

Gauvin, L., Richard, L., Craig, C. L., Spivock, M., Riva, M. and Forster, M. (2005) From walkability to active living potential: An 'ecometric' validation study. *American Journal of Preventive Medicine, 28*(2 (Supplement 2)), 126–33.

George, T. and Feltz, D. L. (1995) Motivation in sport from a collective efficacy perspective. *International Journal of Sport Psychology, 26,* 98–116.

Gettman, L. R. (1996) Economic benefits of physical activity. *The President's Council on Physical Fitness and Sports Physical Activity and Fitness Research Digest, 2*(7), 1–6.

Gibberd, F. B., Page, N. G. R., Spencer, K. M., Kinnear, E. and Hawksworth, J. B. (1981) Controlled trial of physiotherapy and occupational therapy for Parkinson's disease. *British Medical Journal, 282,* 1196.

Giles-Corti, B., Broomhall, M. H., Knuiman, M., Collins, C., Douglas, K. and Ng, K. (2005) Increasing walking: How important is distance to, attractiveness, and size of public open space? *American Journal of Preventive Medicine, 28*(2 (Supplement 2)), 169–76.

Gillies, F. C., Hughes, A. R., Kirk, A. F., Mutrie, N., McCann, G., Hillis, W. S. and MacIntyre, P. D. (in press) Exercise Consultation: An intervention to improve adherence to phase IV cardiac rehabilitation? *British Journal of Sports Medicine.*

Glasgow, R. E., Bull, S. S., Gillette, C., Klesges, L. M. and Dzewaltowski, D. A. (2002) Behavior change intervention research in healthcare settings. A review of recent reports with emphasis on external validity. *American Journal of Preventive Medicine, 23,* 62–9.

Glasgow, R. E., Vogt, T. and Boles, S. (1999) Evaluating the public health impact of health promotion interventions: The RE-AIM framework. *American Journal of Public Health, 89,* 1322–7.

Glasser, W. (1976) *Positive addiction.* New York: Harper and Row.

Gleser, J. and Mendelberg, H. (1990) Exercise and sport in mental health: A review of the literature. *Israel Journal of Psychiatry and Related Sciences, 27,* 99–112.

Gloag, D. (1985) Rehabilitation of patients with cardiac conditions. *British Medical Journal, 290,* 617–20.

Godin, G. (1993) The theories of reasoned action and planned behavior: Overview of findings, emerging research problems and usefulness for exercise promotion. *Journal of Applied Sport Psychology, 5,* 141–57.

Godin, G. (1994) Social-cognitive models. In R. K. Dishman (ed.), *Advances in exercise adherence* (pp. 113–36). Champaign, IL: Human Kinetics.

Godin, G. and Shephard, R. J. (1983) Physical fitness promotion programmes: Effectiveness in modifying exercise behaviour. *Canadian Journal of Applied Sports Sciences, 8,* 104–13.

Godin, G. and Shephard, R. J. (1986a) Importance of type of attitude to the study of exercise behaviour. *Psychological Reports, 58,* 991–1000.

Godin, G. and Shephard, R. J. (1986b) Psychosocial factors influencing intentions to exercise of young students from grades 7 to 9. *Research Quarterly for Exercise and Sport, 57,* 41–52.

Goldberg, D. P., Cooper, B., Eastwood, M. R., Kedward, H. B. and Shephard, M. (1970) A standardized psychiatric interview for use in community surveys. *British Journal of Preventive and Social Medicine, 24,* 18–23.

Gollwitzer, P. M. (1999) Implementation intentions: Strong effects of simple plans. *American Psychologist*, 493–503.

Gomez, J. E., Johnson, B. A., Selva, M. and Sallis, J. F. (2004) Violent crime and outdoor physical activity among inner-city youth. *Preventive Medicine*, *39*(5), 876–81.

Goodwin, R. D. (2003) Association between physical activity and mental disorders among adults in the United States. *Preventive Medicine*, *36*(6), 698–703.

Gordon, J. and Grant, G. (1997) How we feel. London: Jessica Kingsley.

Gordon, N. F. (1993a) *Arthritis: Your complete exercise guide*. Champaign, IL: Human Kinetics.

Gordon, N. F. (1993b) *Breathing disorders: Your complete exercise guide*. Champaign, IL: Human Kinetics.

Gordon-Larsen, P., McMurray, R. G. and Popkin, B. M. (1999) Adolescent physical activity and inactivity vary by ethnicity: The National Longitudinal Study of Adolescent Health. *Journal of Pediatrics*, *135*, 301–6.

Gordon-Larsen, P., McMurray, R. G. and Popkin, B. M. (2000) Determinants of adolescent physical activity and inactivity patterns. *Pediatrics*, *105*(6), www.pediatrics.org/cgi/content/full/105/106/e183.

Gorely, T. and Bruce, D. (2000) A 6-month investigation of exercise adoption from the contemplation stage of the transtheoretical model. *Psychology of Sport and Exercise*, *1*, 89–101.

Gorely, T., Marshall, S. J. and Biddle, S. J. H. (2004) Couch kids: Correlates of television viewing among youth. *International Journal of Behavioural Medicine*, *11*, 152–63.

Gortmaker, S. L., Peterson, K. E., Wiecha, J., Sobol, A. M., Dixit, S., Fox, M. K. and Laird, N. (1999) Reducing obesity via a school-based interdisciplinary intervention among youth: Planet Health. *Archives of Pediatric and Adolescent Medicine*, *153*, 409–18.

Goudas, M. and Biddle, S. J. H. (1994) Perceived motivational climate and intrinsic motivation in school physical education classes. *European Journal of Psychology of Education*, *9*, 241–50.

Goudas, M., Biddle, S. J. H. and Fox, K. (1994a) Perceived locus of causality, goal orientations, and perceived competence in school physical education classes. *British Journal of Educational Psychology*, *64*, 453–63.

Goudas, M., Biddle, S. J. H. and Fox, K. R. (1994b) Achievement goal orientations and intrinsic motivation in physical fitness testing with children. *Pediatric Exercise Science*, *6*, 159–67.

Goudas, M., Biddle, S. J. H., Fox, K. and Underwood, M. (1995) It ain't what you do, it's the way that you do it! Teaching style affects children's motivation in track and field lessons. *The Sport Psychologist*, *9*, 254–64.

Gould, D. (1987) Understanding attrition in children's sport. In D. Gould and M. Weiss (eds), *Advances in pediatric sport sciences: II. Behavioural issues* (pp. 61–85). Champaign, IL: Human Kinetics.

Gould, D. and Petlichkoff, L. (1988) Participation motivation and attrition in young athletes. In F. L. Smoll, R. A. Magill and M. J. Ash (eds), *Children in sport* (pp. 161–78). Champaign, IL: Human Kinetics.

Gould, M. M., Thorogood, M., Iliffe, S. and Morris, J. N. (1995) Promoting physical activity in primary care: Measuring the knowledge gap. *Health Education Journal*, *54*, 304–11.

Grealy, M. A., Johnston, D. A. and Rushton, S. K. (1999) Improving cognitive functioning following brain injury: The use of exercise and virtual reality. *Archives of Physical Medicine and Rehabilitation*, *80*, 661–7.

Green, D. P., Salovey, P. and Truax, K. M. (1999) Static, dynamic, and causative bipolarity of affect. *Journal of Personality and Social Psychology*, *76*, 856–67.

Greenberg, M. R. and Renne, J. (2005) Where does walkability matter the most? An environmental justice interpretation of New Jersey data. *Journal of Urban Health*, *82*(1), 90–100.

Greene, J. G. (1991) *Guide to the Greene Climacteric Scale*. Glasgow: University of Glasgow.

Greer, G. (1992) *The change: Women, ageing and the menopause*. London: Penguin.

Greist, J. H., Klein, M. H., Eischens, R. R., Faris, J. W., Gurman, A. S. and Morgan, W. P. (1979) Running as a treatment for depression. *Comprehensive Psychiatry*, *20*, 41–54.

Greist, J. H., Klein, M. H., Eischens, R. R., Faris, J. W., Gurman, A. S. and Morgan, W. P. (1981) Running through your mind. In M. H. Sacks and M. L. Sacks (eds), *Psychology of running* (pp. 5–31). Champaign, IL: Human Kinetics.

Gruber, J. J. (1986) Physical activity and self-esteem development in children: A meta-analysis. In G. A. Stull and H. M. Eckert (eds), *Effects of physical activity on children* (pp. 30–48). Champaign, IL: Human Kinetics.

Hagger, M. S. and Chatzisarantis, N. L. D. (2005) *The social psychology of sport and exercise.* Milton Keynes: The Open University Press.

Hagger, M. S., Chatzisarantis, N. L. D. and Biddle, S. J. H. (2002) A meta-analytic review of the theories of reasoned action and planned behaviour in physical activity: Predictive validity and the contribution of additional variables. *Journal of Sport and Exercise Psychology, 24,* 3–32.

Hagger, M. S., Biddle, S. J. H., Chow, E. W., Stambulova, N. and Kavussanu, M. (2003) Physical self-perceptions in adolescence: Generalizability of a hierarchical multidimensional model across three cultures. *Journal of Cross-Cultural Psychology, 34,* 611–28.Hale, A. S. (1997) ABC of mental disorders: Depression. *British Medical Journal, 315,* 43–6.

Hall, D. C. and Kaufmann, D. A. (1987) Effects of aerobic and strength conditioning on pregnancy outcomes. *American Journal of Obstetrics and Gynecology, 157,* 1199–203.

Hall, E. E., Ekkekakis, P. and Petruzzello, S. J. (2002) The affective beneficence of vigorous exercise revisited. *British Journal of Health Psychology, 7,* 47–66.

Hamilton, E. R. (1929) *The art of interrogation: Studies in the principles of mental tests and examinations.* London: Kegan Paul, Trench, Trubner and Co Ltd.

Hamilton, M. (1960) A rating scale for depression. *Journal of Neurosurgical Psychiatry, 23,* 56–61.

Han, A., Robinson, V., Judd, M., Taixiang, W., Wells, G. and Tugwell, P. (2004) Tai chi for treating rheumatoid arthritis. *Cochrane Database of Systematic Reviews*(3), CD004849.

Hardman, A. E. (2001) Physical activity and cancer risk. *Proceedings of the Nutrition Society, 60,* 107–13.

Hardman, A. E. and Stensel, D. J. (2003) *Physical activity and health: The evidence explained.* London: Routledge.

Hardy, C. J. and Rejeski, W. J. (1989) Not what, but how one feels: The measurement of affect during exercise. *Journal of Sport and Exercise Psychology, 11,* 304–17.

Harland, J., White, M., Drinkwater, C., Chinn, D., Farr, L. and Howel, D. (1999) The Newcastle exercise project: A randomized controlled trial of methods to promote physical activity in primary care. *British Medical Journal, 319,* 828–32.

Harris, B., Rohaly, K. and Dailey, J. (1993) *Mid-life women and exercise: A qualitative study.* Paper presented at the 12th Congress of the International Association of Physical Education and Sport for Girls and Women, Melbourne, Australia.

Harris, D. V. (1973) *Involvement in sport: A somatopsychic rationale for physical activity.* Philadelphia: Lea and Febiger.

Harris, J. and Cale, L. (1997) How healthy is school PE? A review of the effectiveness of health-related physical education programmes in schools. *Health Education Journal, 56,* 84–104.

Harrison, J. A., Mullen, P. D. and Green, L. W. (1992) A meta-analysis of studies of the Health Belief Model with adults. *Health Education Research: Theory and Practice, 7,* 107–16.

Hart, E. A., Leary, M. R. and Rejeski, W. J. (1989) The measurement of social physique anxiety. *Journal of Sport and Exercise Psychology, 11,* 94–104.

Harter, S. (1978) Effectance motivation reconsidered: Toward a developmental model. *Human Development, 21,* 34–64.

Harter, S. (1985) *Manual for the Self-Perception Profile for Children.* Denver, CO: University of Denver.

Harter, S. and Connell, J. P. (1984) A model of children's achievement and related self perceptions of competence, control and motivational orientations. In J. G. Nicholls (ed.), *Advances in motivation and achievement. III. The development of achievement motivation* (pp. 219–50). Greenwich, CT: JAI Press.

Harter, S. and Pike, R. (1983) *Procedural manual to accompany the Pictorial Scale of Perceived Competence and Social Acceptance for Young Children.* Denver, CO: University of Denver.

Hasler, G., Pine, D. S., Kleinbaum, D. G., Gamma, A., Luckenbaugh, D., Ajdacic, V., Eich, D., Rossler, W. and Angst, J. (2005) Depressive symptoms during childhood and adult obesity: the Zurich Cohort Study. *Molecular Psychiatry, 10*(9), 842–50.

Hasler, T., Fisher, B. M., MacIntyre, P. D. and Mutrie, N. (1997) A counseling approach for increasing physical activity for patients attending a diabetic clinic. *Diabetic Medicine, 4,* S3–4.

Hatfield, B. D. (2005) *Cognitive Neuroscience Aspects of Sport Psychology: Brain Mechanisms Underlying Performance.* Paper presented at the International Society of Sport Psychology 11th World Congress of Sport Psychology, Sydney, Australia.

Hathaway, S. R. and McKinley, J. C. (1943) *Minnesota Multiphasic Personality Inventory.* New York: The Psychological Corporation.

Hausenblas, H. A. and Downs, D. S. (2002a) Exercise dependence: A systematic review. *Psychology of Sport and Exercise, 3*(2), 89–123.

Hausenblas, H. A. and Downs, D. S. (2002b) How much is too much? The development and validation of the exercise dependence scale. *Psychology and Health 17*(4), 387–404.

Hausenblas, H., Carron, A. V. and Mack, D. E. (1997) Application of the theories of reasoned action and planned behavior to exercise behavior: A meta-analysis. *Journal of Sport and Exercise Psychology, 19,* 36–51.

Hayden, J. A., van Tulder, M. W. and Tomlinson, G. (2005) Systematic review: strategies for using exercise therapy to improve outcomes in chronic low back pain. (summary for patients in *Ann Intern Med.* 2005 May 3;142(9):I72; PMID: 15867403). *Annals of Internal Medicine, 142*(9), 776–85.

Hayden, J. A., van Tulder, M. W., Malmivaara, A. and Koes, B. W. (2005) Exercise therapy for treatment of non-specific low back pain. (update of Cochrane Database Syst Rev. 2000;(2):CD000335; PMID: 10796344). *Cochrane Database of Systematic Reviews*(3), CD000335.

Heath, G. W., Brownson, R. C., Kruger, J., Miles, R., Powell, K. E., Ramsey, L. T., Taskforce on Community Preventive Services (2006) The effectiveness of urban design and land use and transport policies and practices to increase physical activity: A systematic review. *Journal of Physical Activity and Health, 3*(Supplement 1), S55–76.

Heather, N., Roberston, I. and Davies, P. (1985) *The misuse of alcohol: Crucial issues in dependance treatment and prevention.* London: Croom Helm.

Henderson, M., Glozier, N. and Elliot, K. H. (2005) Long term sickness absence. *British Medical Journal 330,* 802–3.

Hendry, L. B., Shucksmith, J. and Cross, J. (1989) Young people's mental well-being in relation to leisure. In Health Promotion Research Trust (ed.), *Fit for life* (pp. 129–153). Cambridge: Health Promotion Research Trust.

Higgins, M. W. (1989) Chronic airways disease in the United States: Trends and determinants. *Chest, 96,* 328s–34s.

Hill, A. B. (1965) The environment and disease: Association or causation? *Proceedings of the Royal Society of Medicine, 58,* 295–300.

Hill, J. O., Drougas, H. J. and Peters, J. C. (1994) Physical activity, fitness, and moderate obesity. In C. Bouchard, R. J. Shephard and T. Stephens (eds), *Physical activity, fitness, and health* (pp. 684–95). Champaign, IL.: Human Kinetics.

Hillsdon, M. and Thorogood, M. (1996) A systematic review of physical activity promotion strategies. *British Journal of Sports Medicine, 30,* 84–9.

Hillsdon, M., Foster, C., Naidoo, B. and Crombie, H. (2003) *A review of the evidence on the effectiveness of public health interventions for increasing physical activity amongst adults: A review of reviews.* London: Health Development Agency.

Hillsdon, M., Thorogood, M., White, I. and Foster, C. (2002) Advising people to take more exercise is ineffective: A randomized controlled trial of physical activity promotion in primary care. *International Journal of Epidemiology, 31,* 808–15.

Hillsdon, M., Cavill, N., Nanchahal, K., Diamond, A. and White, I. R. (2001) National level promotion of physical activity: Results from England's *ACTIVE* FOR LIFE campaign. *Journal of Epidemiology and Community Health, 55,* 755–61.

HMSO (1992) *Scotland's Health – a challenge to us all: A policy statement.* Edinburgh: HMSO.

Hodges, P. W. (2003) Core stability exercise in chronic low back pain. *Orthopedic Clinics of North America, 34*(2), 245–54.

Hoffmann, P. (1997) The endorphin hypothesis. In W. P. Morgan (ed.), *Physical activity and mental health* (pp. 163–177). Washington, DC: Taylor & Francis.

Hofstetter, C. R., Hovell, M. F., Macera, C., Sallis, J. F., Spry, V., Barrington, E., Callender, L., Hackley, M. and Rauh, M. (1991) Illness, injury and correlates of aerobic exercise and walking: A community study. *Reserach Quarterly for Exercise and Sport, 62,* 1–9.

Holgate, S. T. (1993) Asthma: Past, present, and future. *European Respiratory Journal, 6,* 1507–20.

Holmes, D. S. (1993) Aerobic fitness and the response to psychosocial stress. In P. Seraganian (ed.), *Exercise psychology: The influence of physical exercise on psychological processes* (pp. 39–63). New York: John Wiley.

Holmes, M. D., Chen, W. Y., Feskanich, D., Kroenke, C. H. and Colditz, G. A. (2005) Physical activity and survival after breast cancer diagnosis. *JAMA, 293*(20), 2479–86.

Hope, S., Wager, E. and Rees, M. (1998) Survey of British women's views on the menopause and HRT. *Journal of the British Menopause Society*(4), 33–6.

Horne, J. A. (1981) The effects of exercise upon sleep: A critical review. *Biological Psychology, 12,* 241–90.

Hospers, H. J., Kok, G. and Strecher, V. J. (1990) Attributions for previous failures and subsequent outcomes in a weight reduction program. *Health Education Quarterly, 17,* 409–15.

Hovland, C. I. and Rosenberg, M. J. (eds) (1960) *Attitudes, organisation and change: An analysis of consistency among attitude components.* New Haven, Conn: Yale University Press.

Hu, L., McAuley, E. and Elavsky, S. (2005) Does the physical self-efficacy scale assess self-efficacy or self-esteem? *Journal of Sport and Exercise Psychology, 27,* 152–70.

Hughes, A. R. and Mutrie, N. (2006) Maintaining physical activity in cardiac rehabilitation. In M. Thow (ed.), *Exercise leadership in cardiac rehabilitation. An evidence-based approach* (pp. 195–219) Chichester: Wiley.

Hughes, A. R., Mutrie, N. and MacIntyre, P. (2007) Effect of an exercise consultation on maintenance of physical activity after completion of phase III exercise-based cardiac rehabilitation. *European Journal of Cardiovascular Prevention and Rehabilitation, 14,* 114–21.

Hughes, A. R., Gillies, F., Kirk, A., Mutrie, N., Hillis, W. and MacIntyre, P. (2002a) Exercise consultation improves exercise adherence in phase IV cardiac rehabilitation. *Journal of Cardiopulmonary Rehabilitation, 22*(6), 421–25.

Humpel, N., Owen, N. and Leslie, E. (2002) Environmental factors associated with adults' participation in physical activity: A review. *American Journal of Preventive Medicine, 22*(3), 188–99.

Hunt, S. M., McEwan, J. and McKenna, S. P. (1986) *Measuring health status.* London: Croom Helm.

Hunter, J. and Schmidt, F. L. (1990). *Methods of meta-analysis: Correcting error and bias in research findings.* Newbury Park, CA: Sage.

Hunter, M. and Whitehead, M. (1989) Psychological experience of the climacteric and post menopause. *Progress in Clinical and Biological Research, 320,* 211–24.

Hunter, M., Battersby, R. and Whitehead, M. (1986) Relationships between psychological symptoms, somatic complaints and menopausal status. *Maturitas, 8,* 217–88.

Hyman, G. P. (1987) *The role of exercise in the treatment of substance abuse.* Unpublished MS thesis, The Pennsylvania State University.

Iannos, M. and Tiggeman, M. (1997) Personality of the excessive exerciser. *Personality and Individual Differences, 22,* 775–8.

Inger, F. and Dahl, H. A. (1979) Dropouts from an endurance training programme: Some histochemical and physiological aspects. *Scandinavian Journal of Sports Sciences, 1,* 20–2.

Institute of Medicine (1990) *Broadening the base of treatment for alcoholism.* New York: Wiley.

Israel, R. G., Sutton, M. and O'Brien, K. F. (1985) Effects of aerobic training on primary dysmenorrhea symptomatology in college females. *Journal of the Amercian College of Health, 33,* 241–4.

Ivarsson, T., Spetz, A. and Hammar, M. (1998) Physical exercise and vasomotor symptoms in postmenopausal women. *Maturitas, 29,* 139–46.

Jago, R. and Baranowski, T. (2004) Non-curricular approaches for increasing physical activity in youth: A review. *Preventive Medicine, 39*(1), 157–63.

Janakiramaiah, N., Gangadhar, B. N., Murthy, P., Harish, M. G., Subbakrishna, D. K. and Vedamurthachar, A. (2000) Antidepressant efficacy of Sudarshan Kriya Yoga (SKY) in melancholia: a randomized comparison with electroconvulsive therapy (ECT) and imipramine. *Journal of Affective Disorders, 57*(1–3), 255–9.

Jankowski, L. W. and Sullivan, S. J. (1990) Aerobic and neuromuscular training: Effect on the capacity, efficiency, and fatigability of patients with traumatic brain injuries. *Archives of Physical Medicine and Rehabilitation, 71,* 500–4.

Janz, N. K. and Becker, M. H. (1984) The Health Belief Model: A decade later. *Health Education Quarterly, 11,* 1–47.

Jenkinson, C., Stewart-Brown, S., Petersen, S. and Paice, C. (1999) Assessment of the SF-36 version 2 in the United Kingdom. *Journal of Epidemiology and Community Health, 53*(1), 46–50.

Jette, A. M., Smith, K., Haley, S. M. and Davis, K. D. (1994) Physical therapy episodes of care for patients with low back pain. *Physical Therapy, 74,* 101–10.

Jolliffe, J., Rees, K., Taylor, R., Thomson, D., Oldridge, N. B. and Ebrahim, S. (2000) Exercise based rehabilitation for coronary heart disease (Cochrane review). *Cochrane Database of Systematic Reviews, 4,* 1–59.

Jones, L. W., Courneya, K. S., Peddle, C. and Mackey, J. R. (2004) Oncologists' attitudes towards recommending exercise to cancer patients: A Canadian national survey. *Journal Of Clinical Oncology, 22*(14), 763S–763S.

Jordan, A. N., Jurca, G. M., Locke, C. T., Church, T. S. and Blair, S. N. (2005) Pedometer indices for weekly physical activity recommendations in postmenopausal women. *Medicine and Science in Sports and Exercise, 37*(9), 1627–32.

Judd, L., Schettler, P. and Akiskal, H. (2002) The prevalence, clinical relevance and public health significance of subthreshold depression. *Psychiatric Clinics North America, 136*(10), 765–76.

Juneau, M., Rogers, F., DeSantos, V., Yee, M., Evans, A. and Bohn, A. (1987) Effectiveness of self-monitored, home-based, moderate intensity exercise training in middle-aged men and women. *American Journal of Cardiology, 60,* 66–70.

Kahn, E. B., Ramsey, L. T., Brownson, R. C., Heath, G. W., Howze, E. H., Powell, K. E., Stone, E. J., Rajab, M. W. and Corso, P. (2002) The effectiveness of interventions to increase physical activity: A systematic review. *American Journal of Preventive Medicine, 22*(4S), 73–107.

Kaiser Family Foundation. (2004) The role of media in childhood obesity. *The Henrry J. Kaiser Family Foundation, February* (Paper #7030 www.kff.org), 1–12.

Kaman, R. L. and Patton, R. W. (1994) Costs and benefits of an active versus an inactive society. In C. Bouchard, R. J. Shephard and T. Stephens (eds), *Physical activity, fitness, and health* (pp. 134–44). Champaign, IL: Human Kinetics.

Kanayama, G., Gruber, A. J., Pope, H. G., Borowiecki, J. J. and Hudson, J. I. (2001) Over-the-counter drug use in gymnasiums: An underrecognized substance abuse problem? *Psychotherapy and Psychosomatics, 70*(3), 137–40.

Kanis, J., Aaron, J., Thavarajah, M., McCluskey, E. V., O'Doherty, D., Hamdy, N. A. T. and Bickerstaff, D. (1990) Osteoporosis: Causes and therapeutic implications. In R. Smith (ed.), *Osteoporosis* (pp. 45–56). London: Royal College of Physicians.

Kaplan, G. A., Roberts, R. E., Camacho, T. C. and Coyne, J. C. (1987) Psychosocial predictors of depression. *American Journal of Epidemiology, 125,* 206–20.

Karageorghis, C. I., Vlachopoulos, S. P. and Terry, P. C. (2000) Latent variable modelling of the relationship between flow and exercise-induced feelings: An intuitive appraisal perspective. *European Physical Education Review, 6,* 230–48.

Karvinen, K. H., Courneya, K. S., Campbell, K. L., Pearcey, R. G., Dundas, G. and Tonkin, K. S. (2005) Individual motivational determinants of exercise in endometrial cancer survivors: An application of the theory of planned behavior. *Journal of Sport and Exercise Psychology, 27,* S84–S84.

Kasimatis, M., Miller, M. and Macussen, L. (1996) The effects of implicit theories on exercise motivation. *Journal of Research in Personality, 30,* 510–16.

Kavale, K. and Mattson, P. D. (1983) 'One jumped off the balance beam': Meta-analysis of perceptual-motor training. *Journal of Learning Disabilities, 16,* 165–73.

Kemmler, W., Lauber, D., Weineck, J., Hensen, J., Kalender, W. and Engelke, K. (2004) Benefits of 2 years of intense exercise on bone density, physical fitness, and blood lipids in early postmenopausal osteopenic women: results of the Erlangen Fitness Osteoporosis Prevention Study (EFOPS) *Archives of Internal Medicine, 164*(10), 1084–91.

Kendzierski, D. (1990) Decision-making vs. decision implementation: An action control approach to exercise adoption and adherence. *Journal of Applied Social Psychology, 20,* 27–45.

Kendzierski, D. and DeCarlo, K. J. (1991) Physical activity enjoyment scale: Two validation studies. *Journal of Sport and Exercise Psychology, 13,* 50–64.

Kenyon, G. S. (1968) Six scales for assessing atitudes toward physical activity. *Reserach Quarterly, 39,* 566–74.

Kettunen, J. A. and Kujala, U. M. (2004) Exercise therapy for people with rheumatoid arthritis and osteoarthritis. *Scandinavian Journal of Medicine and Science in Sports, 14*(3), 138–42.

Killoran, A., Cavill, N. and Walker, A. (1994) Who needs to know what? An investigation of the characteristics of the key target groups for the effective promotion of physical activity in England. In A. Killoran, P. Fentem and C. Caspersen (eds), *Moving on: International perspectives on promoting physical activity* (pp. 149–69). London: Health Education Authority.

Kimiecik, J. C. and Harris, A. T. (1996) What is enjoyment? A conceptual/definitional analysis with implications for sport and exercise psychology. *Journal of Sport and Exercise Psychology, 18,* 247–63.

Kimiecik, J. C. and Stein, G. L. (1992) Examining flow experiences in sport contexts: Conceptual issues and methodological concerns. *Journal of Applied Sport Psychology, 4,* 144–60.

Kimm, S. Y. S., Obarzanek, E., Barton, B. A., Aston, C. E., Similo, S. L., Morrison, J. A., Sabry, Z. I., Schreiber, G. B. and McMahon R. T. (1996) Race, socioeconomic status, and obesity in 9- to 10-year-old girls: The NHLBI growth and health study. *Annals of Epidemiology, 6,* 266–75.

King, A. C. (1991) Community intervention for promotion of physical activity and fitness. *Exercise and Sport Sciences Reviews, 19,* 211–59.

King, A. C. (1994) Are community-wide programmes likely to be effective in getting the message across? Lessons from abroad. In A. J. Killoran, P. Fentem and C. Caspersen (eds), *Moving on: International perspectives on promoting physical activity* (pp. 170–193). London: Health Education Authority.

King, A. C., and Frederiksen, L. W. (1984) Low-cost strategies for increasing exercise behaviour: Relapse prevention training and social support. *Behavior Modification, 8,* 3–21.

King, A. C., Sallis, J. F., Dunn, A. L., Simons-Morton, D. G., Albright, C. A., Cohen, S., Rejeski, W. J., Marcus, B. H. and Coday, M. C. (1998) Overview of activity counseling trial (ACT) intervention or promoting physical activity in primary health care settings. *Medicine and Science in Sports and Exercise, 30,* 1086–96.

King, A. C., Blair, S. N., Bild, D. E., Dishman, R. K., Dubbert, P. M., Marcus, B. H., Oldridge, N. B., Paffenbarger, R. S., Powell, K. E. and Yeager, K. K.(1992) Determinants of physical activity and interventions in adults. *Medicine and Science in Sports and Exercise, 24*(6, Supplement), S221–S36.

Kirk, A., Barnett, J. and Mutrie, N. (in press) Physical activity consultation for people with Type 2 diabetes: evidence and guidelines. *Diabetic Medicine.*

Kirk, A. F., Mutrie, N., MacIntyre, P. and Fisher, B. M. (2004a) Effects of a 12 month physical activity counselling intervention on glycaemic control and cardiovascular risk factors in people with type 2 diabetes. *Diabetologia, 47,* 821–32.

Kirk, A. F., Mutrie, N., MacIntyre, P. D., and Fisher, M. B. (2004b) Promoting and maintaining physical activity in people with Type 2 diabetes. *American Journal of Preventive Medicine, 27*(4), 289–96.

Kirk, A. F., Higgins, L., Hughes, A. R., Mutrie, N., Fisher, M., McLean, J. and MacIntyre, P. (2000) *The effectiveness of exercise consultation on promotion of physical activity in a group of type 2 diabetes patients: A pilot study.* Paper presented at the British Diabetic Association Conference, Brighton.

Kirkendall, D. R. (1986) Effects of physical activity on intellectual development and academic performance. In G. A. Stull and H. M. Eckert (eds), *Effects of physical activity on children* (pp. 49–63). Champaign, IL: Human Kinetics and American Academy of Physical Education.

Klaber Moffet, J. A., Torgerson, D., Bell-Syer, S., Jackson, D., Llewlyn-Philips, H., Farrin, A. *et al.* (1999) Randomized control trial exercise for low back pain: Clinical outcomes, costs, and preferences. *British Medical Journal, 319,* 279–83.

Klaber Moffet, J. A., Richardson, G., Sheldon, T. A. and Maynard, A. (1995) *Back Pain: Its management and cost to society.* York: Centre for Health Economics.

Klein, M. J., Griest, J. H., Gurman, A. S., Neimeyer, R. A., Lesser, D. P., Bushnell, N. J. and Smith R. E. (1985) A comparative outcome study of group psychotherapy vs. exercise treatments for depression. *International Journal of Mental Health, 13,* 148–77.

Knapp, D. N. (1988) Behavioral management techniques and exercise promotion. In R. K. Dishman (ed.), *Exercise adherence: Its impact on public health* (pp. 203–35). Champaign, IL: Human Kinetics.

Koestner, R., Lekes, N., Powers, T. A. and Chicoine, E. (2002) Attaining personal goals: Self-concordance plus implementation intentions equals success. *Journal of Personality and Social Psychology, 83,* 231–44.

Kohl, H. W. (2001) Physical activity and cardiovascular disease: Evidence for a dose-response. *Medicine and Science in Sports and Exercise, 33*(6, Supplement), S472–83.

Koltyn, K. F. (1997) The thermogenic hypothesis. In W. P. Morgan (ed.), *Physical activity and mental health* (pp. 213–26). Washington, DC: Taylor & Francis.

Koplan, J. P., Siscovick, D. S. and Goldbaum, G. M. (1985) The risks of exercise: A public health view of injuries and hazards. *Public Health Reports, 100,* 189–95.

Kranc, V. (2005) In memoriam Precilla Yee Lan Choi. *Women in Sport and Physical Activity Journal, 14*(2), 1–9.

Kraus, H., and Raab, W. (1961) *Hypokinetic disease.* Springfield, IL: C.C. Thomas.

Kriska, A. M., Bayles, C., Cauley, J. A., Laporte, R. E., Sandler, R. B. and Pambianco, G. (1986) A randomized exercise trial in older women: Increased activity over two years and the factors associated with compliance. *Medicine and Science in Sports and Exercise, 18,* 557–62.

Kritz-Silverstein, D., Barrett-Connor, E. and Corbeau, C. (2001) Cross-sectional and prospective study of exercise and depressed mood in the elderly: The Rancho Bernardo study. *American Journal of Epidemiology, 153*(6), 596–603.

Kubitz, K. A. and Landers, D. M. (1993) The effects of aerobic training on cardiovascular responses to mental stress: An examination of underlying mechanisms. *Journal of Sport & Exercise Psychology, 15,* 326–37.

Kubitz, K. A., Landers, D. M., Petruzzello, S. J. and Han, M. (1996) The effects of acute and chronic exercise on sleep: A meta-analytic review. *Sports Medicine, 21,* 277–91.

Kugler, J., Seelbach, H. and Kruskemper, G. (1994) Effects of rehabilitation exercise programmes on anxiety and depression in coronary patients: A meta-analysis. *British Journal of Clinical Psychology, 33,* 401–10.

Kuroda, K. K., Tatara, K., Takatorige, T. and Shinsho, F. (1992) Effect of physical exercise on mortality in patients with Parkinson's disease. *Acta Neurologica Scandinavia, 86,* 55–9.

Kurtz, Z. (1992) *With health in mind.* London: Action for Sick Children.

La Forge, R. (1995) Exercise-associated mood alterations: A review of interactive neurobiological mechanisms. *Medicine, Exercise, Nutrition and Health, 4,* 17–32.

Lacasse, Y., Wong, E., Guyat, G. H., King, D., Cook, D. J. and Goldstein, R. S. (1996) Meta-analysis of respiratory rehabilitation in chronic obstructive pulmonary disease. *Lancet, 348,* 1115–19.

Laitakari, J. and Asikainen, T. (1998) How to promote physical activity through individual counselling: A proposal for a practical model of counselling on health-related physical activity. *Patient Education and Counselling, 33,* S13–24.

Landers, D. and Alderman, B. (2007) Exercise relative to other treatments for reduction of anxiety/depression: overcoming the principle of least effort. In A. Morris, S. Gordon and P. Terry (eds), *Promoting Health and Performance for Life: Invited Papers from the 11th World Congress of Sport Psychology.* Sydney, Australia: Fitness Information Technology.

Landers, D. M. and Arent, S. M. (2001) Physical activity and mental health. In R. N. Singer, H. A. Hausenblas and C. M. Janelle (eds), *Handbook of sport psychology* (2nd edn) (pp. 740–65). New York: John Wiley.

Lankenau, B., Solari, A. and Pratt, M. (2004) International physical activity policy development: a commentary. *Public Health Reports, 119*(3), 352–55.

LaPerriere, A. R., Antoni, M. H., Schneiderman, N., Ironson, G., Klimas, N., Caralis, P. and Fletcher, M. (1990) Exercise intervention attenuates emotional distress and natural killer cell decrements following notification of positive serological status for HIV-1. *Biofeedback and Self Regulation, 15,* 229–42.

LaPerriere, A. R., Fletcher, M. A., Antoni, M. H., Klimas, N. G., Ironson, G. and Schneiderman, N. (1991) Arobic exercise training in an AIDS risk group. *International Journal of Sports Medicine, 12*(1, Supplement), S53–7.

LaPorte, R. E., Montoye, H. J. and Caspersen, C. J. (1985) Assessment of physical activity in epidemiological research: Problems and prospects. *Public Health Reports, 100,* 131–46.

Lawless, D., Jackson, C. and Greenleave, J. (1995) Exercise and human imunodeficiency virus (HIV-1) infection. *Sports Medicine, 19,* 235–9.

Lawlor, D. A., and Hopker, S. W. (2001) The effectiveness of exercise as an intervention in the management of depression: Systematic review and meta-regression analysis of randomised controlled trials. *British Medical Journal, 322*(763) (31 March).

Lawlor, D. A., Ness, A. R., Cope, A. M., Davis, A., Insall, P. and Riddoch, C. (2003) The challenges of evaluating environmental interventions to increase population levels of physical activity: The case of the UK National Cycle Network. *Journal of Epidemiology and Community Health, 57,* 96–101.

Lazarus, R. S. (1991) *Emotion and adaptation.* New York: Oxford University Press.

Le Masurier, G., Sidman, C. and Corbin, C. (2003) Accumulating 10,000 steps: Does this meet current physical activity guidelines? *Research Quarterly for Exercise and Sport, 74*(4), 389–94.

Leary, M. R. (1992) Self presentational processes in exercise and sport. *Journal of Sport and Exercise Psychology, 14,* 339–51.

Leary, M. R. (1995) *Self-presentation: Impression management and interpersonal behavior.* Dubuque, IO: Wm C. Brown.

Leary, M. R., Tchividjian, L. R. and Kraxberger, B. E. (1994) Self-presentation can be hazardous to your health: Impression management and health risk. *Health Psychology, 13,* 461–70.

Lee, I.-M. (1994) Physical activity, fitness, and cancer. In C. Bouchard, R. J. Shephard and T. Stephens (eds), *Physical activity, fitness and health* (pp. 814–31). Champaign, IL: Human Kinetics.

Lee, I.-M. (1995) Exercise and physical health: Cancer and immune function. *Research Quarterly for Exercise and Sport, 66,* 286–91.

Lee, I.-M. and Paffenberger, R. S. (2000) associations of light, moderate, and vigorous intensity physical activity with longevity. The Harvard Alumni Health Study. *American Journal of Epidemiology, 151*(3), 293–9.

Lee, I.-M. and Skerrett, P. J. (2001) Physical activity and all-cause mortality: What is the dose-response relation? *Medicine and Science in Sports and Exercise, 33*(6, Supplement), S459–71.

Leit, R. A., Gray, J. J. and Pope, H. G. (2002) The media's representation of the ideal male body: A cause for muscle dysmorphia? *International Journal of Eating Disorders, 31*(3), 334–8.

Leith, L. (1994) *Foundations of exercise and mental health.* Morgantown, WV: Fitness Information Technology.

Leith, L. and Taylor, A. H. (1990) Psychological aspects of exercise: A decade literature review. *Journal of Sport Behavior, 13,* 219–39.

Lenney, E. (1977) Women's self-confidence in achievement situations. *Psychological Bulletin, 84,* 1–13.

Leon, A. S. (ed.) (1997) *Physical activity and cardiovascular health.* Champaign, IL: Human Kinetics.

Lepper, M. R. and Greene, D. (1975) Turning play into work: Effects of adult surveillance and extrinsic rewards on children's intrinsic motivation. *Journal of Personality and Social Psychology, 31,* 479–86.

Lepper, M. R., Greene, D. and Nisbett, R. E. (1973) Undermining children's intrinsic interest with extrinsic reward: A test of the 'overjustification' hypothesis. *Journal of Personality and Social Psychology, 28,* 129–37.

Levine, M. D., Marcus, M. D. and Moulton, P. (1996) Exercise in the treatment of binge eating disorders. *International Journal of Eating Disorders, 19,* 171–7.

Levy, S. R., Stroessner, S. J. and Dweck, C. S. (1998) Stereotype formation and endorsement: The role of implicit theories. *Journal of Personality and Social Psychology, 74,* 1421–36.

Lewis, F. M. and Daltroy, L. H. (1990) How causal explanations influence behavior: Attribution theory. In K. Glanz, F. M. Lewis and B. K. Rimer (eds), *Health behavior and health education* (pp. 92–114). San Fransisco, CA: Jossey-Bass.

Lindsay-Reid, E. and Osborn, R. W. (1980) Readiness for exercise adoption. *Social Science and Medicine, 14,* 139–46.

Lindsay, R., Aitken, J. M., Anderson, J. B., Hart, D. M., MacDonald, E. B. and Clarke, A. (1976) Long term prevention of postmenopausal osteoporosis by oestrogen. *Lancet, 1*(7968), 1038–41.

Lippke, S. and Plotnikoff, R. C. (2005) Stages of change in physical exercise: A test of stage discrimination and non-linearity. *American Journal of Health Behavior.*

Lippke, S., Ziegelmann, J. P. and Schwarzer, R. (2004) Initiation and maintenance of physical exercise: Stage-specific effects of a planning intervention. *Research in Sports Medicine, 12,* 221–40.

Lippke, S., Ziegelmann, J. P., and Schwarzer, R. (2005) Stage-specific adoption and maintenance of physical activity: Testing a three-stage model. *Psychology of Sport and Exercise, 6,* 585–603.

Liska, A. E. (1984) A critical examination of the causal structure of the Fishbein/Ajzen attitude-behaviour model. *Social Psychology Quarterly, 47,* 61–74.

Lokcy, E. A., Tran, Z. V., Wells, C. L., Myers, B. C. and Tran, A. C. (1991) Effects of exercise on pregnancy outcomes: A meta-analytic review. *Medicine and Science in Sports and Exercise, 23,* 1234–9.

Long, B., Calfas, K. J., Wooten, W., Sallis, J. F., Patrick, K., Goldstein, M., Marcus, B. H., Schwenk, T. L., Chenoworth, J., Carter, R., Torres, T., Palinkas, L. A. and Heath, G. (1996) A multisite field test of the acceptibility of physical activity counseling in primary care: Project PACE. *American Journal of Preventive Medicine, 12*(2), 73–81.

Long, B. C. and van Stavel, R. (1995) Effects of exercise training on anxiety: A meta-analysis. *Journal of Applied Sport Psychology, 7,* 167–89.

Lorr, M. and McNair, D. M. (1984) *Profile of mood states, bipolar form.* San Diego, CA: Educational and Industrial Testing Service.

Lorr, M., Shi, A. Q. and Youniss, R. P. (1989) A bipolar multifactor conception of mood states. *Personality and Individual Differences, 10,* 155–9.

Loughlan, C. and Mutrie, N. (1995) Conducting an exercise consultation: Guidelines for health professionals. *Journal of the Institute of Health Education, 33*(3), 78–82.

Loughlan, C. and Mutrie, N. (1997) A comparison of three interventions to promote physical activity: Fitness assessment, exercise counseling, and information provision. *Health Education Journal, 56,* 154–65.

Lowther, M. and Mutrie, N. (1996) Reliability and concurrent validity of the Scottish Physical Activity Questionnaire. *British Journal of Sports Medicine, 30,* 368.

Lowther, M., Mutrie, N. and Scott, E. M. (1999) Attracting the general public to physical activity interventions: A comparison of fitness assessment and exercise consultations. *Journal of Sports Sciences, 17,* 62–3.

Lowther, M., Mutrie, N. and Scott, E. M. (2007) Identifying key processes of exercise behaviour change associated with movement through the stages of exercise behaviour change. *Journal of Health Psychology*, 12(2), 261–72.

Lowther, M., Mutrie, N., Laughlan, C. and McFarlane, C. (1999a) Development of a Scottish physical activity questionnaire: A tool for use in physical activity interventions. *British Journal of Sports Medicine, 33,* 244–9.

Lox, C. L. McAuley, E., and Tucker, R. S. (1995) Exercise as an intervention for enhancing subjective well-being in an HIV-1 population. *Journal of Sport and Exercise Psychology, 17,* 345–62.

Lubin, B. (1965) Adjective checklists for measurement of depression. *Archives of General Psychiatry, 12,* 57–62.

Lucia, A., Earnest C, Pérez M. (2003) Cancer-related fatigue: Can exercise physiology assist oncologists. *Lancet Oncology, 4,* 616–25.

Mackinnon, L. T. (1989) Exercise and natural killer cells: What is the relationship? *Sports Medicine, 7,* 141–9.

MacMahon, J. R. and Gross, R. T. (1987) Physical and psychological effects of aerobic exercise in boys with learning difficulties. *Developmental and Behavioral Pediatrics, 8,* 274–7.

Maehr, M. L. and Braskamp, L. A. (1986) *The motivation factor: A theory of personal investment.* Lexington, Mass: Lexington Books.

Maehr, M. L. and Nicholls, J. G. (1980) Culture and achievement motivation: A second look. In N. Warren (ed.), *Studies in cross-cultural psychology* (Vol II) (pp. 221–67). New York: Academic Press.

Maibach, E. and Parrott, R. L. (eds) (1995) *Designing health messages.* Thousand Oaks, CA: Sage.

Malina, R. M. (1988) Physical activity in early and modern populations: An evolutionary view. In R. M. Malina and H. M. Eckert (eds), *Physical activity in early and modern populations* (pp. 1–12). Champaign, IL: Human Kinetics and the American Academy of Physical Education.

Malina, R. M. (1996) Tracking of physical activity and physical fitness across the lifespan. *Research Quarterly for Exercise and Sport, 67*(3, Supplement), S48–57.

Malita, F. M., Karelis, A. D., Toma, E. and Rabasa-Lhoret, R. (2005) Effects of different types of exercise on body composition and fat distribution in HIV-infected patients: A brief review. *Canadian Journal of Applied Physiology, 30*(2), 233–45.

Mandela, N. (1994) *Long walk to freedom.* London: Little, Brown and Company.

Manigandan, C., Charles, J., Divya, I., Edward, S. J. and Aaron, A. (2004) Construction of exercise attitude questionnaire-18 to evaluate patients' attitudes toward exercises. *International Journal of Rehabilitation Research, 27*(3), 229–31.

Marcus, B. H. and Owen, N. (1992) Motivational readiness, self-efficacy and decision making for exercise. *Journal of Applied Social Psychology, 22,* 3–16.

Marcus, B. H. and Forsyth, L. H. (2003) *Motivating people to be physically active.* Champaign, IL: Human Kinetics.

Marcus, B. H. and Simkin, L. R. (1994) The transtheoretical model: Applications to exercise behavior. *Medicine and Science in Sports and Exercise, 26,* 1400–1404.

Marcus, B. H., Owen, N., Forsyth, L. H., Cavill, N. and Fridinger, F. (1998) Physical activity interventions using mass media, print media, and information technology. *American Journal of Preventive Medicine, 15,* 362–78.

Marcus, B. H., Rossi, J. S., Selby, V. C., Niaura, R. S. and Abrams, D. B. (1992a) The stages and processes of exercise adoption and maintenance in a worksite sample. *Health Psychology, 11,* 386–95.

Marcus, B. H., Banspach, S. W., Lefebvre, R. C., Rossi, J. S., Carleton, R. A. and Abrams, D. B. (1992b) Using the stages of change model to increase the adoption of physical activity among community participants. *American Journal of Health Promotion, 6,* 424–9.

Marcus, B. H., Goldstein, M. G., Jette, A., Simkin-Silverman, L., Pinto, B. M., Milan, F., Washburn, R., Smith, L., Rakowski, W. and Dub, C. E. (1997) Training physicians to conduct physical activity counseling. *Preventive Medicine, 26,* 382–8.

Marcus, R., Drinkwater, B., Dalsky, G., Dufek, J., Raab, D., Slemenda, C. *et al.* (1992) Osteoporosis and exercise in women. *Medicine and Science in Sports and Exercise, 24*(6, Supplement), S301–S307.

Markland, D. (1999) Self-determination moderates the effects of perceived competence on intrinsic motivation in an exercise setting. *Journal of Sport and Exercise Psychology, 21,* 351–61.

Markland, D., Emberton, M. and Tallon, R. (1997) Confirmatory factor analysis of the Subjective Exercise Experiences Scale among children. *Journal of Sport and Exercise Psychology, 19,* 418–33.

Marks, D. F. (1994) Psychology's role in the Health of the Nation. *The Psychologist: Bulletin of the British Psychological Society, 7*(3), 119–21.

Marlatt, G. A. (1985) Relapse prevention: Theoretical rationale and overview of the model. In G. A. Marlatt and J. R. Gordon (eds), *Relapse prevention: Maintenance strategies in the treatment of addictive behaviours* (pp. 3–70). New York: Guilford Press.

Marlatt, G. A. and Gordon, G. R. (1985) *Relapse prevention.* New York: Guilford Press.

Marsden, E. (1996) *The role of exercise in the well-being of people with insulin dependent diabetes mellitus: Perceptions of patients and health professionals.* Unpublished PhD, University of Glasgow, Glasgow.

Marsden, E. and Kirk, A. (2005) Becoming and staying physically active. In D. Nagi (ed.), *Exercise and sport in diabetes* (pp. 161–92). London: Wiley

Marsh, H. W. and Sonstroem, R. J. (1995) Importance ratings and specific components of physical self-concept: Relevance to predicting global components of self-concept and exercise. *Journal of Sport & Exercise Psychology, 17,* 84–104.

Marsh, H. W., Richards, G. E., Johnson, S., Roche, L. and Tremayne, P. (1994) Physical Self-Description Questionnaire: Psychometric properties and the multitrait-multimethod analysis of relations to existing instruments. *Journal of Sport and Exercise Psychology, 16,* 270–305.

Marshall, S. J. and Biddle, S. J. H. (2001) The transtheoretical model of behavior change: A meta-analysis of applications to physical activity and exercise. *Annals of Behavioral Medicine, 23,* 229–46.

Marshall, S. J., Gorely, T. and Biddle, S. J. H. (2006) A descriptive epidemiology of screen-based media use in youth: A review and critique. *Journal of Adolescence, 29*(3), 333–49.

Marshall, S. J., Biddle, S. J. H., Gorely, T., Cameron, N. and Murdey, I. (2004) Relationships between media use, body fatness and physical activity in children and youth: A meta-analysis. *International Journal of Obesity, 28,* 1238–46.

Marshall, S. J., Biddle, S. J. H., Sallis, J. F., McKenzie, T. L. and Conway, T. L. (2002) Clustering of sedentary behaviours and physical activity among youth: A cross-national study. *Pediatric Exercise Science, 14,* 401–17.

Martin, K. A. and Lutes, L. D. (2000) Group and leadership effects on social anxiety experienced during an exercise class. *Journal of Applied Social Psychology, 30,* 1–18.

Martinsen, E. W. (1989) The role of aerobic exercise in the treatment of depression. *Stress Medicine, 3,* 93–100.

Martinsen, E. W. (1990a) Benefits of exercise for the treatment of depression. *Sports Medicine, 9*(6), 380–9.

Martinsen, E. W. (1990b) Physical fitness, anxiety and depression. *British Journal of Hospital Medicine, 43,* 194; 196; 199.

Martinsen, E. W. (1993) Therapeutic implications of exercise for clinically anxious and depressed patients. *International Journal of Sport Psychology, 24,* 185–99.

Martinsen, E. W. (1994) Physical activity and depression: Clinical experience. *Acta Psychiatrica Scandinavica, 377,* 23–7.

Martinsen, E. W., Hoffart, A. and Solberg, O. (1989a) Aerobic and non-aerobic forms of exercise in the treatment of anxiety disorders. *Stress Medicine, 5*(115–20).

Martinsen, E. W., Hoffart, A., and Solberg, O. (1989b) Comparing aerobic and non-aerobic forms of exercise in the treatment of clinical depression: A randomized trial. *Comprehensive Psychiatry, 30,* 324–31.

Martinsen, E. W., Medhus, A. and Sandvik, L. (1985) Effects of aerobic exercise on depression: A controlled trial. *British Medical Journal, 291,* 100.

Martinsen, E. W., Sandvik, I. and Kolbjornsrud, O. B. (1989) Aerobic exercise in the treatment of non psychotic mental disorders: An exploratory study. *Nordic Journal of Psychiatry, 43,* 411–15.

Martinsen, E. W., Strand, J., Paulson, G. and Kaggestad, J. (1989) Physical fitness level in patients with anxiety and depressive disorders. *International Journal of Sports Medicine, 10,* 58–61.

Mason, V. (1995) *Young people and sport in England, 1994.* London: Sports Council.

Massie, J. F. and Shephard, R. J. (1971) Physiological and psychological effects of training: A comparison of individual and gymnasium programs, with a characterisation of the exercise 'dropout'. *Medicine and Science in Sports, 3,* 110–17.

Mather, A., Rodriguez, C., Guthrie, M. F., McHarg, A. M., Reid, I. C. and McMurdo, M. E. (2002) Effects of exercise on depressive symptoms in older adults with poorly responsive depressive disorder: Randomised controlled trial. *British Journal of Psychiatry, 180,* 411–15.

Mayoux-Benhamou, M. A., Roux, C., Perraud, A., Fermanian, J., Rahali-Kachlouf, H. and Revel, M. (2005) Predictors of compliance with a home-based exercise program added to usual medical care in preventing postmenopausal osteoporosis: an 18-month prospective study. *Osteoporosis International, 16*(3), 325–31.

McArthur, R. D., Levine, S. D. and Berk, T. J. (1993) Supervised exercise training improves cardiopulmonary fitness in HIV infected persons. *Medicine and Science in Sports and Exercise, 25,* 648–88.

McAuley, E. (1991) Efficacy, attributional, and affective responses to exercise participation. *Journal of Sport and Exercise Psychology, 13,* 382–93.

McAuley, E. (1992) Understanding exercise behavior: A self-efficacy perspective. In G. C. Roberts (ed.), *Motivation in Sport and Exercise* (pp. 107–27). Champaign, IL: Human Kinetics.

McAuley, E. and Blissmer, B. (2000) Self-efficacy determinants and consequences of physical activity. *Exercise and Sport Sciences Reviews, 28,* 85–8.

McAuley, E. and Courneya, K. S. (1993a) Adherence to exercise and physical activity as health promoting behaviors: Attitudinal and self-efficacy influences. *Applied and Preventive Psychology, 2,* 65–77.

McAuley, E. and Courneya, K. S. (1993b) Adherence to exercise and physical activity as health-promoting behaviors: Attitudinal and self-efficacy influences. *Applied and Preventive Psychology, 2,* 65–77.

McAuley, E. and Courneya, K. S. (1994) The Subjective Exercise Experiences Scale (SEES): Development and preliminary validation. *Journal of Sport and Exercise Psychology, 16,* 163–77.

McAuley, E. and Mihalko, S. L. (1998) Measuring exercise-related self-efficacy. In J. L. Duda (ed.), *Advances in sport and exercise psychology measurement* (pp. 371–90). Morgantown, WV: Fitness Information Technology.

McAuley, E., Duncan, T. and Russell, D. (1992) Measuring causal attributions: The Revised Causal Dimension Scale (CDSII) *Personality and Social Psychology Bulletin, 18,* 566–73.

McAuley, E., Poag, K., Gleason, A. and Wraith, S. (1990) Attrition from exercise programs: Attributional and affective perspectives. *Journal of Social Behavior and Personality, 5,* 591–602.

McAuley, E., Jerome, G. J., Marquez, D. X., Elavsky, S. and Blissmer, B. (2003) Exercise self-efficacy in older adults: Social, affective, and behavioral influences. *Annals of Behavioral Medicine, 25,* 1–7.

McCann, I. L. and Holmes, D. S. (1984) Influence of aerobic exercise on depression. *Journal of Personality and Social Psychology, 46,* 1142–7.

McDonald, D. G. and Hodgdon, J. A. (1991) *Psychological effects of aerobic fitness training: Research and theory.* New York: Springer-Verlag.

McElroy, M. (2002) *Resistance to exercise: A social analysis of inactivity.* Champaign, IL: Human Kinetics.

McEntee, D. J. and Halgin, R. P. (1996) Therapist's attitudes about addressing the role of exercise in psychotherapy. *Journal of Clinical Psychology, 52,* 48–60.

McGuire, W. J. (1969) The nature of attitudes and attitude change. In G. Lindzey and E. Aronson (eds), *Handbook of social psychology* (Vol III) (pp. 136–314). Reading, MA: Addison-Wesley.

McKee, R., Mutrie, N., Crawford, F. and Green, B. (in press) Promoting walking to school: results of a quasi-experimental trial. *J Epidemiol Community Health.*

McKenzie, T. L., Sallis, J. F., Kolody, B. and Faucette, F. N. (1997) Long-term effects of a physical education curriculum and staff development program: SPARK. *Research Quarterly for Exercise and Sport, 68,* 280–91.

McKenzie, T. L., Nader, P. R., Strikmiller, P. K., Yang, M., Stone, E. J., Perry, C. L., Taylor, W. C., Epping, J. N., Feldman, H. A., Luepker, R. V. and Kelder, S. H. (1996) School physical education: Effect of the Child and Adolescent Trial for Cardiovascular Health. *Preventive Medicine, 25,* 423–31.

McNair, D. M., Lorr, M. and Droppleman, L. F. (1971) *Profile of mood states manual.* San Diego, CA: Educational and Industrial Testing Service.

McTiernan, A., Kooperberg, C., White, E., Wilcox, S., Coates, R., Adams-Campbell, L. L., Woods, N. and Ockene, J. (2003) Recreational physical activity and the risk of breast cancer in postmenopausal women – The Women's Health Initiative cohort study. *Journal of the American Medical Association, 290*(10), 1331–36.

Meltzer, H., Gill, B., Petticrew, M. and Hinds, K. (1995) *The prevalence of psychiatric morbidity among adults living in private households.* London: HMSO.

Merom, D., Miller, Y., Lymer, S. and Bauman, A. (2005) Effect of Australia's Walk to Work Day campaign on adults' active commuting and physical activity behavior. *American Journal of Health Promotion, 19*(3), 159–62.

Merom, D., Rissel, C., Mahmic, A. and Bauman, A. (2005) Process evaluation of the New South Wales Walk Safely to School Day. *Health Promotion Journal of Australia, 16*(2), 100–6.

Messent, P. R., Cooke, C. B. and Long, J. (1999) Primary and secondary barriers to physically activity health lifestyles for adults with learning disabilities. *Disability and Rehabilitation, 21,* 409–19.

Messent, P. R., Cooke, C. B. and Long, J. (2000) Secondary barriers to physical activity for adults with mild and moderate learning disabilities. *Journal of Learning Disabilities, 4,* 247–63.

Messer, B. and Harter, S. (1986) *Manual for the Adult Self-Perception Profile.* Denver, CO: University of Denver.

Metcalf, B., Voss, L., Jeffery, A., Perkins, J. and Wilkin, T. (2004) Physical activity cost of the school run: Impact on schoolchildren of being driven to school (EarlyBird 22) *British Medical Journal,* bmj.38169.688102.F688171.

Mihalik, B., O'Leary, J., Mcguire, F. and Dottavio, F. (1989) Sports involvement across the life span: Expansion and contraction of sports activities. *Research Quarterly for Sport and Exercise, 60,* 396–8.

Miilunpalo, S. (1991) Exercise guidance in primary health care. In P. Oja and R. Telama (eds), *Sport for all* (pp. 185–92). Amsterdam: Elsevier.

Milani, R. V., Lavie, C. J. and Cassidy, M. M. (1996) Effects of cardiac rehabilitation and exercise training on depression in patients after major coronary events. *American Heart Journal, 132,* 726–32.

Miller, W. R. and Rollnick, S. (1991) *Motivational interviewing: Preparing people to change addictive behavior.* New York: The Guilford Press.

Miller, Y. D. and Brown, W. J. (2005) Determinants of active leisure for women with young children: An 'ethic of care' prevails. *Leisure Sciences, 27,* 405–20.

Million Women Study Collaborators (2003) Breast cancer and hormone replacement therapy in the million women study. *Lancet, 362,* 419–27.

Mitchell, S., Grant, S. and Aitchison, T. (1998) Physiological effects of exercise on post-menopausal osteoporotic women. *Physiotherapy, 84*(4), 157–63.

Mobily, K. E., Rubenstein, L. M., Lemke, J. H., O'Hara, M. W. and Wallace, R. B. (1996) Walking and depression in a cohort of older adults: The Iowa 65+ Rural Health Study. *Journal of Aging and Physical Activity, 4,* 119–35.

Moore, G. E. (1997) Introduction. In *ACSM's exercise management for persons with chronic diseases and disabilities* (pp. 3–5). Champaign, IL: Human Kinetics.

Morgan, W. P. (1968) Selected physiological and psychomotor correlates of depression in psychiatric patients. *Research Quarterly, 39,* 1037–43.

Morgan, W. P. (1969) A pilot investigation of physical working capacity in depressed and non-depressed psychiatric males. *Research Quarterly, 40,* 859–61.

Morgan, W. P. (1970a) Physical fitness correlates of psychiatric hospitalization. In G. S. Kenyon (ed.), *Contemporary psychology of sport* (pp. 297–300). Chicago: Athletic Institute.

Morgan, W. P. (1970b) Physical working capacity in depressed and non-depressed psychiatric females: A preliminary study. *American Corrective Therapy Journal, 24,* 14–16.

Morgan, W. P. (1979) Anxiety reduction following acute physical activity. *Psychiatric Annals, 9,* 36–45.

Morgan, W. P. (1985) Affective beneficence of vigorous physical activity. *Medicine and Science in Sports and Exercise, 17,* 94–100.

Morgan, W. P. (1994) Physical activity, fitness and depression. In C. Bouchard, R. J. Shephard and T. Stephens (eds), *Physical activity, fitness and health* (pp. 851–67). Champaign, IL: Human Kinetics.

Morgan, W. P. (ed.) (1997) *Physical activity and mental health.* Washington, DC: Taylor & Francis.

Morgan, W. P. and Goldston, S. E. (eds) (1987) *Exercise and mental health.* Washington: Hemisphere.

Morgan, W. P. and O'Connor, P. J. (1988) Exercise and mental health. In R. K. Dishman (ed.), *Exercise adherence: Its impact on public health* (pp. 91–121). Champaign, IL: Human Kinetics.

Morris, J. N., Heady, J. A., Raffle, P. A. B., Roberts, C. G. and Parks, J. W. (1953) Coronary heart disease and physical activity of work. *The Lancet, ii,* 1053–1057; 1111–20.

Morris, J. N., Kagan, A., Pattison, D. C., Gardner, M. and Raffle, P. A. B. (1966) Incidence and reduction of ischaemic heart disease in London busmen. *The Lancet, ii,* 552–9.

Morris, M., Steinberg, H., Sykes, E. A. and Salmon, P. (1990) Effects of temporary withdrawal from regular running. *Journal of Psychosomatic Research, 34,* 493–500.

Morrison, D., Pettricrew, M. and Thomson, H. (2003) What are the most effective ways of improving population health through transport interventions? Evidence from systematic reviews. *Journal of Epidemiology and Community Health, 57,* 327–33.

Morriss, R. and Mohammed, F. (2005) Metabolism, lifestyle and bipolar affective disorder. *Journal of Psychopharmacology, 19*((6, Supplement)), 94–101.

Moses, J., Steptoe, A., Mathews, A. and Edwards, S. (1989) The effects of exercise training on mental well-being in the normal population: A controlled trial. *Journal of Psychosomatic Research, 33,* 47–61.

Motl, R. W., Birnbaum, A. S., Kubik, M. Y. and Dishman, R. K. (2004) Naturally occurring changes in physical activity are inversely related to depressive symptoms during early adolescence. *Psychosom Med, 66(3),* 336–42.

Moundon, A. V., Lee, C., Cheadle, A. D., Garvin, C., Johnson, D., Schmid, T. L., Weather, R.D. and Lin, L. (2006) Operational definitions of walkable neighborhood: Theoretical and empirical insights. *Journal of Physical Activity and Health, 3*(Supplement 1), S99–S117.

Mueller, C. M. and Dweck, C. S. (1998) Praise for intelligence can undermine children's motivation and performance. *Journal of Personality and Social Psychology, 75,* 33–52.

Muldoon, M. F., Barger, S. D., Flory, J. D. and Manuck, S. B. (1998) What are the quality of life measurements measuring? *British Medical Journal, 316,* 542–5.

Mullan, E. and Markland, D. (1997) Variations in self-determination across the stages of change for exercise in adults. *Motivation and Emotion, 21,* 349–62.

Mullan, E., Markland, D. and Ingledew, D. (1997) A graded conceptualisation of self-determination in the regulation of exercise behaviour: Development of a measure using confirmatory factor analytic procedures. *Personality and Individual Differences, 23,* 745–52.

Mulvihill, C., Rivers, K. and Aggleton, P. (2000) *Physical activity 'at our time': Qualitative research among young people aged 5 to 15 years and parents.* London: Health Education Authority.

Murdoch, F. A. (1988) *Short term interventions for withdrawal from benzodiazepines: A comparative study of group therapy plus exercise vs group therapy.* Unpublished MBCHB Thesis, University of Glasgow.

Murphy, T. J., Pagano, R. R. and Marlatt, G. A. (1986) Lifestyle modification with heavy alcohol drinkers: Effects of aerobic exercise and meditation. *Addictive Behaviors, 11,* 175–86.

Murray, C. J. and Lopez, A. D. (1997) Alernative projections of mortality and disability by 1990–2020: Global burden of disease study, *Lancet, 349,* 1498–1504.

Musgrave, B. and Menell, Z. (1980) *Change and choice: Women and middle-age.* London: Peter Owen.

Mutrie, N. (2000) The relationship between physical activity and clinically defined depression. In S. J. H. Biddle, K. R. Fox and S. H. Boutcher (eds), *Physical activity and psychological well-being* (pp. 46–62). London: Routledge.

Mutrie, N. and Choi, P. Y. L. (1993) *Psychological benefits of physical activity for specific populations.* Paper presented at the 7th Conference of the European Health Psychology Society, Brussels.

Mutrie, N. and Choi, P. Y. L. (2000) Is 'fit' a feminist issue? Dilemmas for exercise psychology. *Feminism and Psychology, 10*(4), 544–51.

Mutrie, N. and Hannah, M. K. (2007) The importance of both setting and intensity of physical activity in relation to non-clinical anxiety and depression. *International Journal of Health Promotion and Education, 45*(1), 24–32.

Mutrie, N. and Knill-Jones, R. (1986) Psychological effects of running: 1985 survey of Glasgow People's Marathon. In J. H. McGregor and J. A. Moncur (eds), *Sport and Medicine: Proceedings of VIII Commonwealth and International Conference on Sport, Physical Education, Dance, Recreation and Health* (pp. 186–90). London: E. and F.N. Spon.

Mutrie, N. and Parfitt, G. (1998) Physical activity and its link with mental, social and moral health in young people. In S. J. H. Biddle, J. F. Sallis and N. Cavill (eds), *Young and active? Young people and health-enhancing physical activity: Evidence and implications* (pp. 49–68). London: Health Education Authority.

Mutrie, N., Wright, A., Wilson, R. and Gunnyeon, K. (2004) Do pedometers motivate people to walk more? *Journal of Sports Sciences, 22*(3), 254.

Mutrie, N., Carney, C., Blamey, A., Crawford, F., Aitchison, T. and Whitelaw, A. (2002) 'Walk in to work out': A randomised controlled trial of self help intervention to promote active commuting. *Journal of Epidemiology and Community Health, 56,* 407–12.

Mutrie, N., Campbell, A. M., Whyte, F., McConnachie, A., Emslie, C., Lee, L., Kearney, N., Walker, A. and Richie, D. (2007) Benefits of supervised group exercise programme for women being treated for early stage breast cancer: pragmatic randomised controlled trial. *British Medical Journal, 334*(7592), 517–520B.

Naidoo, J. and Wills, J. (1994) *Health Promotion Foundations for practice.* London: Bailliere Tindall.

National Health Service (2001) *Exercise referral systems: A national quality assurance framework:* Crown Copyright.

National Institute for Health and Clinical Excellence (2006) *Four commonly used methods to increase physical activity: Brief interventions in primary care, exercise referral schemes, pedometers and community-based exercise programmes for walking and cycling.* London: Author.

Naughton, J. (1985) Role of physical activity as a secondary intervention for healed myocardial infarction. *American Journal of Cardiology, 55,* 210–60.

Neeman, J. and Harter, S. (1986) *Manual for the Self-Perception Profile for college students.* Denver, CO: University of Denver.

Neuberger, G. B., Kasal, S., Smith, K. V. and Hassanein, R. (1994) Determinants of exercise and aerobic fitness in outpatients with arthritis. *Nursing Research, 43,* 11–17.

Newman, A. B., Haggerty, C. L., Kritchevsky, S. B., Nevitt, M. C. and Simonsick, E. M. (2003) Walking performance and cardiovascular response: Associations with age and morbidity: The health, aging and body composition study. *Journals of Gerontology Series A: Biological Sciences and Medical Sciences, 58*(8), 715–20.

NHS Direct (2006) NHS Direct on line health encyclopaedia: anxiety. Retrieved 23 January 2006, from www.nhsdirect.nhs.uk/en.aspx?articleID=28.

Nicholls, J. G. (1989) *The competitive ethos and democratic education.* Cambridge, MA: Harvard University Press.

Nigg, C. R. (2005) There is more to stages of exercise than just exercise. *Exercise and Sport Sciences Reviews, 33,* 32–5.

Nixon, S., O'Brien, K., Glazier, R. H. and Tynan, A. M. (2005) Aerobic exercise interventions for adults living with HIV/AIDS (update of Cochrane Database Syst Rev. 2002;(2):CD001796; PMID: 12076422). *Cochrane Database of Systematic Reviews* (2), CD001796.

Noland, M. and Feldman, R. (1984) Factors related to the leisure exercise behavior of 'returning' women college students. *Health Education, March/April,* 32–6.

Norstrom, J. (1988) Get fit while you sit: Exercise and fitness options for diabetics. *Caring, November,* 52–8.

North, T. C., McCullagh, P. and Tran, Z. V. (1990) Effect of exercise on depression. *Exercise and Sport Sciences Reviews, 18,* 379–415.

Ntoumanis, N. and Biddle, S. J. H. (1999) A review of motivational climate in physical activity. *Journal of Sports Sciences, 17,* 643–65.

O'Brien, K., Nixon, S., Glazier, R. H. and Tynan, A. M. (2004) Progressive resistive exercise interventions for adults living with HIV/AIDS. *Cochrane Database of Systematic Reviews* (4), CD004248.

O'Conner, G., Buring, J., Yusuf, S., Goldhaber, S., Olmstead, E. and Paffenberger, R. (1989) An overview of randomised controlled trials of rehabilitation with exercise after myocardial infarction. *Circulation, 80,* 234–44.

O'Connor, P. J. and Youngstedt, S. D. (1995) Influence of exercise on human sleep. *Exercise and Sport Sciences Reviews, 23,* 105–34.

O'Connor, P. J., Aenchbacher, L. E. and Dishman, R. K. (1993) Physical activity and depression in the elderly. *Journal of Aging and Physical Activity, 1,* 34–58.

O'Connor, P. J., Smith, J. C. and Morgan, W. P. (2000) Physical activity does not provoke panic attacks in patients with panic disorder: A review of the evidence. *Anxiety, Stress, and Coping, 13,* 333–53.

O'Neal, H. A., Dunn, A. L. and Martinsen, E. W. (2000) Depression and exercise. *International Journal of Sport Psychology, 31,* 110–35.

O'Hara, M. and Swain, A. (1996) Rates and risk of postpartum depression: A meta analysis. *International Review of Psychology, 8,* 37–54.

Oatley, K. and Jenkins, J. M. (1996) *Understanding emotions.* Cambridge, MA: Blackwell Scientific.

Office of National Statistics (2004) Social Trends. *32.*

Office of National Statistics (2005) *Social Trends, 35.*

Ogilvie, D., Egan, M., Hamilton, V. and Petticrew, M. (2004) Promoting walking and cycling as an alternative to using cars: Systematic review. *British Medical Journal, 329,* 763–6.

Oja, P. (1995) Descriptive epidemiology of health-related physical activity and fitness. *Research Quarterly for Exercise and Sport, 66,* 303–12.

Oldridge, N. B., Donner, A. and Buck, C. (1983) Predictors of dropout from cardiac exercise rehabilitation: Ontario Exercise Heart Collaborative Study. *American Journal of Cardiology, 51,* 70–4.

Oldridge, N. B., Guyatt, G. H., Fischer, M. E. and Rimm, A. A. (1988) Cardiac rehabilitation after myocardial infarction: Combined experience of randomized clinical trials. *Journal of the American Medical Association, 260,* 945–50.

Olivardia, R., Pope, H. G. and Hudson, J. I. (2000) Muscle dysmorphia in male weightlifters: A case-control study. *American Journal of Psychiatry, 157*(8), 1291–6.

Olson, J. M. and Zanna, M. P. (1993) Attitudes and attitude change. *Annual Review of Psychology, 44,* 117–54.

Orbach, S. (1978) *Fat is a feminist issue: The anti-diet guide to permanent weight loss.* New York: Paddington Press.

Orbell, S. (2000) Motivational and volitional components in action initiation: A field study of the role of implementation intentions. *Journal of Applied Social Psychology, 30,* 780–97.

Orbell, S., Hodgkins, S. and Sheeran, P. (1997) Implementation intentions and the Theory of Planned Behavior. *Personality and Social Psychology Bulletin, 23,* 945–54.

Orwin, A. (1981) The running treatment: A preliminary communication on a new use for an old therapy (physical activity) in the agorophobic syndrome. In M. H. Sacks and M. Sacks (eds), *Psychology of running* (pp. 32–9). Champaign: Human Kinetics.

Ossip-Klein, D. J., Doyne, E. J., Bowman, E. D., Osborn, K. M., McDougall-Wilson, I. B. and Neimeyer, R. A. (1989) Effects of running and weight lifting on self-concept in clinically depressed women. *Journal of Consulting and Clinical Psychology, 57,* 158–61.

Owen, N. and Bauman, A. (1992) The descriptive epidemiology of a sedentary lifestyle in adult Australians. *International Journal of Epidemiology, 21,* 305–10.

Owen, N. and Dwyer, T. (1988) Approaches to promoting more widespread participation in physical activity. *Community Health Studies, 12,* 339–47.

Owen, N., Humpel, N., Leslie, E., Bauman, A. and Sallis, J. F. (2004) Understanding environmental influences on walking: Review and research agenda. *American Journal of Preventive Medicine, 27*(1), 67–76.

Owen, N., Leslie, E., Salmon, J. and Fotheringham, M. J. (2000) Environmental determinants of physical activity and sedentary behavior. *Exercise and Sport Sciences Reviews, 28*(4), 153–8.

Paffenbarger, R. S., Blair, S. N. and Lee, I. (2001) A history of physical activity, cardiovascular health and longevity: The scientific contributions of Jeremy N. Morris, DSc, DPH, FRCP. *International Journal of Epidemiology, 30,* 1184–92.

Paffenbarger, R. S., Lee, I. M. and Leung, R. (1994). Physical activity and personal characteristics associated with depression and suicide in American college men. *Acta Psychiatrica Scandinavia, 89*(s377), 16–22.

Paffenbarger, R. S., Wing, A. L. and Hyde, R. T. (1978) Physical activity as an index of heart attack risk in college alumni. *American Journal of Epidemiology, 108,* 161–75.

Paffenbarger, R. S., Hyde, R. T., Wing, A. L. and Hsieh, C.-C. (1986) Physical activity, all-cause mortality, and longevity of college alumni. *New England Journal of Medicine, 314,* 605–13.

Paffenbarger, R. S., Hyde, R. T., Wing, A. L., Lee, I.-M. and Kampert, J. B. (1994) Some interrelations of physical activity, physiological fitness, health and longevity. In C. Bouchard, R. J. Shephard and T. Stephens (eds), *Physical activity, fitness, and health* (pp. 119–33). Champaign, IL: Human Kinetics.

Paffenbarger, R. S., Hyde, R. T., Wing, A. L., Lee, I.-M., Jung, D. L. and Kampert, J. B. (1993) The association of changes in physical activity level and other lifestyle characteristics with mortality among men. *New England Journal of Medicine, 328,* 538–45.

Palenzuela, D. L. (1988) Refining the theory and measurement of expectancy of internal versus external control of reinforcement. *Personality and Individual Differences, 9,* 607–29.

Palmer, J., Vacc, N. and Epstein, J. (1988) Adult inpatient alcoholics: Physical exercise as a treatment intervention. *Journal of Studies on Alcohol, 49*(5), 418–421.

Palmer, S. S., Mortimer, J. A., Webster, D. D., Bistevins, R. and Dickinson, G. L. (1986) Exercise therapy for Parkinson's disease. *Archives of Physical Medicine and Rehabilitation, 67,* 741–5.

Papaioannou, A. (1994) Development of a questionnaire to measure achievement orientation in physical education. *Research Quarterly for Exercise and Sport, 65,* 11–20.

Papaioannou, A. (1995) Motivation and goal perspectives in children's physical education. In S. J. H. Biddle (ed.) *European perspectives on exercise and sport psychology* (pp. 245–69). Champaign, IL: Human Kinetics.

Papaioannou, A. and Goudas, M. (1999) Motivational climate of the physical education class. In Y. V. Auweele, F. Bakker, S. J. H. Biddle, M. Durand and R. Seiler (eds), *Psychology for physical educators* (pp. 51–68). Champaign, IL: Human Kinetics.

Parfitt, G., Markland, D. and Holmes, C. (1994) Response to physical exertion in active and inactive males and females. *Journal of Sport and Exercise Psychology, 16,* 178–86.

Pate, R. R. (1988) The evolving definition of physical fitness. *Quest, 40,* 174–9.

Pate, R. R. and Macera, C. A. (1994) Risks of exercising: Musculoskeletal injuries. In C. Bouchard, R. J. Shephard and T. Stephens (eds), *Physical activity, fitness, and health* (pp. 1008–18). Champaign, IL: Human Kinetics.

Pate, R. R., Baranowski, T., Dowda, M. and Trost, S. G. (1996) Tracking of physical activity in young children. *Medicine and Science in Sports and Exercise, 28,* 92–6.

Pate, R. R., Trost, S. G., Dowda, M., Ott, A. E., Ward, D. S., Saunders, R. and Felton, G. (1999) Tracking of physical activity, physical inactivity, and health-related physical fitness in rural youth. *Pediatric Exercise Science, 11,* 364–76.

Pate, R. R., Pratt, M., Blair, S. N., Haskel, W. L., Macera, C. A., Bouchard, C., Buchner, D., Ettinger, W., Heath, G., King, A. C., Kriska, A., Leon, A., Marcus, B. H., Morris, J., Paffenbarger, R. S., Patrick, K., Pollock, M. L., Rippe, J. M., Sallis, J. F. and Wilmore, J. H. (1995) Physical activity and public health: A recommendation from the Centers for Disease Control and Prevention and the American College of Sports Medicine. *Journal of the American Medical Association, 273,* 402–7.

Paton, L. (1993) *Barriers and motivation to exercise in osteoporotic post-menopausal women.* Unpublished M.App.Sci, University of Glasgow, Glasgow.

Patrick, K., Sallis, J. F., Long, B. J., Calfas, K. J., Wooten, W. J. and Heath, G. (1994) PACE: Physician-based assessment and counseling for exercise, background and development. *The Physician and Sportsmedicine, 22,* 245–5.

Patton, R. W., Corry, J. M., Gettman, L. R. and Graf, J. S. (1986) *Implementing health/fitness programs.* Champaign, IL: Human Kinetics.

Paykel, E. S. and Priest, R. G. (1992) Recognition and management of depression in general practice: A consensus statement. *British Medical Journal, 305,* 1198–202.

Pelham, T. W. and Campagna, P. D. (1991) Benefits of exercise in psychiatric rehabilitation of persons with schizophrenia. *Canadian Journal of Rehabilitation, 4*(3), 159–68.

Pelham, T. W., Campagna, P. D., Ritvo, P. G. and Birnie, W. A. (1993) The effects of exercise therapy on clients in a psychiatric rehabilitation programme. *Psychosocial Rehabilitation Journal, 16*(4), 75–84.

Pell, J., Pell, A., Morrison, C., Blatchford, O. and Dargie, H. (1996) Retrospective study of influence of deprivation on uptake of cardiac rehabilitation. *British Medical Journal, 313,* 267–8.

Pelletier, L. G., Fortier, M. S., Vallerand, R. J., Tuson, K. M., Briere, N. M. and Blais, M. R. (1995) Toward a new measure of intrinsic motivation, extrinsic motivation, and amotivation in sports: The Sport Motivation Scale (SMS) *Journal of Sport and Exercise Psychology, 17,* 35–53.

Pender, N. J., Sallis, J. F., Long, B. J. and Calfas, K. J. (1994) Health-care provider counseling to promote physical activity. In R. K. Dishman (ed.), *Advances in exercise adherence* (pp. 213–35). Champaign, IL: Human Kinetics.

Peronnet, F. and Szabo, A. (1993) Sympathetic response to psychosocial stressors in humans: Linkage to physical exercise and training. In P. Seraganian (ed.), *Exercise psychology: The influence of physical exercise on psychological processes* (pp. 172–217). New York: John Wiley.

Perugini, M. and Bagozzi, R. P. (2001) The role of desires and anticipated emotions in goal-directed behaviours: Broadening and deepening the theory of planned behavior. *British Journal of Social Psychology, 40,* 79–98.

Peterson, C. and Seligman, M. E. P. (1984) Causal explanations as a risk factor for depression: Theory and evidence. *Psychological Review, 91,* 347–74.

Peterson, C., Maier, S. F. and Seligman, M. E. P. (1993) *Learned helplessness: A theory for the age of personal control.* New York: Oxford University Press.

Petruzzello, S. J. (1995) Does physical exercise reduce anxious emotions? A reply to W. Schlicht's meta-analysis. *Anxiety, Stress and Coping, 8,* 353–6.

Petruzzello, S. J., Landers, D. M., Hatfield, B. D., Kubitz, K. A. and Salazar, W. (1991) A meta-analysis on the anxiety-reducing effects of acute and chronic exercise: Outcomes and mechanisms. *Sports Medicine, 11,* 143–82.

Petty, R. E. and Cacioppo, J. T. (1986) The elaboration-likelihood model of persuasion. In L. Berkowitz (ed.), *Advances in experimental social psychology* (Vol. 19) (pp. 123–205). San Diego, CA: Academic Press.

Petty, T. (1993) Pulmonary rehabilitation in perspective: Historical roots, present status and future projections. *Thorax, 48,* 855–62.

Phillips, K. A., Osullivan, R. L. and Pope, H. G. (1997) Muscle dysmorphia. *Journal of Clinical Psychiatry, 58*(8), 361.

Pickett, T. C., Lewis, R. J., Cash, T. F. and Pope, H. G. (2005) Men, muscles, and body image: comparisons of competitive bodybuilders, weight trainers, and athletically active controls. *Br J Sports Med, 39*(4), 217–22.

Pierce, E. (1994) Exercise dependence syndrome in runners. *Sports Medicine, 18,* 149–55.

Pieron, M., Cloes, M., Delfosse, C. and Ledent, M. (1996) An investigation of the effects of daily physical education in kindergarten and elementary school. *European Physical Education Review, 2,* 116–32.

Pikora, T., Giles-Corti, B., Bull, F., Jamrozik, K. and Donovan, R. (2003) Developing a framework for assessment of the environmental determinants of walking and cycling. *Social Science and Medicine, 56,* 1693–1703.

Pitts, F. N. and McClure, J. N. (1967) Lactate metabolism in anxiety neurosis. *The New England Journal of Medicine, 277,* 1329–36.

Plante, T. G. (1993) Aerobic exercise in prevention and treatment of psychopathology. In P. Seraganian (ed.), *Exercise psychology. The influence of physical exercise on psychological processes* (pp. 358–79). New York: John Wiley.

Polivy, J. (1994) Physical activity, fitness, and compulsive behaviors. In C. Bouchard, R. J. Shephard and T. Stephens (eds), *Physical activity, fitness, and health* (pp. 883–97). Champaign, IL: Human Kinetics.

Pollatschek, J. L. and O'Hagan, F. J. (1989) An investigation of the psycho-physical influences of a quality daily physical education programme. *Health Education Research: Theory and Practice, 4,* 341–50.

Pope, H. G., Katz, D. L. and Hudson, J. I. (1993) Anorexia nervosa and 'reverse anoxeria' among 108 male bodybuilders. *Comprehensive Psychiatry, 34,* 406–9.

Pope, H. G., Olivardia, R., Gruber, A. and Borowiecki, J. (1999) Evolving ideals of male body image as seen through action toys. *International Journal of Eating Disorders, 26*(1), 65–72.

Pope, H. G., Gruber, A. J., Choi, P., Olivardia, R. and Phillips, K. A. (1997) Muscle dysmorphia: An underrecognized form of body dysmorphic disorder. *Psychosomatics, 38*(6), 548–57.

Pope, H. G., Pope, C. G., Menard, W., Fay, C., Olivardia, R. and Phillips, K. A. (in press) Clinical features of muscle dysmorphia amongst males with body dysmorphic disorder. *Body Image.*

Porter, D. E., Kirtland, K. A., Neet, M. J., Williams, J. E. and Ainsworth, B. E. (2004) Considerations for using a geographic information system to assess environmental supports for physical activity. *Preventing Chronic Disease, 1* (www.cdc.gov/pcd/issues/2004/oct/).

Potempa, K. Braun, L. T., Tinkell, T. and Popovich, J. (1996) Benefits of aerobic exercise after stroke. *Sports Medicine, 21,* 337–46.

Powell, K. E. (1988) Habitual exercise and public health: An epidemiological view. In R. K. Dishman (ed.), *Exercise adherence: Its impact on public health* (pp. 15–39). Champaign, IL: Human Kinetics.

Powell, K. E. and Blair, S. N. (1994) The public health burdens of sedentary living habits: Theoretical but realistic estimates. *Medicine and Science in Sports and Exercise, 26,* 851–6.

Powell, K. E., Spain, K. S., Christenson, C. J. and Mollenkamp, M. P. (1986) The status of the 1990 objectives for physical fitness and exercise. *Public Health Reports, 101,* 15–21.

Powell, K. E., Thompson, P. D., Caspersen, C. J. and Kendrick, J. S. (1987) Physical activity and the incidence of coronary heart disease. *Annual Review of Public Health, 8,* 253–87.

Powell, K. E., Stephens, T., Marti, B., Heinemann, L. and Kreuter, M. (1991) Progress and problems in the promotion of physical activity. In P. Oja and R. Telama (eds), *Sport for all* (pp. 55–73). Amsterdam: Elsevier.

Prentice, A. M. and Jebb, S. A. (1995) Obesity in Britain: Gluttony or sloth? *British Medical Journal, 311,* 437–9.

Prentice, A. M. and Jebb, S. A. (2000) Physical activity level and weight control in adults. In C. Bouchard (ed.), *Physical activity and obesity* (pp. 247–61). Champaign, IL: Human Kinetics.

Prentice-Dunn, S. and Rogers, R. (1986) Protection Motivation Theory and preventive health: Beyond the Health Belief Model. *Health Education Research: Theory and Practice, 1,* 153–61.

Prescott-Clarke, P. and Primatesta, P. (1998) *Health survey for England '96: A survey carried out on behalf of the Department of Health. Volume I: findings. (The Health of the Nation.):* The Stationery Office.

Prestwich, A., Lawton, R. and Conner, M. (2003) The use of implementation intentions and the decision balance sheet in promoting exercise behaviour. *Psychology and Health, 18,* 707–21.

Prior, J. C. and Vigna, Y. (1987) Conditioning exercise decreases premenstrual symptoms: A prospective, controlled 6-month trial. *Fertility and Sterility, 47,* 402–8.

Prochaska, J. O. (1994) Strong and weak principles for progressing from precontemplation to action on the basis of twelve problem behaviors. *Health Psychology, 13,* 47–51.

Prochaska, J. O. and DiClemente, C. C. (1982) Transtheoretical therapy: Toward a more integrative model of change. *Psychotherapy: Theory, Research and Practice, 19,* 276–88.

Prochaska, J. O. and Marcus, B. H. (1994) The transtheoretical model: Application to exercise. In R. K. Dishman (ed.), *Advances in exercise adherence* (pp. 161–80). Champaign, IL: Human Kinetics.

Prochaska, J. O. and Velicer, W. (1997) The transtheoretical model of health behavior change. *American Journal of Health Promotion, 12,* 38–48.

Prochaska, J. O., DiClemente, C. C. and Norcross, J. C. (1992) In search of how people change: Applications to addictive behaviors. *American Psychologist, 47,* 1102–14.

Prochaska, J. O., Norcross, J. C. and DiClemente, C. C. (1994) *Changing for good.* New York: Avon.

Prochaska, J. O., Velicer, W. F., Rossi, J. S., Goldstein, M. G., Marcus, B. H., Rakowski, W., Fiore, C., Harlow, L. L., Redding, C. A., Rosenbloom, D. and Rossi, S. R. (1994) Stages of change and decision balance for 12 problem behaviors. *Health Psychology, 13,* 39–46.

Proper, K. I., Hildebrandt, V. H., Van der Beek, A. J., Twisk, J. W. R. and Van Mechelen, W. (2003) Effect of individual counseling on physical activity fitness and health: A randomized controlled trial in a workplace setting. *American Journal of Preventive Medicine, 24*(3), 218–26.

Prosser, G., Carson, P. and Phillips, R. (1985) Exercise after myocardial infarction: Long term rehabilitation effects. *Journal of Psychosomatic Research, 29,* 535–40.

Quaglietti, S. and Froelicher, V. F. (1994) Physical activity and cardiac rehabilitation for patients with coronary heart disease. In C. Bouchard, R. J. Shephard and T. Stephens (eds), *Physical activity, fitness and health* (pp. 591–608). Champaign, IL: Human Kinetics.

Quinney, H. A., Gauvin, L. and Wall, A. E. T. (1994) *Toward active living.* Champaign, IL: Human Kinetics.

Radloff, L. S. (1977) The CES-D scale: A self-report depression scale for research in the general population. *Applied Psychological Measurement, 1,* 385–401.

Raglin, J. S. (1997) Anxiolytic effects of physical activity. In W. P. Morgan (ed.), *Physical activity and mental health* (pp. 107–26) Washington, DC: Taylor & Francis.

Ramirez-Marrero, F. A., Smith, B. A., Melendez-Brau, N. and Santana-Bagur, J. L. (2004) Physical and leisure activity, body composition, and life satisfaction in HIV-positive Hispanics in Puerto Rico. *Journal of the Association of Nurses in AIDS Care, 15*(4), 68–77.

Rankin, J. (2002) *Effects of antenatal exercise on psychological well-being, pregnancy and birth outcomes.* London: Whurr.

Rankin, J., Hillan, E. M. and Mutrie, N. (2000) An historical overview of physical activity and childbirth. *British Journal of Midwifery, 8*(12), 761–4.

Redman, S., Spencer, E. A. and Sanson-Fisher, R. W. (1990) The role of mass media in changing health-related behaviour: A critical appraisal of two models. *Health Promotion International, 5,* 85–101.

Reed, B. D., Jensen, J. D. and Gorenflo, D. W. (1991) Physicians and exercise promotion. *American Journal of Preventive Medicine, 7,* 410–15.

Reed, G. R. (1999) Adherence to exercise and the transtheoretical model of behaviour change. In S. J. Bull (ed.), *Adherence issues in sport and exercise* (pp. 19–46). Chichester: Wiley.

Rejeski, W. J. and Brawley, L. R. (1988) Defining the boundaries of sport psychology. *The Sport Psychologist, 2,* 231–42.

Rejeski, W. J. and Thompson, A. (1993) Historical and conceptual roots of exercise psychology. In P. Seraganian (ed.), *Exercise psychology. The influence of physical exercise on psychological processes* (pp. 3–35). New York: John Wiley.

Rejeski, W. J., Brawley, L. R. and Shumaker, S. A. (1996) Physical activity and health-related quality of life. *Exercise and Sport Sciences Reviews, 24,* 71–108.

Rennie, K. L. and Jebb, S. A. (2005) Prevalence of obesity in Great Britain. *Obesity Reviews, 6,* 11–12.

Research Quarterly for Exercise and Sport (1995) Special issue: Proceedings of the International Scientific Consensus Conference, 'Physical Activity, Health and Well-Being'. *Research Quarterly for Exercise and Sport, 66(4) [Whole].*

Reuter, I., Engelhardt, M., Stecker, K. and Baas, H. (1999) Therapeutic value of exercise training in Parkinson's disease. *Medicine and Science in Sports and Exercise, 31,* 1544–9.

Rhodes, R. E., Courneya, K. S. and Jones, L. W. (2002) Personality, the theory of planned behavior, and exercise: A unique role for extroversion's activity facet. *Journal of Applied Social Psychology, 32,* 1721–36.

Rhodes, S. D., Bowie, D. A. and Hergenrather, K. C. (2003) Collecting behavioural data using the world wide web: considerations for researchers. *J Epidemiol Community Health, 57*(1), 68–73.

Richardson, C. R., Faulkner, G. E. J., McDevitt, J., Skrinar, G. S., Hutchinson, D. S. and Piette, J. D. (2005) Integrating physical activity into mental health services for persons with serious mental illness. *Psychiatric Services, 56*(3), 324–31.

Rickabaugh, T. E. and Saltarelli, W. (1999) Knowledge and attitudes related to diabetes and exercise guidelines among selected diabetic children, their parents, and physical education teachers. *Research Quarterly for Exercise and Sport, 70,* 389–94.

Rickli, R. E. and McManus, R. (1990) The effect of exercise on bone mineral content in post menopausal women. *Research Quarterly for Exercise and Sport, 61,* 243–9.

Riddoch, C. (1998) Relationships between physical activity and physical health in young people. In S. J. H. Biddle, J. F. Sallis and N. Cavill (eds), *Young and active? Young people and health-enhancing physical activity: Evidence and implications* (pp. 17–48). London: Health Education Authority.

Riddoch, C., Puig-Ribera, A. and Cooper, A. (1998) *Effectiveness of physical activity promotion schemes in primary care: A review.* London: Health Education Authority.

Rigby, N. J., Kumanyika, S. and James, W. P. (2004) Confronting the epidemic: the need for global solutions. *Journal of Public Health Policy, 25*(3–4), 418–34.

Rigsby, L., Dishman, R. K., Jackson, W., McClean, G. S. and Rowen, P. B. (1992) Effects of exercise training on men seropositive for HIV-1. *Medicine and Science in Sports and Exercise, 24,* 6–12.

Rippetoe, P. A. and Rogers, R. (1987) Effects of components of protection-motivation theory on adaptive and maladaptive coping with a health threat. *Journal of Personality and Social Psychology, 52,* 596–604.

Rivis, A. and Sheeran, P. (2003) Social influences and the theory of planned behaviour: Evidence for a direct relationship between prototypes and young people's exercise behaviour. *Psychology and Health, 18*(5), 567–83.

Roberts, D., Foehr, U., Rideout, V. and Brodie, M. (1999) *Kids and media @ the new millennium.* Menlo Park, CA: The Henry J. Kaiser Family Foundation.

Robinson, T. N. (1999) Reducing children's television viewing to prevent obesity: A randomized controlled trial. *Journal of the American Medical Association, 282*(16), 1561–7.

Robinson, T. N. and Killen, J. D. (1995) Ethnic and gender differences in the relationships between television viewing and obesity, physical activity, and dietary fat intake. *Journal of Health Education, 26*(2, Supplement), S91–8.

Rodgers, W. M. and Brawley, L. R. (1993) Using both the self-efficacy theory and the theory of planned behavior to discriminate adherers and dropouts from structured programmes. *Journal of Applied Sport Psychology, 5,* 195–206.

Rogers, L., Courneya, K. S., Verhulst, S., Markwell, S., Lanzotti, V. and Shah, P. (2006) Exercise barrier and task self-efficacy in breast cancer patients during treatment. *Supportive Care in Cancer, 14*(1), 84–90.

Rogers, R. W. (1983) Cognitive and physiological processes in fear appeals and attitude change: A revised theory of protection motivation. In J. R. Cacioppo and R. E. Petty (eds), *Social psychology: A sourcebook* (pp. 153–76). New York: Guilford Press.

Rollnick, S. and Miller, W. R. (1995) What is motivational interviewing? *Behavioural and Cognitive Psychotherapy, 23,* 325–34.

Rollnick, S., Mason, P. and Butler, C. (1999) *Health behavior change: A guide for practitioners.* Edinburgh: Churchill Livingstone.

Rollnick, S., Butler, C. C., McCambridge, J., Kinnersley, P., Elwyn, G. and Resnicow, K. (2005) Consultations about changing behaviour. *British Medical Journal, 331*(7522), 961–3.

Rooney, B., Smalley, K., Larson, J. and Havens, S. (2003) Is knowing enough? Increasing physical activity by wearing a pedometer. *Wisconsin Medical Journal, 102*(4), 31–6.

Rosenstock, I. (1974) Historical origins of the health belief model. *Health Education Monographs, 2,* 32835.

Rothman, A. J., Salovey, P., Turvey, C. and Fishkin, S. A. (1993) Attributions of responsibility and persuasion: Increasing mammography utilization among women over 40 with an internally oriented message. *Health Psychology, 12,* 39–47.

Rotter, J. B. (1954) *Social learning and clinical psychology.* Englewood Cliffs, NJ: Prentice-Hall.

Rotter, J. B. (1966) Generalised expectancies for internal versus external control of reinforcement. *Psychological Monographs, 80, Whole No. 609,* 1–28.

Rovario, S., Holmes, D. and Holmsten, D. (1984) Influence of a cardiac rehabilitation program on the cardiovascular, psychological, and social functioning of cardiac patients. *Journal of Behavioral Medicine, 7,* 61–81.

Rowland, D., DiGuiseppi, C., Gross, M., Afolabi, E. and Roberts, I. (2003) Randomised controlled trial of site specific advice on school travel patterns. *Archives of Disease in Childhood, 88*(1), 8–11.

Rudolph, D. L. and McAuley, E. (1995) Self-efficacy and salivary cortisol responses to acute exercise in physically active and less active adults. *Journal of Sport and Exercise Psychology, 17,* 206–13.

Rummel, A. and Feinberg, R. (1988) Cognitive evaluation theory: A meta-analytic review of the literature. *Social Behavior and Personality, 16,* 147–64.

Russell, J. A. (1980) A circumplex model of affect. *Journal of Personality and Social Psychology, 39,* 1161–78.

Russell, J. A. (2003) Core affect and the psychological construction of emotion. *Psychological Review, 110,* 145–72.

Russell, J. A. and Barrett, L. F. (1999) Core affect, prototypical emotional episodes, and other things called emotion: Dissecting the elephant. *Journal of Personality and Social Psychology, 76,* 805–19.

Ryan, R. and Connell, J. (1989) Perceived locus of causality and internalization: Examining reasons for acting in two domains. *Journal of Personality and Social Psychology, 57,* 749–61.

Ryan, R. M. and Deci, E. L. (2000a) Intrinsic and extrinsic motivations: Classic definitions and new directions. *Contemporary Educational Psychology, 25,* 54–67.

Ryan, R. M. and Deci, E. L. (2000b) Self-determination theory and the facilitation of intrinsic motivation, social development, and well-being. *American Psychologist, 55,* 68–78.

Ryan, R. M., Connell, J. P. and Grolnick, W. S. (1992) When achievement is not intrinsically motivated: A theory of internalization and self-regulation in school. In A. K. Boggiano and T. S. Pittman (eds), *Achievement and motivation: A social developmental perspective* (pp. 167–88). Cambridge: Cambridge University Press.

Ryckman, R. M., Robbins, M. A., Thornton, B. and Cantrell, P. (1982) Development and validation of a Physical Self-Efficacy Scale. *Journal of Personality and Social Psychology, 42,* 891–900.

Saelens, B. E. (2003) Helping individuals reduce sedentary behavior. In R. E. Andersen (ed.), *Obesity: Etiology, assessment, treatment, and prevention* (pp. 217–38). Champaign, IL: Human Kinetics.

Sallis, J. F. (1998) Family and community interventions to promote physical activity in young people. In S. J. H. Biddle, J. F. Sallis and N. Cavill (eds), *Young and Active? Young people and health-enhancing physical activity: Evidence and implications* (pp. 150–61). London: Health Education Authority.

Sallis, J. F. and Hovell, M. (1990) Determinants of exercise behavior. *Exercise and Sport Sciences Reviews, 18,* 307–30.

Sallis, J. F. and Owen, N. (1999) *Physical activity and behavioral medicine.* Thousand Oaks, CA: Sage.

Sallis, J. F. and Owen, N. (2002) Ecological models of health behavior. In K. Glanz, B. Rimer and F. Lewis (eds), *Health behavior and health education: Theory, research and practice* (3rd edn) (pp. 403–24). San Francisco: Jossey-Bass.

Sallis, J. F. and Owen, N. (2002a) Ecological models of health behavior. In K. Glanz, F. Lewis and B. Rimer (eds), *Health behaviour and health education* (3rd edn) (pp. 403–24). San Francisco: Jossey-Bass.

Sallis, J. F. and Patrick, K. (1994) Physical activity guidelines for adolescents: Consensus statement. *Pediatric Exercise Science, 6,* 302–14.

Sallis, J. F. and Saelens, B. E. (2000) Assessment of physical activity by self-report: Status, limitations, and future directions. *Research Quarterly for Exercise and Sport, 71,* 1–14.

Sallis, J. F., Bauman, A. and Pratt, M. (1998) Environmental and policy interventions to promote physical activity. *American Journal of Preventive Medicine, 15,* 379–97.

Sallis, J. F., Prochaska, J. J. and Taylor, W. C. (2000) A review of correlates of physical activity of children and adolescents. *Medicine and Science in Sports and Exercise, 32,* 963–75.

Sallis, J. F., Hovell, M. F., Hofstetter, C. R. and Barrington, E. (1992) Explanation of vigorous physical activity during two years using social learning variables. *Social Science and Medicine, 34,* 25–32.

Sallis, J. F., Grossman, R. M., Pinski, R. B., Patterson, T. L. and Nader, P. R. (1987) The development of scales to measure social support for diet and exercise behaviours. *Preventive Medicine, 16,* 825–36.

Sallis, J. F., Pinski, R. B., Grossman, R. M., Patterson, T. L. and Nader, P. R. (1988) The development of self-efficacy scales for health-related diet and exercise behaviors. *Health Education Research: Theory and Practice, 3,* 283–92.

Sallis, J. F., Haskell, W., Fortmann, S., Vranizan, K., Taylor, C. B. and Solomon, D. (1986) Predictors of adoption and maintenance of physical activity in a community sample. *Preventive Medicine, 15,* 331–41.

Sallis, J. F., McKenzie, T. L., Alcaraz, J. E., Kolody, B., Faucette, N. and Hovell, M. F. (1997) The effects of a 2-year physical education program (SPARK) on physical activity and fitness in elementary school students. *American Journal of Public Health, 87,* 1328–34.

Sallis, J. F., Simons-Morton, B. G., Stone, E. J., Corbin, C. B., Epstein, L. H., Faucette, N., Iannotti, R. J., Killen, J. D., Klesges, R. C., Petray, C. K., Rowland, T. W. and Taylor, W. C. (1992) Determinants of physical activity and interventions in youth. *Medicine and Science in Sports and Exercise, 24*(6, Supplement), S248–57.

Salmon, J., Owen, N., Crawford, D., Bauman, A. and Sallis, J. F. (2003) Physical activity and sedentary behavior: A population-based study of barriers, enjoyment, and preference. *Health Psychology, 22,* 178–88.

Salmon, J., Timperio, A., Telford, A., Carver, A. and Crawford, D. (2005) Association of family environment with children's television viewing and with low level of physical activity. *Obesity Research, 13*(11), 1939–51.

Salonen, J. T., Puska, P., Kottke, T. E., Tuomilehto, J. and Nissinen, A. (1983) Decline in mortality from coronary heart disease in Finland from 1969 to 1979. *British Medical Journal, 286,* 1857–60.

Saris, W., Blair, S. N., van Baak, M., Eaton, S., Davies, P., Di Pietro, L., Fogelholm, M., Rissanen, A., Schoeller, D., Swinburn, B. A., Tremblay, A., Westerterp, K. R. and Wyatt, H. (2003) How much physical activity is enough to prevent unhealthy weight gain? Outcome of the IASO 1st Stock Conference and consensus statement. *Obesity Reviews 4,* 101–14.

Sarrazin, P., Biddle, S. J. H., Famose, J. P., Cury, F., Fox, K. and Durand, M. (1996) Goal orientations and conceptions of the nature of sport ability in children: A social cognitive approach. *British Journal of Social Psychology, 35,* 399–414.

Saxton, J., Daley, A., Woodroofe, M. N., Coleman, R., Powers, H., Mutrie, N., Siddal, V. and Crank, H. (2005) Study protocol: The effect of a lifestyle intervention on body weight, psychological health status and risk factors associated with disease recurrence in women recovering from breast cancer treatment [ISRCTN08045231]. *BioMed Central Cancer.*

Scanlan, T. K. and Lewthwaite, R. (1986) Social psychological aspects of competition for male youth sport participants: IV. Predictors of enjoyment. *Journal of Sport Psychology, 8,* 25–35.

Schifter, D. E. and Ajzen, I. (1985) Intention, perceived control, and weight loss: An application of the theory of planned behaviour. *Journal of Personality and Social Psychology, 49,* 843–51.

Schlicht, W. (1994) Does physical exercise reduce anxious emotions? A meta-analysis. *Anxiety, Stress and Coping, 6,* 275–88.

Schlicht, W. (1995) Does physical exercise reduce anxious emotions? A retort to Steven J. Petruzzello. *Anxiety, Stress and Coping, 8,* 357–9.

Schmitz, K. H., Holtzman, J., Courneya, K. S., Masse, L. C., Duval, S. and Kane, R. (2005) Controlled physical activity trials in cancer survivors: A systematic review and meta-analysis. *Cancer Epidemiology Biomarkers and Prevention, 14*(7), 1588–95.

Schnohr, P., Kristensen, T. S., Prescott, E. and Scharling, H. (2005) Stress and life dissatisfaction are inversely associated with jogging and other types of physical activity in leisure time: The Copenhagen City Heart Study. *Scandinavian Journal of Medicine and Science in Sports, 15*(2), 107–12.

Schoeneman, T. J. and Curry, S. (1990) Attributions for successful and unsuccessful health behaviour change. *Basic and Applied Social Psychology, 11,* 421–31.

Schoeneman, T. J., Hollis, J. F., Stevens, V. J., Fischer, K. and Cheek, P. R. (1988) Recovering stride versus letting it slide: Attributions for 'slips' following smoking cessation treatment. *Psychology and Health, 2,* 335–47.

Schoeneman, T. J., Stevens, V. J., Hollis, J. F., Cheek, P. R. and Fischer, K. (1988) Attribution, affect and expectancy following smoking cessation treatment. *Basic and Applied Social Psychology, 9,* 173–84.

Schwarz, L. and Kindermann, W. (1992) Changes in B-endorphin levels in response to aerobic and anaerobic exercise. *Sports Medicine, 13,* 25–36.

Schwarzer, R. (1992) Self-efficacy in the adoption and maintenance of health behaviours: Theoretical approaches and a new model. In R. Schwarzer (ed.), *Self-efficacy: Thought control of action* (pp. 217–43). Bristol, PA: Taylor & Francis.

Schwarzer, R. (2001) Social-cognitive factors in changing health-related behaviors. *Current Directions in Psychological Science, 10*(2), 47–51.

Scott, J. (1996) Cognitive therapy of affective disorders: A review. *Journal of Affective Disorders, 37,* 1–11.

Scottish Executive (2002) *Let's make Scotland more active.* Edinburgh: Author.

Scottish Executive (2003) *Let's make Scotland more active: A strategy for physical activity.* Edinburgh: Author.

Sechrist, K. R., Walker, S. N. and Pender, N. J. (1987) Development and psychometric evaluation of the exercise benefits/barriers scale. *Research in Nursing and Health, 10,* 357–65.

Seligman, M. E. P. (1975) *Helplessness: On depression, development and death.* San Fransisco: Freeman.

Sevick, M. A., Dunn, A. L., Morrow, M. S., Marcus, B. H., Chen, G. J. and Blair, S. N. (2000) Cost-effectiveness of lifestyle and structured exercise interventions in sedentary adults – Results of project ACTIVE. *American Journal of Preventive Medicine, 19*(1), 1–8.

Sexton, H., Maere, A. and Dahl, N. H. (1989) Exercise intensity and reduction in neurotic symptoms: A controlled follow-up study. *Acta Psychiatrica Scandinavica, 80,* 231–5.

Sharratt, M. T. and Sharratt, J. K. (1994) Potential health benefits of active living for persons with chronic conditions. In H. A. Quinney, L. Gauvin and A. E. T. Wall (eds), *Toward active living* (pp. 39–45). Champaign, IL: Human Kinetics.

Shavelson, R. J., Hubner, J. J. and Stanton, G. C. (1976) Self-concept: Validation of construct interpretations. *Review of Educational Research, 46,* 407–41.

Sheeran, P. and Abraham, C. (1996) The Health Belief Model. In M. Conner and P. Norman (eds), *Predicting health behaviour* (pp. 23–61). Buckingham: Open University Press.

Sheeran, P. and Orbell, S. (2000) Self schemas and the theory of planned behaviour. *European Journal of Social Psychology, 30,* 533–50.

Sheeran, P., Norman, P. and Orbell, S. (1999) Evidence that intentions based on attitudes better predict behaviour than intentions based on subjective norms. *European Journal of Social Psychology, 29,* 403–6.

Shephard, R. J. (1985) Motivation: The key to fitness compliance. *The Physician and Sportmedicine, 13*(7), 88–101.

Shephard, R. J. (1989) Current perspectives on the economics of fitness and sport with particular reference to worksite programmes. *Sports Medicine, 7,* 286–309.

Shephard, R. J. (1992) A critical analysis of work-site fitness programs and their postulated economic benefits. *Medicine and Science in Sports and Exercise, 24,* 354–70.

Shephard, R. J. (1997) Curricular physical activity and academic performance. *Pediatric Exercise Science, 9,* 113–26.

Shephard, R. J., Lankenau, B., Pratt, M., Neiman, A., Puska, P., Benaziza, H., Bauman, A. (2004) Physical activity policy development: A Synopsis of the WHO/CDC Consultation, September 29 through October 21 2002, Atlanta, Georgia. *Public Health Reports, 119*(3), 346–51.

Sheppard, B. H., Hartwick, J. and Warshaw, P. R. (1988) The theory of reasoned action: A meta-analysis of past research with recommendations for modifications and future research. *Journal of Consumer Research, 15,* 325–343.

Sher, L. (2005) Type D personality: the heart, stress, and cortisol. *Qjm, 98*(5), 323–9.

Sherer, M., Maddux, J. E., Mercendante, B. and Prentice-Dunn, S. (1982) The Self-Efficacy Scale: Construction and validation. *Psychological Reports, 51,* 663–71.

Sheridan, C. L. and Radmacher, S. A. (1992) *Health psychology: Challenging the biomedical model.* New York: Wiley.

Shimbo, D., Chaplin, W., Crossman, D., Haas, D. and Davidson, K. W. (2005) Role of depression and inflammation in incident coronary heart disease events. *American Journal of Cardiology, 96*(7), 1016–21.

Sibley, B. A. and Etnier, J. L. (2003) The relationship between physical activity and cognition in children: A meta-analysis. *Pediatric Exercise Science, 15,* 243–56.

Simkin, A. J., Ayalon, J. and Leichter, I. (1987) Increased trabecular bone density due to bone-loading exercises in postmenopausal osteoporotic women. *Calcified Tissue International, 40,* 59–63.

Simon, H. B. (1990) Discussion: Exercise, immunity, cancer, and infection. In C. Bouchard, R. J. Shephard, T. Stephens, J. R. Sutton and B. D. McPherson (eds), *Exercise, fitness and health* (pp. 581–588). Champaign, IL: Human Kinetics.

Simons-Morton, D. G., Calfas, K. J., Oldenburg, B. and Burton, N. W. (1998) Effects of interventions in health care settings on physical activity or cardiorespiratory fitness. *American Journal of Preventive Medicine, 15,* 413–30

Singh, N. A., Clements, K. M. and Fiatarone, M. A. (1997) A randomized controlled trial of progressive resistance training in depressed elders. *Journal of Gerontology: Biological Sciences and Medical Sciences, 52A* (1), M27–M35.

Singh, N. A., Clements, K. M. and Singh, M. A. F. (2001) The efficacy of exercise as a long-term antidepressant in elderly subjects: A randomized, controlled trial. *Journals of Gerontology Series A: Biological Sciences and Medical Sciences, 56*(8), M497–M504.

Singh, N. A., Stavrinos, T. M., Scarbek, Y., Galambos, G., Liber, C. and Fiatarone Singh, M. A. (2005) A randomized controlled trial of high versus low intensity weight training versus general practitioner care for clinical depression in older adults. *Journals of Gerontology Series A: Biological Sciences and Medical Sciences, 60*(6), 768–76.

Sinyor, D., Brown, T., Rostant, L. and Seraganian, P. (1982) The role of physical exercise in the treatment of alcoholism. *Journal of Studies on Alcohol, 43,* 380–6.

Siscovick, D. S., Weiss, N. S., Fletcher, R. H. and Lasky, T. (1984) The incidence of primary cardiac arrest during vigorous physical exercise. *New England Journal of Medicine, 311,* 874–7.

Skinner, E. (1995) *Perceived control, motivation, and coping.* Thousand Oaks, CA: Sage.

Skinner, E. (1996) A guide to constructs of control. *Journal of Personality and Social Psychology, 71,* 549–70.

Slavin, J. L., Lutter, J. M., Cushman, S. and Lee, V. (1988) Pregnancy and exercise. In J. Puhl, C. H. Brown and R. O. Voy (eds), *Sport science perspectives for women* (pp. 151–160). Champaign, IL: Human Kinetics.

Smidt, N., de Vet, H. C., Bouter, L. M., Dekker, J., Arendzen, J. H., de Bie, R. A., Bierma-Zeinstra, S. M. Helders, P. J. Keus, S. H. Kwakkel, G. Lenssen, T. Oostendorp, R. A. Ostelo, R. W. Reijman, M. Terwee, C. B. Theunissen, C. Thomas, S. van Baar, M. E. van 't Hul, A. van Peppen, R. P. Verhagen, A. van der Windt, D. A. Exercise Therapy Group (2005) Effectiveness of exercise therapy: a best-evidence summary of systematic reviews. *Australian Journal of Physiotherapy, 51*(2), 71–85.

Smith, D. and Hale, B. (2004) Validity and factor structure of the bodybuilding dependence scale. *British Journal Of Sports Medicine, 38*(2), 177–181.

Smith, D. and Hale, B. (2005) Exercise-dependence in bodybuilders: antecedents and reliability of measurement. *Journal of Sports Medicine And Physical Fitness, 45*(3), 401–8.

Smith, E. L., Smith, K. A. and Gilligan, C. (1990) Exercise, fitness, osteoarthritis, and osteoporosis. In C. Bouchard, R. J. Shephard, T. Stephens, J. R. Sutton and B. D. McPherson (eds), *Exercise, fitness, and health* (pp. 517–28). Champaign, IL: Human Kinetics.

Smith, J. F. (2006) *Is exercise beneficial in the rehabilitation of drug users?* University of Strathclyde, Glasgow.

Smith, R. A. and Biddle, S. J. H. (1995) Psychological factors in the promotion of physical activity. In S. J. H. Biddle (ed.), *European perspectives on exercise and sport psychology* (pp. 85–108). Champaign, Il: Human Kinetics.

Smith, R. A. and Biddle, S. J. H. (1999) Attitudes and exercise adherence: Tests of the Theories of Reasoned Action and Planned Behaviour. *Journal of Sports Sciences, 17,* 269–81.

Smith, R. E. and Smoll, F. L. (1996) *Way to go coach! A scientifically-proven approach to coaching effectiveness.* Portola Valley, CA: Warde Publishers.

Smith, R. E., Smoll, F. L. and Curtis, B. (1979) Coach effectiveness training: A cognitive-behavioral approach to enhancing relationship skills in youth sport coaches. *Journal of Sport Psychology, 1,* 59–75.

Solomon, R. L. (1980). The opponent-process theory of acquired motivation. *American Psychologist, 35,* 691–712

Sonstroem, R. J. (1984) Exercise and self-esteem. *Exercise and Sport Sciences Reviews, 12,* 123–55.

Sonstroem, R. J. (1988) Psychological models. In R. K. Dishman (ed.), *Exercise Adherence: Its Impact on Public Health* (pp. 125–53). Champaign, IL: Human Kinetics.

Sonstroem, R. J. (1997a) Physical activity and self-esteem. In W. P. Morgan (ed.), *Physical activity and mental health* (pp. 127–1–43). Washington, DC: Taylor & Francis.

Sonstroem, R. J. (1997b) The physical self-system: A mediator of exercise and self-esteem. In K. R. Fox (ed.), *The physical self: From motivation to well-being* (pp. 3–26). Champaign, IL: Human Kinetics.

Sonstroem, R. J. and Morgan, W. P. (1989) Exercise and self esteem: Rationale and model. *Medicine and Science in Sports and Exercise, 21,* 329–37.

Sparkes, A. C. (1997) Reflections on the socially constructed physical self. In K. R. Fox (ed.), *The physical self: From motivation to well-being* (pp. 83–110). Champaign, IL: Human Kinetics.

Sparks, P. and Guthrie, C. (1998) Self-identity and the theory of planned behavior: a useful addition or an unhelpful artifice? *Journal of Applied Social Psychology, 28*(15), 1393–1410.

Sparks, P., Guthrie, C. A. and Shepherd, R. (1997) The dimensional structure of the 'perceived behavioural control' construct. *Journal of Applied Social Psychology, 27,* 418–38.

Spence, J. C., McGannon, K. R. and Poon, P. (2005) The effect of exercise on global self-esteem: A quantitative review. *Journal of Sport and Exercise Psychology, 27,* 311–34.

Spielberger, C. D., Gorsuch, R. L. and Lushene, R. (1970) *State-trait anxiety inventory manual.* Palo Alto, CA: Consulting Psychologists Press.

Spitzer, R. L., Endicott, J. and Robins, E. (1978) Research diagnostic criteria. *Archives of General Psychiatry, 35,* 773–82.

Sport & Recreation New Zealand (SPARC) (2002) *Push Play Update: Push Play Facts:* www.pushplay.org.nz.

Sport England (2003) *Young people and sport in England: Trends in participation 1994–2002.* London: Author.

Sports Council and Health Education Authority (1992) *Allied Dunbar National Fitness Survey: Main findings.* London: Author.

Stamatakis, E., Primatesta, P., Chinn, S., Rona, R. J. and Falascheti, E. (2005) Overweight and obesity trends from 1974 to 2003 in English children: What is the role of socioeconomic factors? *Archives of Disease in Childhood, 90,* 999–1004.

Stanger, J. (1997) *Television in the home: The 1997 survey of parents and children:* The Annenberg Public Policy Center of the University of Pennsylvania.

Stanger, J. (1998) *Media in the Home 1998: The third annual survey of parents and children:* The Annenberg Public Policy Center of the University of Pennsylvania.

Stanger, J. and Gridina, N. (1999) *Media in the Home 1999: The fourth annual survey of parents and children:* The Annenberg Public Policy Center of the University of Pennsylvania.

Stanley, M. and Maddux, J. (1986) Cognitive processes in health enhancement: Investigation of a combined protection motivation and self-efficacy model. *Basic and Applied Social Psychology, 7,* 101–13.

Steinhardt, M. A. and Dishman, R. K. (1989) Reliability and validity of expected outcomes and barriers for habitual physical activity. *Journal of Occupational Medicine, 31,* 536–46.

Stenstrom, C. H. (1994) Therapeutic exercise in rheumatoid arthritis. *Arthritis Care and Research, 7*(4), 190–97.

Stephens, T. (1988) Physical activity and mental health in the United States and Canada: Evidence from four population surveys. *Preventive Medicine, 17,* 35–47.

Stephens, T. and Caspersen, C. J. (1994) The demography of physical activity. In C. Bouchard, R. J. Shephard and T. Stephens (eds), *Physical activity, fitness, and health* (pp. 204–13). Champaign, IL: Human Kinetics.

Stephens, T., Jacobs, D. R. and White, C. C. (1985) A descriptive epidemiology of leisure-time phyical activity. *Public Health Reports, 100,* 147–58.

Steptoe, A. and Bolton, J. (1988) The short-term influence of high and low intensity physical exercise on mood. *Psychology and Health, 2,* 91–106.

Steptoe, A. and Butler, N. (1996) Sports participation and emotional well-being in adolescents. *The Lancet, 347,* 1789–92.

Steptoe, A. and Cox, S. (1988) Acute effects of aerobic exercise on mood. *Health Psychology, 7,* 329–40.

Steptoe, A., Moses, J., Edwards, S. and Mathews, A. (1993) Exercise and responsivity to mental stress: Discrepancies between the subjective and physiological effects of aerobic training. *International Journal of Sport Psychology, 24,* 110–29.

Steptoe, A., Docherty, S., Rink, E., Kerry, S., Kendrick, T. and Hilton, S. (1999) Behavioural counselling in general practice for the promotion of healthy behaviour among adults at increased risk of coronary heart disease: Randomised trial. *British Medical Journal, 319,* 943–948.

Stetson, B. A., Beacham, A. O., Frommelt, S. J., Boutelle, K. N., Cole, J. D., Ziegler, C. H., Looney, S. W. (2005) Exercise slips in high-risk situations and activity patterns in long-term exercisers: An application of the relapse prevention model. *Annals of Behavioral Medicine, 30,* 25–35.

Stevinson, C. and Fox, K. (2004) Role of exercise for cancer rehabilitation in UK hospitals: a survey of oncology nurses. *European Journal of Cancer Care, 14,* 63–9.

Stevinson, C. and Fox, K. R. (2006) Feasibility study of an exercise programme for cancer care patients. *European Journal of Cancer Care, 15,* 386–96.

Stevinson, C., Lawlor, D. and Fox, K. (2004) Exercise interventions for cancer patients: systematic review of controlled clinical trials. *Cancer Causes and Control 15,* 1035–56.

Stewart, A. L., Hays, R. D., Wells, K. B., Roger, W. H., Spritzer, K. L. and Greenfield, S. (1994) Long-term functioning and well-being outcomes associated with physical activity and exercise in patients with chronic conditions in the medical outcomes study. *Journal of Clinical Epidemiology, 47,* 719–30.

Stone, E. J., McKenzie, T. L., Welk, G. J. and Booth, M. L. (1998) Effects of physical activity interventions in youth: Review and synthesis. *American Journal of Preventive Medicine, 15,* 298–315.

Stovitz, S., VanWormer, J., Center, B. and Bremer, K. (2005) Pedometers as a means to increase ambulatory activity for patients seen at a family medicine clinic. *Journal of the American Board of Family Practice 18,* 335–43.

Strang, V. R., and Sullivan, P. L. (1985) Body image attitudes during pregnancy and the postpartum period. *Journal of Obstetric Gynecological Neonatal Nursing, 14,* 332–7.

Strawbridge, W. J., Deleger, S., Roberts, R. E. and Kaplan, G. A. (2002) Physical activity reduces the risk of subsequent depression for older adults. *American Journal of Epidemiology, 156*(4), 328–34.

Strecher, V. J., DeVellis, B. E., Becker, M. H. and Rosenstock, I. M. (1986) The role of self-efficacy in achieving health behaviour change. *Health Education Quarterly, 13,* 73–92.

Stricker, C., Drake, D., Hoyer, K. and Mock, V. (2004) Evidence-based practice for fatigue management in adults with cancer: exercise as an intervention. *Oncol Nurs Forum, 31*(5), 963–76.

Strickland, B. (1978) Internal-external expectancies and health-related behaviors. *Journal of Consulting and Clinical Psychology, 46,* 1192–211.

Stringer, W. W. (1999) HIV and aerobic exercise: current recommendations. *Sports medicine, 28,* 389–395.

Stringer, W. W., Berezovskaya, M., O'Brien, W., Beck, C. K. and Casaburi, R. (1998) The effect of exercise training on aerobic fitness, immune indices, and quality of life in HIV+ patients. *Medicine and Science in Sports and Exercise, 30,* 11–16.

Stroebe, W. and Stroebe, M. S. (1995) *Social psychology and health.* Buckingham: Open University Press.

Sturm, R. (2005) Childhood obesity: What we can learn from existing data on societal trends, Part 1. *Preventing Chronic Disease [serial online], 2*(1), January.

Sutherland, I. and Shepherd, J. P. (2001) The prevalence of alcohol, cigarette, and illicit drug use in a stratified sample of English adolescents. *Addiction, 96,* 637–40.

Sutton, S. (2000) Interpreting cross-sectional data on stages of change. *Psychology and Health, 15,* 163–71.

Svebak, S. and Murgatroyd, S. (1985) Metamotivational dominance: A multimethod validation of reversal theory constructs. *Journal of Personality and Social Psychology, 48,* 107–16.

Swift, C. S., Armstrong, J. E., Beerman, K. A., Campbell, R. K. and Pond-Smith, D. (1995) Attitudes and beliefs about exercise among persons with non-insulin-dependent diabetes. *The Diabetes Educator, 21,* 533–40.

Swinburn, B. A. and Egger, G. (2004) The runaway weight gain train: Too many accelerators, not enough brakes. *British Medical Journal, 329*(7468), 736–9.

Swinburn, B. A., Walter, L. G., Arrol, B., Tilyard, M. W. and Russell, D. G. (1997) Green prescriptions: attitudes and perceptions of general practitioners towards prescribing exercise. *British Journal of General Practice, 47,* 567–9.

Swinburn, B. A., Walter, L. G., Arrol, B., Tilyard, M. W. and Russell, D. G. (1998) The green prescription study: A randomized controlled trial of written exercise advice in general practice. *American Journal of Public Health, 88*(2), 288–91.

Szabo, A. (1995) The impact of exercise deprivation on well-being of habitual exercisers. *Australian Journal of Science and Medicine in Sport, 27*(3), 68–75.

Szabo, A. (2000) Physical activity as a source of psychological dysfunction. In S. J. H. Biddle, K. R. Fox and S. H. Boutcher (eds), *Physical activity and psychological well-being* (pp. 130–153). London: Routledge.

Tai, S. S., Gould, M. and Iliffe, S. (1997) Promoting health exercise among older people in general practice: Issues in designing and evaluating therapeutic interventions. *British Journal of General Practice, 47,* 119–22.

Taylor, A. H. (1999) Adherence in primary health care exercise promotion schemes. In S. J. Bull (ed.), *Adherence issues in sport and exercise* (pp. 47–74). Chichester: Wiley.

Taylor, A. H. (2000) Physical activity, anxiety, and stress. In S. J. H. Biddle, K. R. Fox and S. H. Boutcher (eds), *Physical activity and psychological well-being* (pp. 10–45). London: Routledge.

Taylor, A. H. and Ussher, M. H. (2005) Effects of exercise on smoking cessation and coping with withdrawal symptoms and nicotine cravings. In G. E. J. Faulkner and A. H. Taylor (eds), *Exercise, health and mental health. Emerging relationships* (pp. 135–58). London: Routledge.

Taylor, A. H., Doust, J. and Webborn, N. (1998) Randomised controlled trial to examine the effects of a GP exercise referral programme in Hailsham, East Sussex, on modifiable coronary heart disease risk factors. *Journal of Epidemiology and Community Health, 52,* 595–601.

Taylor, W. C., Baranowski, T. and Sallis, J. F. (1994) Family determinants of childhood physical activity: A social cognitive model. In R. K. Dishman (ed.), *Advances in Exercise Adherence* (pp. 319–42) Champaign, IL: Human Kinetics.

Taylor, W. C., Baranowski, T. and Young, D. R. (1998) Physical activity interventions in low-income, ethnic minority, and populations with disability. *American Journal of Preventive Medicine, 15,* 334–43.

Telama, R. and Silvennoinen, M. (1979) Structure and development of 11 to 19 year olds' motivation for physical activity. *Scandinavian Journal of Sports Sciences, 1,* 23–31.

Telama, R., Yang, X., Hirvensalo, M. and Raitakari, O. (2006) Participation in organised youth sport as a predictor of adult physical activity: A 21-year longidudinal study. *Pediatric Exercise Science, 17,* 76–88.

Telama, R., Yang, X., Viikari, J., Valimaki, I., Wanne, O. and Raitakari, O. (2005) Physical activity from childhood to adulthood: A 21-year tracking study. *American Journal of Preventive Medicine, 28*(3), 267–73.

Terry, D. J. and O'Leary, J. E. (1995) The theory of planned behaviour The effects of perceived behavioural control and self-efficacy. *British Journal of Social Psychology, 34,* 199–220.

The Pedestrians' Association (1997) *Did you walk today?* London: The Pedestrians' Association.

The Pedestrians' Association (1998) *Stepping out: Local Authority policies and provision for walking.* London: The Pedestrians' Association.

Theberge, N. (1987) Sport and women's empowerment *Women's Studies International Forum, 10,* 387–93.

Thirlaway, K., and Benton, D. (1996) Exercise and mental health: The role of activity and fitness. In J. Kerr, A. Griffiths and T. Cox (eds), *Workplace health, employee fitness and exercise* (pp. 69–82). London: Taylor & Francis.

Thompson, C. E. and Wankel, L. M. (1980) The effects of perceived activity choice upon frequency of exercise behaviour. *Journal of Applied Social Psychology, 10,* 436–43.

Thompson, J. K. and Blanton, P. (1987) Energy conservation and exercise dependence: A sympathetic arousal hypothesis. *Medicine and Science in Sports and Exercise, 19,* 91–7.

Thompson, J. K. and Pasman, L. (1991) The obligatory exercise questionnaire. *Behavior Therapist, 14,* 137.

Thorsen, L., Nystad, W., Stigum, H., Dahl, O., Klepp, O., Bremnes, R. M., Wist, E. and Fossa, S. D. (2005) The association between self-reported physical activity and prevalence of depression and anxiety disorder in long-term survivors of testicular cancer and men in a general population sample. *Supportive Care in Cancer, 13*(8), 637–46.

Thune, I. and Furberg, A. S. (2001) Physical activity and cancer risk: Dose-response and cancer, all sites and site-specific. *Medicine and Science in Sports and Exercise, 33*(6), S530–S550.

Timm, K. E. (1991) Management of chronic low back patient pain: A retrospective analysis of different treatment approaches. *Isokinetics and Exercise Science, 1,* 44–8.

Tomporowski, P. D. and Ellis, N. R. (1986) Effects of exercise on cognitive processes: A review. *Psychological Bulletin, 99,* 338–46.

Tomson, L. M., Pangrazi, R. P., Friedman, G. and Hutchison, N. (2003) Childhood depressive symptoms, physical activity and health related fitness. *Journal of Sport and Exercise Psychology, 25*(4), 419–39.

Transport 2000 (2000) *Changing journeys to work: An employers' guide to green commuter plans.* London: Transport 2000.

Treiber, F. A., Baranowski, T., Braden, D. S., Strong, W. B., Levy, M. and Knox, W. (1991) Social support for exercise: Relationship to physical activity in young adults. *Preventive Medicine, 20,* 727–50.

Triandis, H. C. (1977) *Interpersonal behaviour.* Monterey, CA: Brooks/Cole.

Trigo, M., Silva, D. and Rocha, E. (2005) Psychosocial risk factors in coronary heart disease: beyond type A behavior. *Revista Portuguesa de Cardiologia, 24*(2), 261–81.

Troiano, R. P., Macera, C. A. and Ballard-Barbash, R. (2001) Be physically active each day: How can we know? *Journal of Nutrition, 131*(Supplement), 451S–60S.

Trost, S. G., Owen, N., Bauman, A. E., Sallis, J. F. and Brown, W. (2002) Correlates of adults' participation in physical activity: Review and update. *Medicine and Science in Sports and Exercise, 34,* 1996–2001.

Tsukue, I. and Shohoji, T. (1981) Movement therapy for alcoholic patients. *Journal of Studies on Alcohol, 42,* 144–9.

Tudor-Locke, C. and Bassett, D. R. (2004) How many steps/day are enough? Preliminary pedometer indices for public health. *Sports Medicine, 34*(1), 1–8.

Tudor-Locke, C., Ainsworth, B. E. and Popkin, B. M. (2001) Active commuting to school: an overlooked source of children's physical activity? *Sports Medicine, 31*(5), 309–13.

Tudor-Locke, C., Williams, J., Reis, J. and Pluto, D. (2002) Utility of pedometers for assessing physical activity: convergent validity. *Sports Medicine, 32*(12), 795–808.

Tudor-Locke, C. E. and Myers, A.M. (2001) Challenges and opportunities for assessing physical activity in sedentary adults. *Sports Medicine,* 31, 92–100.

Tudor-Locke, C. E. and Myers, A. M. (2001) Methodological considerations for researchers and practitioners using pedometers to measure physical (ambulatory) activity. *Research Quarterly for Exercise and Sport,* 72(1), 1–12.

Tunstall-Pedoe, H. and Smith, W. L. S. (1986) Level and trends of coronary heart disease mortality in Scotland compared to other countries. *Health Bulletin, 44,* 153–61.

UK Beam Trial Team (2004) United Kingdom back pain exercise and manipulation (UK BEAM) randomised trial: effectiveness of physical treatments for back pain in primary care. *BMJ, 329*(7479), 1377-.

UK Committee for Safety and Medicine (2003) HRT: update on the risk of breast cancer and long-term safety. *Current Problems Pharmacovigil, 29,* 1–3.

Uston, T. B., Ayuso-Mateos, J. L., Chatterji, S., Mathers, C. and Murray, C. J. L. (2004) Global burden of depressive disorders in the year 2000. *British Journal of Psychiatry, 184,* 386–92.

Vallerand, R. J. (1997) Toward a hierarchical model of intrinsic and extrinsic motivation. In M. P. Zanna (ed.), *Advances in experimental social psychology.* (Vol 29) (pp. 271–360). New York: Academic Press.

Vallerand, R. J. and Blanchard, C. M. (2000) The study of emotion in sport and exercise: Historical, definitional, and conceptual perspectives. In Y. L. Hanin (ed.), *Emotions in sport* (pp. 3–37). Champaign, IL: Human Kinetics.

Vallerand, R. J. and Fortier, M. S. (1998) Measures of intrinsic and extrinsic motivation in sport and physical activity: A review and critique. In J. L. Duda (ed.), *Advances in sport and exercise psychology measurement* (pp. 81–101). Morgantown, WV: Fitness Information Technology.

Vallerand, R. J. and Losier, G. F. (1999) An integrative analysis of intrinsic and extrinsic motivation in sport. *Journal of Applied Sport Psychology, 11,* 142–69.

van Beurden, E., Barnett, L. M., Zask, A., Dietrich, U. C., Brooks, L. O. and Beard, J. (2003) Can we skill and activate children through primary school physical education lessons? 'Move it Groove it' – a collaborative health promotion intervention. *Preventive Medicine, 36,* 493–501.

van Gool, C. H., Kempen, G. I., Penninx, B. W., Deeg, D. J., Beekman, A. T., van Eijk, J. T., Pahor, M. and Messier, S.P. (2003) Relationship between changes in depressive symptoms and unhealthy lifestyles in late middle aged and older persons: results from the Longitudinal Aging Study Amsterdam. *Age and Ageing, 32*(1), 81–7.

van Gool, C. H., Penninx, B. W., Kempen, G. I., Rejeski, W. J., Miller, G. D., van Eijk, J. T. *et al.* (2005) Effects of exercise adherence on physical function among overweight older adults with knee osteoarthritis. *Arthritis and Rheumatism, 53*(1), 24–32.

Van Landuyt, L. M., Ekkekakis, P., Hall, E. E. and Petruzzello, S. J. (2000) Throwing the mountains into the lakes: On the perils of nomothetic conceptions of the exercise-affect relationship. *Journal of Sport and Exercise Psychology, 22,* 208–34.

Van Mechelen, W., Twisk, J. W. R., Post, G. B., Snel, J. and Kemper, H. C. G. (2000) Physical activity of young people: The Amsterdam Longitudinal Growth and Health Study. *Medicine and Science in Sports and Exercise, 32,* 1610–16.

Van Wersch, A. (1997) Individual differences and intrinsic motivations for sport participation. In J. Kremer, K. Trew and S. Ogle (eds), *Young people's involvement in sport* (pp. 57–77). London: Routledge.

Van Wersch, A., Trew, K. and Turner, I. (1992) Post-primary school pupils' interest in physical education: Age and gender diferences. *British Journal of Educational Psychology, 62,* 56–72.

Vasterling, J. J., Sementilli, M. E. and Burish, T. G. (1988) The role of aerobic exercise in reducing stress in diabetic patients. *Diabetic Education, 14*(3), 197–201.

Vaughn, C. C. (1976) Rehabilitation of post-menopausal osteoporosis. *Israeli Journal of Medical Sciences, 12,* 652–9.

Veale, D. M. (1995) Does primary exercise dependence really exist? In J. Annett, B. Cripps and H. Steinberg (eds), *Exercise addiction. Motivations for participation in sport and exercise* (p. 71). Leicester: The British Psychological Society Sport and Exercise Psychology Section.

Veale, D. M. and Le Fevre, K. (1988) *A survey of exercise dependence.* Paper presented at the Sport, Health, Psychology and Exercise Symposium, Bisham Abbey National Sports Centre.

Veale, D. M, Le Fevre, K., Pantelis, C., de Souza, V., Mann, A. and Sargeant, A. (1992). Aerobic exercise in the adjunctive treatment of depression: A randomized controlled trial. *Journal of the Royal Society of Medicine, 85,* 541–4.

Veale, D. M. (1987) Exercise dependence. *British Journal of Addiction, 82,* 735–40.

Vealey, R. S. (1986) Conceptualisation of sport confidence and competitive orientation: Preliminary investigation and instrument development. *Journal of Sport and Exercise Psychology, 8,* 221–53.

Vilhjalmsson, R. and Kristjansdottir, G. (2003) Gender differences in physical activity in older children and adolescents: The central role of organised sport. *Social Science and Medicine, 56,* 363–74.

Vitale, A. E., Sullivan, S. J., Jankowski, L. W., Fleury, J., Lefrancois, C. and Lebouthillier, E. (1995) Screening of health risk factors prior to exercise or a fitness evaluation of adults with traumatic brain injury: A consensus by rehabilitation professionals. *Brain Injury, 10,* 367–75.

Vlachopoulos, S. and Biddle, S. J. H. (1996) Achievement goal orientations and intrinsic motivation in a track and field event in school physical education. *European Physical Education Review, 2,* 158–64.

Vlachopoulos, S. and Biddle, S. J. H. (1997) Modeling the relation of goal orientations to achievement-related affect in physical education: Does perceived ability matter? *Journal of Sport and Exercise Psychology, 19,* 169–87.

Vlachopoulos, S., Biddle, S. and Fox, K. (1996) A social-cognitive investigation into the mechanisms of affect generation in children's physical activity. *Journal of Sport and Exercise Psychology, 18,* 174–93.

Vuori, I. M. (1995) Exercise and physical health: Musculoskeletal health and functional capabilities. *Research Quarterly for Exercise and Sport, 66,* 276–85.

Vuori, I. M. (2001) Dose-response of physical activity and low back pain, osteoarthritis, and osteoporosis. *Medicine and Science in Sports and Exercise, 33*(6, Supplement), S551–S86.

Vuori, I. M., Oja, P. and Paronen, O. (1994) Physically active commuting to work: Testing its potential for exercise promotion. *Medicine and Science in Sports and Exercise, 26,* 844–50.

Waddell, G. (1992) Biopsychosocial analysis of low back pain. *Balliere's Clinical Rheumatology, 6,* 523–57.

Wallace, A. M., Boyer, D. B., Dan, A. and Holm, K. (1986) Aerobic exercise, maternal self-esteem, and physical discomforts during pregnancy. *Journal of Nurse-Midwifery, 31,* 255–62.

Wallace, L., Boxall, M. and Riddick, N. (2004) Influencing exercise and diet to prevent osteoporosis: lessons from three studies. *British Journal of Community Nursing, 9*(3), 102–9.

Wallston, B. S. and Wallston, K. (1978) Locus of control and health: A review of the literature. *Health Education Monographs, 6,* 107–17.

Wallston, B. S. and Wallston, K. A. (1985) Social psychological models of health behaviour: An examination and integration. In A. Baum, S. E. Taylor and J. E. Singer (eds), *Handbook of psychology and health: IV. Social psychological aspects of health* (pp. 23–53). Hillsdale, NJ: Erlbaum.

Wallston, K. A., Wallston, B. S. and DeVellis, R. (1978) Development of the multidimensional health locus of control (MHLC) scales. *Health Education Monographs, 6,* 160–70.

Wang, C. K. J. and Biddle, S. J. H. (2001) Young people's motivational profiles in physical activity: A cluster analysis. *Journal of Sport and Exercise Psychology, 23,* 1–22.

Wang, C. K. J., Liu, W. C., Biddle, S. J. H. and Spray, C. M. (2005) Cross-cultural validation of the Conceptions of the Nature of Athletic Ability Questionnaire Version 2. *Personality and Individual Differences, 38,* 1245–56.

Wankel, L. M. (1997) 'Strawpersons', selective reporting, and inconsistent logic: A response to Kimiecik and Harris's analysis of enjoyment. *Journal of Sport and Exercise Psychology, 19,* 98–109.

Wankel, L. M. and Kreisel, P. S. J. (1985) Factors underlying enjoyment of youth sports: Sport and age group comparisons. *Journal of Sport Psychology, 7,* 51–74.

Wankel, L. M. and Mummery, K. W. (1993) Using national survey data incorporating the theory of planned behavior: Implications for social marketing strategies in physical activity. *Journal of Applied Sport Psychology, 5,* 158–77.

Wankel, L. M. and Sefton, J. M. (1994) Physical activity and other lifestyle behaviors. In C. Bouchard, R. J. Shephard and T. Stephens (eds), *Physical activity, fitness, and health* (pp. 531–50). Champaign, IL: Human Kinetics.

Wanless, D. (2004) *Securing good health for the whole population.* London: Crown.

Ware, J., Snows, K. K., Kosinski, M. and Gandek, B. (1993) *SF36: Health survey manual and interpretation guide.* Boston: Nimrod Press.

Warner, K., Wickizer, T. M., Wolfe, R. A., Schildroth, J. E. and Samuelson, M. H. (1988) Economic implications of workplace health promotion programs: Review of the literature. *Journal of Occupational Medicine, 30,* 106–12.

Wassertheil-Smoller, S., Shumaker, S., Ockene, J., Talavera, G. A., Greenland, P., Cochrane, B., Robbins, J., Aragaki, A. and Dunbar-Jacob, J. (2004) Depression and cardiovascular sequelae in postmenopausal women. The Women's Health Initiative (WHI). *Arch Intern Med, 164*(3), 289–98.

Watson, D., Clark, L. A. and Tellegen, A. (1988) Development and validation of brief measures of positive and negative affect: The PANAS scales. *Journal of Personality and Social Psychology, 54,* 1063–70.

Watson, D., Wiese, D., Vaidya, J. and Tellegen, A. (1999) The two general activation systems of affect: Structural findings, evolutionary considerations, and psychobiological evidence. *Journal of Personality and Social Psychology, 76,* 820–38.

Webb, O. J. and Eves, F. F. (2005) Promoting stair use: single versus multiple stair-riser messages. *American Journal of Public Health, 95*(9), 1543–4.

Weber, J. and Wertheim, E. H. (1989) Relationships of self-monitoring, special attention, body fat percentage, and self-motivation to attendance at a community gymnasium. *Journal of Sport and Exercise Psychology, 11,* 105–14.

Weinberg, R. S., Hughes, H. H., Critelli, J. W., England, R. and Jackson, A. (1984) Effects of pre-existing and manipulated self-efficacy on weight loss in a self-control programme. *Journal of Research in Personality, 18,* 352–8.

Weiner, B. (1979) A theory of motivation for some classroom experiences. *Journal of Educational Psychology, 71,* 3–25.

Weiner, B. (1985) An attributional theory of motivation and emotion. *Psychological Review, 92,* 548–573

Weiner, B. (1986) *An attributional theory of motivation and emotion.* New York: Springer-Verlag.

Weiner, B. (1992) *Human motivation.* Newbury Park, CA: Sage.

Weiner, B. (1995) *Judgements of responsibility.* New York: The Guilford Press.

Weinstein, N. D., Rothman, A. J. and Sutton, S. R. (1998) Stage theories of health behavior: Conceptual and methodological issues. *Health Psychology, 17,* 290–9.

Weismann, M. M. and Klerman, G. L. (1992) Depression: Current understanding and changing trends. *Annual Review Public Health, 13,* 319–39.

Wells, N. (1985) *Back pain.* London: Office of Health Economics.

West, P., Reeder, A. I., Milne, B. J. and Poulton, R. (2002) Worlds apart: A comparison between physical activities among youth in Glasgow, Scotland and Dunedin, New Zealand. *Social Science and Medicine, 54,* 607–19.

Weyerer, S. (1992) Physical inactivity and depression in the community: Evidence from the Upper Bavarian Field Study. *Journal of Sports Medicine, 13,* 492–6.

White, R. W. (1959) Motivation reconsidered: The concept of competence. *Psychological Review, 66,* 297–333.

Whitehead, J. R. (1993) Physical activity and intrinsic motivation. *President's Council on Physical Fitness and Sports Physical Activity and Fitness Research Digest, 1*(2), 1–8.

Whitehead, J. R. (1995) A study of children's physical self-perceptions using an adapted physical self-perception profile questionnaire. *Pediatric Exercise Science, 7,* 132–51.

Whitehead, J. R. and Corbin, C. B. (1988) Multidimensional scales for the measurement of locus of control of reinforcements for physical fitness behaviors. *Research Quarterly for Exercise and Sport, 59,* 108–17.

Whitehead, J. R. and Corbin, C. B. (1991) Youth fitness testing: The effect of percentile-based evaluative feedback on intrinsic motivation. *Research Quarterly for Exercise and Sport, 62,* 225–31.

Whitehead, J. R., Pemberton, C. L. and Corbin, C. B. (1990) Perspectives on the physical fitness testing of children: The case for a realistic educational approach. *Pediatric Exercise Science, 2,* 111–23.

Widmeyer, W. N., Brawley, L. R. and Carron, A. V. (1985) *The measurement of cohesion in sport teams: The Group Environment Questionnaire.* London, Ontario: Sports Dynamics.

Widmeyer, W. N., Carron, A. V. and Brawley, L. R. (1993) Group cohesion in sport and exercise. In R. Singer, M. Murphey and L. K. Tennant (eds), *Handbook of research on sport psychology* (pp. 672–92). New York: Macmillan.

Wiersma, U. J. (1992) The effects of extrinsic rewards in intrinsic motivation: A meta-analysis. *Journal of Occupational and Organizational Psychology, 65,* 101–14.

Williams, G. C., Frankel, R. M., Campbell, T. L. and Deci, E. L. (2000) Research on relationship-centered care and healthcare outcomes from the Rochester Biopsychosocial Program: A Self-Determination Theory integration. *Families, Systems and Health, 18,* 79–90.

Williams, H. G. (1986) The development of sensory-motor function in young children. In V. Seefeldt (ed.), *Physical activity and well-being* (pp. 106–22). Reston, VA: American Alliance for Health, Physical Education, Recreation, and Dance.

Wimbush, E., Macgregor, A. and Fraser, E. (1997) Impacts of a mass media campaign on walking in Scotland. *Health Promotion International, 13,* 45–53.

Wing, R. R., Epstein, L. H., Nowalk, M. P. and Lamparski, D. M. (1986) Behavioral self-regulation in the treatment of patients with diabetes mellitus. *Psychological Bulletin, 99,* 78.

Wold, B. and Hendry, L. (1998) Social and environmental factors associated with physical activity in young people. In S. J. H. Biddle, J. F. Sallis and N. Cavill (eds), *Young and active? Young people and health-enhancing physical activity: Evidence and implications* (pp. 119–32). London: Health Education Authority.

Wollman, R. L., Cornall, C., Fulcher, K. and Greenwood, R. (1994) Aerobic training in brain-injured patients. *Clinical Rehabilitation, 8,* 253–7.

Woodard, E. and Gridina, N. (2000) *Media in the Home 2000: The fifth annual survey of parents and children:* The Annenberg Public Policy Center of the University of Pennsylvania.

Woods, C., Mutrie, N. and Scott, M. (2002) Physical activity intervention: A transtheoretical model-based intervention designed to help sedentary young adults become more active. *Health Education Research: Theory and Practice, 17*(4), 451–60.

World Health Organization (1986) *Targets for Health for All.* Copenhagen: WHO.

World Health Organization (1993) *The ICD–10 classification of mental and behavioral disorders: Diagnostic criteria for research.* Geneva: WHO.

World Health Organization (1996) *Health behaviour in school-aged children: A World Health Organization cross-national study.*

World Health Organization (2000) *Health and health behaviour among young people: WHO Policy Series. Policy for children and adolescents, issue 1.* Geneva: Author.

World Health Organization (2004) Global strategy on diet physical activity and health: World Health Organization.

Writing Group for the Women's Health Initiative Investigators (2002) Risk and benefits of estrogen plus progestin in healthy postmenopausal women; principal results from the Women's Health Initiative randomised controlled trial. . *JAMA, 288,* 321–33.

Wurtele, S. and Maddux, J. (1987) Relative contributions of protection motivation theory components in predicting exercise intentions and behaviour. *Health Psychology, 6,* 453–66.

Yamazaki, S., Ichimura, S., Iwamoto, J., Takeda, T., and Toyama, Y. (2004) Effect of walking exercise on bone metabolism in postmenopausal women with osteopenia/osteoporosis. *Journal of Bone and Mineral Metabolism, 22*(5), 500–8.

Yancy, A. K., Miles, O. and Jordan, A. (1999) Organizational characteristics facilitating initiation and institutionalization of physical activity programs in a multiethnic urban community. *Journal of Health Education, 30,* S44–S51.

Young, D. R. (1997) Community-based interventions for increasing physical activity. In A. S. Leon (ed.), *Physical activity and cardiovascular health: A national consensus* (pp. 252–61) Champaign, Il: Human Kinetics.

Youngstedt, S. D., O'Connor, P. J. and Dishman, R. K. (1997) The effects of acute exercise on sleep: A quantitative synthesis. *Sleep, 20,* 203–14.

Yu, S., Yarnell, J., Sweetnam, P. and Murray, L. (2003) What level of physical activity protects against premature cardiovascular death? The Caerphilly study. *Heart,* 89, 502–6.

Zaitz, D. (1989) Are you an exercise addict? *Idea Today, 7,* 44.

Zigmond, A. S. and Snaith, R. P. (1983) The hospital anxiety and depression scale. *Acta Psychiatrica Scandinavia, 67,* 361–70.

Zlot, A. I., Librett, J. J., Buchner, D. M. and Schmid, T. L. (2006) Environmental, transportation, social, and time barriers to physical activity. *Journal of Physical Activity and Health, 3*(1).

Zuckerman, M. and Lubin, B. (1965) *Manual for the Multiple Affect Adjective Checklist.* San Diego, CA: Educational and Industrial Testing Service.

Zunft, H.-J. F., Friebe, D., Seppelt, B., Widhalm, K., de Winter, A.-M. R., de Almeida, M. D. V., Kearney, J. M. and Gibney, M. 1999) Perceived benefits and barriers to physical activity in a nationally representative sample in the European Union. *Public Health Nutrition, 2*(1a), 153–60.

Zung, W. W. K. (1965) A self-rating depression scale. *Archives of General Psychiatry, 12,* 63–70.

Zung, W. W. K., Richards, C. B. and Short, M. J. (1965) Self-rating depression scale in an outpatient clinic. *Archives of General Psychiatry, 13,* 508–15.

Subject index

Author index

Aaro, L.E. 334
Aarts, H. 68
Abele, A. 170
Abraham, C. 55, 68
Abramson, L.Y. 95, 281
Adamson, M.J. 269
Adler, N. 94
Aenchbacher, L.E. 220
Aggleton, P. 47, 49, 142
Ainsworth, B.E. 26, 297
Aitchison, T. 260, 341
Ajzen, I. 59, 60, 61, 63, 64, 65, 67, 68, 332, 335
Akiskal, H. 220
Alder, B. 191
Alderman, B. 279
Alexander, A.M. 322
Allison, K.R. 208
Almond, L. 318
Ames, C. 149
Andersen, R.E. 28
Anderson, B.L. 255
Andrew, G.M. 50
Anspaugh, D.J. 217
Archer, J. 149
Arent, S.M. 167, 173
Arif, A. 269
Armitage, C. 61
Armstrong, K. 193
Armstrong, N. 27
Asci, F.H. 184
Ashford, B. 58
Asikainen, T. 301
Astrand, P.O. 6
Ayalon, J, 259

Babyak, M. 233, 235
Bachman, G. 194
Backhouse, S.H. 75
Baekeland, F. 181
Bagozzi, R.P. 68
Bailey, C. 303
Baker, G. 298

Bandura, A. 37, 42, 64, 72, 107, 108, 109, 111, 114, 115, 153
Banks, A. 263, 269
Baranowski, T. 52, 63, 145, 312
Barker, D.J.P. 19
Barrett, L.F. 166, 167
Bartholomew, L.K. 138, 354
Bassett, D.R. 7
Bassey, E.J. 22
Battersby, R. 193
Batty, D. 23
Bauman, A. 30, 43, 335, 345
Becker, M.H. 55, 56, 57, 221, 267
Beedie, C.J. 167
Beesley, S. 206
Beh, H.C. 275
Belisle, M. 132
Bell, A.C. 21
Belman, L.J. 247
Bentler, P. 62
Benton, D. 174, 175
Berg, K. 22
Berger, B.G. 166, 169, 173, 251
Berk, T.J. 258
Bernaards, C.M. 225
Bernston, G.G. 167
Bhui, K, 207
Biddle, S. 15, 16, 23, 24, 25, 29, 30, 36, 37, 42, 48, 49, 50, 52, 58, 61, 62, 65, 66, 67, 69, 76, 83, 87, 94, 97, 98, 104, 105, 109, 119, 120, 124, 125, 127, 130, 133, 138, 140, 141, 145, 149, 151, 154, 172, 176, 182, 188, 196, 206, 213, 230, 239, 265, 276, 279, 282, 303, 322, 323, 324, 325, 340
Biering, F.S. 327
Birk, T.J. 257
Blair, S.N. 6, 18, 20, 25, 250
Blamey, A. 313, 341
Blanchard, C.M. 167, 255
Blanton, P. 275
Blissmer, B. 37, 107, 113
Blumenthal, J.A. 50, 233, 235
Boer, H. 72